▶ Eighth Edition

# Human Resource Management

## R. Wayne Mondy, SPHR
*McNeese State University*

## Robert M. Noe, SPHR
*Texas A&M University–Commerce*

## Shane R. Premeaux
*McNeese State University*

*In collaboration with*

## Judy Bandy Mondy
*McNeese State University*

Prentice Hall

*Upper Saddle River, New Jersey  07458*

Mondy, R. Wayne
   Human resource management / R. Wayne Mondy, Robert M. Noe, Shane R.
Premeaux.—8th ed.
      p. cm.
   Includes index.
   ISBN 0-13-032280-6
   1. Personnel management—United States. 2. Personnel management. I. Noe, Robert M.
II. Premeaux, Shane R., III. Title

HF5549.2.U5 M66  2002
658.3—dc21
                                                                          00-065250

Acquisitions Editor: Melissa Steffens
Assistant Editor: Jessica Sabloff
Media Project Manager: Michele Faranda
Marketing Manager: Michael Campbell
Marketing Assistant: Katie Mulligan
Managing Editor (Production): Judy Leale
Production Editor: Emma Moore
Production Assistant: Keri Jean
Permissions Coordinator: Suzanne Grappi
Associate Director, Manufacturing: Vincent Scelta
Production Manager: Arnold Vila
Design Manager: Pat Smythe
Art Director: Cheryl Asherman
Interior Design: Jill Little
Cover Design: Amanda Wilson
Cover Illustration/Photo: Jose Ortega/SIS
Illustrator (Interior): Electra Graphics
Manager, Print Production: Christy Mahon
Full-Service Project Management and Text Composition: Elm Street Publishing Services, Inc.
Printer/Binder: Courier/Kendallville

Credits and acknowledgments borrowed from other sources and reproduced, with permission, in this textbook appear on page 581 within text.

10 9 8 7 6 5 4 3 2
ISBN 0-13-032280-6

*To my daughters, granddaughter, and grandson*

Alyson Lynn, Marianne Elizabeth,
Madison Jon, and Matthew Bryce

*RWM*

*To my wife*

Joanie

*RMN*

*To my best friend*

Wayne Mondy

*who made book writing possible for me*

*SRP*

# ► Brief Contents

# ►Contents

# Preface

## PRACTICAL . . .
## APPLIED . . .
## CONTEMPORARY . . .

Let Mondy, Noe, and Premeaux show your students that **PEOPLE** make the difference between a company's success or failure.

**Today**, while nearly all corporations have access to the same technology, no one can deny it is the human resources who make the real difference in achieving organizational goals. In fact, an organization's unique advantage has become increasingly dependent upon a firm's most valuable asset—its employees.

The eighth edition of this classic, respected text reveals this strategic function practically and realistically while it maintains its balance between pragmatism and theory. The authors vividly illustrate the interrelationship of human resource management functions and the increasing utilization of technology throughout the book while they convey the strategic role of HR in planning and operating organizations.

Current and modern in every way, the text reflects the latest information, including the impact of global competition and rapid technological advances that have accelerated trends such as shared service centers, outsourcing, and just-in-time training. Throughout the book, you'll find a wealth of actual company examples that demonstrate how concepts are being used in today's leading-edge organizations.

Take a look at the features outlined on the next few pages of this preface, and you'll see for yourself why *Human Resource Management, Eighth Edition* is the absolute choice for your course!

# Now the Eighth Edition has been completely updated . . .

### Now available in an affordable new paperback format,

## Human Resource Management, EIGHTH EDITION

*includes many new enhancements and features. For example:*

## HR Trends & Innovations

These unique sections—which appear in each chapter—offer additional insight into various aspects of human resources, both domestically and in other countries. These sections portray the many changes that are currently occurring in the field of human resource management. Some examples of the topics discussed in **HR Trends and Innovations** include *Long Distance Marriages, United Parcel's 360-Degree Evaluation System,* and *The Intranet Comes of Age.*

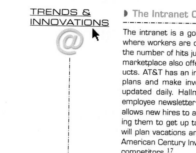

TRENDS & INNOVATIONS

▶ The Intranet Comes of Age

The intranet is a good way to keep everyone up to date, especially in a global age where workers are dispersed. After General Electric revamped its intranet last year, the number of hits jumped from a couple of thousand to 10 million a week. An online marketplace also offers discounts on GE appliances, Dell computers, and other products. AT&T has an intranet where workers can manage benefits, check their 401(k) plans and make investment changes, as well as check company news, which is updated daily. Hallmark Cards even posts the cafeteria menu, as well as the employee newsletter and job-training resources, on the intranet. Texas Instruments allows new hires to access the intranet before their first day on the job, thereby helping them to get up to speed quicker. The site also includes a concierge service that will plan vacations and run errands and a way to pick doctors from the health plan. American Century Investments uses its intranet for classified ads and information on competitors.[17]

(152)   Part Three ▶ Staffing

# ... with exciting new features to make teaching and learning more rewarding

## HR Web Wisdom

In every chapter, you'll find these useful sections that give students suggested topics for Internet surfing. Among the myriad sites listed, the authors include numerous links to sites related to diversity, HR training, professional associations and organizations, HR planning, electronic résumés, compensation and benefits, health and safety, and more. To ensure that the Internet addresses for each topic remains current, Prentice Hall has posted the URL for each on the Web site at **www.prenhall.com/mondy**.

Two sites are particularly helpful: the *Society for Human Resource Management* and the *School of Labor and Industrial Relations at Michigan State University*. The Prentice Hall Internet sites listed are hot-linked to specific Web sites.

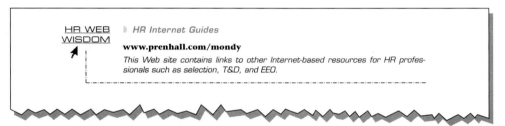

HR WEB WISDOM ▶ *HR Internet Guides*

**www.prenhall.com/mondy**

*This Web site contains links to other Internet-based resources for HR professionals such as selection, T&D, and EEO.*

## Other changes include:

- In Chapter 2, **new sections** include *The Internal Environment*, including topics on Mission, Policies, Corporate Culture, Management Style of Upper Management, Employees, Informal Organization, Other Units of the Organization, and Unions.

- **Global Perspectives** offer additional insight into various global aspects of HR.

- **Chapter 6: Internet Recruiting**, is an entirely new chapter that provides a hands-on appreciation of the importance of Internet Recruiting.

- **Expanded coverage** of Personality Tests, Behavioral Interviews, and Professional References and Background Investigations have been added.

- **A new emphasis on technology** is evident in this edition, in new sections such as *Evaluating Training and Development Programs, A Case for Simplicity, Business/Government/Education Training Partnerships, Workforce Investment Act,* and *Other Partnerships*. Sections that have been extended include *Coaching and Mentoring, Web-Based Training: The Internet, Intranets and Just-in-Time Training, Special Training Areas,* and *Orientation*.

- The authors discuss **new topics** such as *Benefits for Part-Time Employees, Safety: The Economic Impact, Legal Consequences to Workplace Violence, Individual and Organizational Characteristics to Monitor,* and *Internal Employee Relations*.

- **New information** on Global Staffing and Expatriate Development, as well as Global Safety and Health, is now included.

# Ongoing features that make this book a favorite

## HRM in Action

These brief exercises allow students to make decisions regarding real-world situations that take place in the business world. A debriefing guide is provided in the *Instructor's Resource Manual*. In the Eighth Edition, all of the *HRM In Action* features are new.

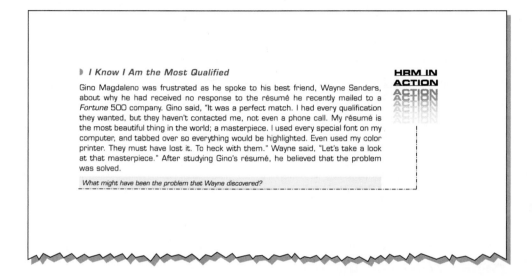

▶ *I Know I Am the Most Qualified*

Gino Magdaleno was frustrated as he spoke to his best friend, Wayne Sanders, about why he had received no response to the résumé he recently mailed to a *Fortune* 500 company. Gino said, "It was a perfect match. I had every qualification they wanted, but they haven't contacted me, not even a phone call. My résumé is the most beautiful thing in the world; a masterpiece. I used every special font on my computer, and tabbed over so everything would be highlighted. Even used my color printer. They must have lost it. To heck with them." Wayne said, "Let's take a look at that masterpiece." After studying Gino's résumé, he believed that the problem was solved.

*What might have been the problem that Wayne discovered?*

## HRM Incidents

Compelling opening cases and two *HRM Incidents*, which appear at the end of each chapter, highlight in greater detail the material covered in that chapter and help students focus on important issues. In this edition, more than 50 percent of the *HRM Incidents* are new.

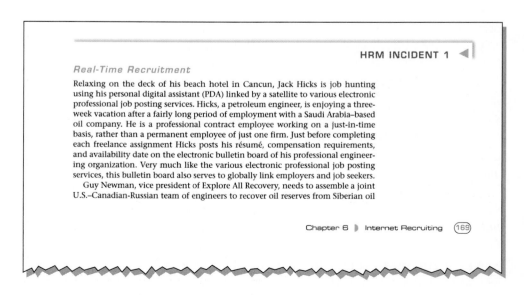

HRM INCIDENT 1 ◀

*Real-Time Recruitment*

Relaxing on the deck of his beach hotel in Cancun, Jack Hicks is job hunting using his personal digital assistant (PDA) linked by a satellite to various electronic professional job posting services. Hicks, a petroleum engineer, is enjoying a three-week vacation after a fairly long period of employment with a Saudi Arabia–based oil company. He is a professional contract employee working on a just-in-time basis, rather than a permanent employee of just one firm. Just before completing each freelance assignment Hicks posts his résumé, compensation requirements, and availability date on the electronic bulletin board of his professional engineering organization. Very much like the various electronic professional job posting services, this bulletin board also serves to globally link employers and job seekers.

Guy Newman, vice president of Explore All Recovery, needs to assemble a joint U.S.–Canadian-Russian team of engineers to recover oil reserves from Siberian oil

Chapter 6 ▶ Internet Recruiting (169)

# . . . of both professors and students

Because of the impact of the global environment on human resource management, new major global topics have been added to each chapter. These *Global Perspective* features offer additional insight into the various global aspects of human resources and cover topics such as *HR Planning at the United Nations, Molex Selects HR Professionals, Global Internet Recruiting: A Fad or the Future?*, and *AIDS: A Global Problem*.

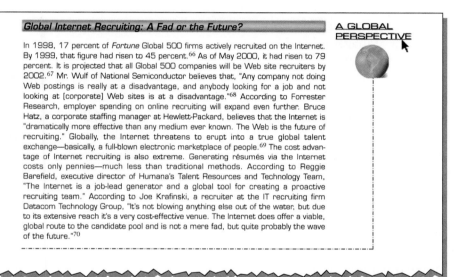

## Global Internet Recruiting: A Fad or the Future?

**A GLOBAL PERSPECTIVE**

In 1998, 17 percent of *Fortune* Global 500 firms actively recruited on the Internet. By 1999, that figure had risen to 45 percent.[66] As of May 2000, it had risen to 79 percent. It is projected that all Global 500 companies will be Web site recruiters by 2002.[67] Mr. Wulf of National Semiconductor believes that, "Any company not doing Web postings is really at a disadvantage, and anybody looking for a job and not looking at [corporate] Web sites is at a disadvantage."[68] According to Forrester Research, employer spending on online recruiting will expand even further. Bruce Hatz, a corporate staffing manager at Hewlett-Packard, believes that the Internet is "dramatically more effective than any medium ever known. The Web is the future of recruiting." Globally, the Internet threatens to erupt into a true global talent exchange—basically, a full-blown electronic marketplace of people.[69] The cost advantage of Internet recruiting is also extreme. Generating résumés via the Internet costs only pennies—much less than traditional methods. According to Reggie Barefield, executive director of Humana's Talent Resources and Technology Team, "The Internet is a job-lead generator and a global tool for creating a proactive recruiting team." According to Joe Krafinski, a recruiter at the IT recruiting firm Datacom Technology Group, "It's not blowing anything else out of the water, but due to its extensive reach it's a very cost-effective venue. The Internet does offer a viable, global route to the candidate pool and is not a mere fad, but quite probably the wave of the future."[70]

## Technology

The *Internet Recruiting* chapter includes an overview of how the Internet is changing HR, specifically in recruiting, not only from the standpoint of the company but also the individual. With links to other Internet-based resources for HR professionals, this chapter now also has useful information on ASCII résumés, scanning résumés, using keywords, and sample electronic résumés.

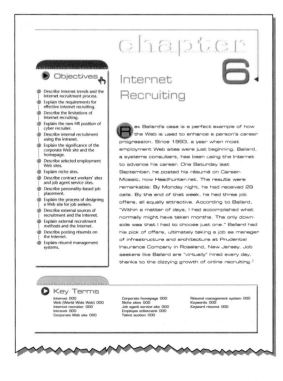

# Instructor's Resources

## INSTRUCTOR'S MANUAL

This helpful *Instructor's Manual* includes sample syllabi, lecture outlines, answers to all end-of-chapter and case questions.

## TEST ITEM FILE

The Test Item File includes multiple-choice and true/false questions for every chapter.

## WINPH CUSTOM TEST MANAGER

The electronic version of the Test Item File includes the Test Manager program.

## POWERPOINT, LECTURE

The PowerPoint program includes more than 20 slides per chapter, all of which highlight important chapter material.

## VIDEOS

These compelling videos include part-ending video segments, made from Skills Live video clips.

## INSTRUCTOR'S RESOURCE CD-ROM

All on one CD! You'll find the *Instructor's Manual*, Test Item File, PowerPoints, and WinPH Custom Test Manager all on this cross-platform CD-ROM.

## HUMAN RESOURCE MANAGEMENT SKILLS CD-ROM

This CD-ROM includes the HR Skills Live! video segments, and a human resources–related quiz game.

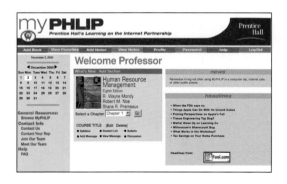

## PHLIP/CW—PRENTICE HALL LEARNING ON THE INTERNET PARTNERSHIP (PHLIP)

This content-rich, multidisciplinary business education Web site was created by professors for professors and their students. PHLIP provides academic support for faculty and students using this text, offering students the Student Study Hall, current events, an Interactive Study Guide, and Internet resources. Instructors can choose from text-specific resources such as the Faculty Lounge, Teaching Archive, Help with Computers, and Internet Skills.

# Acknowledgments

The assistance and encouragement of many people are normally required in the writing of any book. It is especially true in the writing of *Human Resource Management, Eighth Edition*. Although it would be virtually impossible to list each person who assisted in this project, we feel that certain people must be credited because of the magnitude of their contribution. Dr. Judy Bandy Mondy developed the *HR Web Wisdoms* and *PowerPoint®* presentation for this edition. She also provided spiritual inspiration for the new Internet Recruiting chapter. Judy is a true professional.

We would also like to thank Marthanne Lamansky, Kendra Ingram, and Sue Weatherbee, all very competent and professional individuals, who were always available to ensure that our deadlines were met. Two highly qualified graduate assistants, Lili Sugandi and Dikran Jebejian, found numerous errors before they could be published. As with the previous editions, the support and encouragement of many practicing HRM professionals have made this book possible.

We especially appreciate the efforts of the professionals who reviewed this edition. These individuals are Stan Malos, San Jose State University; Dr. Richard Bartlett, Muskingum Area Tech College; Anne Fielder, Barry University; and Paula Silva, University of New Mexico.

R. Wayne Mondy, SPHR
McNEESE STATE UNIVERSITY

Robert M. Noe, SPHR
TEXAS A&M UNIVERSITY–COMMERCE

Shane R. Premeaux
McNEESE STATE UNIVERSITY

## Part One
*Introduction*

## Objectives

- Identify the human resource management functions.
- Explain how organizations are adjusting to human resource restructuring trends.
- Explain the need for human resources to be a strategic partner.
- Distinguish among executives, generalists, and specialists.
- Describe the changes that occur in the human resource function as a firm grows larger and more complex.
- Explain the nature of the professionalization of human resources and the direction it has taken.
- Define *ethics* and relate ethics to human resource management.

# chapter

# 1

# Human Resource Management: An Overview

arl Edwards is the supervisor of 10 Baby Giant convenience stores in Sacramento, California. Because the Baby Giant chain is relatively small (only 40 stores), it has no human resource department. Each supervisor is in charge of all employment activities for his or her store. Carl must ensure that only the best people are recruited for positions as store managers, and then he must properly train these individuals. If one of the managers fails to report for an assigned shift and Carl cannot find a replacement, he is expected to work the shift. On one recent Friday afternoon, Carl is hurriedly attempting to locate a replacement because a store manager quit without giving notice.

Tremika Scott is the industrial relations manager for Axton Pneumotives, a small manufacturer of pumps located in Bangor, Maine. The 65 machine operators in the firm are unionized. Tremika has been negotiating with union leaders for five weeks

## Key Terms

Human resource management (HRM) 2
Staffing 3
Operative employees 4

Human resource manager 7
Shared service centers (SSCs) 8
Outsourcing 8
Executive 11

Generalist 11
Specialist 11
Profession 14
Ethics 16

with little success. The union members have threatened to walk off the job if the contract is not resolved by midnight. However, if Tremika's firm agrees to all the union's demands, it will no longer be competitive in the industry because of the higher wage level.

C arl and Tremika have one thing in common; they are deeply involved with some of the challenges and problems related to human resource management. Managers of human resources must constantly deal with the often volatile, and sometimes unpredictable, human element that makes working in this field very challenging. Managing people in organizations has become more complex than ever because of rapidly changing and increasingly complicated work environments.

In the first part of this chapter, we discuss the basic human resource management functions. Next, we address human resource restructuring trends and the human resource manager as a strategic partner. Then, we review the impact of technology. The distinctions among human resource executives, generalists, and specialists and among the human resource functions in organizations of different sizes are addressed next. We then discuss professionalism and ethics in this dynamic discipline. A description of the scope of the book concludes the chapter.

## EXPLORING WITH "HR WEB WISDOM"

Also included in the eighth edition of *Human Resource Management* is "HR Web Wisdom," found in each chapter, which suggests topics for Internet surfing. To ensure that the Internet addresses for each topic remain current, they are posted on the Prentice Hall Web site at www.prenhall.com/mondy. Two sites are particularly helpful: Society for Human Resource Management and the School of Labor and Industrial Relations at Michigan State University. The Prentice Hall Internet sites listed are hot-linked to specific Web sites.

## HUMAN RESOURCE MANAGEMENT FUNCTIONS

**Human resource management (HRM)**
The utilization of individuals to achieve organizational objectives.

**Human resource management (HRM)** is the utilization of individuals to achieve organizational objectives. Consequently, all managers at every level must concern themselves with human resource management. Basically, managers get things done through the efforts of others; this requires effective human resource management. Today's human resource problems and opportunities are enormous and appear to be expanding. Individuals dealing with human resource matters face a multitude of challenges, ranging from a constantly changing workforce to ever-present government regulations and a major technological revolution. Furthermore, global competition has caused both large and small organizations to be more conscious of costs and productivity. Because of the critical nature of human resource issues, these matters are receiving major attention from upper management.

People who are engaged in the management of human resources develop and work through an integrated human resource management system. As Figure 1-1 shows, five functional areas are associated with effective human resource management: staffing, human resource development, compensation and benefits, safety and health, and employee and labor relations. These functional areas mirror the human resource certification examination format, which is shown in the appendix to this chapter.[1] We discuss these functions next.

▶ Today's human resource problems and opportunities are enormous and appear to be expanding.

## Staffing

**Staffing** is the process through which an organization ensures that it always has the proper number of employees with the appropriate skills in the right jobs at the right time to achieve the organization's objectives. Staffing involves job analysis, human resource planning, recruitment, and selection. Firms must ensure that their workforces are productive today and in the foreseeable future.

Staffing
The process through which an organization ensures that it always has the proper number of employees with the appropriate skills in the right jobs at the right time to achieve the organization's objectives.

**The Human Resource Management System**   Figure 1-1

www.hr-guide.com

*Job analysis* is the systematic process of determining the skills, duties, and knowledge required for performing jobs in an organization. It impacts human resource planning, recruitment, and selection. *Human resource planning (HRP)* is the process of systematically reviewing human resource requirements to ensure that the required numbers of employees, with the required skills, are available when needed. *Recruitment* is the process of attracting qualified individuals and encouraging them to apply for work with the organization. A new chapter entitled "Internet Recruiting" has been added to this edition to reflect the increased emphasis on this method. *Selection* is the process through which the organization chooses, from a group of applicants, those individuals best suited both for open positions and for the company. Successful accomplishment of these three tasks is vital if the organization is to effectively accomplish its mission. Chapters 4, 5, 6, and 7 are devoted to these topics, which are sometimes referred to as *staffing*.

## Human Resource Development

*Human resource development (HRD)* is a major HRM function that consists not only of training and development but also individual career planning and development activities and performance appraisal, an activity that emphasizes T&D needs. *Training* is designed to provide learners with the knowledge and skills needed for their present jobs. *Development* involves learning that goes beyond today's job; it has a more long-term focus. Training and development is covered in Chapter 8.

*Career planning* is an ongoing process whereby an individual sets career goals and identifies the means to achieve them. *Career development* is a formal approach used by the organization to ensure that people with the proper qualifications and experiences are available when needed. Individual careers and organizational needs are not separate and distinct. Organizations should assist employees in career planning so the needs of both can be satisfied. Career planning and development is discussed in Chapter 9.

Through *performance appraisal,* employees and teams are evaluated to determine how well they are performing their assigned tasks. Performance appraisal affords employees the opportunity to capitalize on their strengths and overcome identified deficiencies, thereby becoming more satisfied and productive employees. Performance appraisal is discussed in Chapter 10.

Throughout this text, but especially in the HRD chapters, we use the term *operative employees.* **Operative employees** are all workers in an organization except managers and professionals, such as engineers, accountants, or professional secretaries. Steelworkers, truck drivers, retail clerks, and waiters are examples of operative employees.

**Operative employees**
All workers in an organization except managers and professionals, such as engineers, accountants, and professional secretaries.

## Compensation and Benefits

The question of what constitutes a fair day's pay has plagued management, unions, and workers for a long time. A well-thought-out compensation system provides employees with adequate and equitable rewards for their contributions to meeting organizational goals. As used in this book, the term *compensation* includes all rewards that individuals receive as a result of their employment. The reward may be one or a combination of the following:

- *Pay:* The money that a person receives for performing a job.
- *Benefits:* Additional financial rewards, other than base pay, including paid vacations, sick leave, holidays, and medical insurance.
- *Nonfinancial rewards:* Nonmonetary rewards, such as enjoyment of the work performed or a satisfactory workplace environment that provides flexibility.

Although compensation includes all these rewards, the increasing importance of benefits and incentives warrants separate treatment. We discuss compensation in Chapter 11 and address benefits and other compensation issues in Chapter 12.

## Safety and Health

*Safety* involves protecting employees from injuries caused by work-related accidents. *Health* refers to the employees' freedom from illness and their general physical and mental well-being. These aspects of the job are important because employees who work in a safe environment and enjoy good health are more likely to be productive and yield long-term benefits to the organization. For this reason, progressive managers have long advocated and implemented adequate safety and health programs. Today, because of federal and state legislation that reflects societal concerns, most organizations have become attentive to their employees' safety and health.[2] Chapter 13 is devoted to the topic of safety and health.

## Employee and Labor Relations

Since 1983, union membership has fallen approximately 8 percent, to only 13.9 percent of the workforce—the lowest level since the Great Depression. Subtracting government employees, unions represent only 9.5 percent of the private industry workforce.[3] Even so, a business firm is required by law to recognize a union and bargain with it in good faith if the firm's employees want the union to represent them. In the past, this relationship was an accepted way of life for many employers. But most firms today would like to have a union-free environment.

As Tremika Scott, industrial relations manager for Axton Pneumotives, discovered, dealing with a union often presents difficult problems. During the stressful bargaining process, the union placed Tremika in a difficult position. If the workers walk off the job, production stops; but agreeing to all the union's demands may result in pricing the firm's products out of the market. Tremika must be a skilled negotiator to solve these problems. When a labor union represents a firm's employees, the human resource activity is often referred to as *industrial relations,* which handles the job of collective bargaining. Chapters 14, 15, and 16 address employee and labor relations issues.

## Human Resource Research

Although human resource research is not a distinct HRM function, it pervades all functional areas, and the researcher's laboratory is the entire work environment. For instance, a study related to recruitment may suggest the type of worker most likely to succeed in a particular firm. Research on job safety may identify the causes of certain work-related accidents. The reasons for problems such as excessive absenteeism or excessive grievances may not be readily apparent. However, when such problems occur, human resource research can often shed light on their causes and possible solutions. Human resource research is clearly an important key to developing the most productive and satisfied workforce possible.

## Interrelationships of HRM Functions

All HRM functional areas are highly interrelated. Management must recognize that decisions in one area will affect other areas. For instance, a firm that emphasizes recruiting top-quality candidates but neglects to provide satisfactory compensation is wasting time, effort, and money. In addition, a firm's compensation system will be inadequate unless employees are provided a safe and healthy work environment. The interrelationships among the HRM functional areas will become more obvious as we address each topic throughout the book.

# HOW HUMAN RESOURCE MANAGEMENT IS PRACTICED IN THE REAL WORLD

At the beginning of each chapter, there are one or two lead cases that focus on and are integrated into the chapter material. Sections entitled "HRM in Action" and "HRM Incident" are also included in all chapters. These sections permit you to make decisions about real-world situations. They are designed to put you on the spot and let you think through how you would react in typical human resource management situations. In the "Developing HRM Skills" section, an experiential exercise permits you to see how you would react in simulated real-life situations. Each exercise enables you to understand how the subject matter may be used in making decisions.

# HR RESTRUCTURING TRENDS: WHO PERFORMS THE HUMAN RESOURCE MANAGEMENT TASKS?

The role of HR departments is changing in a dramatic way.[4] This restructuring has often resulted in a shift in who performs each function. Many organizations continue to perform the majority of HR functions inside the firm. However, as internal operations are reexamined, the following questions are raised. Can some HR tasks be performed more efficiently by line managers or outside vendors? Can some HR tasks be automated or eliminated altogether? One apparent fact is that all functions within today's organizations are being scrutinized for cost cutting, and HR is no exception. HR remains an expensive function, costing the average company $1,584 annually per full-time-equivalent (FTE) employee.[5] A study conducted by Mercer Management Consulting revealed three common threads that form a new organizational model for HR. First, strategic recentralization emphasizes that corporate headquarters establishes the direction for HR strategy. Second, there is more of a focus on cost reductions that result in consolidating routine administrative tasks. Third, delivery of many HR functions has shifted to line managers.

All units must operate under a strict budget in this competitive global environment, and HR is no exception. Because of time and budgetary constraints, some company and HR executives have had to make difficult decisions regarding how traditional HR tasks are accomplished. Naturally, the basic HR functions previously discussed must be accomplished, but the person(s) or units accomplishing these functions are being altered.[6] As discussed in the following sections, the traditional human resource manager continues to be in place in most organizations, but some organizations are also using shared service centers, outsourcing, and line managers to assist in the delivery of human resources to better accomplish organizational objectives. Additionally, HR departments are getting smaller because certain functions are now being accomplished by others. This shift permits HR to shed its gatekeeping image to focus on more strategic and mission-oriented activities.

## The Human Resource Manager

A **human resource manager** is an individual who normally acts in an *advisory* or *staff* capacity, working with other managers to help them deal with human resource matters. One general trend is that HR personnel are servicing an increasing number of employees, but the number varies. David Hiborn, an associate with William M. Mercer in Philadelphia, believes the old rule of thumb, one HR person for every 100 employees, does not really hold true today. "Organizations have outsourced, insourced, and taken many different responsibilities within the HR umbrella," he explains. "Every organization is so different, you're never comparing apples to apples."[7]

> **Human resource managers** Individuals who normally act in an advisory (or staff) capacity when working with other managers to help them deal with human resource matters.

Historically, the HR department basically performed the five functions internally.[8] Often, large HR departments were created, with the central figure being the HR manager or executive. The human resource manager is primarily responsible for coordinating the management of human resources to help the organization achieve its goals. There is a shared responsibility between line managers and human resource professionals. The distinction between human resource management and the human resource manager is illustrated by the following account:

> Bill Brown, the production supervisor for Ajax Manufacturing, has just learned that one of his machine operators has resigned. He immediately calls Sandra Williams, the human resource manager, and says, "Sandra, I just had a Class A machine operator quit down here. Can you find some qualified people for me to interview?" "Sure, Bill," Sandra replies. "I'll send two or three down to you within the week, and you can select the one that best fits your needs."

In this instance, both Bill and Sandra are concerned with accomplishing organizational goals, but from different perspectives. As a human resource manager, Sandra identifies applicants who meet the criteria specified by Bill. Yet, Bill will make the final decision as to who is hired because he is responsible for the machine operator's performance. His primary responsibility is production; hers is human resources. As a human resource manager, Sandra must constantly deal with the many problems related to human resources that Bill and the other managers face. Her job is to help them meet the human resource needs of the entire organization. In some firms, her function is also referred to as *personnel, employee relations,* or *industrial relations.*

▌ *SHRM-HR Links*

**www.prenhall.com/mondy**

To facilitate HR excellence, the Society for Human Resource Management has a series of Web Hot Links to topics of particular interest to HR professionals and students.

HR WEB
WISDOM

▶ **IBM's Human Resources Service Center**

When industry migrated from the mainframe to the PC, Big Blue took a tumble; by 1993, its revenue losses swelled to $8 billion. HR did not escape the downsizing that took place. Centralized functional units were formed to provide HR support regionally. In one year the number of IBM HR employees was reduced by 1,400 to a total of 2,000. Instead of praising HR for saving the firm $115 million, management issued a mandate to reduce costs by another 40 to 50 percent. In early 1995, all service functions were consolidated into a centralized Human Resources Service Center (HRSC) based in Raleigh, North Carolina. This center not only helps IBM employees receive information quickly and easily but also frees HR consultants to be more strategic. Today, the HRSC helps more than 700,000 employees, former employees, and their families, and handles more than seven million transactions a year. It has saved IBM an astonishing $180 million since its inception.[9]

## Shared Service Centers

**Shared service centers (SSCs)**
Centers that take routine, transaction-based activities dispersed throughout the organization and consolidate them in one place.

**Shared service centers (SSCs)** take routine, transaction-based activities dispersed throughout the organization and consolidate them in one place. A major advantage of this concept is that HR managers can assume a more strategic role because they are freed from the more routine tasks. For example, a company with 20 strategic business units could consolidate these routine HR tasks and perform them in one location. The increased volume makes the tasks more suitable for automation, which in turn results in the need for fewer HR personnel. For instance, Amoco estimates that the use of shared service centers, combined with selective outsourcing of some functions, achieved $400 million in annual savings for the company.[10]

## Outsourcing Firms

**Outsourcing**
The process of transferring responsibility for an area of service and its objectives to an external provider.

**Outsourcing** is the process of transferring responsibility for an area of service and its objectives to an external provider. By outsourcing certain projects, companies can save time and resources and redirect their energy to more strategic issues.[11] Outsourcing may provide advantages in the form of reduced costs, expanded capacity, and enhanced process flows and efficiencies. It also gives companies the necessary tools to manage the opposing forces of reducing costs while providing excellent service to a changing and dynamic workforce.[12] However, it is important for human resources leaders not to get caught up in the outsourcing trend without taking a serious look at their staffing objectives.[13]

Many companies are focusing their resources on their core businesses and have made the decision to outsource any function that they consider nonstrategic.[14] Outsourcing is a good way to eliminate functions that bog down the department. "At our corporate site, we have about 600 test operators," says Bobbi La Plante, corporate HR manager for Atmel Corporation, a semiconductor manufacturer in San Jose, California. "Because these employees tend to be transient, we did the same thing over and over with them; it was a job that was never done." Five years ago, HR took bids from temporary staffing agencies and sold the idea of outsourcing recruitment of test operators. "Now the company gets more bang for its buck, personnel-wise," says La Plante. "Once we got the administrative load off, we were able to strengthen our recruiting and benefits focus." She adds that the remaining staff has more interesting jobs and better career development because of the decision.[15]

As one might expect, the key to outsourcing success is to determine which functions to outsource, the extent to which they should be outsourced, and which ones to keep in-house. Currently, HR outsourcing use is highest in benefits administration and payroll processes, while use is most limited in hiring administration, recruiting and staffing, and records management.[16] Also, some firms are even questioning the value of having a fully staffed, permanent training function. Ideally, an outsourced training function costs only when it is used.[17]

## Line Managers

Line managers, by the nature of their jobs, are involved with human resources. Carl Edwards, the convenience store supervisor in Sacramento, California, fully understands the challenges a line manager faces with human resources because he will have to work Friday night if he cannot find a replacement. Hiring people with the proper qualifications will make or break any manager. All managers understand that their workers must be continuously trained and developed. Compensation and benefits are important to every member of the workforce. And, if the organization is unionized, the line manager must know how to deal effectively with the union. In organizations that emphasize using line managers to deliver more HR services, the size of the HR department may be reduced.

## HR AS A STRATEGIC PARTNER

The role of HR has changed with the globalization of business. In today's competitive environment, the HR function can no longer afford to be the personnel department of old, whose function was often described as "hire 'em and fire 'em." Rather, it must fulfill a broader and more strategic role in driving business direction.[18] The increasing recognition of HR as a legitimate business unit has made it highly strategic in nature and more critical to achieving corporate objectives.[19] "HR people have become strategic business partners with top management," says Terry Lauter, a principal with the HR consulting firm Humanomics of Granada Hills, California. "They have to make sure that HR activities are aligned with the business goals of the company." To succeed, HR executives must "understand the complex organizational design and be able to determine the capabilities of the company's workforce, both today and in the future."[20] HR involvement in strategy is necessary to ensure that human resources support the firm's mission. Unfortunately, this does not always occur. According to a recent survey, more than a third of responding senior HR professionals say they are always involved in strategic planning; more than 40 percent are sometimes involved; but nearly 25 percent of the respondents are rarely or never involved in strategy.[21]

The HR executive should be a partner to the chief executive officer (CEO) on the deployment of human resources and therefore should be accountable for making today's decisions regarding the company's future workforce.[22] From the CEO on down, management is responsible for implementing the strategic plan.[23] As previously mentioned, a trend has developed whereby more companies are outsourcing some HR tasks, placing other functions with shared service centers, or assigning the function to line managers. As the more routine and mundane tasks are removed from the responsibility of the HR manager, these individuals are better able to focus their attention on issues of greater strategic importance to the

> ▶ *Why Take Those Courses?*

Shamira Jones, a management major at State University, was being advised by her college advisor, Lonnie Barrios, and she was confused. Professor Barrios had just told her that several courses, including Staffing, Collective Bargaining, and Compensation, would be beneficial to her in her major. Shamira said, "But I am a management major. I want to move up the ladder in management. The electives you mentioned are HR courses. I don't need them."

*How do you believe Lonnie should respond?*

organization. The *new* HR executive must fully comprehend his or her company's current and future business challenges.[24] The human resource executive will increasingly become a strategic business partner and decision maker.

Even titles of HR executives are being changed to reflect this new partnership. Peggy Tate is now vice president of human resources strategy for DFS Group Limited, having added the word *strategy* to her title. According to Tate, "I have to be very closely linked to what senior management is thinking in terms of where the business is heading. I have to think about how to recruit the right people and train them; how to reward them; how to hold on to them." The current function of many chief human resource managers is epitomized by a banking executive who states, "I am now a strategic partner with line management and participate in business decisions which bring human resources perspectives to the general management of the company."[25]

The future appears bright for HR managers willing to forge a strategic partnership with other business units. If these managers are to become strategic partners in their organizations, they must run their departments according to the same rigid criteria that apply to other units. They must be able to use data available in

**Table 1-1** **Some Outs and Ins of HR: A List of Trends That Will Affect How Work Is Done in the Future**

| | |
|---|---|
| OUT: | Job titles and labels such as "employee," "manager," "staff," and "professional" |
| IN: | Everyone a businessperson, an "owner" of a complete business process, president of his or her job |
| OUT: | Chain-of-command, reporting relationships, department, function, turf, sign-off, work as imposed-from-above tasks |
| IN: | Self-management, responsiveness, proactivity, initiative, collaboration, egalitarianism, self-reliance, standards of excellence, personal responsibility, work as collection of self-initiated projects and teams |
| OUT: | Stability, order, predictability, structure, better safe than sorry |
| IN: | Flux, disorder, ambiguity, risk, better sorry than safe |
| OUT: | Good citizenship—show up, be a good soldier, stay 9-to-5 in cubicle, don't make waves, wait for someone else to decide your fate, work in same organization for 30 years, retire with gold watch |
| IN: | Make a difference—add value, challenge the process, work 4 hours or 18 hours per day, accept the job site as wherever the action is, learn from mistakes, develop career mobility and fluidity, work your tail off and be intensely loyal to Company X for 1 year or 10 years, and then move on to Company Y, a better, more marketable person |

*Source:* Adapted from Oren Harari, "Back to the Future of Work," *Management Review* 82 (September 1993): 35.

their unit to forecast outcomes and become real partners with upper management. HR units must be able to show how they add value to the company.[26]

Table 1-1, which lists some of the outs and ins of human resources, provides a brief insight into why the profession itself is in a great deal of flux.[27] While several trends are appearing, the only thing certain is that the job of human resource professional is continuously evolving. Yesterday's solutions may not be sufficient for tomorrow's challenges.

## IMPACT OF TECHNOLOGY

It has been estimated that there will be more technological change in the next 50 years than in the last 1,000 years.[28] The world has never before seen technological changes occur as rapidly as they are presently happening in the computer and telecommunications industries. One estimate is that technological changes are coming so fast that a person may have to change his or her entire skill repertoire three or four times in a career.[29] These advances affect every area of a business, including human resource management. For example, Internet recruiting, the topic of Chapter 6, is now being used by many organizations. New technology can potentially affect virtually every major HR task. The impact of technology on these practices is noted throughout the book.

## HUMAN RESOURCE EXECUTIVES, GENERALISTS, AND SPECIALISTS

Various classifications occur within the human resource profession, and you need to recognize and understand them. Among these are human resource executives, generalists, and specialists. An **executive** is a top-level manager who reports directly to the corporation's chief executive officer (CEO) or to the head of a major division. A **generalist,** who often is an executive, performs tasks in a variety of human resource–related areas. The generalist is involved in several, or all, of the five human resource management functions. A change is taking place in some companies. They are assigning a human resource generalist to each line organization and maintaining a smaller core of centralized staff. These individuals then serve the HR needs of a specific department.[30] A **specialist** may be a human resource executive, manager, or nonmanager who is typically concerned with only one of the five functional areas of human resource management. Figure 1-2 helps clarify these distinctions.

The vice president of industrial relations shown in Figure 1-2 specializes primarily in union-related matters. This person is both an executive and a specialist. The human resource vice president is both an executive and a generalist, having responsibility for a wide variety of functions. The manager of compensation and benefits is a specialist, as is the benefits analyst. Whereas an executive is identified by a position level in the organization, the breadth of such positions distinguishes generalists and specialists.

In today's HR environment, there is a trend for human resource professionals to become generalists. This change does not suggest that an HR professional should be a jack of all trades and master of none. The generalist is expected to be capable of working knowledgeably with all aspects of HR. In addition, the HR professional should be familiar with tasks that have been outsourced or placed with shared service centers.

**Executive**
A top-level manager who reports directly to a corporation's chief executive officer or to the head of a major division.

**Generalist**
A person who performs tasks in a variety of human resource–related areas.

**Specialist**
An individual who may be a human resource executive, a human resource manager, or a nonmanager, and who is typically concerned with only one of the five functional areas of human resource management.

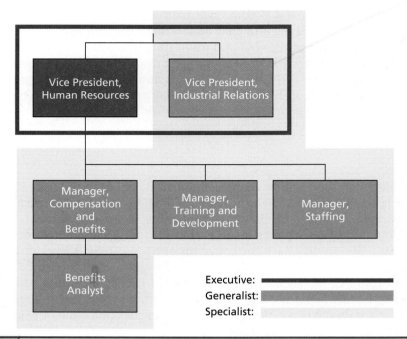

**Figure 1-2** 👆 **Human Resource Executives, Generalists, and Specialists**

## THE HUMAN RESOURCE FUNCTION IN ORGANIZATIONS OF VARIOUS SIZES

As firms grow and become more complex, the human resource function also becomes more complex and achieves greater importance. The basic purpose of human resource management remains the same; the difference is in the approach used to accomplish its objectives.

### Human Resource Functions in Small Businesses

Small businesses seldom have a formal human resource unit and HRM specialists, as Figure 1-3 shows. Rather, other managers handle human resource functions. The focus of their activities is generally on hiring and retaining capable employees.

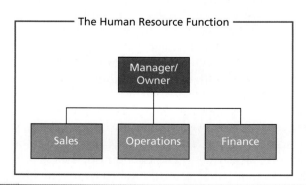

**Figure 1-3** 👆 **The Human Resource Function in a Small Business**

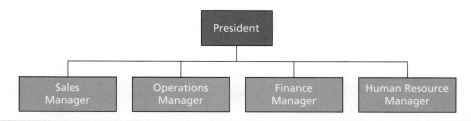

**The Human Resource Function in a Medium-Sized Business** Figure 1-4

Some aspects of human resource functions may actually be more significant in smaller firms than in larger ones. For example, a staffing mistake—hiring an incompetent employee who turns off customers—may cause the business to fail. In a larger firm, such an error might be much less harmful.

## Human Resource Management Functions in Medium-Sized Firms

As a firm grows, a separate staff function may be required to coordinate human resource activities. In a medium-sized firm, the person chosen to fill this role will be expected to handle most of the human resource activities, as Figure 1-4 implies. For these firms, there is little specialization. A secretary may be available to handle correspondence, but the human resource manager is essentially the entire department.

## Traditional Human Resource Functions in a Large Firm

When the firm's human resource function becomes too complex for one person, separate sections are often created and placed under a human resource executive. These sections will typically perform tasks involving training and development, compensation and benefits, staffing, safety and health, and labor relations (if the firm is unionized), as depicted in Figure 1-5. Each human resource function may have a manager and staff reporting to the HR executive. The HR vice president works closely with top management in formulating corporate policy. This basic

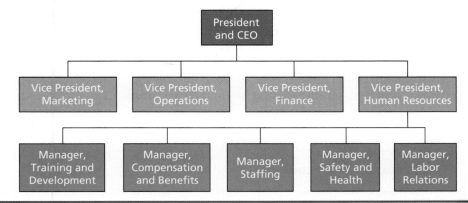

**The Human Resource Function in a Large Firm** Figure 1-5

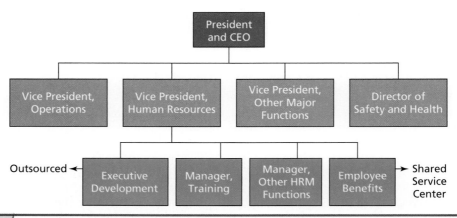

**Figure 1-6** A New HR Organizational Variation for Large Firms

arrangement is the traditional HR model and is used in many, if not most, large organizations today.

## An Evolving HR Organization for Large Firms

The HR organizational structure of large firms changes as firms outsource, use company service centers, and evolve in other ways to make HR more strategic. Regardless of an organization's design, the five human resource functions must still be accomplished. The organizational mission and corporate culture have a major impact in determining a specific HR organization. For example, the company depicted in Figure 1-6 has outsourced executive development, a function previously performed by the training department. As you can see, employee benefits has been placed with a shared service center. Safety and health has been removed from HR and, because of its importance in this particular firm, reports directly to the chief executive officer. Other HR tasks remain under the control of the HR vice president.

## PROFESSIONALIZATION OF HUMAN RESOURCE MANAGEMENT

**Profession**
A vocation characterized by the existence of a common body of knowledge and a recognized procedure for certifying practitioners.

A **profession** is a vocation characterized by the existence of a common body of knowledge and a procedure for certifying members of the profession. Performance standards are established by members of the profession rather than by outsiders; that is, the profession is self-regulated. Most professions also have effective representative organizations that permit members to exchange ideas of mutual concern. These characteristics apply to the field of human resources, and several well-known organizations serve the profession. Among the more prominent are the Society for Human Resource Management (SHRM); Human Resource Certification

Institute (HRCI); American Society for Training and Development (ASTD); the WorldatWork, The Professional Association for Compensation, Benefits, and Total Rewards (formerly the American Compensation Association); and the International Personnel Management Association (IPMA).

## Society for Human Resource Management

The largest national professional organization for individuals involved in all areas of human resource management is the Society for Human Resource Management (SHRM). The name reflects the increasingly important role that human resource management plays in the overall bottom line of organizations. The basic goals of the society include defining, maintaining, and improving standards of excellence in the practice of human resource management. Membership consists of 135,000 professionals, with more than 450 local chapters and numerous student chapters on university campuses across the country.[31] SHRM publishes a monthly journal, *HRMagazine* and a monthly newspaper, *HR News.*

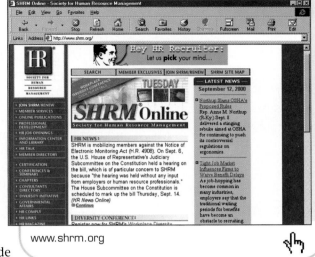

www.shrm.org

## Human Resource Certification Institute

One of the more significant developments in the field of HRM has been the establishment of the Human Resource Certification Institute (HRCI), an affiliate of SHRM.[32] Founded in 1976, HRCI's goal is to recognize human resource professionals through a certification program.[33] This program encourages human resource professionals to update their knowledge and skills continuously. Certification indicates they have mastered a validated common body of knowledge (see appendix at the end of the chapter). A number of years ago, Wiley Beavers, a former national president of SHRM, stated that human resource certification would:

▶ Allow students to focus on career directions earlier in their education.
▶ Provide sound guidelines for young practitioners in important HR areas.
▶ Encourage senior practitioners to update their knowledge.

## American Society for Training and Development

Founded in 1944, the American Society for Training and Development (ASTD) has grown to become the largest specialized professional organization in human resources. Its membership exceeds 55,000, and it has more than 155 local chapters.[34] The membership consists of individuals who are concerned specifically

▶ *HRCI*

**www.prenhall.com/mondy**

The Professional Certification Program in HR Management is for individuals seeking to expand their formal HR training.

HR WEB WISDOM

with training and development. The society publishes a monthly journal, *Training and Development,* to encourage its members to remain current in the field.

## WorldatWork: The Professional Association for Compensation, Benefits, and Total Rewards

WorldatWork was founded in 1955 as the American Compensation Association (ACA) and currently has a membership that exceeds 23,000.[35] This organization consists of managerial and human resource professionals who are responsible for the establishment, execution, administration, or application of compensation practices and policies in their organizations. The WorldatWork's quarterly journal contains information related to compensation issues and its certification program is well known for its quality.

## International Personnel Management Association

The International Personnel Management Association (IPMA) was founded in 1973 and currently has more than 6,500 members. This organization seeks to improve human resource practices by providing testing services, an advisory service, conferences, professional development programs, research, and publications. It sponsors seminars and workshops on various phases of public human resource administration. The organization's journal, *Public Personnel Management,* is published quarterly primarily for those involved in human resource administration in public agencies.[36]

## ETHICS AND HUMAN RESOURCE MANAGEMENT

**Ethics**
The discipline dealing with what is good and bad, or right and wrong, or with moral duty and obligation.

Professionalization of human resource management created the need for a uniform code of ethics. Today, more and more companies are concerned with values and ethics.[37] **Ethics** is the discipline dealing with what is good and bad, or right and wrong, or with moral duty and obligation. Every day, individuals who work in human resources must make decisions that have ethical implications.[38] Ethical dilemmas, such as whether a manager should recommend not hiring a woman applicant strictly because she will be working exclusively with men, occur somewhat frequently and need to be addressed correctly. These issues must be dealt with on the basis of what is ethically correct, not just what will benefit the organization most in the short run.

According to Louis V. Larimer, president of the Larimer Center for Ethical Leadership Inc., HR professionals must take responsibility for the design and implementation of ethics programs. Their first and foremost challenge is to educate and influence the organization's CEO to make ethics a priority. Progressive HR professionals must be the constant voice that calls for ethical commitment, vision, behavior, achievement, and courage. Basically, Larimer recommends that HR be the keeper of the corporate conscience, thereby reminding the organization of the need to err on the side of goodness.[39] When employees perceive that ethics/compliance programs were created to help guide behavior, as well as to establish and reinforce a shared set of company values that are rooted in the company culture, the programs are significantly more successful than ones employees believe were designed primarily for purposes of compliance.[40] Also, a recent study

As a member of the Society for Human Resource Management, I pledge myself to:

✴ Maintain the highest standards of professional and personal conduct.

✴ Strive for personal growth in the field of human resource management.

✴ Support the Society's goals and objectives for developing the human resource management profession.

✴ Encourage my employer to make the fair and equitable treatment of all employees a primary concern.

✴ Strive to make my employer profitable both in monetary terms and through the support and encouragement of effective employment practices.

✴ Instill in the employees and the public a sense of confidence about the conduct and intentions of my employer.

✴ Maintain loyalty to my employer and pursue its objectives in the ways that are consistent with the public interest.

✴ Uphold all laws and regulations relating to my employer's activities.

✴ Refrain from using my official positions, either regular or volunteer, to secure special privilege, gain, or benefit for myself.

✴ Maintain the confidentiality of privileged information.

✴ Improve public understanding of the role of human resource management.

This Code of Ethics for members of the Society for Human Resource Management has been adopted to promote and maintain the highest standards of personal conduct and professional standards among its members. Adherence to this code is required for membership in the Society and serves to assure public confidence in the integrity and service of human resource management professionals.

**SHRM Code of Ethics**  **Figure 1-7**

*Source:* Reprinted from *Who's Who in HR 1992 Directory,* 4. Copyright 1992, The Society for Human Resource Management, Alexandria, Virginia.

revealed a possible link between a company's overall performance and its ethical commitment.[41]

There are many kinds of ethical codes, and most professions have their own. An example is SHRM's Code of Ethics, shown in Figure 1-7. A growing number of firms are establishing ethical codes and communicating these codes to all employees. It is vitally important that those who work with human resource management understand those practices that are unacceptable and ensure that organizational members behave ethically in dealing with others.

## SCOPE OF THIS BOOK

Effective human resource management is crucial to the success of every organization. To be effective, managers must understand and competently practice human resource management. We designed this human resource management book to give you the following:

▶ An insight into the evolving role of human resource management in today's organizations and the impact of technology and global competition.

▶ An understanding of job analysis, human resource planning, recruitment (including Internet recruiting), and selection.

▶ An awareness of the importance of training and developing employees at all levels.

▶ An understanding of performance appraisal and its role in performance management.

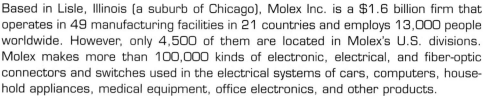

**Molex Selects HR Professionals**

Based in Lisle, Illinois (a suburb of Chicago), Molex Inc. is a $1.6 billion firm that operates in 49 manufacturing facilities in 21 countries and employs 13,000 people worldwide. However, only 4,500 of them are located in Molex's U.S. divisions. Molex makes more than 100,000 kinds of electronic, electrical, and fiber-optic connectors and switches used in the electrical systems of cars, computers, household appliances, medical equipment, office electronics, and other products.

Molex was one of the first U.S.–based firms to do away with the concept of a domestic and international title for HR staff. The assumption was, What's domestic if you're a global organization? This is the kind of attitude that pervades the business. Malou Roth, vice president of human resources for corporate training and development, believes that when you are running an international company, you really cannot or should not expect to have the same HR policies and programs all over the world. HR actually is the most localized of all the functions. "If you're looking at engineering, quality, manufacturing, finance, legal, or other functions, that may be so. However, HR is the one that's the most country-specific," says Roth.

Each local unit has unique needs, so the philosophy for hiring HR staff internationally has been to hire experienced HR professionals from other companies in the same country in which they have operations. Roth figures you need to hire people who know the language, have credibility, know the law, and know how to recruit. "You can't transfer someone in to do that," says Roth. "You can transfer a controller or a quality guy in from someplace else because those operations are much more standardized—but HR isn't." There are 80 HR staff members in 17 countries where Molex operates. "Having guidelines and policies in place is also important because when you hire HR managers from other companies, like Intel or IBM, you run the risk of having them want to implement the same types of policies from their former firms. While you can get good ideas from new blood, you have to protect the investment you've made in forming a culture and your company's way of doing things."[42]

> An appreciation of how compensation and benefits programs are formulated and administered.

> An understanding of safety and health factors as they affect the firm's profitability.

> An opportunity to view employee and labor relations from both unionized and union-free standpoints.

> An appreciation of the global dimension of human resource management.

Students often question whether the content of a book corresponds to the realities of the business world. In writing and revising this book, we have drawn heavily on the comments, observations, and experiences of human resource practitioners as well as our own extensive research efforts. We cite the human resource practices of leading business organizations to illustrate how theory can be applied in the real world. Our intent is to enable you to experience human resource management in action.

This book is organized into eight parts, as shown in Figure 1-8; combined, they provide a comprehensive view of human resource management. As you read this book, we hope you will be stimulated to increase your knowledge in this rapidly changing, expanding, and challenging field.

**Organization of This Book** **Figure 1-8**

# Summary

**1 Identify the human resource management functions.**
The human resource management functions include staffing, human resource development, compensation and benefits, safety and health, and employee and labor relations.

**2 Explain how organizations are adjusting to human resource restructuring trends.**
Shared service centers take routine, transaction-based activities that are dispersed throughout the organization and consolidate them in one place. Outsourcing is the process of transferring responsibility for an area of service and its objectives to an external provider. Line managers in certain firms are being used more frequently than before to deliver HR services.

**3 Explain the need for human resources to be a strategic partner.**
The increasing recognition of HR as a legitimate business unit has made it highly strategic in nature and increasingly critical to achieving corporate objectives. HR involvement in strategy is necessary to ensure that human resources support the firm's mission.

**4 Distinguish among executives, generalists, and specialists.**
Executives are top-level managers who report directly to the corporation's chief executive officer or the head of a major division. Generalists (who are often

executives) are persons who perform tasks in a wide variety of human resource–related areas. A specialist may be either a human resource executive, manager, or nonmanager who typically is concerned with only one of the functional areas of human resource management.

⑤ **Describe the changes that occur in the human resource function as a firm grows larger and more complex.**

As firms grow and become more complex, human resource functions become more complex and achieve greater importance. The basic functions remain essentially the same, but the company changes the approach it uses to accomplish its objectives.

⑥ **Explain the nature of the professionalization of human resources and the direction it has taken.**

A profession is characterized by the existence of a common body of knowledge and a procedure for certifying members of the profession. These characteristics apply to the field of human resources, and several well-known organizations serve the profession.

⑦ **Define *ethics* and relate ethics to human resource management.**

Ethics is the discipline dealing with what is good and bad, or right and wrong, or with moral duty and obligation. Individuals working with human resources face ethical (or unethical) decisions every day.

---

## ▶ Questions for Review

p. 13   1. What human resource management functions must be performed regardless of the organization's size?

p. 6   2. What are the current restructuring trends in human resource management?

3. How should HR act as a strategic partner?

4. Distinguish among human resource executives, generalists, and specialists.

5. How does the implementation of human resource functions change as a firm grows? Briefly describe each stage of development.

6. Define *profession*. Do you believe that the field of human resource management is a profession? Explain your answer.

p. 10   7. Define *ethics*. Why is ethics important to the field of human resource management?

TAKE IT TO THE NET

*We invite you to visit the Mondy homepage on the Prentice Hall Web site at* **www.prenhall.com/mondy**

*for updated information, Web-based exercises, and links to other HR-related sites.*

---

## ▶ Developing HRM Skills

### *An Experiential Exercise*

In many organizations, managers work with both individuals and groups. Cooperation is essential if human resource tasks are to be accomplished effectively.

The Blue-Green exercise provides students with the opportunity to experience some of the interrelationships that occur in a structured setting, such as an organization or work group.

The Blue-Green exercise is one of the best to use when working with a relatively large group. In fact, it is not recommended for groups of fewer than 12 persons. It has been successfully used with groups as large as 40. This exercise works equally well with groups of people who have been working together for some time and with heterogeneous groups whose members barely know one another.

Those who participate in this exercise usually find it quite enlightening. The total group will be divided into four subgroups of as nearly equal size as possible. These subgroups will be called *teams* and designated Team A-1, Team A-2, Team B-1, and Team B-2. Your instructor will provide the additional information necessary to participate. Enjoy the classic Blue-Green exercise.

## HRM INCIDENT 1 ◀

### *An Ethical Dilemma*

Amber Davis had recently graduated from college with a degree in general business. Amber was quite bright, although her grades did not reflect this. She had thoroughly enjoyed school—dating, tennis, swimming, and similar stimulating academic events. When she graduated from the university, she had not found a job. Her dad was extremely upset when he discovered this, and he took it upon himself to see that Amber became employed.

Amber's father, Allen Davis, was executive vice president of a medium-sized manufacturing firm. One of the people he contacted in seeking employment for Amber was Bill Garbo, the president of another firm in the area. Mr. Davis purchased many of his firm's supplies from Garbo's company. After telling Bill his problem, Allen was told to send Amber to Bill's office for an interview. Amber went, as instructed by her father, and before she left Bill's firm, she was surprised to learn that she had a job in the accounting department. Amber may have been lazy, but she certainly was not stupid. She realized that Bill had hired her because he hoped that his action would lead to future business from her father's company. Although Amber's work was not challenging, it paid better than the other jobs in the accounting department.

It did not take long for the employees in the department to discover the reason she had been hired; Amber told them. When a difficult job was assigned to Amber, she normally got one of the other employees to do it, implying that Mr. Garbo would be pleased with that person if he or she helped her out. She developed a pattern of coming in late, taking long lunch breaks, and leaving early. When the department manager attempted to reprimand her for these unorthodox activities, Amber would bring up the close relationship that her father had with the president of the firm. The department manager was at the end of his rope.

### Questions

1. From an ethical standpoint, how would you evaluate the merits of Mr. Garbo employing Amber? Discuss.
2. Now that she is employed, what course would you follow to address her on-the-job behavior?
3. Do you feel that a firm should have policies regarding practices such as hiring people like Amber? Discuss.

## HRM INCIDENT 2

*It Sure Is Different Now!*

Maxine Vincent is the new HR manager of Developmental Technologies, Inc., which was once the research and development division of a large long-distance phone service provider located in Philadelphia. Developmental Technologies, Inc. became a separate business entity so the long-distance provider could prepare for the competitive changes resulting from the deregulation of telecommunication services. Maxine was the assistant to the vice president of HR for the long-distance carrier before the reorganization, so she believed she was well prepared to deal with her new responsibilities as manager. However, the new company does not have the unlimited resources of the older one; therefore, reducing operating costs is a necessity.

Although Maxine was not totally enthusiastic about the idea, outsourcing of certain HR functions appeared to be a solution. Even though Maxine had no previous experience with outsourcing, she believed that it would be one way of relieving the burden on her rather small staff. Just as she was to meet with potential outsourcing providers, her boss called to set up a meeting to discuss her role as a strategic partner in upper-level planning. This was the first Maxine had heard of being a strategic partner and she was both apprehensive and somewhat excited about the opportunity to influence the future direction of Developmental Technologies. Evidently, there would now be a new way of doing things.

### Questions

1. What human resource management function might Maxine outsource? Explain your answer.
2. What should be Maxine's role as a strategic partner?

## Notes

1. David Forman and Debra J. Cohen, "The SHRM Learning System," *Human Resource Management* 38 (Summer 1999): 155.
2. The key law in the area of health and safety is the Occupational Safety and Health Act of 1970. This act is discussed in Chapter 14.
3. Frank Swoboda, "Organized Labor Fights to Recover Strength," *The Washington Post* (October 12, 1999): E:1.
4. Lin Grensing-Pophal, "HR, HEAL THYSELF: Recognizing and Conquering on-the-Job Burnout," *HRMagazine* 44 (March1999): 82–88.
5. "Increased Investment in Human Resources Reaping Benefits for Most," *PR Newswire* (November 3, 1999): 1.
6. "HR's New Role: Creating Value," *HR Focus* 77 (January 2000): 14.
7. Carla Joinson, "Changing Shapes: As Organizations Evolve, HR's Form Follows Its Functions," *HRMagazine* 44 (March 1999): 40–48.
8. Reyer A. Swaak, "Are We Saying Good-bye to HR?" *Compensation & Benefits Review* 28 (September/October 1996): 32+.
9. Gillian Flynn, "Out of the Red, into the Blue," *Workforce* 79 (March 2000): 50–52.

10. Donna Keith and Rebecca Hirschfield, "The Benefits of Sharing," *HR Focus* 73 (September 1996): 15.

11. Stacy VanDerWall, "Strategic Outsourcing: A Structured Approach to Outsourcing Decisions and Initiatives," *HRMagazine* 44 (August 1999): 151–152.

12. Karen Bowman, "Benefits of Outsourcing: Entrusting Employees to a Service Provider," *Employee Benefit News* (April 15, 1999): 1.

13. Jennifer Laabs, "Are You Ready to Outsource Staffing?" *Workforce* 79 (April 2000): 56.

14. Joe Dysart, "Kick Your System Outside," *HRMagazine* 44 (August 1999): 114–122.

15. Joinson, "Changing Shapes."

16. "GartnerGroup's Dataquest Says U.S. Human Resources Outsourcing Market to Exceed $37 Billion in 2003," *Business Wire* (November 22, 1999): 1.

17. Jennifer J. Salopek, "Outsourcing, Insourcing, and In-Between Sourcing," *Training & Development* 52 (July 1998): 51–54+.

18. "RCMS: RCMS Brings 'Advantage' to HR Directors," *M2 PressWIRE* (March 12, 1999).

19. Patricia M. Buhler, "The Changing Role of HR: Partnering with Managers," *Supervision* 60 (June 1999): 16–18.

20. John Case, "HR Learns How to Open the Books in Pursuit of a Common Goal," *HRMagazine* 43 (May 1998): 70–76.

21. Lin Grensing-Pophal, "Taking Your Seat 'At the Table'," *HRMagazine* 44 (March 1999): 90–96.

22. Jac Fitz-Enz, "Top 10 Calculations for Your HRIS," *HR Focus* 75 (April 1998): S3.

23. Diana Kunde, "Cyber-Search: Etiquette Shifts as Job Seekers, Recruiters Head Online," *The Dallas Morning News* (February 3, 1999): 1D.

24. "New Study Finds That Human Resource Professionals Must 'Cross Train' to Break Boardroom Barriers," *Business Wire* (April 27, 1999): 1.

25. Donald McNerney, "Career Development: As HR Changes, so Do HR Career Paths," *HR Focus* 74 (February 1996): 1.

26. Elizabeth Sheley, "Share Your Worth," *HRMagazine* 41 (June 1996): 86.

27. Charlene Marmer Solomon, "Managing the HR Career of the 90's," *Personnel Journal* 73 (June 1994): 62–64+.

28. Richard L. Knowdell, "The 10 New Rules for Strategizing Your Career," *The Futurist* 32 (June 1998): 1.

29. David Snyder, "The Revolution in the Workplace: What's Happening to Our Jobs?" *The Futurist* 30 (March 1996): 8.

30. James Down, "Human Resources Takes a Strategic Role," *Executive Forum* (March 1997): 1.

31. SHRM Customer Service Team, Custsvc@SHRM.org, July 19, 2000.

32. Juanita F. Perry, "Accredited Professionals Are Better Prepared," *Personnel Administrator* 30 (December 1985): 48.

33. Details of the HRCI are shown in the Appendix to this chapter.

34. Tara E. Sheets, ed., and Sarah J. Peters, assoc. ed., *Encyclopedia of Associations*, 35th ed., vol. 1: National Organizations of the United States, Part 1 (Detroit: Gale Research Company, 1999): 808.

35. Ibid., 126.

36. Ibid., 127.

37. Elizabeth Bankowski, "Ethics Must Come from the Top Down," *Compensation And Benefits Review* 29 (March/April 1997): 25–26.

38. Lin Grensing-Pophal, "Walking the Tightrope, Balancing Risks and Gains in Making Judgment Calls on Ethics Issues, HR Needs to Balance the Organization's Fundamental Values, the Needs of Employees and the Bottom Line," *HRMagazine* 43 (October 1, 1998): 112–119.

39. Louis V. Larimer, "Reflections on Ethics and Integrity," *HR Focus* 74 (April 1997): 5.

40. "Beware the Bad Ethics Program," *HR Focus* 76 (July 1999): 5.

41. Louisa Wah, "Ethics Linked to Financial Performance," *Management Review* 88 (July/August 1999): 7.

42. Jennifer Laabs, "Molex Makes Global HR Look Easy," *Workforce* 78 (March 1999): 42–46.

# PROFESSIONAL CERTIFICATION

The Human Resource Certification Institute (HRCI) is an affiliate of the Society for Human Resource Management. Since its inception in 1976, the HRCI has granted certification to many human resource professionals.

The Human Resource Certification Institute program provides for two levels of certification: Professional in Human Resources (PHR), and Senior Professional in Human Resources (SPHR). These two levels recognize degrees of expertise and responsibility.

## ELIGIBILITY

The HRCI grants certification after an applicant has:

1. verified current professional exempt-level experience in the HR field as either a practitioner, educator, researcher, or consultant, and
2. passed a comprehensive written examination to demonstrate mastery of knowledge.

**To earn either the Professional in Human Resources (PHR) or the Senior Professional in Human Resources (SPHR) certification, candidates must have two (2) years of HR exempt-level experience and pass a comprehensive examination.** The PHR examination focuses more on technical/operational aspects of HR, whereas the SPHR examination focuses more on strategic/HR policy issues.

Candidates may select the level of certification they feel best represents their mastery of the HR body of knowledge. Candidate performance has shown that appropriate HR experience and educational background contribute significantly to success on the examinations. It is strongly recommended that candidates attempting the PHR exam have two to four years of HR exempt-level experience. Likewise, it is strongly recommended that candidates attempting the SPHR examination have six to eight years of HR exempt-level experience. Success depends on mastery of the entire body of HR knowledge as reflected in the Content Outline shown later in this appendix. Therefore, candidates should carefully assess their qualifications, using the previous guidelines, prior to selecting the level of certification desired.

**Note:** Students are allowed to take the PHR examination within one year of graduation even if they do not have the required experience. If they pass the exam, they receive notification of the results. They then have five years in which to complete the two-year experience requirement for certification. They receive the PHR certification when they submit evidence of meeting the work experience requirements.

## DEFINITIONS

The credentialing program established and administered by the HRCI is intended for those professionals who are currently working in the field. While the work need not always be exclusively in the HR field, it is expected that work in the field be the dominating thrust. Therefore, the following general definitions apply:

*Practitioner:* One whose duties are those normally found in the typical HR/Personnel activity.

*Educator:* One whose principal area of instruction is in the HR/Personnel field in an accredited institution of higher education.

*Researcher:* One whose research activities are restricted primarily to the HR/Personnel field.

*Consultant:* One whose consulting activities are predominantly in the HR/Personnel field.

The HRCI defines professional HR exempt-level experience as "work that would meet the test for 'exempt' as defined by the Fair Labor Standards Act and its amendments."

## EXAM COMPOSITION

## Functional Areas

1. Staffing
2. Human resource development
3. Compensation and benefits
4. Health, safety, and security
5. Employee and labor relations
6. Management practices
7. General employment practices

The content of HRCI's comprehensive examinations is divided up (by percentage) as follows:

| Functional Content Area | PHR Level | SPHR Level |
|---|---|---|
| Staffing | 19% | 15% |
| Human resource development | 11% | 12% |
| Compensation and benefits | 19% | 15% |
| Employee and labor relations | 11% | 14% |
| Health, safety, and security | 6% | 6% |
| Management practices | 15% | 21% |
| General employment practices | 19% | 17% |

In addition:

- Both exams have a four-hour time limit.
- Both exams have 250 multiple-choice questions, with each question having four possible answers.
- Passing or failing is based on the examinees' scaled score for the total test. A scaled score of at least 500 is needed to pass.
- Unanswered questions are counted as incorrect.

## Recertification

Certification is earned by individuals who demonstrate their mastery of the defined body of knowledge. The human resources field, however, is not static. Rapid changes require new and more sophisticated knowledge and behaviors by human resource professionals who wish to grow and develop with their field. Recertification is a method that certified individuals can use to demonstrate their accomplishments in keeping abreast of these changes and to update their knowledge in the field.

Recertification is required within three years of certification. Each subsequent recertification period is also three years. There are two ways to become recertified. Testing is one method. The other method involves continuing one's educational and professional experience.

Certification examinations are given on the first Saturday of each May and December at designated test sites. Applications must be submitted at least 10 weeks in advance of the examination date. For additional certification information, contact the Human Resource Certification Institute, 1800 Duke Street, Alexandria, VA 22314 (703) 548-3440. Fax: (703) 836-0367; TDD (703) 548-6999; E-mail: hrci@shrm.org at HRCI homepage: www.shrm.org/hrci

The video cases you will be seeing in each of the remaining parts of this text show realistic human resource situations that many managers face daily. Each case is accompanied by questions that will help you focus on the cases' relevant points, and in answering them you will apply some of the principles and concepts about which you are learning. You may be asked to provide written responses or to discuss the situations in class.

You should not be surprised if everyone in your class or discussion group does not come up with the same solution. Remember that in many interpersonal situations such as you'll see in these videos, there are no absolute right or wrong answers. Your goals in working with these cases are to broaden your experience in tackling human-resource problem solving, to widen the range of issues you feel comfortable addressing, and to test possible solutions to typical human resource situations.

With one exception, the cases deal with human resource challenges faced by the management of Quicktakes, a small television production company that produces short films and videos for corporate and entrepreneurial clients.

The one exception is the case for Part 6, which explores the issue of job stress in the context of another small company that operates a fictitious Web site called allaboutself.com.

As you watch each video, you might want to take a few notes about the issues in each case, and the actions taken by each of the people involved in the problem. Look for clues to the origin of the problem, and see whether you can determine the advantages and disadvantages of the manager's attempted solution. Each set of questions will ask you to critique the solution and, if you can, propose a better one.

Here is a brief description of the upcoming cases.

### Part 2—The Legal Aspects of HRM
An employee complains of sexual harassment by a fellow worker.

### Part 3—Staffing
A manager interviews a candidate for a job opening.

### Part 4—Human Resource Development
A manager must give an employee a negative performance review.

### Part 5—Compensation and Benefits
An employee unexpectedly asks for an unscheduled raise.

### Part 6—Safety and Health
An entrepreneur feels stress when an employee turns in inadequate work.

### Part 7—Employee and Labor Relations
A manager suspends a union worker, who threatens to file a grievance.

### Part 8—Operating in a Global Environment
The European employee of a firm expects differential treatment.

Part Two

*The Environment and Legal Aspects of Human Resource Management*

##  Objectives

- Describe the dynamics of the human resource management environment.
- Identify the external environmental factors that affect human resource management.
- Distinguish between a proactive and a reactive response to the external environment.
- Explain internal environmental factors.
- Describe the diverse workforce that management now confronts.
- Describe human resource management and the small business.
- Define *corporate culture*.

chapter
chapterchapterchapterchapterchapterchapter

2

# The Environment of Human Resource Management

s Wayne Simmons, vice president of human resources for Lone Star Manufacturing, returned to his office from the weekly executive staff meeting, he was visibly disturbed. Lone Star, a producer of high-quality telecommunications equipment, is headquartered in Longview, Texas, and has manufacturing plants throughout Texas, Louisiana, and Oklahoma. Wayne had just heard a rumor that an overseas firm had developed a new manufacturing process that had the potential to cut costs substantially. Should this report prove true, customers might switch to the cheaper product. The three plants in the Longline Division that produce similar products would then be in serious trouble.

The Longline Division had been expanding rapidly, but Wayne knew that demand for Lone Star's products was far from automatic. If the new technology was superior, he also knew Lone Star might have to

##  Key Terms

| | | |
|---|---|---|
| External environment 31 | Reactive response 35 | Informal organization 38 |
| Social responsibility 32 | Internal environment 36 | Diversity 39 |
| Union 33 | Mission 36 | Dual-career family 41 |
| Shareholders 33 | Policy 37 | |
| Proactive response 35 | Corporate culture 37 | |

cut back production severely or even close the three plants in the Longline Division. Lone Star's mission has always been to produce high-quality telecommunications equipment using older technology. Lone Star's plants were constructed during the 1970s and the layouts were not sufficiently flexible to permit effective use of certain state-of-the-art equipment. Plant closings would have a devastating effect on many longtime employees. A few workers could be transferred to other locations, but most would have to be laid off. Thus, Wayne is now keenly aware of how the external environment can impact the operations of Lone Star Manufacturing.

**I**n this chapter, we first discuss the dynamics of the human resource management environment. Then, we describe the means by which specific external environmental factors can influence human resource management and distinguish between a proactive and reactive response to the external environment. Next, we describe the internal environmental factors, the diverse workforce that management now confronts, and human resource management in the small business environment. We end the chapter with a discussion of corporate culture.

## THE DYNAMIC HUMAN RESOURCE MANAGEMENT ENVIRONMENT

Many interrelated factors affect human resource management. Such factors are part of either the firm's external environment or its internal environment (see Figure 2-1). The firm often has little, if any, control over how the external environment affects management of its human resources. These factors impinge on the organization from outside its boundaries. Moreover, important factors within the firm itself, especially corporate culture, also have an impact on how the firm manages its human resources.

Certain interrelationships tend to complicate the management of human resources. For instance, human resource professionals constantly work with people who represent all organizational levels and functional areas. Therefore, they must recognize the different perspectives that these individuals bring to HRM if they are to perform their human resource tasks properly.

Understanding the many interrelationships implied in Figure 2-1 is essential in order for the human resource professional to help other managers resolve issues and problems. For instance, a production manager may want to give a substantial pay raise to a particular employee. The human resource manager may know that this employee does an exceptional job; he or she should also be aware that granting the raise may affect pay practices in the production department and set a precedent for the entire firm. The human resource manager may have to explain to the production manager that such an action is not an isolated decision. If the firm is not in danger of losing a top-notch employee with critical skills, it may

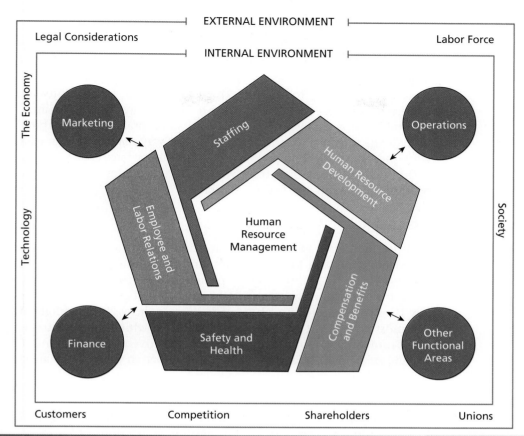

The Environments of Human Resource Management    **Figure 2-1**

consider alternative means of rewarding the employee for superior performance, without upsetting the organization's reward system. One solution may be for the human resource manager to point to a higher paying position the employee is qualified to fill.

Whatever the case, the implications of a particular act must be considered in light of its potential impact on a department and the entire organization. Those involved in human resource management must realize the overwhelming importance of the big picture, rather than concentrating on a narrow phase of the company's operation. The basic HRM tasks remain essentially the same regardless of the situation; however, the manner in which those tasks are accomplished may be altered substantially by factors in the external environment. Wayne Simmons is fully aware of the external environment, particularly the overall impact of new technology on the Longline Division.

## EXTERNAL ENVIRONMENT FACTORS

Factors outside its boundaries that affect a firm's human resources make up the **external environment**. As illustrated in Figure 2-1, external factors include the labor force, legal considerations, society, unions, shareholders, competition, customers, technology, and the economy. Each factor, either separately or in combination with others, can place constraints on how human resource management tasks are accomplished.

**External environment**
Factors outside its boundaries that affect a firm's human resources.

## The Labor Force

The labor force is a pool of individuals external to the firm from which the organization obtains its workers. The capabilities of a firm's employees determine to a large extent how well the organization can perform its mission. Since new employees are hired from outside the firm, the labor force is considered an external environmental factor. The labor force is always changing, and these shifts inevitably cause changes in the workforce of an organization. In turn, changes in individuals within an organization affect the way management must deal with its workforce. In short, changes in the country's labor force create dynamic situations within organizations. This topic will be discussed later in this chapter under the heading "Managing the Diverse Workforce."

## Legal Considerations

Another significant external force affecting human resource management relates to federal, state, and local legislation and the many court decisions interpreting this legislation. In addition, many presidential executive orders have had a major impact on human resource management. These legal considerations affect virtually the entire spectrum of human resource policies. We highlight in Chapter 3 the most significant of these considerations, which affect equal employment opportunity. Laws, court decisions, and executive orders affecting other human resource management activities will be described in the appropriate chapters.

## Society

Society may also exert pressure on human resource management. The public is no longer content to accept, without question, the actions of business. Individuals and special-interest groups have found that they can effect change through their voices, votes, and other actions. The influence of activists is obvious by the large number of regulatory laws that have been passed since the early 1960s. To remain acceptable to the general public, a firm must accomplish its purpose while complying with societal norms.

**Social responsibility**
The implied, enforced, or felt obligation of managers, acting in their official capacities, to serve or protect the interests of groups other than themselves.

The attitudes and beliefs of the general public can affect the firm's behavior, because those attitudes and beliefs often directly affect profitability. When a corporation behaves as if it has a conscience, it is said to be socially responsible. **Social responsibility** is an implied, enforced, or felt obligation of managers, acting in their official capacities, to serve or protect the interests of groups other than themselves. Many companies develop patterns of concern for moral and social issues. Wayne Simmons was aware, and apparently concerned about, the impact that the possible closure of the three plants in the Longline Division would have on their employees. Companies can show social concern through policy statements, their practices, and leadership over time. Open-door policies, grievance procedures, and employee benefit programs often stem as much from a desire to do what is right as from a concern for productivity and avoidance of strife.

You may well ask, "Why should a business be concerned with the welfare of society? Its goal is to make a profit and grow." Obviously, a business must make a profit over the long run if it is to survive. But you should also remember another basic point: If a firm does not satisfy society's needs, then it will ultimately cease to exist. A firm operates by public consent to satisfy society's requirements. The organization is a member of the community in which it operates. Just as citizens work to improve the quality of life in their community, the organization should also respect and work with the other members of its community. For instance, a high unemployment rate among a certain minority group may exist within the firm's service area. A philosophy of hiring workers who are capable of being trained, in addition to qualified applicants, may help to reduce unemployment for that minority group. In the long run, this philosophy will certainly enhance the firm's image and may actually improve profitability.

In recent years, companies have been struggling with how they will compete in the new global environment. They are constantly looking for new ideas that will make them more efficient. In view of this new environment, some are questioning whether or not efficiency and social responsibility can be married. For example, IBM once had the reputation of never laying off workers. This reputation was shattered when many workers were laid off in the early 1990s. In view of these layoffs, IBM's reputation for being socially responsible may have been tarnished. Firms may need to carefully consider costs and benefits to determine if a certain socially responsible action actually assists them in remaining competitive in this ever-expanding global environment. Only time will tell how the concept of social responsibility fares in this new environment.

## Unions

Wage levels, benefits, and working conditions for millions of employees now reflect decisions made jointly by unions and management. A **union** is a group of employees who have joined together for the purpose of dealing with their employer. Unions are treated as an environmental factor because, essentially, they become a third party when dealing with the company. In a unionized organization, the union rather than the individual employee negotiates an agreement with management. As mentioned in Chapter 1, union membership as a percentage of the nonagricultural workforce slipped from 33 percent in 1955 to 13.9 in 1999. When government employees are subtracted, unions represent about 9.5 percent of the private industry workforce.[1] If this trend continues, and if the power and influence of unions decline further, the emphasis will likely shift further to a human resource system that deals directly with the individual worker and his or her needs.[2]

**Union**
A group of employees who have joined together for the purpose of dealing collectively with their employer.

## Shareholders

The owners of a corporation are called **shareholders**. Because shareholders, or stockholders, have invested money in the firm, they may at times challenge programs considered by management to be beneficial to the organization. Managers may be forced to justify the merits of a particular program in terms of how it will affect future projects, costs, revenues, and profits. For instance, $500,000 spent on implementing a management development program may require more justification than simply stating that "managers should become more open and adaptive to the needs of employees." Shareholders are concerned with how such expenditure decisions will increase revenues or decrease costs. Thus, management must be prepared to explain the merits of a particular program in terms of its economic costs and benefits. Stockholders are wielding increasing influence. They have even filed lawsuits against managers and directors, claiming they failed to look out for stockholder interests.

**Shareholders**
The owners of a corporation.

## Competition

Firms may face intense competition in both their product or service and labor markets. Unless an organization is in the unusual position of monopolizing the market it serves, other firms will be producing similar products or services. A firm must maintain a supply of competent employees if it is to succeed, grow, and

WANTED
• $1,000 in cash less taxes, for the referral and subsequent hire of all exempt engineers and any technically related positions of non-exempt Grade 9 or above; i.e., technical writers, draftspersons, etc.
• New employee must be employed 180 days before "bounty" is paid.
• In order to qualify, the person referred must indicate the Ampex employee's name on the Ampex employment application under the column headed "Referred By," and Ampex must be free of any obligation to pay an agency or any other fee upon employment of the person.
• Non-eligible persons for this "bounty" are Department Managers, exempt Personnel Department employees, and managers directly involved in the selection of the person for the opening to be filled.
$1,000
REWARD

**Figure 2-2** A Recruitment Poster

prosper. But other organizations are also striving for that same objective. A firm's major task is to ensure it obtains and retains a sufficient number of employees in various career fields to allow the firm to compete effectively. A bidding war often results when competitors attempt to fill certain critical positions in their firms. Because of the strategic nature of their needs, firms are sometimes forced to resort to unusual means to recruit and retain such employees. The poster shown in Figure 2-2 exemplifies the extreme approaches some organizations have used to recruit qualified workers. In today's tight job market, bonuses are often paid.[3]

## Customers

The people who actually use a firm's goods and services also are part of its external environment. Because sales are crucial to the firm's survival, management has the task of ensuring that its employment practices do not antagonize the customers it serves. Customers constantly demand high-quality products and after-purchase service. Therefore, a firm's workforce should be capable of providing top-quality goods and services. Sales are often lost or gained because of variances in product quality and follow-up service. These conditions relate directly to the skills, qualifications, and motivations of the organization's employees.

## Technology

The rate of technological change is accelerating, and as a result, few firms operate today as they did even a decade ago. In fact, corporate leaders are putting more emphasis on recruiting individuals with an understanding of computers and information systems.[4] Of major concern to those dealing with human resource management is the effect that technological changes have had, and will have, on businesses. Products that were not envisioned only a few years ago are now being mass-produced, substantially enlarging the tasks of all managers. New skills are typically not in large supply; recruiting qualified individuals in areas that demand them is often difficult. Technology is changing so rapidly that it is difficult to keep track of the new jobs associated with it.[5] Today, computer-literacy skills are required for most jobs.

Only a few years ago, the lack of computer-literacy skills was said to separate the haves and have-nots. Now the *digital divide* is the term used to describe the difference between households with Internet access and those without. Some believe that those without Internet access are limited from gaining information available on the Web, and that the United States is split between technological haves and have-nots.[6]

The trend toward a service economy affects the type and amount of technology needed. The Bureau of Labor Statistics has projected that service-producing establishments will account for virtually all of the job growth over the next 10 years. Services jobs are expected to increase by 3.9 million over the next decade. Among occupations, professional specialties will increase the fastest and add the most jobs, about 5.3 million by 2008. These two groups are at the opposite ends of the educational attainment and earnings spectrum.[7]

## The Economy

The economy of the nation, on the whole and in its various segments, is a major environmental factor affecting human resource management. As a generalization, when the economy is booming, recruiting qualified workers is more difficult than in less prosperous times. This was the case in the spring of 2000 when the national unemployment rate was under 4 percent. On the other hand, when a downturn is experienced, more applicants are typically available. To complicate this situation even further, one segment of the country may be experiencing a downturn, another a slow recovery, and another a boom.

## THE EXTERNAL ENVIRONMENT: A PROACTIVE VERSUS REACTIVE RESPONSE

Managers approach changes in the external environment proactively or reactively. A **proactive response** involves taking action in anticipation of environmental changes. A **reactive response** involves simply responding to environmental changes after they occur. For example, while the Americans with Disabilities Act (ADA) was weaving its way through Congress, some companies had already implemented its anticipated provisions. Managers of these companies were being proactive. Those who waited until the law went into effect to even plan the required changes were being reactive.

**Proactive response**
Taking action in anticipation of environmental changes.

**Reactive response**
Simply reacting to environmental changes after they occur.

Organizations exhibit varying degrees of proactive and reactive behavior. When the Occupational Health and Safety Act (OSHA) was enacted, some firms did only what the letter of the law required. Others went far beyond that and allocated significant resources to create a safe and healthful environment for employees. The response to Title VII of the Civil Rights Act of 1964 provides another example. Prior to passage of that law, many firms were inactive with regard to equal employment opportunity. However, many of these same companies later became aggressive in promoting equal opportunity. Convinced that the national agenda was to eliminate discrimination in employment based on race, color, sex, religion, or national origin, they went beyond the explicit requirements of the law. Those dealing with human resource management discovered that a proactive attitude leads to performance improvements and reduces the level of damaging discrimination suits.[8]

A firm may be either reactive or proactive in any matter, legal or otherwise. For example, reactive managers may demonstrate concern for employee welfare only after a union-organizing attempt starts. Proactive managers try to spot early signs of discontent and correct the causes of that discontent before matters get out of hand. Proactive managers prevent customer complaints rather than *handle* them. In the markets they serve, proactive managers tend to set the prices competitors must match. They install scrubbers on exhaust stacks before environmental groups begin picketing the plant and before federal regulators file suit. In all matters, proactive managers initiate rather than respond. When an unanticipated environmental change occurs, proactive managers go beyond what the change forces them to do.

## THE INTERNAL ENVIRONMENT

**Internal environment**
Factors inside a firm's boundaries that affect its human resources.

As with the external environment, the internal environment also exerts considerable pressure on human resource management (refer back to Figure 2-1). Factors inside its boundaries that affect a firm's human resources comprise the **internal environment**. The primary internal factors include the firm's mission, policies, corporate culture, management style of upper managers, employees, the informal organization, other units of the organization, and the labor-management agreement. These factors have a major impact on determining the interaction between HRM and other departments within the organization. This interaction has a major effect on overall organizational productivity, so it is vital that the interaction be positive and supportive of the firm's mission.

### Mission

**Mission**
The organization's continuing purpose or reason for being.

**Mission** is the organization's continuing purpose or reason for being. Each management level should operate with a clear understanding of the firm's mission. In fact, each organizational unit (division, plant, department) should clearly understand objectives that coincide with that mission. The specific company mission must be regarded as a major internal factor that affects the tasks of human resource management. Consider two companies, each having a broadly based mission, and envision how certain tasks might differ from one firm to the other. Company A's goal is to be an industry leader in technological advances. Its growth occurs through the pioneering of new products and processes. Company B's goal is one of conservative growth, which involves little risk taking. Only after another company's product or process has proven itself in the marketplace will Company B commit itself. Lone Star's Longline Division is an example of this type of company.

Company A needs a creative environment to encourage new ideas. Highly skilled workers must be recruited to foster technological advancements. Constant attention to workforce training and development is essential. A compensation program designed to retain and motivate the most productive employees is especially important. The basic tasks of human resource management are the same for Company B, but the mission dictates that they be altered somewhat. A different kind of workforce will likely be needed. Highly creative individuals may not want to work for Company B. Perhaps because the mission encourages little risk taking, most of the major decisions will be made at higher levels in the organization. Thus, management development at lower levels in the organization may receive less emphasis. The compensation program may reflect the different requirements of this particular workforce. As this comparison indicates, a human resource manager must clearly understand the company's mission.

## Policies

A **policy** is a predetermined guide established to provide direction in decision making. As guides, rather than as hard-and-fast rules, policies are somewhat flexible, requiring interpretation and judgment in their use. They can exert significant influence on how managers accomplish their jobs. For instance, many firms have an open-door policy that permits an employee to take a problem to the next higher level in the organization if it can't be solved by the immediate supervisor. Knowing that their subordinates can take problems to a higher echelon tends to encourage supervisors to try harder to resolve problems at their levels.

**Policy**
A predetermined guide established to provide direction in decision making.

Many larger firms have policies related to every major operational area. Although policies are established for marketing, production, and finance, the largest number of policies often relate to human resource management. Some potential policy statements that affect human resource management are as follows:

- Provide employees with a safe place to work.
- Encourage all employees to achieve as much of their human potential as possible.
- Provide compensation that will encourage a high level of productivity in both quality and quantity.
- Ensure that current employees are considered first for any vacant position for which they may be qualified.

Because policies have a degree of flexibility, the manager is not necessarily required to adhere strictly to the policy statement. Often the tone of a policy guides managers as much as the actual words. Consider, for instance, a policy that ensures that "all members of the labor force have equal opportunity for employment." This policy implies more than merely adhering to certain laws and government regulations. Confronted with this policy, the human resource manager will likely do more than merely conform to the law. Perhaps the manager will initiate a training program to permit the hiring of minorities or women who are not immediately qualified to perform available jobs. Rather than just seeking qualified applicants, a firm that actively implements this policy goes beyond the minimum required by law.

## Corporate Culture

When being considered as an internal environmental factor affecting human resource management, corporate culture refers to the firm's social and psychological climate. **Corporate culture** is defined as the system of shared values,

**Corporate culture**
The system of shared values, beliefs, and habits within an organization that interacts with the formal structure to produce behavioral norms.

beliefs, and habits within an organization that interacts with the formal structure to produce behavioral norms.[9] Managers can, and should, determine the kind of corporate culture they wish to work with and strive to make sure that this kind of culture develops. This topic will be discussed later in the chapter.

## Management Style of Upper Managers

Closely related to corporate culture is the way in which the attitudes and preferences of one's superiors affect how a job is done. This situation deserves special emphasis here because of the problems that can result if the managerial style of upper-level managers differs from that of lower-level managers. In general, a lower-level manager must adapt to the style of the boss. It is hard to be open and considerate when the boss believes in just giving orders and having them followed. A lower-level manager's concerns about involving employees in decision making and giving them freedom may be seen as a lack of decisiveness. Even the company president must deal with the management style and attitudes of superiors—in this case, the board of directors. The president may be a risk taker and want to be aggressive in the marketplace, but the board may prefer a more conservative approach.

## Employees

Employees differ in many ways including their capabilities, attitudes, personal goals, and personalities. As a result, behavior that a manager finds effective with one worker may not be effective with another. In extreme cases, employees can be so different that it is virtually impossible for them to be managed as a group. In order to be effective, the manager must consider both individual and group differences. A supervisor of experienced workers, for instance, may pay less attention to the technical details of the job and more to encouraging group cooperation, while a supervisor of inexperienced workers may focus mainly on the technical aspects of the task.

## Informal Organization

New managers quickly learn that there are two organizations they must deal with in the firm: one formal, the other informal. The formal organization is usually described by an organizational chart and job descriptions. Managers know the official reporting relationships. But an informal organization exists alongside the formal one. The **informal organization** is the set of evolving relationships and patterns of human interaction within an organization that are not officially prescribed. Such informal relationships are quite powerful. Assume, for instance, that top management has expressed total commitment to equal employment opportunity. An all-male or all-white work group may still resist the assignment of women or blacks to the group. Unwanted workers may be ostracized or refused the usual friendly assistance in adapting to a new job. In extreme cases, derogatory jokes may be told within earshot of such employees. This kind of behavior places the supervisor in a difficult position, caught between a formal policy and aggressive action arising from the informal organization.

**Informal organization**
The set of evolving relationships and patterns of human interaction within an organization that are not officially prescribed.

## Other Units of the Organization

Managers must be keenly aware of interrelationships that exist among divisions or departments and should use such relationships to their best advantage. The human resource department helps maintain a competent workforce; the purchasing department buys materials and parts. Because one department precedes another in the flow of work, that department's output becomes the other department's input. Most managers soon discover that cooperation with other departments is necessary if the system is to work efficiently. Managers who fail to develop positive relationships with other managers may jeopardize the productivity of several departments.

## Labor-Management Agreement

In a unionized company, upper management typically negotiates labor-management agreements, but managers throughout the organization must implement the terms of the agreements. In most instances, agreements place restrictions on the manager's actions. For example, a manager may want to shift a maintenance worker to an operator's job temporarily, but if the labor-management agreement specifies the tasks that can and cannot be performed in each job, the supervisor may not be able to make the temporary assignment.

## MANAGING THE DIVERSE WORKFORCE

From McDonald's to Holiday Inn, AT&T to Levi Strauss, managers are learning not only to understand their kaleidoscopic workforce, but also to effectively manage diverse environments. Managing diversity presents new challenges in the workplace. Not only are more businesses expanding their operations overseas, but many workers in the United States are working alongside individuals whose cultures differ substantially from their own, as more ethnic minorities enter the workforce. Managers must be knowledgeable about common group characteristics to manage diversity effectively. Diversity is becoming a key hiring and retention tool for staff-starved companies, as well for international organizations that must meld workers from different backgrounds to achieve maximum productivity.[10]

**Diversity** refers to any perceived difference among people: age, functional specialty, profession, sexual orientation, geographic origin, lifestyle, tenure with the organization, or position.[11] Diversity aims to create workforces that mirror the populations and customers that organizations serve.[12] R. Roosevelt Thomas Jr., president of the American Institute for Managing Diversity, clarified some misconceptions about diversity in corporate America when he said, "People vary along an infinite number of possibilities." Thomas also believes, "They vary according to race and gender, but they also vary according to age, sexual orientation, and when they joined the company. Some workers are union members; some are not. Some are exempt; some are nonexempt. The variety is endless. Your definition has to be sufficiently broad to encompass everyone."[13]

In 1999, the U.S. labor force was 139 million people with a national unemployment rate of under 4 percent.[14] Size alone, however, does not tell the whole story. The labor force now includes more women and older persons than ever before. Employees with disabilities are being included in increasing numbers. Many immigrants from developing areas, especially Southeast Asia and Latin America, are joining the labor force. The challenge for managers in the coming decades will be to recognize that people with common, but different, characteristics from the mainstream often think differently, act differently, learn differently,

**Diversity**
Any perceived difference among people: age, functional specialty, profession, sexual orientation, geographic origin, lifestyle, tenure with the organization, or position.

and communicate differently. Because every person, culture, and business situation is unique, there are no simple rules for managing diversity, but diversity experts say that employees need to develop patience, open-mindedness, acceptance, and cultural awareness. Only by such measures can productivity be maximized.

## Single Parents and Working Mothers

The number of nontraditional, single-parent households in the United States is growing.[15] Since more than half of all marriages today end in divorce, this trend is expected to continue. Often, one or more children are involved. Of course, there are always widows and widowers who have children, as well, and there are some men and women who choose to raise children outside of wedlock.

Traditionally, child-care needs were viewed as being outside the realm of the business world—a responsibility workers had to bear and manage alone. This situation was particularly difficult for single parents, but even working parent couples often cannot afford a full-time live-in housekeeper. For many workers, child care has been managed with the help of family or friends. The need for alternative arrangements is evidenced by the fact that in 1950, only 12 percent of women with children under age six were in the labor force. Today, 63 percent of mothers of small children and 78 percent of mothers of school-aged children work outside the home.[16] Working mothers are increasingly likely to be primary caregivers for aging parents and relatives, as well as children.

Today, business has begun to see that providing child-care services and workplace flexibility may influence workers' choice of employers. Many companies have begun providing day care services for employees. Some companies located in the same building or facility provide joint day care service. Other companies, such as IBM, provide day care referral services. More and more companies provide paid maternity leave, and some offer paternity leave. Still other firms give time off for children's visits to doctors, which can be charged against the parents' sick leave or personal time. Managers need to be sensitive to the needs of working parents. At times, management also needs to be creative in accommodating this most valuable segment of the workforce.

▶ Diversity aims to create workforces that mirror the populations and customers that organizations serve.

## Women in Business

Women represent 11.9 percent of corporate officers (1,386 out of 11,681) at America's 500 largest companies.[17] However, the number of women in entry- and mid-level managerial positions has risen from 34 percent in 1983 to 46 percent in 1998, meaning many more women are in the pipeline to executive spots. Today, there are more than nine million women-owned businesses, up from 400,000 in 1972.[18] Because of the critical mass of talent, many believe that the first decade of the twenty-first century will be remembered as the decade that saw women en masse break through to upper-level management.

Because of the number of women who are entering the workforce, there is an increasing number of nontraditional households in the United States. These households include those headed by single parents and those in which both partners work full time. Many women, who formerly remained at home to care for children and the household, today need and want to work outside the home. If this valuable segment of the workforce is to be effectively utilized, organizations must fully recognize the importance of addressing work/family issues.

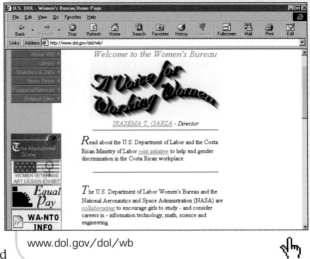

www.dol.gov/dol/wb

## Dual-Career Families

The increasing number of **dual-career families**, where both the husband and wife have jobs and family responsibilities, presents both challenges and opportunities for organizations. In fact, 53 percent of marriages are dual career.[19] In a study by the Conference Board, a New York business research group, more than 50 percent of employers said employees in their organizations have turned down relocations because of spouses' jobs and concerns about their children.[20] As a result of this trend, some firms have revised their policies against nepotism to allow both partners to work for the same company. Other firms have developed polices to assist the spouse of an employee who is transferred. When a firm wishes to transfer an employee to another location, the employee's spouse may be unwilling to give up a good position or may be unable to find an equivalent position in the new location. Some companies are offering assistance in finding a position for the spouse of a transferred employee.

As the number of dual-career families increases, organizations must become even more flexible. For example, cafeteria benefit plans may need to be more flexible for today's worker. With dual-career families, only one of the spouses might pick up a health care plan, and additional vacation might be selected by the second spouse. Some companies are actually designing their buildings to help dual-career families. At Procter & Gamble, the company specifically incorporated into

**Dual-career family**
A situation in which both husband and wife have jobs and family responsibilities.

▶ **Long-Distance Marriages**

The military is not the only career affected by long-distance marriages. These unconventional relationships are also occurring in corporate America as more women advance in their own careers. More couples are choosing to live in separate cities so both partners can get ahead. No one knows how many couples sustain long-distance relationships, but researchers at Loyola University in Chicago estimate about 6 to 8 percent of all job relocations today result in commuting relationships. "It would be so hard to be a trailing spouse. I would feel second class," says Kathleen Gilbert, 49, a family studies professor in Bloomington, Indiana. Her husband, Steven, is a professor in Kokomo, Indiana. "But it's emotionally challenging, like when my daughter was younger and came to me and said, 'Mom, did Dad divorce us?'" For 11 years they have sustained a long-distance marriage. Now, they see each other every weekend and keep in touch by e-mail. Some employers are taking steps to help by encouraging telecommuting or paying for occasional visits home.[21]

TRENDS & INNOVATIONS

the plant a dry cleaner, a shoe repair shop, and a cafeteria that prepares food that employees can take home at night, relieving them of the need to prepare an evening meal.[22]

Many dual-career families have established long-distance careers to ensure that both couples are able to advance in their careers. The shift is coming as job relocations create a mobile workforce, leaving many professional couples grappling with career tracks that diverge. More are choosing to live in separate cities so both partners can get ahead.[23] According to one survey, more than anything, dual-career families want flexibility in their workplaces and careers. Flexible hours topped the list, with cafeteria-style benefits, family leave, customizable career paths, the ability to telecommute from a home office, formal flexible work programs, and company-supported child care also being important.[24]

## Workers of Color

Workers of color (including Hispanics, African Americans, and Asians) are often stereotyped. At times, they encounter misunderstandings and expectations based on ethnic or cultural differences. Members of ethnic or racial groups are socialized within their particular culture. Many are socialized as members of two cultural groups—the dominant culture and their racial or ethnic culture. Ella Bell, professor of organizational behavior at MIT, refers to this dual membership as *biculturalism*. In her study of African American women, Bell identifies the stress of coping with membership in two cultures simultaneously as *bicultural stress*. She indicates that *role conflict*—competing roles from two cultures—and *role overload*—too many expectations to comfortably fulfill—are common characteristics of bicultural stress. Although these issues can be applied to other minority groups, they are particularly intense for women of color. This is because this group experiences dynamics affecting *both* minorities and women.[25]

Socialization in one's culture of origin can lead to misunderstandings in the workplace. This is particularly true when the manager relies solely on the cultural norms of the majority group. According to these norms, within the American culture it is acceptable, even considered positive, to publicly praise an individual for a job well done. However, in cultures that place primary value on group harmony and collective achievement, this method of rewarding an employee may cause emotional discomfort. Some employees feel that, if praised publicly, they will lose face within their group.

## Older Workers

The U.S. population is growing older, a trend that is expected to continue into the twenty-first century. The nation's workforce is hitting middle age, and the threat of a long-term labor shortage is developing. Nearly half of U.S. workers now fit in the 35–54 age group. By 2006, the median age of the labor force is expected to peak at 40.6 years. The first boomers will hit 65 in 2011, and if all of them retire between then and 2030, there will not be nearly enough new workers to take their places. Lower birthrates, coupled with job expansion, has created a serious shortfall of workers that could last through the first half of the twenty-first century. The growing segment of Americans 65 and older is widely considered to be one of the most important groups in the labor force. Since 1900, the percentage of Americans 65 and older has more than tripled.[26]

The United States's 20-year pattern of early retirement is about to reverse itself. Many older persons do not want to retire—or even slow down. *Workforce 2020* argues that older men and women will stay in the workforce longer. They will want to keep working, either for enjoyment or to supplement their pensions.[27] As the workforce grows older, its needs and interests may change. Many will become bored with their present careers and desire different challenges. The graying of the workforce has required some adjustments. Some older workers favor less demanding full-time jobs, others choose semiretirement, and still others prefer part-time work. Many of these individuals require retraining as they move through the various stages of their careers.

## People with Disabilities

Common disabilities include limited hearing or sight, limited mobility, mental or emotional deficiencies, and various nerve disorders. Such disabilities limit the amount or kind of work a person can do or make its achievement unusually difficult. In jobs for which they are qualified, however, disabled workers do as well as the unimpaired in terms of productivity, attendance, and average tenure. In fact, in certain high-turnover occupations, handicapped workers have had lower turnover rates. The Americans with Disabilities Act (ADA), passed in 1990, prohibits discrimination against *qualified individuals with disabilities* and will be discussed in detail in Chapter 3.

A serious barrier to effective employment of disabled persons is bias, or prejudice. Managers should examine their own biases and preconceived attitudes toward such individuals. Many individuals experience anxiety around workers with disabilities, especially if the disabilities are severe. Fellow workers may show pity or feel that a disabled worker is fragile. Some even show disgust. The manager can set the tone for proper treatment of workers with disabilities. If someone is unsure about how to act or how much help to offer, the disabled person should be asked for guidance. Managers must always strive to treat employees with disabilities as they treat other employees and must hold them accountable for achievement.

## Immigrants

The permitted level of legal immigration in the United States is one million per year.[28] Large numbers of immigrants from Asia and Latin America have settled in many parts of the United States. Some are highly skilled and well educated, and others are only minimally qualified and have little education. They have one thing in common: an eagerness to work. They have brought with them attitudes, values, and mores particular to their home country cultures.

After the end of hostilities in Vietnam, Vietnamese immigrants settled along the Mississippi, Louisiana, and Texas Gulf Coast. At about the same time, thousands of Thais fleeing the upheaval in Thailand came to the Boston area to work and live. New York's Puerto Rican community has long been an economic and political force there. Cubans who fled Castro's regime congregated in southern Florida, especially Miami. A flood of Mexicans and other Hispanics continues across the southern border of the United States. The Irish, the Poles, the Italians, and others who came here in past decades have long since assimilated into, and indeed become, the culture. Newer immigrants require time to adapt. Meanwhile, they generally take low-paying and menial jobs, live in substandard housing, and form enclaves where they cling to some semblance of the cultures they left.

Wherever they settle, members of these ethnic groups soon begin to become part of the regular workforce in certain occupations and break out of their isolation. They begin to adopt the English language and American customs. They learn new skills and adapt old skills to their new country. Human resource managers can place these individuals in jobs appropriate to their skills, with excellent results for the organization. As corporations employ more foreign nationals in this country, managers must work to understand the different cultures of their employees.

## Young Persons with Limited Education or Skills

A shortage of skilled workers is the greatest challenge facing U.S. businesses, according to a national survey. Additionally, the skills needed to maintain a competitive edge are outpacing the skill sets of their workforce.[29] Each year, thousands of young, unskilled workers are hired, especially during peak periods, such as holiday buying seasons. These workers generally have limited education, sometimes even less than a high school diploma. Those who have completed high school often find that their education hardly fits the work they are expected to do. Most, for example, lack familiarity with computers. Many of these young adults and teenagers have poor work habits; they tend to be tardy or absent more often than experienced or better-educated workers.

Although the negative attributes of these workers at times seem to outweigh the positive ones, they are a permanent part of the workforce. There are many jobs they can do well. And more jobs can be de-skilled, making it possible for lower-skilled workers to do them. A well-known example of de-skilling is McDonald's substitution of pictures for numbers on its cash register keys. Managers should also look for ways to train unskilled workers and to further their formal education.

## Educational Level of Employees

Another form of diversity now found in the workplace concerns the educational level of employees. The United States is becoming a bipolar country with regard to education, with a growing number of very educated people on one side and an alarming increase in the illiteracy rate on the other. These functionally illiterate people want to join the workforce.[30] Complicating this situation even more is the estimate that more than half of the new jobs created through 2005 will require

HR WEB WISDOM

▶ *Business Owner's Toolkit*

**www.prenhall.com/mondy**

Offers detailed instructions for the small business owner on how to hire, manage, and retain employees.

some education beyond high school.[31] Adding even more complexity is the trend in the workplace to empower workers. Empowerment is possible because of the advanced educational level required of the new workforce; however, those with limited education will be left out of this empowerment effort.[32]

## HUMAN RESOURCE MANAGEMENT AND THE SMALL BUSINESS

Every year, thousands of individuals—motivated by a desire to be their own boss, to earn a better income, and to realize the American dream—launch new business ventures. These individuals, often referred to as *entrepreneurs,* have been essential to the growth and vitality of the American free enterprise system. Entrepreneurs develop or recognize new products or business opportunities, secure the necessary start-up capital, and organize and operate the business. Most people who start their own businesses get a great deal of satisfaction from owning and managing them. Almost every large corporation began as a small business. If small businesses are successful, they can become big businesses.

There is no commonly agreed-on definition of what constitutes a small business. The Small Business Act of 1953 defines a small business as one that is independently owned and operated and not dominant in its field. Basically, a small business is one in which the owner-operator knows personally the key personnel. In most small businesses, this key group would ordinarily not exceed 12 to 15 people. Regardless of the specific definition of a small business, this category certainly makes up the overwhelming majority of business establishments in the United States. Smaller manufacturers—those with 500 employees or less—make up almost 99 percent of all U.S. manufacturers, which produce more than half of our value-added goods and employ about 12 million Americans. These firms generated about three-fourths of all new manufacturing jobs and account for 55 percent of all value-added manufacturing.[33]

Small businesses are ideal for implementing human resource initiatives because of their lack of bureaucracy and their ability to involve all individuals in the business process. Some aspects of the human resource function may actually be more significant in smaller firms than in larger ones. For instance, if the owner of a small business hires her first and only full-time salesperson and this individual promptly alienates the firm's customers, the business might actually fail. Also, no firm is too small to ignore the laws relating to human resource issues. The violation of some employment laws or acts carries heavy financial penalties whether the firm has 1, 15, 50, or 500 employees.

As will be seen in Chapter 3, small businesses are impacted substantially by federal, state, and local laws. In fact, the laws are structured in a manner that may have an uneven effect on small businesses. Typically, smaller companies have the same HR requirements as larger employers but often lack the experience, resources, or time needed to manage HR functions in-house.[34] Small businesses usually do not have a formal HR unit; therefore, line managers have to be aware of the many pitfalls associated with employment legislation. For instance, a business with 4 or more employees is covered under the Immigration Reform and Control Act. Under the Civil Rights Act, a company with 15 or more workers is covered, and the Americans with Disabilities Act applies to a company with 20 or more workers. Probably no company with fewer than 20 workers will have a formal human resource area; consequently, line managers will be required to ensure adherence to the law.

The environment of managers in large and small businesses is often quite different. Managers in large firms may be separated from top management by

**www.prenhall.com/mondy**

This Web site offers a wide array of surveys, software, videos, books, reprints, training, coaching, and consulting. These resources incorporate wisdom from more than 1,000 culture change applications.

numerous managerial layers. They may have difficulty seeing how they fit into the overall organization. They often know managers one or two layers above them, but seldom those higher up. In some large companies, supervisors are restricted by many written guidelines, and they may feel more loyalty to their workers than to upper management. Managers in small businesses often identify more closely with the goals of the firm. They can readily see how their efforts affect the firm's profits. In many instances, lower-level managers know the company executives personally. These supervisors know that the organization's success is closely tied to their own effectiveness.

## CORPORATE CULTURE

When beginning a new job, an employee may soon hear, "This is the way we do things around here." This bit of informal communication refers to something more formally known as corporate culture. As previously defined, corporate culture is the system of shared values, beliefs, and habits within an organization that interacts with the formal structure to produce behavioral norms. It is the pattern of basic assumptions, values, norms, and artifacts shared by organizational members. Corporate culture embodies the values and standards that guide people's behavior.[35] It determines the organization's overall direction. Corporate culture governs what the company stands for, how it allocates resources, its organizational structure, the systems it uses, the people it hires, the fit between jobs and people, and the results it recognizes and rewards. The culture also decides what the company defines as problems and opportunities and how it deals with them. As human resource executives become more like strategic partners, they will be major players in shaping the cultures of organizations.

www.healthyculture.com

Each individual forms perceptions of the job and organization over a period of time as he or she works under the general guidance of a superior and a set of organizational policies. For example, employees rapidly discover if the firm has a goal of having a diverse workplace. A firm's culture has an impact on employee job satisfaction as well as on the level and quality of employee performance. Each employee may assess the nature of an organization's culture differently, however. One person may perceive the culture negatively, and another may view it positively. Employees who are quite dissatisfied may even leave an organization in the hope of finding a more compatible culture.

Businesses are being forced to make many changes to stay competitive, including changes in corporate culture. A means of shaping corporate culture

When companies expand internationally, they typically take great care to study foreign markets and ways of competing with them. But they often forget to consider a very important element: how to maintain their corporate culture. Failure to consider bringing their corporate culture with them can affect a company's success in the international marketplace. "Companies need to be global today . . . and culture is a key way to bring about globalization," says Alan Brache, director of consulting services at the management consulting firm of Kepner-Tregoe Inc., Princeton, New Jersey. Letting everyone know that the corporate culture remains "serves as a moral compass for employees, but also allows far-flung employees to work in concert." According to Peter Pribilla, executive vice president and a member of the corporate executive committee at Siemens AG in Munich, Germany, which has 438,000 employees in more than 190 countries, "Our corporate culture expresses the shared identity of our entire global company. It binds us together and fosters all our activities. It helps ensure that we all pursue the same goals and that we all pull in the same direction, irrespective of our individual tasks and ranks."

A firm's culture may bind, but it must also be willing to adapt somewhat to the local culture. There are parts that must be distinctively local. A global company that successfully takes its culture across international borders usually ends up with a mosaic, not a melting pot. Gary Weaver, a professor of intercultural communications at American University in Washington, D.C., and executive director of its Intercultural Management Institute, believes that "the biggest problem that companies, particularly American companies, have is the assumption that organizational culture is all there is. [That it] somehow supersedes the local culture." Companies with global experience understand that while it is important to have one umbrella culture, there are and will always be differences in how that culture is carried out locally. According to Joan Gallagher, vice president of public affairs at the Gillette Company in Boston, Massachusetts, "We have been an international business since 1905 when we opened a manufacturing facility in Paris. We realize that our business is made up of many other businesses. We have a common core set of values, but we appreciate and understand the distinctions between our various subsidiaries."[36]

is through organizational development, a topic of Chapter 8. Companies must find ways to improve quality, increase speed of operations, and adopt a customer orientation. These changes are so fundamental that they must take root in a company's very essence, which means in its culture.[37] Corporate culture is an integral part of accomplishing an organization's mission and objectives.

Environmental factors, such as governmental action, workforce diversity, and global competition, often require a firm to change its culture and even make a clean break with the past. A diverse American workforce reflects the increasing diversity of the country's population. To maximize the advantages of diversity, particularly the talents of women and minorities, companies are trying to create cultures in which each employee has the opportunity to contribute and to advance in the organization based on excellent performance. Human resource professionals know that critical factors, such as retention, motivation and advancement, are highly dependent on how employees react to their firm's culture.

A survey of a group of managers with high representations of women and minorities identified several problem areas inherent in counterproductive cultures.[38]

- *Stereotypes.* The number one problem faced by women and minority managers is related to frustrations in coping with gender and race stereotypes.
- *Discrimination and harassment.* Whether experiencing discrimination personally or witnessing it, managers reported that such incidents caused them to question whether they fit in with the firm.
- *Exclusion and isolation.* Women and minority managers are often excluded from social activities and left out of informal communication networks.
- *Poor work-family balance.* Women managers expressed the view that "playing the game" often requires compromising personal values and conforming to the expectations of others.
- *Lack of career development.* Observing how few women and minority managers there are in the organization can result in concerns about opportunities for career advancement.

These problem areas illustrate legitimate concerns that organizations must consider in revamping their corporate cultures. Taken together, women and minorities represent the majority of employees entering the workforce. If the talents of these key groups are to be utilized to the fullest, corporate cultures of the future must reflect their needs.

## ▶ Summary

**①  Describe the dynamics of the human resource management environment.**

Understanding the many interrelationships that exist today is essential in order for the human resource professional to help other managers resolve issues and problems.

**②  Identify the external environmental factors that affect human resource management.**

External environmental factors include the labor force, legal considerations, society, unions, shareholders, competition, customers, technology, and the economy.

**③  Distinguish between a proactive and a reactive response to the external environment.**

A proactive response involves taking action in anticipation of environmental changes. A reactive response involves simply reacting to environmental changes after they occur.

**④  Explain internal environmental factors.**

The primary internal factors include the firm's mission, policies, corporate culture, management style of upper managers, employees, the informal organization, other units of the organization, and labor-management agreement.

**⑤  Describe the diverse workforce that management now confronts.**

Diversity refers to any perceived difference among people: age, functional specialty, profession, sexual orientation, geographic origin, lifestyle, tenure with the organization, or position. The workforce is made up of the following: dual-career families, workers of color, older workers, people with disabilities, immigrants, young persons with limited education or skills, and employees with varying educational levels.

**⑥  Describe human resource management and the small business.**

Some aspects of the human resource function may actually be more significant in smaller firms than in larger ones. Small businesses typically do not have a formal HR unit, and therefore, line managers have to be aware of the many pitfalls associated with employment legislation.

**7** **Define corporate culture.**
Corporate culture is the system of shared values, beliefs, and habits within an organization that interacts with the formal structure to produce behavioral norms.

## Questions for Review ◀

*P-3\* 1. What factors make up the external environment of human resource management? Briefly describe each of these factors.

*P-352* 2. Distinguish between a proactive and reactive response. Give an example of each.

*P-36* 3. What factors comprise the internal environment?

*P-39* 4. Define *diversity*.

5. What is the composition of the U.S. labor force?

6. How important is small business to our economy?

*P-46* 7. Define *corporate culture*. What effect could it have on human resource management?

*We invite you to visit the Mondy homepage on the Prentice Hall Web site at*

**www.prenhall.com/mondy**

*for updated information, Web-based exercises, and links to other HR-related sites.*

TAKE IT TO
THE NET

---

## Developing HRM Skills ◀

### An Experiential Exercise

Judy Flack has just been promoted from assistant to the human resource director to assistant general manager. Although the general manager, Jerry Connors, has mixed feelings about Judy, he did not directly oppose the promotion, but he did express his concerns to his immediate boss, Mr. Samuelson. Jerry's boss told him that he could *handle* her, and that the company needed more female managers. Now, Jerry and Judy are about to have their first meeting since the promotion, which should prove very interesting.

If you like a little excitement, you will enjoy this exercise. It is obvious that Jerry and Judy will disagree on many aspects of supervision, and that could lead to some interesting interactions. If you want to be in Jerry's shoes, or if you'd like to be Judy, volunteer quickly. Everyone else, observe carefully. Your instructor will provide the participants with additional information.

---

## HRM INCIDENT 1 ◀

### Downsizing

As the largest employer in Ouachita County, Arkansas, International Forest Products Company (IFP) is an important part of the local economy. Ouachita County is a mostly rural area of south-central Arkansas. It employs almost 10 percent of the local workforce, and few alternative job opportunities are available in the area.

Scott Wheeler, the human resource director at IFP, tells of a difficult decision he once had to make. According to Scott, everything was going along pretty well despite the economic recession, but he knew that sooner or later the company would be affected. "I got the word at a private meeting with the president, Mr. Deason, that we would have to cut the workforce by 30 percent on a crash basis. I was to get back to him within a week with a suggested plan. I knew that my plan would not be the final one, since the move was so major, but I knew that Mr. Deason was depending on me to provide at least a workable approach.

"First, I thought about how the union would react. Certainly, workers would have to be let go in order of seniority. The union would try to protect as many jobs as possible. I also knew that all management's actions during this period would be intensely scrutinized. We had to make sure that we had our act together.

"Then there was the impact on the surrounding community to consider. The economy of Ouachita County had not been in good shape recently. Aside from the influence on the individual workers who were laid off, I knew that our cutbacks would further depress the area's economy. I knew that there would be a number of government officials and civic leaders who would want to know how we were trying to minimize the harm done to the public in the area.

"We really had no choice but to make the cuts, I believed. First of all, I had no choice because Mr. Deason said that we were going to do it. Also, I had recently read a news account that one of our competitors, Johns Manville Corporation in West Monroe, Louisiana, had laid off several hundred workers in a cost-cutting move. To keep our sales from being further depressed, we had to ensure that our costs were just as low as those of our competitors. The wood products market is very competitive and a cost advantage of even 2 or 3 percent would allow competitors to take many of our customers.

"Finally, a major reason for the cutbacks was to protect the interests of our shareholders. A few years ago a shareholder group disrupted our annual meeting to insist that IFP make certain antipollution changes. In general, though, the shareholders seem to be more concerned with the return on their investment than with social responsibility. At our meeting, the president reminded me that, just like every other manager in the company, I should place the shareholders' interest above all else. I really was quite overwhelmed as I began to work up a personnel plan that would balance all of the conflicting interests that I knew about."

### Questions

1. List the elements in the company's environment that will affect Scott's suggested plan. How legitimate is the interest of each of these?
2. Is it true that Scott should be concerned first and foremost with protecting the interests of shareholders? Discuss.

---

▶ **HRM INCIDENT 2**

*Moving to Vance*

As Nathaniel Jones, vice president of strategic human resources for Automotive Elements & Design (AED), headquartered in New Jersey, walked to his office after the executive meeting, he realized that his job would be even busier than usual during the next nine months.

AED produces automotive trim and interior components for luxury automobiles. The company had recently signed an exclusive 10-year contract with a luxury sport utility manufacturer. Because of the just-in-time requirements of the manufacturer and the frequent interactions necessary between the manufacturer's design people and AED's design people, AED must locate a new design and production facility in Vance, Alabama.

Nathaniel and other members of the executive committee analyzed various alternative plans involving expansion of the current New Jersey facility to avoid building an additional production and design facility. However, the luxury sport utility manufacturer's requirements made the development of a new facility in Vance the only viable alternative.

In the year when the plant is completed, 300 new employees must be available and trained in the advanced methods utilized at the new high-tech design and production facility in Vance. In addition, 70 employees at the New Jersey facility will be transferred to Vance, necessitating their retraining. Nathaniel is responsible for ensuring that qualified new workers are hired and trained and that the transferred workers are retrained and are effectively integrated into the new workforce.

### Question

**1.** What external environmental factors confront Nathaniel?

## Notes

1. Bureau of Labor Statistics, 1999.
2. Frank Swoboda, "Organized Labor Fights to Recover Strength," *The Washington Post* (October 12, 1999): E:1.
3. "Companies Sign on to Signing Bonuses," *HR Focus* 76 (June 1999): 4.
4. Philip Davis, "What Computer Skills Do Employees Expect from Recent College Graduates?" *T.H.E. Journal* 25 *(Technological Horizons In Education)* (September 1997): 74.
5. Jonathan Sidener, "Pace of Net Technology Means Redefining Jobs Quickly," *The Arizona Republic* (May 14, 2000): S13.
6. "Digital Divide Likely to Widen," *United Press International* (December 9, 1999).
7. "Services Sector Jobs Will Dominate the Employment Landscape," *HR Focus* 77 (April 2000): 8.
8. Sinclair E. Hugh, "Observations from the Witness Stand," *HRMagazine* 39 (August 1994): 176.
9. R. Wayne Mondy and Shane R. Premeaux, *Management: Concepts, Practices, and Skills,* 8th ed. (Cincinnati, OH: Thompson Learning, 2000): 345.
10. "Diversity: A 'New' Tool for Retention," *HR Focus* 77 (June 2000): 14.
11. Matti F. Dobbs, "Managing Diversity: Lessons from the Private Sector," *Public Personnel Management* 25 (September 1996): 351.
12. Robert J. Grossman, "Is Diversity Working?" *HR Magazine* 45 (March, 2000): 46–50.
13. Barbara Ettorre, Donald J. McNerne, and Bob Smith, "HR's Shift to a Center of Influence," (American Management Association's 67th Annual Human Resources Conference and Exposition) *HR Focus* 73 (June 1996): 12.
14. Robert J. Samuelson, "Our Lifetime Job Prospects," *Newsweek* 133 (June 28, 1999): 33.
15. "Don't Forget the 9.8 Million Single Moms This Mother's Day; Match.Com Invites Friends and Family to 'Give a Single Mom a Break' on Saturday, May 8," *Business Wire* (April 29, 1999): 1.

16. "Mother's Day 1999 Finds 63% of Mothers of Small Children in the Workforce; Caregiving Still Goes Largely Unrecognized," *PR Newswire* (May 3, 1999).

17. "Few Women Corporate Officers Hold Key Line Officer Posts," *HR Focus* 77 (February 2000): 8.

18. Leah K. Glasheen and Susan L. Crowley, "More Women in Driver's Seat; But Barriers Hinder Many in Midcareer," *AARP Bulletin* (November 1999): 3.

19. Mary Beth Grover, "Financial Chemistry," *Forbes Magazine* (June 1999): 238.

20. Amy Saltzman, "A Family Transfer," *U.S. News & World Report* 122 (February 10, 1997): 60–62.

21. Stephanie Armour, "Married . . . with Separation: More Couples Live Apart as Careers Put Miles between Them," *USA Today* (November 23, 1998): 1B.

22. Joan Hamilton, Stephen Baker, and Bill Vlasic, "The New Workplace," *Business Week* (April 29, 1996): 106.

23. Armour, "Married . . . with Separation: More Couples Live Apart as Careers Put Miles between Them."

24. Robert Bellinger, "The Profession: New Survey Finds Men and Women Embrace Common Goals—Dual-Career Couples Crave Flexible Hours and Jobs," *Electronic Engineering Times* (October 1998): 121.

25. Ella Bell, "The Bicultural Life Experience of Career Oriented Black Women," *Journal of Organizational Behavior* 11 (November 1990): 459–478.

26. Jennifer Arend, "The Golden Years: Often Ignored, Mature Employees Are a Vital Part of the Workforce," *The Dallas Morning News* (August 11, 1999): 1D.

27. Michele Himmelberg, "Workforce Is Aging, Shrinking," *The Arizona Republic* (March 3, 1999): A1.

28. Yeh Ling-Ling, "Immigration Injures U.S. Environment," *Newsday* (March 1995): A42.

29. "Skills Gap Jeopardizing U.S. Companies' Ability to Compete; Executives Cite Shortage of Skilled Workers as the Greatest Challenge Facing U.S. Industry," *Business Wire* (May 5, 1999): 1.

30. Patricia Buhler, "Managing in the 90s," *Supervision* 58 (March 1997): 24.

31. Laurie J. Bassi, George Benson, and Scott Cheney, "The Top Ten Trends," *Training & Development* 50 (November 1996): 28.

32. Ibid.

33. Raymond G. Kammer, "Future of Small Manufacturers," *Congressional Testimony* (March 1999).

34. "HR Support for Small Business," *Business Wire* (March 1, 2000).

35. Mondy and Premeaux, *Management: Concepts, Practices, and Skills.*

36. Jenny McCune, "Exporting Corporate Culture," *Management Review* 88 (December 1999): 52–56.

37. Mondy and Premeaux, *Management: Concepts, Practices, and Skills.*

38. Benson Rosen and Kay Lovelace, "Fitting Square Pegs into Round Holes," *HRMagazine* 39 (January 1994): 86–93.

# 3

  objectivesobjectivesobjectives

## ▶ Objectives

- Identify the major laws affecting equal employment opportunity.
- Explain presidential Executive Orders 11246 and 11375.
- Identify some of the major Supreme Court decisions that have had an impact on equal employment opportunity.
- Describe the Equal Employment Opportunity Commission.
- Explain the purpose of the *Uniform Guidelines on Employee Selection Procedures.*
- Explain adverse impact.
- Describe the *Uniform Guidelines* related to sexual harassment, national origin, and religion.
- Explain affirmative action programs.

# Equal Employment Opportunity and Affirmative Action

L eroy Hasty was faced with a dilemma. He supervised 12 process technicians at the Indestro Chemical plant in Los Angeles, California, but was being transferred to a new job. The production manager, Jack Richards, had just asked Leroy to nominate one of his subordinates as a replacement. Two possible choices immediately came to mind, Carlos Chavez and James Mitchell.

Carlos was a very capable worker. He was 24 years old and married, and he had earned his bachelor's degree in management by attending night school. His heritage was Mexican American. He had done an excellent job on every assignment Leroy had given him. He had all the qualifications Leroy believed a good supervisor should have, including solid technical expertise. Leroy considered Carlos punctual, diligent, mature, and intelligent. A serious sort, Carlos often came to work early and stayed late and seemed to spend most of his spare time with his family.

keytermskeytermskeyterms

## ▶ Key Terms

Glass ceiling 61
Executive Order (EO) 61

Affirmative action 62
Adverse impact 69

Affirmative action program (AAP) 73

James was a 25-year-old high school graduate. He was single, and Hasty knew he often went hunting or partying with several of the other technicians. Like most of his fellow workers, James was a WASP (white Anglo-Saxon Protestant). He was a hard worker and was liked and respected by the others, including Carlos. On the basis of objective factors, Leroy believed James ran second to Carlos, although the call was a close one.

However, there was the race issue. Several times Leroy had heard fellow workers refer to Carlos as a "wetback." Leroy believed some of the workers would prefer to have James as a supervisor, purely because of his national origin. In fact, he thought one or two of them might resist Carlos's authority to try to make him look bad. And if productivity in the section fell off because of administrative problems, Leroy knew his own record with the company might be tarnished.

At that moment, the phone rang. It was Jack Richards. "Leroy," he said, "I need to see you. Could you come to my office in a few minutes?" As Leroy hung up the phone, he thought, "I know Jack is going to want to talk about my replacement."

**H**iring decisions such as the one that Leroy will make occur every day and impact the field of study called equal employment opportunity (EEO). In this chapter, we provide an overview of the major EEO legislation that impacts human resource management. We first discuss the significant equal employment opportunity laws affecting human resource management. Then, we describe the importance of presidential Executive Orders 11246 and 11375. Next, we review significant Supreme Court decisions and describe the Equal Employment Opportunity Commission. We then discuss the Uniform Guidelines on Employee Selection Procedures and address the issues of adverse impact and additional guidelines. We devote the remainder of the chapter to affirmative action programs.

## EQUAL EMPLOYMENT OPPORTUNITY: AN OVERVIEW

The concept of equal employment opportunity has undergone much modification and fine-tuning since the passage of the Civil Rights Act of 1964. Congress has passed numerous amendments to that act, as well as other acts in response to oversights in the initial legislation. Major Supreme Court decisions interpreting

▶ *HR Law*

**www.prenhall.com/mondy**

This site provides a monthly update of federal and state HR laws.

HR WEB
WISDOM

the provisions of the act have also been handed down. Executive orders were signed into law that further strengthened equal employment opportunity. Nearly four decades have passed since the introduction of the first legislation, and equal employment opportunity has become an integral part of the workplace.

Although equal employment opportunity has come a long way since the early 1960s, continuing efforts are required. The Bureau of Justice Statistics reports that employment discrimination lawsuits more than tripled in the private sector during the 1990s, climbing from 6,936 cases filed in U.S. district courts in 1990 to 21,450 cases in 1998.[1] While perfection is elusive, the majority of businesses today do attempt to make employment decisions based on who is the best qualified, as opposed to whether an individual is of a certain gender, race, religion, color, national origin, or age. By and large, legislation, Supreme Court decisions, and executive orders have encouraged both public and private organizations to tap the abilities of a workforce that was largely underutilized before the mid-1960s.

## LAWS AFFECTING EQUAL EMPLOYMENT OPPORTUNITY

Numerous national laws have been passed that have had an impact on equal employment opportunity. The passage of these laws reflects society's attitude toward the changes that should be made to give everyone an equal opportunity for employment. We briefly describe the most significant of these laws in the following sections.

## Civil Rights Act of 1866

The oldest federal legislation affecting staffing is the Civil Rights Act of 1866, which is based on the Thirteenth Amendment to the U.S. Constitution. Specifically, this act provides that all citizens have the same right "as enjoyed by white citizens . . . to inherit, purchase, . . . hold, and convey . . . property, [and that] all persons . . . shall have the same right to make and enforce contracts . . . as enjoyed by white citizens." As interpreted by the courts, employment as well as membership in a union is a contractual arrangement. Blacks and Hispanics are covered by this act if they are discriminated against on the basis of race. Until 1968, it was assumed that the act was applicable only when action by a state or state agency, and not by private parties, was involved. That year the Supreme Court overruled this assumption and broadened the interpretation of the act to cover all contractual arrangements. There is no statute of limitations to the act.

## Title VII of the Civil Rights Act of 1964— Amended 1972

The statute that has had the greatest impact on human resource management is Title VII of the Civil Rights Act of 1964, as amended by the Equal Employment Act of 1972. Under Title VII, it is illegal for an employer to discriminate in hiring, firing, promoting, compensating, or in terms, conditions, or privileges of employment on the basis of race, color, sex, religion, or national origin.

Title VII covers employers engaged in or affecting interstate commerce who have 15 or more employees for each working day in each of 20 calendar weeks in the current or preceding calendar year. Also included in the definition of employers are state and local governments, schools, colleges, unions, and private employment agencies that procure employees for an employer with 15 or more employees.

Three notable exceptions to discrimination as covered by Title VII are bona fide occupational qualifications (BFOQs), seniority and merit systems, and testing and educational requirements. According to the act it is not:

> an unlawful employment practice for an employer to hire and employ employees . . . on the basis of his religion, sex, or national origin in those certain instances where religion, sex, or national origin is a bona fide occupational qualification reasonably necessary to the normal operation of the particular business or enterprise.

Thus, for example, religious institutions, such as churches or synagogues, may legally refuse to hire professors whose religious persuasion is different from that of the hiring institution. Likewise, a maximum security correctional institution housing only male inmates may decline to hire females as security guards. The concept of bona fide occupational qualification was designed to be narrowly, not broadly, interpreted and has been so construed by the courts in a number of cases. The burden of proving the necessity for a BFOQ rests entirely on the employer.

The second exception to discrimination under Title VII is a bona fide seniority system such as the type normally contained in a union contract. Differences in employment conditions among workers are permitted "provided that such differences are not the result of an intention to discriminate because of race, color, religion, sex, or national origin." Even if a bona fide seniority system has an adverse impact on those individuals protected by Title VII (i.e., it affects a class or group), the system can be invalidated only by evidence that the actual motives of the parties to the agreement were to discriminate.

In the matter of testing and educational requirements, Title VII states that it is not "an unlawful employment practice for an employer to give, and to act upon, the results of any professionally developed ability test provided that such test, its administration, or action upon the results is not designed, intended or used to discriminate because of race, color, religion, sex, or national origin." Employment testing and educational requirements must be job related, and the burden of proof is on the employer to show that a demonstrable relationship exists between actual job performance and the test or educational requirement.

**HRM IN ACTION**

▶ *An Equal Employment Dilemma*

Bob Lewis, the personnel manager for Jessup Manufacturing Company, was meeting with Aaron Denney, the production manager. Aaron began the conversation by stating, "Bob, one of our first-line supervisors has applied for the new departmental job. This guy would be great and is the best qualified. But, I don't want to put a 62-year-old person in the position. I'd rather fill the vacancy with someone who will be with us for a while. Also, our competition is so great that we must absolutely have a person in this job who has the energy to work long hours."

"Aaron," Bob said, "I guess you don't realize that our company has always had a policy against age discrimination. Not only that, it's illegal. I suggest that if age is your only hang-up, the worker should be promoted."

*Do you agree with Bob's assessment of the situation?*

Persons not covered by Title VII include aliens not authorized to work in the United States and members of the communist party. Homosexuals are also not protected under Title VII. The courts have consistently ruled that where the term *sex* is used in any federal statute, that term refers to biological gender and not to sexual preference.

The Civil Rights Act of 1964 also created the Equal Employment Opportunity Commission (EEOC) and assigned enforcement of Title VII to this agency. Consisting of five presidentially appointed members, the EEOC is empowered to investigate, conciliate, and litigate charges of discrimination arising under provisions of Title VII. Additionally, the commission has the responsibility of issuing procedural regulations and interpretations of Title VII and the other statutes it enforces. The most significant regulation issued by the EEOC is the *Uniform Guidelines on Employee Selection Procedures*.

## Age Discrimination in Employment Act of 1967—Amended in 1978 and 1986

As originally enacted, the Age Discrimination in Employment Act (ADEA) prohibited employers from discriminating against individuals who were 40 to 65 years old. The 1978 amendment provided protection for individuals who were at least 40, but less than 70 years old. In a 1986 amendment, employer discrimination against anyone over 40 years old became illegal. The EEOC is responsible for administering this act.

The act pertains to employers who have 20 or more employees for 20 or more calendar weeks (either in the current or preceding calendar year); unions with 25 or more members; employment agencies; and federal, state, and local government subunits. An exception was recently created when the Supreme Court ruled that states cannot be sued for violating a federal age discrimination law. Members of the group claimed in their suit that a state Board of Regents' failure to adjust professors' and librarians' salaries was aimed at them, since it had a *disproportionate impact* on those over 40. An appeals court eventually rejected that claim, citing the state's sovereign immunity. The Supreme Court decision affirmed the appeal.[2]

Enforcement begins when a charge is filed, but the EEOC can review compliance even if no charge is filed. The Age Discrimination in Employment Act differs from Title VII of the Civil Rights Act in providing for a trial by jury and carrying a possible criminal penalty for violation of the act. The trial-by-jury provision is important because juries may have great sympathy for older people who may have been discriminated against. The criminal penalty provision means that a person may receive more than lost wages if discrimination is proved. The 1978 amendment also makes class action suits possible.

The Older Workers Benefit Protection Act (OWBPA), an amendment to the Age Discrimination in Employment Act, prohibits discrimination in the administration of benefits on the basis of age but also permits early retirement incentive plans as long as they are voluntary.[3] The act establishes wrongful termination waiver requirements as a means of protecting older employees by ensuring that waiver acceptance is made by fully informed and willful personnel.[4]

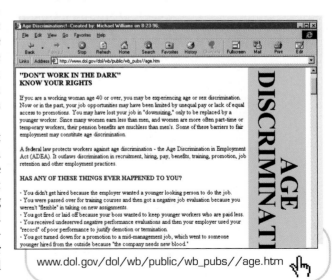

www.dol.gov/dol/wb/public/wb_pubs//age.htm

Age can be a bona fide occupational qualification where it is reasonably necessary to the essence of the business, and the employer has a rational or factual basis for believing that all, or substantially all, people within the age class would not be able to perform satisfactorily. In 1997, the U.S. Federal Court of Appeals ruled that the Federal Aviation Administration adequately explained its long-standing rule that it can force pilots to retire at age 60. The age 60 rule was first imposed in 1959 and had long been controversial.[5]

This ruling supported the 1974 Seventh Circuit Court decision that Greyhound did not violate the ADEA when it refused to hire persons 35 years of age or older as intercity bus drivers. Again, the likelihood of risk or harm to its passengers was involved. Greyhound presented evidence concerning degenerative physical and sensory changes that humans undergo at about age 35 that have a detrimental effect upon driving skills, and that the changes are not detectable by physical tests.[6]

## Rehabilitation Act of 1973

The Rehabilitation Act prohibits discrimination against disabled workers who are employed by certain government contractors and subcontractors and organizations that receive federal grants in excess of $2,500. Individuals are considered disabled if they have a physical or mental impairment that substantially limits one or more major life activities or if they have a record of such impairment. Protected under the act are diseases and conditions such as epilepsy, cancer, cardiovascular disorders, AIDS, blindness, deafness, mental retardation, emotional disorders, and dyslexia.

There are two primary levels of the act. All federal contractors or subcontractors exceeding the $2,500 base are required to post notices that they agree to take affirmative action to recruit, employ, and promote qualified disabled individuals. If the contract or subcontract exceeds $50,000, or if the contractor has 50 or more employees, the employer must prepare a written affirmative action plan for review by the Office of Federal Contract Compliance Programs (OFCCP), which administers the act. In it, the contractor must specify that reasonable steps are being taken to hire and promote disabled persons.

## Pregnancy Discrimination Act of 1978

Passed as an amendment to Title VII of the Civil Rights Act, the Pregnancy Discrimination Act prohibits discrimination in employment based on pregnancy, childbirth, or related medical conditions. The basic principle of the act is that women affected by pregnancy and related conditions must be treated the same as other applicants and employees on the basis of their ability or inability to work. A woman is therefore protected against such practices as being fired or refused a job or promotion merely because she is pregnant or has had an abortion. She usually cannot be forced to take a leave of absence as long as she can work. If other employees on disability leave are entitled to return to their jobs when they are able to work again, so too are women who have been unable to work because of pregnancy.

The same principle applies in the benefits area, including disability benefits, sick leave, and health insurance. A woman unable to work for pregnancy-related reasons is entitled to disability benefits or sick leave on the same basis as employees unable to work for medical reasons. Also, any health insurance provided must cover expenses for pregnancy-related conditions on the same basis as expenses for other medical conditions. However, health insurance for expenses arising from an abortion is not required except where the life of the mother would be endangered if the fetus were carried to term or where medical complications have arisen from an abortion.

In a class action suit originally filed in 1978 but not settled until July 1991, American Telephone & Telegraph Company (AT&T) agreed to settle a pregnancy discrimination suit with the EEOC for $66 million. This suit was the largest cash recovery in the agency's history and involved more than 13,000 then-present and former female AT&T workers. The 1978 suit charged that Western Electric required pregnant workers to leave their jobs at the end of their sixth month of pregnancy, denied them seniority credit, and refused to guarantee them a job when they returned.[7]

## Immigration Control Acts

Three immigration control acts deserve mention as related to human resource management. These are the Immigration Reform and Control Act of 1986, the Immigration Act of 1990, and the Illegal Immigration Reform and Immigrant Responsibility Act of 1996.

**Immigration Reform and Control Act (IRCA).** The Immigration Reform and Control Act (IRCA) established criminal and civil sanctions against employers who knowingly hire an unauthorized alien. The act also makes unlawful the hiring of anyone unless the person's employment authorization and identity are verified. When dealing with the national origin provision of the Civil Rights Act, IRCA reduces the threshold coverage from 15 to 4 employees. The effect of this extension of the 1964 law is to curtail hiring actions of some businesses. They often choose to hire only U.S. citizens and, thereby, avoid any potential violation of IRCA. However, many foreign nationals are in this country legally (many are legal immigrants awaiting citizenship); refusing to hire them would violate their civil rights.[8]

**Immigration Act.** The Immigration Act of 1990 significantly revised U.S. policy on legal immigration. The law increased levels of immigrations, particularly employment-based immigration of highly skilled professionals and executives. Apparently a problem resulted from this act. It opened the front door on immigration but, as some say, it did not close the back door, and illegal immigration continued.[9]

**Illegal Immigration Reform and Immigrant Responsibility Act.** The Illegal Immigration Reform and Immigrant Responsibility Act was signed into law in 1996. The law places severe limitations on persons who have come to the United States and remain in the country longer than permitted by their visas and/or persons who have violated their nonimmigrant status. Anyone unlawfully present in the United States for 180 days, but less than one year, will be subject to a three-year ban for admission to the United States. Anyone unlawfully present in the United States for one year or more is subject to a 10-year ban for admission to the United States. There are certain exceptions, however, such as extreme hardship.[10]

## Americans with Disabilities Act (ADA)

The Americans with Disabilities Act (ADA), passed in 1990, prohibits discrimination against *qualified individuals with disabilities*. Persons discriminated against because they have a known association or relationship with a disabled individual are also protected. The ADA defines an *individual with a disability* as a person who has, or is regarded as having, a physical or mental impairment that substantially limits one or more major life activities, and has a record of such an impairment, or is regarded as having such an impairment. However, the Supreme Court recently ruled that people with correctable physical limitations, like poor eyesight or high blood pressure, may not seek the protection of the Americans with Disabilities Act. The ruling means more than 100 million Americans with correctable impairments are not covered by antidiscrimination law.[11]

The ADA prohibits discrimination in all employment practices, including job application procedures, hiring, firing, advancement, compensation, training, and other terms, conditions, and privileges of employment. It applies to recruitment, advertising, tenure, layoffs, leaves, fringe benefits, and all other employment-related activities. The employment provisions apply to private employers, state and local governments, employment agencies, and labor unions. Employers with 15 or more employees are covered.

The Equal Employment Opportunity Commission (EEOC) guidelines on pre-employment inquiries and tests regarding disabilities clarify provisions in the ADA that prohibit inquiries and medical examinations intended to gain information about applicants' disabilities before a conditional job offer. The guiding principle is to ask only about potential employees' ability to do the job, and not about their disabilities.[12] Lawful inquiries include those regarding performance of specific functions or possession of training, while illegal inquiries include those that ascertain previous medical conditions or extent of prior drug use. The ADA does not protect people currently using illegal drugs. It does protect those in rehabilitation programs that are not currently using illegal drugs, those that have been rehabilitated, and those erroneously labeled as drug users.[13]

## Civil Rights Act of 1991

During its 1988–1989 term, the Supreme Court rendered six employment discrimination decisions of such magnitude that a congressional response was provoked.[14] The result was passage of the Civil Rights Act of 1991. The Act amended five statutes: (1) the Civil Rights Act of 1866; (2) Title VII of the Civil Rights Act of 1964, as Amended; (3) the Age Discrimination in Employment Act of 1967, as Amended; (4) the Rehabilitation Act of 1973; and (5) the Americans with Disabilities Act of 1990.

The Civil Rights Act of 1991 had the following purposes:

▷ To provide appropriate remedies for intentional discrimination and unlawful harassment in the workplace.
▷ To codify the concepts of *business necessity* and *job related* pronounced by the Supreme Court in *Griggs v Duke Power Co.*
▷ To confirm statutory authority and provide statutory guidelines for the adjudication of disparate impacts under Title VII of the Civil Rights Act of 1964.
▷ To respond to recent decisions of the Supreme Court by expanding the scope of relevant civil rights statutes in order to provide adequate protection to victims of discrimination.

Under this act, a complaining party may recover punitive damages if the complaining party demonstrates that the company engaged in a discriminatory practice with malice or with reckless indifference to the law. However, the following limits, based on the number of people employed by the company, were placed on the amount of the award:

▷ Between 15 and 100 employees—$50,000
▷ Between 101 and 200 employees—$100,000

- Between 201 and 500 employees—$200,000
- More than 500 employees—$300,000

In each case, aggrieved employees must be with the firm for 20 or more calendar weeks in the current or preceding calendar year.

With regard to burden of proof, a complaining party must show that a particular employment practice causes a disparate impact on the basis of race, color, religion, sex, or national origin. It must also be shown that the company is unable to demonstrate that the challenged practice is job related for the position in question and consistent with business necessity. The act also extends the coverage of the Civil Rights Act of 1964 to extraterritorial employment. However, the act does not apply to U.S. companies operating in another country if it would violate the law of the foreign country. The act also extends the nondiscrimination principles to Congress and other government agencies, such as the General Accounting Office and the Government Printing Office.

Also included in the Civil Rights Act of 1991 is the Glass Ceiling Act. The **glass ceiling** is the invisible barrier in organizations that prevents many women and minorities from achieving top-level management positions. This act established a Glass Ceiling Commission to study the manner in which businesses fill management and decision-making positions, the developmental and skill-enhancing practices used to foster the necessary qualifications for advancement to such positions, and the compensation programs and reward structures currently utilized in the workplace. It was also to study the limited progress made by minorities and women. It established an annual award for excellence in promoting a more diverse skilled workforce at the management and decision-making levels in business.

**Glass ceiling**
The invisible barrier in organizations that prevents many women and minorities from achieving top-level management positions.

## State and Local Laws

Numerous state and local laws also affect equal employment opportunity. A number of states and some cities have passed fair employment practice laws prohibiting discrimination on the basis of race, color, religion, gender, or national origin. Even prior to federal legislation, several states had antidiscrimination legislation relating to age and gender. For instance, New York protected individuals between the ages of 18 and 65 prior to the 1978 and 1986 ADEA amendments, and California had no upper limit on protected age. In 2000, San Francisco voted to ban weight discrimination. The Board of Supervisors added body size to city laws that already bar discrimination based on race, color, religion, age, ancestry, sex, sexual orientation, disability, place of birth, or gender identity.[15] When EEOC regulations conflict with state or local civil rights regulations, the legislation more favorable to women and minorities applies.

## EXECUTIVE ORDER 11246, AS AMENDED BY EXECUTIVE ORDER 11375

An **executive order (EO)** is a directive issued by the president and has the force and effect of a law enacted by Congress as they apply to federal agencies and federal contractors. In 1965 President Lyndon B. Johnson signed EO 11246, which establishes the policy of the U.S. government as providing equal opportunity in federal employment for all qualified people. It prohibits discrimination in employment because of race, creed, color, or national origin. The order also requires promoting the full realization of equal employment opportunity through

**Executive Order (EO)**
Directive issued by the president that has the force and effect of a law enacted by the Congress.

## HR WEB WISDOM

> *SHRM-HR Links*

**www.prenhall.com/mondy**

The diversity hot link covers various issues including affirmative action and equal employment opportunity.

a positive, continuing program in each executive department and agency. The policy of equal opportunity applies to every aspect of federal employment policy and practice.

A major provision of EO 11246 requires adherence to a policy of nondiscrimination in employment as a condition for the approval of a grant, contract, loan, insurance, or guarantee. Every executive department and agency that administers a program involving federal financial assistance must include such language in its contracts. Contractors must agree not to discriminate in employment because of race, creed, color, or national origin during performance of a contract.

**Affirmative action**, stipulated by EO 11246, requires covered employers to take positive steps to ensure employment of applicants and treatment of employees during employment without regard to race, creed, color, or national origin. Covered human resource practices relate to employment, upgrading, demotion, transfer, recruitment or recruitment advertising, layoffs or termination, rates of pay or other forms of compensation, and selection for training, including apprenticeships. Employers are required to post notices explaining these requirements in conspicuous places in the workplace. In the event of contractor noncompliance, contracts can be canceled, terminated, or suspended in whole or in part, and the contractor may be declared ineligible for future government contracts. In 1968, EO 11246 was amended by EO 11375, which changed the word *creed* to *religion* and added sex discrimination to the other prohibited items. These EOs are enforced by the Department of Labor through the Office of Federal Contract Compliance Programs (OFCCP).

**Affirmative action**
Stipulated by Executive Order 11246, it requires covered employers to take positive steps to ensure employment of applicants and treatment of employees during employment without regard to race, creed, color, or national origin.

## SIGNIFICANT U.S. SUPREME COURT DECISIONS

Knowledge of the law is obviously important for human resource managers; however, they must be aware of and understand much more than the words in the law itself. The manner in which the courts interpret the law is also vitally important. Also, interpretation continuously changes, even though the law may not have been amended. Discussions of some of the more significant U.S. Supreme Court decisions affecting equal employment opportunity follow.

## Griggs v Duke Power Company

A major decision affecting the field of human resource management was rendered in 1971. A group of black employees at Duke Power Company had charged job discrimination under Title VII of the Civil Rights Act of 1964. Prior to Title VII, the Duke Power Company had two workforces, separated by race. After passage of the act, the company required applicants to have a high school diploma and pass a paper-and-pencil test to qualify for certain jobs. The plaintiff was able to demonstrate that, in the relevant labor market, 34 percent of the white males but only 12 percent of the black males had a high school education. The plaintiff was also able to show that people already in those jobs were performing successfully even though they did not have high school diplomas. No business necessity could be shown for this educational requirement.

In an 8-0 vote, the Supreme Court ruled against Duke Power Company and stated, "If an employment practice which operates to exclude Negroes cannot be shown to be related to job performance, the practice is prohibited." A major implication of the decision is that when human resource management practices eliminate substantial numbers of minority or women applicants, the burden of proof is on the employer to show that the practice is job related. This court decision significantly affected the human resource practices of many firms. Questions in employment procedures that should be avoided if not job related include credit record, arrest record, conviction record, garnishment record, and education. Even work experience requirements that are not job related should be avoided.

## Albermarle Paper Company v Moody

In 1966, a class action suit was brought against Albermarle Paper Company and the plant employees' labor union. A permanent injunction was requested against any policy, practice, custom, or usage at the plant that violated Title VII. In 1975, the Supreme Court, in *Albermarle Paper Co. v Moody,* reaffirmed the idea that any test used in the selection process or in promotion decisions must be validated if it is found its use has had an adverse impact on women and minorities. The employer has the burden of proof for showing that the test is valid. Subsequently, the employer must show that any selection or promotion device actually measures what it is supposed to measure.

## Phillips v Martin Marietta Corporation

In 1971, the Court ruled that Martin Marietta had discriminated against a woman because she had young children. The company had a rule prohibiting the hiring of women with school-age children. The company argued that it did not preclude all women from job consideration, only those women with school-age children. Martin Marietta contended that this was a business requirement. The argument was obviously based on stereotypes and was rejected. A major implication of this decision is that a firm cannot impose standards for employment only on women. For example, a firm cannot reject divorced women if it does not also reject divorced men. Neither application forms nor interviews should contain questions for women that do not also apply to men. Therefore, questions concerning marital status ("Do you wish to be addressed as Ms., Miss, or Mrs.?") should not be asked.

## Espinoza v Farah Manufacturing Company

In 1973, the Court ruled that Title VII does not prohibit discrimination on the basis of lack of citizenship. The EEOC had previously said that refusing to hire anyone who was a noncitizen was discriminatory as this selection standard was likely to have an adverse impact on individuals of foreign national origin. Because 92 percent of the employees at the Farah facility in question were Hispanics who had become American citizens, the Court held that the company had not discriminated on the basis of national origin when it refused to hire a Hispanic who was not a U.S. citizen.

## Weber v Kaiser Aluminum and Chemical Corporation

In 1974, the United Steelworkers of America and Kaiser Aluminum and Chemical Corporation entered into a master collective bargaining agreement covering terms and conditions of employment at 15 Kaiser plants. The agreement contained an affirmative action plan designed to eliminate conspicuous racial imbalances in Kaiser's then almost exclusively white craft workforce. Black craft hiring goals equal to the percentage of blacks in the respective local labor forces were set for each Kaiser plant. To enable the plants to meet these goals, on-the-job training programs were established to teach unskilled black and white production workers the skills necessary to become craft workers. The plan reserved 50 percent of the openings in the newly created in-plant training programs for black employees.

In 1974, only 1.83 percent (5 out of 273) of the skilled craft workers at the Gramercy, Louisiana, plant were black, even though the labor force in the Gramercy area was approximately 39 percent black. Thirteen craft trainees, of whom seven were black and six were white, were selected from Gramercy's production workforce. The most junior black selected for the program had less seniority than several white production workers whose bids for admission were rejected. Brian Weber subsequently instituted a class action suit alleging that the action by Kaiser and USWA discriminated against him and other similarly situated white employees in violation of Title VII. Although the lower courts ruled that Kaiser's actions were illegal because they fostered reverse discrimination, the Supreme Court reversed that decision, stating that Title VII does not prohibit race-conscious affirmative action plans. Because the affirmative action plan was voluntarily agreed to by the company and the union, it did not violate Title VII.

## Dothard v Rawlingson

At the time Rawlingson applied for a position as correctional counselor trainee, she was a 22-year-old college graduate whose major course of study had been correctional psychology. She was refused employment because she failed to meet the minimum height and weight requirements. In this 1977 case, the Supreme Court upheld the U.S. District Court's decision that Alabama's statutory minimum height requirement of five feet two inches and minimum weight requirement of 120 pounds for the position of correctional counselor had a discriminatory impact on women applicants. The contention was that minimum height and weight requirements for the position of correctional counselor were job related. However, the Court stated that this argument does not rebut *prima facie* evidence showing these requirements have a discriminatory impact on women, whereas no evidence was produced correlating these requirements with a requisite amount of strength thought essential to good performance. The impact of the decision was that height and weight requirements must be job related.

## University of California Regents v Bakke

This Supreme Court decision involved the first major test involving reverse discrimination. The University of California had reserved 16 places in each beginning medical school class for minorities. Allen Bakke, a white man, was denied admission even though he scored higher on the admission criteria than some minority applicants who were admitted. The Supreme Court ruled 5–4 in Bakke's favor. As a result, Bakke was admitted to the university and later received his degree. But, at the same time, the Court reaffirmed that race may be taken into account in admission decisions.

## American Tobacco Company v Patterson

This 1982 Supreme Court decision allows seniority and promotion systems established since Title VII to stand, although they unintentionally hurt minority workers. Under *Griggs v Duke Power Co.,* a *prima facie* violation of Title VII may be established by policies or practices that are neutral on their face and in intent, but that nonetheless discriminate against a particular group. A seniority system would fall under the *Griggs* rationale if it were not for Section 703(h) of the Civil Rights Act, which provides:

> Notwithstanding any other provision of this subchapter, it shall not be an unlawful employment practice for an employer to apply standards of compensation, or different terms, conditions, or privileges of employment pursuant to a bona fide seniority or merit system . . . provided that such differences are not the result of an intention to discriminate because of race, color, religion, sex, or national origin, nor shall it be an unlawful employment practice for an employer to give and to act upon the results of any professionally developed ability test provided that such test, its administration or action upon the results is not designed, intended or used to discriminate because of race, color, religion, sex, or national origin. . . .

Thus, the court ruled that a seniority system adopted after Title VII may stand even though it has an *unintended* discriminatory impact.

## City of Richmond v J. A. Croson Co.

The City of Richmond adopted a Minority Business Utilization Plan requiring prime contractors awarded city construction contracts to subcontract at least 30 percent of the dollar amount of each contract to one or more Minority Business Enterprises (MBEs). The plan defined MBEs to include a business from anywhere in the country that was at least 51 percent owned and controlled by black, Spanish-speaking, Oriental, Native American, Eskimo, or Aleut citizens. After J. A. Croson Co. was denied a waiver and lost its contract, it brought suit alleging that the plan was unconstitutional under the Fourteenth Amendment's Equal Protection Clause. The Supreme Court affirmed a Court of Appeals ruling that the city's plan was not justified by a compelling governmental interest because the record revealed no prior discrimination by the city itself in awarding contracts, and the 30 percent set-aside was not narrowly tailored to accomplish a remedial purpose. The decision forced 36 states and many cities and counties to review their policies.

## Adarand Constructors v Pena

In a 5–4 opinion, the U.S. Supreme Court in 1995 criticized the moral justification for affirmative action, saying that race-conscious programs can amount to unconstitutional reverse discrimination and even harm those they seek to advance. The Adarand case concerned a Department of Transportation policy that gave contractors a bonus if they hired minority subcontractors. A white contractor challenged the policy in court after losing a contract to build guardrails, despite offering the lowest bid. A federal appeals court upheld the program as within the proper bounds of affirmative action. The Supreme Court decision did not uphold or reject that ruling, but instead sent the case back for further review under new, tougher rules. As a result, the ruling seems to invite legal challenges to other federal affirmative action programs.

Since Adarand, racial or ethnic preferences in scholarships, employment, contracting, and education have been universally denounced by federal appellate courts as affronts to the equal protection clause of the Fourteenth Amendment.[16] For the past decade, the Supreme Court has ruled consistently that government at

HR WEB WISDOM

▶ *The EEOC*

**www.prenhall.com/mondy**

The home page for the Equal Employment Opportunity Commission is presented.

all levels cannot make race the primary reason for discrimination unless it can demonstrate it has some *compelling state interest* for doing so.[17]

## O'Connor v Consolidated Coin Caterers Corp.

In 1996, the U.S. Supreme Court unanimously ruled that an employee does not have to show that he or she was replaced by someone younger than 40 to bring suit under the ADEA. The High Court declared that discrimination is illegal even when all the employees are members of the protected age group. The case began in 1990 when James O'Connor's job as a regional sales manager was eliminated. The company did not select O'Connor, age 56, to manage either of its two remaining sales territories. He later was fired. His replacement was 40 years old. O'Connor was evidently doing so well that he earned a bonus of $37,000 the previous year. Apparently, O'Connor's new boss told him he was "too damn old" for the kind of work he was doing and that what the company needed was "new blood."

Writing for the Court, Justice Scalia stated, "The ADEA does not ban discrimination against employees because they are aged 40; it bans discrimination against employees because of their age, but limits the protected class to those who are 40 or older." Thus, it is not relevant that one member in the protected class has lost out to another member in that class, so long as the person lost out because of his or her age. The Court also found that being replaced by someone substantially younger was a more reliable indicator of age discrimination than being replaced by someone outside the protected class.[18]

## EQUAL EMPLOYMENT OPPORTUNITY COMMISSION

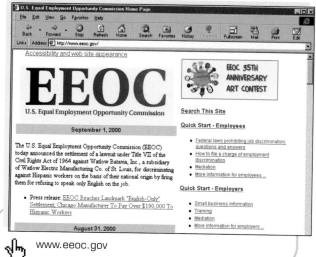

www.eeoc.gov

Title VII of the Civil Rights Act, as amended, created the Equal Employment Opportunity Commission. It was initially charged with administering the act. Under Title VII, filing a discrimination charge initiates EEOC action. The EEOC continually receives complaints. In 1998, 79,591 employees filed complaints with the Equal Employment Opportunity Commission. Employers paid more than $169 million in damages to employees who won claims.[19] Charges may be filed by one of the presidentially appointed EEOC commissioners, by any aggrieved person, or by anyone acting on behalf of an aggrieved person. Charges must be filed within 180 days of the alleged act; however, the time is extended to 300 days if a state or local agency is involved in the case.

Figure 3-1 shows that when a charge is filed, the EEOC typically proceeds in the following manner. First, an attempt at no-fault settlement is made. Essentially, the organization charged with the

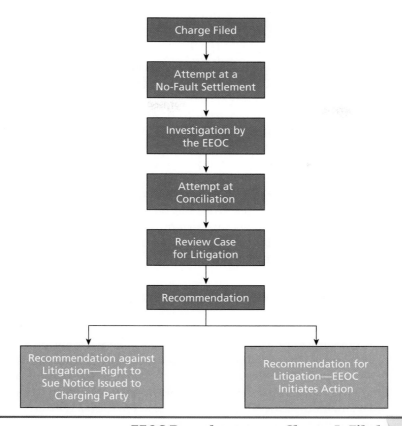

**EEOC Procedure once a Charge Is Filed**　　**Figure 3-1**

violation is invited to settle the case with no admission of guilt. Most charges are settled at this stage.

Failing settlement, the EEOC investigates the charges. Once the employer is notified that an investigation will take place, no records relating to the charge may be destroyed. During the investigative process, the employer is permitted to present a position statement. After the investigation has been completed, the district director of the EEOC will issue a *probable cause* or a *no probable cause* statement.

In the event of a probable cause statement, the next step involves attempted conciliation. In the event this effort fails, the case will be reviewed for litigation potential. Some of the factors that determine whether the EEOC will pursue litigation are (1) the number of people affected by the alleged practice; (2) the amount of money involved in the charge; (3) other charges against the employer; and (4) the type of charge. Recommendations for litigation are then passed on to the general counsel of the EEOC. If the recommendation is against litigation, a right to sue notice will be issued to the charging party. Note that the Civil Rights Act of 1964 prohibits retaliation against employees who have opposed an illegal employment practice. The act also protects those who have testified, assisted, or participated in the investigation of discrimination.

Recently, the EEOC began a new strategy. Burdened with thousands of backlogged employment discrimination cases, it is trying a new approach. The enforcement agency formally launched a voluntary mediation program in cities around the country. The goal, officials said, is to resolve a significant number of disputes before the EEOC even starts to investigate by bringing the contesting parties together in a neutral forum.[20]

### ▶ EEO and the Internet

For the minority job hunter, there are both advantages and drawbacks to Internet recruiting. Some Internet applications include standardized tests, which are notorious for their alleged biases. In addition, Internet recruiting can be seen as discriminatory against those who do not have Internet access. On the other hand, Internet recruiting can also be a deterrent to discrimination because computers are blind to such factors as race, age, and disability status. A primary concern is whether the standardized tests are fair to minority applicants.

According to Nathan Mondragon, director of research and measurement at SHL Aspen Tree, a custom Internet recruiting software development company, "We gather EEO data for research purposes only. The recruiter is not told the race, gender, or age of the applicant. That information goes directly to us, and we track it to make sure our tests do not inadvertently screen out protected groups." The ACLU's Lewis Maltby agrees that this Internet recruiting software "shouldn't create EEO problems as long as it's done carefully."[21]

## UNIFORM GUIDELINES ON EMPLOYEE SELECTION PROCEDURES

Prior to 1978, employers were faced with complying with several different selection guidelines. In 1978, the Equal Employment Opportunity Commission, the Civil Service Commission, the Department of Justice, and the Department of Labor adopted the *Uniform Guidelines on Employee Selection Procedures*. These guidelines cover several federal equal employment opportunity statutes and executive orders including Title VII of the Civil Rights Act, EO 11246, and the Equal Pay Act. They do not apply to the Age Discrimination in Employment Act or the Rehabilitation Act.

The *Uniform Guidelines* provide a single set of principles that were designed to assist employers, labor organizations, employment agencies, and licensing and certification boards in complying with federal prohibitions against employment practices that discriminate on the basis of race, color, religion, gender, and national origin. The *Uniform Guidelines* provide a framework for making legal employment decisions about hiring, promotion, demotion, referral, retention, licensing and certification, the proper use of tests, and other selection procedures. Under the *Uniform Guidelines,* recruiting procedures are not considered selection procedures and therefore are not covered.

Regarding selection procedures, the *Uniform Guidelines* state that a test is

> any measure, combination of measures, or procedures used as a basis for any employment decision. Selection procedures include the full range of assessment techniques from traditional paper and pencil tests, performance tests, testing programs or probationary periods and physical, education, and work experience requirement through informal or casual interviews and unscored application forms.

Using this definition, virtually any instrument or procedure used in the selection decision is considered a test.

## THE CONCEPT OF ADVERSE IMPACT

Prior to the issuance of the *Uniform Guidelines,* the only way to prove job relatedness was to validate each test. The *Uniform Guidelines* do not require validation in all cases. Essentially, it is required only in instances where the test or other selection device produces an adverse impact on a minority group. Under the *Uniform Guidelines,* adverse impact has been defined in terms of selection rates, the selection rate being the number of applicants hired or promoted, divided by the total number of applicants. **Adverse impact**, a concept established by the *Uniform Guidelines,* occurs if women and minorities are not hired at the rate of at least 80 percent of the best-achieving group. This has also been called the four-fifths rule, which is actually a guideline subject to interpretation by the EEOC. The groups identified for analysis under the guidelines are (1) blacks, (2) Native Americans (including Alaskan natives), (3) Asians, (4) Hispanics, (5) women, and (6) men.

The following formula is used to compute adverse impact for hiring:

$$\frac{\text{Success rate for women and minority applicants}}{\text{Success rate for best-achieving group applicants}} = \frac{\text{Determination of}}{\text{adverse impact}}$$

The success rate for women and minority applicants is determined by dividing the number of members of a specific group *employed* in a period by the number of women and minority *applicants* in a period. The success rate of best-achieving group applicants is determined by dividing the number of people in the best-achieving group *employed* by the number of the best-achieving group *applicants* in a period.

Using the formula, let us determine whether there has been an adverse impact in the following case. During 2001, 400 people were hired for a particular job. Of the total, 300 were white and 100 were black. There were 1,500 applicants for these jobs, of whom 1,000 were white and 500 were black. Using the adverse formula, we have:

$$\frac{100/500}{300/1,000} = \frac{0.2}{0.3} = 66.67\%$$

We conclude that adverse impact exists.

Evidence of adverse impact involves more than the total number of minority workers *employed*. Also considered are the total number of qualified *applicants*. For instance, assume that 300 blacks and 300 whites were hired. But there were 1,500 black applicants and 1,000 white applicants. Putting these figures into the adverse impact formula, we conclude that adverse impact still exists.

$$\frac{300/1,500}{300/1,000} = \frac{0.2}{0.3} = 66.67\%$$

Thus, it is clear that firms must monitor their recruitment efforts very carefully. Obviously, firms should attempt to recruit qualified individuals because once in the applicant pool, they will be used in computing adverse impact.

Assuming that adverse impact is shown, employers have two avenues available to them if they still desire to use a particular selection standard. First, the employer may validate a selection device by showing that it is indeed a predictor of success. The employer can show a strong relationship between the selection device and job performance, and that if it did not use this procedure, the firm's training costs would become prohibitive. If the device has proved to be a predictor of job performance, business necessity has been established. If the firm's selection device has not been validated, business necessity may be demonstrated in another manner.

The second avenue available to employers should adverse impact be shown is the *bona fide occupational qualification (BFOQ)* defense. The BFOQ defense means that only one group is capable of performing the job successfully. As you might expect, courts have narrowly interpreted this defense because it almost always

**Adverse impact**
A concept established by the *Uniform Guidelines;* it occurs if women and minorities are not hired at the rate of at least 80 percent of the best-achieving group.

relates to sex discrimination. For instance, courts have rejected the concept that because most women cannot lift 50 pounds, all women should be eliminated from consideration for a job requiring heavy lifting.

Creators of the *Uniform Guidelines* adopted the bottom-line approach in assessing whether a firm's employment practices are discriminatory. For example, if a number of separate procedures are used in making a selection decision, the enforcement agencies will focus on the end result of these procedures to determine whether adverse impact has occurred. Essentially, the EEOC is concerned more with what is occurring than how it occurred. It admits that discriminatory employment practices that cannot be validated may exist; however, the net effect—or the bottom line—of the selection procedures is the focus of the EEOC's attention.

## ADDITIONAL GUIDELINES

Since the *Uniform Guidelines* were published in 1978, they have been modified several times. Some of these changes reflect Supreme Court decisions; others clarify implementation procedures. The three major changes discussed are the *Interpretative Guidelines on Sexual Harassment, Guidelines on Discrimination because of National Origin,* and *Guidelines on Discrimination because of Religion.*

### Interpretative Guidelines on Sexual Harassment

One of the most fervently pursued civil rights issues today relates to sexual harassment.[22] From 1990 to 1998, the number of sexual harassment complaints filed with the Equal Employment Opportunity Commission more than doubled, climbing from 6,100 to 15,500.[23] As previously mentioned, Title VII of the Civil Rights Act generally prohibits discrimination in employment on the basis of gender. The EEOC has also issued interpretative guidelines that state that employers have an affirmative duty to maintain a workplace free from sexual harassment. The OFCCP has also issued similar guidelines. Managers in both for-profit and not-for-profit organizations should be particularly alert to the issue of sexual harassment. The EEOC issued the guidelines because of the belief that sexual harassment continued to be a widespread problem. Table 3-1 contains the EEOC's definition of sexual harassment.

According to these guidelines, employers are totally liable for the acts of their supervisors, regardless of whether the employer is aware of the sexual harassment act.[24] Where co-workers are concerned, the employer is responsible for such acts if the employer knew, or should have known, about them. The employer is not responsible when it can show that it took immediate and appropriate corrective action on learning of the problem.

Another important aspect of these guidelines is that employers may be liable for acts committed by nonemployees in the workplace if the employer

▶ One of the most fervently pursued civil rights issues today relates to sexual harassment.

Unwelcome sexual advances, requests for sexual favors, and verbal or physical conduct of a sexual nature that occur under any of the following situations:

1. When submission to such contact is made either explicitly or implicitly a term or condition of an individual's employment
2. When submission to or rejection of such contact by an individual is used as the basis for employment decisions affecting such individual
3. When such conduct has the purpose or effect of unreasonably interfering with an individual's work performance or creating an intimidating, hostile, or offensive working environment

knew, or should have known, of the conduct and failed to take appropriate action. Firms are responsible for developing programs to prevent sexual harassment in the workplace.[25] They must also investigate all formal and informal complaints alleging sexual harassment. After investigating, a firm must take immediate and appropriate action to correct the situation.[26] Failure to do so constitutes a violation of Title VII, as interpreted by the EEOC. To prevail in court, companies must have clear procedures for handling sexual harassment complaints. Typically, employers choose an impartial ombudsperson to hear and investigate charges before lawyers get involved. If the sexual harassment complaint appears legitimate, the company must take *immediate and appropriate action.*

There have been numerous sexual harassment court cases. In *Miller v Bank of America,* a U.S. Circuit Court of Appeals held an employer liable for the sexually harassing acts of its supervisors, even though the company had a policy prohibiting such conduct, and even though the victim did not formally notify the employer of the problem. Another U.S. Circuit Court of Appeals ruled that sexual harassment, in and of itself, is a violation of Title VII. The court ruled that the law does not require the victim to prove that she or he resisted harassment and was penalized for that resistance. The first sexual harassment case to reach the U.S. Supreme Court was the case of *Meritor Savings Bank v Vinson.* In the Vinson decision, the Supreme Court recognized for the first time that Title VII could be used for offensive environment claims.[27] According to the EEOC, specific actions that could create a hostile workplace include a pattern of threatening, intimidating, or hostile acts and remarks, negative sexual stereotyping, or the display of written or graphic materials considered degrading. The Supreme Court decision of *Harris v Forklift Systems, Inc.* expanded the hostile workplace concept and made it easier to win sexual harassment claims. In a unanimous decision, the Supreme Court held that "to be accountable as abusive work environment harassment, conduct need not seriously affect . . . the psychological well-being or lead the plaintiff to suffer injury." No longer does severe psychological injury have to be proved. Under this ruling, plaintiffs need to show only that their employer allowed a hostile to abusive work environment to exist.[28]

Complaints still occur all too regularly. In 1999, Ford Motor Co. agreed to pay $7.5 million in damages and millions more in training costs to settle a sexual harassment complaint brought by the U.S. Equal Employment Opportunity Commission on behalf of female workers at the company's two Chicago-area plants. The $7.5 million settlement was the fourth-largest sexual harassment case in EEOC history and the second major damages award in the auto industry in little more than a year. The largest harassment settlement was an agreement in 1999 by Mitsubishi Motor Manufacturing Company to pay $34 million to settle a similar case. As part of the Ford settlement, the company also agreed to spend as much as $10 million to train approximately 40,000 employees, including managers, at 23 stamping and assembly plants nationwide on how to prevent sexual harassment and job discrimination. The auto maker also agreed to increase the number of women entering supervisory positions to 30 percent over the next three years at the two Chicago plants. Women now make up about 15 percent of the supervisors at the two plants. Ford also promises *substantial discipline,* including dismissal, for any managers who allow discrimination or harassment to take place against workers under their supervision.[29]

For a long time an unresolved question in employment law has been whether same-sex harassment (for example, males harassing males) is unlawful under Title VII of the Civil Rights Act of 1964. The Supreme Court in the case of *Oncale v Sundowner Offshore Services* held that same-sex sexual harassment may be unlawful under Title VII. The Court emphasized that Title VII does not prohibit all verbal or physical harassment in the workplace—only that which constitutes discrimination because of sex.[30] In 1999, an El Paso jury awarded $7.3 million to shoe salesman David Gonzalez, who claimed he was sexually harassed by his male supervisor. The decision against Little Rock–based Dillard's Inc. department stores is believed to be one of the largest sums returned in a same-sex harassment case.[31]

## Guidelines on Discrimination because of National Origin

Both EEOC and the courts have interpreted national origin protection under Title VII as extending far beyond discrimination against individuals who came from, or whose forebears came from, a particular country. National origin protection also covers (1) marriage or association with a person of a specific national origin; (2) membership in, or association with, an organization identified with, or seeking to promote the interests of national groups; (3) attendance at, or participation in, schools, churches, temples, or mosques generally used by persons of a national origin group; and (4) use of an individual's or spouse's name that is associated with a national origin group.[32] As Table 3-2 shows, the EEOC has identified certain selection procedures that may be discriminatory.

Harassment on the basis of national origin is a violation of Title VII. Employers have an affirmative duty to maintain a working environment free from such harassment. Ethnic slurs and other verbal or physical conduct relating to an individual's national origin constitute harassment when this conduct (1) has the purpose or effect of creating an intimidating, hostile, or offensive working environment; (2) has the purpose or effect of unreasonably interfering with an individual's work performance; or (3) otherwise adversely affects an individual's employment opportunity.

**Table 3-2**    **Selection Procedures That May Be Discriminatory with Regard to National Origin**

1. Fluency in English requirements: One questionable practice involves denying employment opportunities because of an individual's foreign accent or inability to communicate well in English. When this practice is continually followed, the Commission will presume that such a rule violates Title VII and will study it closely. However, a firm may require that employees speak only in English at certain times if business necessity can be shown.
2. Training or education requirements: Denying employment opportunities to an individual because of his or her foreign training or education, or practices that require an individual to be foreign trained or educated may be discriminatory.

Of current interest with regard to national origin is the English-only rule. Courts have generally ruled in the employer's favor if the rule would promote safety and product quality and stop harassment. For example, suppose a company has a rule that only English must be spoken except during breaks. That rule must be justified by a compelling business necessity. In *Garcia v Spun Steak,* the Ninth Circuit Court of Appeals (the Supreme Court refused to review) concluded that the rule did not necessarily violate Title VII. Spun Steak's management implemented the policy after some workers complained they were being harassed and insulted in a language they could not understand. The rule allowed workers to speak Spanish during breaks and lunch periods.[33] However, English-only policies that are not job related have been challenged and eliminated.

## Guidelines on Discrimination Because of Religion

The number of religious discrimination charges filed with the EEOC has increased every year but one since 1991. In 1998, 1,786 religion-related charges were filed, 43 percent more than in 1991.[34] Employers have an obligation to accommodate religious practices unless they can demonstrate a resulting hardship. The most common claims filed under the religious accommodation provisions involve employees objecting to either Sabbath employment or membership in or financial support of labor unions.[35] Consideration is given to identifiable costs in relation to the size and operating costs of the employer and the number of individuals who actually need the accommodation. These guidelines recognize that regular payment of premium wages constitutes undue hardship, whereas these payments on an infrequent or temporary basis do not. Undue hardship would also exist if an accommodation required a firm to vary from its bona fide seniority system.

These guidelines identify several means of accommodating religious practices that prohibit working on certain days. Some of the methods suggested included voluntary substitutes, flexible scheduling, lateral transfer, and change of job assignments. Some collective bargaining agreements include a provision that each employee must join the union or pay the union a sum equivalent to dues. When an employee's religious beliefs prevent compliance, the union should accommodate the employee by permitting that person to make an equivalent donation to a charitable organization.

## AFFIRMATIVE ACTION PROGRAMS

An **affirmative action program (AAP)** is an approach developed by organizations with government contracts to demonstrate that workers are employed in proportion to their representation in the firm's relevant labor market. The need for affirmative action programs was created by EO 11246, as amended by EO 11375, which places enforcement with the Office of Federal Contract Compliance Programs (OFCCP). An affirmative action program may also be voluntarily implemented by an organization. In such an event, goals are established and action is taken to hire and move minorities and women up in the organization. In other situations, an AAP may be mandated by the OFCCP. The degree of control the OFCCP will impose depends on the size of the contract, with contracts of $10,000 or less not covered. The first level of control involves contracts that exceed $10,000 but are less than $50,000. These contractors are governed by the equal opportunity clause, as shown in Table 3-3.

**Affirmative action program (AAP)**
A program that an organization with government contracts develops to employ women and minorities in proportion to their representation in the firm's relevant labor market.

**Table 3-3** Equal Opportunity Clause—Government Contracts

1. The contractor will not discriminate against any employee or applicant for employment because of race, color, religion, sex, or national origin. The contractor will take affirmative action to ensure that applicants are employed, and that employees are treated during employment, without regard to their race, color, religion, sex, or national origin. Such action shall include, but not be limited to the following: employment, upgrading, demotions, or transfer; recruitment or recruitment advertising, layoff or termination; rates of pay or other forms of compensation; and selection for training, including apprenticeship. The contractor agrees to post in conspicuous places, available to employees and applicants for employment, notices to be provided by the contracting officer setting forth the provisions for this nondiscrimination clause.

2. The contractor will in all solicitations or advertisements for employees placed by or on behalf of the contractor, state that all qualified applicants will receive consideration for employment without regard to race, color, religion, sex, or national origin.

3. The contractor will send to each labor union or representative of workers with which he or she has a collective bargaining agreement or other contract or understanding, a notice to be provided by the agency contracting officer, advising the labor union or workers' representative of the contractor's commitments under section 202 of Executive Order 11246 of September 24, 1965, and shall post copies of the notice in conspicuous places available to employees and applicants for employment.

4. The contractor will comply with all provisions of Executive Order 11246 of September 24, 1965, and the rules, regulations, and relevant orders of the Secretary of Labor.

5. The contractor will furnish all information and reports required by Executive Order 11246 of September 24, 1965, and by the rules, regulations, and orders of the Secretary of Labor, or pursuant thereto, and will permit access to his or her books, records, and accounts by the contracting agency and the Secretary of Labor for purposes of investigation to ascertain compliance with such rules, regulations, and orders.

6. In the event of the contractor's noncompliance with the nondiscrimination clauses of this contract or with any of such rules, regulations, or orders, this contract may be canceled, terminated, or suspended in whole or in part and the contractor may be declared ineligible for further Government contracts in accordance with procedures authorized in Executive Order 11246 of September 24, 1965, or by rule, regulation, or order of the Secretary of State, or as otherwise provided by law.

7. The contractor will include the provisions of paragraphs (1) through (7) in every subcontract or purchase order unless exempted by rules, regulations, or orders of the Secretary of Labor issued pursuant to section 204 of Executive Order 11246 of September 24, 1965, so that such provisions will be binding upon each subcontractor or vendor. The contractor will take such action with respect to any subcontract or purchase order as may be directed by the Secretary of Labor as a means of enforcing such provisions including sanctions for noncompliance: Provided, however, that in the event the contractor becomes involved in, or is threatened with litigation with a subcontractor or vendor as a result of such direction, the contractor may request the United States to enter into such litigation to protect the interests of the United States.

*Source: Federal Register,* 45, no. 251 (Tuesday, December 30, 1980): 86230.

The second level of control occurs if the contractor (1) has 50 or more employees; (2) has a contract of $50,000 or more; (3) has contracts which, in any 12-month period, total $50,000 or more or reasonably may be expected to total $50,000 or more; or (4) is a financial institution that serves as a depository for government funds in any amount, acts as an issuing or redeeming agent for U.S. savings bonds and savings notes in any amount, or subscribes to federal deposit or share insurance. Contractors meeting these criteria must develop a written affirmative action program for each of their establishments and file an annual EEO-1 report (see Figure 3-2). The affirmative action program is the major focus of EO 11246. It requires specific steps to guarantee equal employment opportunity.

## EQUAL EMPLOYMENT OPPORTUNITY

**EMPLOYER INFORMATION REPORT EEO—1**

**1997**

Joint Reporting
Committee

- Equal Employment Opportunity Commission
- Office of Federal Contract Compliance Programs (Labor)

Standard Form 100
(Rev. 4–92)

O.M.B. No. 3048–0007
EXPIRES 12/31/93
100-213

---

### Section A—TYPE OF REPORT
Refer to instructions for number and types of reports to be filed.

1. Indicate by marking in the appropriate box the type of reporting unit for which this copy of the form is submitted (MARK ONLY ONE BOX).

(1) ☐ Single-establishment Employer Report

Multi-establishment Employer:
(2) ☐ Consolidated Report (Required)
(3) ☐ Headquarters Unit Report (Required)
(4) ☐ Individual Establishment Report (submit one for each establishment with 50 or more employees)
(5) ☐ Special Report

2. Total number of reports being filed by this Company (Answer on Consolidated Report only) _____

### Section B—COMPANY IDENTIFICATION (To be answered by all employers)

OFFICE USE ONLY

1. Parent Company

   a. Name of parent company (owns or controls establishment in item 2) omit if same as label

   a.

   Address (Number and street)

   b.

   | City or town | State | ZIP code |
   |---|---|---|

   c.

2. Establishment for which this report is filed. (Omit if same as label)

   a. Name of establishment

   d.

   | Address (Number and street) | City or town | County | State | ZIP code |
   |---|---|---|---|---|

   e.

   b. Employer identification No. (IRS 9-DIGIT TAX NUMBER)

   f.

   Was an EEO–1 report filed for this establishment last year? ☐ Yes ☐ No

### Section C—EMPLOYERS WHO ARE REQUIRED TO FILE (To be answered by all employers)

☐ Yes ☐ No   1. Does the entire company have at least 100 employees in the payroll period for which you are reporting?

☐ Yes ☐ No   2. Is your company affiliated through common ownership and/or centralized management with other entitles in an enterprise with a total employment of 100 or more?

☐ Yes ☐ No   3. Does the company or any of its establishments (1) have 50 or more employees AND (b) is not exempt as provided by 41 CFR 60–1.5, AND either (1) is a prime government contractor or first-tier subcontractor, and has a contract, subcontract, or purchase order amounting to $50,000 or more, or (2) serves as a depository for Government funds in any amount or is a financial institution which is an issuing and paying agent for U.S. Savings Bonds and Savings Notes?

If the response to question C–3 is yes, please enter your Dun and Bradstreet Identification number (if you have one): ☐☐☐☐☐☐☐☐☐

NOTE: If the answer is yes to questions 1, 2, or 3, complete the entire form, otherwise skip to Section G.

NSN 7540–00–180–6384

---

**Equal Opportunity Employer Information Report**    **Figure 3-2**

Prerequisite to development of a satisfactory AAP is identification and analysis of problem areas inherent in employment of minorities and women, and an evaluation of opportunities for utilizing minority and women employees.

The third level of control on contractors is in effect when contracts exceed $1 million. All previously stated requirements must be met, and in addition, the OFCCP is authorized to conduct pre-award compliance reviews. The purpose of a compliance review is to determine whether the contractor is maintaining

## Section D—EMPLOYMENT DATA

Employment at this establishment—Report all permanent full-time and part-time employees including apprentices and on-the-job trainees unless specifically excluded as set forth in the instructions. Enter the appropriate figures on all lines and in all columns. Blank spaces will be considered as zeros.

| JOB CATEGORIES | | OVERALL TOTALS (SUM OF COL. B THRU K) | MALE | | | | | FEMALE | | | | |
|---|---|---|---|---|---|---|---|---|---|---|---|---|
| | | | WHITE (NOT OF HISPANIC ORIGIN) | BLACK (NOT OF HISPANIC ORIGIN) | HISPANIC | ASIAN OR PACIFIC ISLANDER | AMERICAN INDIAN OR ALASKAN NATIVE | WHITE (NOT OF HISPANIC ORIGIN) | BLACK (NOT OF HISPANIC ORIGIN) | HISPANIC | ASIAN OR PACIFIC ISLANDER | AMERICAN INDIAN OR ALASKAN NATIVE |
| | | A | B | C | D | E | F | G | H | I | J | K |
| Officials and Managers | 1 | | | | | | | | | | | |
| Officials and Managers | 2 | | | | | | | | | | | |
| Officials and Managers | 3 | | | | | | | | | | | |
| Officials and Managers | 4 | | | | | | | | | | | |
| Officials and Managers | 5 | | | | | | | | | | | |
| Officials and Managers | 6 | | | | | | | | | | | |
| Officials and Managers | 7 | | | | | | | | | | | |
| Officials and Managers | 8 | | | | | | | | | | | |
| Service Workers | 9 | | | | | | | | | | | |
| TOTAL | 10 | | | | | | | | | | | |
| Total employment reported in previous EEO–1 report | 11 | | | | | | | | | | | |

NOTE: Omit questions 1 and 2 on the Consolidated Report.

1.  Date(s) of payroll period used: 

2.  Does this establishment employ apprentices?
    1 ☐ Yes    2 ☐ No

### Section E—ESTABLISHMENT INFORMATION (Omit on the Consolidated Report)

1.  What is the major activity of this establishment? (Be specific, i.e., manufacturing steel castings, retail grocer, wholesale plumbing supplies, title insurance, etc. Include the specific type of product or type of service provided, as well as the principal business or industrial activity.)

OFFICE USE ONLY

g.

### Section F—REMARKS

Use this item to give any identification data appearing on last report which differs from that given above, explain major changes in composition or reporting units and other pertinent information.

### Section G—CERTIFICATION (See Instructions G)

Check one

1 ☐ All reports are accurate and were prepared in accordance with the instructions. (Check on consolidated only)
2 ☐ This report is accurate and was prepared in accordance with the instructions.

| Name of Certifying Official | Title | Signature | Date |
|---|---|---|---|
| Name of person to contact regarding this report (Type or print) | Address (Number and Street) | | |
| Title | City and State | ZIP code | Telephone Number (including Area Code) | Extension |

All reports and information obtained from individual reports will be kept confidential as required by Section 709(e) of Title VII.
WILLFULLY FALSE STATEMENTS ON THIS REPORT ARE PUNISHABLE BY LAW, U.S. CODE, TITLE 18, SECTION 1001.

---

**Figure 3-2** 🖐 **Equal Opportunity Employer Information Report** (*continued from page 75*)

nondiscriminatory hiring and employment practices. The review also ensures that the contractor is utilizing affirmative action to guarantee that applicants are employed, placed, trained, upgraded, promoted, terminated, and otherwise treated fairly without regard to race, color, religion, gender, national origin, veteran status, or disability during employment. In determining whether to conduct a pre-award review, the OFCCP may consider, for example, the items presented in Table 3-4.

1. The past EEO performance of the contractor, including its current EEO profile and indications of underutilization
2. The volume and nature of complaints filed by employees or applicants against the contractor
3. Whether the contractor is in a growth industry
4. The level of employment or promotional opportunities resulting from the expansion of, or turnover in, the contractor's workforce
5. The employment opportunities likely to result from the contract in issue
6. Whether resources are available to conduct the review

If an investigation indicates a violation, the OFCCP first tries to secure compliance through persuasion. If persuasion fails to resolve the issue, the OFCCP serves a notice to show cause or a notice of violation. A show cause notice contains a list of the violations, a statement of how the OFCCP proposes that corrections be made, a request for a written response to the findings, and a suggested date for a conciliation conference. The firm usually has 30 days to respond. Successful conciliation results in a written contract between the OFCCP and the contractor. In a conciliation agreement, the contractor agrees to take specific steps to remedy noncompliance with an EO. Firms that do not correct violations can be passed over in the awarding of future contracts. The procedures for developing affirmative action plans were published in the *Federal Register* of December 4, 1974. These regulations are referred to as Revised Order No. 4. The OFCCP guide for compliance officers, outlining what to cover in a compliance review, is known as Order No. 14.

The OFCCP is very specific about what should be included in an affirmative action program. A policy statement has to be developed that reflects the CEO's attitude regarding equal employment opportunity, assigns overall responsibility for preparing and implementing the affirmative action program, and provides for reporting and monitoring procedures. The policy should state that the firm intends to recruit, hire, train, and promote persons in all job titles without regard to race, color, religion, gender, or national origin, except where gender is a *bona fide organizational qualification (BFOQ)*. The policy should guarantee that all human resource actions involving such areas as compensation, benefits, transfers, layoffs, return from layoffs, company-sponsored training, education, tuition assistance, and social and recreational programs will be administered without regard to race, color, religion, gender, or national origin. Revised Order No. 4 is quite specific with regard to dissemination of a firm's EEO policy, both internally and externally. An executive should be appointed to manage the firm's equal employment opportunity program. This person should be given the necessary support by top management to accomplish the assignment. Revised Order No. 4 specifies the minimum level of responsibility associated with the task of EEO manager.

An acceptable AAP must include an analysis of deficiencies in the utilization of minority groups and women. The first step in conducting a utilization analysis is to make a workforce analysis. The second step involves an analysis of all major job groups. An explanation of the situation is required if minorities or women are currently being underutilized. A job group is defined as one or more jobs having similar content, wage rates, and opportunities. Underutilization is defined as having fewer minorities or women in a particular job group than would reasonably be expected by their availability. The utilization analysis is important because the calculations determine whether underutilization exists.

For example, if the utilization analysis shows that the availability of blacks for a certain job group is 30 percent, the organization should have at least 30 percent black employment in that group. If actual employment is less than 30 percent, underutilization exists, and the firm should set a goal of 30 percent black employment for that job group.

The primary focus of any affirmative action program is on goals and timetables, with the issue being how many and by when. Goals and timetables developed by the firm should cover its entire affirmative action program, including correction of deficiencies. These goals and timetables should be attainable; that is, they should be based on results that the firm, making good-faith efforts, could reasonably expect to achieve. Goals should be significant and measurable, as well as attainable. Two types of goals must be established regarding underutilization: annual and ultimate. The annual goal is to move toward elimination of underutilization, whereas the ultimate goal is to correct all underutilization. Goals should be specific in terms of planned results, with timetables for completion. However, goals should not establish inflexible quotas that must be met. Rather, they should be targets that are reasonably attainable.

Employers should also conduct a detailed analysis of job descriptions to ensure that they accurately reflect job content. Job specifications should be validated, with special attention given to academic, experience, and skill requirements. If a job specification screens out a disproportionate number of minorities or women, the requirements must be professionally validated in relation to job performance. Thus, a comprehensive job analysis program is required.

When an opening occurs, everyone involved in human resource recruiting, screening, selection, and promotion should be aware of the opening. In addition, the firm should evaluate the entire selection process to ensure freedom from bias. Individuals involved in the process should be carefully selected and trained to minimize bias in all human resource actions.

## A GLOBAL PERSPECTIVE

### EEO Is Embraced by the United Kingdom

The EEO movement has always been led by the United States, but now the United Kingdom (UK) appears to be following. Historically, American firms often find their human resource policies in conflict with the laws and accepted norms of the host country, including the UK. For instance, the influence of Title VII of the Civil Rights Act of 1964, as amended, has been felt by virtually all firms operating in the United States, but most countries in the world do not have laws prohibiting discrimination. In fact, some countries practice overt discrimination against certain groups whose members would be protected if employed in America.

Now, American-style EEO is gaining support in Britain. According to Andrew Smith, UK Employment and Equal Opportunities Minister, "Our vision on equality is clear—to create a society where every individual, regardless of their background, has the same opportunities and respect as his or her neighbor." Smith also believes that "there is no place for any unjustified discrimination in today's workplace." In addition, under Smith's leadership the government enacted a new Code for Age Diversity in the Workplace, aimed at giving many older workers a fairer deal in competing for jobs in the workplace.[36] The UK's ratification of the International Labor Organization's position on discrimination in employment at the International Labor Conference in Geneva signals that Britain intends to become an equality beacon to the world. Britain aims to make equality in the workplace a reality.[37]

▶ Identify referral organizations for minorities and women.
▶ Hold formal briefing sessions with representatives of referral organizations.
▶ Encourage minority and women employees to refer applicants to the firm.
▶ Include minorities and women on the Personnel Relations staff.
▶ Permit minorities and women to participate in Career Days, Youth Motivation Programs, and related activities in their community.
▶ Actively participate in job fairs and give company representatives the authority to make on-the-spot-commitments.
▶ Actively recruit at schools having predominant minority or female enrollments.
▶ Use special efforts to reach minorities and women during school recruitment drives.
▶ Undertake special employment programs whenever possible for women and minorities. These might include technical and nontechnical co-op programs, after-school and/or work-study jobs, summer jobs for underprivileged individuals, summer work-study programs, and motivation, training, and employment programs for the hardcore unemployed.
▶ Pictorially present minorities and women in recruiting brochures.
▶ Include the minority news media and women's interest media when expending help wanted advertising.

*Source: Federal Register,* 45, no. 251 (Tuesday, December 30, 1980): 86243.

Firms should observe the requirements of the *Uniform Guidelines.* Selection techniques other than paper-and-pencil tests can also be used improperly, and thus discriminate against minorities and women. Such techniques include unscored interviews, unscored or casual application forms, use of arrest records and credit checks, and consideration of marital status, dependency, and minor children. Where data suggest that discrimination or unfair exclusion of minorities and women exists, the firm should analyze its unscored procedures and eliminate them if they are not objective and valid. Some techniques that can be used to improve recruitment and increase the flow of minority and women applicants are shown in Table 3-5.

As previously discussed in the *Adarand Constructors v Pena* Supreme Court decision, affirmative action programs are presently receiving court challenges. As a result of this case, the future of affirmative action is yet to be determined. From now on, federal affirmative action programs will be subject to the most rigorous level of court review.[38]

## Summary ◀

**①  Identify the major laws affecting equal employment opportunity.**
Major laws include the Civil Rights Act of 1866; Title VII of the Civil Rights Act of 1964, as Amended in 1972; Age Discrimination in Employment Act of 1967, as Amended in 1978 and 1986; Rehabilitation Act of 1973; Pregnancy Discrimination Act of 1978; Immigration Reform and Control Act (IRCA) of 1986; Immigration Act of 1990; Illegal Immigration Reform and Immigrant Responsibility Act of 1996; and the Civil Rights Act of 1991.

**②  Explain presidential Executive Orders 11246 and 11375.**
By EO 11246, the policy of the government of the United States expanded to provide equal opportunity in federal employment for all qualified persons. The order prohibited discrimination in employment because of race, creed, color, or national origin. EO 11246 was amended by EO 11375, which changed the word *creed* to *religion* and added sex discrimination to the other prohibited items.

**③** Identify some of the major Supreme Court decisions that have had an impact on equal employment opportunity.

Major decisions include *Griggs v Duke Power Company, Albermarle Paper Company v Moody, Phillips v Martin Marietta Corporation, Espinoza v Farah Manufacturing Company, Weber v Kaiser Aluminum and Chemical Corporation, Dothard v Rawlingson, University of California Regents v Bakke, American Tobacco Company v Patterson, Meritor Savings Bank v Vinson, City of Richmond v J. A. Croson Co., Adarand Constructors v Pena,* and *O'Connor v Consolidated Coin Caterers Corp.*

**④** Describe the Equal Employment Opportunity Commission.

Title VII of the Civil Rights Act, as amended, created the Equal Employment Opportunity Commission. It was initially charged with administering the act.

**⑤** Explain the purpose of the *Uniform Guidelines on Employee Selection Procedures.*

The guidelines adopted a single set of principles that were designed to assist employers, labor organizations, employment agencies, and licensing and certification boards to comply with requirements of federal law prohibiting employment practices that discriminated on the basis of race, color, religion, sex, and national origin. They were designed to provide a framework for determining the proper use of tests and other selection procedures.

**⑥** Explain adverse impact.

Adverse impact is a concept established by the *Uniform Guidelines* and occurs if women and minorities are not hired at the rate of at least 80 percent of the best-achieving group.

**⑦** Describe the *Uniform Guidelines* related to sexual harassment, national origin, and religion.

The EEOC has also issued interpretive guidelines that state that employers have an affirmative duty to maintain a workplace free from sexual harassment. The EEOC broadly defined discrimination on the basis of national origin as the denial of equal employment opportunity because of an individual's ancestors or place of birth or because an individual has the physical, cultural, or linguistic characteristics of a national origin group. Employers have an obligation to accommodate religious practices unless they can demonstrate a resulting hardship.

**⑧** Explain affirmative action programs.

An affirmative action program (AAP) is an approach that an organization with government contracts develops to demonstrate that women or minorities are employed in proportion to their representation in the firm's relevant labor market.

---

## ▶ Questions for Review

1. Briefly describe the following laws:

   a. Civil Rights Act of 1866
   b. Title VII of the Civil Rights Act of 1964, as amended in 1972
   c. Age Discrimination in Employment Act of 1967, as amended in 1978 and 1986
   d. Rehabilitation Act of 1973
   e. Pregnancy Discrimination Act of 1978
   f. Immigration Control Acts
   g. Americans with Disabilities Act of 1990
   h. Civil Rights Act of 1991.

2. What is a presidential executive order? Describe the major provisions of EO 11246, as amended by EO 11375.

3. What is the purpose of the Office of Federal Contract Compliance Programs?

4. What are the significant U.S. Supreme Court decisions that have had an impact on equal employment opportunity?

5. What is the purpose of the *Uniform Guidelines on Employee Selection Procedures?*

6. Distinguish between adverse impact and affirmative action programs.

7. How does the Equal Employment Opportunity Commission (EEOC) define sexual harassment?

*We invite you to visit the Mondy homepage on the Prentice Hall Web site at*

**www.prenhall.com/mondy**

*for updated information, Web-based exercises, and links to other HR-related sites.*

TAKE IT TO
THE NET

## Developing HRM Skills ◄

### An Experiential Exercise

Many laws have been passed and court decisions rendered that affect the everyday actions of human resource management. But past decisions may no longer apply. Managers have a responsibility to ensure that actions affecting human resource management adhere to both the letter and intent of the law. Unfortunately, not everyone may share this view, which is when problems occur. Against this backdrop, the human resource manager and a dock foreman for New York–based Hoffa Loading and Storage Company are having an employment disagreement.

Two individuals will participate in this exercise in which a potential for conflict exists. One person will serve as the human resource manager, and the other will play the role of dock foreman. All students not playing a role should carefully observe the behavior of both participants. Your instructor will provide the participants with the necessary additional information that they will need.

## HRM INCIDENT 1 ◄

### I Feel Great

Les Partain, supervisor of the training and development department for Gazelle Corporation, was 64 years old and had been with the firm for over thirty years. For the past twelve years he had served as Gazelle's training and development manager and felt that he had been doing a good job. This belief was supported by the fact that during the last five years he had received excellent performance reports from his boss, Bennie Helton, director of personnel.

Six months before Les's birthday, he and Bennie were enjoying a cup of coffee together. "Les," said Bennie, "I know that you're pleased with the progress our T&D section has made under your leadership. We're really going to miss you when you retire this year. You'll certainly live the good life because you'll receive the maximum retirement benefits. If I can be of any assistance to you in developing the paperwork for your retirement, please let me know."

"Gee, Bennie," said Les. "I really appreciate the good words, but I've never felt better in my life, and although our retirement plan is excellent, I figure that I have at least five more good years. There are many other things I would like to do for the department before I retire. I have some excellent employees, and we can get many things done within the next five years."

After finishing their coffee, both men returned to their work. As Bennie left, he was thinking, "My gosh, I had no idea that character intended to hang on. The only reason I gave him those good performance appraisals was to make him feel better before he retired. He was actually only an average worker and I was anxious to move a more aggressive person into that key job. We stand to lose several good people in that department if Les doesn't leave. From what they tell me, he's not doing too much of a job."

### Questions

1. From a legal viewpoint, what do you believe Bennie can do regarding this situation? Discuss.
2. What actions should Bennie have taken in the past to avoid his current predicament?

## ► HRM INCIDENT 2

### *So, What's Affirmative Action?*

Supreme Construction Company began as a small commercial builder located in Baytown, Texas. Until the 1990s, Alex Boyd, Supreme's founder, concentrated his efforts on small, freestanding shops and offices. Up to that time, Alex had never employed more than 15 people.

In 1992, Alex's son, Michael, graduated from college with a degree in construction management and immediately joined the company full time. Michael had worked on a variety of Supreme jobs while in school, and Alex felt his son was really cut out for the construction business. Michael was given increasing responsibility, and the company continued its success, although with a few more projects and a few more employees than before. In 1999, Mike approached his father with a proposition: "Let's get into some of the bigger projects now. We have the capital to expand and I really believe we can do it." Alex approved, and Supreme began doing small shopping centers and multistory office buildings in addition to work in its traditional area of specialization. Soon, employment had grown to 75 employees.

In 2001, the National Aeronautics and Space Administration (NASA) released construction specifications for two aircraft hangars to be built southeast of Houston. Although Supreme had never done any construction work for the government, Michael and Alex considered the job within the company's capabilities. Michael worked up the $1,982,000 bid and submitted it to the NASA procurement office.

Several weeks later the bids were opened. Supreme had the low bid. However, the acceptance letter was contingent on submission of a satisfactory affirmative action program.

### Questions

1. Explain why Supreme must submit an affirmative action program.
2. Generally, what should the program be designed to accomplish?

1. Wendy Bliss, "The Wheel of Misfortune," *HRMagazine* 45 (May 2000): 207.

2. "Court Says Age Bias Law Doesn't Affect States," *United Press International* (January 11, 2000): 1.

3. Robert J. Noble, Esq., "To Waiver or Not to Waiver Is the Question of OWPWA," *Personnel* 68 (June 1991): 11.

4. Kate Colborn, "You Want Me to Sign What?" *EDN* 38 (March 11, 1993): 69.

5. Carol J. Castaneda, "Panel Backs FAA on Retire-at-60 Rule," *USA Today* (July 16, 1997): 6A.

6. Donald L. Caruth, Robert M. Noe III, and R. Wayne Mondy, *Staffing the Contemporary Organization* (New York: Quorum Books, 1988): 49.

7. John J. Keller, "AT&T Will Settle EEOC Lawsuit for $66 Million," *Wall Street Journal* 88, no. 13 (July 18, 1991): B8.

8. Art L. Bethke, "The IRCA: What's an Employer to Do?" *Wisconsin Small Business Forum* 6 (Fall 1987): 26.

9. Susan Martin, "U.S. Immigration Policy," *National Forum* 74 (June 1994): 12.

10. Dan P. Danilow, "New Immigration Law Signed," *Northwest Asian Weekly* (November 15, 1996): PG.

11. Susan E. Long, "Supreme Court Issues Several Key ADA Decisions," *HR Focus* 76 (September 1999): 3.

12. Gary H. Anthes, "The Invisible Workforce," *Computerworld* 34 (May 2000): 50–54.

13. Eric Minton, "The ADA and Records Management," *Records Management Quarterly* 28 (January 1994): 12.

14. The six cases are *Ward Cove Packing Co., Inc., v Antonio, Price Waterhouse v Hopkins, Patterson v McClean Credit Union, Martin v Wilks, West Virginia Hospitals v Casey,* and *Lorence v AT&T.*

15. Andrew Quinn, "San Francisco Comes Down Hard on Weightism," *Reuters* (May 8, 2000): 1.

16. Bruce Fein, "Preferences Fading Away," *The Washington Times* (August 3, 1999): A16.

17. Michael Kirkland, "Court: No Bias Suit Under Objective Rules," *United Press International* (November 29, 1999).

18. Constance B. DiCesare, "Age Discrimination *(O'Connor v Consolidated Coin Caterers Corp.),*" *Monthly Labor Review* 119 (July 1996): 51.

19. Donald Caruth and Gail Handlogten, "Avoiding HR Lawsuits," *Credit Union Executive Journal* 39 (November-December 1999): 25.

20. Diana Kunde, "Heading Off Trouble: EEOC Turns to Mediation to Resolve Backlog of Cases," *The Dallas Morning News* (February 24, 1999): 1D.

21. "The Online Job Hunt: No Tie Required," *EEO BiMonthly, Equal Employment Opportunity Career Journal* (December 31, 1998): 34.

22. "Job Bias Suits and Jury Awards Are Souring," *HR Focus* 77 (March 2000): 2.

23. Susan E. Long and Catherine G. Leonard, "The Changing Face of Sexual Harassment," *HR Focus* 76 (October 1999): S1.

24. "Complying with EEOC Anti-Harassment Guidelines: Supervisor Training and Communications Prove Crucial," *PR Newswire* (June 23, 1999): 1.

25. Debbie Rodman Sandler, "Sexual Harassment Rulings: Less Than Meets the Eye," *HRMagazine* 43 (October 1, 1998): 136–143.

26. Theresa Brady, "Added Liability: Third-Party Sexual Harassment," *Management Review* 86 (April 1997): 45–47.

27. Stacey J. Garvin, "Employer Liability for Sexual Harassment," *HRMagazine* 36 (June 1991): 107.

28. Larry Reynolds, "Sex Harassment Claims Surge," *HR Focus* 74 (March 1997): 8.

29. Frank Swoboda, "Ford to Pay Fine in Harassment Settlement," *The Washington Post* (September 8, 1999): E:1.

30. Mary-Kathryn Zachary, "Supreme Court Clarifies Same-Sex Harassment," *Supervision* 59 (July 1998): 20–21.

31. Jennifer Laabs, "News Digest," *Workforce* 78 (July 1999): 22.

32. Barbara Lindemann Schlei and Paul Grossman, *Employment Discrimination Law,* 2nd ed. (Washington, D.C.: Bureau of National Affairs, 1983): 423.

33. Theresa Brady, "The Downside of Diversity," *Management Review* 85 (June 1996): 29.

34. "Religious Diversity: A Handle-with-Care Challenge," *HR Focus* 77 (March 2000): 3.

35. Stephanie Overman, "Good Faith Is the Answer," *HRMagazine* 39 (January 1994): 76.

36. "UK Government: Smith at International Labour Conference—UK Ratifies ILO on Discrimination," *M2 Press Wire* (June 8,1999).

37. Ibid.

38. Melinda-Hawkeye Carlton, Philip Hawkey, Douglas Watson, William Donahue, Bobby Garcia, and Dan Johnson, "Affirmative Action," *Public Management* 79 (January 1997): 19.

This video begins with a brief dramatized incident that presents one or more of a firm's employees with a problem to resolve. After you have seen how the employee reacts to the challenge, you will be ready to address the questions following each case. Use what you have learned, both from the textbook chapters in each part and from your own experience, to fashion a suggested solution to the problem.

This first video introduces some of the staff members at Quicktakes Video, a small television production company that produces short films and videos for various corporate and entrepreneurial clients. Most of the videos that accompany this text also relate incidents that occur at Quicktakes.

Quicktakes is owned by Hal Boylston, who manages most of the administrative tasks for the firm, and Karen Jarvis, who functions as the director of sales, managing the sales people and bringing new clients to the firm.

The firm employs 40 people, among them script writers, producers, union actors (known in the business as "talent"), salespeople, editors, and support staff including clerical workers and accounting professionals. Its mission is fairly specialized, but you'll see in the video segments that its staff must deal with the same strategic, legal, and personal issues that people typically face in many work environments. The experiences of Quicktakes' employees will demonstrate why it's important for everyone to have basic human resource skills, whether the company has a formal Human Resource Department or not. (Quicktakes does not.)

This segment presents Kim, Quicktakes' chief writer, and Brad, a successful Quicktakes salesperson. We'll also meet Hal Boylston and observe how he interacts with each of these employees when a conflict arises between them.

While you watch the video, keep in mind that, as you read in Chapter 3, the Equal Employment Opportunity Commission (EEOC) charges employers with an affirmative duty to maintain a workplace free of sexual harassment and intimidation. Harassment on the basis of sex is a violation of Title VII (of the 1964 Civil Rights Act) when its purpose or effect is to substantially interfere with a person's work performance *or* to create a hostile work environment. Of particular concern to Hal should be the law's provision that an employer is liable for the sexually harassing acts of its nonsupervisory employees if they knew or should have known about them.

### Discussion Questions

1. Has Brad sexually harassed Kim? Why or why not?
2. If Kim believes she has been sexually harassed, how should she react now? Is there anything she should do that she has not done?
3. Hal has made at least one mistake already. What was it, and how can he correct it? How will that help him resolve the difference between Brad's and Kim's accounts of the reason for their disagreement?
4. Does the quality of Kim's work have any bearing on the eventual resolution?
5. In trying to resolve the issue, what weight should Hal give to Brad's skill at bringing new business to the firm?

**Part Three**

*Staffing*

objectivesobjectivesobjectives

# Objectives

- Describe why job analysis is a basic human resource tool.
- Explain the reasons for conducting job analysis.
- Describe the types of information required for job analysis.
- Describe the various job analysis methods.
- Describe the components of a well-designed job description.
- Identify the other methods available for conducting job analysis.
- Describe how job analysis helps satisfy various legal requirements.
- Explain the human resource planning process.
- Describe some human resource forecasting techniques.
- Define *requirements* and *availability forecasts.*
- Identify what a firm can do when either a surplus or a shortage of workers exists.
- Distinguish between succession planning and succession development.
- Describe job design.

chapter
chapterchapterchapterchapterchapterchapter

# 4

# Job Analysis and Human Resource Planning

**B**rian Charles, the vice president of marketing for Sharpco Manufacturing, commented at the weekly executive directors' meeting, "I have good news. We can get the large contract with Medord Corporation. All we have to do is complete the project in one year instead of two. I told them we could do it."

Charmagne Powell, vice president of human resources, brought Brian back to reality by reminding him, "Remember our strategic plan that we all agreed to? Our present workers do not have the expertise required to produce the quality that Medord's particular specifications require. Under the two-year project timetable, we planned to retrain our present workers gradually. With this new time schedule, we will have to go into the job market and recruit workers who are already experienced in

keytermskeytermskeyterms

# Key Terms

Job analysis 87
Job 87
Position 88
Job description 88
Job specification 88
Job analysis schedule (JAS) 98
Functional job analysis (FJA) 99

Position analysis questionnaire (PAQ) 100
Management position description questionnaire (MPDQ) 100
Guidelines-oriented job analysis (GOJA) 100
Strategic planning 102

Human resource planning (HRP) 102
Zero-base forecasting 103
Bottom-up approach 104
Simulation 105
Requirements forecast 105
Availability forecast 105
Succession planning 108

Succession development 110
Job design 110
Job enrichment 110
Job enlargement 110
Total quality management (TQM) 111
Reengineering 111

this process. We all need to study your proposal further. Human resource costs will rise considerably if we attempt to complete the project in one year instead of two. Sure, Brian, we can do it, but with these constraints, will the project be cost effective?"

**I**n this instance, Charmagne considered the strategic nature of human resource planning when she challenged Brian's "good news" forecast. In today's fast-paced, competitive environment, failure to recognize the strategic nature of human resource planning will often destroy an otherwise well-thought-out plan.

We begin the chapter by describing why job analysis is a basic human resource management tool and explaining the reasons for conducting job analysis. Next, we review the types of job analysis information required and discuss job analysis methods. Then, we explain the components of a well-designed job description and describe other methods for conducting job analysis and the ways job analysis helps to satisfy various legal requirements. We then examine the human resource planning process and some human resource forecasting techniques. Next, we discuss forecasting human resource requirements and availability and describe what actions could be taken should either a surplus or a shortage of workers exist. The chapter ends with a discussion of succession planning and development and job design.

## JOB ANALYSIS: A BASIC HUMAN RESOURCE MANAGEMENT TOOL

**Job analysis** is the systematic process of determining the skills, duties, and knowledge required for performing jobs in an organization.[1] It is an essential and pervasive human resource technique. In today's rapidly changing work environment, the need for a sound job analysis system is extremely critical. New jobs are being created, and old jobs are being redesigned or eliminated. A job analysis that was conducted only a few years ago quite probably includes inaccurate data. Some have even suggested that changes are occurring too fast to maintain an effective job analysis system.

A **job** consists of a group of tasks that must be performed for an organization to achieve its goals. A job may require the services of one person, such as that of

**Job analysis**
The systematic process of determining the skills, duties, and knowledge required for performing specific jobs in an organization.

**Job**
A group of tasks that must be performed if an organization is to achieve its goals.

▶ *Bureau of Labor Statistics*

**www.prenhall.com/mondy**

Vital information related to human resource planning is available on this site.

HR WEB
WISDOM

president, or the services of 75, as might be the case with data entry operators in a large firm. A **position** is the collection of tasks and responsibilities performed by one person; there is a position for every individual in an organization. In a work group consisting of a supervisor, two senior clerks, and four word processing operators, there are three jobs and seven positions. For instance, a small company might have 25 jobs for its 75 employees, whereas in a large company 2,000 jobs may exist for 50,000 employees. In some firms, as few as 10 jobs constitute 90 percent of the workforce.

The purpose of job analysis is to obtain answers to six important questions:

1. What physical and mental tasks does the worker accomplish?
2. When is the job to be completed?
3. Where is the job to be accomplished?
4. How does the worker do the job?
5. Why is the job done?
6. What qualifications are needed to perform the job?

Job analysis provides a summary of a job's duties and responsibilities, its relationship to other jobs, the knowledge and skills required, and working conditions under which it is performed. Job facts are gathered, analyzed, and recorded as the job exists, not as the job should exist. This function is most often assigned to industrial engineers, methods analysts, or others. Job analysis is conducted after the job has been designed, the worker has been trained, and the job is being performed.

Job analysis is performed on three occasions. First, it is done when the organization is founded and a job analysis program is initiated for the first time. Second, it is performed when new jobs are created. Third, it is used when jobs are changed significantly as a result of new technologies, methods, procedures, or systems. Job analysis is most often performed because of changes in the nature of jobs. Job analysis information is used to prepare both job descriptions and job specifications.

The **job description** is a document that provides information regarding the tasks, duties, and responsibilities of the job. The minimum acceptable qualifications that a person should possess in order to perform a particular job are contained in the **job specification**. We discuss both types of documents in greater detail later in the chapter.

## REASONS FOR CONDUCTING JOB ANALYSIS

As Figure 4-1 shows, data derived from job analysis can have an impact on virtually every aspect of human resource management. A major use of job analysis data is in the area of human resource planning (to be discussed later in this chapter). Merely knowing that the firm will need 1,000 new employees to produce goods or services to satisfy sales demand is insufficient. Each job requires different knowledge, skill, and ability levels. Obviously, effective human resource planning must take these job requirements into consideration.

### Staffing

All areas of staffing would be haphazard if the recruiter did not know the qualifications needed to perform the various jobs. Lacking up-to-date job descriptions and specifications, a firm would have to recruit and select employees for jobs without having clear guidelines; this practice could have disastrous consequences.

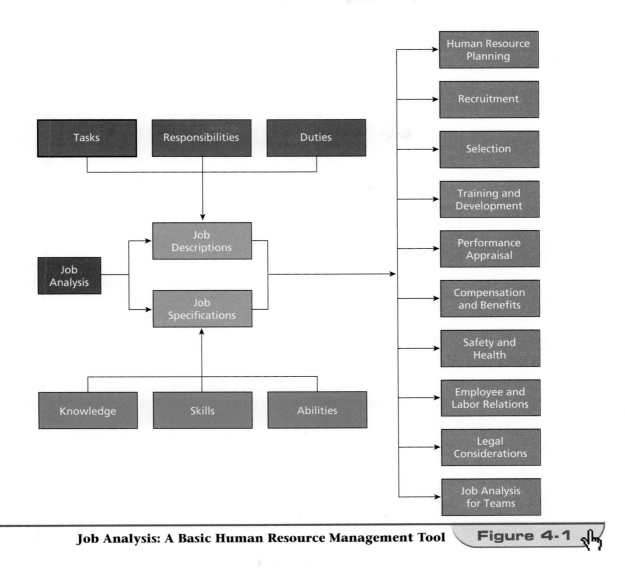

**Job Analysis: A Basic Human Resource Management Tool** — **Figure 4-1**

Such a practice is virtually unheard of when firms procure raw materials, supplies, or equipment. For example, even when ordering personal computers, the purchasing department normally develops precise specifications. Surely, the same logic should apply when recruiting and selecting a firm's most valuable asset!

## Training and Development

Job specification information often proves beneficial in identifying training and development needs. If the specification suggests that the job requires a particular knowledge, skill, or ability and the person filling the position does not possess all the qualifications required, training and/or development is probably in order. It should be directed at assisting workers in performing duties specified in their present job descriptions or preparing them for broader responsibilities. With regard to performance appraisal, employees should be evaluated in terms of how well they accomplish the duties specified in their job descriptions and any specific goals that may have been established. A manager who evaluates an employee on factors not clearly predetermined is left wide open to allegations of discrimination.

## Compensation and Benefits

In the area of compensation, the relative value of a particular job to the company must be known before a dollar value can be placed on it. From an internal perspective, the more significant its duties and responsibilities, the more the job is worth. Jobs that require greater knowledge, skills, and abilities should be worth more to the firm. For example, the relative value of a job calling for a master's degree normally would be higher than that of a job that requires a high school diploma. This might not be the case if the market value of the job requiring only a high school diploma was higher, however. Such a situation occurred in a major West Coast city a number of years ago. It came to light that city "sanitation engineers" were paid more than better-educated public schoolteachers.

## Safety and Health

Information derived from job analysis is also valuable in identifying safety and health considerations. For example, employers are required to state whether a job is hazardous.[2] The job description/specification should reflect this condition. In addition, in certain hazardous jobs, workers may need specific information about the hazards in order to perform the jobs safely.

## Employee and Labor Relations

Job analysis information is also important in employee and labor relations. When employees are considered for promotion, transfer, or demotion, the job description provides a standard for comparison of talent. Regardless of whether the firm is unionized, information obtained through job analysis can often lead to more objective human resource decisions.

## Legal Considerations

Having properly accomplished a job analysis is particularly important for supporting the legality of employment practices. In fact, the importance of job analysis is well documented in the *Uniform Guidelines on Employee Selection Procedures*.[3] Job analysis data are needed to defend decisions involving promotion, transfers, and demotions, for example. Thus far, we have described job analysis as it pertains to specific HRM functions. In practice, however, these functions are interrelated. Job analysis provides the basis for tying the functional areas together and the foundation for developing a sound human resource program.

## Job Analysis for Teams

Historically, companies established permanent jobs and filled these jobs with people who best fit the job description. The jobs were then maintained for years to come.[4] In some firms today, people are being hired and paid on a project basis. Better performance produces better income. Today, whenever someone asks, "What is your job description?" the reply might well be "Whatever." What this means is that if a project has to be completed, individuals do what has to be done to complete the task.[5]

In a traditional organization, work was compartmentalized into jobs or positions defined by functional and occupational domains. The result was disjointed execution, high unit cost, and long, noncompetitive cycle times. With team design, there are no narrow jobs. Today, departments and functional domains have disappeared in some organizations and work is bundled into teams. The

## ▶ The End of the Job as We Know It

William Bridges wrote *JobShift*, a book proposing that traditional jobs were radically changing. Bridges foresees a shift away from narrow job classifications and descriptions to a work world in which dejobbing is prevalent and the emphasis is placed on the distribution of work. According to Bridges, "What I'm calling the JobShift is the migration of work away from the fixed boxes that we've always called jobs. American and Western organizations are very job centered. I don't want to say that no job will exist in 20 years. There's a continuum, with work at one end that probably needs to be spelled out in very specific duties. For example, nuclear power plant workers should have clear job descriptions—no messing around. On the other hand, there are whole industries, such as filmmaking and consulting, in which job descriptions don't play any real role. Jobs are not the way work gets done, but instead, work gets done in cross-functional teams. It's outsourced to a group that isn't even made up of employees; it's done by temps. Now we can extend the word job to cover all those conditions, but notice what we're doing. We can't say, That's my job anymore."[6]

members of these teams have a far greater depth and breadth of skills than would have been required in traditional jobs. In addition, the teams often include employees from more than one company. This versatility allows an employee to take an entire business process from start to finish in one rapid, seamless flow. Formerly, there might have been 100 separate job classifications in a facility. With team design, there may be just 10 or fewer broadly defined roles of teams.[7] Another dimension is added to job analysis when groups or teams are considered: Job analysis may determine how important it is for employees to be team players and work well in group situations. Other traits that might be discovered through job analysis include the ability to work in more than one system.[8]

## TYPES OF JOB ANALYSIS INFORMATION

Considerable information is needed for the successful accomplishment of job analysis. The job analyst identifies the job's actual duties and responsibilities and gathers the other types of data shown in Table 4-1. Essential functions of the job are determined in this process. Note that work activities, worker-oriented activities, and the types of machines, tools, equipment, and work aids used in the job are important. This information is used later to help determine the job skills needed. In addition, the job analyst looks at job-related tangibles and intangibles, such as the knowledge needed, the materials processed, and the goods made or services performed.

Some job analysis systems identify job standards. Work measurement studies may be needed to determine how long it takes to perform a task. With regard to job content, the analyst studies the work schedule, financial and nonfinancial incentives, and physical working conditions. Specific education, training, and work experience pertinent to the job are identified. Because many jobs are often performed in conjunction with others, organizational

www.nationjob.com

**Table 4-1** Types of Data Collected in Job Analysis

### Summary of Types of Data Collected through Job Analysis[a]

1. **Work activities**
   a. Work activities and processes
   b. Activity records (in film form, for example)
   c. Procedures used
   d. Personal responsibility

2. **Worker-oriented activities**
   a. Human behaviors, such as physical actions and communicating on the job
   b. Elemental motions for methods analysis
   c. Personal job demands, such as energy expenditure

3. **Machines, tools, equipment, and work aids used**

4. **Job-related tangibles and intangibles**
   a. Knowledge dealt with or applied (as in accounting)
   b. Materials processed
   c. Products made or services performed

5. **Work performance[b]**
   a. Error analysis
   b. Work standards
   c. Work measurements, such as time taken for a task

6. **Job context**
   a. Work schedule
   b. Financial and nonfinancial incentives
   c. Physical working conditions
   d. Organizational and social contexts

7. **Personal requirements for the job**
   a. Personal attributes such as personality and interests
   b. Education and training required
   c. Work experience

[a] This information can be in the form of qualitative, verbal, narrative descriptions or quantitative measurements of each item, such as error rates per unit of time or noise level.
[b] All job analysis systems do not develop the work performance aspects.
*Source:* Reprinted by permission of Marvin D. Dunnette.

and social contexts are also noted. Subjective skills required, such as strong interpersonal skills, should be identified if the job requires that the jobholder be personable.[9]

## JOB ANALYSIS METHODS

Job analysis has traditionally been conducted in a number of different ways because organizational needs and resources for conducting job analysis differ. Selection of a specific method should be based on the purposes for which the information is to be used (job evaluation, pay increases, development, and so on) and the approach that is most feasible for a particular organization. We describe the most common methods of job analysis in the following sections.

## Questionnaires

Questionnaires are typically quick and economical to use. The job analyst may administer a structured questionnaire to employees, who identify the tasks they perform. In some cases, employees may lack verbal skills, a condition that makes this method less useful. Also, some employees may tend to exaggerate the significance of their tasks, suggesting more responsibility than actually exists.

## Observation

When using the observation method, the job analyst usually watches the worker perform job tasks and records his or her observations. This method is used primarily to gather information on jobs emphasizing manual skills, such as those of a machine operator. It can also help the analyst identify interrelationships between physical and mental tasks. Observation alone is usually an insufficient means of conducting job analysis, however, particularly when mental skills are dominant in a job. Observing a financial analyst at work would not reveal much about the requirements of the job.

## Interviews

An understanding of the job may also be gained through interviewing both the employee and the supervisor. Usually the analyst interviews the employee first, helping the worker describe the duties performed. Then, the analyst normally contacts the supervisor for additional information, to check the accuracy of the information obtained from the worker, and to clarify certain points.

## Employee Recording

In some instances, job analysis information is gathered by having employees describe their daily work activities in a diary or log. With this method, the problem of employees exaggerating job importance may have to be overcome. Even so, valuable understanding of highly specialized jobs, such as recreational therapist, may be obtained in this way.

## Combination of Methods

Usually an analyst does not use one job analysis method exclusively. A combination of methods is often more appropriate. In analyzing clerical and administrative jobs, the analyst might use questionnaires supported by interviews and limited observation. In studying production jobs, interviews, supplemented by extensive work observations, may provide the necessary data. Basically, the analyst should employ the combination of techniques needed for accurate job descriptions/specifications.

## Conducting Job Analysis

The person who conducts job analysis is interested in gathering data on what is involved in performing a particular job. The people who participate in job analysis should include, at a minimum, the employee and the employee's immediate supervisor. Large organizations may have one or more job analysts, but in small organizations line supervisors may be responsible for job analysis. Organizations that lack the technical expertise often use outside consultants to perform job analysis.

▶ *To Heck with the Job Description!*

"Carlos, I'm having trouble figuring out what kind of machine operators you need," said John Anderson, the human resource manager at Phillips Machinery. "I've sent four people for you to interview who seemed to meet the requirements outlined in the job description. You rejected all of them."

"To heck with the job description," replied Carlos. "What I'm concerned with is finding someone who can do the job. The people you sent me couldn't do the job. Besides, I've never even seen the job description."

*How do you believe that John should respond?*

Regardless of the approach taken, before conducting job analysis, the analyst should learn as much as possible about the job by reviewing organizational charts and talking with individuals acquainted with the jobs to be studied. Before beginning, the supervisor should introduce the analyst to the employees and explain the purpose of the job analysis. Although employee attitudes about the job are beyond the job analyst's control, the analyst must attempt to develop mutual trust and confidence with those whose jobs are being analyzed. Failure in this area will detract from an otherwise technically sound job analysis. Upon completion of the job analysis, two basic human resource documents—job descriptions and job specifications—can be prepared.

## JOB DESCRIPTION

Information obtained through job analysis is crucial to the development of job descriptions. Earlier, *job description* was defined as a document that states the tasks, duties, and responsibilities of the job. It is vitally important that job descriptions are both relevant and accurate. They should provide concise statements of what employees are expected to do on the job and indicate what employees do, how they do it, and the conditions under which the duties are performed.

Job descriptions take on an even greater importance under the Americans with Disabilities Act (ADA) because the identification of essential job functions may be critical to a defense regarding reasonable accommodation.[10] Although there is no legal mandate to do so, some firms present essential job functions in a separate section of the job description. In an interesting definition of an *essential function,* the U.S. Court of Appeals for the First Circuit held that working more than 40 hours per week is an essential function of an HR manager's job; therefore a request for an accommodation of a limited 40-hour week was unreasonable and not required under the Americans with Disabilities Act.[11] However, Peggy Mastroianni, the Equal Employment Opportunity Commission's associate legal counsel, predicts that reasonable accommodation of workers with disabilities will be the next hot issue in ADA employment litigation.[12]

Among the items frequently included in a job description are these:

▶ Major duties performed.
▶ Percentage of time devoted to each duty.
▶ Performance standards to be achieved.
▶ Working conditions and possible hazards.
▶ Number of employees performing the job and to whom they report.
▶ The machines and equipment used on the job.

The contents of the job description vary somewhat with the purpose for which it will be used. Job descriptions are also of increased importance when dealing with recruitment on the Internet. Today's workforce superstars know their value in this competitive employment marketplace, and getting their attention given the numerous online opportunities available can be the most difficult task of all. Effective job descriptions can increase a firm's ability to attract talent and can create excitement and interest about the position and the company.[13] The next section addresses the parts of a job description.

## Job Identification

The job identification section includes the job title, the department, the reporting relationship, and a job number or code. A good title will closely approximate the nature of the work content and will distinguish that job from others. Unfortunately, job titles are often misleading. An executive secretary in one organization may be little more than a highly paid clerk, whereas a person with the same title in another firm may practically run the company. For instance, one former student's first job after graduation was with a major tire and rubber company as an *assistant district service manager.* Because the primary duties of the job were to unload tires from trucks, check the tread wear, and stack the tires in boxcars, a more appropriate title would probably have been *tire checker and stacker.*

One information source that assists in standardizing job titles is the *Dictionary of Occupational Titles (DOT).*[14] The *DOT* includes standardized and comprehensive descriptions of job duties and related information for over 200,000 occupations. Such standardization permits employers in different industries and parts of the country to match job requirements with worker skills more accurately.

An example of a *DOT* definition, for a *branch manager*, occupational code 183.137-010, is provided in Figure 4-2. The first digit of the code identifies one of the following major occupations:

| 0/1 | Professional, technical, and managerial |
|---|---|
| 2 | Clerical and sales |
| 3 | Service |
| 4 | Farming, fishing, forestry, and related |
| 5 | Processing |
| 6 | Machine trade |
| 7 | Bench work |
| 8 | Structural work |
| 9 | Miscellaneous |

For the branch manager, the major classification would be *managerial* occupations. Thus, this example has a code 1.

The next two digits represent breakdowns of the general occupation category. Digits four through six describe the job's relationship to data, people, and things. For the branch manager, a code 1 for data would be *coordinating,* a code 3 for people would be *supervising,* and a code 7 for things would be *handling.*

The final three digits indicate the alphabetical order of titles within the six-digit code group. These codes assist in distinguishing a specific occupation from other similar ones. The alphabetical order for *branch manager* is indicated by the digits 010.

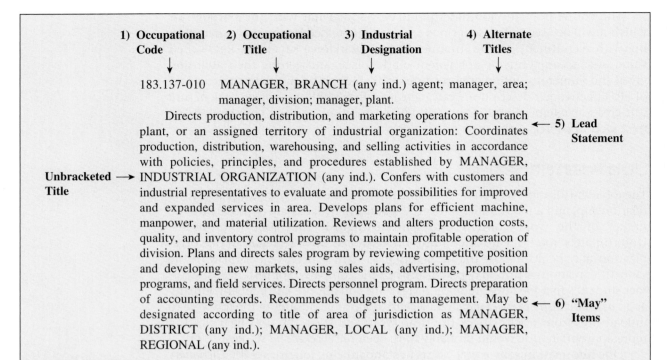

**Figure 4-2** The Parts of the *Dictionary of Occupational Titles* Definition

*Source:* U.S. Department of Labor, *Dictionary of Occupational Titles.*

## Date of the Job Analysis

The job analysis date is placed on the job description to aid in identifying job changes that would make the description obsolete. Some firms have found it useful to place an expiration date on the document. This practice ensures periodic review of job content and minimizes the number of obsolete job descriptions.

## Job Summary

The job summary provides a concise overview of the job. It is generally a short paragraph that states job content.

## Duties Performed

The body of the job description delineates the major duties to be performed. Usually one sentence beginning with an action verb such as *receives, performs, establishes,* or *assembles* adequately explains each duty. As stated earlier, essential functions may be shown in a separate section to aid in complying with the Americans with Disabilities Act.

## Job Specification

Recall that we defined *job specification* as a document containing the minimum acceptable qualifications that a person should possess in order to perform a particular job. Items typically included in the job specification are educational requirements, experience, personality traits, and physical abilities. In practice, job specifications are often included as a major section of job descriptions.

Figure 4-3 is an actual job description provided by Conoco for an Administrative Support position. Some of the critical skills needed for the job include interpersonal skills/team player, ability to influence others, and knowledge of software applications. This type of information is extremely valuable in the recruiting and selection process.

After jobs have been analyzed and the descriptions written, the results should be reviewed with the supervisor and the worker to ensure that they are accurate, clear, and understandable. The courtesy of reviewing results with employees also helps to gain their acceptance. Because the job description and job specification are often combined into one form, we use the term *job description* in this book to include both documents.

| Position Title:  Administrative Support | Code: | Salary Grade: |
|---|---|---|
| Work Location: | Report To: | Function: |

**Basic Purpose/Accountabilities:**
Responsible for providing and coordinating administrative support to assigned functional groups. Focus is on aligning contributions to department needs and company goals.

| Primary Functions/Responsibilities: | Critical Skills/Leadership Criteria: |
|---|---|
| —Preparation of time sheets | **CRITICAL SKILLS** |
| —Track employee attendance | |
| —Manage fixtures, furniture, and equipment necessary to support the function | —Interpersonal skills/team player |
| —Process invoices, monitor expenditures | —Ability to influence others |
| —Coordinate and support meetings | |
| —Participate in planning process on projects | —Knowledge of business software applications |
| —Type documentation to individuals external to Conoco | —Confidentiality |
| —Assist with presentation preparation and planning | —Planning, organizing, and time management |
| —Coordinate large scale documentation reproduction | —Written and oral communication |
| —External mailing/facsimile transmission | —Customer orientation |
| —Coordinate central office supplies | |
| —Resource computer software applications | —Knowledge of operations and organization |
| —Coordinate work activities with other functions | **LEADERSHIP CRITERIA** |
| —Generate alternatives and make recommendations on improving area work process | —Able to lead others |
| —Record retention/filing | —Engenders trust |
| | —Understands and uses functional expertise to contribute |
| | —Accepts ownership, is accountable, and delivers on commitments |
| | —Oriented towards continuous learning |

**Quantitative Factors/Business Model Activities:**

| Quantitative | Business Model |
|---|---|

**A Conoco Job Description**     **Figure 4-3**

*Source:* Conoco Inc.

## The Expanded Job Description

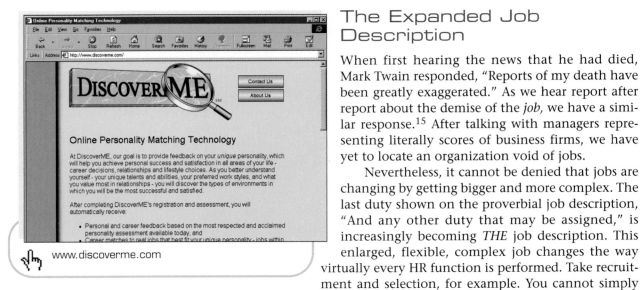

www.discoverme.com

When first hearing the news that he had died, Mark Twain responded, "Reports of my death have been greatly exaggerated." As we hear report after report about the demise of the *job,* we have a similar response.[15] After talking with managers representing literally scores of business firms, we have yet to locate an organization void of jobs.

Nevertheless, it cannot be denied that jobs are changing by getting bigger and more complex. The last duty shown on the proverbial job description, "And any other duty that may be assigned," is increasingly becoming *THE* job description. This enlarged, flexible, complex job changes the way virtually every HR function is performed. Take recruitment and selection, for example. You cannot simply look for an individual who possesses narrow skills required to perform a job. You must go deeper and seek competencies, intelligence, ability to adjust, and ability and willingness to work in teams. Today more than ever, people go from project to project and from team to team. Job definitions become blurred, and titles become almost meaningless. Basically, what matters is what you know and how well you apply it to the business.[16]

## Timeliness of Job Analysis

The rapid pace of technological change makes the need for accurate job analysis even more important now and in the future. Historically, job analysis could be conducted and then set aside for a reasonable time. Today, however, job requirements are changing so rapidly that they must be constantly reviewed to keep them relevant. By one estimate, technological change is occurring so rapidly that people may have to change their entire skills set three or four times during their career.[17] If this projection is accurate, the need for accurate and timely job analysis is becoming even more important.

On the downside, because of rapid technological changes, companies that do not constantly monitor their job analysis program will be placed in a difficult position. Recruiting for a position with an inaccurate job description may result in a poor match of skills possessed and skills needed. Also, training may be irrelevant and the compensation system may be flawed. Thus, job analysis is likely to be even more important in today's environment.

## OTHER JOB ANALYSIS METHODS

Over the years, attempts have been made to provide more systematic methods of conducting job analysis. We describe several of these approaches next.

## Department of Labor Job Analysis Schedule

**Job analysis schedule (JAS)**
A systematic method of studying jobs and occupations; developed by the U.S. Department of Labor.

The U.S. Department of Labor established a method of systematically studying jobs and occupations called the **job analysis schedule (JAS)**. When the JAS method is used, information is gathered by a trained analyst. A major component of the JAS is the Work Performed Ratings section. Here, what workers do in performing a job with regard to data (D), people (P), and things (T) is evaluated. Each is viewed as a hierarchy of functions, with the items higher in the category being more difficult. The codes in the worker functions section represent the highest level of involvement in each of the three categories.

The JAS component Worker Traits Ratings relates primarily to job requirement data. The topics general education designation (GED), specific vocational preparation (SVP), aptitudes, temperaments, interests, physical demands, and environmental conditions are included. The Description of Tasks section provides a specific description of the work performed. Both routine tasks and occasionally performed tasks are included.

## Functional Job Analysis

**Functional job analysis (FJA)** is a comprehensive job analysis approach that concentrates on the interactions among the work, the worker, and the organization. This approach is a modification of the job analysis schedule. It assesses specific job outputs and identifies job tasks in terms of task statements.[18] The fundamental elements of FJA follow:

1. A major distinction is made between what gets done and what workers do to get things done. It is more important in job analysis to know the latter. For instance, a word processing operator does not just keep the system running; a number of tasks must be performed in accomplishing the job.
2. Each job is concerned with data, people, and things.
3. Workers function in unique ways as they relate to data, people, and things.
4. Each job requires the worker to relate to data, people, and things in some way.
5. Only a few definite and identifiable functions are involved with data, people, and things (refer to Table 4-2).
6. These functions proceed from the simple to the complex. The least complex form of data would be comparing, and the most complex would be synthesizing. In addition, the assumption is that if an upper-level function is required, all the lower-level functions are also required.
7. The three hierarchies for data, people, and things provide two measures for a job. First, there is a measure of relative complexity in relation to data, people, and things—in essence, the amount of interrelationship among the three functions. Second, there is a measure of proportional involvement for each function. For instance, 50 percent of a person's time may be spent in analyzing, 30 percent in supervising, and 20 percent in operating.

**Functional job analysis (FJA)**
A comprehensive approach to formulating job descriptions that concentrates on the interactions among the work, the worker, and the work organization.

## Worker Function Scale for Job Analysis Schedule  Table 4-2

| Data (4th digit) | | People (5th digit) | | Things (6th digit) | |
|---|---|---|---|---|---|
| 0 | Synthesizing | 0 | Monitoring | 0 | Setting up |
| 1 | Coordinating | 1 | Negotiating | 1 | Precision working |
| 2 | Analyzing | 2 | Instructing | 2 | Operating—controlling |
| 3 | Compiling | 3 | Supervising | 3 | Driving—operating |
| 4 | Computing | 4 | Diverting | 4 | Manipulating |
| 5 | Copying | 5 | Persuading | 5 | Tending |
| 6 | Comparing | 6 | Speaking—signaling | 6 | Feeding—offbearing |
| 7 | No significant relationship | 7 | Serving | 7 | Handling |
| | | 8 | No significant relationship | 8 | No significant relationship |

*Source:* U.S. Department of Labor, *Dictionary of Occupational Titles.*

# Position Analysis Questionnaire

**Position analysis questionnaire (PAQ)**
A structured job analysis questionnaire that uses a checklist approach to identify job elements.

The **position analysis questionnaire (PAQ)** is a structured job analysis questionnaire that uses a checklist approach to identify job elements. It focuses on general worker behaviors instead of tasks. Some 194 job descriptors relate to job-oriented elements. Advocates of the PAQ believe that its ability to identify job elements, behaviors required of job incumbents, and other job characteristics makes this procedure applicable to the analysis of virtually any type of job. Each job descriptor is evaluated on a specified scale such as extent of use, amount of time, importance of job, possibility of occurrence, and applicability.

Each job being studied is scored relative to the 32 job dimensions. The score derived represents a profile of the job; this can be compared with standard profiles to group the job into known job families—that is, jobs of a similar nature. In essence, the PAQ identifies significant job behaviors and classifies jobs. Using the PAQ, job descriptions can be based on the relative importance and emphasis placed on various job elements. The PAQ has been called one of the most useful job analysis methods.[19]

# Management Position Description Questionnaire

**Management position description questionnaire (MPDQ)**
A form of job analysis designed for management positions that uses a checklist method to analyze jobs.

The **management position description questionnaire (MPDQ)** is a method of job analysis designed for management positions; it uses a checklist to analyze jobs. The MPDQ has been used to determine the training needs of individuals who are slated to move into managerial positions. It has also been used to evaluate and set compensation rates for managerial jobs and to assign the jobs to job families.

# Guidelines-Oriented Job Analysis

**Guidelines-oriented job analysis (GOJA)**
A method that responds to the growing amount of legislation affecting employment decisions by utilizing a step-by-step procedure to describe the work of a particular job classification.

The **guidelines-oriented job analysis (GOJA)** responds to the legislation affecting staffing and involves a step-by-step procedure for describing the work of a particular job classification.[20] It is also used for developing selection tools, such as application forms, and for documenting compliance with various legal requirements. The GOJA obtains the following types of information: (1) machines, tools, and equipment; (2) supervision; (3) contacts; (4) duties; (5) knowledge, skills, and abilities; (6) physical and other requirements; and (7) differentiating requirements.

# Descriptions Now

KnowledgePoint, a developer of human resource management software, has released a powerful new upgrade to its job description–writing tool, *Descriptions Now*. *Descriptions Now* has a library of over 3,500 jobs to help managers and HR professionals clearly define job requirements and qualifications. The expanded library includes over 1,000 new and enhanced jobs that reflect the changing job market and employment needs of organizations in every industry. It allows a company to access a continually updated job library over the Internet. The knowledge-based software provides an easy-to-use question-and-answer format to create comprehensive job descriptions that help address ADA-compliance issues. Based on the user's input, the technology automatically writes sections defining qualifications, supervisory responsibilities, physical demands, and work environment.[21]

Effective job analysis is essential to sound human resource management as an organization recruits, selects, and promotes employees. In particular, human resource management has focused on job analysis because selection methods need to be clearly job related.[22] Legislation requiring thorough job analysis includes the following acts.

*Fair Labor Standards Act:* Employees are categorized as exempt or nonexempt, and job analysis is basic to this determination. Nonexempt workers must be paid time and a half when they work more than 40 hours per week. Overtime pay is not required for exempt employees.

*Equal Pay Act:* Men are often paid higher salaries than women, even though they perform essentially the same job. If jobs are not substantially different, the employees performing them must receive similar pay. When pay differences exist, job descriptions can be used to show whether jobs are substantially equal in terms of skill, effort, responsibility, or working conditions.

*Civil Rights Act:* As with the Equal Pay Act, job descriptions may provide the basis for an equitable compensation system and an adequate defense against unfair discrimination charges in initial selection, promotion, and all other areas of human resource administration. When job analysis is not performed, defending certain qualifications established for the job is usually difficult. For instance, stating that a high school diploma is required without having determined its necessity through job analysis makes the firm vulnerable in discrimination suits.

*Occupational Safety and Health Act (OSHA):* Job descriptions are required to specify elements of the job that endanger health or are considered unsatisfactory or distasteful by the majority of the population. Showing the job description to the employee in advance is a good defense.

*The Americans with Disabilities Act (ADA):* Employers are required to make reasonable accommodations for workers with disabilities who are able to perform the essential functions of a job. It is important that organizations distinguish these essential functions from those that are marginal. The EEOC defines *reasonable accommodation* as any modification or adjustment to a job, an employment practice, or the work environment that makes it possible for an individual with a disability to enjoy an equal employment opportunity. What constitutes reasonable accommodation depends on the disability and the skills of the person in question.[23]

## STRATEGIC PLANNING AND THE HUMAN RESOURCE PLANNING PROCESS

In Chapter 1, we stressed that HR executives are now focusing their attention on how human resources can help the organization achieve its strategic objectives.[24] This is precisely what Charmagne did when she critically analyzed the proposal that Brian made with regard to completing the Medord Corporation project in

❱ *HR Planning Organization*

**www.prenhall.com/mondy**

This is the Web site for the Human Resource Planning Society.

HR WEB
WISDOM

one year instead of two. Without this strategic outlook and attitude, Charmagne might have just gone along with Brian's proposal and tried to make the best out of a bad situation. As with Charmagne, HR executives now have the role of a strategic partner with line executives in assuring that the organization achieves its mission. Thus, HR must now be highly involved in the strategic planning process. Essentially, HR is moving from a *micro* to a *macro* view of its mission.[25] **Strategic planning** is the process by which top management determines overall organizational purposes and objectives and how they are to be achieved.

**Strategic planning**
The determination of overall organizational purposes and goals and how they are to be achieved.

When a firm's mission is clearly defined and its guiding principles understood, employees and managers are likely to put forth maximum effort in pursuing company objectives. Top management expects HR activities to be closely aligned to this mission and strategic goals and to add value toward achieving these goals.[26] Brian Charles of Sharpco Manufacturing tried to exclude HR from the strategic planning process and wanted to accept a contract that would not be cost effective because of HR constraints. Charmagne, acting in her strategic planning role, did not accept his proposal. The advantage of strategic planning is most evident as firms respond to rapidly changing environments.

Corporate-level executives such as Brian, Charmagne, and the CEO and other vice presidents first agree upon a broad company strategy. **Human resource planning (HRP)**—the process of systematically reviewing human resource requirements to ensure that the required number of employees, with the required skills, are available when and where they are needed—can then be accomplished.[27] Human resource planning involves matching the internal and external supply of people with job openings anticipated in the organization over a specified period of time. The human resource planning process is illustrated in Figure 4-4. Note that strategic planning precedes human resource planning.

**Human resource planning (HRP)**
The process of systematically reviewing human resource requirements to ensure that the required number of employees with the required skills are available when and where they are needed.

Specific quantitative and qualitative human resource plans are determined from the organizational plans. Note in Figure 4-4 that human resource planning has two components: requirements and availability. Forecasting human resource requirements involves determining the number and type of employees needed, by skill level and location. These projections will reflect various factors, such as production plans and changes in productivity. In order to forecast availability, the human resource manager looks to both internal sources (presently employed employees) and external sources (the labor market). When employee requirements and availability have been analyzed, the firm can determine whether it will have a surplus or shortage of employees. Ways must be found to reduce the number of employees if a surplus is projected. Some of these methods include restricted hiring, reduced hours, early retirements, and layoffs. If a worker shortage is forecast, the firm must obtain the proper quantity and quality of workers from outside the organization. In this case, external recruitment and selection are required.

▶ Because conditions in the external and internal environments can change quickly, the human resource planning process must be continuous.

Because conditions in the external and internal environments can change quickly, the human resource planning process must be continuous.

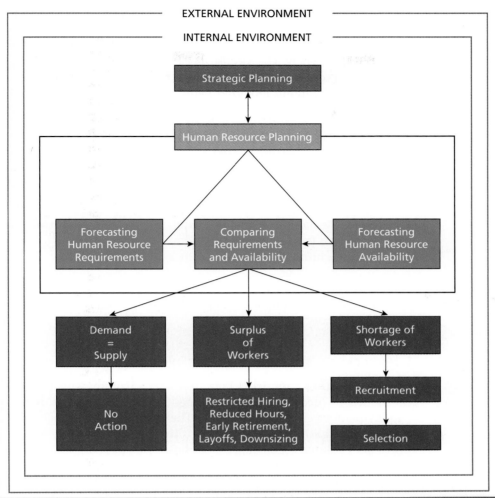

**The Human Resource Planning Process** | **Figure 4-4**

Changing conditions could affect the entire organization, thereby requiring extensive modification of forecasts. Planning, in general, enables managers to anticipate and prepare for changing conditions, and HR planning in particular allows flexibility in the area of human resource management.

## HUMAN RESOURCE FORECASTING TECHNIQUES

Several techniques for forecasting human resource requirements and availability are currently used by HR professionals. Some of the techniques are qualitative in nature, and others are quantitative. Several of the better-known methods are described in this section.

## Zero-Base Forecasting

The **zero-base forecasting** approach uses the organization's current level of employment as the starting point for determining future staffing needs. Essentially the same procedure is used for human resource planning as for zero-base budgeting, whereby each budget must be justified each year. If an employee

**Zero-base forecasting**
A method for estimating future employment needs using the organization's current level of employment as the starting point.

retires, is fired, or leaves the firm for any other reason, the position is not automatically filled. Instead, an analysis is made to determine whether the firm can justify filling it. Equal concern is shown for creating new positions when they appear to be needed. The key to zero-base forecasting is a thorough analysis of human resource needs. In today's globally competitive environment, an open position is thoroughly analyzed before a replacement is approved. More often than not, the position is not filled and the work is spread out among remaining employees.

## Bottom-Up Approach

**Bottom-up approach**
A forecasting method beginning with the lowest organizational units and progressing upward through an organization ultimately to provide an aggregate forecast of employment needs.

Some firms use what might be called the bottom-up approach to employment forecasting. It is based on the reasoning that the manager in each unit is most knowledgeable about employment requirements. In the **bottom-up approach**, each successive level in the organization—starting with the lowest—forecasts its requirements, ultimately providing an aggregate forecast of employees needed. Human resource forecasting is often most effective when managers periodically project their human resource needs, comparing their current and anticipated levels, and giving the human resource department adequate lead time to explore internal and external sources.

## Use of Mathematical Models

Another means of forecasting human resource requirements is to use mathematical models to predict future requirements. One of the most useful predictors of employment levels is sales volume. The relationship between demand and the number of employees needed is a positive one. As you can see in Figure 4-5, a firm's sales volume is depicted on the horizontal axis, and the number of employees actually required is shown on the vertical axis. In this illustration, as sales decrease, so does the number of employees. Using such a method, managers can approximate the number of employees required at different demand levels.

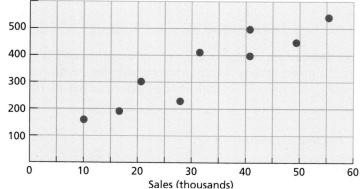

**Figure 4-5**  **The Relationship of Sales Volume to Number of Employees**

# Simulation

**Simulation** is a technique for experimenting with a real-world situation through a mathematical model representing that situation. A model is an abstraction of the real world. Thus, a simulation model is an attempt to represent a real-world situation through mathematical logic to predict what will occur. Simulation assists human resource managers by permitting them to ask many *what if* questions without having to make a decision resulting in real-world consequences.

In human resource management, a simulation model might be developed to represent the interrelationships among employment levels and many other variables. The manager could then ask *what if* questions such as these:

- What would happen if we put 10 percent of the present workforce on overtime?
- What would happen if the plant utilized two shifts? Three shifts?

The purpose of the model is to permit managers to gain considerable insight into a particular problem before making an actual decision.

**Simulation**
A technique for experimenting with a real-world situation by means of a mathematical model that represents the actual situation.

## FORECASTING HUMAN RESOURCE REQUIREMENTS

A **requirements forecast** is an estimate of the numbers and kinds of employees the organization will need at future dates in order to realize its stated goals. Before human resource requirements can be projected, demand for the firm's goods or services must first be forecast. This forecast is then converted into people requirements for the activities necessary to meet this demand. For a firm that manufactures personal computers, activities might be stated in terms of the number of units to be produced, number of sales calls to be made, number of vouchers to be processed, or a variety of other activities. For example, manufacturing 1,000 personal computers each week might require 10,000 hours of work by assemblers during a 40-hour week. Dividing the 10,000 hours by the 40 hours in the workweek gives 250 assembly workers needed. Similar calculations are performed for the other jobs needed to produce and market the personal computers.

**Requirements forecast**
An estimate of the numbers and kinds of employees an organization will need at future dates to realize its stated objectives.

## FORECASTING HUMAN RESOURCE AVAILABILITY

Forecasting requirements provide managers with the means of estimating how many and what types of employees will be required. But there is another side to the coin, as this example illustrates:

A large manufacturing firm on the West Coast was preparing to begin operations in a new plant. Analysts had already determined there was a large long-term demand for the new product. Financing was available and equipment was in place. But production did not begin for two years! Management had made a critical mistake: It had studied the demand side of human resources but not the supply side. There were not enough qualified workers in the local labor market to operate the new plant. New workers had to receive extensive training before they could move into the newly created jobs.

Determining whether the firm will be able to secure employees with the necessary skills, and from what sources, is called an **availability forecast**. It helps to show whether the needed employees may be obtained from within the company, from outside the organization, or from a combination of the two sources.

**Availability forecast**
A process of determining whether a firm will be able to secure employees with the necessary skills from within the company, from outside the organization, or from a combination of the two sources.

Many of the workers that will be needed for future positions may already work for the firm. If the firm is small, management probably knows all the workers sufficiently well to match their skills and aspirations with the company's needs. Suppose the firm is creating a new sales position. It may be common knowledge in the company that Mary Garcia, a five-year employee, has both the skills and the desire to take over the new job. This unplanned process of matching people and positions may be sufficient for smaller firms. As organizations grow, however, the matching process becomes increasingly difficult. Databases are being used by organizations that take human resources seriously. Also, succession planning helps ensure an internal supply of highly qualified management personnel.

Databases include information on all managerial and nonmanagerial employees. Information generally provided for nonmanagerial employees includes the following:

- Background and biographical data
- Work experience
- Specific skills and knowledge
- Licenses or certifications held
- In-house training programs completed
- Previous performance appraisal evaluations
- Career goals

Firms may maintain additional databases for their managers. Essentially, this type of inventory provides information for replacement and promotion decisions. It would likely include data such as these:

- Work history and experience
- Educational background
- Assessment of strengths and weaknesses
- Developmental needs
- Promotion potential at present, and with further development
- Current job performance
- Field of specialization
- Job preferences
- Geographic preferences
- Career goals and aspirations
- Anticipated retirement date
- Personal history, including psychological assessments

## SURPLUS OF EMPLOYEES FORECASTED

When a comparison of requirements and availability indicates a worker surplus will result, restricted hiring, reduced hours, early retirements, and layoffs may be required to correct the situation. Downsizing, one result of worker surpluses, will be discussed as a separate topic.

## Restricted Hiring

When a firm implements a restricted hiring policy, it reduces the workforce by not replacing employees who leave. New workers are hired only when the overall performance of the organization may be affected. For instance, if a quality control department that consisted of four inspectors lost one to a competitor, this individual probably would not be replaced. If the firm lost all its inspectors, however, it would probably replace at least some of them to ensure continued operation.

## Reduced Hours

A company can also react to a reduced workload requirement by reducing the total number of hours worked. Instead of continuing a 40-hour week, management may decide to cut each employee's time to 30 hours. This cutback normally applies only to hourly employees because management and other professionals typically are salaried and therefore not paid on an hourly basis.

## Early Retirement

Early retirement of some present employees is another way to reduce the number of workers. Some employees will be delighted to retire, but others will be somewhat reluctant. However, the latter may be willing to accept early retirement if the total retirement package is made sufficiently attractive. A key point to remember is that because of the Age Discrimination in Employment Act, as amended, retirement can no longer be mandated by age.

## Layoffs

At times, a firm has no choice but to lay off part of its workforce. A layoff is not the same as a firing, but it has the same basic effect—the worker is no longer employed. When the firm is unionized, layoff procedures are usually stated clearly in the labor-management agreement. Typically, workers with the least seniority are laid off first. If the organization is union free, it may base layoffs on a combination of factors, such as seniority and productivity level. When managers and other professionals are laid off, the decision is likely to be based on ability, although internal politics may be a factor. Layoffs on a large scale are referred to as *downsizing* and will be discussed in greater detail in Chapter 16.

## SHORTAGE OF WORKERS FORECASTED

Unemployment in the United States was at an all-time low in the summer of 2000. Faced with a shortage of workers, many organizations had to intensify their efforts to recruit the necessary people to meet their needs. Some actions that were taken included the following.

## Creative Recruiting

A shortage of personnel often means that new approaches to recruiting must be used. The organization may have to recruit in different geographic areas than in the past, explore new methods of recruitment, and seek different kinds of candidates. Chapter 6 is devoted to a discussion of Internet recruiting.

## Compensation Incentives

Firms competing for workers in a high-demand situation may have to rely on compensation incentives. Premium pay is one obvious method; however, this approach may trigger a bidding war that the organization cannot sustain for an extended period. More subtle forms of rewards may be required to attract employees to a firm, such as four-day workweeks, flexible working hours, telecommuting, part-time employment, and child-care centers. Compensation incentives are discussed in Chapters 11 and 12.

## Training Programs

Special training programs may be needed to prepare previously unemployable individuals for positions with a firm. Remedial education and skills training are two types of programs that may help attract individuals to a particular company.

## Different Selection Standards

Another approach for dealing with shortages of workers is the lowering of employment standards. Selection criteria that screen out certain workers may have to be altered to ensure that enough people are available to fill jobs. For instance, instead of desiring extensive work experience, a firm may be willing to hire an inexperienced worker and train him or her to do the job.

## SUCCESSION PLANNING AND DEVELOPMENT

**Succession planning**
The process of ensuring that a qualified person is available to assume a managerial position once the position is vacant.

The fatal crash of Commerce Secretary Ron Brown's plane in 1996 with 16 corporate executives on board suddenly brought major attention to succession planning and development across the nation.[28] Were replacements ready to take over these leadership positions? Unfortunately, it does not take something as rare as a plane crash to cause a company's sudden loss. A month later, Texas Instruments CEO Jerry Junkins, with no history of heart disease, died suddenly of a heart attack at age 58. Fortunately, Junkins had personally groomed his successor, and continuity was assured.[29] **Succession planning** is the process of ensuring that a qualified person is available to assume a managerial position once the position is vacant. This definition includes untimely deaths, resignations, terminations, or the orderly retirements of company officials. William Byham, CEO of Development Dimensions International, a global HR consulting firm, said, "The avoidance of succession planning is a costly time bomb."[30]

Because of the tremendous changes that will confront management this century, succession planning is taking on more importance than ever before. It is not only deaths that have created an increased focus on succession planning. CEOs are being terminated faster than previously. Jill Barad's hasty departure from Mattel came just three years after she had ascended to the top. Shortly after that announcement, Douglas Ivester left Coca-Cola after 2½ years at the helm. Two weeks later, Robert Annunziata was gone from Global Crossing after only 53 weeks. The following week Robert Ayling was abruptly ousted from British Airways after only four years on the job. Then, Dale Morrison of Campbell Soup was out after less than three years. Many expect the tenure for CEOs to continue to grow shorter.[31]

One of the outcomes of a management database is a succession plan. Detroit Edison calls its plan a Career Planning Inventory Organization Review Chart. In

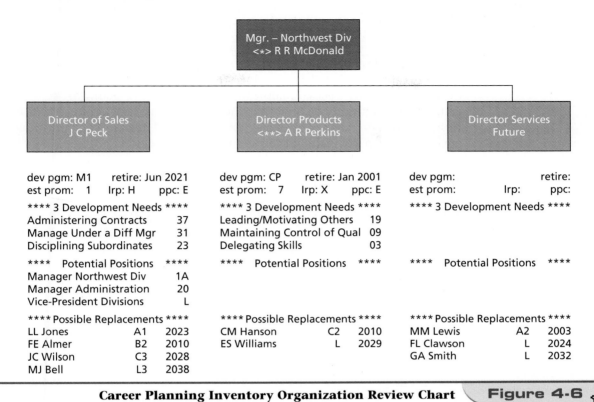

**Career Planning Inventory Organization Review Chart** | **Figure 4-6**

Figure 4-6, the chart shows a manager in the top box, with immediate subordinates in the lower boxes. Information shown on the chart includes the following:

*Position box:* Each box shows the position title and the incumbent's name. The symbol * preceding the name identifies incumbents who will retire between 2001 and 2007, indicating that short-range planning is required. The symbol ** preceding the name identifies incumbents who will retire between 2004 and 2011, indicating that long-range planning is required. If the word *open* appears in the box, the position is unfilled. If *future* appears, the position is anticipated but does not yet exist.

*dev pgm:* Identifies the particular development program in which the employee participates.

*retire:* Indicates the month and year of the employee's planned retirement.

*est prom:* Indicates the employee's estimated potential for promotion.

*lrp:* Indicates the employee's long-range career potential with the company.

*ppc:* Indicates the incumbent's current organizational level.

*3 Development Needs:* Describes three priority development needs that have been identified.

*Potential Positions:* Shows the title of each position to which the incumbent is potentially promotable, along with codes that indicate an estimate of when the employee would be ready.

*Possible Replacements:* Lists the names of up to 10 possible replacements for the incumbent, with codes indicating when the replacements would be ready for promotion to this position.

A concept related to succession planning is succession development. **Succession development** is the process of determining a comprehensive job profile of the key positions and then ensuring that key prospects are properly developed to match these qualifications. In succession planning, replacement candidates often do not know that they are in consideration for a future position, whereas in succession development, candidates are kept informed and encouraged to participate in their development process.[32]

## JOB DESIGN

**Job design** is the process of determining the specific tasks to be performed, the methods used in performing these tasks, and how the job relates to other work in the organization. Four concepts related to job design—job enrichment, job enlargement, total quality management, and reengineering—will be discussed next.

## Job Enrichment

In the past two decades, there has been considerable interest in and application of job enrichment in a wide variety of organizations. Strongly advocated by Frederick Herzberg, **job enrichment** consists of basic changes in the content and level of responsibility of a job so as to provide greater challenge to the worker. Job enrichment provides a vertical expansion of responsibilities. The worker has the opportunity to derive a feeling of achievement, recognition, responsibility, and personal growth in performing the job. Although job enrichment programs do not always achieve positive results, they have often brought about improvements in job performance and in the level of worker satisfaction in many organizations. One group that appears to be particularly receptive to job enrichment is Generation X employees (to be discussed in Chapter 9).

According to Herzberg, five principles should be followed when implementing job enrichment:

1. *Increasing job demands:* The job should be changed in such a way as to increase the level of difficulty and responsibility.
2. *Increasing the worker's accountability:* More individual control and authority over the work should be allowed, while the manager retains ultimate accountability.
3. *Providing work scheduling freedom:* Within limits, individual workers should be allowed to schedule their own work.
4. *Providing feedback:* Timely periodic reports on performance should be made directly to workers rather than to their supervisors.
5. *Providing new learning experiences:* Work situations should encourage opportunities for new experiences and personal growth.[33]

Today, job enrichment is moving toward the team level, as more teams become autonomous, or self-managed.[34]

## Job Enlargement

There is a clear distinction between job enrichment and job enlargement. **Job enlargement** involves changes in the scope of a job to provide greater variety to the worker. It provides a horizontal expansion of duties. For example, instead of knowing how to operate only one machine, a person is taught to operate two or even three, but no higher level of responsibility is required. A recent study of three work design variables, including job enlargement, indicates that it is a key organizational predictor of employees' perceived capability of carrying out a broader and more proactive set of work tasks. So, normally, job enlargement expands an employee's overall performance capabilities.[35]

## Total Quality Management

**Total quality management (TQM)** is a commitment to excellence by everyone in an organization that emphasizes excellence achieved by teamwork and a process of continuous improvement. Today, many companies have total quality programs that integrate every department from manufacturing to marketing in the effort to improve. Implied in the concept is a commitment to be the best and provide the highest quality products and services that meet or exceed the customer's expectations. Businesses are making many changes to stay competitive and are constantly seeking ways to improve quality, increase speed of operations, and adopt a customer orientation. These changes are so fundamental that they must take root in a company's very essence, which means in its *culture*. TQM often involves major cultural changes, which require new ways of thinking and strong leadership at all levels. Individuals throughout the organization must be inspired to do things differently.

Job design should precede or accompany the introduction of total quality management. Since TQM is a fundamental organizational change, job design considerations cannot be ignored. With cultural and organizational changes comes the need to reevaluate how tasks are performed, the methods used in performing these tasks, and how jobs relate to other work.[36] At times, TQM works, and at other times, it is unsuccessful. According to one researcher, "TQM is not synonymous with quality. Quality is essential for organizational success and competitive advantage. TQM is only one of many possible means to attain quality. In other words, quality is sacred; TQM is not."[37]

## Reengineering

When business problems occur, workers are often blamed, even though the real obstacle lies in process design. Unfortunately, rather than looking for process problems, managers often focus on worker deficiencies, at least initially. If process is the problem, it might be reengineered for a substantial improvement in productivity. Reengineering essentially involves the firm rethinking and redesigning its business system to become more competitive. **Reengineering** is "the fundamental rethinking and radical redesign of business processes to achieve dramatic improvements in critical contemporary measures of performance, such as cost, quality, service, and speed."[38]

Reengineering emphasizes the radical redesign of work in which companies organize around process instead of by functional departments. Incremental change is not what is desired, as with TQM; instead, radical changes are wanted that will alter entire operations at one time. Essentially, the firm must rethink and redesign its business system from the ground up.

Reengineering focuses on the overall aspects of job designs, organizational structures, and management systems. It stresses that work should be organized around outcomes as opposed to tasks or functions. Reengineering should never be confused with downsizing (discussed in Chapter 16), even though a workforce reduction often results from this strategy.[39] Naturally, job design considerations are of paramount concern because as the process changes, so do essential

**Total quality management (TQM)**
A commitment to excellence by everyone in an organization that emphasizes excellence achieved by teamwork and a process of continuous improvement.

**Reengineering**
The fundamental rethinking and radical redesign of business processes to achieve dramatic improvements in critical, contemporary measures of performance such as cost, quality, service, and speed.

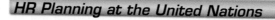

The United Nations (UN) has 188 member nations that attempt to maintain international peace and security. To help accomplish their mission, the UN Office of HR Management (OHRM) spearheaded a quiet revolution in its global HR practices. It is hard to imagine a more complex HR challenge than maintaining a worldwide staff of 8,500 representing the interests of more than 5.7 billion people in 188 nations, with employees from cultures that are openly hostile towards each other. That is the everyday HR challenge at the UN. Recently, OHRM added a full-time post in HR planning and then asked the private sector for assistance. Corporate experts from companies like General Electric made concrete recommendations for overhauling HR planning. The primary shortcoming identified was inadequate HR planning, which impaired the UN's ability to identify and move the right person into the right job at the right time.

Currently, HR planning is taking the lead at the UN. Now, virtually all UN employees complete a detailed online survey of their skills and experience. This skills inventory will assist in HR planning by providing a clear analysis of what skills are needed and help guide future recruitment. Even now, some key appointments—such as leading an overseas peacekeeping mission—are given only to available employees. Ultimately, though, OHRM hopes to properly plan to identify and reach the most qualified candidates. To align the competency data, OHRM developed an HR forecasting and modeling system to further integrate HR planning with program, organizational, and financial planning. These HR planning efforts have been so successful that the UN won the Workforce Optimas Award for Global Outlook.[40]

elements of jobs. Like TQM, reengineering can be effective in certain instances. There are numerous examples of very successful implementations. The use of reengineering at IBM to significantly change its benefit center is a high-profile example of success.[41] There are other instances of failure, with Levi Strauss having a very disappointing and costly experience.[42]

## ▶ Summary

**❶ Describe why job analysis is a basic human resource tool.**
Job analysis is the systematic process of determining the skills, duties, and knowledge required for performing jobs in an organization. It is an essential and pervasive human resource technique. In today's rapidly changing work environment, the need for a sound job analysis system is extremely critical. New jobs are being created, and old jobs are being redesigned or eliminated.

**❷ Explain the reasons for conducting job analysis.**
Without a properly conducted job analysis, it would be difficult, if not impossible, to satisfactorily perform the other human resource–related functions.

**❸ Describe the types of information required for job analysis.**
Work activities, worker-oriented activities, and the types of machines, tools, equipment, and work aids used in the job are important. This information is used to help determine the job skills needed. In addition, the job analyst looks at job-related tangibles and intangibles.

**❹ Describe the various job analysis methods.**
The job analyst may administer a structured questionnaire, witness the work being performed, interview both the employee and the supervisor, or ask them to

describe their daily work activities in a diary or log. A combination of methods is often used.

**5** **Describe the components of a well-designed job description.**
Components include the job identification section, which includes the job title, department, reporting relationship, and a job number or code; the job analysis date; the job summary; and the body of the job description, which delineates the major duties to be performed.

**6** **Identify the other methods available for conducting job analysis.**
The U.S. Department of Labor job analysis schedule (JAS), functional job analysis (FJA), the position analysis questionnaire (PAQ), the management position description questionnaire (MPDQ), and guidelines-oriented job analysis (GOJA) are other available methods.

**7** **Describe how job analysis helps satisfy various legal requirements.**
Legislation requiring thorough job analysis includes the following acts: Fair Labor Standards Act, Equal Pay Act, Civil Rights Act, Occupational Safety and Health Act, and the Americans with Disabilities Act.

**8** **Explain the human resource planning process.**
After strategic plans have been formulated, human resource planning can be undertaken. Human resource planning has two components: requirements and availability.

**9** **Describe some human resource forecasting techniques.**
Forecasting techniques include zero-base forecasting, the bottom-up approach, and the use of predictor variables.

**10** **Define *requirements* and *availability forecasts*.**
A *requirements forecast* is an estimate of the numbers and kinds of employees the organization will need at future dates in order to realize its goals. Determining whether the firm will be able to secure employees with the necessary skills and from what sources these individuals may be obtained is called an *availability forecast*.

**11** **Identify what a firm can do when either a surplus or a shortage of workers exists.**
When a surplus of workers exists a firm may implement one or more of the following: restricted hiring, reduced hours, early retirement, and layoffs. When a shortage of workers exists, creative recruiting, compensation incentives, training programs, and different selection standards are possible.

**12** **Distinguish between succession planning and succession development.**
Succession planning is the process of ensuring that a qualified person is available to assume a managerial position once the position is vacant. Succession development is the process of determining a comprehensive job profile of the key positions, then ensuring that key prospects are properly developed to match these qualifications.

**13** **Describe job design.**
Job design is the process of determining the specific tasks to be performed, the methods used in performing the tasks, and how the job relates to other work in the organization.

---

## Questions for Review ◄

1. What is the distinction between a job and a position? Define *job analysis*.
2. Describe the traditional methods used to conduct job analysis.
3. List and briefly describe the types of data that are typically gathered when conducting job analysis.

4. What are the basic components of a job description? Briefly describe each.

5. What are the items typically included in a job specification?

6. Briefly define each of the following: (a) the U.S. Department of Labor job analysis schedule (JAS); (b) functional job analysis (FJA); (c) the position analysis questionnaire (PAQ); (d) the management position description questionnaire (MPDQ); and (e) guidelines-oriented job analysis (GOJA).

7. Describe how effective job analysis can be used to satisfy each of the following statutes: (a) Fair Labor Standards Act, (b) Equal Pay Act, (c) Civil Rights Act, (d) Occupational Safety and Health Act, and (e) Americans with Disabilities Act.

8. Describe the human resource planning process.

9. What are the human resource forecasting techniques?

10. Distinguish between forecasting human resource requirements and availability. Use definitions and examples.

11. What actions could a firm take if it had a worker surplus?

12. What actions could a firm take if it forecasted a shortage of workers?

13. Why is it important to have succession planning?

14. Define each of the following:
    a. job design
    b. job enrichment
    c. job enlargement
    d. total quality management (TQM)
    e. reengineering

TAKE IT TO THE NET

*We invite you to visit the Mondy homepage on the Prentice Hall Web site at*

**www.prenhall.com/mondy**

*for updated information, Web-based exercises, and links to other HR-related sites.*

## ▶ Developing HRM Skills

### An Experiential Exercise

This exercise is designed to give participants experience in dealing with some aspects of planning that a typical human resource manager faces. Students will also be exposed to some of the activities that human resource managers confront on a daily basis. The old axiom, "Plan your work and work your plan" will probably have new meaning after this exercise.

You are the human resource manager at a large canning plant. Your plant produces several lines of canned food products that are shipped to wholesale distributors nationwide.

It is Monday morning, August 30. You have just returned from a weeklong corporate executives' meeting at the home office. The meeting was attended by all human resource managers from each of the company's plants. You returned with notes from the meeting and other materials concerning the company's goals and plans for the next six months. When you arrive at your office (an hour early), you find your in-basket full of notes, messages, and other correspondence.

Your instructor will provide you with additional information necessary to participate.

HRM INCIDENT 1

### This Whole Thing Is a Can of Worms!

John Case, accounting supervisor, was clearly annoyed as he approached his boss, Gerald Jones. He began, "Gerald, this note you sent me says I have to update descriptions for all 10 of the jobs in my department within the next two weeks."

"Well, what's the problem with that?" asked Gerald.

John explained, "This is a waste of time, especially since I have other deadlines. It will take at least 30 hours. We still have two weeks of work left on the internal audit reviews. You want me to push that back and work on job descriptions? No way."

"We haven't looked at these job descriptions in years. They will need a great deal of revision. And as soon as they get into the hands of the employees, I'll get all kinds of flack."

"Why would you get flack for getting the job descriptions in order?" asked Gerald.

John answered, "This whole thing is a can of worms. Just calling attention to the existence of job descriptions will give some people the idea that they don't have to do things that aren't in the description. And if we write what the people in my division really do, some jobs will have to be upgraded and others downgraded, I'll bet. I just can't afford the morale problem and the confusion right now."

Gerald replied, "What do you suggest, John? I have been told just to get it done, and within two weeks."

"I don't want to do it at all," said John, "But certainly not during the audit period. Can't you just go back up the line and get it put off until next month?"

#### Questions

1. What have John and Gerald forgotten to do prior to the creation of job descriptions? Why is that step important?
2. Evaluate John's statement, "Just calling attention to the existence of job descriptions will give some people the idea that they don't have to do things that aren't in the description."

HRM INCIDENT 2

### The Announcement

Dave Johnson, human resource manager for Eagle Aircraft, had just returned from a brief vacation in Cozumel, Mexico. Eagle is a Wichita, Kansas, maker of small commercial aircraft. Eagle's workforce in 2001 totaled 236. Dave's friend Carl Edwards, vice president for marketing, stopped by to ask Dave to lunch, as he often did. In the course of their conversation Carl asked Dave's opinion on the president's announcement concerning expansion. "What announcement?" was Dave's response.

Carl explained that there had been a special meeting of the executive council to announce a major expansion involving a new plant to be built near St. Louis, Missouri. He continued, "Everyone at the meeting seemed to be completely behind the president. Joe Davis, the controller, stressed our independent financial position. The production manager had written a complete report on the equipment we are going to need, including availability and cost information. And I have been pushing for this expansion for some time. So I was ready. I think it will be good for you too, Dave. The president said he expects employment to double in the next year."

As Carl left, Rex Schearer, a production supervisor, arrived. "Dave," said Rex, "the production manager jumped on me Friday because Maintenance doesn't have anybody qualified to work on the new digital lathe that's being installed."

"He's right," Dave replied. "Maintenance sent me a requisition last week. We'd better get moving and see if we can find someone." Dave knew that it was going to be another busy Monday.

### Questions

1. What should Dave do, if anything, about being kept in the dark regarding the expansion? Explain.
2. Discuss any additional problems highlighted by the case. What should be done to solve them?

## ▶ Notes

1. R. Wayne Mondy, Robert M. Noe, and Robert E. Edwards, "What the Staffing Function Entails," *Personnel* 63 (April 1986): 55–58.
2. Michael J. Blotzer, "Job Hazard Analysis and More," *Occupational Hazards* 60 (July 1, 1998): 25(3).
3. *Uniform Guidelines on Employee Selection Procedures, Federal Register* (Friday, August 25, 1978), Part IV.
4. IBM Human Resources Conference, "IT Should Support HR Changes" (October 23, 1996).
5. Mary Molina Fitzer, "Managing from Afar: Performance and Rewards in a Telecommmuting Environment," *Compensation & Benefits Review* 29 (January/February 1997): 65–73.
6. Caitlin P. Williams, "The End of the Job as We Know It," *Training & Development* 53 (January 1, 1999): 52–54.
7. N. Fredric Crandall and Marc J. Wallace Jr., "Inside the Virtual Workplace: Forging a New Deal for Work and Rewards," *Compensation & Benefits Review* 29 (January/February 1997): 27–36.
8. Gilbert B. Siegel, "Job Analysis in the TQM Environment," *Public Personnel Management* 25 (December 1996): 493.
9. Jonathan A. Segal, "Brains in a Jar," *HRMagazine* 44 (April 1999): 130.
10. Stuart Silverstein, "Guidelines for Disability Cases," *Newsday* (May 11, 1997): F12.
11. Susan E. Long, "Long Hours Can Be Essential Job Function," *HR Focus* 76 (June 1999): 3.
12. "Accommodation Will Be the Next ADA Issue," *Workforce* 79 (March 2000): 2.

13. Diane Mary Propsner, "How to Write Online Job Descriptions," *Workforce* 79 (August 1999): 1.

14. U.S. Department of Labor, *Dictionary of Occupational Titles,* 4th ed. (Washington, DC: U.S. Government Printing Office, 1977).

15. Howard Risher, "The End of Jobs: Planning and Managing Rewards in the New Work Paradigm," *Compensation & Benefits Review* 29 (January/February 1997): 13–17.

16. Anne Fisher, "Six Ways to Supercharge Your Career," *Fortune* 135 (January 13, 1997): 46+.

17. David Snyder, "The Revolution in the Workplace: What's Happening to Our Jobs?" *Futurist* 30 (March 1996): 8.

18. Jodi Barnes Nelson, "The Boundaryless Organization: Implications for Job Analysis, Recruitment, and Selection," *Human Resource Planning* 20 (1997): 39–49.

19. Ibid.

20. Stephen E. Bemis, Ann Holt Belenky, and Dee Ann Soder, *Job Analysis: An Effective Management Tool* (Washington, DC: The Bureau of National Affairs, 1983): 42.

21. "Writing and Managing Job Descriptions Just Got Easier," *Business Wire* (October 10, 1997).

22. James P. Clifford, "Job Analysis: Why Do It, and How Should It Be Done?" *Public Personnel Management* 23 (Summer 1994): 324.

23. Eric Minton, "The ADA and Records Management," *Records Management Quarterly* 28 (January 1994): 12.

24. Connie Freeman, "Strategy: Training HR Pros to Fit Your Culture," *HR Focus* 74 (May 1997): 9.

25. James Down, "From Paper Pushing to Strategic Planning," *Boston Business Journal* 16 (January 24, 1997): 6.

26. Melody Jones, "Four Trends to Reckon With," *HR Focus* 73 (July 1996): 22.

27. Mondy, Noe, and Edwards, "What the Staffing Function Entails."

28. Robert J. Grossman, "Heirs Unapparent as the Next Millennium Begins, Leaders Will Have to Be Made Because Not Enough Have Been Born," *HRMagazine* 44 (February 1999): 36–44.

29. Gale Dutton, "Future Shock: Who Will Run the Company?" *Management Review* 85 (August 1996): 19.

30. Grossman, "Heirs Unapparent," 25.

31. Ram Charan and Geoffrey Colvin, "The Right Fit: Most Boards Handle CEO Succession Poorly," *Fortune* 141 (May 17, 2000): 226+.

32. Kenneth Nowack, "The Secrets of Succession," *Training & Development* 48 (November 1994): 49.

33. Frederick Herzberg, "One More Time: How Do You Motivate Employees?" *Harvard Business Review* 65 (September/October 1987): 109–120.

34. Patricia M. Buhler, "Managers: Out with the Old and in with the New—Skills That Is," *Supervision* 59 (June 1998): 22–26.

35. Sharon K. Parker, "Enhancing Role Breadth Self-Efficacy: The Roles of Job Enrichment and Other Organizational Interventions," *Journal of Applied Psychology* (December 1998): 835–852.

36. Ellis Pines, "TQM Training: A New Culture Sparks Change at Every Level," *Aviation Week and Space Technology* 132 (May 21, 1990): S38.

37. Oren Harari, "Ten Reasons TQM Doesn't Work," *Management Review* 86 (January 1997): 38–41.

38. Michael Hammer and James Champy, *Reengineering the Corporation: A Manifesto for Business Revolution* (New York: Harper Collins Publishers, 1993): 32.

39. "The Malapropian 'R' Word," *Industry Forum* prepared by the American Management Association (September 1993): 1.

40. Brenda Paik Sunoo, "Around the World in HR Ways," *Workforce* (March 2000): 54–58.

41. Edward Shugrue, Joan Berland, and Bob Gonzales, "Case Study: How IBM Reengineered Its Benefits Center into a National HR Service Center," *Compensation & Benefits Review* 29 (March/April 1997): 41–48.

42. Stratford Sherman and Eanne C. Lee, "Levi's as Ye Sew, So Shall Ye Reap Vastly Successful, Immensely Rich, a Little Smug, the World's Premier Blue Jeans Maker Has Created a Unique Bond with Employees. Will Layoffs Wreck It?" *Fortune* 135 (May 1997): 104.

# chapter

chapterchapterchapterchapterchapterchapter

# 5

## Recruitment

## ▶ Objectives

- Explain alternatives to recruitment.
- Explain the external and internal environment of recruitment.
- Describe the recruitment process.
- Describe internal recruitment methods.
- Identify external sources of recruitment.
- Identify external recruitment methods.
- Describe how recruitment methods and sources are tailored to each other.
- Explain how to recruit for diversity.

orothy Bryant, recruiting supervisor for International Manufacturing Company in Salt Lake City, Utah, had been promoted to her position after several years as a group leader in the production department. One of Dorothy's first assignments was to recruit two software design engineers for International. After considering various recruitment alternatives, Dorothy placed the following ad in a local newspaper with a circulation in excess of 1,000,000:

EMPLOYMENT OPPORTUNITY
FOR SOFTWARE DESIGN ENGINEERS
2 positions available for software design engineers
desiring career in growth industry.
Prefer recent college graduates with good appearance.
Apply today! Send your résumé,
in confidence, to: D. A. Bryant
International Manufacturing Co., P.O. Box 1515
Salt Lake City, UT 84115

## ▶ Key Terms

More than 300 applications were received in the first week, and Dorothy was elated. When she reviewed the applicants, however, it appeared that few people possessed the desired qualifications for the job.

**D**orothy learned—the hard way—the importance of proper recruiting practices. She obviously failed to include specific job requirements in her newspaper ad. As a result, an excessive number of unqualified persons applied. Also, the road is paved for a potential legal problem because Dorothy uses a subjective criterion, *good appearance,* which may not be job related. In addition, stating a preference for a *recent college graduate* may also prove to be ill-advised because of the age implication. Adding further to Dorothy's dilemma is the potential liability her ad creates for the firm by implying a *career* for employees. Her corporate attorney will probably advise her to avoid any semblance of creating an implied contract for a candidate who is hired. The individual may later be discharged, then sue the company for breach of contract. Dorothy has found that preparing an effective, legally sound recruitment ad is not as simple as it once was.

**Recruitment**
The process of attracting individuals on a timely basis, in sufficient numbers, and with appropriate qualifications, and encouraging them to apply for jobs with an organization.

**Recruitment** is the process of attracting individuals on a timely basis, in sufficient numbers, and with appropriate qualifications, and encouraging them to apply for jobs with an organization. Finding the appropriate way of encouraging qualified candidates to apply for employment is extremely important when a firm needs to hire employees. Tapping productive sources of applicants and using suitable recruitment methods are essential to maximizing recruiting efficiency and effectiveness. Some firms, however, may prefer options other than recruitment. We begin this chapter by discussing alternatives to recruitment and the external and internal environments of recruitment. We then present the recruitment process. Internal recruitment methods, external recruitment sources, and external recruitment methods follow this section. Finally, recruitment for diversity is discussed.

## ALTERNATIVES TO RECRUITMENT

Even when human resource planning indicates a need for additional or replacement employees, a firm may decide against increasing the size of its workforce. Recruitment and selection costs are significant when all the related expenses are considered: the search process, interviewing, agency fee payment, and relocation and processing of a new employee. Although selection decisions are not irreversible, once employees are placed on the payroll, they may be difficult to remove, even if their performance is marginal. Therefore, a firm should consider its alternatives carefully before engaging in recruitment. Alternatives to recruitment commonly include outsourcing, use of contingent workers, employee leasing, and overtime.

## Outsourcing

As defined in Chapter 1, *outsourcing* is the process of transferring responsibility for an area of service and its objectives to an external provider. Subcontracting of various functions to other firms has been a common practice in industry for decades. This decision is usually made when the subcontractor is viewed as an organization that can perform a given function, such as maintenance, with perhaps even greater efficiency and effectiveness. Within the past few years, this practice has become a widespread and increasingly popular alternative involving virtually every business area, including human resources.

## Contingent Workers

Described by the Secretary of Labor as the "disposable American workforce," **contingent workers**—also known as part-timers, temporaries, and independent contractors—work for staffing companies or are classified as independent contractors. According to a study by the Bureau of Labor Statistics, they comprise the fastest-growing segment of the U.S. economy, about 12.6 million people.[1] According to a Conference Board survey, over 80 percent of the respondents indicated the number one reason for the rapid growth of jobs for these workers was to achieve flexibility. Global competition and changing technology prevent employers from accurately forecasting their employment needs months in advance. To avoid hiring people one day and resorting to layoffs the next, firms look to a temporary workforce as a buffer.[2]

**Contingent workers** Also known as part-timers, temporaries, and independent contractors, individuals who work for staffing companies or are classified as independent contractors.

In addition to the need for flexibility, another factor is cost. The total cost of a permanent employee is generally estimated at 30 to 40 percent above gross pay. This figure does not include, among other things, the costs of recruitment.

To avoid some of these costs and to maintain flexibility as workloads vary, many organizations utilize part-time or temporary employees. Companies that provide temporary workers assist their clients in handling excess or special workloads. These companies assign their own employees to their customers and fulfill all the obligations normally associated with an employer. The expenses of recruitment, absenteeism and turnover, and employee benefits are avoided by the client firms.

Contingent workers are the human equivalents of just-in-time inventory. These *disposable workers* permit maximum flexibility for the employer and lower labor costs.[3] The main unanswered question is whether this approach to staffing is healthy for our society in the long run. In the shorter term, the advantages gained by using contingent workers may be essential for success or even survival of many companies.

## Professional Employer Organizations: Employee Leasing

**Professional employer organizations (PEOs)** are essentially off-site human resources departments that put a client firm's employees on their payroll, then lease the employees back to the company. PEOs typically charge from 1 to 4 percent of the customer's gross wages, with percentages based on the number of

**Professional employer organizations (PEOs)** Off-site human resources departments that puts a client firm's employees on its payroll, then leases the employees back to the company.

employees being leased. The organization handles the company's payroll, benefits, human resources, and risk management.[4] PEOs are typically used with small- and medium-sized firms.[5]

Leasing has advantages for employees also. Because leasing companies provide workers for many companies, they often enjoy economies of scale that permit them to offer excellent, low-cost benefit programs. In addition, workers frequently have greater opportunities for job mobility. Some leasing firms operate throughout the nation. If one employed spouse in a dual-career family is relocated, the leasing company may offer the other a job in the new location too. Also, if a client organization suffers a downturn in business, the leasing company can transfer employees to another client, avoiding both layoffs and loss of seniority. A potential disadvantage to the client is erosion of employee loyalty because workers receive pay and benefits from the leasing company. Regardless of any shortcomings, use of employee leasing is growing. By 2005, the industry could have $185 billion in revenues and more than nine million employees.[6]

## Overtime

Perhaps the most commonly used method of meeting short-term fluctuations in work volume is overtime. Overtime may help both employer and employee. The employer benefits by avoiding recruitment, selection, and training costs. The employee gain from increased income during the overtime period.

There are potential problems with overtime, however. Many managers believe that when they work employees for unusually long periods of time, the company pays more and receives less in return. Employees may become fatigued and lack the energy to perform at a normal rate, especially when excessive overtime is required. Two additional possible problems are related to the use of prolonged overtime. Employees may, consciously or not, pace themselves so that overtime will be assured. They may also become accustomed to the added income resulting from overtime pay. Employees may even elevate their standard of living to the level permitted by this additional income. Then, when overtime is no longer required and their paychecks shrink, employees may become disgruntled.

## EXTERNAL ENVIRONMENT OF RECRUITMENT

Like other human resource functions, the recruitment process does not take place in a vacuum. Factors external to the organization can significantly affect the firm's recruitment efforts. Of particular importance is the demand for and supply of specific skills in the labor market. If demand for a particular skill is high relative to supply, an extraordinary recruiting effort may be required.

## Labor Market Conditions

As the unemployment rate nears record lows nationwide, some small business firms have implemented creative approaches to recruitment. For example, certain business owners in Milwaukee are paying bonuses to churches where pastors will work the pews to recruit entry-level workers. Another small firm in Los Angeles, Benji Electronics Inc., has expanded its labor market by hiring people with few, if any, qualifications. The firm is then willing to spend much time and money training them, often in remedial subjects.[7]

When the unemployment rate in an organization's labor market is high, the firm's recruitment process may be simplified. The number of unsolicited applicants is usually greater, and the increased size of the labor pool provides a better opportunity for attracting qualified applicants. Conversely, as the unemployment rate drops, recruitment efforts must be increased and new sources explored.

Local labor market conditions are of primary importance in recruitment for most nonmanagerial, many supervisory, and even some middle-management positions. However, recruitment for executive and professional positions often extends to national or even global markets. Although the recruiter's day-to-day activities provide a *feel* for the labor market, accurate employment data—found in professional journals and U.S. Department of Labor reports—can be extremely useful.

## Legal Considerations

Legal matters also play a significant role in recruitment practices in the United States. The individual and the employer first make contact during the recruitment process. One survey found that about one-fourth of all discrimination claims resulted from the employers' recruitment and selection actions.[8] Therefore, nondiscriminatory practices at this stage are absolutely essential. We discuss this topic later in this chapter.

## Corporate Image

The firm's corporate image is another important factor that affects recruitment. If employees believe that their employer deals with them fairly, the positive word-of-mouth support they provide is of great value to the firm. It assists in establishing credibility with prospective employees. Good reputations earned in this manner may help attract more and better qualified applicants. Prospective employees are more inclined to respond positively to the organization's recruitment efforts if the firm is praised by its employees. The firm with a positive public image is one believed to be a *good place to work,* and its recruitment efforts are often greatly enhanced.

## INTERNAL ENVIRONMENT OF RECRUITMENT

The labor market and the government exert powerful external influences on recruitment practices; however, the organization's own practices and policies also affect recruitment.

## Human Resource Planning

In most cases, a firm cannot attract prospective employees in sufficient numbers and with the required skills overnight. Examining alternative sources of recruits and determining the most productive sources and methods for obtaining them often requires planning time. After identifying the best alternatives, managers can make better recruitment decisions.

## Promotion Policies

An organization's promotion policy can also have a significant impact on recruitment. An organization can stress a policy of promotion from within its own ranks or a policy of filling positions from outside the organization. Depending on the circumstances, either approach may have merit.

**Promotion from within (PFW)** is the policy of filling vacancies above entry-level positions with current employees. When an organization emphasizes promotion from within, its workers have an incentive to strive for advancement.

**Promotion from within (PFW)**
The policy of filling vacancies above entry-level positions with employees presently employed by a company.

**www.prenhall.com/mondy**

This site covers various recruitment issues including career management and planning, interviewing, and directories and reviews for online computing services.

When employees see co-workers being promoted, they become more aware of their own opportunities. Motivation provided by this practice often improves employee morale. Today's *flatter* organizational structures, with fewer levels of management, restrict upward mobility to a degree. However, the opportunity to move up in an organization will continue to serve as a motivating factor for some employees.

It is unlikely, however, that a firm can (or would even desire to) adhere rigidly to a practice of promotion from within. The vice president of human resources for a major automobile manufacturer offers this advice: "A strictly applied 'PFW' policy eventually leads to inbreeding, a lack of cross-fertilization, and a lack of creativity. A good goal, in my opinion, is to fill 80 percent of openings above entry-level positions from within." Frequently, new blood is needed to provide new ideas and innovation that must take place for firms to remain competitive. In such cases, even organizations with promotion from within policies may opt to look outside the organization for new talent. In any event, a promotion policy that first considers insiders is great for employee morale and motivation and is often beneficial to the organization.

## The Firm's Knowledge of Employees

Another advantage of internal recruitment is that the organization is usually well aware of its employees' capabilities. An employee's job performance may not, by itself, be a reliable criterion for promotion. Nevertheless, many of the employee's personal and job-related qualities will be known. The employee has a track record, as opposed to being an *unknown quantity*. Also, the company's investment in the individual may yield a higher return. Still another positive factor is the employee's knowledge of the firm, its policies, and its people.

## Nepotism

Policies related to the employment of relatives may also affect a firm's recruitment efforts. The content of such policies varies greatly, but it is not uncommon for companies to have antinepotism policies that discourage the employment of close relatives, especially when related employees would be placed in the same department, under the same supervisor, or in supervisor-subordinate roles.

When internal alternatives to hiring additional employees are considered but determined to be inappropriate, organizations—with due consideration to environmental factors—turn to recruitment to attract potential employees and encourage them to apply for open positions.

## THE RECRUITMENT PROCESS

As previously defined, *recruitment* is the process of attracting individuals on a timely basis, in sufficient numbers, and with appropriate qualifications, and encouraging them to apply for jobs with an organization. Applicants with qualifications most closely related to job specifications may then be selected. Dorothy Bryant was quite disappointed when she reviewed over 300 applicants and only a few had the desired qualifications.

Finding the appropriate way of encouraging qualified candidates to apply for employment is extremely important when a firm needs to hire employees. Tapping productive sources of applicants and using suitable recruitment methods are essential to maximizing recruiting efficiency and effectiveness. As Jim Goodnight, CEO of the software giant SAS Institute Inc., stated, "Ninety-five percent of our assets drive out the gate every afternoon at five. I want them to come back in the morning. I need them to come back in the morning."[9] In an April 2000 survey, nearly two-thirds of respondents said that recruiting, selecting, and placing employees are among their top three priorities for 2000.[10]

How many times do we hear CEOs state, "Our most important assets are human"? While this adage has probably always been true, an increasing number of executives are beginning to actually believe it. Hiring the best people available has never been more critical than today because of global competition. Furthermore, hiring decisions can be no better than the alternatives presented through recruitment efforts.

Figure 5-1 shows that when human resource planning indicates a need for employees, the firm may evaluate alternatives to hiring. If these alternatives are found to be inappropriate, the recruitment process starts. Frequently, recruitment

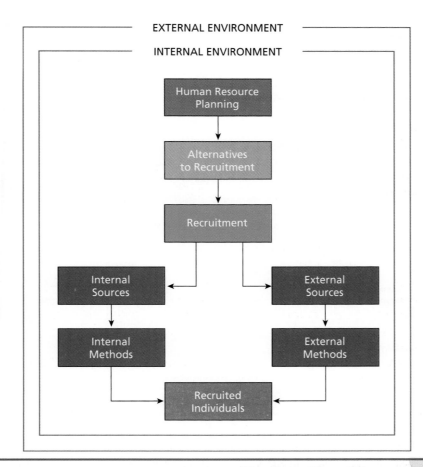

**The Recruitment Process**   **Figure 5-1**

## EMPLOYMENT REQUISITION - Greenville

*(This Document Must Be Typed)*

Requisition Number: № 30560

| Title Of Position | Job Code | Date Needed | ☐ Supervisory<br>☐ Non-Supervisory |
|---|---|---|---|

**Job Status (Please Check One)**

☐ Regular (Standard Hours)_____ am/pm to_____ am/pm

☐ Part-Time (Less Than 40 Hours/Week)

☐ Temporary For _____ days

☐ Co-Op Alternating

☐ Co-Op Parallel (part time)

☐ Temporary For _____ days

☐ Job Shop / Consultant

☐ New Grad

☐ ICT or VOE Trainee

Department Name:

Account Number

| Department Number | CBN Number | Extension of Time (Temp)<br>☐ Yes  ☐ No |
|---|---|---|

Please Check One:

☐ Indirect   ☐ Direct Contract Number _____

Department Interviewer

1._____ Ext. _____

2._____ Ext. _____

**Justification**

☐ Addition ☐ Replacement For (Name) _____

**Security Clearance**

Level _____ Access _____

Recommended Billed Hourly Rate

(Temps only) _____ / Hr.

Not to Exceed $ _____ / Total Effort

Per Diem Authorized ☐ Yes ☐ No

**Knowledge and Skills**

Indicate Type(s) of Computer

☐ Mainframe

☐ IBM PC

☐ Macintosh

☐ Other _____

Indicate Type(s) of Software

☐ MS Word

☐ Excel

☐ Power Point

☐ Other _____

Other Skills Required _____

_____

_____

## APPROVALS

Section/Department Head _____ Date _____

VP Organization _____ Date _____

VP Finance _____ Date _____

Vice President and General Manager _____ Date _____

## FOR HUMAN RESOURCES USE ONLY

☐ Received In Labor Relations   Date _____

☐ Released In Labor Relations   Date _____

Temporary Agency _____

Date Approval for Staffing _____

☐ Reviewed For ETOP   Posted ☐ Yes ☐ No

8-98999-1 (June 1996)

**Figure 5-2** An Employee Requisition for Raytheon

*Source:* Courtesy of Raytheon.

begins when a manager initiates an **employee requisition**, a document that specifies job title, department, the date the employee is needed for work, and other details. An employee requisition for Raytheon is provided in Figure 5-2. With this information, managers can refer to the appropriate job description to determine the qualifications the recruited person needs. These qualifications, however, are becoming less clear-cut. According to Joanne Jorz, vice president of program development for Conceptual Systems Inc., an HRM consulting firm, "Job descriptions aren't cleanly defined any longer. When you recruit and hire for task X, it won't be long before the employee will be asked to do A, B, C, and D as well."[11] With such broad expectations from the company, the employee will obviously need a broader range of skills and abilities. Some firms are dealing with this situation by striving to employ individuals who are bright, adaptable, and can work effectively in teams. Hiring for organizational *fit* is discussed in Chapter 7.

The next step in the recruitment process is to determine whether qualified employees are available within the firm (the internal source) or must be recruited from external sources, such as colleges, universities, and other organizations. Because of the high cost of recruitment, organizations need to utilize the most productive recruitment sources and methods available. Both the Saratoga Institute and the independent human resources consulting company Hewitt Association have estimated that the cost of replacing a worker runs between 1 and 2½ times the salary of the open job; the more sophisticated the job, the higher the cost.[12]

**Recruitment sources** are the locations where qualified individuals can be found. **Recruitment methods** are the specific means by which potential employees can be attracted to the firm. When the sources of potential employees have been identified, appropriate methods for either internal or external recruitment are used to accomplish recruitment objectives.

Companies may discover that some recruitment sources and methods are superior to others for locating and attracting potential talent. For instance, one large equipment manufacturer determined that medium-sized, state-supported colleges and universities located in rural areas were good sources of potential managers. Other firms may arrive at different conclusions. To maximize recruiting effectiveness, utilizing recruitment sources and methods tailored to a specific organization's needs is vitally important.

## INTERNAL RECRUITMENT METHODS

Management should be able to identify current employees who are capable of filling positions as they become available. Helpful tools used for internal recruitment include employee databases, job posting, and job bidding procedures. As we mentioned in Chapter 4, employee databases permit organizations to determine whether current employees possess the qualifications for open positions. As a recruitment device, these databases have proved to be extremely valuable to organizations when they are kept current. Databases can be of tremendous value in locating talent internally and supporting the concept of promotion from within.

**Job posting** is a procedure for informing employees that job openings exist. **Job bidding** is a technique that permits employees who believe that they possess the required qualifications to apply for a posted job. Table 5-1 shows the procedure a medium-sized firm might use. As seen in Chapter 6, the intranet is also used to provide an up-to-date list of job openings for which any qualified employee is encouraged to apply.

| Responsibility | Action Required |
|---|---|
| Human Resource Assistant | 1. Upon receiving an employee requisition, post opening on intranet or send an e-mail or memo to each appropriate supervisor stating that a job opening exists. The message should include a job title, job number, pay grade, salary range, summary of the basic duties performed, and the essential qualifications required for the job (data to be taken from the job description/specification). |
| Supervisors | 2. Ensure that the message is communicated to all within their section. |
| Interested Employees | 3. Contact Human Resources. |

The job posting and bidding procedure can help minimize the commonly heard complaint that insiders never hear of a job opening until it has been filled. It reflects an openness that most employees generally value highly. A firm that offers freedom of choice and encourages career growth has a distinct advantage over firms that do not. However, a job posting and bidding system does have some negative features. An effective system requires the expenditure of considerable time and money. When bidders are unsuccessful, someone must explain to them why they were not chosen. If care has not been taken to ensure that the most qualified applicant is chosen, the system will lack credibility. Even successful implementation of such a system cannot completely eliminate complaints.

## EXTERNAL RECRUITMENT SOURCES

At times, a firm must look beyond its own borders to find employees, particularly when expanding its workforce. The following needs require external recruitment: (1) to fill entry-level jobs; (2) to acquire skills not possessed by current employees; and (3) to obtain employees with different backgrounds to provide a diversity of ideas. As Figure 5-3 shows, even when promotions are made internally, entry-level jobs must be filled from the outside. Thus, after the president of a firm retires, a series of internal promotions is made. Ultimately, however, the firm has to recruit externally to fill the entry-level position of salary analyst. If the president's position had been filled from the outside, the chain reaction of promotions from within would not have occurred. Depending on the qualifications desired, employees may be attracted from a number of outside sources.

## High Schools and Vocational Schools

Organizations concerned with recruiting clerical and other entry-level operative employees often depend heavily on high schools and vocational schools. Many of these schools have outstanding training programs for specific occupational skills, such as home appliance repair and small-engine mechanics. Some companies work with schools to ensure a constant supply of trained individuals with specific job skills. In some areas, companies even loan employees to schools to assist in the training programs. Business support of education is covered in Chapter 8.

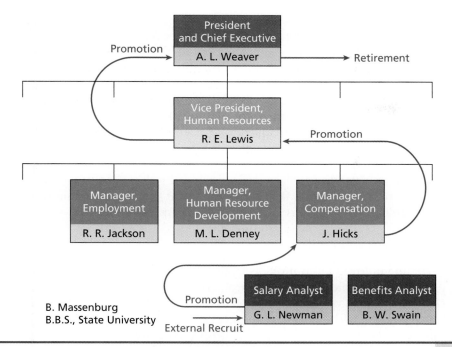

**Internal Promotion and External Recruitment** | **Figure 5-3**

## Community Colleges

Many community colleges are sensitive to the specific employment needs in their local labor markets and graduate highly sought after students with marketable skills. Typically, community colleges have two-year programs designed for both a terminal education and preparation for a four-year university degree program. Many community colleges also have excellent mid-management programs combined with training for specific trades. In addition, career centers often provide a place for employers to contact students, thereby facilitating the recruitment process.

## Colleges and Universities

Colleges and universities represent a major recruitment source for many organizations. Potential professional, technical, and management employees are typically found in these institutions. Many firms routinely utilize this source for prospective employees.

Placement directors, faculty, and administrators can be helpful to organizations in their search for recruits. Because on-campus recruitment is mutually beneficial, both employers and universities should take steps to develop and maintain close relationships. When a company establishes recruitment programs with educational institutions, it should continue those programs year after year to maintain an effective relationship with each school. It is important that the firm knows the school and that the school knows the firm.[13]

## Competitors and Other Firms

Competitors and other firms in the same industry or geographic area may be the most important source of recruits for positions in which recent experience is required. The fact that approximately 5 percent of the working population is, at any one time, either actively seeking or receptive to a change of position emphasizes the importance of these sources. Even organizations that have policies of promotion from within occasionally look elsewhere to fill important positions. Hardly a day goes by that we don't read about an executive leaving one company for another, often at a large salary increase. Although the ethics of corporate raiding may be debatable, it is apparent that competitors and other firms do serve as external sources of recruitment for high-quality talent.

Smaller firms in particular look for employees who have been trained by larger organizations that have greater developmental resources. For instance, an optical firm located in the Midwest believes that its own operation is not large enough to provide extensive training and development programs. Therefore, a person recruited by this firm for a significant management role is likely to have held at least two previous positions with a competitor.

## The Unemployed

The unemployed often provide a valuable source of recruits. Qualified applicants join the unemployment rolls every day for various reasons. Companies may go out of business, cut back operations, or be merged with other firms, leaving qualified workers without jobs. Employees are also fired sometimes merely because of personality differences with their bosses. Not infrequently, employees become frustrated with their jobs and simply quit.

Many organizations are coaxing former employees out of retirement for part-time or temporary contracts. Retirees and people nearing retirement used to have a great deal of difficulty finding work. The situation is not the same today. For instance, Ralph Calcavecchio worked at IBM for 38 years, setting industrywide standards for electromagnetic compatibility before retiring. Today, Calcavecchio continues his work as a freelance consultant and in fact is under contract to IBM. The work is the same, except that Calcavecchio works out of his home.[14]

## Older Individuals

Older workers, including those who are retired, may also represent a valuable source of employees. Although these workers are often victims of negative stereotyping, the facts support the notion that older people can perform many jobs extremely well. When Kentucky Fried Chicken Corporation had difficulty recruiting younger employees, it turned to older individuals and those with disabilities. The results included a dramatically reduced turnover rate and vacancies. Management surveys indicate that most employers have high opinions of their older workers. They value them for many reasons, including having better work habits than younger workers, having lower absenteeism rates, and having higher levels of commitment to the organization.[15]

## Military Personnel: Operation Transition

Operation Transition is a program that offers employers two vehicles for tapping into the military labor pool at no cost: the Defense Outplacement Referral System (DORS) and the Transition Bulletin Board (TBB). DORS is an automated résumé and referral system that allows employers to request résumés for open positions. Companies can register for the program at www.dmdc.osd.mil. The TBB, www.dmdc.osd.mil/tbb, is a bulletin board where companies can post jobs online. Jobseekers at military bases around the world see these listings.[16]

**www.prenhall.com/mondy**

These job agent service sites permit jobseekers to specify parameters for their ideal job and to receive job opening information only on the opportunities that fit these restrictions.

Hiring of former service members may make sense to many employers because these individuals typically have a proven work history and are flexible, motivated, and drug free. Another valuable characteristic of veterans is their goal and team orientation.[17] As skills possessed by veterans are wide ranging, this source of employees should not be overlooked.

## Self-Employed Workers

Finally, the self-employed worker may also be a good potential recruit. Such individuals may constitute a source of applicants for any number of jobs requiring technical, professional, administrative, or entrepreneurial expertise within a firm.

## EXTERNAL RECRUITMENT METHODS

By examining recruitment sources, a firm determines the location of potential job applicants. It then seeks to attract these applicants by specific recruitment methods. Some conventional external methods of recruitment are discussed next.

## Advertising

**Advertising** communicates the firm's employment needs to the public through media such as radio, newspapers, television, and industry publications. Advertising on the Internet will be discussed in the next chapter. In determining the content of an advertising message, a firm must decide on the corporate image it wants to project. Obviously, the firm should give prospective employees an accurate picture of the job and the organization. Dorothy's ad did not provide an accurate picture of the job and was flawed in other ways, including legal aspects and the use of subjective criteria. At the same time, the firm should attempt to appeal to the self-interest of prospective employees, emphasizing the job's unique qualities. The ad must tell potential employees why they should be interested in that particular job and organization. The message should also indicate how an applicant is to respond: apply in person, apply by telephone, apply on firm's Web site, or submit a résumé by fax or e-mail. An advertisement that sells applicants on joining a company is presented in Figure 5-4.

The firm's previous experience with various media should suggest the approach to be taken for specific types of jobs. A common form of advertising

> **Advertising**
> A way of communicating the firm's employment needs to the public through media such as radio, newspaper, or industry publications.

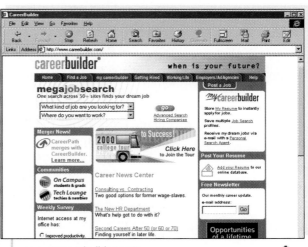

www.careerbuilder.com
*Source:* Courtesy of CareerBuilder.com

**Are you spending the best years of your life with an organization that has your best interest at heart?**

**If not, check us out!**

Our mid-sized electronics firm is looking for a professional recruiter with at least two years experience in HR or a bachelor's degree in that field. Must have extensive knowledge in recruitment sources and methods used in recruiting professional employees. General knowledge in human resources and performance management are a definite plus.

Consider these company practices:

✱ Three weeks of paid vacation
✱ Ten paid holidays each year
✱ Five personal days each year
✱ Professional education opportunities
✱ Performance-based pay and excellent benefits
✱ Casual dress policy every day

If interested, e-mail resume to rwmondy@argontech.net or fax to 555-123-4567.

**Primono Electronics**

You may learn more about our firm at www.prenhall.com/mondy

**We are an Equal Opportunity Employer**

**Figure 5-4** **A Job Advertisement**

that provides broad coverage is the newspaper ad. The greatest problem with this method of external recruitment is the large number of unqualified individuals who respond to such ads. This situation increases the likelihood of poor selection decisions.

Although few base their decision to change jobs on advertising, an ad creates awareness, generates interest, and encourages a prospect to seek more information about the firm and the job opportunities that it provides. Examination of the Sunday edition of any major newspaper reveals the extensive use of advertising in recruiting. Certain media attract audiences that are more homogeneous in terms of employment skills, education, and orientation. Advertisements placed in such publications as *The Wall Street Journal* relate primarily to managerial, professional, and technical positions. The readers of these publications are generally individuals qualified for many of the positions advertised. Focusing on a specific labor market minimizes the likelihood of receiving marginally qualified or even totally unqualified applicants.

Virtually every professional group publishes a journal that is widely read by its members. Advertising for a marketing executive position in *Marketing Forum,* for example, would hit the target market because it is read almost exclusively by marketing professionals. Trade journals are also widely utilized. The use of journals does, however, present some problems. For example, they lack scheduling flexibility; their publishing deadlines may be weeks prior to the issue date and may be even further in advance for four-color material. Because staffing needs cannot always be anticipated far in advance, the use of journals for recruitment has obvious limitations.

Qualified prospects who read job ads in newspapers and professional and trade journals may not be so dissatisfied with their present jobs that they will pursue opportunities advertised. Therefore, in high-demand situations, a firm needs to consider all available media resources.

Other media that can also be used include radio, billboards, and television. These methods are likely to be more expensive than newspapers or journals, but they have been used with success in specific situations. For instance, a regional medical center used billboards successfully to attract registered nurses. One large manufacturing firm achieved considerable success in advertising for production trainees by means of spot advertisements on the radio. A large electronics firm used television to attract experienced engineers when it opened a new facility and needed more engineers immediately. Thus, in situations where hiring needs are urgent, television and radio may provide good results even though these media may not be sufficient by themselves. Broadcast messages can let people know that an organization is seeking recruits. They are, however, limited in the amount of information they can transmit.

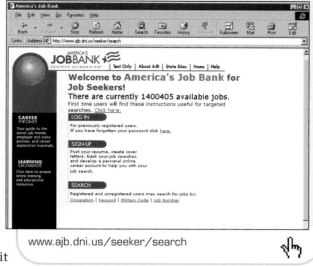

www.ajb.dni.us/seeker/search

## Private and Public Employment Agencies

An **employment agency** is an organization that helps firms recruit employees and at the same time aids individuals in their attempt to locate jobs. These agencies perform recruitment and selection functions that have proven quite beneficial to many organizations.

Firms utilize *private employment agencies* for virtually every type of position. However, these agencies are best known for recruiting white-collar employees and offer an important service in bringing qualified applicants and open positions together. Neither the organization nor the job applicant should overlook this method. The one-time fees that some agencies charge often turn off candidates; however, many private employment agencies deal primarily with firms that pay the fees.

The *public employment agencies* operated by each state receive overall policy direction from the U.S. Employment Service. Public employment agencies are best known for recruiting and placing individuals in operative jobs, but they have become increasingly involved in matching people with technical, professional, and managerial positions. Some public agencies use computerized job-matching systems to aid in the recruitment process. Public employment agencies provide their services without charge to either the employer or the prospective employee.

**Employment agency**
An organization that assists firms in recruiting employees and also aids individuals in their attempts to locate jobs.

▶ *Niche Recruitment Sites*

**www.prenhall.com/mondy**
Several niche recruitment sites are presented.

HR WEB WISDOM

## Recruiters

Recruiters most commonly focus on technical and vocational schools, community colleges, colleges, and universities. Employers rank on-campus recruiting as the number one method for snaring students.[18] The key contact for recruiters on college and university campuses is often the student placement director. This administrator is in an excellent position to arrange interviews with students possessing the qualifications desired by the firm. Placement services help organizations utilize their recruiters efficiently. Qualified candidates are identified, interviews are scheduled, and suitable rooms are provided for interviews.

The company recruiter plays a vital role in attracting applicants. The interviewee often perceives the recruiter's actions as a reflection of the character of the firm. If the recruiter is dull, the interviewee may think the company dull; if the recruiter is apathetic, discourteous, or vulgar, the interviewee may well attribute all these negative characteristics to the firm. Recruiters must always be aware of the image they present at the screening interview because it makes a lasting impression.

Some American firms have discovered an innovative use of recruiters. All it takes is a computer system with a terminal at both corporate headquarters and on a college campus. Recruiters can communicate with college career counselors and interview students through a video conferencing system without leaving the office. Connie Thanasoulis-Cerrachio of Citibank states that "$1,000 versus the cost of $12 or $13 an interview is an amazing savings." According to Citibank, these systems have grown fivefold to more than 150 on campuses in the past year.[19]

## Special Events

Holding **special events** is a recruiting method that involves an effort on the part of a single employer or group of employers to attract a large number of applicants for interviews. Job fairs, for example, are designed to bring together applicants and representatives of various companies. From an employer's viewpoint, a primary advantage of job fairs is the opportunity to meet a large number of candidates in a short time. More than a dozen commercial firms operate job fairs, but

## TRENDS & INNOVATIONS

### ▶ *Keiretsu*

Technology workers have quite a list of party options in the Washington, D.C., area these days, thanks to employee-hungry companies. They can head out to Fairfax County, Virginia, tonight for free pool and beer, courtesy of WHFS-FM, Techies.com, and nearly 20 area high-tech firms. Thursday night, they can schmooze with executives from Roku Technologies and a handful of other companies at a Herndon, Virginia, coffeehouse—and get a free beer glass. Tomorrow night, the company is holding "*Keiretsu*," a networking event at Revolution Coffee Lounge in Herndon, where Roku will buy all comers two free drinks. The evening's event is co-sponsored by ITrecruitermag.com and other technology firms.

*Keiretsu* is a Japanese word, and though there's no literal English translation, it's basically a network of people who use their personal relationships to help each other professionally. The emphasis is on a casual atmosphere, more of a situation where people are really interacting with each other, feeling at ease.[20]

government agencies, charitable organizations, and business alliances also frequently sponsor them. As a recruitment method, job fairs offer the potential for a much lower cost per hire than traditional approaches.

## Internships

An **internship** is a special form of recruiting that involves placing a student in a temporary job. Internships are now being used by more and more companies as a recruiting technique.[21] Many companies are recruiting students through internships in their sophomore and junior years.[22] In this arrangement, there is no obligation by the company to hire the student permanently or by the student to accept a permanent position with the firm following graduation. An internship typically involves a temporary job for the summer months or a part-time job during the school year. It may also take the form of a student working full time one semester and going to school full time the next.

▶ A primary advantage of job fairs is the opportunity to meet a large number of candidates in a short time.

During the internship, the student gets to view business practices firsthand. At the same time, the intern contributes to the firm by performing needed tasks. Through this relationship, a student can determine whether a company would be a desirable employer. Similarly, having a relatively lengthy period of time to observe the student's job performance, the firm can make a better judgment regarding the person's qualifications. Studies show that students with internship and co-op experience are able to find jobs more easily and progress much further and faster in the business world than those without.[23]

In addition to other benefits, internships provide opportunities for students to bridge the gap from business theory to practice. For many employers, an internship enhances an application by demonstrating a solid commitment to a career choice. More than half the employers surveyed by the National Association of Colleges and Employers say their recent hires out of college had internship experience.[24] Firms have learned that student interns can also serve as effective recruiters. If the intern has a good experience, he or she will tell other students about it. Internships also serve as an effective public relations tool that provides visibility for the company and assists in recruitment.

**Internship**
A special form of recruitment that involves placing students in temporary jobs with no obligation either by the company to hire the student permanently or by the student to accept a permanent position with the firm following graduation.

## Executive Search Firms

Executive search firms may be used by organizations in their recruitment efforts to locate experienced professionals and executives when other sources prove inadequate. **Executive search firms** are organizations that seek the most qualified executive available for a specific position and are generally retained by companies needing specific types of individuals.

Fees for *contingency searches* were forecast to increase 24 percent to $8.6 billion in 2000. These fees are paid only upon successful placement of a candidate in a job opening. Fees for *retainer searches,* typically utilized for top business executives, were expected to increase 22 percent to $4.5 billion in 2000.[25] The executive

**Executive search firms**
Organizations retained by a company to search for the most qualified executive available for a specific position.

search industry has evolved from a basic recruitment service to a highly sophisticated profession serving a greatly expanded role. Search firms now assist organizations in determining their human resource needs, establishing compensation packages, and revising organizational structures.

An executive search firm's representatives often visit the client's offices and interview the company's management. This enables them to gain a clear understanding of the company's goals and the job qualifications required. After obtaining this information, they contact and interview potential candidates, check references, and refer the best-qualified person to the client for the selection decision. Search firms maintain databases of résumés that are used during this process. Other sources used include networking contacts, files from previous searches, specialized directories, personal calls, previous clients, colleagues, and unsolicited résumés. The search firm's fee is generally a percentage of the individual's compensation for the first year. The client pays expenses, as well as the fee.

The relationship between a client company and a search firm should be based on mutual trust and understanding. Both parties gain the most from their relationship when they interact often and maintain good communication. To be successful, the search firm must understand in detail the nature of the client's operations, the responsibilities of the position being filled, and the client's corporate culture. Similarly, the client must understand the search process, work with the consultant, and provide continuous, honest feedback.

## Professional Associations

Many professional associations in business areas including finance, marketing, accounting, and human resources provide recruitment and placement services for their members. The Society for Human Resource Management, for example, operates a job referral service for members seeking new positions and employers with positions to fill.

## Employee Referrals

Many organizations have found that their employees can serve an important role in the recruitment process by actively soliciting applications from their friends and associates. It is a fact that employee referrals are better qualified and stay on the job longer than any other candidate source.[26] Many companies recruit new hires through employee-referral incentive programs. Current employees typically have a good idea of what kind of people and skills an organization needs.[27]

## Unsolicited Walk-in Applicants

If an organization has the reputation of being a good place to work, it may be able to attract qualified prospects even without extensive recruitment efforts. Acting on their own initiative, well-qualified workers may seek out a specific company to apply for a job. Unsolicited applicants who apply because they are favorably impressed with the firm's reputation often prove to be valuable employees.

## Open Houses

Open houses are a valuable recruiting tool, especially during days of low unemployment. Here, firms pair potential hires and managers in a warm, casual environment that encourages on-the-spot job offers. Open houses are cheaper and faster than hiring through recruitment agencies, and they also beat out career fairs in popularity. There are pros and cons of holding a truly *open* house. If the event is open, it may draw a large turnout, but it also may attract more unqualified candidates. Some companies prefer to control the types of candidates they host, and so they conduct invitation-only sessions. In this scenario, the HR staff screens résumés in response to ads, then invites only preselected candidates.[28] Open houses are advertised in both conventional manners and through the Internet. Major open houses may be featured on the homepage of the company's Web site. For example, Sabre, Inc. advertised an open house on Monster.com in June 2000. People who could not attend the open house could apply through the Web site.

## Event Recruiting

Cisco pioneered event recruiting as a recruitment approach and it has brought the company some success. The concept is very simple: Attend the events that the people you are seeking go to. In the case of programmers in Silicon Valley, the choice spots have been microbreweries, marathons, and bike races. Companies that participate in these events should become involved in some way that promotes their name and cause. For example, they might sponsor or cosponsor an event, pass out refreshments, and give away prizes. Individuals should know that the company is recruiting and what type of workers are being sought.

Event recruiting gives a company the opportunity to create an image of the kind of company it is. For example, Cisco quickly became known as the company with *cool* recruiters that, therefore, must be a *cool* place to work. Everyone was aware of it. Even if a participant was not interested, he or she probably knew someone who was. It became obvious to lots of people that companies such as IBM and Hewlett Packard were not there, and therefore could not be *cool* places to work. And *cool* is big for some employees. They want an atmosphere of youth, excitement, growth, and—perhaps most of all—permission to experiment and make mistakes.[29]

## Virtual Job Fairs

In a **virtual job fair** individuals meet recruiters face to face in interviews conducted over special computers that transmit head-and-shoulder images of both parties. This recruitment method is a project of VIEWnet Inc., producer of the technology, and career centers in 21 universities from the Atlantic Coast and Southeastern Conferences. In what was advertised as the nation's first Virtual Job Fair, recruiters at 20 major corporations chose 1,000 students from 12,000 résumés to interview for 300 jobs. Recruiters can visit all schools without leaving their offices.[30]

**Virtual job fair**
A recruitment method in which individuals meet recruiters face to face in interviews conducted over special computers that transmit head-and-shoulder images of both parties.

### ▌ *The Right Source?*

"I just don't understand it," said Freddy Rivera, recruitment specialist for Tandem Computers. "I have been recruiting like mad for those senior systems analysts that management said we need, and I just haven't had any luck."

"Where have you been trying to locate them?" said Erm Chen, the HR director.

Freddy replied, "I have recruited at every college in the region, but none of the applicants has the experience level required for a senior analyst."

*How do you believe that Erm should respond?*

**HRM IN ACTION**

## Sign-on Bonuses

Some firms are following the practice of the sports industry by offering sign-on bonuses to high-demand prospects. In a recent survey, nearly three out of five companies now use the signing bonus as a recruitment tool.[31] This strategy is especially prevalent in industries where severe shortages of highly skilled workers, such as information systems, exist. The amounts being offered vary dramatically depending on the worker's position and line of work. Prospective retail clerks at some Macy's department stores, for example, are being offered sign-on bonuses ranging from $100 to $400 to staff the stores during the busy holiday season. College students with technical degrees being recruited for their first jobs are getting $5,000 to $10,000. At the top end of the scale, David A. Neuman, a former Walt Disney Company executive, received a $1 million signing bonus as part of his new pay package at Digital Entertainment Network Inc., an Internet start-up in Santa Monica, California.[32]

The trend is still relatively new, and human resources executives say there is no simple formula for computing hiring bonuses. As discussed in Chapter 12, lump-sum payments have broad appeal because they provide a means for companies to compensate employees (in this case recruit them) while controlling fixed pay rates.[33]

## TAILORING RECRUITMENT METHODS TO SOURCES

Because each organization is unique in many ways, so are the types and qualifications of workers needed to fill positions. Thus, to be successful, recruitment must be tailored to the needs of each firm. In addition, recruitment sources and methods often vary according to the type of position being filled.

Figure 5-5 shows a matrix that depicts methods and sources of recruitment for an information systems manager. Managers must first identify the *source* (where prospective employees are) before choosing the *methods* (how to get them). Suppose, for example, that a large firm has an immediate need for an accounting manager with a minimum of five years' experience, and no one within the firm has these qualifications. It is most likely that such an individual is employed by another firm—very possibly, a competitor—or is self-employed. After considering the recruitment source, the recruiter must then choose the method (or methods) of recruitment that offers the best prospects for attracting qualified candidates. Perhaps the job can be advertised in the classified section of the *Wall Street Journal, National Employment Weekly,* or *The CPA Journal.* Alternatively, an executive search firm may be used to locate qualified candidates. In addition, the recruiter may attend meetings of professional accounting associations. One or more of these methods will likely yield a pool of qualified applicants.

In another scenario, consider a firm's need for 20 entry-level machine operators, who the firm is willing to train. High schools and vocational schools would probably be good recruitment sources. Methods of recruitment might include newspaper ads, public employment agencies, sending recruiters to vocational schools, and employee referrals.

The specific recruitment methods used will be affected by external environmental factors, including market supply and job requirements. Each organization should maintain employment records and conduct its own research in order to determine which recruitment sources and methods are most appropriate under various circumstances.

| External Recruitment Methods | Advertising | Private and public employment agencies | Recruiters | Special events | Internships | Executive search firms | Professional associations | Employee referrals | Unsolicited walk-in applicants | Open houses | Event recruiting | Virtual job fairs | Sign-on bonuses |
|---|---|---|---|---|---|---|---|---|---|---|---|---|---|
| High schools | | | | | | | | | | | | | |
| Vocational schools | | | | | | | | | | | | | |
| Community colleges | | | | | | | | | | | | | |
| Colleges and universities | | | | | | | | | | | | | |
| Competitors and other firms | X | X | | | | X | X | | | | | | |
| Unemployed | | | | | | | | | | | | | |
| Self-employed | | | | | | | | | | | | | |

**Methods and Sources of Recruitment for an Information Systems Manager**

**Figure 5-5**

## RECRUITMENT FOR DIVERSITY

Equal opportunity legislation outlaws discrimination in employment based on race, religion, sex, color, national origin, age, disability, and other factors. Some firms abide by these laws solely to avoid the legal consequences of violating them. Others, however, also recognize the inherent advantages of heterogeneous groups: greater creativity and the ability to help a firm expand its customer base. Global competition mandates that firms be innovative. Therefore, forward-thinking organizations actively engage in acquiring a workforce that reflects society and helps the company expand into untapped markets.[34] To accomplish this objective, firms may need to use nontraditional recruitment approaches.

Because of past unequal opportunity, women, minorities, and individuals with disabilities may not respond to traditional recruitment methods. These groups may be omitted altogether from the typical recruitment process unless specific action is taken to attract them. Therefore, any organization that seeks diversity must implement recruitment and other employment programs that assure women, minorities, and those with disabilities are included in the decision-making processes. Otherwise, organizations will overlook a great deal of much-needed talent.

## Analysis of Recruitment Procedures

To ensure that its recruitment program is diversity oriented, a firm must analyze its recruitment procedures. In identifying sources of continuing discrimination, a helpful approach is to develop a *record of applicant flow*. This record may be mandatory if the firm has been found guilty of discrimination or operates under an affirmative action program. An applicant flow record includes personal and job-related data concerning each applicant. It indicates whether a job offer was extended and, if no such offer was made, an explanation of the decision. Such records enable the organization to analyze its recruitment and selection practices and take corrective action when necessary.

## Utilization of Minorities, Women, and Individuals with Disabilities

Recruiters should be trained in the use of objective, job-related standards because these individuals occupy a unique position in terms of encouraging or discouraging minorities, women, and the disabled to apply for jobs. Qualified members of these groups may be used effectively in key recruitment activities, such as visiting schools and colleges and participating in career days. They also are in an excellent position to provide valuable input for recruitment planning and can effectively serve as referral sources. Pictures of minority, women, and disabled employees in help-wanted advertisements and company brochures give credibility to the message, "We are an equal opportunity employer."

## Advertising

With few exceptions, jobs must be open to all individuals. Therefore, gender-segregated ads, for example, should not be used unless gender is a bona fide occupational qualification (BFOQ). The BFOQ exception provided in Title VII of the Civil Rights Act requires that qualifications be job related. This definition is narrowly interpreted by EEOC and the courts. The burden of proof is on the employer to establish that the requirements are essential for successful performance of the job. Dorothy may have a problem with her ad specifying someone with a "good appearance," since this criterion is subjective and may not be job related. Other advertising practices designed to provide equal opportunity include the following:

- Ensuring that the content of advertisements does not indicate preference for any race, gender, or age or that these factors are a qualification for the job.
- Utilizing media that are directed toward minorities, such as appropriate radio stations.
- Emphasizing the intent to recruit without regard to race, gender, or disabled status by placing appropriate statements in job ads. Remember from Figure 5-4 that the statement "We are an Equal Opportunity Employer" was in the ad.

## Employment Agencies

An organization should emphasize its nondiscriminatory recruitment practices when utilizing employment agencies.[35] Even when a business works with private agencies, which are also covered under Title VII, jobs at all levels should be listed with the state employment service. These agencies can provide valuable assistance to organizations seeking to fulfill diversity goals. In addition, agencies and consultant firms that specialize in minority and women applicants should be contacted.

## Other Suggested Recruitment Approaches

Personal contact should be made with counselors and administrators at high schools, vocational schools, and colleges with large minority and/or female enrollments. Counselors and administrators should be made aware that the

## Expanding the Search

In the summer of 2000, U.S. companies were struggling to find enough qualified workers in America to staff U.S. jobs. Many HR managers had to expand their search area to attract qualified candidates. For some, recruitment now encompasses the entire world. Therefore, the methods HR professionals use are changing.

A major recruiting plus for many U.S. firms is the prestige of an American address. Many citizens of other countries are interested in a job with a U.S. company because it is increasingly seen as a résumé-builder and a necessary step on the global management track. Having an employment tour with a U.S. firm makes most candidates more attractive in the international business market. But American recruiters cannot count on that alone to sell a U.S. job to a worker who lives abroad. According to Jo Bredwell, senior vice president of Bernard Hodes Advertising, a major player in the recruitment advertising industry, "Many American advertisers seem to believe that advertising over there is enough." They often assume that the best strategy is to recruit the same way they do in the United States: place an ad, collect résumés, interview, then hire. The distance factor makes the recruitment process difficult for U.S. firms that do not have offices in the markets in which they are recruiting. Bredwell advises American firms to make it easy for indigenous applicants in foreign areas to make contact. That could mean sending someone from your own firm to that location to receive calls and to conduct interviews. Or, a go-between could make contact with someone abroad.

It is important to be available to applicants during their nonworking hours. Those aspects of your company that will appeal to candidates from other countries should be marketed. The benefits of the location should be highlighted. Do not assume that people will already know the benefits simply by seeing an American address "unless you're in a city that most people would know, like New York City or Los Angeles." According to Bredwell, "Don't presume that people know what it's like to live where you're located or that everyone knows the name of your company. American companies, especially major multinational corporations, tend to make the mistake of thinking people everywhere are familiar with who they are."

New technology also supports global recruiting. In the old days, companies were lucky if they had a teletype machine to send messages globally. Now there are fax machines, laptop computers, and videoconferencing. This technology makes the recruiting process easier, especially in the global arena. However, the Internet is perhaps the best thing to hit global recruitment. Bredwell believes that "it's a tool that will continue to be well-used to speed global communication." Indeed, not only can HR managers and job candidates e-mail each other to set up interviews, but they can also discover each other in the first place through the various Web sites directed at linking jobseekers and firms with job openings.[36]

organization is actively seeking minorities, women, and disabled individuals for jobs that they have not traditionally held. Also, counselors and administrators should be familiar with the types of jobs available and the training and education needed to perform these jobs. The possibilities for developing internships and summer employment should be carefully investigated. Firms should develop contacts with minority, women's, and other community organizations. These organizations include the National Association for the Advancement of Colored People (NAACP), the League of United Latin American Citizens, the

National Urban League, the American Association of University Women, the Federation of Business and Professional Women's Talent Bank, the National Council of Negro Women, and the Veterans Administration. The EEOC's regional offices will assist employers in locating appropriate local agencies.

## ▶ Summary

**①  Explain alternatives to recruitment.**
Alternatives include outsourcing, contingent workers, employee leasing, and overtime.

**②  Explain the external and internal environment of recruitment.**
Factors external to the organization can significantly affect the firm's recruitment efforts. The organization's own practices and policies also affect recruitment.

**③  Describe the recruitment process.**
Recruitment frequently begins when a manager initiates an employee requisition. Next, the firm determines whether qualified employees are available from within (the internal source) or must be recruited externally from sources such as colleges, universities, and other firms. Sources and methods are then identified.

**④  Describe internal recruitment methods.**
Job posting is a method of internal recruitment that is used to communicate the fact that job openings exist. Job bidding is a system that permits individuals in an organization to apply for a specific job within the organization.

**⑤  Identify external sources of recruitment.**
External sources of recruitment include high schools and vocational schools, community colleges, colleges and universities, competitors and other firms, the unemployed, older individuals, military personnel, and self-employed workers.

**⑥  Identify external recruitment methods.**
External recruitment methods include advertising, employment agencies, recruiters, special events, internships, executive search firms, professional associations, employee referrals, unsolicited walk-in applicants, open houses, event recruiting, virtual job fairs, and sign-on bonuses.

**⑦  Describe how recruitment methods and sources are tailored to each other.**
Recruitment must be tailored to the needs of each firm. In addition, recruitment sources and methods often vary according to the type of position being filled.

**⑧  Explain how to recruit for diversity.**
Forward-thinking organizations actively engage in acquiring a workforce that reflects society and helps the company expand into untapped markets. To accomplish this objective, firms may need to use nontraditional recruitment approaches.

## ▶ Questions for Review

1. What are the typical alternatives to recruitment a firm may use?

2. Describe the basic components of the recruitment process.

3. List and discuss the various external and internal factors that may affect recruitment.

4. What is meant by the term *internal recruitment?* Describe the advantages and disadvantages of internal recruitment.

5. Describe the methods commonly used in internal recruitment. Briefly define each.

6. Discuss the reasons for an external recruitment program.

7. Distinguish between sources and methods of external recruitment.

8. How can a firm improve its recruiting efforts to achieve diversity?

*We invite you to visit the Mondy homepage on the Prentice Hall Web site at*

**www.prenhall.com/mondy**

*for updated information, Web-based exercises, and links to other HR-related sites.*

TAKE IT TO
THE NET

---

## Developing HRM Skills ◀

### An Experiential Exercise

Human resource managers have the responsibility for preparing job descriptions. From these job descriptions, profiles of the types of individuals needed to fill various positions in the firm can be developed and recruitment efforts can be designed. The human resource manager must determine where the best applicants are located (recruitment sources) and how to entice them to join the organization (recruitment methods). This exercise is designed to provide an understanding of the relationship between recruitment sources and methods.

Participants will attempt to determine the most appropriate recruitment sources and methods for the job description that will be given to them. Your instructor will provide the participants with additional information necessary to complete the exercise.

---

## HRM INCIDENT 1 ◀

### The Wrong Approach

Eric Ardoin is a human resource manager at Epler Manufacturing Company in Greenfield, Wisconsin. He was considering the need to recruit qualified blacks for Epler when Shontae Blount walked into his office. "Got a minute?" asked Shontae. "I need to talk to you about the recruiting trip to Michigan State next week."

"Sure," Eric replied, "but, first I need your advice about something. How can we get more blacks to apply for work here? We're running ads on WBEZ radio along with the classified ads in the *Tribune*. I think you and John have made recruiting trips to every community college within 200 miles. We've encouraged employee referral, too, and I still think that's our most reliable source of new workers. But we just aren't getting any black applicants."

From the president on down, the management at Epler claimed commitment to equal employment opportunity. According to Eric, the commitment went much deeper than posting the usual posters and filing an affirmative action program with the federal government. However, the percentage of black employees at Epler remained at only 5 percent, while the surrounding community was 11 percent black. Epler paid competitive wages and had a good training program.

Epler had a particular need for machine operator trainees. The machines were not difficult to operate, and there was no educational requirement for the job. There were also several clerical and management trainee positions open.

### Question

1. Evaluate the current recruitment effort. How could Eric better the firm's goal of equal employment?

---

▶ **HRM INCIDENT 2**

### I Am Qualified—Why Not Me?

Five years ago, when Bobby Bret joined Crystal Productions as a junior accountant, he felt that he was on his way up. He had just graduated with a B+ average from college, where he was well liked by his peers and by the faculty and had been an officer in several student organizations. Bobby had shown a natural ability to get along with people as well as to get things done. He remembered what Roger Friedman, the controller at Crystal, had told him when he was hired: "I think you will do well here, Bobby. You've come highly recommended. You are the kind of guy that can expect to move right on up the ladder."

Bobby felt that he had done a good job at Crystal and everybody seemed to like him. In addition, his performance appraisals had been excellent. However, after five years he was still a junior accountant. He had applied for two senior accountant positions that had come open, but they were both filled by people hired from outside the firm. When the accounting supervisor's job came open two years ago, Bobby had not applied. He was surprised when his new boss turned out to be a hotshot graduate of State University whose only experience was three years with a large accounting firm. Bobby had hoped that Ron Greene, a senior accountant he particularly respected, would get the job.

On the fifth anniversary of his employment at Crystal, Bobby decided it was time to do something. He made an appointment with the controller. At that meeting Bobby explained to Mr. Friedman that he had worked hard to obtain a promotion and shared his frustration about having been in the same job for so long. "Well," said Mr. Friedman, "you don't think that you were all that much better qualified than the people that we have hired, do you?" "No," said Bobby, "but, I think I could have handled the senior accountant job. Of course, the people you have hired are doing a great job too." The controller responded, "We just look at the qualifications of all the applicants for each job, and considering everything, try to make a reasonable decision."

### Questions

1. Do you believe that Bobby has a legitimate complaint? Explain.
2. Explain the impact of a promotion-from-within policy on outside recruitment.

- Everybody works will complain
- Impact on organization

1. Timothy Burn, "Part-Time, Flexible Work Wave Has Yet to Crest; Numbers Keep Swelling, and Not Everybody's Happy about It," *The Washington Times* (May 9, 1999): C1.

2. Cassandra Hayes and Charlene Solomon, "The Lure of Temping," *Black Enterprise* 26 (February 1996): 120–122.

3. Mark Harrington, "Permanent Need for Temp Help/Contingent Workers Are the Rage at Sizzling Tech Companies," *Newsday* (June 20, 1999): F6.

4. Andrea C. Bassoff, "Staff Leasing Firm Markets Fewer Hassles with Workers," *The Washington Times* (September 20, 1999): D3.

5. William Flannery, "PEOS Change the Face of Human Resources," *St. Louis Post-Dispatch* (August 24, 1999): C6.

6. Jay Finegan, "Look before You Lease," *Inc.* 19 (February 1997): 106.

7. Dale D. Buss, "Help Wanted Desperately," *Nation's Business* 84 (April 1996): 17–19.

8. Ken Dubrowski, "What Employers Can and Cannot Ask," *HR Focus* 72 (June 1995): 3.

9. Charles Fishman, "Moving Toward a Balanced Work Life," *Workforce* 79 (March 2000): 40.

10. "The Top HR Issues of 2000," *HR Focus* 77 (April 2000): 1.

11. Martha I. Finney, "Playing a Different Tune: Using the Hidden Assets of Employees," *HRMagazine* 41 (December 1996): 73.

12. "Don't Let the Talent Crunch Hurt Your Company's Chance for Success; Seven Tips to Reduce Employee Attrition," *PR Newswire* (June 8, 1999): 1.

13. Sandra Grabczynski, "Nab New Grads by Building Relationships with Colleges," *Workforce* 79 (May 2000): 98.

14. Michael Hickins, "Recruitment: The Silver Solution," *HR Focus* 76 (May 1999): 1.

15. Phaedra Brotherton, "Tapping into an Older Workforce," *Mosaics* 6 (March/April 2000): 4.

16. Miles Z. Epstein and David G. Epstein, "Hiring Veterans: A Cost-Effective Staffing Solution," *HRMagazine* 43 (November 1998): 108.

17. Stephanie Overman, "Heroes for Hire," *HRMagazine* 38 (December 1993): 61–62.

18. Andrea C. Poe, "Face Value," *HRMagazine* 45 (May 2000): 60.

19. Fred Katayama, "Recruiting in the 90s," *CNNfn, Digital Jam,* cnnfn.com/digital-jam/9701/29/job_pkg/index.htm (May 24, 1997).

20. Julie Hyman, "Technology Firms Fish for Recruits in Unusual Waters," *The Washington Times* (February 23, 2000): B8.

21. Carla D'Nan Bass and Vikas Bajaj, "Internships Give Students Job Skills While Businesses Get Recruiting Edge," *The Dallas Morning News* (January 9, 2000): 1H.

22. Julie Hyman, "Grads Have Easy Time in Tight Job Market; Better Pay, Benefits Await Class of 2000," *The Washington Times* (May 13, 2000): A1.

23. Rebecca Simmons, "Internship Experience Invaluable," *University Wire* (July 19, 1999).

24. Jill M. Singer, "Students Leap into Internships and Land Jobs after College," *USA Today* (February 21, 2000): 6D.

25. "Staffing Industry Assisted and Restrained by Tight Job Market," *Business Wire* (May 17, 2000).

26. "Don't Let the Talent Crunch Hurt Your Company's Chance for Success."

27. Keith Swenson, "Maximizing Employee Referrals," *HRMagazine* 76 (January 1999): 9.

28. Monica Fuertes, "Open Sesame," *HRMagazine* 44 (April 1, 1999): 58–64.

29. Kevin Wheeler, "Non-Traditional Recruiting Method," *Electronic Recruiting Daily* (March 29, 2000).

30. Beth Ashley, "Job Interview Comes to Cyberspace," *USA Today,* wsf2.usatoday.com/life/cyber/tech/ct351.htm (May 30, 1997).

31. "Companies Sign on to Signing Bonuses," *HR Focus* 76 (June 1999): 4.

32. Kirstin Downey Grimsley, "No Simple Formula for a Signing Bonus," *The Washington Post* (November 17, 1999): E1.

33. Carrie Mason-Draffen, "Companies Find New Ways to Pay/Workers' Performance Tied to Stock Options, Bonuses, Raises," *Newsday* (January 5, 1997): F8.

34. Jim Roberts, "Workforce Diversity Helping Companies Boost Bottom Line," *Fairfield County Business Journal* 34 (December 11, 1995): 8.

35. "Are Your Recruiting Methods Discriminatory?" *Workforce* 79 (May 2000): 105.

36. Jennifer J. Laabs, "Like Finding a Needle in a Haystack: Recruiting in the Global Village," *Workforce* 77 (April 1998): 30–33.

# Internet Recruiting

objectivesobjectivesobjectives

 ▶ Objectives

- Describe Internet trends and the Internet recruitment process.
- Explain the requirements for effective Internet recruiting.
- Describe the limitations of Internet recruiting.
- Explain the new HR position of cyber recruiter.
- Describe internal recruitment using the intranet.
- Explain the significance of the corporate Web site and the homepage.
- Describe selected employment Web sites.
- Explain niche sites.
- Describe contract workers' sites and job agent service sites.
- Describe personality-based job placement.
- Explain the process of designing a Web site for jobseekers.
- Describe external sources of recruitment and the Internet.
- Explain external recruitment methods and the Internet.
- Describe posting résumés on the Internet.
- Explain résumé management systems.

ex Ballard's case is a perfect example of how the Web is used to enhance a person's career progression. Since 1993, a year when most employment Web sites were just beginning, Ballard, a systems consultant, has been using the Internet to advance his career. One Saturday last September, he posted his résumé on Career-Mosaic, now Headhunter.net. The results were remarkable: By Monday night, he had received 29 calls. By the end of that week, he had three job offers, all equally attractive. According to Ballard, "Within a matter of days, I had accomplished what normally might have taken months. The only down-side was that I had to choose just one." Ballard had his pick of offers, ultimately taking a job as manager of infrastructure and architecture at Prudential Insurance Company in Roseland, New Jersey. Job-seekers like Ballard are "virtually" hired every day, thanks to the dizzying growth of online recruiting.[1]

keytermskeytermskeyterms

## ▶ Key Terms

**F**or experienced and talented individuals like Ballard, the career opportunities offered on the Web are striking. For companies like Prudential, the speed and expanded talent pool offered by the Web help make their recruiting processes more efficient and cost effective. Basically, recruiting on the Web expands individual employment options, as well as improving the recruitment process for businesses. The age-old task of matching candidates with jobs is being revolutionized. Unfortunately, Internet recruiting is changing so fast that it is virtually impossible to keep up to date. New Web sites are constantly being created, sites are merging, sites are expanding, and some are even being dissolved. To stay abreast of these changes and those that impact other HR areas, please consult our Web site at www.prenhall.com/mondy for continual updates.

**Internet**
The large system of many connected computers around the world that individuals and businesses use to communicate with each other.

**Web (World Wide Web)**
The system of connected documents on the Internet, which often contains color pictures, video, and sound and can be searched for information about a particular subject.

The **Internet** is the large system of many connected computers around the world that individuals and businesses use to communicate with each other.[2] The **Web (World Wide Web)** is the system of connected documents on the Internet, which often contains color pictures, video, and sound and can be searched for information about a particular subject.[3] Although these two terms are different in several respects, in this text the terms will be used interchangeably, unless otherwise indicated.

In this chapter we will first describe Internet trends and the Internet recruitment process. Then, the requirements for effective Internet recruiting will be explained. The limitations of Internet recruiting, the new HR position of cyber recruiter, and internal recruitment using the intranet will then be examined. Next, corporate Web sites and the homepage, employment Web sites, niche sites, sites for contract workers, and job agent service sites will be described, followed by personality-based job placement on the Web and how to design your own Web site. External sources and methods of recruitment and the Internet will be explained next. Finally, posting résumés on the Internet and résumé management systems will be discussed.

## INTERNET TRENDS AND THE RECRUITMENT PROCESS

What do Kforce.com, HotJobs.com, and Monster.com have in common? During the 2000 Superbowl, they advertised their employment Web sites on national television, reaching audiences around the world. Soon after, these Web sites became major players in the Internet-based employment business. There are millions of candidates online, reviewing hundreds of thousands of job openings listed at thousands of career sites on the Web.[4] The Association for Internet Recruiting conducted a recent poll on the Internet recruiting practices of 1,000 organizations. The study revealed some interesting trends.

- Over 70 percent of organizations will be spending more next year on Internet recruiting.
- Almost half of the companies polled had hired 1 to 20 percent of this year's workforce as a direct result of Internet recruiting.
- Almost 35 percent of companies with over 10,000 employees had at least one recruiter dedicated strictly to Internet recruiting.
- Over 80 percent of the organizations studied had an employment section within their company's Web site.[5]

According to a survey released by SBC Internet Services, 82 percent of college graduates will use the Internet to search for job openings or information on careers, and 66 percent will actually e-mail a résumé to prospective employers. The Internet is a valuable recruiting tool, especially for reaching prospective employees in their twenties and thirties.[6] Initiating contact with prospective employers by telephone or through the U.S. Postal Service is fast becoming an outmoded technique for finding jobs. The survey also revealed the following:

- 75 percent of 1999 spring/summer college graduates used the Internet to research a specific career or job.
- 79 percent researched a specific prospective employer on the Internet.
- 74 percent used the Internet to search for a job in a specific geographic location.
- 55 percent posted their résumé through an online job service.[7]

In the last few years, the manner in which recruiting is conducted has changed dramatically. Although the basic recruitment philosophy remains the same, the technology used has had a tremendous impact on how recruitment is accomplished. Today, chefs, secretaries, firefighters, construction workers, accountants, reporters, and marketing and advertising executives, as well as people in just about every profession, use the Internet to identify job prospects. Even though the technology is still relatively new and changing quickly, it is without a doubt the wave of the future.

As defined in the previous chapter, *recruitment* is the process of attracting individuals on a timely basis, in sufficient numbers, with appropriate qualifications, and then encouraging them to apply for jobs with an organization. When the Internet is involved in the recruitment process, the definition itself does not change. However, words within the definition may take on different meanings. For example, *on a timely basis* may mean within a month or two with traditional recruitment methods. With the Internet, *timely* may be within a week, a day, or almost immediately. Now consider the term *in sufficient numbers* and see the power of the Internet. Even in days of low unemployment, large numbers of qualified applicants may be identified. Internet recruiting can effectively identify both active and passive applicants. Dissecting the definition still further, we deal with the term *appropriate qualifications*. With the Internet, there are numerous ways to screen applicants to determine if they have the appropriate qualifications for the job. Finally, *applying for a job with the organization* is easy. Individuals can wake up at midnight, decide to change jobs, and have new résumés out for review before going back to bed. Companies can also place a new job advertisement on a Web site at any time during the workday. Both employees and employers are embracing the Internet, and this trend will probably expand dramatically in the future.

According to Darlene Chapin, recruiting manager at Cheetah Technologies, a $50 million computer network management company, the Internet will be the most effective recruiting and staffing tool in the future. Chapin also believes that "like anything else, it's no be-all and end-all. It takes practice, training, and commitment to make it pay off." Currently, Web recruiting is a supplement, rather than a replacement, for traditional recruiting methods. Cheetah Technologies embraces Internet recruiting as well as other approaches including newspaper and technical publication ads, job fairs, college outreach, employee-referral programs, and the occasional headhunter. Chapin says, "You need a complete recruiting process wrapped around it."[8]

The complexity of online recruiting is grossly exaggerated and can be overcome by utilizing certain tips for Internet recruiting success. Although Internet recruiting will not replace traditional recruiting in the near future, it is quickly becoming an essential aid for today's recruiters. HR managers using the following steps will be better able to facilitate their own recruiting efforts. To maximize recruiting success HR managers must:

- Embrace Internet technology, because it is quickly becoming a central part of doing business in America. Effective recruiting is the most obvious and long-term contribution HR professionals can make to organizational success, and Internet recruiting improves their efforts.
- Research Internet employment sites and become familiar with the options available online, which include thousands of employment-related Web sites, ranging from commercial-free and fee-based job and résumé databases to elaborate corporate employment Web sites.
- Establish a budget and set aside necessary funds for Internet recruiting (starting with 10 percent of the annual recruitment advertising budget is common).
- Develop an Internet Web site that is upbeat and informative, as well as a selling device that promotes the company to prospective job candidates. HR professionals must be heavily involved in developing the recruiting section of the corporate Web page. They must provide all the data that candidates need, including information about the job, company, work environment, and how candidates may apply online.
- Write effective online ads that are not like the short, one-column-inch ads in the Sunday newspaper. The Internet provides enough space to fully describe the job, location, and company. Also, once a recruiting Web page has been established, include the Web address in job ads placed in other media.
- Experiment with various advertising approaches by placing ads in several relevant sites across the Internet, including the company homepage, free state and federal job-posting services, and/or several of the commercial online employment sites.
- Monitor both traditional and Internet advertisements to judge the cost-effectiveness of each approach. Internet recruiting advertisements can be tracked with tags that monitor the number of times the ad is viewed.
- Experiment with various Web sites to determine which sites contain pools of the skill sets necessary for open positions. HR managers must master database search techniques to learn how to conduct the most effective searches and return to preferred Web employment sites on a regular basis to evaluate new résumé postings.

- Become a sleuth on the Internet by searching for data on applicants with critically needed skills. There is information about each individual somewhere online, and more and more candidates in the future will have their own Web sites to provide information directly to employers, including e-mail addresses and referrals.

- Do not neglect traditional recruiting methods, such as referrals and ads in professional periodicals and newspapers, as well as job fairs. Coordinate the recruiting strategy so that successes in one area complement the recruiting efforts in another.[9]

Because Internet technology and services offered on the Web evolve so quickly, it is vitally important that HR professionals remain technologically savvy. Since Web-based recruiting changes so rapidly, tomorrow's changes could greatly simplify recruiting, affording a more cost-effective and efficient approach.

## LIMITATIONS OF INTERNET RECRUITING

According to Paul Paez, vice president of marketing for Source Services Corporation, it would be unwise for human resources professionals to rely solely on the Internet to attract candidates. At this point in time, the Internet's true recruiting value is its immediacy and ability to interact digitally with potential employees. Employers can post jobs on either a company Web site or sites for newsgroups, commercial job hunting, and staffing or recruiting firms. The paperless platform offers companies a way to target talented professionals. Jobseekers can communicate via e-mail and even conduct online interviews. Although the Internet can help gather, scan, and sort data, it does have certain limitations that must be taken into account.[10]

First, the Internet is not a selection tool. It does not replace conducting background checks, face-to-face interviews, and other steps to assess attitudes and behavior that are vital to finding qualified employees. Second, according to a survey by Kforce.com, a Web-based staffing company, HR professionals are frustrated with the Internet's lack of a personal touch. Third, the number of résumés that must be reviewed is growing dramatically. Larger organizations now dedicate more than two in-house recruiters to deal with Internet recruiting activities. Fourth, there is more competition for qualified employees from small and medium, as well as global, companies. In the past year, one out of every 10 hires was a direct result of Internet recruiting. Fifth, spending on Internet recruiting is increasing, but often at the expense of other, more traditional approaches. Over the next year, two out of five companies will increase Internet recruitment spending. Finally, confidentiality could be a problem, since all of the applicant's information is on one or more Web sites, which could be violated by hackers.[11]

## A NEW HR POSITION—CYBER RECRUITER

Jobs that were not even considered five years ago have been created because of the Internet revolution. Certainly this is true with regard to the new position that has emerged in human resources. The **Internet recruiter**, also called *cyber recruiter,* is a person whose primary responsibility is to use the Internet in the recruitment process. With over 80 percent of surveyed companies currently posting jobs on their organization's Web site and more expected in the near future, it is important to note that a company's Web site is not just for selling products or services. A Web site is also an excellent way to display an organization's employment

**Internet recruiter**
Also called *cyber recruiter;* a person whose primary responsibility is to use the Internet in the recruitment process.

opportunities.[12] Individuals must be in place to monitor and coordinate these activities. The more a company recruits on the Internet, the greater the need for Internet recruiters. For instance, Texas Instruments has three full-time cyber recruiters.[13] Currently, high-tech firms have the greatest needs, but that is quickly changing as more traditional firms are also getting into the act.

Once the need for Internet recruiters was recognized, a professional organization was established. Recruitersnetwork.com is the Web site for the Association for Internet Recruiting. The organization is for recruiting and human resource professionals and consists of over 16,000 members. Membership includes a free monthly newsletter, access to an extensive online resource directory, participation in an interactive list of services, and more.[14]

## INTERNAL RECRUITMENT—USING THE INTRANET

**Intranet**
A system of computers that enables people within an organization to communicate with each other.

Job posting and job bidding have changed significantly as companies and employees continue to expand usage of the intranet. The **intranet** is a system of computers that enables people within an organization to communicate with each other.[15] In the past, many a disgruntled employee has discovered that a vacancy existed in another location a month after it was filled. Posted jobs often did not find their way to the bulletin boards in all locations. This approach has changed in many companies across the nation and internationally with the use of the intranet.[16] Now, if a worker does not know about a new vacancy, it is because he or she did not check the intranet posting regularly.

Assume that a vacancy occurs in the Chicago office and permission is granted to fill the position. The position announcement and qualifications required are placed on the company intranet. That very day, an employee in San Francisco may see the posting and apply for this position, using the company résumé format. The common format approach permits each applicant to be analyzed on an equal basis. Many organizations have already had all of their employees complete a standardized application form. In this case, the applicant merely submits the completed application when applying for a vacant position. Distance is not a factor when using the intranet for internal recruiting. Assuming that several qualified applications exist, the company has the option of using teleconferencing to conduct the

## TRENDS & INNOVATIONS

### ▶ The Intranet Comes of Age

The intranet is a good way to keep everyone up to date, especially in a global age where workers are dispersed. After General Electric revamped its intranet last year, the number of hits jumped from a couple of thousand to 10 million a week. An online marketplace also offers discounts on GE appliances, Dell computers, and other products. AT&T has an intranet where workers can manage benefits, check their 401(k) plans and make investment changes, as well as check company news, which is updated daily. Hallmark Cards even posts the cafeteria menu, as well as the employee newsletter and job-training resources, on the intranet. Texas Instruments allows new hires to access the intranet before their first day on the job, thereby helping them to get up to speed quicker. The site also includes a concierge service that will plan vacations and run errands and a way to pick doctors from the health plan. American Century Investments uses its intranet for classified ads and information on competitors.[17]

initial screening. Or, the screening may actually result in an immediate hiring. This type of technology is beginning to revolutionize internal recruiting.

## THE CORPORATE WEB SITE AND HOMEPAGE

The **corporate Web site** is a virtual medium that presents information about the company, often including human resources information, and possibly even allowing individuals to apply for jobs. The **corporate homepage** is the initial page of the Web site, used by an organization to present itself to viewers on the Internet. The growth in the use of the Web site and homepage as recruiting devices has been dramatic. The Web site provides a place to post an unlimited number of openings with detailed job descriptions and helps to tell the benefits of joining the company. Individuals desiring jobs with a particular organization discover job opportunities on the Web site. As competition for talent becomes aggressive, the Web provides companies with an edge in attracting corporate talent. A recent study reports that more than 90 percent of job applicants check out a company's Web site before taking the job. The Web helps bring qualified individuals together with corporations in need of talent.[18] Take the case of Shamira Hardy.

> Shamira Hardy had a desire to work for a particular company located in Denver, Colorado. She went to its Web site and searched the "Positions Available" section. Finding a proper job match, she e-mailed a letter of application and attached a copy of her résumé to the e-mail. Upon receipt of the e-mail, the cyber recruiter read the résumé, decided that a proper match existed, e-mailed Shamira a message signifying interest, and ultimately hired a happy new employee. Without the Web site, she may never have known about the job opening, and the company would not have so easily and inexpensively found a new employee.

Examples of the successful use of Web sites for recruiting abound. Recently, Hewlett-Packard's job listing page received a total of 105,000 résumés that resulted in approximately 1,400 new hires.[19] In the first three months, the job listing page for Taco Bell received approximately 500 résumés, which was double the normal flow of managerial résumés.[20]

McDonald's Web site covers several topics, ranging from job responsibilities to the chain's extensive training programs. It features an icon of a U.S. map where jobseekers can click on their home state and find the address of the nearest McDonald's regional office. Candidates can either mail or fax their résumés to the company. According to Lisa Howard, a media relations manager for McDonald's, "It expands our ability to reach applicants." Through its Internet site, McDonald's recently recruited a manager-trainee who lived in a rural area of Florida. Without McDonald's exposure on the Web, the applicant probably would not have known about the job opening. Howard further stated that the company has extensive plans to expand the online career section to include a list of hourly positions and the ability for applicants to respond through e-mail.[21]

Humana Inc., one of the country's largest publicly traded managed health companies, exchanged its paper-based recruiting process for an automated electronic system tied to its own custom-made job site on the Web. According to Reggie Barefield, executive director of Humana's Talent Resources and Technology Team, generating résumés via the Internet "costs pennies, while using newspaper ads averages about $128 per résumé received. The Internet is a job-lean generator and a global tool for creating a proactive recruiting team." Job candidates may

**Corporate Web site**
A virtual medium that presents information about the company, often including human resources information, and possibly even allowing individuals to apply for jobs.

**Corporate homepage**
The initial page of the Web site, used by an organization to present itself to viewers on the Internet.

**www.prenhall.com/mondy**

This Web site contains links to other Internet-based resources for HR professionals such as selection, T&D, and EEO.

browse for jobs by location, corporate division, and keywords, and then post résumés. The résumé databases are checked daily to identify qualified candidates.[22]

A Web site is essential, but creating a site that is easy to use and that produces good results is not easy. It takes time and experimentation to create a really successful site. Cisco's ([www.cisco.com](http://www.cisco.com)), Federated Department Store's ([www.retailology.com](http://www.retailology.com)), and Goldman-Sachs's ([www.goldmansachs.com](http://www.goldmansachs.com)) provide examples of well-designed Web sites.[23] The Web site presents an image of how well a company is organized. On Texas Instruments Inc.'s site, applicants can search for specific job openings, fill out electronic résumés, and even take an interactive quiz that tests how well they would fit into Texas Instrument's corporate culture.[24] (The importance of organizational fit is emphasized in the next chapter.) Applicants can also check out benefits packages and even calculate cost-of-living adjustments and relocation expenses.[25]

## EMPLOYMENT WEB SITES

According to a 1999 survey of HR professionals by the Society for Human Resource Management, while nearly two-thirds of human resources professionals placed classified ads in Sunday newspapers, almost 40 percent relied on Internet job postings as well. It was estimated that 32 percent of all recruitment advertising budgets in the year 2000 would be spent on the Internet, while the share that went to newspapers would shrink from 70 percent to 52 percent.[26]

Many companies have experienced excellent results through Internet recruiting on their own Web site. However, other firms also utilize employment Web sites by simply typing in key job criteria, skills, and experience and indicating their geographic location. They next click *Search for Candidates* and in seconds have a ranked list of résumés from candidates that match the firm's requirements. Fees vary from one employment Web site to another, and the number of sites has expanded dramatically in recent years. It would be virtually impossible to list and discuss all of the sites, and therefore, only the most widely recognized employment Web sites will be briefly discussed. These include Monster.com, Headhunter.net, HotJobs.com, and CareerBuilder.com.

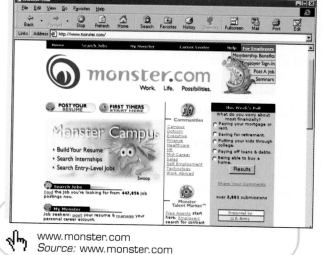

www.monster.com
*Source:* www.monster.com

## Monster.com

Currently, more people are visiting Monster.com than any other career-related site. Monster's global network consists of local content and language sites in the United States, United Kingdom, Australia, Canada, the Netherlands, Belgium, New Zealand, Singapore, Hong Kong, and France. In December 1999, Monster partnered with America

Online to become its exclusive career channel.[27] *Forbes* magazine recognized Monster's leadership position by naming it the best job hunting site on the Web from among more than 3,000 sites devoted to careers. *Forbes*'s "Best of the Web" award is based on five criteria: design, navigation, content, speed, and customization. *Forbes*'s judges said of Monster, "Every function, from storing your résumé to researching jobs, is simple and intuitive."[28] Also, Monster can be very cost effective since a 60-day job ad on Monster costs roughly $200 to $300, while an employment ad in one issue of the Sunday *New York Times* business section costs $917 per column inch.[29]

## Monster Campus: The Student Alternative

Monster Campus ([campus.monster.com](campus.monster.com)), a subdivision of Monster, helps students looking for internship programs or their first career opportunity to define and achieve their career goals. It provides a comprehensive resource for jobs, as well as an online community support system for the anxiety associated with the entire career advancement process. Regardless of whether the student is a freshman just starting to think about a career or a senior about to enter the "real world," this site will be helpful. Monster Campus features are organized in sequential steps that group related tools, quizzes, advice, and resources. From *Self-Assessment* to *The Real World*, Monster Campus content is an easy-to-navigate guide to finding a first job.

> Professionals searching for freelance work are increasingly turning to the Web sites that let them market themselves globally as for-hire help.

The features of Monster Campus include the following. *General Resources* includes information on résumé preparation, cover letters, interviewing, compensation, and networking. This feature provides step-by-step instructions to teach first-time jobseekers how to build a résumé, and how to market their university and other experiences. Jobseekers can post their résumé in Monster's database, enabling quick and easy access by employers. *Research Companies* permits students to find out about companies by location or key word. *Toolkits* provides students with targeted information and special networking. *Chat Rooms* allow students to communicate with peers, to share intern experiences, to post queries for job opportunities in the U.S. and abroad, and to network with thousands of alumni.[30]

## Headhunter.net

This company has challenged Monster's leadership position by acquiring rival CareerMosaic.com.[31] The acquisition created a major U.S. online recruiting service.[32] The online job site created by the merger of Headhunter.net and CareerMosaic offers postings of more than 250,000 open positions in a variety of job categories, postings of about 450,000 résumés, and online recruitment services for 11,000 business customers. Expected traffic of more than 7 million hits per month is anticipated.[33] Headhunter.net CEO and president Robert Montgomery says the two companies have little overlap among jobseekers and business customers. CareerMosaic's clientele includes some of the nation's largest companies, and it offers college and international recruiting; Headhunter.net has been more successful with recruiting for midsize companies and attracting candidates with two to ten years of work experience. The merger was completed in July of 2000.[34]

Headhunter.net posts basic job listings for only $20 per month. *VIP Résumé Reserve* offers employers a "sneak peek" at résumés before general posting. Jobseekers will find more than 25,000 financial listings among employer postings.[35] Headhunter.net is targeted at virtually any size business because it delivers cost-effective convenience, with no registration required. The credit card–based *EaseEPost* is a good option for companies posting fewer than 10 jobs a month; *Performance Posting* maximizes the reach and visibility of individualized company profile Web sites. Headhunter.net allows employers to write and post detailed job listings directly online and instantly modifies them to correct job criteria. Utilizing a proprietary database, Headhunter.net delivers a unique and powerful geographical search capability enabling jobseekers to request specific positions within 30 miles of a desired city. A variety of user-friendly services assists individuals in posting their résumés online, offers upgrade options for maximum visibility, and provides educational resources for developing effective job searches.

## HotJobs.com

HotJobs.com is a leading Internet-based recruiting solutions company that provides a direct exchange of information between jobseekers and employers. Over 5,000 member employers subscribe to the HotJobs.com online employment exchange. HotJobs.com also provides employers with additional recruiting solutions, such as its proprietary Softshoe® and Shoelace™ recruiting software, its *WorkWorld* career expos, and online advertising and consulting services. New York–based Hot Jobs, Inc., charges an annual fee of $3,000 for unlimited access. However, a single 30-day job posting costs $195.[36] One recruiter avoided a $12,000 recruiting firm fee for a $60,000-per-year information technology position by hiring someone through HotJobs. According to Tim Vasquez, a senior recruiter at Oracle, "I paid the $3,000 already. Now anyone else I get is gravy. HotJobs has cut my cost of hires down, and I expect to increase my number of hires from the Internet this year."[37] Another merger resulted from the online recruiting consolidation in 2000 for HotJobs.com. It recently merged with Resumix Inc., a leading developer of staffing management software.[38]

## CareerBuilder.com

In another online recruiting consolidation of late 2000, CareerBuilder Inc., CareerPath.com Inc., Knight Ridder, and Tribune Company announced their merger effective October 31, 2000. The transactions bring together CareerBuilder's patented e-cruiting technology, talent and substantial syndicated career network with the local market strength of Knight Ridder and Tribune and the significant content and audience reach of CareerPath. According to Chairman and CEO Rob McGovern, "The company's goal is to be the consumer's first and only choice for finding new jobs and obtaining advice and information on career management and advancement throughout one's career-building experience.[39] It is expected that the new site will attract more than 5 million monthly visitors which would place CareerBuilder in the Number 2 position among industry leaders. Although CareerBuilder is now a major player in Internet recruiting, it began its career as a job agent service site (discussed later in this chapter).

Knight Ridder is the nation's second-largest newspaper publisher. The company publishes 32 daily newspapers in 28 U.S. markets, with a readership of 8.7 million daily and 12.9 million Sunday. Tribune is a leading multimedia company with businesses in 23 major U.S. markets. Many of CareerBuilder's job listings are from Knight Ridder and Tribune. The newspaper job database is searchable by geography, newspaper, job type, and keyword. The employers' listing database is searchable by geography, employer, job type, and keyword. According to Chairman McGovern, the CareerBuilder Network includes CareerBuilder.com, the flagship career center, and over 60 affiliate career sites including MSN, Bloomberg, USATODAY.com, NBC, iVillage.com, and the nation's leading local online employment centers.[40]

## NICHE SITES

Thus far our discussion has focused on Web sites that contain every conceivable type of job. **Niche sites** are Web sites that cater to a specific profession; a few of these sites will be discussed next. Many recruiters and jobseekers are migrating to niche sites. Job sites for technical employees are expanding quickly. Sites such as Dice.com, Techies.com, and Techjobbank.com are booming. Techies.com carries only technology-based job openings. It requires visitors to register and become a member before they can view job postings.[41] There appears to be a site for everyone. For dreamers, there is Coolworks.com, which lists adventure jobs such as park ranger, and the self-explanatory Sixfigurejobs.com.[42] A Web site that caters to black applicants is Blackvoices.com. Looking for a job in broadcasting? Check out www.TVjobs.com. How about trucking? Check out www.Layover.com.

**Niche sites**
Web sites that cater to a specific profession.

Jobtrak.com's job listings and résumé services target college students and alumni. Jobtrak has formed partnerships with more than 900 college and university career centers, alumni associations, and M.B.A. programs nationwide. More than 400,000 employers have utilized Jobtrak to target college students and alumni for full- or part-time employment opportunities. There are more than 35,000 jobseeking students, graduates, and experienced professionals accessing the Jobtrak.com Web site daily.[43]

Suppose that you are a professor and desire to change jobs. It used to be that you had to go to the library and thumb frantically through the many pages of *The Chronicle of Higher Education*. Now, sitting in the comfort of your own home, you can enter www.chronicle.com, which takes you to *The Chronicle of Higher Education* Web site. All the jobs listed with the *Chronicle* are available to view for free. Each position announcement has a hot link to a university homepage where additional information can be obtained. The universities pay the fee.

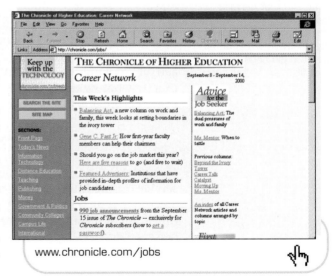

www.chronicle.com/jobs

## SITES FOR CONTRACT WORKERS

In Chapter 4, contract workers were mentioned as an alternative to recruitment. Recently, sites have been developed to assist this segment of the workforce. Professionals searching for freelance work are increasingly turning to Web sites that let them market themselves globally as for-hire help. The trend is fast erasing the traditional and geographic boundaries separating employers and millions of contract workers. Now specialized Web sites let workers advertise their skills, set their price, and pick an employer. Some Web sites, including Guru.com, let independent professionals search a database of jobs and post a profile that employers can view. The site also has resources that allow freelancers to sign up for health insurance, participate in chats with other contractors, and incorporate online. "It opens me up to a network of something like 70,000 people," says Rob Weinberg, a strategic marketing consultant in Beverly, Massachusetts, who has found jobs through Guru.

FreeAgent.com lets contractors search in fields such as technical writing, customer support, and real estate. They can also network online with other freelancers and showcase their skills to employers with an online portfolio. Ants.com is an online site linking businesses looking for freelancers with independent professionals who can do the job from remote locations. A company posts a project, and freelancers around the world bid on the job. Project prices range from a few hundred dollars for a small job to more than $26,000 for a two-month technical job. These online sites are creating a convenience for employers who are finding they can get the workers they need for specific jobs despite an agonizingly tight labor market.[44]

## JOB AGENT SERVICE SITES

**Job agent service site**
Web site that permits job-seekers to specify parameters for their ideal job and to receive information on only the job opportunities that fit these restrictions.

The previous section was devoted to a discussion of posting résumés on the Web. Sites such as Monster.com, HotJobs.com, and Headhunter.net are excellent means of shopping résumés to hundreds of employers at once. This approach is a double-edged sword, however. Privacy is lost as soon as résumés are posted, and excessive visibility may result. Sometimes résumés seem to float through the Web forever.[45] To overcome this, individuals can use a **job agent service site** that permits job-seekers to specify parameters for their ideal job and to receive information on only the job opportunities that fit these criteria. NationJob.com and Jobs.com are job agent service sites. This approach is effective for a passive jobseeker (a person who is not actively looking for a job). With a job agent, a person who is not actively looking for a job can leave the door open to opportunities by indicating exactly what he or she wants in a dream job, then forgetting about it until something becomes available that fits the description.

## PERSONALITY-BASED JOB PLACEMENT

DiscoverMe (www.discoverme.com) is the first personality-based job placement service on the Internet available to both jobseekers and *Fortune* 1000 companies. Since few résumés, especially ones downloaded from the Internet, tell recruiters much about a candidate's personality, some method is needed to help recruiters better understand applicants. An important key to successful job fit is often first having a more complete understanding of who a person is, not just what he or she has done. According to Gerry Crispin, co-author of *CareerXRoads,* an annual directory of career-management Web sites, "Personality assessment has been around for many years, but being able to do this on the Net, in real time, is obviously the next generation."[46]

The DiscoverMe site allows individuals to complete a personality assessment online (which takes about an hour), then receive a one-page personality summary. They can be contacted later if they match the profile of a job opening from a DiscoverMe client-employer. DiscoverMe gives recruiters more insight into candidates' personalities before they spend valuable interview time. Surprisingly, it costs about the same as or less than using a headhunter or a recruitment agency. Client companies develop a "role profile" for each job, which is all the information on that particular position, including the job description, salary, location, requirements, and a top-performer personality profile. This is a composite of all the personality profiles for a given role. Candidates are sought that have not only the skills, but also similar profiles.

Recently, recruiters for the Abbott Laboratories diagnostics division used the DiscoverMe approach as a source for its hardest-to-fill and hardest-to-keep position: sales representative. According to Nancy Baker-Buckman, manager of USO human resources for Abbott Laboratories, "It's the job that we have the most turnover in. It's something we're always searching for, so we felt DiscoverMe would be a good tool to try in finding candidates."[47] Basically, the DiscoverMe approach helps isolate such intangibles as leadership ability and aggressiveness that may identify sales representatives with staying power.

Personality profiling and testing has been used in the employment arena for years. Some HR professionals embrace these techniques, while others do not. Although these tests can be quite useful, companies must be aware that predicting the job behavior of future employees is quite difficult. However, knowing as much as possible about job candidates, particularly in high turnover jobs, seems prudent.[48]

## DESIGNING A WEB SITE FOR JOBSEEKERS

Recently, job applicants have discovered that establishing their own Web site can be very useful in their job search. According to Donna Peerce of the Heart and Soul Career Center in Nashville, Tennessee, "To have your own Web site—it's like you're putting out an advertisement for yourself." Recruiters and HR professionals like them because they are an easy way to get more information about a job candidate. According to Peerce, "Web sites are convenient for companies. They can really look at you and your background and they don't have to make the commitment about calling on the phone. People are so busy that they do not want to take time to telephone you if they're not really interested."[49]

Web sites allow jobseekers to expand their résumés beyond the traditional format. For instance, a Web site could contain a list of projects the individual managed and details about each one. A Web site is also a good place to post letters of reference and biographical details that might be of interest to employers, but that are not job related, such as volunteer work and a list of recent awards. An effective Web site should have a simple design, consisting of a homepage with an executive summary, home address, phone numbers, and an e-mail address. Links to other pages, such as chronological work history, educational background, career highlights and accomplishments, photo and personal biographical sketch, and references and letters of recommendation, are often quite useful. The two most popular Internet browsers, Netscape and Internet Explorer, offer free tutorials.[50]

## EXTERNAL SOURCES OF RECRUITMENT AND THE INTERNET

In the previous chapter, external sources of recruitment included high schools and vocational schools, community colleges, colleges and universities, competitors and other firms, the unemployed, older individuals, military personnel, and self-employed workers. All of these recruitment sources remain viable today, and they all have one thing in common. Attracting candidates from these sources is enhanced and altered through use of the Internet. A computer with a modem and an Internet connection makes the recruitment methods used unique to this time in history.

In the previous chapter, the section entitled "External Recruitment Methods" included such topics as advertising, private and public employment agencies, recruiters, special events, internships, executive search firms, professional associations, employee referrals, unsolicited walk-in applicants, open houses, event recruiting, virtual job fairs, and signing bonuses. As Internet recruitment is described, some of these general topics will again be discussed and others will be added.

## Advertising

Print advertising will probably not be abandoned soon. However, go to any of the major Web recruiting sites and it will become readily apparent that advertising plays a major role in financing the site. Advertising job openings on the Internet is becoming increasingly popular. The homepage of most Web sites makes a person feel like studying the information presented. For example, the friendly site Monster.com seems to invite visitors to stay longer, with icons that are very eye appealing. Because of the differences in traditional and Internet advertising, an entire new field of study has developed which requires new research and writing.[51]

Advertising on the Internet requires new insight. Certainly the classified section of the Sunday newspaper provides a valuable source of available jobs. But now these same jobs are also being placed on the Internet. All major newspapers now have their jobs advertised on the Internet and at no additional cost to the companies placing the ads. A positive aspect of this form of advertising is that the total number of ads placed has increased. Trade journals have also benefited from the Internet. For example, *HRMagazine*, the journal of the Society for Human Resource Management, has significantly increased its advertising activities because help wanted ads are included both in the journal and on the homepage.

## Private Employment Agencies

Employment agencies often have their own Web site to show prospective employees the array of jobs available through their agency. Rather than bombard the agency representative with phone calls, a searcher can review the site to see what jobs might provide a fit, then contact the agency. Jobseekers are matched with a personal recruiter who can help them sort through job opportunities and give career advice over the phone.

## Public Employment Agencies

America's Job Bank is a partnership between the U.S. Department of Labor and the state-operated public Employment Service. The public Employment Service provides labor exchange services to employers and jobseekers through a network of 1,800 offices throughout the United States. The service of posting résumés from jobseekers was initiated in 1998. Publicizing job listings on a national basis has helped employers recruit the employees they need to help their businesses succeed, while providing the American labor force with an increased number of opportunities to find work and realize career goals. The America's Job Bank computerized network links various state Employment Service offices to provide jobseekers with the largest pool of active job opportunities available anywhere and nationwide exposure for their résumés. For employers, it provides rapid, national exposure for job openings and an easily accessible pool of candidates. In addition, the job openings and résumés found in America's Job Bank are available on computer systems in public libraries, colleges and universities, high schools, shopping malls, transition offices on military bases worldwide, and other places of public access. America's Job Bank many be reached at www.ajb.dni.us. There is no charge to either employers who list their job vacancies or to jobseekers who utilize America's Job Bank to locate employment.

## College Recruiters

The Internet is a dramatic tool for recruiting college students. According to Mark Mehler, co-author of *CareerXroads,* a book that rates job sites, "It's definitely replacing the career-planning and placement offices on campuses."[52] While that statement may sound excessively harsh, the job of the college recruiter is changing drastically. As discussed in the previous chapter, some recruiters are using computers to communicate with college career counselors and interview students through a video conferencing system without leaving the office.

## Online Job Fairs

The Internet provides a special opportunity to conduct online job fairs, which are quickly becoming commonplace. Most major job sites regularly conduct online job fairs targeting major U.S. and international job markets. The fairs are featured on the Web's homepage as well as on various other pages. Each corporate logo takes a user to a page with information on each company, job openings, and an online response form. A fair may include 25 or more companies. Each company tells a little about itself and lists the jobs available. Each job can be viewed, and if the applicant believes he or she is qualified, an application can be immediately processed.

## Internships

Currently, students find out about many internship programs by using the Internet. Numerous job sites focus on assisting students in obtaining internships. For example, internshipprograms.com focuses on student internship programs.[53] USInterns.com provides a database of more than 65,000 opportunities from nearly 2,500 employers, a résumé builder, and career content. The site enables students to search for internships by salary, industry, and geography, as well as by keyword, skills set, and organization.[54]

## Executive Search Firms

The primary difference between traditional work done by executive search firms before and after the Internet is one of speed. Often searches now take weeks instead of months. For instance, Futurestep Inc., Korn/Ferry's new Internet subsidiary, promises to help companies line up candidates in four short weeks rather than the months it typically takes. Candidates who come to the Futurestep.com site receive an assessment of their market value and other customized career feedback, based on a lengthy questionnaire. Besides listing job preferences and credentials, candidates indicate the kind of environment they are used to working in.[55]

NETSHARE (www.netshare.com) is a Web-based service that offers a comprehensive career management approach. NETSHARE specializes in online career management resources that cater exclusively to senior executives and recruiters. According to NETSHARE president David Theobald, "The current online *classified bulletin board* approach of listing thousands of jobs at all levels doesn't work for jobseekers or those looking to fill senior-level positions." NETSHARE caters exclusively to the $100,000+ executive and offers members the option of reviewing all 1,500 daily updated senior-level positions or receiving targeted, matched positions via e-mail. NETSHARE also offers subscribers access to extensive market intelligence, industry trend information, and feedback from career coaches and résumé writers.[56]

## Professional Associations

Professional associations can combine the print and online components better than anyone. In SHRM's monthly *HR News,* for example, paid job advertisements now fill a dozen or more pages, triple the amount of a year before. Encouraging that growth was a promise to place print ads online on SHRM's Web site in 24 to 48 hours, then notify thousands of registered jobseekers. Neither print nor online strategies alone could have produced this result. Hundreds of small and large associations are beginning to realize the unique opportunity for revenue and added service to their members. Recruiters should poll employees to identify all professional associations relevant to their organization, then contact those groups to post appropriate job openings or link their sites together.[57]

## Employee Enlistment

**Employee enlistment** is a recruitment method whereby every employee becomes a company recruiter. This is not the same as asking employees to refer friends to the company. Employees are given simple business cards that do not have anyone's name on them. Instead, these cards say something like: "We are always looking for great _____. To find out more, log onto our Web site." These cards are to be given out at parties, sports events, family gatherings, picnics, the park, or wherever an employee goes. They are used to let people know that the company really does want people to apply. Employees can use the cards as a way to talk about what they do and how great their company is. When this method is used, all employees should know that recruiting is critical to the firm's success.[58]

## Unsolicited Walk-In Applicants

If an organization has the reputation of being a good place to work, it may be able to attract qualified prospects even without extensive recruitment efforts. With the Internet, it is now much easier for unsolicited walk-in applicants to apply for a job. A person merely has to pull up a firm's homepage to find out more about a company. For example, suppose that Ford Motor Company has the reputation of being a good place to work, and therefore, you decide to visit its homepage. Immediately you see *Careers* and you click on the icon. Then, you can paste your résumé with Ford's normal application information. You can search for a job with Ford worldwide and access a tremendous amount of company information, the work environment, career programs, and recruiting schedules. At the General Motors homepage, you will find out about thousands of career opportunities, job fairs, internship programs available worldwide, as well as how to prepare for one or several of these careers while you are still a student.

## Talent Auctions

A **talent auction** in Web terminology, the act of a person or persons placing their qualifications on a site and having organizations bid on their services. In

## ▶ *I Know I Am the Most Qualified*

Gino Magdaleno was frustrated as he spoke to his best friend, Wayne Sanders, about why he had received no response to the résumé he recently mailed to a *Fortune* 500 company. Gino said, "It was a perfect match. I had every qualification they wanted, but they haven't contacted me, not even a phone call. My résumé is the most beautiful thing in the world; a masterpiece. I used every special font on my computer, and tabbed over so everything would be highlighted. Even used my color printer. They must have lost it. To heck with them." Wayne said, "Let's take a look at that masterpiece." After studying Gino's résumé, he believed that the problem was solved.

*What might have been the problem that Wayne discovered?*

early 2000, a group of 16 trailblazing engineers tried to sell their services on the auction site eBay.com for a starting bid of more than $3.14 million. They eventually withdrew their offer, but the idea of people auctioning themselves on the Internet was born. It continues to be used today primarily by free agents and consultants. One talent auction site, Bid4Geeks.com, is a silent auction where IT recruiters can bid on individual employees or a combined talent pool. The search engine allows recruiters to find prospects by keyword or geographic location. ITAuctionHouse.com uses an auction format, where placement agencies and employers bid on the services of IT professionals. Once a successful match is made, an ITAuctionHouse representative facilitates job negotiations. TalentMarket.Monster.com is a sleek, professionally designed site that hosts more than 34,000 live auctions and provides access to nearly 200,000 independent pros who are mostly free agents and consultants.[59]

## ▶ *Electronic Résumés*

HR WEB
WISDOM

**www.prenhall.com/mondy**

ASCII résumés, scanning résumés, using keywords, and sample electronic résumés are the topics discussed.

## POSTING RÉSUMÉS ON THE INTERNET

According to a newly released study by the Society for Human Resource Management, most HR professionals now prefer to receive résumés via e-mail.[60] Many Web sites are available for use by applicants in securing jobs. But, how does a person get his or her résumé from his or her computer to an employment site? Each day millions of people and thousands of companies exchange information over computer networks such as the Internet. The different types of computers and computer languages are sometimes overwhelming; therefore, a special format is used to help accommodate these differences. This common format is known as ASCII which stands for "American Standard Code for Information Interchange." ASCII text is the simplest form of text, meaning there is no formatting mechanism within the document and the text is not application specific. ASCII is the text format widely used when you read and write e-mail. Because of its simplicity, ASCII text enables anyone to construct an online résumé prospective employers can view over the Internet no matter what kind of computer software is being used.[61]

In creating an ASCII résumé, type your résumé using a word-processing application such as Word or WordPerfect, and then save it as a text-only document. This should be an option under your *Save* or *Save as* command. Since your résumé will appear as ASCII text, it will not recognize special formatting commands specific to your word-processing program. Therefore, you must watch for these common mistakes:

▶ Avoid special characters.
▶ Do not use tabs; use your space bar.
▶ Do not use the word wrap feature when composing your résumé; instead, use hard carriage returns to insert line breaks.
▶ Use the default font and size.
▶ Do not use boldface and italics.[62]

## RÉSUMÉ MANAGEMENT SYSTEMS

**Résumé management systems**
Systems that scan résumés into databases, search the databases on command, and rank the résumés according to the number of resulting hits they receive.

Several electronic résumé databases have been developed by a myriad of associations, groups, and companies. They vary widely in size, content, accessibility, and cost, but they all search in one way or another by computers. **Résumé management systems** scan résumés into databases, search the databases on command, and rank the résumés according to the number of resulting hits they receive. At times such searches utilize multiple (10–20) criteria. Major corporations and recruitment firms usually use résumé management systems to do a better job of prescreening résumés arriving in response to Web ads. At Humana, the system ranks the résumés in order, from most likely to match the company's requirements to least likely to match.[63]

The reliance upon résumé management systems, coupled with the downsizing of human resource departments in many corporations, has resulted in a situation whereby many résumés are never seen by human eyes once they enter the system. Therefore, a job applicant should make their résumé as computer/scanner friendly as possible so that its life in a database will be extended and its likelihood of producing hits enhanced.

**Keywords**
Those words or phrases that are used to search databases for résumés that match.

**Keyword résumé**
A résumé that contains an adequate description of the jobseeker's characteristics and industry-specific experience presented in keyword terms in order to accommodate the electronic/computer search process.

To make the process work, a new résumé style should be used. **Keywords** refer to those words or phrases that are used to search databases for résumés that match. This match is called a *hit* and occurs when one or more résumés are selected as matching the various criteria (keywords) used in the search. Keywords tend to be more of the noun or noun phrase type (*Word 97, UNIX, Biochemist*) as opposed to action verbs often found in traditional résumés (*developed, coordinated, empowered, organized*). Another way to look at keyword phrases is to think in terms of job duties. Detailing an individual's job duties may require a change in mindset away from traditional résumé writing. The **keyword résumé** is one that contains an adequate description of the jobseeker's characteristics and industry-specific experience presented in keyword terms in order to accommodate the electronic/computer search process. These are the words and phrases that employers and recruiters use to search the databases for hits. Failure to provide sufficient hits may limit the usefulness of the résumé.[64]

The following preparation guidelines are recommended if it is suspected that his or her résumé will be scanned by an electronic system.

- Left-justify the entire document.
- Utilize a size 10 sans serif font.
- Avoid tabs.
- Avoid italic text, script, underlining, graphics, bold text, and shading.
- Avoid horizontal and vertical lines.
- Avoid parentheses and brackets.
- Avoid compressed lines of print.
- Avoid faxed copies that become fuzzy.

An example of a keyword résumé may be seen in Figure 6-1. Jobseekers usually need to prepare two versions of their résumés, a keyword résumé and a traditional one. The traditional résumé, as seen in Figure 6-2, will continue to be

---

HENRY SANCHEZ
1508 Westwood Drive
New York, NY  20135
(914) 555-3869

OBJECTIVE:

To obtain an entry-level position in a public accounting firm.

EMPLOYMENT HISTORY:

11/2000–Present, Assistant Administrator at Touch of Class Foods Corporation
**Built Accounts Payable and Accounts Receivable ledgers.
**Originated a responsive invoice program.
**Prepared corporate tax returns and all schedules.
**Oversaw intern program.
**Initiated ISO-9002 Certifications in all areas of plant production.
05/1998–11/2000 — *Personal Assistant* at Park Board of Trustees
**Research and Development with City Sewer District.
**Assisted with general accounting procedures.
**Assisted with customer-related issues.
**Assisted with the allocation of public funds.

EDUCATION:
**M.B.A., University of New York, 2000, GPA: 3.8
**B.S. in Business Administration, concentration in Individual and
Corporate Taxation with an emphasis in Management Information Systems, 1997, GPA: 3.2

COMPUTER SKILLS:
**Microsoft Word 97, AmiPro, WordPerfect 7.0
**Lotus 123, Microsoft Excel, Quattro Pro, Quicken
**Windows and Windows 2000 Application

AFFILIATIONS:
**ISO-9002
**TQM National Association

---

**Sample Keyword Résumé**     **Figure 6-1**

**Henry Sanchez**

*Current Address:*
1508 Westwood Dr.
New York, NY 20135
914/555-3869

| | |
|---|---|
| **OBJECTIVE:** | To obtain an entry-level position in a public accounting firm. |
| **EDUCATION:** | University of New York<br>**Master of Business Administration, December 2000**<br>**Bachelor of Science, Business Administration, May 1997**<br>Concentration: Individual and Corporate Tax<br>with emphasis on Management Information Systems<br>GPA: 3.2 / 4.0 |
| **HONORS:** | Honors in Accounting and Finance<br>Full academic scholarship<br>President of Summer Conference Program |
| **ACCOMPLISHMENTS:** | Conducted TQM seminars<br>Successfully completed ISO-9002 courses<br>Graduate Assistant to the Dean |
| **EXPERIENCE:**<br>*November 2000*<br>*Present* | **ASSISTANT ADMINISTRATOR**<br>Touch of Class Foods Corporation<br>Accounting Department<br>• Responsible for building A/P and A/R ledgers<br>• Originated a responsive invoice program<br>• Prepared corporate tax returns and all schedules<br>• Oversaw intern program<br>• Initiated ISO-9002 Certifications in all areas of plant production |
| *May 1998*<br>*November 2000* | **PERSONAL ASSISTANT**<br>Mr. Charles Brandon<br>Park Board of Trustees<br>• Research and Development with City Sewer District<br>• Assisted with general accounting procedures<br>• Assisted with customer-related issues<br>• Assisted with the allocation of public funds |
| **COMPUTER SKILLS:** | Microsoft Word, AmiPro, WordPerfect 7.0<br>Lotus 123, Microsoft Excel, Quattro Pro, Quicken<br>Windows and Windows 2000 Applications |
| **AFFILIATIONS:** | ISO-9002 Certified Consultant<br>TQM National Association |

**Figure 6-2** **Example of Traditional Résumé**

designed to be read by real people in 20 seconds or less and will follow the various formats presented by untold numbers of résumé writers and résumé writing programs. The keyword résumé, however, should be added to the jobseeker's arsenal and utilized in any situation where computer scanning or posting online might possibly be involved. Comparing the résumés in Figures 6-1 and 6-2 provides real insight into the differences between keyword résumés and traditional résumés. The key to success in the future is to prepare both correctly, and then get them to prospective employers.[65]

## Global Internet Recruiting: A Fad or the Future?

In 1998, 17 percent of *Fortune* Global 500 firms actively recruited on the Internet. By 1999, that figure had risen to 45 percent.[66] As of May 2000, it had risen to 79 percent. It is projected that all Global 500 companies will be Web site recruiters by 2002.[67] Mr. Wulf of National Semiconductor believes that, "Any company not doing Web postings is really at a disadvantage, and anybody looking for a job and not looking at [corporate] Web sites is at a disadvantage."[68] According to Forrester Research, employer spending on online recruiting will expand even further. Bruce Hatz, a corporate staffing manager at Hewlett-Packard, believes that the Internet is "dramatically more effective than any medium ever known. The Web is the future of recruiting." Globally, the Internet threatens to erupt into a true global talent exchange—basically, a full-blown electronic marketplace of people.[69] The cost advantage of Internet recruiting is also extreme. Generating résumés via the Internet costs only pennies—much less than traditional methods. According to Reggie Barefield, executive director of Humana's Talent Resources and Technology Team, "The Internet is a job-lead generator and a global tool for creating a proactive recruiting team." According to Joe Krafinski, a recruiter at the IT recruiting firm Datacom Technology Group, "It's not blowing anything else out of the water, but due to its extensive reach it's a very cost-effective venue. The Internet does offer a viable, global route to the candidate pool and is not a mere fad, but quite probably the wave of the future."[70]

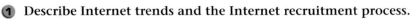

## Summary

**1** **Describe Internet trends and the Internet recruitment process.**

There are millions of candidates online, reviewing hundreds of thousands of job openings listed at thousands of career sites on the Web. When the Internet is involved in the recruitment process, the definition itself does not change; however, words within the definition may take on different meanings.

**2** **Explain the requirements for effective Internet recruiting.**

The requirements for effective Internet recruiting are to research Internet employment sites, establish a budget, develop an Internet Web site that is upbeat and informative, write effective online ads, experiment with various advertising approaches, monitor both traditional and Internet advertisements, experiment with various Web sites, and become a sleuth on the Internet. In addition, do not neglect traditional recruiting methods and coordinate the recruiting strategy.

**3** **Describe the limitations of Internet recruiting.**

First, the Internet does not replace doing background checks, skills tests, face-to-face interviews, and other steps to assess attitudes and behavior that are vital to finding qualified employees. Second, HR professionals are frustrated with the Internet's lack of a personal touch. Third, the number of résumés that must be reviewed is growing dramatically. Fourth, there is more competition for qualified employees from small and medium, as well as global, companies. Fifth, spending on Internet recruiting is increasing, but often at the expense of other, more traditional approaches. Finally, confidentiality could be a problem.

**4** **Explain the new HR position of cyber recruiter.**

The Internet recruiter, also called cyber recruiter, is a person whose primary responsibility is to use the Internet in the recruitment process.

**⑤ Describe internal recruitment using the intranet.**

Job posting and job bidding have changed significantly as companies and employees continue to expand usage of the intranet. Now, if a worker does not know about a new vacancy, it is because the intranet posting was not checked regularly.

**⑥ Explain the significance of the corporate Web site and the homepage.**

The corporate Web site is a virtual media format that presents information about the company, often including human resources information, and possibly even allowing individuals to apply for jobs. The corporate homepage is the initial page of the Web site, used by an organization to present itself to viewers on the Internet.

**⑦ Describe selected employment Web sites.**

The most widely recognized employment Web sites are Monster.com, HotJobs.com, Headhunter.net, and CareerBuilder.com.

**⑧ Explain niche sites.**

Sites that cater to a specific profession are called niche sites.

**⑨ Describe contract workers sites and job agent service sites.**

Specialized Web sites let contract workers advertise their skills, set their price, and pick who they will work for. Job agent service sites permit jobseekers to specify parameters for their ideal job and to receive job-opening information only on the opportunities that fit these restrictions.

**⑩ Describe personality-based job placement.**

DiscoverMe is the first personality-based job placement service on the Internet available to both jobseekers and *Fortune* 1000 companies.

**⑪ Explain the process of designing a Web site for jobseekers.**

Job applicants have discovered that establishing their own Web site can be very useful in their job search.

**⑫ Describe external sources of recruitment and the Internet.**

External sources of recruitment include high schools and vocational schools, community colleges, colleges and universities, competitors and other firms, the unemployed, older individuals, military personnel, and self-employed workers. Attracting these sources is enhanced and altered through use of the Internet.

**⑬ Explain external recruitment methods and the Internet.**

In the previous chapter, a section entitled "External Recruitment Methods" was presented. These and additional topics are also used with Internet recruiting.

**⑭ Describe posting résumés on the Internet.**

In creating an ASCII résumé, type your résumé using a personal word-processing application such as Word or WordPerfect, and then save it as a text-only document.

**⑮ Explain résumé management systems.**

Résumé management systems scan résumés into databases, search the databases on command, and rank the résumés according to the number of resulting hits they receive.

## ▶ Questions For Review

1. How does Internet recruiting differ from traditional recruiting?
2. What are the requirements for effective Internet recruitment?
3. What are the limitations of Internet recruiting?
4. What is the responsibility of the cyber recruiter?

5. How is internal recruitment conducted through the use of the intranet?

6. What is the significance of the corporate Web site and homepage?

7. Define the following:

   a. Niche sites
   b. Contract workers sites
   c. Job agent service sites

8. How might a person conduct personality assessment on the Web?

9. In seeking a job, what is the value of designing your own Web page?

10. How do traditional external recruiting sources differ from Internet recruitment sources?

11. What are the rules to follow in posting résumés on the Internet?

12. Define *résumé management systems*. How do they work?

*We invite you to visit the Mondy homepage on the Prentice Hall Web site at*
**www.prenhall.com/mondy**
*for updated information, Web-based exercises, and links to other HR-related sites.*

TAKE IT TO
THE NET

## Developing HRM Skills ◀

### *An Experiential Exercise*

After studying Chapters 5 and 6 of this text, students should have a much better appreciation of what is involved in recruiting. After reading Chapter 6, you might even begin to believe that traditional recruitment methods may become a thing of the past. In this exercise, participants will develop an understanding of which recruitment methods will be best to use both with and without the Internet.

## HRM INCIDENT 1 ◀

### *Real-Time Recruitment*

Relaxing on the deck of his beach hotel in Cancun, Jack Hicks is job hunting using his personal digital assistant (PDA) linked by a satellite to various electronic professional job posting services. Hicks, a petroleum engineer, is enjoying a three-week vacation after a fairly long period of employment with a Saudi Arabia–based oil company. He is a professional contract employee working on a just-in-time basis, rather than a permanent employee of just one firm. Just before completing each freelance assignment Hicks posts his résumé, compensation requirements, and availability date on the electronic bulletin board of his professional engineering organization. Very much like the various electronic professional job posting services, this bulletin board also serves to globally link employers and jobseekers.

Guy Newman, vice president of Explore All Recovery, needs to assemble a joint U.S.–Canadian-Russian team of engineers to recover oil reserves from Siberian oil fields. Newman is assembling the remaining specialists needed for the team with specialized software capable of searching online databases for keywords related to job experience and training. Once individuals with the needed specialties are isolated from databases compiled by various bulletin boards and electronic job posting services, they are downloaded into Newman's desktop computer. Newman then reviews the various matches and isolates individuals with the skills and experiences needed and who have reasonable compensation requirements and are available immediately. Hicks's résumé is directly in line with Newman's needs and he is familiar with Hicks's excellent reputation. In addition, Hicks has experience working in the inhospitable conditions of Siberia.

Newman e-mails Hicks indicating a strong interest in working with him on the upcoming Siberian project. The e-mail reaches Hicks, who is still relaxing in his lounge chair. Hicks is interested in the Siberian project, also having heard good things about Newman. Hicks uses his PDA to call Newman and leaves a voice-mail message indicating his strong interest. Newman e-mails Hicks an employment contract via his PDA. Newman and Hicks discuss the possibilities utilizing their visual/voice/data link capabilities. Several contractual changes are made and Hicks initials them onscreen. Both Hicks and Newman sign the revised contract with their styluses, completing the deal. Newman goes back to work assembling the remaining team members, while Hicks heads back to the beach.[71]

### Question

1. What traditional recruiting methods might have been used to get Jack Hicks to join Guy Newman?

---

### ▶ HRM INCIDENT 2

#### Can the Internet Help Us?

Shane Bordeaux is the HR director for a medium-size chemical company located on the outskirts of Baton Rouge, Louisiana. Although the company is relatively small, it has a reputation for being quite innovative. The firm employs 15 engineers, most of whom graduated from colleges in the general area. It pays its employees well, benefits are far better than most in the Southeast, and there has been little turnover, with only three engineers being hired in the last two years.

For several years the company has been bidding on a major government contract that could thrust it into the forefront of chemical processing technology. A decision on the contract is expected soon. As Shane sits in his office one morning, he receives a call from company president Dave Louder, who tells him to come down to his office. When he arrives, Dave excitedly tells him that it has happened, the contract is theirs! They now have to get everything in gear and begin production. Successful completion of the contract would make them a major player in the industry. Things have to move fast now. Shane is excited until he realizes that the company will need at least 20 new engineers immediately. Shane then says, "I don't believe I can get those engineers on board that fast. The college placement centers at most of the colleges where I recruit don't have a lot of people graduating this semester, and the demand for engineers is real high these days." Dave replies, "Well, we have to have those people fast or the government will yank the contract. Get to it."

That night Shane discusses his dilemma with his friend Natalie Villamizar. He says, "All my recruitment methods are going to take longer than Dave will allow.

We advertise in *Chemical Monthly,* but that takes a long time to get published. Our internship program has been successful, but it takes way too much time. We have gotten one worker from an employment agency, but that individual just wanted to get back to the Baton Rouge area. Primarily, I have been recruiting on college campuses in the region." Natalie leans back in her chair and says, "Have you tried recruiting on the Internet? My company has been really successful at recruiting on the Web. Maybe you should give it a shot."

## Questions

1. What would be the advantages of Shane's company using the Internet for recruiting?
2. What type of Web sites do you believe would be the most productive?

## Notes

1. "The Web Is Supplementing Help-wanted Ads," *The Patriot Ledger Quincy* (March 16, 1998): 9.

2. "Internet," Cambridge International Dictionaries, *Cambridge University Press* (2000).

3. Ibid.

4. "To Keep Pace with Rapid Growth, CapitalStream Depends on Webhire Internet Recruiting Solutions," *Business Wire* (February 2, 2000).

5. "Internet Recruiting Study Uncovers Latest Trends," *Business Wire* (September 1, 1999).

6. "Online Recruiting: What Works, What Doesn't," *HR Focus* 77 (March 2000): 1.

7. "SBC Finds That More Than 80 Percent of Class of `99 Using the Internet to Search for Work," *Business Wire* (May 13, 1999): 1.

8. Christopher Caggiano, "The Truth about Internet Recruiting," *Inc.* (December 1999): 156–57.

9. Adapted from articles by Ray Schreyer and John McCarter, "10+ Steps to Effective Internet Recruiting," *HR Focus* (September 1998): S6; and Scott Hays, "Hiring on the Web," *Workforce* (August 1999): 76–84.

10. Brenda Paik Sunoo, "Internet Recruiting Has Its Pros and Cons," *Workforce* (April 1998): 17–18.

11. Ibid.; and "More Pros and Cons to Internet Recruiting," *HR Focus* (May 2000): 8–9.

12. "Internet Recruiting Study Uncovers Latest Trends."

13. Shelley Donald Coolidge, "Why More Job Hunters Are Stalking the Web," *The Christian Science Monitor* (August 16, 1999): 11.

14. "Internet Recruiting Study Uncovers Latest Trends."

15. "Intranet," Cambridge International Dictionaries, *Cambridge University Press* (2000).

16. "Web Technology Dominates HR Delivery," *HR Focus* 77 (May 2000): 9.

17. Stephanie Armour, "Corporate Intranets Help Bring Employees into the Loop," *USA Today* (March 20, 2000): 3B.

18. "Why Your Web Site Is More Important Than Ever to New Hires," *HR Focus* 77 (June 2000): 9.

19. Leyla Kokmen, "Online Recruiting on the Rise," *Denver Post* (June 1, 1998): E-6.

20. Jennifer D'Alessandro, "Editor's Choice: Video Goes Corporate—Cvideo Now Is a Twofold Opportunity for VARs," *VarBusiness* (October 1, 1997): 53.

21. Amy Zuber, "Workers Catch Wave, Surf Net for Employment," *Nation's Restaurant News* 32 (February 9, 1998): 1.

22. Judith N. Mottl, "Managing Change: Employers Head to the Web," *InternetWeek* (August 10, 1998): 29.

23. Kevin Wheeler, "Five Tips for Getting Started in E-Recruiting," *An e-Recruiting Primer* (April 5, 2000).

24. Diana Kunde, "Cyber-Search: Etiquette Shifts as Job Seekers, Recruiters Head Online," *The Dallas Morning News* (February 3, 1999): 1D.

25. Coolidge, "Why More Job Hunters Are Stalking the Web."

26. Alan S. Kay, "Employers Tout the Lower Cost, Wider Reach, and Targeting Ability of Online Job Boards," *InformationWeek* (March 20, 2000): 72.

27. "Breakaway Run in Fourth Quarter 1999 Takes TMP Interactive and Monster.com to Super Bowl Victory and Beyond," *Business Wire* (March 7, 2000).

28. Ibid.

29. Elisabeth Eaves, "Online Job Sites Deliver Too Little—and Too Much," *Reuters Business Report* (April 30, 2000).

30. content.monster.com/jobseekerresources/generalresources (October 27, 2000).

31. "The Internet Analyst News—Headhunter.net Burnishes Its C.V.," *Business Wire* (May 9, 2000).

32. "Headhunter.net to Buy CareerMosaic for $109 Million," *Reuters* (April 17, 2000).

33. Chris Murphy, "Online Recruiters to Consolidate," *Informationweek* (April 24, 2000): 165.

34. www.careermosaic.com (August 25, 2000).

35. www.Headhunter.net (August 26, 2000).

36. "Post a Single Job," www.hotjobs.com (March 8, 2000).

37. Tim Ouellette, "Internet Job Sites Get Lean to Win Back Recruiters," *Computerworld* 32 (February 2, 1998): 6.

38. "HotJobs.com, Ltd. and Resumix Inc. to Merge," www.hotjobs.com (October 24, 2000).

39. "CareerBuilder, CareerPath, Knight Ridder, and Tribune Create New Online Career Network," www.careerbuilder.com/merger/facts.html (October 25, 2000).

40. Ibid.

41. Eric Wieffering, "Online Headhunting // Techies.Com, an Online Job Service That Was Developed in the Twin Cities, Began Rolling Out across the Country Late Last Year," *Minneapolis Star Tribune* (April 14, 1999): 1D.

42. "The Best of the Web Gets Better," *U.S. News & World Report* (November 15, 1999): 113.

43. "Corporate Profile for JOBTRAK.COM, Dated Jan. 14, 2000," *Business Wire* (January 14, 2000): 1.

44. Stephanie Armour, "Web Sites Play Matchmaker to Freelancers, Employers," *USAToday* (April 19, 2000):10B.

45. Jerry Useem, "Cyberspace Is a Job Jungle," *Fortune* 139 (May 24, 1999): 290.

46. Jennifer Laabs, "Personality Fit: A New Approach to Recruiting," *Workforce* (August 1999): 89–90.

47. Ibid.

48. Ibid.

49. Vicky Uhland, "Web Page Aids in Job Search Personal Internet Site Helps Candidate Stand Out in Crowd," *Denver Rocky Mountain News* (April 30, 2000): 1J.

50. Ibid.

51. Zeff Robbin and Brad Aronson, *Advertising on the Internet,* 2nd ed. (John Wiley & Sons, 1999).

52. Coolidge, "Why More Job Hunters Are Stalking the Web."

53. Jill M. Singer, "Students Leap into Internships and Land Jobs after College," *USA Today* (February 21, 2000): 6D.

54. "USInterns.com Partners with First E-Transcript Service to Ease Cumbersome Process for Students, Schools, Employers," *Business Wire* (May 9, 2000).

55. Jennifer Reingold, "Executive Search: Headhunting 2000," 3629 *Business Week* (May 17, 1999): 74.

56. "Add Career Planning to Your Y2K Resolutions," *PR Newswire* (October 11, 1999): 1.

57. Gerry Crispin and Mark Mehler, "Recruiting Rockets Through Cyberspace: The World Wide Web Has Opened a New Universe for Recruiting and Job-Hunting—and the Best May Be Yet to Come," *HRMagazine* 42 (December 1997): 72.

58. Kevin Wheeler, "Non-Traditional Recruiting Method," *Electronic Recruiting Daily* (March 29, 2000).

59. Jim Battey, "IT Online Recruitment Auctions," *InfoWorld* 22 (May 8, 2000): 137.

60. "SHRM Survey Finds Preference for E-Mailed Resumes," *HR News* 19 (June 2000): 23.

61. "ASCII Resumes," www.careermosaic.com (February 28, 2000).

62. Kunde, "Cyber-Search: Etiquette Shifts as Job Seekers, Recruiters Head Online."

63. Barb Cole-Gomolski, "Recruiters Who Use Web Tighten Focus," *Computerworld* (April 5, 1999): 40–41.

64. Taunee Bensson, "Does Your Résumé Vanish into a Black Hole?" www.careers.wsj.com (March 3, 2000).

65. Wayne M. Gonyea, "Tips on Using Keywords for Electronic Résumés," www.careermosaic.com (February 28, 2000).

66. Daniel Eisenberg, "We're for Hire, Just Click," *Time* 154 (August 16, 1999): 46–47.

67. "79% of Global 500 Recruiting on Corporate Web Sites," *Business Wire* (May 10, 2000).

68. Diana Kunde, "Search Engines: Groups Spring Forward to Help Job Hunters Sift Through Heap of Online Postings," *The Dallas Morning News* (April 7, 1999): 1D.

69. Jerry Useem and Wilton Woods, "For Sale Online: The New Way to Look for a Job is also the New Way for Companies like Cisco, Marriott, Motorola, and Prudential," *Fortune* 140 (July 5, 1999): 66+.

70. Mottl, "Managing Change: Employers Head to the Web."

71. Adapted from Lyle M. Spencer, Jr., *Reengineering Human Resources* (New York: Wiley, 1995): 6–7.

objectivesobjectivesobjectives

## ▶ Objectives

- Explain the significance of employee selection.
- Identify environmental factors that affect the selection process.
- Describe the general selection process.
- Explain the importance of the preliminary interview.
- Describe the importance of the application for employment.
- Describe the advantages, potential problems, and characteristics of properly designed selection tests.
- Explain the types of validation studies.
- Describe types of employment tests.
- Explain the importance of interview planning and describe the content of the interview.
- Describe the basic types of interviewing.
- Describe the various methods of interviewing.
- Explain the legal implications of interviewing.
- Describe assessment centers as a means of selection.
- Explain why personal and professional references are requested and background investigations are conducted.
- Explain negligent hiring and retention and the use of polygraph tests.
- Describe the selection decision, the physical examination, and notification of candidates.

# chapter

chapterchapterchapterchapterchapterchapter

# 7

# Selection

**B**ill Jenkins is the owner/manager of Quality Printing Company on the outskirts of Chicago. Because of an increase in business, shop employees have been working overtime for almost a month. Last week Bill put an ad in the newspaper to hire a printer. Three people applied for the job. Bill considered only one of them, Mark Ketchell, to be qualified. Bill called Mark's previous employer in Detroit, who responded, "Mark is a diligent, hardworking person. He is as honest as the day is long. He knows his trade, too." Bill also found that Mark had left Detroit after he was divorced a few months ago and that his work had deteriorated slightly prior to the divorce. The next day, Bill asked Mark to operate one of the printing presses. Mark did so competently, and Bill immediately decided to hire him.

Mary Howard is the shipping supervisor for McCarty-Holman Warehouse, a major food distributor in Seattle. One of Mary's truck drivers just quit.

keytermskeytermskeyterms

## ▶ Key Terms

Selection 175
Selection ratio 177
Standardization 185
Objectivity 185
Norm 185
Reliability 185
Validity 186
Criterion-related validity 186
Concurrent validity 186

Predictive validity 186
Content validity 186
Construct validity 187
Cognitive aptitude tests 187
Psychomotor abilities tests 187
Job-knowledge tests 187
Work-sample tests 187
Vocational interest tests 188

Personality tests 188
Genetic testing 190
Employment interview 190
Organizational fit 192
Unstructured interview 193
Structured interview 194
Behavioral interview 194
Group interview 195
Board interview 196

Stress interview 196
Realistic job preview (RJP) 196
Assessment center 199
Reference checks 199
Negligent referral 200
Negligent hiring 201
Negligent retention 201

She spoke to the human resource manager, Tom Sullivan, who said that he would begin the search right away. The next day an ad appeared in the local paper for the position. Tom considered three of the fifteen applicants to be qualified and called them in for an initial interview. The next morning Tom called Mary and said, "I have three drivers who look like they can do the job. When do you want me to set up an interview for you with them? I guess you'll want to give them a driving test at that time." Mary interviewed the three drivers and gave them each a driving test; then she called Tom to tell him her choice. The next day the new driver reported to Mary for work.

**T**hese incidents provide only a brief look at the all-important selection process. In the first case, Bill, as owner/manager of a small printing shop, handled the entire selection process himself. In the second case, Tom, the human resource manager, was heavily involved in the selection process, but Mary, the shipping supervisor, made the actual decision. However, it was important for all parties involved to have a thorough knowledge of how employees are selected.

We begin the chapter with a discussion of the significance of employee selection and the environmental factors that affect it. Then, we describe the selection process, the preliminary interview, and review of the application for employment. Next, we cover the administration of selection tests. In the ensuing sections, we present the types of validation studies and describe types of employment tests. Next, we explain the employment interview, the types of interviews, and the various methods of interviewing. We follow those topics with a discussion of the legal implications of interviewing, assessment centers, personal reference checks, and professional references and background investigations. Negligent hiring and retention and polygraph tests are then discussed. We end the chapter with sections related to the selection decision, physical examination, and notification of candidates.

## THE SIGNIFICANCE OF EMPLOYEE SELECTION

Whereas recruitment encourages individuals to seek employment with a firm, the purpose of the selection process is to identify and employ the best-qualified individuals. **Selection** is the process of choosing from a group of applicants the individual best suited for a particular position and organization. As might be expected, a firm's recruitment success has a significant impact on the quality of the selection decision. The organization may be forced to employ marginally qualified workers if recruitment efforts do not result in some qualified applicants.

**Selection**
The process of choosing from a group of applicants those individuals best suited for a particular position and organization.

There are many ways to improve productivity, but none is more powerful than making the right hiring decision. Superior performers are often two or three times more productive than those who are barely acceptable.[1] A firm that selects qualified employees can reap substantial benefits, which may be repeated every year the employee is on the payroll.

Most managers recognize employee selection as one of their most difficult and most important business decisions. Hiring people has never been easy. Around two thousand years ago, officials in the Han dynasty tried to make a science of the selection process by creating long and detailed job descriptions for civil servants. Archaeological records suggest that these officials were frustrated by the results of their efforts as new hires seldom worked out as well as anticipated.[2] Michael J. Lotito, chair of the SHRM board of directors for 2000, declared, "HR has traditionally been seen as the soft side of business, but I submit that attracting and retaining the right people for your organization is the hard side of business because that is the *foundation upon which everything is based*."[3] Libby Sartain, vice president of human resources for Southwest Airlines, provides another perspective. She states, "We would rather go short and work overtime than hire one bad apple."[4] If a firm hires *many* bad apples, it cannot be successful long even if it has perfect plans, a sound organizational structure, and finely tuned control systems. Competent people must be available to ensure that organizational goals are attained. Today, with many firms having access to the same technology, it is the *people* who make the real difference. An organization's distinctive advantage has become increasingly dependent upon its human resources.

As mentioned in Chapter 2, small businesses, especially, cannot afford to make hiring mistakes. One incompetent person's foul-up in a large firm may have insignificant consequences. A similar error in a small company may be devastating, however. In the smaller, less specialized firm, each person typically accounts for a larger part of the business's activity. Bill Jenkins's small print shop business could suffer greatly if Bill selects an unskilled printing press operator. The impact of Mary hiring one inept driver would probably have a negative, but lesser, impact on McCarty-Holman Warehouse's entire operation.

The selection process affects, and is also affected by, the other HR functions. For instance, if the selection process provides the firm with only marginally qualified workers, the organization may have to intensify its training efforts. If the compensation package is inferior to those provided by the firm's competition, hiring the best-qualified applicants will be difficult or impossible.

The goal of the selection process is to properly match people with jobs and the organization. If individuals are overqualified, underqualified, or for any reason do not *fit* either the job or the organization's culture, they will probably leave the firm.

## ENVIRONMENTAL FACTORS AFFECTING THE SELECTION PROCESS

A standardized screening process that can be followed consistently would greatly simplify the selection process; however, circumstances may require exceptions to be made. The following sections describe environmental factors that affect the selection process.

## Legal Considerations

As previously described, human resource management is greatly influenced by legislation, executive orders, and court decisions. Hiring managers must have extensive knowledge of the legal aspects of selection. It is important for them to see the relationship between useful and legally defensible selection tools. Although interpretation of legislation by the courts and federal agencies has often created controversy and been met with opposition by the private sector, the *intent* of federal legislation is generally not at odds with good business sense.

## Speed of Decision Making

The time available to make the selection decision can also have a major effect on the selection process. Suppose, for instance, that the production manager for a manufacturing firm comes to the human resource manager's office and says, "My only quality control inspectors just had a fight and both resigned. I can't operate until those positions are filled." In this instance speed is crucial and a few phone calls, two brief interviews, and a prayer may constitute the entire selection procedure. On the other hand, conducting a national search to select a chief executive officer may take months. In bureaucracies, the selection process often requires a considerable amount of time. However, as discussed in a later section, if the selection process takes too long, the best candidates will be working for another, more efficient employer.

## Organizational Hierarchy

Different approaches to selection are generally taken for filling positions at varying levels in the organization. For instance, consider the differences in hiring a chief executive officer and a person to fill a clerical position. Extensive background checks and interviewing would be conducted for the executive position. On the other hand, an applicant for a clerical position would most likely take a word processing test and perhaps have a short employment interview.

## Applicant Pool

The number of qualified applicants for a particular job can also affect the selection process. The process can be truly selective only if there are several qualified applicants. Yet only a few applicants with the required skills may be available. The selection process then becomes a matter of choosing from whoever is at hand. Expansion and contraction of the labor market also exert considerable influence on availability, and thus, the selection process. This was the problem confronting many businesses in the spring of 2000, when the unemployment rate was under 4 percent—the lowest in over three decades.

The number of people hired for a particular job compared to the individuals in the applicant pool is often expressed as a **selection ratio**, or

$$\text{Selection ratio} = \frac{\text{Number of open positions}}{\text{Number of available applicants}}$$

**Selection ratio**
The number of people hired for a particular job compared to the total number of individuals in the applicant pool.

A selection ratio of 1.00 indicates that there is only one qualified applicant for each position. An effective selection process is impossible if this situation exists. People who might otherwise be rejected are often hired. The lower the ratio falls below 1.00, the more alternatives the manager has in making a selection decision. For example, a selection ratio of 0.10 indicates that there are 10 qualified applicants for each position.

## Type of Organization

The sector of the economy in which individuals are to be employed—private, governmental, or not for profit—can also affect the selection process. A business in the private sector is heavily profit oriented. Prospective employees are screened with regard to how they can help achieve profit goals. Consideration of the total individual, including personality factors that are job related, is involved in the selection of future employees for this sector.

Government civil service systems typically identify qualified applicants through competitive examinations. Often a manager is allowed to select from among only the top three applicants for a position. A manager in this sector frequently does not have the prerogative of interviewing other applicants.

Individuals being considered for positions in not-for-profit organizations (such as the Boy Scouts, Girl Scouts, YMCA, or YWCA) confront still a different situation. The salary level may not be competitive with those of private and governmental organizations. Therefore, a person who fills one of these positions must be not only qualified but also dedicated to this type of work.

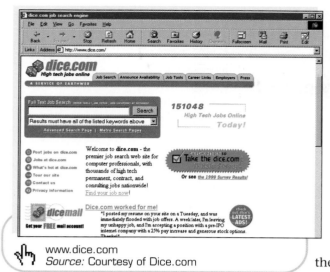

www.dice.com
*Source:* Courtesy of Dice.com

## Probationary Period

Many firms use a probationary period that permits them to evaluate an employee's ability based on established performance. This practice may be either a substitute for certain phases of the selection process or a check on the validity of the process. The rationale is that if an individual can successfully perform the job during the probationary period, other selection tools are not needed. In any event, newly hired employees should be monitored to determine whether the hiring decision was a good one.

Even in unionized firms, a new employee typically is not protected by the union-management agreement until after a certain probationary period. This period is typically from 60 to 90 days. During that time, an employee may be terminated with little or no justification. Terminating a marginal employee may prove to be quite difficult after the probationary period. When a firm is unionized, it becomes especially important for the selection process to identify the most productive workers. Once the probationary period is completed, workers are under the union-management agreement and its terms must be followed in changing the status of a worker.

## THE SELECTION PROCESS

Figure 7-1 illustrates a generalized selection process that may vary by organization. It typically begins with the preliminary interview, after which obviously unqualified candidates are quickly rejected. Next, applicants complete the firm's application for employment. Then, they progress through a series of selection tests, the employment interview, and reference and background checks. The successful applicant receives a company physical examination. The individual is employed if results of the physical examination are satisfactory. The environmental factors previously

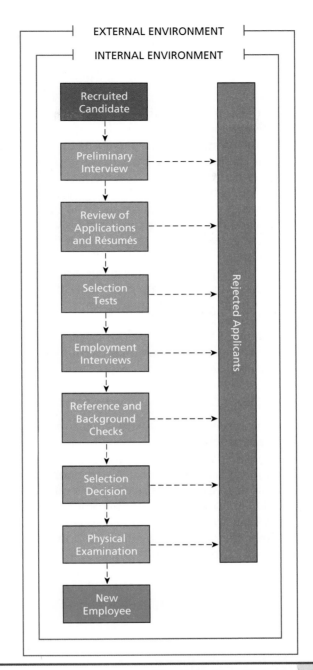

**The Selection Process**   **Figure 7-1**

---

▶ *Prescreening*

**www.prenhall.com/mondy**

Prescreening for a productive, dependable, customer- and sales-oriented work-force is briefly reviewed.

mentioned impact the selection process, and the manager must take them into account in making selection decisions.

## THE PRELIMINARY INTERVIEW

The selection process often begins with a preliminary interview. The basic purpose of this initial screening of applicants is to eliminate those who obviously do not meet the position's requirements. At this stage, the interviewer asks a few straightforward questions. For instance, a position may require a specific certification such as certified public accountant (CPA). If the interview determines that the candidate is not so certified, any further discussion regarding this particular position wastes time for both the firm and the applicant.

In addition to eliminating obviously unqualified job applicants quickly, a preliminary interview may produce other positive benefits for the firm. It is possible the position for which the applicant applied is not the only one available. A skilled interviewer will know about other vacancies in the firm and may be able to steer the prospective employee to another position. For instance, a skilled interviewer may decide that an applicant is not a good fit for the applications-engineering job that requires contact with customers but is an excellent candidate for an internal R&D position.[5] This type of interviewing not only builds goodwill for the firm but also can maximize recruitment and selection effectiveness. The types of preliminary interviews are discussed next.

### Telephone Interview

Organizations are always struggling to keep selection costs down. While there is nothing new in using telephone interviews, they are now being considered more carefully. This method obviously lacks the advantages of face-to-face contact. For example, it is not possible to observe nonverbal cues from the candidate that may give hints to aspects of the candidate's interpersonal skills.[6] Also, while the interviewer cannot be biased by the candidate's physical appearance, the candidate's voice—particularly any regional accent—may have a greater effect.[7] Nevertheless, the telephone may be the most economically feasible way to exchange information with applicants in distant locations. In addition, a larger number of candidates can be screened using this method.

### Videotaped Interview

A videotaped interview is another method that may be used to reduce selection costs and fit some situations. Consulting firms that have many interviewers available throughout the nation are available to assist with this method. Using a structured interview format designed by the hiring firm, the interviewer can videotape the candidate's responses. To assure standardized treatment of other similarly conducted interviews, the interviewer may not interact with the candidate, but only repeat the question, if necessary. The videotaped interview has definite shortcomings and is not intended to replace personal interviews. However, as with the telephone interview, it does allow a firm to conduct a broader search and get more people involved in the selection process.[8]

### Computer Interview

At times, the computer is used for interviewing. A major clothing manufacturer used computer-assisted interviewing to screen out inappropriate applicants. This approach saved the firm $2.4 million during a three-year period by reducing turnover from 87 to 51 percent.[9]

Coopers & Lybrand is the first firm to put its computer-assisted interviewing system on the Internet, using a Web site called Springboard. Students in the business areas of accounting, auditing, and computers can complete an employment application and four screening modules at their convenience by accessing the Web site. The program compares a student's work preferences and education with results from studies of the firm's culture and the profiles of its most successful partners and managers. It helps students determine whether Coopers & Lybrand would be the right fit for a career and enables recruiters to focus on candidates most likely to succeed at the firm.[10]

www.resume-center.com
*Source:* Courtesy of Resume-Center.com

## REVIEW OF APPLICATIONS

Another early step in the selection process, which may either precede or follow the preliminary interview, is having the prospective employee complete an application for employment. The employer then evaluates it to see whether there is an apparent match between the individual and the position. A well-designed and properly used application form can be helpful since essential information is included and presented in a standardized format (see Figure 7-2). Applications may not be required for many management and professional positions. In these cases, a firm will most likely deal with the résumé, which was discussed in the previous chapter.

The specific information requested on an application for employment may vary from firm to firm, and even by job type within an organization. An application form typically contains sections for name, address, telephone number, military service, education, and work history. Preprinted statements that are very important when the applicant signs the form include certification that everything on the form is true; if not, the candidate can be released. When not prohibited by state law, the form should also state that the position is *employment at will* and that the employer or the employee can terminate employment at any time for any reason or no reason. Finally, the form should contain a statement whereby the candidate gives permission to have his or her references checked.

An employment application form must reflect not only the firm's informational needs but also EEO requirements. Conoco provides an example of a well-designed application form (see Figure 7-2). Notice the following statement in the employee release and privacy section: "I agree and understand that any employment which may be offered to me will not be for any definite period of time and that such employment is subject to termination by me or by Conoco Inc. at any time, with or without cause." Potentially discriminatory questions inquiring about such factors as gender, race, age, and number of children living at home do not appear on the form.

The information contained in a completed application for employment is compared to the job description to determine whether a potential match exists between the firm's requirements and the applicant's qualifications. As you might

## Application for Employment

Application No. **125413**

**Equal Employment Opportunity**—It is our policy to provide equal employment opportunity throughout the Company for all qualified persons without regard to race, color, religion, age, sex, national origin, disability, or veteran status.

**Instructions**
• **Please print in black ink or type information.**

| Name (Last, First, Middle) | Are you over 18 years of age? ☐ Yes ☐ No | Social Security Number |
|---|---|---|

| Present Address (Street, City, State, ZIP Code) | Phone Number (Area Code First) ( ) |
|---|---|

| Permanent Address (Street, City, State, ZIP Code) | Phone Number (Area Code First) ( ) |
|---|---|

| Date Available for Employment | Employment Desired ☐ Temporary ☐ Regular, Full-Time | Would you accept temporary employment? ☐ Yes ☐ No | Will you perform shift work? ☐ Yes ☐ No |
|---|---|---|---|

| Position Desired—First Preference | Second Preference |
|---|---|

| Geographical Location Preferred | Geographical Location Where You Will Not Consider Employment |
|---|---|

| Will you work overtime? ☐ Yes ☐ No | Are you legally authorized to work in the United States on a regular, full-time basis? ☐ Yes ☐ No |
|---|---|

Have you been previously employed by Conoco?
☐ No ☐ Yes   If yes, where _____ when _____

Do you have relatives currently employed by Conoco?
☐ No ☐ Yes   If yes, Name _____

Relationship _____ Department _____ Location _____

If you are presently employed, may we contact your employer for a reference?
☐ Yes ☐ No

**Indicate Source Which Referred You**

☐ Campus Placement Office   ☐ Walk-in   ☐ Private Employment Agency   ☐ Published Advertisement
☐ Employee Referral   ☐ Write-In   ☐ Governmental Employment Agency   ☐ Other (Specify)
   ☐ Rehire

**Employment Record** (List below your employment in reverse chronological order. Include part-time and summer experience)

| From Mo./Yr | To Mo./Yr | / | / | / | / | / | / | / | / |
|---|---|---|---|---|---|---|---|---|---|
| Employer | | | | | | | | | |
| Address | | | | | | | | | |
| | | | | | | | | | |
| Supervisor's Name and Telephone No. (Area Code First) | | ( ) | ( ) | | ( ) | | ( ) | | |
| Position(s) Held | | | | | | | | | |
| Reason for Leaving | | | | | | | | | |

Identify and explain any time lapses in your above employment record.

**Figure 7-2** 🖱 **An Application for Employment: Conoco, Inc.**
*Source:* Courtesy of Conoco, Inc.

| Education—Circle Highest Grade Completed<br>1  2  3  4  5  6  7  8  9  10  11  12 | Course of Study<br>Major—Minor | Degree<br>Received | Grade Average | | Degree<br>Date |
|---|---|---|---|---|---|
| | | | Overall | Major | |
| High School Attended and Location | | Diploma<br>☐ Yes<br>☐ No | | | |
| Vocational or Technical School Attended | | Completed<br>☐ Yes<br>☐ No | | | |
| College or University | | | | | |
| College or University | | | | | |
| College or University | | | | | |

Other—1) Include information you believe is important, such as: special training, apprenticeships completed, military experience, other education, or foreign language fluency.

—2) List those machines and/or equipment you are qualified to operate and any other skills you possess.

—3) Titles of these and special research projects.

**Completion of this section is optional.**

Conoco Inc. is a government contractor subject to Section 503 of the Rehabilitation Act and Section 402 of the Veterans Readjustment Act. As such, we must take affirmative action to employ and advance in employment individuals with disabilities, special disabled veterans, and veterans of the Vietnam era. If you are such an individual and would like to be considered under the affirmative action program, please indicate below.

☐ I am a **special disabled veteran** because **either:** (1) I am entitled to compensation under VA law for disability rated at 30% or more, or for disability rated at 10% or 20% for a serious employment handicap; **or** (2) I was discharged or released from active duty because of a service-connected disability.

☐ I am a **veteran of the Vietnam era** because part or all of my active military service occured between 8/5/64 and 5/7/75 **and either:** (1) I was on active duty for more than 180 days and my discharge or release was not dishonorable; **or** (2) I was discharged or released from active duty because of a service-connected disability.

**Submission of this information is voluntary,** and disclosure or refusal to provide it will not subject you to adverse treatment. This information shall be used only as allowed by law and shall be kept confidential except that (i) supervisors and managers may be informed about restrictions on work or job duties and necessary accommodations, (ii) first aid or safety personnel may be informed where appropriate in case of an emergency, and (iii) government officials investigating compliance with the law shall be informed.

You may omit references in this section which you feel might reveal age, race, color, sex, national origin, or handicap.

Name and description of scholastic honors received including scholarships.

Name honorary, technical and professional organizations of which you have been a member, or other extracurricular activities in which you have participated, including offices held. (List professional licenses held.)

This form will usually provide the necessary information. It may be supplemented, however, by a letter or personal resume.

**PLEASE READ THE FOLLOWING CAREFULLY BEFORE SIGNING.**

I authorize any third parties, including former employers, schools, law enforcement authorities, and any persons named above, to give to Conoco Inc. any information they may have regarding me and my background, whether or not such information is contained in written records. I hereby release these third parties from all liability for any damage whatsoever for providing information to Conoco Inc. in connection with this application. I also release Conoco Inc., its agents, employees, and representatives from any liability in connection with their collection and use of information obtained from third parties during the application process. I certify that all information furnished in this application, signed and dated by me this date, is true and complete to the best of my knowledge and belief and that falsification or omission of information requested in this application or in the application process shall be grounds for disqualification from further consideration or for termination.

I understand that if an employment offer is extended, I may be required to undergo a physical examination and/or drug screen test at the expense of Conoco Inc. I further understand that if I do not successfully complete the physical examination or drug screen test, Conoco Inc. may refuse to hire me, and I agree to hold Conoco Inc. harmless for such refusal. I also understand that employment is conditional on my ability to verify my identity and eligibility for employment as required by the Immigration Reform and Control Act of 1986.

I agree and understand that any employment which may be offered to me will not be for any definite period of time and that such employment is subject to termination by me or by Conoco Inc. at any time, with or without cause. I also agree and understand that nothing contained in this application nor any verbal statements made during the application process or during my employment shall be deemed to constitute an employment contract between me and Conoco Inc.

| Signature | Date |
|---|---|

12-21 (R), 3-92

**An Application for Employment: Conoco Inc. (*continued*)**   **Figure 7-2**

expect, this comparison is often difficult. Applicants frequently attempt to present themselves in an exaggerated, somewhat unrealistic light, and this often complicates the selection process.

Some companies now have computer terminals in their lobbies on which applicants can complete a job application form. Also, optical scanning programs that can handle the first-level screening of applications may be used. These programs may scan applications for other jobs that the applicants do not know they are qualified to fill. This comprehensive approach reduces the expense of selecting employees.

## ADMINISTRATION OF SELECTION TESTS

Evidence suggests that the use of tests is becoming more prevalent for assessing an applicant's qualifications and potential for success. In one study, more than half of the organizations surveyed require skills tests for hourly jobs. Twenty-three percent of firms use skills tests for management jobseekers.[11] Tests are used more in the public sector than in the private sector and more in medium-sized and large companies than in small companies. Large organizations are likely to have trained specialists to run their testing programs. Employers should be aware that tests might be unintentionally discriminatory. When they exclude a protected category at a significant rate, the test is unlawful unless the employer can show the test is job related for the position in question and consistent with business necessity.[12] The topic of adverse impact was discussed in Chapter 3. Specifics regarding tests are reviewed next.

## Advantages of Selection Tests

Selection testing can be a reliable and accurate means of selecting qualified candidates from a pool of applicants. Each hiring decision will ultimately cost tens of thousands of dollars in salary, training, and benefits. The cost of employment testing is small in comparison, and a successful program will ultimately bolster a firm's bottom line.[13] The main reason organizations use tests is to identify attitudes and job-related skills that cannot be identified in interviews. They are a more efficient way to get at that type of information and may result in an increase in quality of the people hired. This has been true at Cox Communications, a telecommunications company in Rancho Santa Margarita, California. Tests have been used in this firm since 1996 and have proven to be an effective part of its screening process. Tests are used to measure honesty, safety, work values, drug avoidance, customer service skills, and attitude toward supervision.[14]

Some employers favor tests because of deficiencies in other techniques. For example, Hank Plotkin, president and founder of the Plotkin Group in Carlsbad, California, believes that while some financial institutions are obsessed with credit checks, these checks do not reduce the risk of on-the-job theft. He states that "all they show is whether people pay their bills on time. It can't tell you if they pay those bills with stolen money."[15] As with all selection procedures, it is important to identify the essential functions of each job and determine the skills needed to perform it. Selection tests must be job related and must meet the standards outlined in the EEOC's *Uniform Guidelines on Employee Selection Procedures*.

## Potential Problems Using Selection Tests

Job performance is related primarily to an individual's ability and motivation to do the job. Selection tests may accurately predict an applicant's ability to perform the job—the *can do*—but they are less successful in indicating the extent to which the individual will be motivated to perform it—the *will do*. The most successful employees have two things in common: they identify with their firm's goals and they are highly motivated. For one reason or another, many employees with high potential never seem to reach it. The factors related to success on the job are so numerous and complex that selection may always be more of an art than a science.

Test anxiety can also be a problem. Applicants often become quite anxious when confronting yet another hurdle that might eliminate them from consideration. The test administrator's reassuring manner and a well-organized testing operation should serve to reduce this threat. Actually, although a great deal of anxiety is detrimental to test performance, a slight degree is helpful.

The dual problems of hiring unqualified or less qualified candidates and rejecting qualified candidates will continue regardless of the procedures followed. Organizations can minimize such errors through the use of well-developed tests administered by competent professionals. Nevertheless, selection tests rarely, if ever, are perfect predictors. Using even the best test, errors will be made in predicting success. For this reason, tests should not be used alone in the selection process but rather in conjunction with other tools.

## Characteristics of Properly Designed Selection Tests

Properly designed selection tests are standardized, objective, based on sound norms, reliable, and—of utmost importance—valid. We discuss the application of these concepts next.

Standardization. **Standardization** is the uniformity of the procedures and conditions related to administering tests. In order to compare the performance of several applicants on the same test, it is necessary for all to take the test under conditions that are as close to identical as possible. For example, the content of instructions provided and the time allowed must be the same, and the physical environment must be similar. If one person takes a test in a room with jackhammers operating just outside and another takes it in a more tranquil environment, differences in test results are likely.

Objectivity. **Objectivity** in testing is achieved when everyone scoring a test obtains the same results. Multiple-choice and true-false tests are said to be objective. The person taking the test either chooses the correct answer or does not.

Norms. A **norm** is a frame of reference for comparing an applicant's performance with that of others. Specifically, a norm reflects the distribution of many scores obtained by people similar to the applicant being tested. A score by itself is insignificant. It becomes meaningful only when it can be compared with other applicants' scores.

When a sufficient number of employees are performing the same or similar work, employers can standardize their own tests. Typically, this is not the case, and a national norm for a particular test must be used. A prospective employee takes the test, the score obtained is compared to the norm, and the significance of the test score is determined.

Reliability. **Reliability** is the extent to which a selection test provides consistent results. Reliability data reveal the degree of confidence that can be placed in a test. If a test has low reliability, its validity as a predictor will also be low. The existence of reliability does not in itself guarantee validity, however.

**Standardization**
Uniformity of the procedures and conditions related to administering tests.

**Objectivity**
The condition that is achieved when all individuals scoring a given test obtain the same results.

**Norm**
A frame of reference for comparing an applicant's performance with that of others.

**Reliability**
The extent to which a selection test provides consistent results.

Validity. The basic requirement for a selection test is that it be valid. **Validity** is the extent to which a test measures what it is supposed to measure. If a test cannot indicate ability to perform the job, it has no value as a predictor and, if used, will result not only in poor hiring decisions but also a serious legal liability for the employer.

Validity is commonly reported as a correlation coefficient, which summarizes the relationship between two variables. For example, these variables may be the score on a selection test and some measure of employee performance. A coefficient of 0 shows no relationship, while coefficients of either +1.0 or –1.0 indicate a perfect relationship, one positive and the other negative. Naturally, no test will be 100 percent accurate, yet organizations strive for the highest feasible coefficient. If a test is designed to predict job performance, and validity studies of the test indicate a high correlation coefficient, most prospective employees who score high on the test will probably later prove to be high performers.

Employers are not required to validate their selection tests automatically. Generally, validation is required only when the selection process as a whole results in an adverse impact on women or minorities. Validation of selection tests is expensive; however, an organization cannot know whether the test is actually measuring the qualities and abilities being sought without validation.

## TYPES OF VALIDATION STUDIES

The *Uniform Guidelines* established three approaches that may be followed to validate selection tests: criterion-related validity, content validity, and construct validity.

### Criterion-Related Validity

**Criterion-related validity** is determined by comparing the scores on selection tests to some aspect of job performance determined, for example, by performance appraisal. Performance measures might include quantity and quality of work, turnover, and absenteeism. A close relationship between the score on the test and job performance suggests that the test is valid.

The two basic forms of criterion-related validity are concurrent and predictive validity. **Concurrent validity** means the test scores and the criterion data are obtained at essentially the same time. For instance, all currently employed telemarketers may be given a test. Company records contain current information about each employee's job performance. If the test is able to identify productive and less productive workers, one could say that it is valid. A potential problem in using this validation procedure results from changes that may have occurred within the work group. For example, the less productive workers may have been fired, and the more productive employees may have been promoted out of the group.

**Predictive validity** involves administering a test and later obtaining the criterion information. For instance, a test might be administered to all applicants but the test results not used in the selection decision; employees would be hired on the basis of other selection criteria. After employee performance has been observed over a period of time, the test results are analyzed to determine whether they differentiate the successful and less successful employees. Predictive validity is considered to be a technically sound procedure. Because of the time and cost involved, however, its use is often not feasible.

### Content Validity

Although statistical concepts are not involved, many practitioners believe that content validity provides a sensible approach to validating a selection test. **Content validity** is a test validation method whereby a person performs certain tasks that are actually required by the job or completes a paper-and-pencil test that measures relevant job knowledge. Thorough job analysis and carefully prepared job descriptions are needed when this form of validation is used. An example of the use of content validity is giving a data-entering test to an applicant whose primary job would be to enter data. Court decisions have supported the concept of content validity.

## Construct Validity

**Construct validity** is a test validation method that determines whether a test measures certain traits or qualities that are important in performing the job. For instance, if the job requires a high degree of teamwork, a test would be used to measure the applicant's ability to work effectively in teams. Traits or qualities such as teamwork, leadership, and planning or organization ability must first be carefully identified through job analysis. Remember from Chapter 4 that job analysis often determines what traits are needed for the job.

**Construct validity**
A test validation method to determine whether a selection test measures certain traits or qualities that have been identified as important in performing a particular job.

**TOPIC**
### TYPES OF EMPLOYMENT TESTS

Individuals differ in characteristics related to job performance. These differences, which are measurable, relate to cognitive abilities, psychomotor abilities, job knowledge, work samples, vocational interests, and personality. Other tests that may be administered include drug and alcohol testing and genetic testing, which is a controversial issue. Also, Internet testing is being used to test various skills.

## Cognitive Aptitude Tests

**Cognitive aptitude tests** are tests that determine general reasoning ability, memory, vocabulary, verbal fluency, and numerical ability. They may be helpful in identifying job candidates who have extensive knowledge bases. As the content of jobs becomes broader and more fluid, employees must be able to adapt quickly to job changes and rapid technological advances. It is likely that more general selection methods will be needed to determine the broader range of characteristics required for success.

**Cognitive aptitude tests**
Tests that measure general reasoning ability, memory, vocabulary, verbal fluency, and numerical ability.

## Psychomotor Abilities Tests

**Psychomotor abilities tests** measure strength, coordination, and dexterity. The development of tests to determine these abilities has been accelerated by miniaturization in assembly operations. Much of this work is so delicate that magnifying lenses must be used, and the psychomotor abilities required to perform the tasks are critical. Standardized tests are not available to cover all these abilities, but those that are involved in many routine production jobs and some office jobs can be measured.

**Psychomotor abilities tests**
Aptitude tests that measure strength, coordination, and dexterity.

## Job-Knowledge Tests

**Job-knowledge tests** measure a candidate's knowledge of the duties of the job for which he or she is applying. Such tests are commercially available but may also be designed specifically for any job, based on data derived from job analysis.

**Job-knowledge tests**
Tests designed to measure a candidate's knowledge of the duties of the job for which he or she is applying.

## Work-Sample Tests (Simulations)

**Work-sample tests**, or simulations, are tests that require an applicant to perform a task or set of tasks representative of the job. Therefore, such tests by their

**Work-sample tests**
Tests requiring an applicant to perform a task or set of tasks that are representative of a particular job.

nature are job related. Not surprisingly, the evidence to date concerning this type of test is that it produces a high predictive validity, reduces adverse impact, and is more acceptable to applicants. If a position requires writing quickly on short deadlines, for example, a simulation would require the applicant to take a writing test. The applicant can then demonstrate his or her ability to write satisfactorily under the pressure imposed by time and the interview environment itself. A real test with validity, in the opinion of some experts, should be a performance assessment: Take individuals to a job and give them the opportunity to perform it.[16]

## Vocational Interest Tests

**Vocational interest tests** indicate the occupation a person is most interested in and likely to receive satisfaction from. These tests compare the individual's interests with those of successful employees in a specific job. Although interest tests may have application in employee selection, their primary use has been in counseling and vocational guidance.

## Personality Tests

**Personality tests** are self-reported measures of traits, temperaments, or dispositions. Because American businesses lose from $15 to $25 billion per year from employee theft, personality tests—especially those measuring honesty and integrity—are being used more frequently.[17] Personality tests have also been used to identify individuals who are highly motivated, flexible, and able to work well in teams. Some firms use these tests to classify personality types. With this information, firms can create diverse teams for creativity or homogeneous teams for compatibility. The use of personality tests as selection tools has been controversial because they lack face validity. Nevertheless, a study indicated that the use of personality tests was on the rise. Eighteen percent of the responding firms ask hourly workers to take a personality test, and 22 percent of the firms ask managers to take one.[18]

### Drug and Alcohol Testing

Few issues generate more controversy today than drug testing. And drug and alcohol abuse are definitely workplace issues. According to the federal government, about 71 percent of alcohol and drug abusers are employed.[19] Since most individuals in our country work for small businesses, the problem for these organizations is particularly acute since they often lack the resources for drug testing.

Proponents of drug testing programs contend that they are necessary to ensure workplace safety, security, and productivity. The U.S. Postal Service did a study in which it tracked both employees who passed its drug test and those who failed. Drug users were found to be absent 66 percent more and spent 84 percent more on health benefits. They were also disciplined more often and had a significantly higher turnover rate.[20] Drug testing is viewed as an accurate measure of drug use and a means to deter it. Critics of drug testing argue just as vigorously that drug testing is an unjustifiable intrusion into private lives.

Although the controversy remains, along with legal questions, it appears that drug testing is becoming more commonplace in the United States. Even so, U.S. drug testing reveals only about a two to six percent positive rate among tested applicants. This low rate is partially attributed to the fact that many applicants who use hard drugs avoid their use for several days prior to the test. In addition, there are several well-publicized and easily available means of eluding positive urine test results.[21] One creative approach to beating the test comes from an individual who, for $69 plus postage, sells five ounces of his urine in a small plastic bag, along with 30 inches of plastic tubing and a tiny heat pack designed to keep the fluid at body temperature. By taping it to his or her body, an individual is able to substitute this urine during workplace drug testing.[22]

In addition to concerns about privacy, some employers worry that applicants denied employment after taking drug tests may seek protection as persons with a disability under the American with Disabilities Act. The act, however, is actually supportive of testing when it is carefully performed. Persons engaging in the illegal use of drugs are excluded from the act's definition of *qualified individual with a disability*. It is important to note, however, that persons who have successfully completed or are participating in a supervised drug-rehabilitation program and who no longer engage in illegal drug use are not automatically excluded from this definition.

Preemployment alcohol testing may also be accomplished by means of breath, urine, blood, saliva, or hair samples. The method of choice by law enforcement agencies and the transportation industry is breath alcohol analysis. However, most experts regard blood tests as the forensic benchmark against which others should be compared. The problem with this approach is that it is an invasive method and requires trained personnel for administration and analysis. The use of hair samples is unique in that drug traces will remain in the hair and will not likely diminish over time. While urine and blood testing can detect only current drug use, makers of hair sample analysis claim it can detect drug use from 3 days to 90 days after drug consumption. This would prohibit an applicant from beating the test by short-term abstinence. From a prospective employee's viewpoint, hair testing may be less embarrassing than a urine test. For example, it is pretty humiliating to hear, "We're happy to have you on board. Here, will you take this cup and fill it?"[23]

There is controversy as to which type of testing is preferable and most effective. However, an American Medical Association study revealed that 92 percent of testing companies use urine sampling, 15 percent use blood sampling, 2 percent use hair sampling, and 2 percent use nonmedical performance testing. From the statistics, it is obvious that some companies use multiple methods.[24]

Prevalence of drug and alcohol testing varies across industry groups. Mining and construction have the highest prevalence of drug testing (69.6 percent) and finance, real estate, and insurance have the lowest (22.6 percent). Communications, utilities, and transportation have the highest alcohol testing rates (34.9 percent) and finance, real estate, and insurance industries have the lowest rates (7.8 percent).[25]

Failure to test for drugs can have a disastrous effect. For instance, Cake for You is a small specialty bakery. Its service includes delivering wedding cakes to reception sites. In hiring a delivery driver, Cake for You owners were always careful to determine that the potential candidate had a valid driver's license. The owners were quite pleased with their new employee, Mike. He was prompt, neatly attired, and seemed to have a pleasant demeanor. Unfortunately, while making a delivery one morning, Mike was involved in—and in fact caused—a four-vehicle accident that resulted in one fatality. During the course of the investigation it was discovered that Mike was "high" on marijuana. Had the owners of the firm included drug testing as part of their screening process, they might not be facing a huge lawsuit.[26]

## Genetic Testing

As genetic research progresses, confirmed links between specific gene mutations and diseases are emerging. Scientists have assembled the entire set of genetic instructions for building a human body; world leaders likened this achievement to putting a human being on the moon.[27] This announcement brings both hope and concerns to the forefront in employment testing.

**Genetic testing** determines whether a person carries the gene mutation for certain diseases, including heart disease, colon cancer, breast cancer, and Huntington's disease.[28] Gene tests may predict a predisposition to having a disease. Usually such tests cannot tell whether a person is certain to get the disease or would become ill at age 30 or 90. In addition, everyone has some disposition to genetic disease, and a genetic predisposition is not the same as a preexisting condition. Protective laws recognize that there is a difference between a present medical condition and a genetic tendency towards a certain illness.[29] Nevertheless, a survey conducted by the American Management Association indicated that from 6 to 10 percent of employers were conducting genetic tests.[30]

There are two primary reasons for genetic testing. Predictive testing allows employers to reject certain employees and maintain a more productive workforce. It also enables therapeutic intervention, allowing carriers to get appropriate therapy. The major concerns about genetic testing all relate to possible misuse of information. The process is perceived as being highly invasive and communicating to employees that the firm really does not care about them.[31] Also, once the results of a genetic test are in a medical record, they may be made available to employers and insurers without an individual's knowledge or consent.

Guidelines issued by the EEOC interpreted the Americans with Disabilities Act as covering discrimination on the basis of genetic information. In addition, states have begun to act. Twelve states have passed laws against genetic discrimination in employment, and similar bills are pending in at least 13 more. Several bills on genetic privacy issues have been introduced in Congress, but no action has yet been taken. However, an executive order applicable to every aspect of federal employment was issued in 2000 that prohibits discrimination against employees based on genetic information.[32]

## Internet Testing

The Internet is increasingly being used to test various skills required by applicants. For example, a new type of Web service is available that tests job applicants on their alleged technical abilities. Know It All, Inc. in Philadelphia ([www.proveit.com](www.proveit.com)) and New Art Technologies in Edgewater, New Jersey, ([www.test-and-train.com](www.test-and-train.com)) offer job-skills testing as a service to firms that lack the resources to evaluate candidates on their own. For less than $100 per prospect, you can confirm job candidates' skills online without ever laying eyes on them. The tests are not merely pass-fail, but rather measure applicants' skill levels.[33]

## THE EMPLOYMENT INTERVIEW

The **employment interview** is a goal-oriented conversation in which the interviewer and applicant exchange information. Historically, interviews have not been shown to be valid predictors of success on the job. Nevertheless, they continue to be the primary method companies use to evaluate applicants. As we discuss later in the chapter, some firms have made progress in improving the validity of interviews. The employment interview is especially significant because the applicants who reach this stage are the survivors. They have endured the preliminary interview and scored satisfactorily on selection tests. At this point, the candidates appear to be qualified, at least on paper. Every seasoned manager knows,

## ▶ Graphoanalysis (Handwriting Analysis)

In the United States, handwriting analysis is often put in the same context as psychic readings or astrology. In Europe, however, a large number of employers use graphoanalysis to help screen and place job applicants. For example, over 80 percent of employers in Israel and Switzerland use graphoanalysis, and in France the percentage of employers using the technique is almost as high.

There are two distinct schools of handwriting analysis: the gestalt theory, developed in Germany, and the trait method, developed mainly in France, England, and the United States. The latter method examines handwriting for certain defined traits such as how people cross their "ts" or make loops for letters such as "ls."

Although no definitive study has been done on the extent of its use in the United States, according to some handwriting experts, graphoanalysis is becoming more common. A basic reason for the reluctance of U.S. employers to use this approach appears to be a concern over the ability to validate such tests. This and the worry about possible legal action seem to make many American employers wary of the process.[34]

however, that appearances can be quite misleading. Additional information is needed to indicate whether the individual is willing to work and can adapt to that particular organization.

## Interview Planning

Interview planning is essential to effective employment interviews. A primary consideration should be the speed in which the process occurs. Many studies have demonstrated that the top candidates for nearly any job are hired and off the job market within anywhere from 1 to 10 days.[35] It is imperative that interview scheduling be done with this in mind.

The physical location of the interview should be both pleasant and private, providing for a minimum of interruptions. The interviewer should possess a pleasant personality, empathy, and the ability to listen and communicate effectively. He or she should become familiar with the applicant's qualifications by reviewing the data collected from other selection tools. As preparation for the interview, a job profile should be developed based on the job description. After job requirements have been listed, it is helpful to have an interview checklist that includes these hints:

▶ Compare an applicant's application and résumé with job requirements.

▶ Develop questions related to the qualities sought.

▶ Prepare a step-by-step plan to present the position, company, division, and department.

▶ Determine how to ask for examples of past applicant behavior, not what future behavior might be.

▶ Interviews continue to be the primary method companies use to evaluate new applicants.

# Content of the Interview

Both the interviewer and the candidate have agendas for the interview. After establishing rapport with the applicant, the interviewer seeks additional job-related information to complement data provided by other selection tools. The interview permits clarification of certain points, the uncovering of additional information, and the elaboration of data needed to make a sound selection decision. The interviewer should provide information about the company, the job, and expectations of the candidate. However, candidates who do not check the firm's Web site, stock performance, and annual report are foolish, according to Sean Sweeney, president of the Mid-Atlantic Association of Personnel Consultants.[36] Other areas typically included in the interview are discussed next.

**Occupational Experience.** The interviewer will explore the candidate's knowledge, skills, abilities, and willingness to handle responsibility. Although successful performance in one job does not guarantee success in another, it does provide an indication of the person's ability and willingness to work.

**Academic Achievement.** In the absence of significant work experience, a person's academic record takes on greater importance. A grade point average, however, should be considered in light of other factors; for example, involvement in work or extracurricular activities may have affected an applicant's grades.

**Interpersonal Skills.** An individual may possess important technical skills significant to accomplishing a job; however, if the person cannot work well with others, chances for success are slim. This is especially true in today's world with the increasing use of teams. According to Atlanta-based R. Wendell Williams, managing director of the Emergenetics Consulting Group, the biggest mistake an interviewee can make is thinking that people are hired only for their technical skills. He says that the personal impact made on the recruiter is equally important.[37]

**Personal Qualities.** Personal qualities normally observed during the interview include physical appearance, speaking ability, vocabulary, poise, adaptability, and assertiveness. As with all selection criteria, these attributes should be considered only if they are relevant to job performance, however.

**Organizational Fit.** A hiring criterion not prominently mentioned in the literature is *organizational fit*. Using fit as a criterion raises legal and diversity questions, and perhaps this explains the low profile. Nevertheless, there is evidence that it is used in making selection decisions.

**Organizational fit**
Management's perception of the degree to which the prospective employee will fit in with the firm's culture or value system.

    **Organizational fit** refers to management's perception of the degree to which the prospective employee will fit in with the firm's culture or value system. Dr. Elisabeth Marx, director of Norman Broadbent International, executive recruitment consultants, is familiar with many instances where a company has failed to match a candidate to its culture. The result is that the working relationship ends with the candidate's dismissal or hasty departure.[38] Russell Yaquinto, who coaches managerial jobseekers for the outplacement firm Right Management Consultants in Dallas, states that, "There's very widespread agreement . . . that you can have the credentials, but if you aren't going to fit [the culture], it doesn't matter. Before long, you'll be out of there."[39] This may be especially true for CEOs, because it seems that they are getting the boot faster than ever. Chief executives at Coca-Cola, Global Crossing, Campbell Soup, and British Airways all exited their firms after a short tenure. Why the fast exodus? Time and again the boards of directors are not selecting executives who *fit*. If you can define the culture, you can hire for it, and many businesses today are investing time and effort in doing just that.[40]

**Candidates' Objectives.** It is important to remember that interviewees also have objectives for the interview. One objective might be to determine what the firm is willing to pay as a starting salary. A recent survey conducted by the Society for Human Resource Management indicated that 8 out of 10 recruiters were willing to negotiate pay and benefits with job applicants. However, only one-third of the job applicants surveyed said they felt comfortable negotiating.[41] Jobseekers have other goals that may include the following:

- To be listened to and understood
- To have ample opportunity to present their qualifications
- To be treated fairly and with respect
- To gather information about the job and the company
- To make an informed decision concerning the desirability of the job

The specific content of employment interviews varies greatly by organizational strategic mission and the nature of the job. For example, David Pritchard, director of recruiting for Microsoft, has stated, "The best thing we can do for our competitors is hire poorly." Two of the things Microsoft looks for in a candidate are intelligence and experience. But it also wants to know what a prospective employee will bring to the firm in the long term. Because of the dynamic nature of the industry, where things change virtually daily, Microsoft must have people who are flexible and capable of learning new things.[42]

After the interview is concluded, the interviewer must determine whether the candidate is suitable for the open position. If the conclusion is positive, the process continues; if there appears to be no match, the candidate is eliminated from consideration.

# TYPES OF INTERVIEWS

"Tell me about yourself" was a standard question asked in interviews during the 1980s. However, it has become quite outdated. Even if it or a similar question is asked, it is likely to be followed up by more probing questions in a variety of interview approaches.[43] Interviews may be broadly classified as structured or unstructured. The differences between these two formats are discussed next.

## The Unstructured (Nondirective) Interview

An **unstructured interview** is one in which the interviewer asks probing, open-ended questions. This type of interview is comprehensive, and the interviewer encourages the applicant to do much of the talking. The nondirective interview is often more time consuming than structured interviews and results in obtaining different information from different candidates. This adds to the potential legal woes of organizations using this approach. Compounding the problem is the likelihood of ill-advised, potentially discriminatory information being discussed. The applicant who is being encouraged to pour his heart out may volunteer information that the interviewer does not need or want to know. Unsuccessful applicants subjected to this interviewing approach may later claim in court that the reason for their failure to get the job was the employer's use of this information. Angela Baron, policy adviser at the Institute of Personnel and Development (IPD), voices this opinion: "Untrained interviewers who hold unstructured interviews might just as well be tossing a coin."[44]

**Unstructured interview**
A meeting with a job applicant during which the interviewer asks probing, open-ended questions.

# The Structured (Directive or Patterned) Interview

**Structured interview**
A process in which an interviewer consistently presents the same series of job-related questions to each applicant for a particular job.

The **structured interview** is a series of job-related questions that are consistently asked of each applicant for a particular job. Although interviews have historically been very poor predictors for making selection decisions, use of structured interviews increases reliability and accuracy by reducing the subjectivity and inconsistency of unstructured interviews.

A structured job interview typically contains four types of questions.

▶ *Situational questions* are those that pose a typical job situation to determine what the applicant did in a similar situation.

▶ *Job-knowledge questions* are those that probe the applicant's job-related knowledge; these questions may relate to basic educational skills or complex scientific or managerial skills.

▶ *Job-sample simulation questions* involve situations in which an applicant may be required to actually perform a sample task from the job.

▶ *Worker requirements questions* are those that seek to determine the applicant's willingness to conform to the requirements of the job. For example, the interviewer may ask whether the applicant is willing to perform repetitive work or move to another city.

## Behavioral Interviews

**Behavioral interview**
A structured interview that uses questions designed to probe the candidate's past behavior in specific situations.

The **behavioral interview** is a structured interview that uses questions designed to probe the candidate's past behavior in specific situations. The technique is derived from the work of industrial psychologist Bill Owens, who suggested that past behavior is the best predictor of future behavior.[45] It has become a primary interviewing tool. The reason for behavioral interviewing's rise, according to Marc Blessing, vice president of the Cleveland search and recruiting firm Management Recruiters International Inc., is that the older methods have proven to be rotten predictors of a candidate's success.[46] The premise that past behavior is the best predictor of future behavior avoids having to make judgments about applicants' personalities and precludes hypothetical and self-evaluative questions.

In the behavioral interview, the situational behaviors are carefully selected for their relevance to job success. Questions are formed from the behaviors by asking applicants how they performed in the described situation. For example, a candidate for an engineering position might be asked, "Tell me about a time when you had to make an important decision without having all the information you needed." Benchmark answers derived from behaviors of successful employees are prepared for use in rating applicant responses. A candidate's response to a given situation provides the means to develop an insight into his or her job potential. Behavioral interviewing allows candidates to unwittingly reveal information about their attitudes, intelligence, and truthfulness. Arrogance, lack of cooperation with team members, and anger can all spill out during such an interview. While some candidates may think the interview is all about technical skills, it's as much about them as anything. This aspect of a candidate is important, as evidenced in one study's finding that 97 percent of job failures could be attributed, not to technical deficiencies, but to personality clashes.[47]

Developing a behavior-based interview would likely include these steps:[48]

▶ Analyze the job to determine the knowledge, skills, abilities, and behaviors important for job success.

- Determine which behavioral questions to ask about the particular job to elicit the desired behaviors.
- Develop a structured format tailored for each job.
- Set benchmark responses: examples of *good, average,* and *bad* answers to questions.
- Train the interviewers.

Questions asked in behavior description interviewing are legally safe since they are job related. Equally important, since both questions and answers are related to successful job performance, they are more accurate in predicting whether applicants will be successful in the job they are hired to perform. Research indicates that while traditional interviewing has a success rate of about 14 percent, behavioral interviewing has a success rate of around 55 percent.[49]

A rating scale may be helpful in comparing several candidates. The same individuals who develop the interview questions can determine the appropriate responses for each level of the scale. These people are thoroughly familiar with the job for which the interview was developed. The scale may have only three levels; for example, 5—Excellent (responses that reflect probable success); 3—Marginal (probable difficulty in performing the task); and 1—Poor (probable failure). A total score for each applicant can then be obtained.[50] A positive feature of behavioral interviewing is its ability to serve as a tiebreaker. When several candidates appear to possess similar skills, experiences, and qualifications, this technique can help select the one who is most likely to excel in the job. It answers the one question both the hiring manager and the candidate want to know most: Is this a good *fit?*[51]

Although behavioral interviewing was once used exclusively for senior executive positions, it is now a popular technique for lower-level positions. At CIGNA Corporation, headquartered in Philadelphia, all candidates for positions hired through the company's corporate staffing department undergo behavioral interviewing. Whether applying for a clerical or management position, each candidate will be put through the process.[52]

One fly in the ointment for behavioral interviewing is that some jobseekers have gotten wise to the process. A growing number of candidates, especially those coming from business and law schools, deliberately misrepresent themselves during the interview. The stories some tell about who they are and what they did in real-life situations are pure fiction.[53]

## METHODS OF INTERVIEWING

Interviews may be conducted in several ways. The level of the position to be filled and the labor market to be tapped determine the most appropriate approach. The methods of interviewing are discussed next.

## One-on-One Interview

In a typical employment interview, the applicant meets one-on-one with an interviewer. As the interview may be a highly emotional occasion for the applicant, meeting alone with the interviewer is often less threatening. The environment this method provides may allow an effective exchange of information to take place.

## Group Interview

In a **group interview**, several applicants interact in the presence of one or more company representatives. This approach, while not mutually exclusive of other

**Group interview**
A meeting in which several job applicants interact in the presence of one or more company representatives.

interview types, may provide useful insights into the candidates' interpersonal competence as they engage in a group discussion. Another advantage of this technique is that it saves time for busy professionals and executives.

## Board Interview

**Board interview**
A meeting in which one candidate is interviewed by several representatives of a company.

In a **board interview**, several of the firm's representatives interview one candidate. At Texas Instruments, the prospective employee is interviewed by the potential hire's peers, subordinates, and supervisors. James Mitchell, vice president of corporate staff, claims that using multiple interviewers not only leads to better hiring decisions, it also begins the transition process. The candidate has learned a lot about the company, the strong team culture, its people, and the job by the time interviewing is completed.[54]

## Stress Interview

**Stress interview**
A form of interview that intentionally creates anxiety to determine how a job applicant will react in certain types of situations.

Most interview sessions are designed to minimize stress on the part of the candidate. In the **stress interview**, however, anxiety is intentionally created to determine how an applicant will react to stress on the job. The interviewer deliberately makes the candidate uncomfortable by asking blunt and often discourteous questions. The purpose is to determine the applicant's tolerance for stress. Knowledge of this factor may be important if the job requires the ability to deal with a high level of stress. While some degree of stress may be felt in any job, it seems clear that the stress interview is not appropriate for the majority of situations.

## Realistic Job Previews

Many applicants have unrealistic expectations about the prospective job and employer. This inaccurate perception may have negative consequences, yet it is often encouraged when interviewers paint false, rosy pictures of the job and company. This practice leads to mismatches of people and positions. The problem is compounded when candidates exaggerate their own qualifications. To correct this situation from the employer's side, a realistic job preview should be given to applicants early in the selection process and definitely before a job offer is made.

**Realistic job preview (RJP)**
A method of conveying both positive and negative job information to an applicant in an unbiased manner.

A **realistic job preview (RJP)** involves conveying both positive and negative job information to the applicant in an unbiased manner. An RJP conveys information about tasks the person would perform and the behavior required to fit into the organization and adhere to company policies and procedures.[55] This approach helps applicants develop a more accurate perception of the job and the firm. While not all research confirms the effectiveness of realistic job previews,

**HRM IN ACTION**

▶ *But I Didn't Mean To!*

David Corbello, the office manager of the *Daily Gazette*, a Midwestern newspaper, was flabbergasted as he spoke with the HR manager, Amanda Dervis. He had just discovered that he was the target of a lawsuit filed by an applicant who had not been selected. "All I did was make friendly inquiries about her children. I thought I was merely breaking the ice and setting the tone for an effective dialogue. I thought nothing of it when she told me that she needed a day care facility when she went to work. A year later she claims to have been the victim of sexual discrimination because she believes that a man would not have been asked questions about his children. There's nothing to this lawsuit, is there, Amanda?"

*How should Amanda respond?*

proponents of the approach maintain that RJPs are relatively inexpensive to develop and implement and that the payoff can be significant in terms of lower selection and turnover costs.[56] In addition, there are benefits from being an up-front, ethical employer.[57]

## LEGAL IMPLICATIONS OF INTERVIEWING

The definition of a test in the *Uniform Guidelines* includes "physical, education, and work experience requirements from informal or casual interviews." Because the interview is considered to be a test, it is subject to the same validity requirements as any other step in the selection process, should adverse impact be shown. For unstructured interviews, this constraint presents special difficulties. Historically, improper use of the interview has caused more charges of discrimination than any other tool used in the selection process. Interviewing is primarily governed by one simple rule: all questions must be job related. In addition to being a waste of time, irrelevant or personal questions are dangerous and often improper.[58] Since behavioral interviews necessarily consist of job-related questions, their popularity is understandable.

To elicit needed information in any type of interview, the interviewer must create a climate that encourages the applicant to speak freely. However, the conversation should not become too casual. Whereas engaging in friendly chitchat with candidates might be pleasant, in our litigious society, it may be the most dangerous thing an interviewer can do.

To avoid the appearance of discrimination, employers should ask all applicants for a position the same questions.[59] It is also critical to record the applicant's responses. If a candidate begins volunteering personal information that is not job related, the interviewer should steer the conversation back on course. It might do well to begin the interview by tactfully stating, "This selection decision will be based strictly on qualifications. Let's not discuss topics such as religion, social activities, national origin, gender, or family situations. We are definitely interested in you, personally. However, these factors are not job related and will not be considered in our decision." Table 7-1 shows potential problems that can threaten the success of employment interviews.

The Americans with Disabilities Act also provides caveats for interviewers. There are only a few situations in which interviewers should inquire about the need for reasonable accommodations. For example, the topic should be brought up if the applicant is in a wheelchair and has an obvious disability that will require an accommodation. Also, the applicant may voluntarily disclose a disability or even ask for some reasonable accommodation. Otherwise, employers should refrain from broaching the subject. Instead, interviewers should frame questions in terms of whether applicants can perform the essential functions of the jobs they are applying for.[60]

When the interviewer has obtained the necessary information and answered the applicant's questions, the interview should be concluded. At this point, the interviewer should tell the applicant that he or she will be notified of the selection decision shortly. Keeping this promise helps maintain a positive relationship with the applicant.

▶ *Selection Web Sites*

**www.prenhall.com/mondy**

Several professional selection sites are presented.

HR WEB
WISDOM

**Table 7-1** Potential Interviewing Problems

### Inappropriate Questions

Although no questions are illegal, many are clearly inappropriate. When they are asked, the responses generated create a legal liability for the employer. The most basic interviewing rule is this: "Ask only job-related questions!"

### Premature Judgments

Research suggests that interviewers often make judgments about candidates in the first few minutes of the interview. When this occurs, a great deal of potentially valuable information is not considered.

### Interviewer Domination

In successful interviews, relevant information must flow both ways. Therefore, interviewers must learn to be good listeners as well as suppliers of information.

### Inconsistent Questions

If interviewers ask all applicants for a given job essentially the same questions and in the same sequence, all the applicants are judged on the same basis. This enables better decisions to be made while decreasing the likelihood of discrimination charges.

### Central Tendency

When interviewers rate virtually all candidates as average, they fail to differentiate between strong and weak candidates.

### Halo Error

When interviewers permit only one or a few personal characteristics to influence their overall impression of candidates, the best applicant may not be selected.

### Contrast Effects

An error in judgment may occur when, for example, an interviewer meets with several poorly qualified applicants and then confronts a mediocre candidate. By comparison, the last applicant may appear to be better qualified than he or she actually is.

### Interviewer Bias

Interviewers must understand and acknowledge their own prejudices and learn to deal with them. The only valid bias for an interviewer is to favor the best-qualified candidate for the open position.

### Lack of Training

When the cost of making poor selection decisions is considered, the expense of training employees in interviewing skills can be easily justified.

### Behavior Sample

Even if an interviewer spent a week with an applicant, the sample of behavior might be too small to judge the candidate's qualifications properly. In addition, the candidate's behavior during an interview is seldom typical or natural.

### Nonverbal Communication

Interviewers should make a conscious effort to view themselves as applicants do to avoid sending inappropriate or unintended nonverbal signals.

An **assessment center** is a selection technique used to identify and select employees for positions in the organization that requires individuals to perform activities similar to those they might encounter in an actual job. Because assessment centers are expensive to conduct, they are more commonly used as an internal selection and development device for managerial positions.[61]

**Assessment center**
A selection technique used to identify and select employees for positions in the organization that requires individuals to perform activities similar to those they might encounter in an actual job.

In an assessment center, candidates are subjected to a number of exercises that simulate the tasks they will perform in the job for which they are being considered. Various tests may be administered; the applicants may be subjected to in-basket exercises, management games, leaderless discussion groups, mock interviews, and other simulations. The traditional in-basket may be given a technological boost by replacing the paper memos with e-mail messages, faxes, or voice mail. Assessment centers measure candidates' skills in prioritizing, delegating, and decision making. The professional assessors who evaluate the candidates' performances usually observe them away from the workplace over a certain period of time, perhaps a single day. The assessors selected are typically experienced managers who may not only evaluate performances, but also participate in the exercises. Assessment centers are used by numerous organizations, including small firms and such large corporations as General Electric Company, JCPenney Company, Ford Motor Company, and AT&T.

Assessment centers for executives are considerably different from those used by firms 40 years ago. Weeks in advance, the executive candidate may receive such information about the organization as its key employees and future plans. Candidates may also receive a videotape to help them visualize the firm's outputs and acquaint them with hypothetical fellow workers. The candidates may be provided with modern communication devices and receive an outline of activities and scheduled meetings. When not tackling these duties, the candidate has time to handle the in-basket items. Professional assessors assist with role-playing in meetings and in other settings. For example, when a candidate is required to deal with a difficult employee, an assessor may fill this role.[62] The candidate might have to deal with a subordinate's performance problem, cope with a harassment case, or work out conflicts between a peer and a superior. Assessors give the candidate a rating and observe other personal characteristics that people reveal when responding to those situations.[63]

An advantage of the assessment center approach is the increased reliability and validity of the information provided. Research has shown that the in-basket exercise, a typical component of assessment centers, is a good predictor of management performance. Its face validity provides an alternative to paper-and-pencil tests.[64]

## PERSONAL REFERENCE CHECKS

**Reference checks** are validations that may provide additional insight into the information furnished by the applicant and allow verification of its accuracy. In fact, applicants are often required to submit the names of several references that can provide additional information about them. The basic flaw with this step in the selection process is that virtually every living person can name three or four individuals willing to make favorable statements about him or her. Even so, there is anecdotal evidence that personal references do not always sugarcoat the information they provide. They may not necessarily be committed to shading the

**Reference checks**
A way to gain additional insight into the information provided by an applicant and to verify the accuracy of the information provided.

truth for the applicant. Still, it appears that most organizations place more emphasis on professional references included in background investigations.

## PROFESSIONAL REFERENCES AND BACKGROUND INVESTIGATIONS

Background investigations primarily seek data from various sources, including professional references. An effective and comprehensive background investigation will include verification/examination of the following elements:[65]

- previous employment
- education
- personal references
- criminal history
- driving record
- civil litigation
- workers' compensation history
- credit history
- Social Security number

The principal reason for conducting background investigations is to hire better workers.[66] As we shall see, however, there are other critical reasons as well. The intensity of background investigations depends on the level of responsibility inherent in the position to be filled. The employer faces several potential problems at this stage of the selection process. If a *reasonable* background investigation is not conducted, the employer may be legally liable for negligent hiring; or, if the investigation reveals negative information about the applicant, invasion of privacy or defamation charges may be filed. A potential catch-22 situation is created for employers. Carefully checking references reduces the risk of a lawsuit stemming from the failure to exercise reasonable care when selecting new employees. Reasonable care varies according to the job. The risk of harm to third parties, for example, requires a higher standard of care when hiring a taxi driver as opposed to a bank teller.

A related problem in obtaining information from previous employers is their general reluctance to reveal such data. The Privacy Act of 1974, although limited to the public sector, provides a major reason for this hesitancy. Employers and employees in the private sector have become very sensitive to the privacy issue. There are two schools of thought with regard to supplying information about former employees. One is, "Don't tell them anything." The other is, "Honesty is the best policy." In the more conservative approach, the employer typically provides only basic data, such as starting and termination dates and last job title. The honesty approach is based on the reality that facts honestly given or opinions honestly held constitute a solid legal defense. When former employers are unwilling to give any information about a job applicant, both the potential employer and the applicant are at a disadvantage. A red flag is quickly raised when a former employer refuses to talk about a onetime employee. A relatively new concept, negligent referral, has added still another dimension to the investigation process. **Negligent referral** is when a former employer fails to offer a warning about a particularly severe problem with a past employee. Though this concept is not yet widely accepted, some courts have recognized a cause of action for negligent references.[67]

Regardless of the difficulties encountered in background investigations and reference checks, employing organizations have no choice but to engage in them. And, recognizing the importance of investigations in selecting employees, at least

**Negligent referral**
When a former employer fails to offer a warning about a particularly severe problem with a past employee.

26 states have passed laws offering varying degrees of protection to employers who provide good-faith references and who release truthful information about current or former employees.[68] The intent of this legislation is to make it easier for employers to give and receive meaningful information. However, there has been some hesitancy on the part of firms to take advantage of it. Apparently, there is a wait-and-see attitude that, although a protective law does exist, it takes litigation and a court ruling before the statute is fully understood.

One compelling reason for needing accurate reference information is that credential fraud has increased in recent years. Some applicants are not even who they say they are. They may also exaggerate their skills, education, and experience when given the opportunity. To be legally safe, employers should ask applicants to sign a liability waiver permitting a background investigation. A comprehensive waiver releases former employers, business references, and others from liability. The waiver can also authorize checks of court records and the verification of the applicant's educational history and other credentials. The results of all reference and background checks should be fully documented.

Small firms may not possess the staff to screen backgrounds of prospective employees thoroughly. Even large organizations may prefer to utilize the specialized services of professional screening firms. Firms can outsource their background-checking duties to a handful of third-party investigators who are regulated by the Fair Credit Reporting Act. They also require a signed release from the applicant. Such firms charge an average of $40 to $50 per inquiry, but their fee may exceed $100 if a complicated search is required.[69]

Regardless of how they are accomplished, background investigations have become increasingly important in making sound selection decisions and avoiding charges of negligent hiring and retention. The investigations may provide information critical to selection decisions since virtually every qualification an applicant lists can be verified.

## NEGLIGENT HIRING AND RETENTION

Negligent hiring has become a critical concern in the selection process. **Negligent hiring** is the liability an employer incurs when it does not reasonably investigate an applicant's background and then assigns a potentially dangerous person to a position where he or she can inflict harm. The employer can be held responsible for the employee's unlawful acts even if the employee's actions are not job related. A related potential liability, **negligent retention**, occurs when a company keeps persons on the payroll whose records indicate strong potential for wrongdoing.

Employers are beginning to be held responsible for actions outside the scope of their employees' duties. For example, if an employer hired a manager of an apartment complex without investigating the person's background and the individual later assaulted a tenant, the employer could be held responsible for the action. Employers are required by law to provide employees a safe place to work. This duty has been extended to providing safe employees because the courts have reasoned that a dangerous worker is comparable to a defective machine.

Negligent hiring cases often involve awards in the hundreds of thousands of dollars. In addition, they are likely to be upheld on appeal. The primary consideration in negligent hiring is whether the risk of harm from a dangerous employee was reasonably foreseeable. The nature of the job also has a critical bearing on the employer's obligation. Don Cross, a labor law specialist for Overton & Feeley, a Denver law firm, emphasizes the danger in not performing background checks. He

**Negligent hiring**
The liability an employer incurs when it does not reasonably investigate an applicant's background and then assigns a potentially dangerous person to a position where he or she can inflict harm.

**Negligent retention**
When a company keeps persons on the payroll whose records indicate strong potential for wrongdoing.

states that this practice not only fails to hire top-notch people, but more seriously, the firm is at risk for potentially catastrophic losses from negligent hiring. Those who operate home-service businesses, day care centers, and home health care operations are particularly at risk as are those with employees who drive company vehicles, visit customer locations, handle money, or work with children, the elderly, or the impaired.[70] Beverly California Corporation recently learned this lesson the hard way. A Virginia jury found that the nursing home chain was liable for $4.5 million in punitive damages and $518,000 in compensatory damages for negligently hiring and retaining a nursing aide without checking his references, which would have revealed prior wrongdoing.[71]

Trusted Health Resources, Inc., hired a male applicant as an aide in a home health care program run by the Visiting Nurses Association of Boston. The firm did not request a criminal background report, which would have turned up six larceny-related convictions. It also did not check his false claims that he had previously worked for a state agency and attended nursing classes at Northeastern University. This hiring turned out to be a tragic mistake. Eventually, the employee beat and stabbed to death a 32-year-old quadriplegic in his care and his 77-year-old grandmother. The victim's parents sued Trusted Health and VNA, alleging the defendants were negligent in allowing a convicted felon to care for their son, a cerebral palsy victim. The panel agreed, awarding $26.5 million in compensatory and punitive damages.[72] Hiring organizations cannot avoid the possibility of legal action. However, following sound selection procedures and keeping written records of the investigations will serve them well.

## POLYGRAPH TESTS

For many years, another means used to verify background information has been the polygraph, or lie detector test. One purpose of the polygraph was to confirm or refute the information contained in the application. However, the Employee Polygraph Protection Act of 1988 severely limited the use of polygraph tests in the private sector. It made unlawful the use of a polygraph test by any employer engaged in interstate commerce. Even so, the act does not apply to governmental employers, and there are limited exceptions. The act permits polygraph tests to be administered in the private sector to certain prospective employees of security service firms and pharmaceutical manufacturers, distributors, and dispensers. The act also permits, with certain restrictions, polygraph testing of certain employees who are reasonably suspected of involvement in a workplace incident, such as theft or embezzlement. Persons who take polygraph tests have a number of specific rights. For example, they have the right to a written notice before testing, the right to refuse or discontinue a test, and the right not to have test results disclosed to unauthorized persons.[73]

## THE SELECTION DECISION

After a company has obtained and evaluated information about the finalists in a job selection process, the buck stops with the manager, who must take the most critical step of all: the actual hiring decision. The final choice will be made from among those still in the running after reference checks, selection tests, background investigations, and interview information have been evaluated. The individual with the best overall qualifications may not be hired. Rather, the person whose qualifications most closely conform to the requirements of the open position and the organization should be selected. If a firm is going to invest thousands of dollars to recruit, select, and train an employee, it is important for the manager to hire the most qualified available candidate for the position.

Human resource professionals may be involved in all phases leading up to the final employment decision. However, especially for higher-level positions, the person who normally makes the final selection is the manager who will be responsible for the new employee's performance. In making this decision, the operating manager will review results of the selection methods used. All will not likely be weighted the same. The question then becomes, "Which data are most predictive of job success?" For each firm or group of jobs, the optimum selection method may be different.

## PHYSICAL EXAMINATION

The Americans with Disabilities Act (ADA) does not prohibit preemployment testing. However, it does determine what tests may be permitted and at what point during the selection process they may be administered. ADA explicitly states that all exams must be directly relevant to the job requirements and that a medical exam cannot be given until an offer of employment has been extended.[74] Typically, a job offer is contingent on the applicant's passing of this examination. The basic purpose of the physical examination is to determine whether an applicant is physically capable of performing the work.

Managers must be aware of the legal liabilities related to physical examinations. The *Uniform Guidelines* state that these examinations should be used to reject applicants only when the results show that job performance would be adversely affected. The Rehabilitation Act of 1973 and the Americans with Disabilities Act of 1990 require employers to take affirmative action to hire qualified disabled persons who, with reasonable accommodation, can perform the essential components of a job.

## NOTIFICATION OF CANDIDATES

The selection process results should be made known to both successful and unsuccessful candidates as soon as possible. Any delay may result in the firm losing a prime candidate, as top prospects often have other employment options. The unsuccessful candidates should also be promptly notified as a matter of courtesy and good public relations.

If currently employed by another firm, the successful candidate customarily gives between two and four weeks' notice. Even after this notice, the individual may need some personal time to prepare for the new job. This transition time is particularly important if the new job requires a move to another city. Thus the amount of time before the individual can join the firm is often considerable.

Applicants may be rejected during any phase of the selection process. Research has indicated that most people can accept losing if they lose fairly.[75] Problems occur when the selection process appears to be less than objective. It is therefore important for firms to develop and utilize rational selection tools. Increasingly, time constraints prevent firms from spending much time explaining why a candidate was not selected. A rejection letter is a more likely method. However, the letter can still be personalized. A personal touch will often reduce the stigma of rejection and the chance that the applicant will have negative feelings about the company. An impersonal letter is likely to have the opposite effect. The best an organization can do is to make selection decisions objectively. Hopefully, most unsuccessful individuals can, with time, accept the fact that they were not chosen.

## *Different Qualities Are Needed for Global HR*

International human resource management is becoming a management challenge of major proportions. Not only does a person have to know HR well, but a world of knowledge beyond that. However, international HR is still in its infancy and few HR professionals have had the opportunity to develop these skills. International HR is not a career that most HR professionals head into when they first enter the HR field. More often, it is by chance. "It's just one of those accidental things that happens. Companies start sending people overseas, then all of a sudden they have international questions, like how to pay their first expat going to France," says Dennis Briscoe, professor of international HR management at the Ahler Center for International Business & School of Business Administration at the University of San Diego.

Global HR managers need effective communication skills, including the ability to listen well, says John de Leon, regional director of international HR for Deloitte & Touche LLP's international assignment services group. Communication skills also are highly valued at Westinghouse Energy Systems. Gordon Beecher, manager of services and projects/international, agrees that communication skills are the most important for international HR professionals. He says, "Not only because international HR managers have to overcome language barriers, but also they have to be able to express themselves to multiple audiences, much more than a U.S. human resource person does." On top of that, most of the HR professionals employed by the division's European offices are required to speak other languages. "We prefer people who can speak French, Flemish, or Spanish there, whereas my U.S. HR reps don't [have to speak another language]," says Beecher.

Furthermore, good international HR professionals must have a comprehensive understanding of the international business environment. In the United States, a business model to fit most situations has usually been developed. "But offshore there tend to be as many models as there are countries," says de Leon. "So, although partnering with line management is critical for U.S. HR, it's a much greater challenge to achieve in the international arena because there just aren't as many models as there are in the domestic environment."[76]

## ▶ Summary

**①  Explain the significance of employee selection.**

Selection is the process of choosing from a group of applicants those individuals best suited for a particular position. There are many ways to improve productivity, but none is more powerful than making the right hiring decision.

**②  Identify environmental factors that affect the selection process.**

The environmental factors that affect the selection process include legal considerations, speed of decision making, organizational hierarchy, applicant pool, type of organization, and probationary period.

**③  Describe the general selection process.**

The selection process typically begins with the preliminary interview, where obviously unqualified candidates are rejected. Next, applicants complete the firm's application blank; this is followed by the administration of selection tests and a series of employment interviews with reference and background checks. Once the selection decision has been made, the prospective employee may be given a company physical examination.

**④ Explain the importance of the preliminary interview.**

The selection process begins with an initial screening of applicants to remove individuals who obviously do not fulfill the position requirements.

**⑤ Describe the importance of the application for employment.**

A well-designed and properly used application form can be helpful because essential information is included and presented in a standardized format.

**⑥ Describe the advantages, potential problems, and characteristics of properly designed selection tests.**

Selection testing can be a reliable and accurate means of selecting qualified candidates from a pool of applicants. Selection tests may accurately predict an applicant's ability to perform the job, the "can do," but they are less successful in indicating the extent to which the individual will be motivated to perform it, the "will do." Properly designed selection tests are standardized, objective, based on sound norms, reliable, and—of utmost importance—valid.

**⑦ Explain the types of validation studies.**

Criterion-related validity is determined by comparing the scores on selection tests to some aspect of job performance as determined, for example, by performance appraisal. Concurrent validity is where the test scores and the criterion data are obtained at essentially the same time. Predictive validity is administering a test and later obtaining the criterion information.

**⑧ Describe types of employment tests.**

Types of employment tests include cognitive aptitude, psychomotor abilities, job-knowledge, work-sample, and vocational interest tests. Few issues generate more controversy today than alcohol and drug testing. Genetic testing can now determine a predisposition to numerous diseases. The Internet is increasingly being used to test various skills required by applicants.

**⑨ Explain the importance of interview planning and describe the content of the interview.**

Interview planning is essential to effective employment interviews. Both the interviewer and the candidate have agendas for the interview. After establishing rapport with the applicant, the interviewer seeks additional job-related information to complement data provided by other selection tools. The interview permits clarification of certain points, the uncovering of additional information, and the elaboration of data needed to make a sound selection decision. The interviewer should provide information about the company, the job, and expectations of the candidate.

**⑩ Describe the basic types of interviewing.**

Basic types of interviews include the unstructured interview, the structured interview, and the behavior interview. The interviewer should provide information about the company, the job, and expectations of the candidate.

**⑪ Describe the various methods of interviewing.**

The methods of interviewing include meeting one on one with an interviewer, a group interview, the board interview, a stress interview, and computer-assisted interview.

**⑫ Explain the legal implications of interviewing.**

Because the interview is considered to be a test, it is subject to the same validity requirements as any other step in the selection process, should adverse impact be shown.

**⑬ Describe assessment centers as a means of selection.**

An assessment center is a selection technique used to identify and select employees for positions in the organization. Candidates are subjected to a number of exercises that simulate tasks they will perform in the job for which they are being considered.

**14** Explain why personal and professional references are requested and background investigations are conducted.

Personal reference checks may provide additional insight into the information furnished by the applicant and allow verification of its accuracy. Background investigations primarily seek data from various sources, including professional references. An effective and comprehensive background investigation will include an examination/verification of the following elements: previous employment, education, personal references, criminal history, driving record, civil litigation, workers' compensation history, credit history, and Social Security number.

**15** Explain negligent hiring and retention and the use of polygraph tests.

An employer can be held responsible for an employee's unlawful acts if it does not reasonably investigate applicants' backgrounds, then assigns potentially dangerous persons to positions where they can inflict harm. Negligent retention involves keeping persons on the payroll whose records indicate strong potential for wrongdoing. One purpose of the polygraph is to confirm or refute the information contained in the application blank.

**16** Describe the selection decision, the physical examination, and notification of candidates.

The selection decision is when the final choice is made from among those still in the running after reference checks, selection tests, background investigations, and interview information are evaluated. The physical is used to screen out individuals who have a contagious disease and to determine if an applicant is physically capable of performing the work. The physical examination information may be used to determine if there are certain physical capabilities that differentiate between successful and less-successful employees. The selection process results should be made known to both successful and unsuccessful candidates as soon as possible.

## ▶ Questions for Review

1. What basic steps normally are followed in the selection process?

2. Identify and describe the various environmental factors that could affect the selection process.

3. What would be the selection ratio if there were 15 applicants to choose from and only one position to fill? Interpret the meaning of this selection ratio.

4. If a firm wants to use selection tests, how should these tests be used to avoid discriminatory practices?

5. What is the general purpose of the preliminary interview?

6. What types of questions should be asked on an application form?

7. What basic conditions should be met if selection tests are to be used in the screening process? Briefly describe each.

8. What approaches do the *Uniform Guidelines* say should be followed to validate selection tests?

9. Identify and describe the various types of employment tests.

10. What information should be gained from the interview?

11. What are the basic types of interviews?

12. Describe the various methods of interviewing.

13. What is a realistic job preview?

14. What are the legal implications of interviewing?

15. What is the purpose of personal references, professional references, and background investigations?

16. Why should an employer be concerned about negligent hiring and retention?

17. What are the reasons for administering a physical examination?

*We invite you to visit the Mondy homepage on the Prentice Hall Web site at*

**www.prenhall.com/mondy**

*for updated information, Web-based exercises, and links to other HR-related sites.*

**TAKE IT TO THE NET**

## Developing HRM Skills ◄

### *An Experiential Exercise*

Selecting the best person to fill a vacant position is one of the most important tasks of human resource management. As all managers recognize, many factors must be considered to ensure proper selection. The selection decision you will be dealing with in this exercise is necessary because George Winston has just been promoted, and before he starts his new job, he must select his replacement. George's firm is an affirmative action employer, and presently there are few women in management. George has some excellent employees to choose from, but there are many factors to consider before he makes a decision. The people upstairs made it perfectly clear that they expect George to select an individual who can perform as well as he did over the last six years.

Four individuals will have roles in this exercise: one to serve as George Winston, the current supervisor, and three to be the candidates for promotion. Your instructor will provide the participants with additional information necessary to complete the exercise.

## HRM INCIDENT 1 ◄

### *A Matter of Priorities*

As production manager for Thompson Manufacturing, Jack Stephens has the final authority to approve the hiring of any new supervisors who work for him. The human resource manager performs the initial screening of all prospective supervisors, then sends the most likely candidates to Jack for interviews.

One day recently, Jack received a call from Pete Peterson, the human resource manager: "Jack, I've just spoken to a young man who may be just who you're looking for to fill the final line supervisor position. He has some good work experience and it appears as if his head is screwed on straight. He's here right now and available if you could possibly see him."

Jack hesitated a moment before answering. "Gee, Pete" he said, "I'm certainly busy today, but I'll try to squeeze him in. Send him on down."

A moment later Allen Guthrie, the applicant, arrived at Jack's office and introduced himself. "Come on in, Allen," said Jack. "I'll be right with you after I make a few phone calls." Fifteen minutes later Jack finished the calls and began talking with Allen. Jack was quite impressed. After a few minutes Jack's door opened and a supervisor yelled, "We have a small problem on line number 1 and need your help." Jack stood up and said, "Excuse me a minute, Allen." Ten minutes later Jack returned, and the conversation continued for ten more minutes before a series of phone calls again interrupted the pair.

The same pattern of interruptions continued for the next hour. Finally, Allen looked at his watch and said, "I'm sorry, Mr. Stephens, but I have to pick up my wife." "Sure thing, Allen," Jack said as the phone rang again. "Call me later today."

### Questions

1. What specific policies should a company follow to avoid interviews like this one?
2. Explain why Jack, not Pete, should make the selection decision.

---

▶ **HRM INCIDENT 2**

### Is Something Wrong?

Pat Swain, district sales manager for Avco Electronics, was preparing to interview her first applicant, Ray Wyscup, for a sales representative position. She had advertised for an individual with detailed knowledge of computers and spreadsheet software in addition to a minimum of five years' sales experience.

"Hello, Ray. I'm Pat Swain. I've looked at your résumé and am anxious to talk to you about this job. You have a very impressive sales record."

"It's nice to meet you, Pat. Your ad in the *Journal* certainly caught my attention. I would like to be with a firm offering such a promising career."

"Glad you saw it, Ray. We like to believe that our firm is unique and truly has something to offer top-caliber people such as you. Why don't you begin this session by telling me all about yourself? We are a very close-knit group here, and I would like to learn about you and your family."

Ray appeared to be very relaxed and comfortable in Pat's presence. He began, "Well, you see, I'm a single parent with two preschool children. Since I'm only 41 years old, I'm pretty well able to keep up with their various activities. Of course, you understand that one gets sick occasionally, and this causes me to take a few personal days off. But, I've always been able to handle it. This circumstance wouldn't affect my job performance."

"Well, I'm sure it wouldn't. I also have some youngsters at home," Pat replied. "Would you now tell me about your last job with IBX?"

Ray, feeling more confident than ever, began, "Well, Pat, I had a brief, but very successful stint with them. But I had rather you not contact them about me. You see, my regional manager and I had a personality conflict, and I'm afraid he might not tell a straight story."

"I see," Pat said. "What about your position before that, your job with Uniserv?"

"I did well there too," Ray stated. "But that outfit went belly up. I have no idea where any of those people are now."

After the interview had continued for about an hour, Pat said, "Well, I guess that about wraps it up, Ray, unless you have questions for me."

"No," Ray responded, "I believe I understand the nature of the position, and I can assure you that I will do a great job for you."

Pat smiled and nodded and the two shook hands as Ray departed.

## Questions

**1.** Do you agree with the interview format followed by Pat Swain? Explain.
**2.** How will Pat handle a background investigation of Ray Wyscup?

1. Clyde E. Witt, "Get Smart about Productivity," *Material Handling Engineering* 51 (January 1996): 22.

2. Claudio Fernandez-Araoz, "Hiring without Firing," *Harvard Business Review* 77 (July 1999): 108.

3. Bill Leonard, "Our Horizons Are Limitless," *HRMagazine* 45 (January 2000): 44–49.

4. Katrina Brooker, "Can Anyone Replace Herb?" *Fortune* 141 (April 17, 2000): 192.

5. Robert Bellinger, "The Profession: In Behavioral Interviews, You Should 'Tell a Story'— Job Interviews Get More Specific," *Electronic Engineering Times* (July 20, 1998): 122.

6. Nancee V. Sneed, Barbara Edlund, and Margaret Ann Kerr, "Telephone Interviews: A Cost-Effective Way to Select Faculty," *Journal of Nursing Education* 36 (February 1997): 87.

7. Clive Fletcher, "Just How Effective Is a Telephone Interview?" *People Management* 3 (June 26, 1997): 49.

8. Robin Rimmer Hurst, "Video Interviewing," *HRMagazine* 41 (November 1996): 101–104.

9. Linda Thornburg, "Computer-Assisted Interviewing Shortens Hiring Cycle," *HRMagazine* 43 (February 1998): 73–79.

10. Ibid.

11. Ellen Neuborne, "Putting Job Seekers to the Test: Employers Score New Hires," *USA Today* (July 9, 1997): 1B.

12. Gillian Flynn, "Pre-Employment Testing Can Be Unlawful," *Workforce* 78 (July 1999): 82.

13. Brenda Paik Sunoo, "The Pros and Cons of Pre-employment Testing," *Workforce* 76 (March 1997): 125.

14. Kathryn Tyler, "Put Applicants' Skills to the Test," Supplement *HRMagazine* 45 (January 2000): 74–75.

15. Patrick Totty, "Find the Best Employees with Screening Software," *Credit Union Magazine* 65 (February 1999): 65.

16. Carla Joinson, "Is After-Hire Testing the Best Solution?" *HRMagazine* 42 (July 1997): 122.

17. David J. Shaffer and Ronald A. Schmidt, "Personality Testing in Employment," *Legal Report,* published by the Society for Human Resource Management (September-October 1999): 1.

18. Neuborne, "Putting Job Seekers to the Test."

19. Janet Forgrieve, "Small Firms Aided in Drug War," *The Tampa Tribune* (January 10, 2000): 8.

20. Ibid.

21. "New Study Shows No Race Bias with Hair Testing," *PR Newswire* (June 14, 1999): 1.

22. Peter Carlson, "Foiling Drug Tests Has Become His Business," *Minneapolis Star Tribune* (September 3, 1999): 11A.

23. Stephanie Overman, "Splitting Hairs," *HRMagazine* 44 (August 1, 1999): 42–48.

24. Jane Easter Bahls, "Drugs in the Workplace," *HRMagazine* 43 (February 1998): 80–87.

25. Tyler D. Hartwell, Paul D. Steele, and Michael T. French, "Prevalence of Drug Testing in the Workplace," *Monthly Labor Review* 119 (November 1996): 35.

26. Jane H. Philbrick, Barbara D. Bart, and Marcia E. Hass, "Pre-employment Screening: A Decade of Change," *American Business Review* 17 (June 1999): 75.

27. "Genetic Milestone: Creation of Human Blueprint Hailed as among Greatest Feats of Science," *The Dallas Morning News* (June 27, 2000): 1A.

28. Maureen Minehan, "The Right to Medical Privacy," *HRMagazine* 42 (March 1997): 160.

29. "Genetic Breakthrough May Open Door to New Workplace Bias Worries," *CCH NetNews:* Human Resources Management, C:\Program Files\Qualcomm\Eudora Pro\Attach\HRMNNO724.htm (July 24, 2000): 1.

30. "Genetic Tests by Employers Should Be Banned," *The Michigan Daily,* www.pub.umich.edu/daily/1999/jul/07-06-99/edit/edit2.html (April 30, 2000).

31. "Does Genetic Testing Send the Wrong Message?" *Workforce* 78 (November 1999): 88.

32. "Executive Order to Prohibit Discrimination in Federal Employment Based on Genetic Information," *Regulatory Intelligence Data,* Industry Group 91 (February 8, 2000): 1.

33. Sarah Fister, "Separating Liars from Hires," *Training* 36 (July 1999): 22.

34. Bill Leonard, "Reading Employees," *HRMagazine* 44 (April 1999): 67–73.

35. John Sullivan, "Death by Interview," *Electronic Recruiting Exchange* (December 3, 1999): 1. www.erexchange.com/articles/printer.asp?d=H&CID={EDE5EF09-DB24-11D3-82E2-00105A12D660} (June 19, 2000).

36. Kim Clark, Joellen Perry, and Marissa Melton, "Why It Pays to Quit," *U.S. News & World Report* 127 (November 1, 1999): 74.

37. Bob Weinstein, "Acing Interview Takes More than Technical Know-How," *Minneapolis Star Tribune* (July 18, 1999): 1J.

38. Al Senter, "Recruiting to Stop the Revolving Door," *Management Today* (February 1999): 80.

39. Diana Kunde, "Interview Techniques Changing," *The Dallas Morning News* (August 11, 1999): 1D.

40. Lin Grensing-Pophal, "Hiring to Fit Your Corporate Culture," *HRMagazine* 44 (August 1999): 50–54.

41. Kim Clark, "Gimme, Gimme, Gimme," *U.S. News & World Report* 127 (November 1, 1999): 88.

42. Erin M. Davies, "Wired for Hiring: Microsoft's Slick Recruiting Machine," *Fortune* 133 (February 5, 1996): 123–124.

43. Kunde, "Interview Techniques Changing."

44. Maureen Moody, "Ready Aim Hire," *Director* 52 (July 1999): 50.

45. Jim Kennedy, "What to Do When Job Applicants Tell Tales of Invented Lives," *Training* 36 (October 1999): 110.

46. Bellinger, "The Profession: In Behavioral Interviews, You Should 'Tell a Story.'"

47. Ibid.

48. Alice M. Starcke, "Tailor Interviews to Predict Performance," *HRMagazine* 41 (July 1996): 49.

49. Jay Zack and Mark Van Beusekom, "Making the Right Hire: Behavioral Interviewing," *The Tax Advisor* 27 (September 1996): 570.

50. Arthur H. Bell, "How to Score a Behavior-Based Structured Interview," *Personic, Workforce On Line,* www.workforce.com/archive/article/000/48/82.xci?topicname=staffing (April 24, 2000).

51. Debbie Veney Robinson, "Behavioral Interviewing at CIGNA," *HR Focus* 75 (December 1998): 6.

52. Ibid.

53. Kennedy, "What to Do When Job Applicants Tell Tales of Invented Lives."

54. Kitty Winkler and Inez Janger, "You're Hired! Now How Do We Keep You?" *Across the Board* 35 (July/August 1998): 17.

55. John P. Wanous, "Tell It Like It Is at Realistic Job Previews," in Kendrith M. Rowland, Manual London, Gerald R. Ferris, and Jay L. Sherman (eds.), *Current Issues in Personnel Management* (Boston: Allyn & Bacon, 1980): 41–50.

56. Jean M. Phillips, "Effects of Realistic Job Previews on Multiple Organizational Outcomes: A Meta-Analysis," *Academy of Management Journal* (December 1, 1998): 673.

57. M. Ronald Buckley, Donald B. Fedor, Shawn M. Carraher, Dwight D. Frink, and David Marvin, "The Ethical Imperative to Provide Recruits Realistic Job Previews," *Journal of Managerial Issues* 9 (December 22, 1997): 468–484.

58. Ellen C. Auwarter, Esq., and Darlene Orlov, "How to Screen without Getting Sued," *Industry Forum* (January 1997), 12.

59. Jonathan A. Segal, "Looking for Trouble?" *HRMagazine* 42 (July 1997): 76–83.

60. Ibid.

61. Donald L. Caruth and Gail D. Handlogten, *Staffing the Contemporary Organization: A Guide to Planning, Recruiting, and Selecting for Human Resource Professionals* (Westport, CT: Quorum Books, 1997): 178.

62. William C. Byham, "How to Create a Reservoir of Ready-Made Leaders," *Training and Development* 54 (March 2000): 32.

63. "Lifetime Hire," *Chief Executive* (The Chief Executive Guide: The War for Talent, Supplement 1999): 11–14.

64. Lizabeth A. Barclay and Kenneth M. York, "Electronic Communication in the Classroom: An E-mail In-Basket Exercise," *Journal of Education for Business* 74 (March 1999): 249.

65. Edward Niam, "Check before You Hire," *HR Focus* 75 (December 1998): S10.

66. Edward Niam, "Do You Know Who You Are Hiring?" *USA Today Magazine* 126 (July 1, 1997): 1.

67. David W. Arnesen, C. Patrick Fleenor, and Marlin Blizinsky, "Name, Rank, and Serial Number? The Dilemma of Reference Checks," *Business Horizons* 41 (July/August 1998): 71–78.

68. Paul W. Barada, "Check Please: Thorough Reference Checking Should Be Central to the Hiring Process in Order to Provide Legal Protection for Employers and to Ensure That the Best Person Is Hired," *Financial Planning* (September 1, 1998): 172.

69. Jerome R. Stockfisch, "Background Checks Can Be Costly, Incomplete," *The Tampa Tribune* (January 11, 2000): 1.

70. Jack Sommers, "The Truth Is Out There: How to Check Job Applicants' Backgrounds," *Colorado Business Magazine* 25 (June 1, 1998): 70(2).

71. Douglas M. Nabhan, "Avoiding the 'Negligent Hiring' Trap," *Nursing Homes* 47 (April 1998): 36.

72. William C. Smith, "Victims of Omission," *ABA Journal, the Lawyer's Magazine* 85 (March 1999): 32.

73. Larry Drake and Rachel Moskowitz, "Your Rights in the Workplace," *Occupational Outlook Quarterly* 41 (June 22, 1997): 22.

74. Kristina Rundquist, "Pre-Employment Testing: Making It Work for You," *Occupational Hazards* 59 (December 1, 1997): 38.

75. Ken Jordan, "Play Fair and Square When Hiring from Within," *HRMagazine* 42 (January 1997): 49.

76. Jennifer J. Laabs, "Must-Have Global HR Competencies," *Workforce* 44 (March 1999): 30.

You'll recall from the video for Part 2 that Quicktakes Video is a small television production company that produces short films and videos for various corporate and entrepreneurial clients. Quicktakes is owned by Hal Boylston, who manages most of the administrative tasks for the firm, and Karen Jarvis, who functions as the director of sales, managing the sales people and bringing new clients to the firm. In this video Hal is seeking to hire a new employee.

Job interviews are among the most stressful situations most of us face at work. While we normally think of how "on the spot" we feel as the job applicant, remember that the interviewer, too, can be under a certain amount of stress. As you know from reading Chapter 7, interviews are a flawed selection tool, but are still the primary method of evaluating job candidates. Interview planning is essential for getting the most useful information from the encounter. And it's important for the interviewer to remember that the candidate will have his or her own agenda for the interview as well.

Structured interviews, with their prepared situational, job knowledge, job-sample, and worker requirements questions, are designed to assist interviewers in reaching objective conclusions about candidates. The questions are what-if questions with predetermined answers that the interviewer asks all applicants for the job. When applicants' answers are compared, the result is usually an unbiased basis for comparing their job skills, willingness and motivation to work, and quality of judgment and decision-making skill.

You may already have interview experience, perhaps on the other side of the desk. Have you ever interviewed for a job and been nervous and anxious to make a good impression? You may have worried about saying too much or too little, or you may have felt unprepared for the questions you were asked.

While you might at first identify with Quicktakes' new job applicant, Mary Byrns, you should also try to see the situation in the video from Hal's point of view. He is looking for a new producer, and in a small company such as Quicktakes it is difficult to invest a great deal of time in training new employees who have little or no experience. Hal therefore needs someone who can get off to a quick start and maintain a high degree of self-motivation. Try to evaluate Mary's potential as a self-starter based on her behavior in the interview.

Be prepared, too, to evaluate Hal's interviewing skills. Since there is no Human Resource Department at Quicktakes, Hal, like managers at many small to medium sized firms, has the responsibility both for screening job candidates and for making the final hiring decision. How well does he put Mary at ease, and how does he react to her volunteering information about herself? Does he make any interviewing errors?

Although Hal does not administer any employment tests, Mary has brought a sample of her work in the form of a videotape. What function do you think it serves? What, if anything, does it tell Hal about Mary's work?

### Discussion Questions

1. Did Hal conduct a structured interview? Justify your answer.
2. Hal has rated Mary "a strong candidate for the job." How do you think he arrived at this conclusion? Do you agree with his assessment? Why or why not?
3. What other facts about Mary's background and experience do you think Hal should have before he makes a decision about whether to hire her? (Assume that her resume provides a brief job history and basic personal data.) How should Hal go about finding this information?
4. What should Mary know about Quicktakes before she decides whether to accept any offer that Hal may make? How can she find this out?
5. How could Hal have better prepared himself for the interview? How could Mary?

chapter
chapterchapterchapterchapterchapterchapter

8

# Training and Development

 Objectives

- Define *training and development (T&D)*.
- Explain the relationship between organization change and training and development.
- Explain factors influencing T&D.
- Describe the T&D process and how training needs are determined and objectives established.
- Identify the various training and development methods.
- Describe management development.
- Identify special training needs.
- Identify the means by which T&D programs are implemented and evaluated.
- Describe the training partnerships that exist between business, government, and education.
- Define *orientation* and identify its purposes.
- Define *organization development (OD)* and describe various OD techniques.

ou McGowen was worried as she approached the training director's office. She is the supervisor of six punch press operators at Keller-Globe, a maker of sheet metal parts for the industrial refrigeration industry. She had just learned that her punch presses would soon be replaced with a continuous-feed system that would double the speed of operations. She was thinking about how the workers might feel about the new system when the training director, Bill Taylor, opened the door and said, "Come on in, Lou. I've been looking forward to seeing you."

After a few pleasantries, Lou told Bill of her concerns. "The operators really know their jobs now. But this continuous-feed system is a whole new ball game. I'm concerned, too, about how the workers

# Key Terms

Training and development (T&D) 214
Human resource development (HRD) 214
Training 215
Development 215
Learning organizations 215
Business games 223

Case study 223
Behavior modeling 224
In-basket training 224
Role playing 224
Job rotation 224
Computer-based training 225
Multimedia 225

Virtual reality 225
On-the-job training (OJT) 227
Apprenticeship training 227
Simulators 228
Vestibule training 228
Management development 229

Orientation 235
Organization development (OD) 238
Survey feedback 239
Quality circles 239
Team building 240
Sensitivity training 241

will feel about it. The new presses are going to run faster. They may think that their job is going to be harder."

Bill replied, "After talking with the plant engineer and the production manager, I have made up a tentative training schedule that might make you feel a little better. I think we first have to let the workers know why this change is necessary. You know that both of our competitors changed to this new system last year. After that, we will teach your people to operate the new presses."

"Who's going to do the teaching?" Lou asked. "I haven't even seen the new system."

"Well, Lou," said Bill, "the manufacturer has arranged for you to visit a plant with a similar system. They'll also ship one of the punch presses in early so you and your workers can learn to operate it."

"Will the factory give us any other training help?" Lou asked.

"Yes, I have asked them to send a trainer down as soon as the first press is set up. He will conduct some classroom sessions and then work with your people on the new machine."

After further discussion about details, Lou thanked Bill and headed back to the production department. She was confident that the new presses would be a real benefit to her section and that her workers could easily learn the skills required.

L ou was lucky enough to have a training professional help her prepare the operators for the change in their jobs. Often, managers themselves perform the training.

**Training and development**
The heart of a continuous effort designed to improve employee competency and organizational performance.

**Human resource development**
A major HRM function that consists not only of T&D but also individual career planning and development activities and performance appraisal.

As we see in this chapter, **training and development (T&D)** is the heart of a continuous effort designed to improve employee competency and organizational performance. **Human resource development (HRD)** is a major HRM function that consists not only of T&D but also individual career planning and development activities and performance appraisal.

We devote the first portion of this chapter to explaining the scope of training and development and its relationship to organizational change. Then, we discuss factors that influence T&D. Next, the T&D process is described along with how training needs are determined and objectives established. Then, we look at the numerous T&D methods and management development. Next, special training areas are described, and the means by which T&D programs are implemented and evaluated are discussed. The partnership that exists among business, government, and education is then explored, followed by sections describing employee orientation. Organization development is the final topic of the chapter.

## TRAINING AND DEVELOPMENT

While the terms *training* and *development* may be used interchangeably, a distinction is sometimes made between the two. **Training** is designed to provide learners with the knowledge and skills needed for their present jobs. Showing a worker how to operate a lathe or a supervisor how to schedule daily production are examples of training. Lou McGowen and her punch press operators will receive training in preparation for the new press. On the other hand, **development** involves learning that goes beyond today's job; it has a more long-term focus. It prepares employees to keep pace with the organization as it changes and grows. Training and development activities have the potential to align employees of a firm with its corporate strategies.[1]

In virtually every market, customers are demanding higher quality, lower costs, and faster cycle times. To meet these requirements, firms must continually improve their overall performance. Rapid advances in technology and improved processes have been important factors in helping businesses meet this challenge. However, the most important competitive advantage for any firm is its workforce—one that must remain competent through continuous training and development efforts. Improved performance—the bottom-line purpose of T&D—is a strategic goal for organizations. A number of forward-thinking firms have become or are striving to become learning organizations. A **learning organization** is one with the capacity to continuously adapt and change. Such a firm views training as a strategic investment rather than a budgeted cost.

It is important to note that *formal* training refers to training activity that is planned, structured, and occurs when people are called away from their workstation to participate in it. It does not include informal on-the-job-training or the increasing numbers of free agent learners who seek development on their own. Continued growth in all forms of training appears to be a given. Most organizations invest in T&D because they believe that higher profits will result; they often do. Training

**Training**
Activities designed to provide learners with the knowledge and skills needed for their present jobs.

**Development**
Learning that goes beyond today's job; it has a more long-term focus.

**Learning organizations**
Firms with the capacity to continuously adapt to change.

www.astd.org
*Source:* Courtesy of ASTD.

▶ *American Society for Training and Development*

**www.prenhall.com/mondy**

The homepage for the American Society for Training and Development (ASTD) is presented.

HR WEB
WISDOM

frequently improves workers' skills and boosts their motivation. This, in turn, leads to higher productivity and increased profitability.

In a recent year, budgeted formal training expenditures were estimated to be over $62 billion.[2] A recent survey found that 75 percent of U.S. firms plan to increase their funding for workforce development over the next two years. Why the increased interest? In its annual coverage of the "100 Best Companies to Work for in America," *Fortune* magazine noted that extensive and ongoing training and development is second only to stock options as a primary means of attracting and retaining talented workers. On average, in 1998, the "100 Best" provided 43 hours of training for each employee—a full day more than the previous year. Some of these firms have begun to include their T&D programs in recruitment materials.[3] Don Harris, manager of staff development for Belk's Store Services, a regional department store chain, believes that "one of the best ways to recruit and retain people is through training and career development."[4] A national study by Interim Services, Inc., which combined information from its Saratoga Institute, provides valuable data about the benefits of offering mentoring, training, and growth opportunities. Interim estimates that by providing these opportunities, companies with over 1,000 employees save up to $40 million, largely due to reduced turnover.[5] A firm that provides poor training and education risks losing 41 percent of its workforce within 12 months compared to only 12 percent where good T&D is offered.[6] Training and development costs should be accepted for what they are: an investment in human resources. It is clear that T&D is not merely a nice thing to provide; it is a strategic resource that firms must tap to energize their organizations in the twenty-first century.[7]

## ORGANIZATION CHANGE AND TRAINING AND DEVELOPMENT

The basic purpose of training and development is to anticipate change and to respond proactively to it. Change involves moving from one condition to another, and it will affect individuals, groups, and entire organizations. All organizations experience change of some sort, and the rate at which change takes place is accelerating. The most prominent changes affecting T&D that have been prophesied and are actually occurring today in business include the following:

▷ Changes in organization structure caused by mergers, acquisitions, rapid growth, downsizing, and outsourcing
▷ Changes in technology and the need for more highly skilled workers
▷ Changes in the educational level of employees—some more highly educated, others needing remedial training
▷ Changes in human resources, creating a diverse workforce consisting of many groups
▷ Competitive pressures necessitating flexible courses and just-in-time and just-what's-needed training
▷ Increased emphasis on learning organizations and human performance management

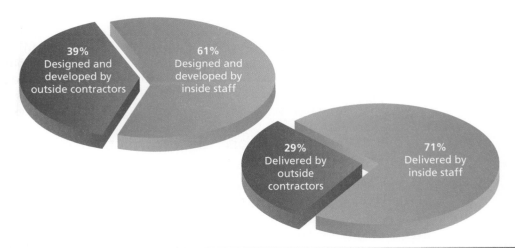

**Training Designed and Delivered by Outside Sources and Inside Staff**

**Figure 8-1**

*Source:* Reprinted with permission from the October 1999 issue of *TRAINING* Magazine. Copyright 1999. Bill Communications, Minneapolis, MN. All rights reserved. Not for resale.

Predictions about the future are not always accurate. For example, a prediction that outsourced training would increase has proved to be wrong. As you can see in Figure 8-1, outside contractors design and deliver only about one-third of training services. This proportion has remained constant since 1997.[8] Nevertheless, it behooves managers to keep an eye to the future in order to anticipate changes and to behave proactively.

Every human is affected by change. As change agents, managers and staff specialists involved with T&D must understand the difficulties associated with change and the ways to reduce resistance to change. Remember that Lou McGowen was worried about how the workers would feel about the new system.

Because of the impact change has on the organization and its employees, it should be undertaken only when a real need exists. Of course, circumstances in the internal or external environments may make change desirable or even necessary. Basically, the impetus for change comes from a belief that the organization and its human resources can be more productive and successful. If change is to be successfully implemented, however, it must be approached systematically. There may be a tendency to feel, "We have always done it this way, so why argue with success?" However, a firm's past success guarantees neither future prosperity nor even survival.

Reducing resistance to change is crucial to success. At times, this may be extremely difficult because it usually requires shifts in attitudes. However, if resistance to it can be reduced or even eliminated, change can be implemented more effectively. Bringing about a change in attitude requires trust and respect between the people attempting to implement the change and the individuals affected by it. Often, an important factor in this attitudinal transformation is active involvement in planning the change by the people who will be affected by it. This creates a feeling of ownership, and who wants to see their own plans go down the tubes?

## FACTORS INFLUENCING TRAINING AND DEVELOPMENT

Change is obviously one factor that impacts and is impacted by T&D. Other issues that often determine whether a firm achieves its T&D objectives are discussed next.

## Top Management Support

Top management support is perhaps the most basic training and development requirement. Without it, a T&D program is up the creek without a paddle. Moreover, this support must be real—not merely lip service. It should be communicated to the entire organization. The most effective way to do this is for executives to take an active part in the training and provide the needed resources.

## Commitment from Specialists and Generalists

In addition to top management, all managers—whether they be specialists or generalists—should be committed to and involved in the T&D process. According to one prominent director of corporate management development, "The primary responsibility for training and development lies with line managers, from the president and chairman of the board on down. T&D professionals merely provide the technical expertise."

## Technological Advances

Perhaps no factor has influenced T&D more than technology. The computer and the Internet, in particular, are dramatically affecting the way all business functions are being conducted. As emphasized throughout this chapter, technology has played a huge role in changing the way knowledge is being delivered to employees, and this change is constantly being extended.

## Organization Complexity

Flatter organization structures resulting from fewer managerial levels give the appearance of a simpler arrangement of people and tasks. Nothing could be further from the truth. The tasks of individuals and teams have been enlarged and enriched with the result that American workers are spending more time on the job and performing more complex tasks than ever before. Also, the interactions between individuals and groups have become more complicated. The traditional chain of command, which provides a sense of stability at the expense of efficiency, is outdated in many modern organizations. Other time-honored concepts have also been laid by the wayside.

In recent years, the increasingly rapid changes in technology, products, systems, and methods have had a significant impact on job requirements. Thus, employees face the need to constantly upgrade their skills and to develop an attitude that permits them not only to adapt to change, but also to accept and even seek it. Many organizations have changed dramatically as a result of downsizing, technological innovations, and customer demands for new and better products and services. The result is often that fewer people must accomplish more work at a more complex level. Supervisors and operative employees performing in self-directed teams are taking up much of the slack from dwindling middle-management ranks. All these changes translate into a greater need for training and development.

## Learning Principles

The purpose of training is to change employee behavior, and information must be learned if change is to occur. Although much remains to be discovered about the learning process, a number of generalizations stemming from the behavioral sciences have affected the way training is conducted. Some examples follow:

◗ Learners progress in an area of learning only as far as they need to in order to achieve their purposes.

◗ The best time to learn is when the learning can be useful.

◗ Depending on the type of training, a wise move may be to space out the training sessions.

Computer technology, the Internet, and intranets have made these approaches economically feasible to a degree never before possible. The ability to deliver knowledge to employees on an as-needed basis, anywhere on the globe, and at a pace consistent with their learning styles greatly enhances T&D's value to organizations.

## Other Human Resource Functions

Successful accomplishment of other human resource functions can also have a crucial impact on T&D. For instance, if recruitment and selection efforts attract only marginally qualified workers, a more extensive T&D program will be needed to train entry-level workers. Training and development efforts may also be influenced by the firm's compensation package. Firms with competitive pay systems or progressive health and safety programs will find it easier to attract workers who are capable of hitting the ground running and to retain employees who require less training.

## THE TRAINING AND DEVELOPMENT PROCESS

Major adjustments in the external and internal environments necessitate corporate change. The general training and development process that anticipates or responds to change is shown in Figure 8-2. Once the need for change is recognized and the factors that influence T&D are considered, the process of determining training and development needs begins. Essentially, two questions must be asked: "What are our training needs?" and "What do we want to accomplish through our T&D efforts?" The objectives might be quite narrow if limited to the supervisory ability of a manager. Or, they might be broad enough to include improving the management skills of all first-line supervisors.

In exemplary organizations, there is a close linkage between the firm's strategic mission and the objectives of the T&D program. These objectives are reviewed and updated periodically to conform to the changing strategic needs of the organization.[9] After stating the T&D objectives, management can determine the appropriate methods for accomplishing them. Various methods and media are available to implement T&D programs. Naturally, T&D must be continuously evaluated to ensure its value in achieving organizational objectives.

Global competition has dramatically increased the need for efficiency. One way this has impacted T&D is the requirement for *just-in-time training*—training made available when and where needed—more closely related to organizational goals and specific needs. Recognizing that T&D must be a nonstop process, there is a trend for firms to become learning organizations. In a dynamic environment, firms must provide training initiatives that address several critical needs:

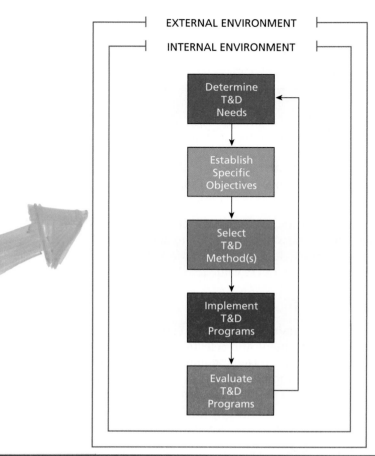

EXTERNAL ENVIRONMENT

INTERNAL ENVIRONMENT

Determine
T&D
Needs

Establish
Specific
Objectives

Select
T&D
Method(s)

Implement
T&D
Programs

Evaluate
T&D
Programs

**Figure 8-2** **The Training and Development (T&D) Process**

- To guide individual employees in planning and managing their careers
- To help managers coach and mentor employees
- To help managers and employees deal with change

The only constant in our lives is said to be change, and change is the force that brings about the need for T&D. Determining training and development needs is discussed next.

## DETERMINING TRAINING AND DEVELOPMENT NEEDS

The first step in the T&D process is to determine specific training and development needs. In today's highly competitive business environment, undertaking programs simply because other firms are doing it is asking for trouble. A systematic approach to addressing bona fide needs must be undertaken.

Training and development needs may be determined by conducting analyses on several levels. From an *overall organizational* perspective, the firm's strategic mission, goals, and corporate plans should be studied, along with the results of human resource planning. The next level of analysis focuses on the *tasks* that must be accomplished in order to achieve the firm's purposes. Job descriptions, performance appraisals, and interviews or surveys of supervisors and job incumbents are important data sources for this analysis level. Finally, *individual training needs* must be addressed. The relevant questions are, "Who needs to be trained?" and "What kind of training is needed?"

Sky Foster, manager for training and associate development for South Carolina–based BMW, emphasizes the need for input from everyone at all levels to determine training needs. He states, "We are now training for need, as opposed to rolling out a number of courses. First it was a check-off list for many of the courses, but now they have more impact and meaning. We specifically ask, 'What knowledge do you want your people to have? What skills do they need? What do they need to do differently from what they're doing today?' We ask more pointed questions and find out exactly what job knowledge and skills the person must have to perform."[10]

## ESTABLISHING TRAINING AND DEVELOPMENT OBJECTIVES

Clear and concise objectives must be formulated for T&D. Without them, designing meaningful T&D programs would not be possible. Worthwhile evaluation of a program's effectiveness would also be difficult at best. Consider these purposes and objectives for a training program involving employment compliance:

### Training Area: Employment Compliance

**Purpose.** To provide the supervisor with
1. Knowledge and value of consistent human resource practices
2. The intent of EEO legal requirements
3. The skills to apply them

**Objectives.** To be able to
1. Cite the supervisory areas affected by employment laws on discrimination.
2. Identify acceptable and unacceptable actions.
3. State how to get help on equal employment opportunity matters.
4. Describe why we have discipline and grievance procedures.
5. Describe our discipline and grievance procedures, including who is covered.

As you can see, the purpose is clearly established first. The specific learning objectives that follow leave little doubt about what should be learned from the training. With these objectives, managers may determine whether a person has obtained the necessary knowledge. For instance, a trainee either can or cannot state how to get help on equal employment opportunity matters.

## TRAINING AND DEVELOPMENT METHODS

When a person is working on a car, some tools are more helpful in doing certain tasks than others. The same logic applies when considering various T&D methods. Note the diverse methods shown in Table 8-1. A few methods are more applicable to managers and professionals and others to operative employees. As you see, however, the majority of T&D methods generally apply to all employees.

Again referring to Table 8-1, note that T&D methods are used both on and off the job. Often, it is not feasible to learn while at the same time performing jobs. Thus, although an increasing amount of training takes place on the job at the time the employee needs the training, many T&D programs occur away from the work setting.

Regardless of whether programs are presented in-house or by an outside source, a number of methods are utilized in imparting knowledge and skills to managers and operative employees. We discuss these methods next.

## Table 8-1  Training and Development Methods

| Method | Utilized Generally for | | | Conducted Primarily | |
|---|---|---|---|---|---|
| | Managers and Professionals | Operative Employees | All Employees | On the Job | Off the Job |
| Coaching and mentoring | X | | | X | |
| Business games | X | | | | X |
| Case study | | | X | | X |
| Videotapes | | | X | | X |
| In-basket training | X | | | | X |
| Internships | X | | | X | |
| Role playing | | | X | | X |
| Job rotation | | | X | X | |
| Computer-based training | | | X | X | |
| Web-based training: the Internet, intranets, and just-in-time training | | | X | X | |
| Distance learning and videoconferencing | | | X | | X |
| Classroom programs | | | X | | X |
| On-the-job training | | | X | X | |
| Apprenticeship training | | X | | X | |
| Simulators | | | X | | X |
| Vestibule training | | X | | | X |
| Corporate universities | | | X | | X |
| Community colleges training | | | X | | X |

## Coaching and Mentoring

Coaching and mentoring are primarily on-the-job development approaches emphasizing learning on a one-to-one basis. Coaching is often considered a responsibility of the immediate boss, who has greater experience or expertise and is in the position to offer sage advice. The same is true with a mentor, but this person may be located elsewhere in the organization or even in another firm. The relationship may be established formally or may develop on an informal basis. Because the two approaches are so similar in concept and the terms often used interchangeably in the literature, they are dealt with together here.

Depending on their organizational relationship, mentors may perform these kinds of roles: They provide coaching, sponsor advancement, provide challenging assignments, protect employees from adverse forces, and encourage positive visibility. They also provide personal support, friendship, acceptance, counseling, and role modeling.[11] How important is it for a manager to have a mentor? It has been suggested that having a mentor is essential to make it to the top, and the lack of one explains the difficulty women and minorities have encountered with the glass ceiling. In addition, mentoring has other advantages for new hires. A study sponsored by Deloitte & Touche found that Generation Xers were entrepreneurial, hardworking, confident, and committed. However, they were less loyal to their employers than their predecessors. What makes a difference for them? The study found that it was mentoring.[12]

While it is helpful for mentors to level with their protégés, this practice can be risky, as the topics that arise often involve gender and race. Discussion of EEO topics would no doubt be helpful, but potential legal dangers discourage the practice.

As a result, mentors tend to seek out their mirror images. Since women and minorities are not equally represented at the firm's top levels, they are often left without a mentor. No action can guarantee freedom from lawsuits. Still, some formal guidelines might provide a degree of legal protection. The main point is that women and minorities need to have advantages provided by mentors to effectively use their talents and realize their potential, not only for their personal benefit but to assist their firm.[13]

Coaching is one of the hottest things going in HR today, although the formal HR unit is often not involved. AT&T, IBM, and Kodak are among large firms that believe in the approach. Also, less-structured programs are popping up in smaller, high-growth companies across the nation.[14] While some companies have become too lean to provide inside coaches, individual managers have independently sought out their own. Today's coaches are often different from those of the past because of a vastly changed environment. "You can't turn to your nice, gray-haired mentor and say, 'From your 30 years of experience, how do you handle a dot-com?'"[15] On the other hand, it seems reasonable that "new economy" managers and "old economy" managers can learn from each other. A classic example is provided by the relationship of Scott McNealy, youthful CEO of Sun Microsystems, and a more seasoned Jack Welch, CEO of General Electric. These executives share their expertise and agree that "dot-coming" your business—essential in today's economy—is not that hard; it is getting the fundamentals down that is the most difficult. Another example is Microsoft's CEO Bill Gates, who regularly consults business guru Warren Buffett for advice.[16]

Although mentoring has many obvious advantages, there are two reasons why the process is not foolproof. One reason is the mentor; the other is the protégé. Some managers do not have the temperament to become a mentor or coach. The role imposes additional work, and some literally have no time. Others just do not want to be bothered. On the other side, some new hires are argumentative or just plain uninterested. Even if both parties are generally willing for the relationship, there may be a personality conflict. Ultimately, the proper pairing of individuals in a mentoring/protégé relationship is critical to its success.[17]

## Business Games

**Business games** are simulations that attempt to duplicate selected factors in a particular business situation, which are then manipulated by the participants. Business games involve two or more hypothetical organizations competing in a given product market. The participants are assigned roles such as president, controller, and marketing vice president. They make decisions affecting price levels, production volumes, and inventory levels. A computer program manipulates their decisions, with the results simulating those of an actual business situation. Participants are able to see how their decisions affect other groups and vice versa. The best part about this type of learning is that if a decision costs the company $1 million, no one gets fired, yet the business lesson is learned.

**Business games**
Simulations that attempt to duplicate selected factors in a particular business situation, which are then manipulated by the participants.

## Case Study

The **case study** is a training method in which trainees are expected to study the information provided in the case and make decisions based on it. If the student is given a case involving an actual company, he or she would be expected to research the firm to gain a better appreciation of its financial condition and environment. Typically, the case study method is used in the classroom with an instructor who serves as a facilitator.

**Case study**
A training method in which trainees are expected to study the information provided in the case and make decisions based on it.

## Videotapes

The use of videotapes continues to be a popular training method. This method may be especially appealing to small businesses that cannot afford more expensive approaches.[18] In addition, videotapes provide the flexibility desired by any firm. Behavior modeling—long a successful training approach—provides an illustration of the use of videotapes. **Behavior modeling** utilizes videotapes to illustrate effective interpersonal skills and how managers function in various situations. The trainees observe the model's actions. Behavior modeling has been used to train supervisors in such tasks as conducting performance appraisal reviews, correcting an unacceptable performance, delegating work, improving safety habits, handling discrimination complaints, overcoming resistance to change, orienting new employees, and mediating between individuals or groups in conflict.

**Behavior modeling**
A training method that utilizes videotapes to illustrate effective interpersonal skills and how managers function in various situations.

## In-Basket Training

**In-basket training** is a simulation in which the participant is given a number of business papers or e-mail messages including memoranda, reports, and telephone messages that would typically be sent to a manager or team leader. The messages, presented in no particular order, call for anything from urgent action to routine handling. The participant is required to act on the information contained in these messages. In this method, the trainee assigns a priority to each particular situation before making any decisions. This training method is commonly used in assessment centers, which were discussed in Chapter 7.

**In-basket training**
A simulation in which the participant is given a number of business papers or e-mail messages including memoranda, reports, and telephone messages that would typically be sent to a manager or team leader.

## Internships

As we mentioned in Chapter 5, an internship program is a recruitment method typically involving university students who divide their time between attending classes and working for an organization. Internships also serve as an effective training method. From the employer's viewpoint, an internship provides an excellent means of viewing a potential permanent employee at work. Internships also provide advantages for students. The experience they obtain through working enables them to integrate theory learned in the classroom with the practice of management.

## Role Playing

In **role playing**, participants are required to actually respond to specific problems they may encounter in their jobs. Rather than hearing about how a problem might be handled or even discussing it, they learn by doing. Role playing is often used to teach such skills as interviewing, grievance handling, performance appraisal reviews, team problem solving, effective communication, and leadership style analysis. The "Developing HRM Skills" section at the end of each chapter is a role-playing exercise that demonstrates the benefits of this training approach.

**Role playing**
A training method in which participants are required to respond to specific problems they may actually encounter in their jobs.

## Job Rotation

In **job rotation**, employees move from one job to another to broaden their experience. This breadth of knowledge is often needed for performing higher-level tasks. Rotational training programs help new employees understand a variety of jobs and their interrelationships. Many of today's jobs are quite broad in scope.

**Job rotation**
A training method that involves moving employees from one job to another to broaden their experience.

Individuals performing in these enlarged and enriched jobs may have the feeling that they are engaged in job rotation. A current job incumbent is certainly receiving a broader exposure to knowledge than in the past, and that is the basic purpose of job rotation.

## Computer-Based Training

**Computer-based training** takes advantage of the speed, memory, and data manipulation capabilities of the computer for greater flexibility of instruction. Some forms of this training reflect a technology upgrade of an earlier training method called *programmed instruction*. The increased speed of presentation is an advantage of this training approach. Another advantage is less dependence on an instructor, although some students may object to the absence of a human facilitator.

Computer-based training may also utilize multimedia. **Multimedia** enhances computer-based learning with audio, animation, graphics, and interactive video. Instruction can be provided either in a central location or a satellite office. While the expense of hardware and software may be significant, with enough trainees the cost may quickly reach an acceptable level. Multimedia also lends itself to Web-based training, as discussed in a later section.

**Virtual reality** is a unique computer-based approach that permits trainees to view objects from a perspective otherwise impractical or impossible. For example, it is not feasible to turn a drill press on its side so it can be inspected from the bottom. A computer easily permits this type of manipulation.

Technology is revolutionizing the way training and development programs can be delivered. It allows a human resources department to provide on-demand information that can be updated constantly and distributed nationally or globally. Computer-based training is clearly more than a fad. In fact, a vast majority of large organizations use computers in training.

Computer training can be delivered in several ways. The most common delivery methods are shown in Figure 8-3. Note that online training using the Internet and intranet is currently the most popular delivery method, accounting for 38 percent of computer training. This approach is closely followed by the use of CD-ROMs, at 37 percent.[19]

**Computer-based training**
A teaching method that takes advantage of the speed, memory, and data manipulation capabilities of the computer for greater flexibility of instruction.

**Multimedia**
An application that enhances computer-based learning with audio, animation, graphics, and interactive video.

**Virtual reality**
A unique computer-based approach that permits trainees to view objects from a perspective otherwise impractical or impossible.

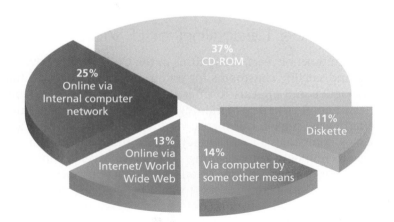

**How Computer-Delivered Training Breaks Down**

**Figure 8-3**

*Source:* Reprinted with permission from the October 1999 issue of *TRAINING* Magazine. Copyright 1999. Bill Communications, Minneapolis, MN. All rights reserved. Not for resale.

# Web-Based Training: The Internet, Intranets, and Just-in-Time Training

E-mail on the Internet is not just an effective and efficient way to exchange memoranda. It may also be used for accessing course material and sharing other information. Interactive tutorials permit trainees to take courses online. This practice has become common. An overwhelming advantage of using Web-based training is that it can be provided anytime when needed, anywhere in the world, and in different languages. Animation, video, and multimedia make presentations vivid and appealing.

In the hotel industry, where the average employee turnover is 120 percent a year for hourly employees, Days Inn of America Inc. had to find a way to train a workforce of 18,000 people at 1,800 locations worldwide with a budget limited to 11 trainers. The answer has been interactive Web-based training using the Internet and the firm's intranets to educate employees, distributors, and others. Although there is a large up-front cost, it is estimated that computer-based training will cost about half as much as classroom training.[20]

DigitalThink, Inc., the leading producer and distributor of Web-based information technology training for professionals worldwide, has an agreement to provide information technology training for up to 11,000 Motorola employees. The training allows Motorola employees to learn the latest technologies at their own pace, from wherever they have a Web connection. Doug Ferguson, training operations specialist for Motorola, stated, "Students can train at their desktops, without having to go to a learning lab, on any computer that runs a standard Web browser."[21]

An innovative way to reduce training costs is for firms to join together, as some have done to form LearnShare, a consortium of large, noncompeting manufacturing companies. This group, which includes Owens Corning, General Motors, Motorola, 3M, and three research universities, has combined resources to buy a Web site and the materials required for multimedia training. Although the firms are in different types of businesses, a survey indicated that 74 percent of their training needs were the same. For example, diversity training for GM employees should vary little from that needed by Reynolds Metals, Deere & Company, or others in the consortium. As these participants consolidate their power to take advantage of technology, their consortium can distribute educational materials anywhere on earth almost instantly and with less cost than if each company acted alone.[22]

## Distance Learning and Videoconferencing

For a number of years, many firms in the United States have used videoconferencing and satellite classrooms for training. This approach to training is now going interactive and appears to offer the flexibility and spontaneity of a traditional classroom. A great deal of training is beginning to take place using this technology, offering the prospect of increasing the number of trainees and at the same time saving companies a lot of money. Global firms in particular can benefit from this new technology. With far-flung operations, travel expenses are getting more and more out of hand. Distance learning, videoconferencing, and similar technology can be used to increase access to training, ensure consistency of instruction, and reduce the cost of delivering training and development programs.

## Classroom Programs

Classroom programs continue to be effective for certain types of employee training. In fact, they continue to head the list of training delivery methods used by

American firms. Ninety percent of respondents to a recent survey stated an intention to use classroom programs, although more are using assistance provided by technology as well.[23] For example, computer software such as Microsoft *PowerPoint* can enhance a presentation.

One advantage of classroom programs is that the instructor may convey a great deal of information in a relatively short period of time. The effectiveness of classroom programs can be improved when groups are small enough to permit discussion, when the instructor is able to capture the imagination of the class, and when multimedia can be used in an appropriate manner. You may recall that Lou McGowen, the supervisor mentioned at the beginning of the chapter, planned to have her workers attend classroom sessions.

## On-the-Job Training

**On-the-job-training (OJT)** is an informal approach to training that permits an employee to learn job tasks by actually performing them. It is the most commonly used approach to T&D. With OJT, there is no problem in later transferring what has been learned to the task. Individuals may also be more highly motivated to learn because it is clear to them that they are acquiring the knowledge needed to perform their jobs. At times, however, the emphasis on production may tend to detract from the training process. The trainee may feel so much pressure to perform that learning is negatively affected. Firms should be selective about who provides on-the-job-training. The trainers can be either supervisors or peers; however, they must have a good work ethic and correctly model desired behavior.

> **On-the-job training (OJT)**
> An informal approach to training in which an employee learns job tasks by actually performing them.

## Apprenticeship Training

**Apprenticeship training** combines classroom instruction with on-the-job training. Such training is traditionally used in craft jobs, such as those of plumber, barber, carpenter, machinist, and printer. While in training, the employee earns less than the master craftsperson who is the instructor. The training period varies according to the craft. For instance, the apprenticeship training period for barbers is two years; for machinists, four years; and for pattern makers, five years.

> **Apprenticeship training**
> A combination of classroom instruction and on-the-job training.

German-owned Siemens Stromberg-Carlson has a background in apprenticeship training that spans 100 years. A program at its Lake Mary, Florida, plant involves both high school students and students from Seminole Community College. The high school students work at Siemens three hours a day, twice a week. Community college students complete a two-and-a-half-year curriculum while working 20 hours a week.[24] Employees recruited from the apprenticeship program are expected to hit the ground running. Siemens's experience had shown that this was not possible with other recruits.[25]

**HRM IN ACTION**

### ▶ *Who Should I Train?*

"This new position of Internet recruiter is really giving me heartburn," said Andrew Alexander, HR director for IT Electronics to the general manager, Gina Magdaleno. "I can find people who are great at working on the Internet but know little about recruiting. I can find HR people who are weak in working on the Internet but have a good HR background. Whatever I do, I am going to have to train the person, and the type of training we need to use will depend on the person hired." Gina replied, "What type of training would be required in both instances?"

*How should Andrew reply?*

## Simulators

**Simulators**
Training devices of varying degrees of complexity that duplicate the real world.

**Simulators** are training devices of varying degrees of complexity that model the real world. They range from simple paper mock-ups of mechanical devices to computerized simulations of total environments. Training and development specialists may use simulated sales counters, automobiles, and airplanes. Although simulator training may be less valuable than on-the-job training for some purposes, it has certain advantages. A prime example is the training of airline pilots: Simulated crashes do not cost lives or deplete the firm's fleet of jets.

## Vestibule Training

**Vestibule training**
Training that takes place away from the production area on equipment that closely resembles the actual equipment used on the job.

**Vestibule training** takes place away from the production area on equipment that closely resembles equipment actually used on the job. For example, a group of lathes may be located in a training center where the trainees will be instructed in their use. A primary advantage of vestibule training is that it removes the employee from the pressure of having to produce while learning. The emphasis is on learning the skills required by the job.

## Corporate Universities

The corporate training institution differs from many traditional training programs in that its focus is on creating organizational change and it is proactive and strategic rather than reactive and tactical. In 1988, there were about 400 corporate universities; in 2000, it was estimated that there were more than 1,600. If this growth rate continues, the roughly 3,700 traditional universities will someday be outnumbered. The best-known corporate universities include those at McDonalds, Disney, Motorola, Sears, and Intel. Intel University in Arizona administers programs developed by 73 training groups located worldwide. Intel offers technology courses ranging from using Microsoft *Word* to training in lithography, one of the stages of computer-chip manufacturing. The university also teaches nontechnical skills such as dealing with conflict and harassment avoidance.[26]

Growth in the number of corporate universities may be attributed to their flexibility, which permits students to learn on their own time, and the use of various modes including CD-ROM programs, audio- and videotapes and, of course, the Internet.[27] Also, firms are better able to control the quality of training and to ensure that their employees receive the same message. The remarkable growth rate of corporate universities clearly illustrates that they have something going for them. However, many public and private colleges and universities are taking similar approaches to training and education. And corporate training programs often partner with colleges and universities or other organizations, such as the American Management Association, in delivering training.[28]

## Community College Training

Some employers, including giant General Motors, have discovered that community colleges can provide certain types of training better and more cost effectively than can alternatives. Rapid technological changes and corporate restructuring have created a new demand by industry for community college training resources. Here are some examples:[29]

▶ Some employees have discovered that community colleges can provide certain types of training better and more cost effectively than can alternatives.

- ▶ Sematech, the semiconductor industry association, is working with Maricopa County Community College in Phoenix to develop a national curriculum for training manufacturing technicians.
- ▶ Pennsylvania Power & Light has created a technology demonstration center with Northampton County Area Community College in Bethlehem, Pennsylvania, to test-run new developments.
- ▶ Aegon US, the Cedar Rapids insurer, built a $10 million corporate data center at Kirkwood Community College in Cedar Rapids, Iowa, to be shared by college students and company employees.
- ▶ General Motors and Toyota donated $2 million of equipment and 75 demonstration cars to Gateway Community Technical College in North Haven, Connecticut, to prepare service technicians to work at area car dealerships. GM has similar programs at more than 50 other schools.

## MANAGEMENT DEVELOPMENT

A firm's future lies largely in the hands of its managers. This group performs certain functions essential to the organization's survival and prosperity. Managers must make the right choices in most of the numerous decisions they make. Otherwise, the firm will not grow and may even fail. Therefore, it is imperative that managers keep up with the latest developments in their respective fields and, at the same time, manage an ever-changing workforce operating in a dynamic environment. **Management development** consists of all learning experiences provided by an organization resulting in an upgrading of skills and knowledge required in current and future managerial positions. Whereas critical knowledge and skills are provided by organizations in development programs, the process also requires personal commitment of the individual manager. In fact, taking responsibility for one's own development may be the most important aspect.

**Management development** Learning experiences provided by an organization for the purpose of upgrading skills and knowledge required in current and future managerial positions.

First-line supervisors, middle managers, and executives may all be expected to participate in management development programs. These programs are offered in-house, by professional organizations, and at colleges and universities. In-house programs are often planned and presented by a firm's T&D specialists in conjunction with line managers. Organizations such as the Society for Human Resource Management and the American Management Association conduct conferences and seminars in a number of specialties. Numerous colleges and universities also provide management training and development programs. At times, colleges and universities possess expertise not available within business organizations. In some cases, academicians and management practitioners can advantageously present

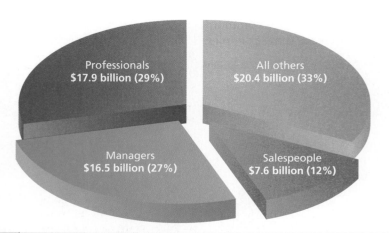

T&D programs jointly. The most frequently mentioned reasons to conduct management training outside the company include these:

- An outside perspective
- New viewpoints
- Exposure to faculty experts and research
- Broader vision

The most frequently mentioned reasons for keeping management training inside the company are the following:

- Training that is more specific to needs
- Lower costs
- Less time
- Consistent, relevant material
- More control of content and faculty
- Development of organizational culture and teamwork

Organizations in the United States focus training efforts on managers and professionals. In fact, better than half their training dollars are spent on these two types of employees. As you can see in Figure 8-4, training for professionals accounts for 29 percent of the total; training for managers, 27 percent; and sales training, 12 percent.[30]

## EXECUTIVE AND MANAGEMENT DEVELOPMENT AT IBM

At IBM, formal management development programs are conducted for various organizational levels. These programs vary from three-day sessions for recently appointed managers to two-week programs designed for newly named executives having worldwide responsibilities. Specifically, the following programs are provided: New Manager Training—U.S. Policy and Practices; New Manager School—IBM Leadership Program; IBM Business Management Institute; and IBM Global Executive Program.

New Manager Training—U.S. Policy and Practices is provided for newly appointed managers at various locations. This three-day program's purpose is to develop an understanding of IBM's basic management policies, practices, and skills. It focuses on performance management, compensation, diversity, career development, and management of individuals.

New Manager School—IBM Leadership Program is designed for all individuals appointed to the initial level of management responsibility. The three-and-a-half-day school normally begins within 60 to 90 days after the appointment and is held at the Central Headquarters Management Development Center in Armonk, New York.

IBM Business Management Institute is an eight-day program held worldwide. It is for individuals newly appointed to responsibility for an organization having significant impact on IBM's success in the marketplace. The program focuses on profitability and customer satisfaction. Case studies and business models are utilized to work on actual IBM business problems.

IBM Global Executive Program is for newly named executives with worldwide responsibilities. This two-week program is conducted in New York and La Hulpe, Belgium. The program focuses on building global perspectives, fostering performance and change, and leveraging IBM's capabilities. A significant part of the program involves addressing a strategic business issue, including the presentation of results to the sponsoring senior executive.

## SPECIAL TRAINING AREAS

As noted, the bulk of training and development programs have historically been provided for managers, professionals, and salespersons. Of course, many organizations also have extensive programs for supervisors and operative employees. These programs are often built around specific tasks required to perform given jobs. Other programs may deal with critical areas that surround the job. Included in the latter category are training involving telecommuting, diversity, customer service, conflict resolution, values, teamwork, empowerment, and remedial training.

- *Telecommuter training* is needed for both the telecommuter and her or his supervisor. The primary challenge for the telecommuter is to be able to work without direct supervision; the challenge for the supervisor is to make a shift from *activity-based management* to *results-based management*.[31] This is a difficult transition for the many managers who feel that you cannot be productive unless you are at your workplace.
- *Diversity training* attempts to develop sensitivity among employees about the unique challenges facing women and minorities and strives to create a more harmonious working environment. This popular training is viewed as essential by many firms that recognize the significance of today's highly diverse workforce.
- *Customer service training* teaches employees the skills needed to meet and exceed customer expectations. Emphasis is given to communication skills, including listening skills, and the recognition of diverse customer needs and requirements.
- *Conflict resolution training* focuses on developing the communication skills needed to resolve gridlock in relationships. While a degree of conflict can be constructive when it improves the quality of decisions and stimulates creativity, uncontrolled conflict is eventually destructive.
- *Values training* educates employees about the firm's most prized values relating to such areas as teamwork, trust, and respect for the individual and quality. Values are important because they generally influence attitudes and behavior.

- *Teamwork training* strives to teach employees how to work in groups that have often been given considerable authority in making decisions. This type of training is essential because our culture has historically nurtured individual accomplishments, yet organizations are increasingly using teams.
- *Empowerment training* teaches employees and work teams how to make decisions and accept responsibility for results. It is often given in conjunction with teamwork training because some firms have delegated considerable authority to teams. For example, work teams may actually hire employees for their group and determine pay increases and work schedules.
- *Remedial training* focuses on foundation skills such as basic literacy and mathematics skills. A large percentage of individuals are entering the workforce without the requisite skills to handle the jobs that technology has produced. David Kearns, former CEO of Xerox, believes that the failure of public school education costs industry at least $50 billion a year. It is estimated that as many as one-third of new employees require remedial training after high school to become qualified for work.[32]

## IMPLEMENTING TRAINING AND DEVELOPMENT PROGRAMS

A perfectly conceived training program can fail if management cannot convince the participants of its merits. Participants must believe that the program has value and will help them achieve their personal and professional goals. T&D's credibility in a firm may not be realized until a number of successful programs have been presented.

Implementing traditional T&D programs is often difficult. One reason is that managers are typically action oriented and feel that they are too busy for T&D. According to one management development executive, "Most busy executives are too involved chopping down the proverbial tree to stop for the purpose of sharpening their axes." Another difficulty in program implementation is that qualified trainers must be available. In addition to possessing communication skills, the trainers must know the company's philosophy, its objectives, its formal and informal organization, and the goals of the training program. Training and development requires more creativity than perhaps any other human resource function.

Implementing training programs presents unique problems. Training implies change, which employees may resist vigorously. Participant feedback is vital at this stage because there are often bugs in new programs. It may be difficult to schedule the training around present work requirements. Unless the employee is new to the firm, he or she undoubtedly has specific full-time duties to perform.

Another difficulty in implementing T&D programs is record keeping. Records should be maintained on all training the employee receives and how well he or she performs during training and on the job. This information is important in terms of measuring program effectiveness and charting the employee's progress in the company. The problems mentioned are certainly not insurmountable; however, the more effectively and efficiently they are resolved, the better the chances for success.

## EVALUATING TRAINING AND DEVELOPMENT

Although corporate America spends billions of dollars a year on employee training, there is no clear consensus within the training community on how to determine its value. Obviously, the credibility of T&D can be greatly enhanced if the tangible benefits to the organization can be shown. Thus, the training and development department must document its efforts and attempt to show that it provides a valuable service. Organizations have taken several approaches to determining the worth of specific programs.

## Participants' Opinions

Evaluating a training and development program by asking the participants' opinions of it is an inexpensive approach that provides a response and suggestions for improvements. You cannot always rely on such responses, however. The training may have taken place in an exotic location with time for golfing and other fun activities, and the overall experience may bias some reports. Nevertheless, this approach is a good way to obtain feedback and to get it quickly.

## Extent of Learning

Some organizations administer tests to determine what the participants in a T&D program have learned. The pretest-posttest control group design is one evaluation procedure that may be used. In this procedure, the same test is administered before and after training. It also calls for both a control group (which does not receive the training) and an experimental group (which does). Trainees are randomly assigned to each group. Differences in pretest and posttest results between the groups are then attributed to the training provided.

## Behavioral Change

Tests may indicate fairly accurately what has been learned, but they give little insight into whether the training leads participants to change their behavior. For example, it is one thing for a manager to learn about motivational techniques but quite another matter for this person to apply the new knowledge. A manager may sit in the front row of a training session dealing with empowerment of subordinates, absorb every bit of the message, understand it totally, and then return the next week to the workplace and continue behaving in the same old autocratic way.

## Accomplishment of T&D Objectives

Still another approach to evaluating T&D programs involves determining the extent to which stated objectives have been achieved. For instance, if the objective of an accident prevention program is to reduce the number and severity of accidents by 15 percent, comparing accident rates before and after training provides a useful measurement of success. The problem is that many programs dealing with broader topics are more difficult to evaluate.

## Benchmarking

Benchmarking uses exemplary practices of other organizations to evaluate and improve training and development programs. By some estimates, up to 70 percent of American firms engage in a type of benchmarking. Most of this effort involves monitoring and measuring a firm's internal processes, such as operations, and then comparing the data with data on companies that excel in those areas.

Benchmarking has been expanded beyond core business operations and is now being used by training functions. Because training programs for individual firms are unique, the training measures should be broad. For example, benchmarking questions often ask about the cost of training, the ratio of training staff to employees, and whether new or more traditional delivery systems are used. Information derived from these questions probably lacks the detail to permit

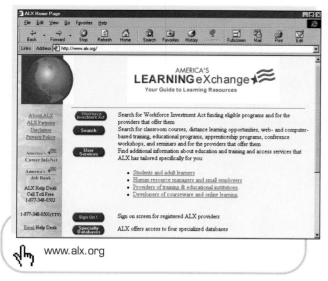

www.alx.org

specific improvements of the training curricula. However, a firm may recognize, for example, that another organization is able to deliver a lot of training for relatively little cost. This information could then trigger the firm to follow up with interviews or site visits to determine whether that phenomenon represents a "best practice." As training and development becomes more crucial to organizational success, determining model training practices and learning from them will become increasingly important.[33]

## A Case for Simplicity

Joe Furando, manager of organization development at Merck-Medco, votes for simplicity in evaluating T&D programs. He thinks that trainers need to understand that value is not determined by after-program evaluations or pre- or posttests. Rather, value is the measure of impact and positive change elicited by the training. Permitting input from numerous sources is an excellent way to determine whether co-workers have experienced a difference in the performance of the training participants.[34] The approach he favors is similar to the 360-degree performance appraisal system that is discussed in Chapter 10.

In evaluating T&D programs, managers should strive for proof that they are effective. Although such proof may be difficult to establish, the effect on performance should at least be estimated to show whether the training achieved its desired purpose. In spite of problems associated with evaluation, managers responsible for T&D must continue to strive for solid evidence of its contributions in achieving organizational goals.

## BUSINESS/GOVERNMENT/EDUCATION TRAINING PARTNERSHIPS

Government funds to support training have been dwindling. However, one federal program that has promise while eliminating much bureaucracy is the Workforce Investment Act. Another partnership was created when Congress passed the School-to-Work Opportunities Act. The overriding purpose of these and other partnerships is to develop a skilled workforce for tomorrow.

### Workforce Investment Act

In 1998, the Workforce Investment Act (WIA) was signed into law. The new law replaces the problem-riddled Job Training Partnership Act (JTPA) and consolidates more than 70 federal job-training programs. It provides states with the flexibility to develop streamlined systems in partnership with local governments. A primary focus of WIA is to meet the needs of business for skilled workers and to satisfy the training, education, and employment needs of individuals.[35]

One-stop service centers are at the heart of the new system. These centers provide jobseekers with a range of services including career counseling, skill assessments, training, job search assistance, and referrals to programs and services depending on need. As with the Job Training Partnership Act, the WIA is led by participants from the private sector. For ASTD's summary of the law and direct links to governors' offices, go to www.astd.org/virtual_community/public_policy. The Department of Labor's summary may be found at usworkforce.org.

## School-to-Work Opportunities Act and Other Partnerships[36]

A retired BellSouth CEO, John Clendenin, says that "the bottom line in America's fight for long-term competitiveness ultimately will be won or lost not in the halls of Congress, not in the boardrooms around the world, but in America's classrooms." In meeting this challenge, the School-to-Work Opportunities Act provides seed money for states to implement school-to-work plans. The National School-to-Work Office, a collaboration between the Departments of Education and Labor, administers grants and coordinates communication between the states and local partnerships. Organizations such as the National Employer Leadership Council are helping companies tailor their participation in school-to-work activities.

An example of how a partnership might function occurred with a prominent telecommunications firm. When a new state-appointed district superintendent, Dr. Beverly Hall, decided to close an old vocational education school that was not preparing youngsters for the workplace, she turned to a corporation for help. One firm—Bell Atlantic—came to the rescue. The school now has state-of-the-art labs and rooms outfitted such that Bell Atlantic actually uses them after hours to train its workers. Creation of the new Technology High School has been just one way that the company has helped itself by assisting schools. The firm sponsors 11 TEC2000 technology education centers in New Jersey that prepare students and other people entering the job market for jobs in the telecommunications industry. Furthermore, Bell Atlantic hires 80 percent of the graduates coming out of these programs. The other 20 percent find jobs elsewhere. The firm claims savings of thousands of dollars in training and retraining result from hiring the graduates.[37]

## ORIENTATION

First impressions are the most lasting. We have been taught this since childhood, and this philosophy can apply to new employees' impressions of their employers.[38] Because of this, many firms have orientation programs for new hires. **Orientation** is the initial T&D effort for new employees that strives to inform them about the company, the job, and the work group. It is a common type of formal training in U.S. organizations, and some firms have developed sophisticated approaches. For example, Federal Express uses computer-based training for orienting new employees in a two-hour program that offers detailed information on the corporate culture, benefits, policies, and procedures. It also outlines the company's organizational structure and features a video message from the chief executive officer. Orientation has the potential to positively impact a firm's operations. For example, one survey of 1,400 financial officers resulted in an overwhelming 83 percent of respondents indicating that formal orientation programs are effective in retaining and motivating personnel.[39]

In a typical orientation program, company policies and rules are spelled out along with the mechanics of promotion, demotion, transfer, resignation, discharge, layoff, and retirement. Also, a summary of employee benefits is often provided. These data are also likely to be included in handbooks given to each new employee or placed on the company's Web site.

To perform effectively, new employees need information that not only permits them to do their jobs but also helps them understand their co-workers'

**Orientation**
The initial T&D effort for new employees that strives to inform them about the company, the job, and the work group.

behavioral patterns. Although orientation is often the joint responsibility of the training staff and the line supervisor, peers often serve as excellent information agents. There are several reasons for peers' success in performing this function. For one thing, they are accessible to newcomers, often more so than the boss. Peers also tend to have a high degree of empathy for new people. In addition, they have the organizational experience and technical expertise to which new employees need access.

A new employee's first few days on the job may be spent in orientation. However, some firms feel that learning is more effective if spread out over a period of time. For example, a program may be delivered in a system of 20 one-hour sessions over a period of several weeks. Some firms are sensitive to information overload and make information available to employees on an "as needed" basis. For example, a new supervisor may eventually have the responsibility for evaluating his or her subordinates. But the knowledge of how to do this may not be needed for six months. A training segment on performance evaluation may be placed on the firm's intranet and be available to the supervisor when the need arises. This approach is consistent with "just-in-time training," discussed earlier in the chapter.

## PURPOSES OF ORIENTATION

Orientation formats are unique to each firm. However, some basic purposes include explaining the employment situation (the job, department, and company), company policies and rules, compensation and benefits, corporate culture, team membership, employee development, dealing with change, and socialization.

### The Employment Situation

At an early point in time, it is helpful for the new employee to know how his or her job fits into the firm's organizational structure and goals. This knowledge tends to clarify the significance of the job and provides meaning to the work.

### Company Policies and Rules

Every job within an organization must be performed within the guidelines and constraints provided by policies and rules. Employees must have an understanding of these to permit a smooth transition to the workplace. Again, it may be advisable to avoid cluttering the new employee's mind with details that will not be remembered. The important point is to have this information in a medium that is readily accessible.

### Compensation and Benefits

Employees will have a special interest in obtaining information about the reward system. This information is usually provided during the recruitment and selection process. A review of the data is appropriate during orientation.

### Corporate Culture

The firm's culture reflects, in effect, "how we do things around here." This relates to everything from the way employees dress to the way they talk. Companies have a number of ways to communicate their culture, and knowledge of it is critical to a new employee's orientation. Remember our earlier discussion of the importance of *organizational fit* to an employee's success.

## Team Membership

A new employee's ability and willingness to work in teams have most likely been determined before he or she was hired. In orientation, the importance of becoming a valued member of the company team may again be emphasized. Even though the individual is now and will always be important to organizations, many processes can be more effectively accomplished through teams. It is imperative that team spirit be instilled in each employee, and the sooner the better.

## Employee Development

Employee development in many cases is a do-it-yourself process. As previously noted, however, some firms do invest heavily in this area. Employees should know exactly what is expected of them and what is required for advancement in the job or for promotion. An individual's employment security is increasingly becoming dependent upon his or her ability to acquire needed knowledge and skills that are constantly changing. Thus, employees should be kept aware of company-sponsored developmental programs and those available externally, and they should receive encouragement and support to take advantage of any appropriate opportunities.

## Dealing with Change

The significance of change was discussed at the beginning of this chapter. Simply put, employees at all levels must learn to deal effectively with change to survive in their jobs. The best way individuals can be prepared for change is to continually expand their skills. It is mutually advantageous for both employee and employer for this to occur as it provides security for the employee and a more valuable performer for the firm.

One specialty parts manufacturer uses a new employee's first week on the job to help him or her adjust to its *change* culture. This particular firm needs to regularly change techniques, rapidly adjust to market needs, and quickly find cost-effective ways to build products. The company values initiative, hard work, innovation, and ability to accept and lead change. To develop an appreciation for accepting and creating change, a three-part orientation program is offered emphasizing these areas:[40]

▶ Recent company achievements, decisions made, expectations for creativity, and existing boundary limits
▶ The importance of working as a team
▶ The need for employee involvement with the business (every new employee is required to offer a suggestion to improve operations)

This firm's culture recognizes and rewards people for using their heads. The purpose of its orientation program is to ensure that each new hire begins employment doing just that.

## Socialization

To reduce the anxiety that new employees may experience, attempts should be made to integrate them into the informal organization. Some firms have found that employees subjected to socialization programs perform better than those who have not undergone such training.

Orientation programs are important to the success of any employee. As in other areas, technology has given a big boost to this organizational effort.

**▶ A Twenty-First Century Orientation Program**

Ernst & Young, headquartered in New York, has hired its first national director of orientation. The firm employs 68,000 people worldwide; 27,000 of these are in the United States. Ernst & Young hires over 5,000 people a year and has found that new employees who go through orientation are twice as likely to remain with the company longer than two years. New employees get a fully loaded computer and access to the company intranet. Online instructions here replace what Mike Egan, an Ernst & Young veteran of some 30 years, calls "those big, big books we used to load them down with." Now, he says, "everything we know is immediately available to them as they need it." Starting dates for new employees are limited to two a month, and a three-day orientation begins on these days to ensure that 100 percent of new hires go through the program. At the end of the program, which includes technology training, company history, and diversity, new hires are given the names of their peer adviser—an individual who is compensated with an extra bonus. New employees are given a customized guidebook that tells them what they are expected to learn and where they are supposed to be over the next six to nine months. Those nine months complete the employee's initial training.[41]

While much training and development effort is directed at individuals or groups of employees, some firms believe that to achieve needed change, the entire organization must be moved in the desired direction. Efforts to achieve this are referred to as *organization development,* and this topic is discussed next.

## ORGANIZATION DEVELOPMENT

**Organization development (OD)**
An organizationwide application of behavioral science knowledge to the planned development and support of organizational strategies, structures, and processes for improving a firm's effectiveness.

Remember from the discussion of corporate culture in Chapter 2 that various factors affect employees' behavior on the job. To bring about desired changes in these factors and behavior, organizations must be transformed into market-driven, innovative, and adaptive systems if they are to survive and prosper in today's highly competitive global environment. Many firms are beginning to face this urgent need by practicing organization development, a human resource development approach that involves the entire system. **Organization development (OD)** is an organizationwide application of behavioral science knowledge to the planned development and support of organizational strategies, structures, and processes for improving a firm's effectiveness.[42] Organization development is a major means of achieving change in the corporate culture. This type of development is increasingly important as both work and the workforce diversify and change.

Organization development applies to an entire system, such as a company or a plant. Although OD does not produce a blueprint for how things should be done, it does provide an adaptive strategy for planning and implementing change and strives for a long-term reinforcement of change.

Numerous organization development interventions are available to the practitioner.[43] Interventions discussed elsewhere in this book include performance appraisal, reward systems, career planning and development, and employee wellness. Interventions covered in the following section include survey feedback—a technique that may be combined with other interventions—quality circles, team building, and sensitivity training.

## Survey Feedback

**Survey feedback** is a process of collecting data from an organizational unit through the use of questionnaires, interviews, and objective data from other sources such as records of productivity, turnover, and absenteeism.[44] It enables management teams to help organizations create working environments that lead to better working relationships, greater productivity, and increased profitability.[45] A developing trend has been to combine survey feedback with other organization development interventions including work design, structural change, and intergroup relations.[46]

Survey feedback generally involves the following steps:

- Members of the organization, including top management, are involved in planning the survey.
- The survey instrument is administered to all members of the organizational unit.
- The OD consultant usually analyzes the data, tabulates results, suggests approaches to diagnosis, and trains participants in the feedback process.
- Data feedback usually begins at the top level of the organization and flows downward to groups reporting at successively lower levels.
- Feedback meetings provide an opportunity to discuss and interpret data, diagnose problem areas, and develop action plans.[47]

**Survey feedback**
A process of collecting data from an organizational unit through the use of questionnaires, interviews, and objective data from other sources such as records of productivity, turnover, and absenteeism.

## Quality Circles

The concept of quality circles was transported to America from Japan over 20 years ago and is used, in one form or another, by most *Fortune* 500 companies. This version of employee involvement is alive and well today, improving quality, increasing motivation, boosting productivity, and adding to the bottom line. **Quality circles** are groups of employees who voluntarily meet regularly with their supervisors to discuss their problems, investigate causes, recommend solutions, and take corrective action when authorized to do so.[48] The team's recommendations are presented to higher-level management for review, and the approved actions are implemented with employee participation.

In order to implement a successful quality circle program, the firm must set clear goals for the program, gain top management's support, and create a climate conducive to participative management. In addition, a qualified manager must be selected for the program and the program's goals must be communicated to all concerned. Individuals participating in the program must receive quality circle training. Most organizations that implement continuous improvement cultures, or team systems, teach their employees tools to use in reaching decisions and solving problems. The tools include four basic steps: problem definition, data collection to confirm the root cause of the problem, solution generation, and action planning. In addition, a tracking system is designed to determine results of the action taken.[49]

Honda of America Manufacturing, Inc., located in Marysville, Ohio, has a most impressive employee involvement effort called Voluntary Improvement Program (VIP). Rewards for participating in the program are very generous and include trips, cash, and points that provide even greater rewards. The VIP consists of the firm's special initiatives for involving employees (called *associates*) in quality circles, in their community, and in the firm's suggestion system. The incentives are based on annual involvement activity and accumulated career involvement. For example, the very top contributors who have accumulated the most

**Quality circles**
Groups of employees who voluntarily meet regularly with their supervisors to discuss problems, investigate causes, recommend solutions, and take corrective action when authorized to do so.

points can receive six months' use of a new Honda Accord or two airline tickets to anywhere in the continental United States. Others may receive restaurant or movie certificates. An associate who has accumulated 5,000 points can receive an Accord four-door LXAT, four weeks' base pay, two airline tickets to anywhere in the world, plus another two weeks' vacation.[50]

One thing seems certain: If employee interest and enthusiasm for quality circle activities are to be sustained, the employees must share in the economic gain. Nonfinancial rewards are great; however, if over the long run they are given to the exclusion of monetary rewards, the employees will wonder who really benefits from the programs.[51]

## Team Building

According to the American Society for Training and Development, team training is one of the hottest trends in human resources. However, while more and more firms are changing to team cultures, some employees—especially older workers—are accustomed to working on their own.[52] Individualism has deep roots in American culture. This trait has been a virtue and will continue to be an asset in our society. Now, however, there are work situations that make it imperative to subordinate individual autonomy in favor of cooperation with a group. Teams have been shown to be clearly superior in performing many of the tasks required by organizations. The building of effective teams, therefore, has become a business necessity.

Much training effort must be expended prior to efficient and effective functioning of work teams. Fortunately, most managers know this. A conscious effort to develop effective work groups throughout the organization is referred to as **team building**. Team building utilizes *self-directed teams* each composed of a small group of employees responsible for an entire work process or segment. Team members work together to improve their operation or product, to plan and control their work, and to handle day-to-day problems. They may even become involved in broader, companywide issues, such as vendor quality, safety, and business planning.

Team building may begin as soon as an employee is added to the payroll. At Southwest Airlines, the firm divides new employees into teams and gives them a raw egg in the shell, a handful of straws, and some masking tape. Their task is, in a limited amount of time, to protect that delicate cargo from an eight-foot drop. The exercise is intended to prepare teams of employees for creative problem solving in a fast-paced environment.[53]

A few years ago, physical-challenge exercises were the rage in team building. These activities have their place but are not suited for every team-building need. As a result, some new, inventive concepts have emerged, from building towers to cooking up a feast.

The Lake Forest Graduate School of Management has developed an approach it calls Team Banquets. This program was developed with an internationally recognized executive chef to bring together people with different knowledge, skills, and experience to accomplish a single goal: create a banquet. This exercise is based on the discovery that some of the most effective, efficient teams in the world are in the kitchens of fine restaurants. These settings serve as models of organization, communication, and results-oriented processes. The Team Banquet brings together 25 to 30 employees and challenges them to prepare a gourmet banquet within two hours. Only the raw ingredients and equipment are provided. The assigned roles may put a mail clerk in charge while a group manager serves as an assistant. Each team is assigned a specific portion of the banquet preparation,

**Team building**
A conscious effort to develop effective work groups throughout an organization.

An understanding of the effect of culture on training success is still often realized only after an experience of culture clash in a training setting. John Mirocha, head of a Minneapolis-based consulting firm, says, "When I first began my training adventures in cross-border settings, my assumption was that because I had studied abroad and worked cross-culturally in the United States, it would be similar [elsewhere]. Boy, was I wrong! I didn't really grasp the depth of the issues." For example, many Asians are reluctant to ask questions in front of a group. Mirocha suggests, "If you let them speak their own language in small groups, they can have the multilingual people report to the whole group. That way, more learning transpires because they're using their first language." In Asia, religion, history, economics, class systems, and politics have a deep impact on how life and work issues are perceived and programmed. According to Mirocha, "Once during a leadership development program in Bangkok, a participant asked me if she could consult her spirit advisors as part of the homework assignment to write a vision statement. Because I understood the religious history of Thailand, I said, 'Fine.'"

Phillip Hoffman, director of training and staff development for General Motors China in Shanghai, says, "It's particularly important to understand your own culture— how others see your culture's influence on your behavior and attitude." To trainers going abroad, Hoffman recommends reading the cultural orientation materials their hosts have read about them.

Kathleen Terry, president of Participative Management Systems, says, "Be willing to modify your ideas and approach. When in Singapore, I had participants write down their ideas, and then I asked them for feedback. Even though that had worked in the United States, no one responded. Later, someone explained to me that, in their culture, to volunteer their response would have been considered bragging. I would have been better off calling on them instead."

Milford Clarke, CEO of Clarke Consulting Group, says, "We assumed that Japanese trainers would be extemporaneous. But, we found that they are expected to 'blend' into a rigorous manual and follow it to the letter. They are also expected to follow an exact time schedule and work through all of the material without veering too far from the lesson plan, even to respond to trainees' questions. What's more, we American trainers were criticized for our behavior in the training sessions. We thought we were being professional. But, to the Japanese trainers, anything that wasn't in the manual was considered 'out of form.'"[54]

from main entrée to decorations and food presentation. Safety instructions are provided but recipes are not. Teams must rely on their own knowledge and creativity in devising the dishes they serve. The initial response to this approach was skepticism. However, it was soon discovered that the exercise provided an excellent analogy to the workplace and provided an outstanding means for developing teamwork.[55]

## Sensitivity Training

**Sensitivity training**, or the T-group, is designed to help participants learn about themselves and how others perceive them. It differs from many traditional forms of training, which stress the learning of a predetermined set of concepts. When sensitivity training begins, there is no agenda, no leaders, no authority, and no power positions. Essentially, a vacuum exists until participants begin to talk.

**Sensitivity training**
An organizational development technique that is designed to make people aware of themselves and their impact on others.

Through dialogue people begin to learn about themselves and others. The trainer's purpose is to serve as a facilitator in this unstructured environment. Participants are encouraged to learn about themselves and others in the group. Some objectives of sensitivity training are to increase the participants' self-awareness and sensitivity to the behavior of others. The training also strives to develop an awareness of the processes that facilitate or inhibit group and intergroup functioning and to increase the participants' ability to achieve more effective interpersonal relationships. T-group training was once a prominent OD intervention. Today, the National Training Laboratories and UCLA are among the few organizations that continue to offer this training.

# ▶ Summary

**①** **Define *training* and *development* (T&D).**

Training is designed to permit learners to acquire knowledge and skills needed for their present jobs. Development involves learning that goes beyond today's job.

**②** **Explain the relationship between organization change and training and development.**

The basic purpose of training and development is to anticipate change and to respond proactively to it. Change involves moving from one condition to another, and it will affect individuals, groups, and entire organizations.

**③** **Explain factors influencing T&D.**

Increasingly rapid changes in technology, products, systems, and methods have had a significant impact on job requirements, making T&D a must. Training and development programs must have top management's full support. All managers should be committed to and involved in the T&D process. They must be convinced that there will be a tangible payoff if resources are committed to this effort.

**④** **Describe the T&D process and how training needs are determined and objectives established.**

Once the need for change has been recognized and the factors that influence intervention considered, the process of determining training and development needs begins. After stating the T&D objectives, management can determine the appropriate methods for accomplishing them. Various training methods are available to use. T&D must be continuously evaluated. Training and development needs may be determined by conducting analyses on several levels. Clear and concise objectives must be formulated for T&D. Without them, designing meaningful T&D programs would not be possible.

**⑤** **Identify the various training and development methods.**

Training and development methods include coaching and mentoring, business games, case study videotapes, in-basket training, internships, role playing, job rotation, programmed instruction, computer-based training, web-based training, distance learning and videoconferencing, classroom programs, on-the-job training, apprenticeship training, simulators, vestibule training, corporate universities, and community college training.

**⑥** **Describe management development.**

Management development consists of all learning experiences provided by an organization for the purpose of providing and upgrading skills and knowledge required in current and future managerial positions.

**⑦** **Identify special training needs.**

Special training needs include training involving telecommuting, diversity, customer service, conflict resolution, values, teamwork, empowerment, and remedial training.

**8** **Identify the means by which T&D programs are implemented and evaluated.**

Means by which T&D programs are evaluated include participants' opinions, extent of learning, behavioral change, accomplishment of T&D objectives, and benchmarking.

**9** **Describe the training partnerships that exist between business, government, and education.**

Federal programs include the Workforce Investment Act and the School-to-Work Opportunities Act.

**10** **Define *orientation* and identify its purposes.**

Orientation is the guided adjustment of new employees to the company, the job, and the work group. Orientation acquaints employees with the employment situation, company policies and rules, compensation and benefits, and corporate culture.

**11** **Define *organization development (OD)* and describe various OD techniques.**

Organization development is an organizationwide application of behavioral science knowledge to the planned development and reinforcement of a firm's strategies, structures, and processes for improving its effectiveness. OD techniques include survey feedback, quality circles, sensitivity training, and team building.

## Questions for Review ◀

1. Distinguish between training and development.

2. What are some factors that influence T&D?

3. Describe the training and development process.

4. List and describe the primary training and development methods.

5. Define *management development*. Why is it important?

6. List and explain some special training needs.

7. What are some of the means of evaluating human resource development programs? Discuss.

8. What type of training partnerships exist between business, government, and education?

9. Define *orientation* and explain the purposes of orientation.

10. Define each of the following:

    a. *organization development*
    b. *survey feedback*
    c. *quality circles*
    d. *sensitivity training*
    e. *team building*

*We invite you to visit the Mondy homepage on the Prentice Hall Web site at*

**www.prenhall.com/mondy**

*for updated information, Web-based exercises, and links to other HR-related sites.*

**TAKE IT TO THE NET**

# ▶ Developing HRM Skills

## An Experiential Exercise

Training and development is very important to any organization as it faces change and deals with the continual development of its employees. Training can often be used to improve employee productivity. However, effective training cannot occur in a vacuum; therefore, training requires the support and understanding of the entire organization.

Two individuals will play roles in this exercise: one as the training specialist and the other as the supervisor. Each participant should carefully follow his or her role. All students not playing roles should carefully observe the behavior of both participants. Your instructor will provide the participants with additional information necessary to complete the exercise.

# ▶ HRM INCIDENT 1

## A Strange Pairing

General Motors and the Army National Guard are trying to solve one of the growing challenges of the Information Age: helping workers keep pace with the exponential growth of on-the-job knowledge. As Kevin Rogers, president of Interactive Solutions, said, "People can't remember all the information they learn in a classroom. They have to put it on their hip and take it with them wherever they go." GM and the military came together to solve their common training problem and brought Rogers into the group. The company has designed a wearable, multimedia, voice-controlled computer that provides on-the-spot training for technicians under the hood of a car or a tank. Users speak into the computer, the heart of which is a 7½-inch by 5½-inch black box packed with a Pentium microprocessor and multimedia cards that process applications such as speech recognition and video. It is equipped with software designed for on-the-job training or instant tutorials.

Training people for a high-tech world is a growing problem. By 2005, three-quarters of all new jobs will require technical skills, according to a spokesman for Interactive Solutions. It's impossible to put a price on what it will cost to address that training crisis nationwide, but it will be expensive if the auto industry is any indication. Interactive Solutions claims that 30 percent of the automotive industry's warranty repair costs are the result of faulty diagnoses by technicians. That creates billions of dollars a year in waste associated with unnecessary labor and parts. "We have literally hundreds of thousands of pages we have to reference. It's becoming more of an issue in the technical world," says Jim Roach, head of service technology research at GM. Some new GM car models have as many as 19 microprocessors, testing traditional training methods. At a model GM car dealership in Warren, Michigan, mechanics are testing five of Interactive Solutions's Mentis computers to see how well they work in the field. If all goes well, GM will distribute computers to car dealers around the country within 12 months, Roach says. Wearable computers could find a much broader application in medicine, education, and other knowledge-rich fields.[56]

### Questions

1. What do General Motors and the Army National Guard have in common?
2. In what other areas might this form of training be valuable?

*Solving a Disciplinary Action Problem Over the Intranet*

Roy Jackson, a recent business school graduate, is in his first job as a district sales manager. He hasn't been in this position nearly long enough to feel confident in confronting one of his top sales reps, Jim Orrin. Jim has led the district in sales for the past eight years and is currently on track for a record year. Jim has a serious problem with alcohol abuse, however, and came to the office drunk for the third time this month.

Uncertain as to his next action, Roy turns to his PC and clicks on an icon that takes him to his firm's intranet program "Management Advisor/Drug and Alcohol Abuse/Confronting an Employee." This program, developed by the training department and several line managers, plays a video that describes the firm's policy on providing help to an employee with a substance abuse problem. It also details the steps of a confrontation interview.

The program then asks if the viewer would like to see an example of a confrontation interview. When Roy clicks on "yes," he sees a 10-minute tape of a confrontation interview showing the steps and points the manager should make, typical employee responses, and how a manager can deal with each.

Orrin, suspecting that he may be fired, uses a company kiosk and clicks on the HR icon. He reaches a program on "Employee Assistance/Drug Abuse & Alcohol/Telling Your Boss You Have a Problem." He then views a tape advising him how to inform his boss that he needs assistance for a personal problem and how he can get help without being terminated.[57]

### Question

**1.** Do you believe that this is a realistic approach to training regarding disciplinary action?

**Notes** ◄

1. Richard Koonce, "How to Find the Right Organizational Fit," *Training & Development* 51 (April 1997): 15.

2. "Industry Report 1999," *Training* 36 (October 1999): 44.

3. Lynn E. Densford, "Star Wars: Employers Are Increasing Their Reliance on Training and Development Programs to Attract, Retain and Further Enhance the Productivity of Prized Employees," *Employee Benefit News* (May 1, 1999): 1.

4. Tom Barron, "Wooing IT Workers," *Training and Development* 53 (April 1999): 22.

5. "Do Perks and Bonuses Really Help Retain Employees? National Study by Interim Services, Inc., Unveils True Drivers of Retention," *PR Newswire* (May 1999): 1.

6. "Saratoga Institute: The 1999 Emerging Workforce Study," *M2 PressWire* (March 25, 1999): 1.

7. Martha H. Peak, "Go Corporate U," *Management Review* 86 (February 1997): 37.

8. "Industry Report 1999."

9. Judy D. Olian, Cathy C. Durham, and Amy L. Kristof, "Designing Management Training and Development for Competitive Advantage: Lessons from the Best," *Human Resource Planning* 21 (1998): 20–21.

10. Holly Ann Suzik, "Built from Scratch," *Quality* 38 (October 1999): 32–34.

11. Jack L. Simonetti, Sonny Ariss, and Joan Martinez, "Through the Top with Mentoring," *Business Horizons* 42 (November 1999): 42.

12. "Money Isn't Everything," *The Journal of Business Strategy* 21 (March/April 2000): 4.

13. Jonathan A. Segal, "Mirror-Image Mentoring," *HRMagazine* 45 (March 2000): 157–166.

14. "Mentoring Takes Off," *HR Focus* 76 (February 1999): 2.

15. Betsy Morris, "So You're a Player. Do You Need a Coach?" *Fortune* 141 (February 21, 2000): 145–146.

16. Brent Schlender, "The Odd Couple," *Fortune* 141 (May 1, 2000): 106–114.

17. Marilyn Moats Kennedy, "Will You Be My Mentor?" *Across the Board* 36 (May 1999): 56.

18. Tim McCollum, "Handy Tools for Training," *Nation's Business* 85 (April 1997): 49.

19. "Industry Report 1999."

20. Bill Roberts, "://Training Via the Desktop," *HRMagazine* 43 (August 1998): 99.

21. "Motorola Selects DigitalThink to Provide Web-Based Training for up to 11,000 Employees Worldwide; Web-Based Training Leader Provides Platform-Independent, High Quality Courses," *Business Wire* (June 2, 1998): 1.

22. Michael Blumfield, "Learning to Share," *Training* 34 (April 1997): 38.

23. "Where the Training Dollars Go," *Training* 36 (October 1999): 54.

24. After eleven months' training in Siemens's Florida program, American apprentices scored higher on their intermediary tests than their German counterparts. This finding suggests that American youths may be more talented than they are often given credit for.

25. Beth Rogers, "The Making of a Highly Skilled Worker," *HRMagazine* 39 (July 1994): 62–63.

26. Glen Creno, "More Companies Serving up Training/Corporate 'Colleges' Take Lead from McDonald's Hamburger University," *The Arizona Republic* (May 16, 1999): AZ4.

27. Russell V. Gerbman, "Corporate Universities 101," *HRMagazine* 45 (February 2000): 101–106.

28. Peak, "Go Corporate U."

29. Susan Jackson, "Your Local Campus: Training Ground Zero," *Business Week* (September 1996): 68.

30. "Where the Training Dollars Go," *Training* 36 (October 1999): 60.

31. Lin Grensing-Pophal, "Training Supervisors to Manage Teleworkers," *HRMagazine* 44 (January 1999): 67.

32. Martin L. Gross, *The Conspiracy of Ignorance: The Failure of American Public Schools* (New York: HarperCollins, 1999): 6.

33. Leslie E. Overmyer Day, "Benchmarking Training," *Training & Development* 49 (November 1995): 27–30.

34. Donna J. Abernathy, "Thinking Outside the Evaluation Box," *Training & Development* 53 (February 1999): 22.

35. Cynthia Pantazis, "The New Workforce Investment Act," *Training & Development* 53 (August 1999): 48–49.

36. Stephanie Overman, "Gearing up for Tomorrow's Workforce," *HR Focus* 76 (February 1999): 1.

37. Ibid., 15.

38. John McGillicuddy, "Making a Good Impression," *Public Management* 81 (January 1999): 15.

39. Max Messmer, "Orientation Programs Can Be Key to Employee Retention," *Strategic Finance Magazine* 81 (February 2000): 12.

40. David K. Lindo, "New Employee Orientation Is Your Job," *Supervision* 60 (August 1999): 6–9.

41. Rebecca Ganzel, "Putting Out the Welcome Mat," *Training* 35 (March 1998): 58–60.

42. Thomas G. Cummings and Christopher G. Worley, *Organization Development and Change* (Cincinnati: South-Western College Publishing, 1997): 2.

43. Ibid., 147.

44. Ibid., 133.

45. Peter B. Stark, "Finding the Pulse," *Credit Union Management* 21 (November 1998): 24–27.

46. Cummings and Worley, *Organization Development and Change,* 133.

47. Ibid., 135–136.

48. "Quality Circles Are Alive and Well," *Office Systems* 16 (February 1999): 12.

49. Helene F. Uhlfelder, "It's All about Improving Performance," *Quality Progress* 33 (February 2000): 47.

50. Sara R. Olderding, "Mitsubishi and Honda on Competition and Quality Circles," *Journal for Quality & Participation* 21 (May/June 1998): 55–59.

51. Ron Mitchell, "Quality Circles in the U.S.: Rediscovering Our Roots," *Journal for Quality & Participation* 22 (November/December 1999): 28.

52. Howard Prager, "Cooking up Effective Team Building," *Training & Development* 53 (December 1999): 14.

53. Kathryn Tyler, "Take New Employee Orientation off the Back Burner," *HRMagazine* 43 (May 1998): 49.

54. Cynthia L. Kemper, "Global Training's Critical Success Factors," *Training & Development* 52 (February 1998): 35–37.

55. Prager, "Cooking up Effective Team Building," 14–15.

56. Steve Rosenbush, "Mechanics Road Test Mentis," *USA Today* (August 12, 1997): 6B.

57. Lyle M. Spencer, Jr., *Reengineering Human Resources* (New York: John Wiley & Sons, 1995): 8–9.

# Career Planning and Development

  ## Objectives

- Define *career planning* and *career development*.
- Distinguish between job security and career security.
- Describe career-impacted life stages and career anchors.
- Explain individual and organizational career planning.
- Describe the various types of career paths.
- Explain the importance of career development.
- Describe career planning and development methods.
- Describe unique segments of the workforce that need to be developed.

**E**ven little shops like Northeast Tool & Manufacturing Company, outside Charlotte, North Carolina, are making the commitment to innovate. Rote assembly-line work is being replaced with an industrial vision that requires skilled and nimble workers to think while they work. This move toward innovation has made career planning and development essential. The past nature of work has little bearing on the future of work. Factory workers at Northeast Tool now must deal with industrial robots and computers that control massive steel casters and stamp presses. Factory workers are constantly funneling information through computers so they can work on the floor and even perform some duties previously performed by management.

Fred Price is being impacted as others are on the line. Fred leaves for work at 4 A.M., and while on the job, this 29-year-old North Carolina factory

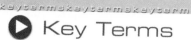

## Key Terms

Career 250
Career planning 250
Organizational career planning 250
Career path 251
Career development 251
Job security 251
Career security 251

Self-assessment 256
Strength/weakness balance sheet 256
Likes and dislikes survey 258
Traditional career path 262
Network career path 262
Lateral skill path 263

Dual career path 263
Career development tools 266
Generation X 269
Generation Y 270
Generation I 271

worker schedules orders as usual for the tiny tool-and-die shop, where he doubles as a supervisor when he's not bending metal. At midday today, test results are coming in from the state Labor Department in Raleigh. These aptitude exams for all 43 workers at Northeast Tool will measure everything from math and mechanical skills to leadership and adaptability. Fred's life is about to change—less leisure and less family time—because Fred, like tens of thousands of employees across America, is going back to school. Because even factory work is increasingly defined by blips on a computer screen, a structured developmental program designed to retrain, reeducate, and continually prepare Fred and his co-workers for future careers is essential. Fred Price realizes that in order to develop to his full potential he must go beyond Northeast's requirements because his career plan is to some-day actually manage the plant.[1]

**T**he impact of innovations on Northeast Tool's workforce will be dramatic. Obviously, Northeast Tool has a well-thought-out career planning and development program. Career planning and development are important to companies like Northeast because they must ensure that people with the necessary skills and experience will be available to adapt with the changing nature of work. This planning and developmental process is continuous for the workforce of this company, which is innovating for future survival.

In this chapter, we first discuss the concept of career planning and development. Next, we distinguish between job security and career security. Then, we identify several factors that affect career planning and discuss both individual and organizational career planning. We next address career paths and discuss career development. Then, career planning and development methods are described. We devote the last part of the chapter to a discussion of developing unique segments of the workforce.

▶ *SHRM-HR Links*

**www.prenhall.com/mondy**

This site covers various issues dealing with careers, including career planning.

**Career**
A general course of action a person chooses to pursue throughout his or her working life.

A **career** is a general course that a person chooses to pursue throughout his or her working life. Of course, the career may change once or many times due to technological changes or the individual's desire to do something different. Fred Price's career is in an extreme state of flux as the process at Northeast Tool becomes more innovative. Historically, a career was a sequence of work-related positions an individual occupied during a lifetime, although often not with the same company. However, the days are numbered for relatively static jobs that require infrequent training and virtually no development for maintaining acceptable productivity levels. Such jobs are going overseas in great numbers; others are simply disappearing.

In a recent article in *Time* entitled, "What Will Be the 10 Hottest Jobs?. . . and What Jobs Will Disappear?" the primary jobs identified for extinction included stockbrokers, auto dealers, mail carriers, and insurance and real estate agents. The reason given for the predicted demise of these jobs was that the Internet will eliminate the middlemen.[2] Other predictions for ultimate career demise include telephone linemen (wireless technology will take over), computer data entry personnel (voice recognition technology and scanning devices will eliminate the manual effort), and library researchers. The researcher of yesterday pulled journals and books from the shelves, copied pertinent pages, and turned them over to the investigator. Today, the investigator sits at his or her computer and accesses any library in the world through the Internet.[3] Because of the rapid rate of technological change, individuals are likely to have several careers during their work lives.

**Career planning**
An ongoing process through which an individual sets career goals and identifies the means to achieve them.

**Organizational career planning**
The process of the organization identifying paths and activities for individual employees as they develop.

**Career planning** is an ongoing process whereby an individual sets career goals and identifies the means to achieve them. Career planning by Fred Price includes a career path that he expects to take him from the factory floor to the plant manager's office. The major focus of career planning should be on matching personal goals with opportunities that are realistically available. Career planning should not concentrate only on advancement opportunities since the present work environment has reduced many of these opportunities. At some point, career planning needs to focus on achieving successes that do not necessarily entail promotions.

In **organizational career planning**, the organization identifies paths and activities for individual employees as they develop. Northeast Tool is committed to innovation that necessitates organizational career planning for all of its employees, including Fred Price. Organizational career planning is necessary to help ensure that a firm improves its ability to perform by identifying needed capabilities and the type of people needed to perform in an ever-evolving business environment.[4] Perhaps it is because of the tight labor market in 2000, but 74 percent of employees surveyed said their companies were helping them develop in their current role and/or achieve their career goals.[5]

Individual and organizational career planning are not separate and distinct. A person whose individual career aspirations cannot be realized within the organization will probably leave the firm sooner or later. If career opportunities are not available

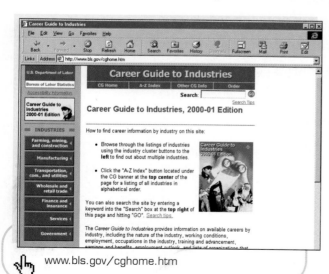

www.bls.gov/cghome.htm

elsewhere, employees may, in effect, leave the firm by letting productivity decline. Thus, organizations should assist employees in career planning so both parties can satisfy their needs. A **career path** is a flexible line of movement through which an employee may move during employment with a company. Following an established career path, the employee can undertake career development with the firm's assistance. From a worker's perspective, following a career path may involve weaving from company to company and from position to position as he or she obtains greater knowledge and experience.

**Career development** is a formal approach used by the organization to help people acquire the skills and experiences needed to perform current and future jobs. Formal career development is important to maintain a motivated and committed workforce.[6] Northeast Tool did extensive employee testing to isolate the developmental needs of its current workforce. Career development tools, which are specified during career planning and utilized in the career development program, most notably include various types of training and the application of organizational development techniques (discussed in Chapter 8). Career planning and development benefit both the individual and the organization and must therefore be carefully considered by both.

**Career path**
A flexible line of progression through which an employee may move during his or her employment with a company.

**Career development**
A formal approach taken by an organization to help people acquire the skills and experiences needed to perform current and future jobs.

## JOB SECURITY VERSUS CAREER SECURITY

There was a time when most people remained with one company and career for the majority of their adult years. Those days are now over. Downsizing, reorganization, and refocusing business strategies changed the way workers look at employers. "People became more loyal to their career than to the organization," said Patricia Bethke, managing consultant at human resources consulting firm Watson Wyatt Worldwide.[7]

In the past, workers planned for a single career. In doing so, it was easier for them to identify their strengths and weaknesses, their likes and dislikes, what they were good and less good at, and the employment opportunities available. A basic assumption was that change would not occur or would occur slowly. But, for most workers today, this assumption is not valid.[8] The old social contract between employers and employees no longer exists.[9] "Downsizing changed all the old rules," says Roger Herman, owner of The Herman Group, a management consulting firm in Greensboro, North Carolina. It fundamentally altered the employer-employee relationship. Employers once preached job security, but the message of downsizing in many firms was that corporate loyalty to employees was dead. Therefore, employee loyalty to these organizations also died.[10] According to Charles W. Sweet, president of A.T. Kearney's executive recruiting firm in Chicago, Illinois, "The way people approached their careers in the past is history. It will never, never, never return."[11] For many workers, career planning involves planning ways to improve their career security as opposed to ensuring job security within one organization.

Fewer and fewer companies offer real **job security** by protecting employees against job loss. Instead of job security, workers strive for career security. **Career security** is the development of marketable skills and expertise that

**Job security**
Protection against job loss within the company.

**Career security**
The development of marketable skills and expertise that help ensure employment within a range of careers.

## ▶ Evolution of Jobs

Five years ago, there were no personal computers for cars, so there were no jobs designing them. And many companies had no Web site, so they had no need for a Web designer. All that has changed quickly. Intel product line engineer Patrick Johnson helped design Intel's Connected Car PC and the company's Internet appliances, computing devices designed specifically for the Internet. Now he's working on a chip to process images and other media for a future generation of copy machines, computerized cash registers, ATMs, and other appliances.

A 12-year Intel employee, Johnson was part of the small group that came up with the idea of a PC for the car. The group was then given the job of designing it. According to Johnson, "We had never built a computer for the car before. We had to decide what goes into it, how it gets packaged." After spending three years on the car computer, Johnson worked for nine months overseeing development of two Internet appliances. One is a set-top box to bring the Internet to television. The other is a countertop appliance, essentially a PC optimized for Internet access. "Five years ago, only a handful of people would have predicted how important the Internet would become," he said. "Not too many people know how it's going to evolve over the next five."

As another example, the title of marketing director has also existed for years, but today's Internet marketers have little in common with their analog counterparts. Robert Danoff, senior vice president of marketing for Tempe-based NeoPlanet, has worked on both sides of the digital divide and says they are much different. In traditional marketing, research would lead to meetings with an advertising agency in a six- to eight-week process before ads are published. On the Internet, the process can happen in 48 hours. According to Danoff, "There's been a dramatic time compression." As these jobs have evolved, so will others in the future, and probably the not-too-distant future.[12]

help ensure employment within a range of careers. Career security is different from job security in that job security implies security in one job, often with one company. Career security results from the ability to perform within a career designation well enough to be marketable to more than one organization. Refer to HRM Incident 2, at the end of the chapter, for an excellent real-life example of an individual's approach to career security. Stephen Bookbinder, a principal at Towers Perrin, believes, "People are pushing for nontraditional benefits that will help them advance their career—even if their job blows up. They aren't looking for job security; they want career security. And companies had better realize this, if they want to attract the people who can take them where they need to go."[13]

With career security, workers are offered opportunities to improve their skills—and thus their employability—in an ever-changing work environment. Under this so-called *employability doctrine*, employees owe the company their commitment while on board and the company owes its workers the opportunity to learn new skills—but that is as far as the commitment goes. As previously mentioned, the loyalty once expected has slipped away.[14] In a recent survey, only 42 percent of surveyed workers felt that their employers deserved their loyalty.[15] Under the employability doctrine, loyalty in either direction is not expected. Even with the employability doctrine, career planning and development is essential to ensure a qualified internal workforce is available.

Several factors affect a person's view of a career. Beyond the environmental and business conditions that shape the future of work—such as the rise of technology-based jobs versus physically demanding labor—two major factors affect career planning: career-impacted life stages and career anchors.

## Career-Impacted Life Stages

Each person's career goes through stages that influence an individual's knowledge of and preference for various occupations. People change and subsequently view their careers differently at various stages of their lives. Some of these changes result from the aging process and others from opportunities for growth and status. The basic life stages are shown in Figure 9-1. The main stages of the career cycle include growth, exploration, establishment, maintenance, and decline.[16]

**Growth Stage.** The growth stage is roughly from birth to age 14 and is a period during which an individual develops a self-concept by identifying and interacting with other people. Toward the beginning of this period, children experiment with different ways of acting. What they observe from these experiences helps them learn how other people react to different behaviors and contributes to their developing, unique personalities. Toward the end of this stage, adolescents begin to think realistically about alternative occupations. During this stage, teenagers establish their own identities.

**Exploration Stage.** The exploration stage is the period from roughly 15 to 24 years of age; during this time, an individual seriously explores various occupational alternatives. The person attempts to match these occupational alternatives with his or her own interests and abilities formed or discovered through education, leisure activities, and work. Young people generally make tentative and broad occupational choices during the beginning of this period. Near its end, they make what seems to them an appropriate choice and try to secure a beginning job. Probably the individual's most important accomplishment at this point is developing a realistic understanding of his or her abilities and talents. Also, he or she makes educational decisions based on credible sources of information about occupational alternatives. During this stage young people explore career alternatives and begin to move into the adult world.

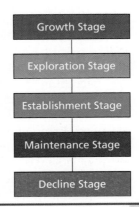

**Career-Impacted Life Stages** **Figure 9-1**

**Establishment Stage.** A person goes through the establishment stage when he or she is roughly 25 to 44 years of age; this period is the major part of most people's work lives. The fortunate individuals find a suitable occupation during this period and engage in those activities that help establish a career. Although a permanent career may be a somewhat outdated concept, during this period a more fluid and ever-evolving career should be nurtured. In these years, people are continually testing their personal capabilities and ambitions against the requirements of their initial occupational choice. The establishment stage itself has three substages: the trial substage, the stabilization substage, and the midcareer crisis.

The *trial substage* lasts from about age 25 to age 30. In these years the person determines whether the chosen field is suitable; if it is not, he or she will probably try to change directions. Between 30 and 40, the individual goes through a *stabilization substage*. At this time, he or she will set more rigid occupational goals and engage in explicit career planning to determine the sequence of promotions, job changes, and/or any educational activities necessary for accomplishing these goals. Then, somewhere in the thirties and forties, the individual may enter the *midcareer crisis substage*. During this period, many people make a major reassessment of their career progress relative to their original ambitions and goals. Also at this point, individuals decide the importance of family and leisure versus career. Frequently, this is the time when people must deal with the difficult choices among what is really important to them, what they can realistically accomplish, and how much they must sacrifice to achieve reevaluated goals.

**Maintenance Stage.** Between the ages of 45 and 65, many people move from the stabilization substage into the maintenance stage. By now, the individual has usually created a place in the work world, and most efforts are directed at maintaining the career gains. Today, this stage may also be characterized by ongoing training and development needed to continually nurture ever-evolving careers.

**Decline Stage.** As retirement becomes an inevitable reality, in the decline stage, there is frequently a period of adjustment; at this time, many begin to accept reduced levels of power and responsibility. During this period individuals either withdraw from the work environment or accept new roles such as mentoring younger employees. Diminishing physical and mental capabilities may accelerate this stage. A person may have lower aspirations and less motivation during the decline stage, resulting in additional career adjustments. However, technological advancements can now overcome the physical limitations that once impeded careers. Now individuals in this stage may evolve with the job. Technology also offers completely new employment alternatives, so when one career declines, another can evolve.

Even though most individuals have career development needs throughout their working lives, the majority of developmental activities were previously directed at new, younger workers. Today, in each stage, developmental activities are becoming more common. Since the last amendment to the Age Discrimination in Employment Act, there has been no mandatory retirement age, and therefore, the self-maintenance and self-adjustment stage is likely to be extended. Future employees will probably need career development as much in their later years as they do in the initial years of their working lives. Also, as a result of downsizing and eliminating layers of management in organizations, development has become much more important as workers are expected to accomplish a wider variety of tasks. It is also important as individuals decide to change careers later in their life because of job elimination, a personal desire to do something different, or the different career opportunities that develop because of technological advancements.

## Career Anchors

All of us have different aspirations, backgrounds, and experiences. Our personalities are molded to a certain extent by the results of our interactions with our environments, as well as the career-impacted life stages we experience. Edgar Schein's research identified five different motives that account for the way people select and prepare for a career. He called them *career anchors*.[17] One additional anchor has been added to better reflect the evolving nature of the new workforce.

1. *Managerial competence.* The career goal of managers is to develop qualities of interpersonal, analytical, and emotional competence. People using this anchor want to manage people.
2. *Technical/Functional competence.* The anchor for technicians is the continuous development of technical talent. These individuals do not seek managerial positions.
3. *Security.* The anchor for security-conscious individuals is to stabilize their career situations. They often see themselves as tied to a particular organization or geographic location. Individuals with this anchor may experience stress as we enter the volatile new century.
4. *Creativity.* Creative individuals are somewhat entrepreneurial in their attitude. They want to create or build something that is entirely their own.
5. *Autonomy and independence.* The career anchor for independent people is a desire to be free from organizational constraints. They value autonomy and want to be their own boss and work at their own pace. This also includes an entrepreneurial spirit exhibited by many Generation X workers.
6. *Technological competence.* This is a natural affinity for technology and a desire to work with technology whenever possible, which is also a characteristic of Generation X workers. These individuals often readily accept change and therefore are very adaptable.

One of the primary implications of career-impacted life stages and career anchors is that companies must be flexible enough to provide alternative career paths to satisfy people's varying needs at various times during their lives.

## CAREER PLANNING

As Alice said in *Through the Looking Glass,* "If you don't know where you're going, any road will get you there." Such is the case with career planning.[18] Career planning must now accommodate a number of objectives and enable us to prepare for each on a contingency basis. It will need updating to accommodate changes in our own interests as well as in the work environment.[19] Historically, it was thought that career planning was logical, linear, and indeed planned.[20] That is not the case today, as individuals have experienced or seen downsizing, job creation, and job elimination. Tom Peters, the well-known management guru, has predicted that during the next 10 to 15 years more than 90 percent of white-collar positions "will disappear or be reconfigured beyond recognition."[21] Predictions such as these have a profound impact on career planning. Because of the many changes that are occurring such as mergers, acquisitions, and spin-offs, career planning is essential for survival for individuals and organizations.[22]

As previously discussed, organizational career planning involves the identification of paths and activities for employees as they develop. Career planning at the individual level and organizational career planning are interrelated and interdependent; therefore, success requires parallel planning at both levels.

## Individual Career Planning: The Self-Assessment

Through career planning, a person continuously evaluates his or her abilities and interests, considers alternative career opportunities, establishes career goals, and plans practical developmental activities. Individual career planning must begin with self-understanding or self-assessment.[23] Then, the person is in a position to establish realistic goals and determine what to do to achieve these goals. This action also lets the person know whether his or her goals are realistic. In addition to a self-assessment, an individual would be wise to follow the guidelines presented in Table 9-1 to prepare for a new career path.

**Self-assessment**
The process of learning about oneself.

**Self-assessment** means learning about oneself. Anything that could affect one's performance in a future job should be considered. Realistic self-assessment may help a person avoid mistakes that could affect his or her entire career progression. Often an individual accepts a job without considering whether it matches his or her interests and abilities. This approach often results in failure. A thorough self-assessment will go a long way toward helping match an individual's specific qualities and goals with the right job or profession.

Some useful tools include a strength/weakness balance sheet and a likes and dislikes survey. However, any reasonable approach that assists self-understanding is helpful.

**Strength/weakness balance sheet**
A self-evaluation procedure, developed originally by Benjamin Franklin, that helps people to become aware of their strengths and weaknesses.

Strength/Weakness Balance Sheet. A self-evaluation procedure, developed originally by Benjamin Franklin, that assists people in becoming aware of their strengths and weaknesses is the **strength/weakness balance sheet.** Employees who understand their strengths can use them to maximum advantage. By recognizing their weaknesses, they are in a better position to overcome them.[24] This attitude is summed up by the statement, "If you have a weakness, understand it and make it work for you as a strength; if you have a strength, do not abuse it to the point where it becomes a weakness."

To use a strength/weakness balance sheet, the individual lists strengths and weaknesses as he or she perceives them. This is quite important because believing, for example, that a weakness exists even when it does not can equate to a real weakness. Thus, a person who believes that he or she will make a poor first impression when meeting someone will probably make a poor impression. The perception of a weakness often becomes a self-fulfilling prophesy.

The mechanics for preparing the balance sheet are quite simple. To begin, draw a line down the middle of a sheet of paper. Label the left side *Strengths* and the right side *Weaknesses*. Record all perceived strengths and weaknesses. You may find it difficult to write about yourself. Remember, however, that no one else need see the results. The primary consideration is complete honesty.

Figure 9-2 shows an example of a strength/weakness balance sheet. Obviously, Wayne (the person who wrote the sheet) did a lot of soul searching in making these evaluations. Typically, a person's weaknesses will outnumber strengths in the first few iterations. However, as the individual repeats the process, some items that first appeared to be weaknesses may eventually be recognized as strengths and should then be moved from one column to the other. A person should devote sufficient time to the project to obtain a fairly clear understanding of his or her

1. **Accept the new values of the workplace by showing how you can help a company meet its bottom-line needs:** increasing profits, cutting costs, increasing productivity and efficiency, improving public relations, even getting new clients. . . .

2. **Continually look for newer and better ways to be of more value to your employer.** Too many who did a good job 15 or 20 years ago are today doing the same thing and thinking that they are still doing a good job. Your company has changed; you need to change with it.

3. **Don't keep yourself stuck in an "information vacuum."** Today you can no longer afford to be unaware of what is happening to your company, industry, your community, your country, or, for that matter, the world. . . .

4. **Don't be reactive.** Those who are successful today are those who prepare ahead of time, anticipate problems and opportunities, and get ready.

5. **Continually seek out a new education.** Expanded knowledge, increased information, and new skills are appearing at record pace. Those who are successful are those who find out what new skills and knowledge they need and who are taking the extra time and trouble to learn them. The others simply will not be competitive.

6. **Develop significant career and financial goals and detailed plans to reach them.** Otherwise, you are vulnerable.

7. **Avoid a state of denial.** When a person is in denial, he or she will ignore signs that something is wrong. Denial is one of the major reasons why people become immobilized and are not prepared for a problem or a change in the company.

8. **Prepare for survival in your present career and for taking the next job or career step.** Have you explored alternatives? Are your job search skills those of today, or are you using antiquated job search methods?

9. **Become motivated by your goals, not by anger, fear, or hopelessness.** In difficult and uncertain career situations, it is human nature to have strong feelings. The problem is that too many of us let those feelings guide our actions and our words.

10. **Market yourself aggressively.** Whether you have a job or are looking for a job, today's world demands that in order to survive and be successful, you must learn to market yourself; network with others, let others know the good work that you do, and don't burn your bridges by making unnecessary enemies. In particular, learn to market within your present company.

11. **Improve your motivation and commitment.** Employers are no longer looking for those who are good enough, they are looking for those who are the most highly motivated. Demand and get the best out of yourself. Go to seminars and get counseling if there is a motivational block. Rejuvenate your enthusiasm and demonstrate it at work.

12. **Place your weaknesses and inadequacies in perspective;** do not allow them to loom so large in your mind that all you can see when you look in the mirror is failure. Remember that no one is without weaknesses, inadequacies, and mistakes.

13. **Realize that to survive and prosper in today's world, your primary job is to change yourself.** You are the one who has to keep up with your training and education. You are the one who has to learn new skills in networking. You are the one who has to develop a different perspective on your career and your employment.

14. **There's no reason HR professionals can't take advantage of the same professional counseling and guidance available to others.** Give yourself the edge and you can confidently move forward to define the career path you want.

*Source:* Sander I. Marcus and Jotham G. Friedland, "Fourteen Steps on a New Career Path," *HRMagazine* 38 (March 1993): 55–56.

strengths and weaknesses. Typically, the process should take a minimum of one week. The balance sheet will not provide all the answers regarding a person's strengths and weaknesses, but many people have gained a better understanding of themselves by completing it.

| Strengths | Weaknesses |
|---|---|
| Work well with people. | Get very close to few people. |
| Like to be given a task and get it done in my own way. | Do not like constant supervision. |
| Good manager of people. | Don't make friends very easily with individuals classified as my superiors. |
| Hard worker. | Am extremely high-strung. |
| Lead by example. | Often say things without realizing consequences. |
| People respect me as being fair and impartial. | Cannot stand to look busy when there is no work to be done. |
| Tremendous amount of energy. | Cannot stand to be inactive. Must be on the go constantly. |
| Function well in an active environment. | |
| Relatively open-minded. | Cannot stand to sit at a desk all the time. |
| Feel comfortable in dealing with high-level businesspersons. | Basically a rebel at heart but have portrayed myself as just the opposite. |
| Like to play politics. (This may be a weakness.) | My conservatism has gotten me jobs that I emotionally did not want. |
| Get the job done when it is defined. | Am sometimes nervous in an unfamiliar environment. |
| Excellent at organizing other people's time. Can get the most out of people who are working for me. | Make very few true friends. |
| | Not a conformist but appear to be. |
| Have an outgoing personality—not shy. | Interest level hits peaks and valleys. |
| Take care of those who take care of me. (This could be a weakness.) | Many people look on me as being unstable. Perhaps I am. Believe not. |
| Have a great amount of empathy. | Divorced. |
| Work extremely well through other people. | Not a tremendous planner for short range. Long-range planning is better. |
| | Impatient—want to have things happen fast. |
| | Do not like details. |
| | Do not work well in an environment where I am the only party involved. |

## Figure 9-2  Strength/Weakness Balance Sheet
*Source:* Wayne Sanders.

**Likes and dislikes survey**
A procedure that helps individuals recognize restrictions they place on themselves.

**Likes and Dislikes Survey.** An individual should also consider likes and dislikes as part of a self-assessment. A **likes and dislikes survey** assists individuals in recognizing restrictions they place on themselves. For instance, some people are not willing to live in certain parts of the country, and such feelings should be noted as a constraint. Some positions require a person to spend a considerable amount of time traveling. Thus, an estimate of the amount of time a person is willing to travel would also be helpful. Recognition of such self-imposed restrictions may reduce future career problems. Another limitation is the type of firm an individual will consider working for.

The size of the firm might also be important. Some like a major organization whose products are well known; others prefer a smaller organization, believing that the opportunities for advancement may be greater or that the environment is better suited to their tastes. All factors that could affect an individual's work performance should be listed in the likes and dislikes survey. An example of this type of survey is shown in Figure 9-3.

A self-assessment such as this one helps a person understand his or her basic motives, setting the stage for pursuing a management career or seeking further technical competence. A person with little desire for management responsibilities

| Likes | Dislikes |
| --- | --- |
| Like to travel.<br>Would like to live in the East.<br>Enjoy being my own boss.<br>Would like to live in a medium-size city.<br>Enjoy watching football and baseball.<br>Enjoy playing racquetball. | Do not want to work for a large firm.<br>Will not work in a large city.<br>Do not like to work behind a desk all day.<br>Do not like to wear suits all the time. |

**Likes and Dislikes Survey**     **Figure 9-3**

*Source:* Wayne Sanders.

should probably not accept a promotion to supervisor or enter management training. People who know themselves can more easily make the decisions necessary for successful career planning. Many people get sidetracked because they choose careers based on haphazard plans or the wishes of others rather than on what they believe to be best for themselves.

Getting to know oneself is not a singular event. As individuals progress through life, priorities change. Individuals may think that they know themselves quite well at one stage of life and later begin to see themselves quite differently. Therefore, self-assessment should be viewed as a continuous process. Career-minded individuals must heed the Red Queen's admonition to Alice: "It takes all the running you can do, to keep in the same place."[25] This admonition is so very true in today's work environment.

## Career Assessment on the Web

The Web has numerous test and assessment sites available to assist jobseekers. For instance, the John Holland's Self-Directed-Search Web site (www.self-directed-search.com) is based on the theory that people and work environments can be classified into six basic types: realistic, investigative, artistic, social, enterprising, and conventional. The test determines which three types describe you, and it suggests occupations that could be a good match. The Keirsey Character Sorter (www.keirsey.com) sorts people into four temperaments: idealists, rationals, artisans, and guardians. It not only places individuals in an overall category, but it also offers a more detailed evaluation of their personality traits.[26]

The Web can also help a person find information regarding organizations that best suit him or her. With WetFeet.com, a jobseeker can research hundreds of companies and more than 34 industries. If a person wants to know what it is really like to work in a certain business, the *Industry Quicks* section should be checked to determine who the major players are and what they do. The site's *What's Great and What's to Hate* section tells an individual just that. And the *Real People Profile* section offers an interview with a real person in a specific industry. Interviews provide valuable insights from those with experience: how they got their job, what a typical day is like for them, what career aspirations they have for the future, and the biggest misconceptions about their business. The site's *Company Q&A* can help you understand the interviewer's point of view. Besides getting an overview of a company's performance data, an applicant can also get information on its strategy (what the company does, who its competitors are, how it differs from the competition), careers (job opportunities, based on level of education and experience; how long most people stay; the skills needed to succeed), culture and lifestyle (what working at this particular company is like), and recruiting (what the application process is like, what to expect during an interview, some pitfalls to avoid).[27] These Internet sites offer helpful interactive information to assist in career assessments.

## Organizational Career Planning

As previously defined, the process of establishing career paths and activities for individuals within a firm is referred to as *organizational career planning*. Organizational career planning should begin with a person's placement in an entry-level job and initial orientation. Management will observe the employee's job performance and compare it with job standards. At this stage, strengths and weaknesses will be noted, enabling management to assist the employee in making a tentative career decision. Naturally, this decision can be altered later as the process continues. This tentative career decision is based on a number of factors, including personal needs, abilities and aspirations, and the organization's needs. Management can then schedule development programs that relate to the employee's specific needs.

Remember that career planning is an ongoing process. It takes into consideration the changes that occur in people, in organizations, and in the environment. This type of flexibility is absolutely necessary in today's dynamic organizational environment. Not only do the firm's requirements change, but individuals may also choose to revise their career expectations. Some prefer the old-fashioned way—up. But in today's horizontal corporate world, workers will likely have to consider other directions that may eventually lead to a higher plane. For example, they can move sideways—with no change in salary or title—to a more dynamic department; leave the company perhaps for a more rewarding career elsewhere; remain in the same position and try to enhance their skills and explore new horizons; or move down to a job that may carry less weight but promise more growth. These options will be discussed later in the section entitled "Career Paths."

Although the primary responsibility for career planning rests with the individual, organizational career planning must closely parallel individual career planning if a firm is to retain its best and brightest workers. Employees must see that the firm's organizational career planning effort is directed toward furthering their specific career objectives. Companies must, therefore, help their employees obtain their career objectives and, most notably, career security. They must provide them with a diversity of opportunities to learn and do different things. Performing the same or similar task over and over provides little development.

Organizational career planning must begin with a virtual redefinition of the way work is done. The once stable, well-defined jobs of years past are now continually evolving, with the overall purpose of making the organization more adaptable in changing markets. Creativity, resourcefulness, flexibility, innovation, and adaptability are becoming much more important than the ability to perform a precisely specified job. Through effective organizational career planning a pool of men and women can be developed who can thrive in any number of organizational structures in the future.

Firms should undertake organizational career planning programs only when the programs contribute to achieving current and future organizational goals. Therefore, the rationale and approach to career planning programs vary among firms. This rationale is more important in today's environment, in which traditional vertical mobility has been stifled in most organizations. Career planning programs are expected to achieve one or more of the following objectives:

‣ Effective development of available talent. Individuals are more likely to be committed to development that is part of a specific career plan. This way, they can better understand the purpose of development.

‣ Self-appraisal opportunities for employees considering new or nontraditional career paths. Some excellent workers do not view traditional upward mobility as a career option since firms today have fewer promotion options available. Other workers see themselves in dead-end jobs and seek relief. Rather than lose these workers, a firm can offer career planning to help them identify new and different career paths.

‣ Development of career paths that cut across divisions and geographic locations. The development should not be limited to a narrow spectrum of one part of a company.

‣ A demonstration of a tangible commitment to EEO and affirmative action. Adverse impact can occur at virtually any level in an organization. Firms that are totally committed to reducing adverse impact often cannot find qualified women and minorities to fill vacant positions. One means of overcoming this problem is an effective career planning and development program.

‣ Satisfaction of employees' specific development needs. Individuals who see their personal development needs being met tend to be more satisfied with their jobs and the organization. They tend to remain with the organization.

‣ Improvement of performance. The job itself is the most important influence on career development. Each job can provide different challenges and experiences.

‣ Increased employee loyalty and motivation, leading to decreased turnover. Individuals who believe that the firm is interested in their career planning are more likely to remain with the organization.

‣ A method of determining training and development needs. If a person desires a certain career path and does not presently have the proper qualifications, this identifies a training and development need.[28]

All these objectives may be desirable. But successful career planning depends on a firm's ability to satisfy those objectives that it considers most crucial to employee development and the achievement of organizational goals.

## CAREER PATHS

Recall that a career path is a flexible line of progression through which an employee typically moves during employment. Information regarding career options and opportunities must be available before individuals can begin to set realistic career objectives. One way to provide this information is to develop career path data for each job group. This information can be developed from job descriptions, based on historic trends within the organization or on similarities to other jobs in the same job family. All of this information must be reevaluated in line with the changing nature of work. Career path information is particularly useful because it shows each employee how his or her job relates to other jobs, presents career alternatives, describes educational and experience requirements for a career change, and points out the orientations of other jobs.[29] Career paths have historically focused on upward mobility within a particular occupation, a choice not nearly as available as in the past. Other career paths include the network, lateral skill, dual career paths, adding value to your career, and even demotion. Typically, these career paths are used in combination and may be more popular at various stages of a person's career.

## Traditional Career Path

The following is a quote from a recent *Fortune* magazine article:

> Close your eyes and picture an object that embodies the word *career*. If you joined the workforce, say, 15 or 20 or 25 years ago, you're probably hard-wired, as the techies say, to visualize your working life as a predictable series of narrow and distinctly separate rungs that lead straight up (or down)—in other words, a ladder. Ha! Ha, ha, ha! My friend, the ladder has been chopped up into little pieces and dumped in the garbage pile. A team of sanitation engineers disposed of it at dawn, while you were dreaming.[30]

Although the traditional career path is somewhat dated, understanding it furthers one's comprehension of the various career path alternatives.

**Traditional career path**
A vertical line of career progression from one specific job to the next.

The **traditional career path** is one in which an employee progresses vertically upward in the organization from one specific job to the next. The assumption is that each preceding job is essential preparation for the next-higher-level job. Therefore, an employee must move, step by step, from one job to the next to gain needed experience and preparation. One of the biggest advantages of the traditional career path is that it is straightforward. The path is clearly laid out, and the employee knows the specific sequence of jobs through which he or she must progress.

Today, the old model of a career in which an employee worked his way up the ladder in a single company is becoming somewhat rare.[31] Some of the factors contributing to this situation include the following:

- A massive reduction in management ranks due to mergers, downsizing, stagnation, growth cycles, and reengineering
- Extinction of paternalism and job security
- Erosion of employee loyalty
- A work environment where new skills must constantly be learned

The certainties of yesterday's business methods and growth have disappeared in many industries, and neither organizations nor individuals can be assured of ever regaining them. However, the one certainty that still remains is that there will always be top-level managers and individuals who strive to achieve these positions. Unfortunately, it is just more difficult to obtain one of these positions.

## Network Career Path

**Network career path**
A method of job progression that contains both vertical and horizontal opportunities.

The **network career path** contains both a vertical sequence of jobs and a series of horizontal opportunities. The network career path recognizes the interchangeability of experience at certain levels and the need to broaden experience at one level before promotion to a higher level. Often, this approach more realistically represents opportunities for employee development in an organization than does the traditional career path. For instance, a person may work as an inventory manager for a few years and then move to a lateral position of shift manager before being considered for a promotion. The vertical and horizontal options lessen the probability of blockage in one job. One major disadvantage of this type of career path is that it is more difficult to explain to employees the specific route their careers may take for a given line of work.

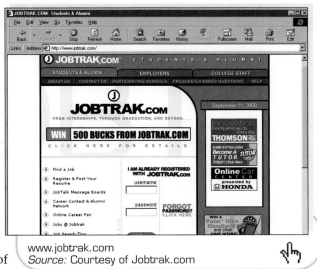

www.jobtrak.com
*Source:* Courtesy of Jobtrak.com

## Lateral Skill Path

Traditionally, a career path was viewed as moving upward to higher levels of management in the organization. The previous two career path methods focused on such an approach. The availability of these two options has diminished considerably in recent years, but this does not mean that an individual has to remain in the same job for life. The **lateral skill path** allows for lateral moves within the firm that are taken to permit an employee to become revitalized and find new challenges. Neither pay nor promotion may be involved, but by learning a different job, an employee can increase his or her value to the organization and also become revitalized and reenergized.

Although status or pay may remain unchanged, the employee is given the opportunity to develop new skills. Firms that want to encourage lateral movement may choose to utilize a skill-based pay system that rewards individuals for the type and number of skills they possess. Another approach, which we discussed in Chapter 4, is job enrichment. This approach rewards (without promotion) an employee by increasing the challenge of the job, giving the job more meaning, and giving the employee a greater sense of accomplishment.

**Lateral skill path**
A career path that allows for lateral moves within the firm; these permit an employee to become revitalized and find new challenges.

## Dual Career Path

The dual career path was originally developed to deal with the problem of technically trained employees who had no desire to move into management through the normal procedure for upward mobility in an organization. The **dual career path** recognizes that technical specialists can and should be allowed to contribute their expertise to a company without having to become managers. In organizations such as National Semiconductor, a worldwide high-tech firm headquartered in Santa Clara, California, a dual career approach was set up to encourage and motivate individual contributors in engineering, sales, marketing, finance, human resources, and other areas.[32] Individuals in these fields can increase their specialized knowledge, make contributions to their firms, and be rewarded without entering management. Whether on the management or technical path, compensation would be comparable at each level.

The dual career path is becoming increasingly popular at some firms. At AlliedSignal Inc. in Morristown, New Jersey, turnover among the top technical performers traditionally has hovered around 25 percent. Technical people were leaving because they felt they had nowhere to go unless they went into management. Since the company created a dual career system, no top talent has been lost. [33] Dow Corning has created what it describes as multiple ladders. As may be seen in Figure 9-4, individuals can progress upward in research, technical service

**Dual career path**
A method of rewarding technical specialists and professionals who can and should be allowed to contribute significantly to a company without having to become managers.

| Level | Managerial | Research | Technical Service and Development (TS&D) | Process Engineering |
|---|---|---|---|---|
|  | Vice President, R&D Director |  |  |  |
| VIII | Manager | Senior Research Scientist | Senior Development Scientist | Senior Process Engineering Scientist |
| VII | Manager | Research Scientist | Development Scientist | Process Engineering Scientist |
| VI | Section Manager | Associate Research Scientist | Associate Development Scientist | Associate Process Engineering Scientist |
| V | Group Leader | Senior Research Specialist | Senior TS&D Specialist | Senior Engineering Specialist |
| IV |  | Research Specialist | TS&D Specialist | Senior Project Engineer |
| III |  | Project Chemist | TS&D Representative | Project Engineer |
| II |  | Associate Project Chemist | TS&D Engineer | Development Engineer |
| I |  | Chemist | Engineer | Engineer |

**Figure 9-4**  **Multiple Ladders at Dow Corning**

*Source:* Charles W. Lentz, "Dual Ladders Become Multiple Ladders at Dow Corning," *Research Technology Management* 33 (May–June 1990): 28.

and development, and process engineering without being forced into management roles. The dual system is also used in higher education, where individuals can move through the ranks of instructor, assistant professor, associate professor, and professor without having to go into administration.

## Adding Value to Your Career

Adding value to your career may appear to be totally self-serving, but nevertheless, it is a logical and realistic career path. John Humphrey, CEO of executive-training powerhouse Forum Corporation, talks about adding value as if it were a toolbox that you carry with you to work each day. According to Humphrey, "The old ladder was a rigid thing. Now the question is, what skills have you got in your toolbox so that you can carry them anywhere and ply your craft?"[34] In today's environment, many workers tend to view themselves as independent contractors who must constantly improve their skills. The better their qualifications, the greater the opportunities in the job market.

Regardless of the career pursued, today's workers need to develop a plan whereby they are viewed as continually *adding value* to their careers. Otherwise, their value to a company diminishes. Workers must anticipate what tools and knowledge will be needed for future success and constantly strive to obtain these skills. They must look across company lines to other organizations to determine what skills are needed, and then go and get them. If their present organization does not provide them with the necessary skills, they will look elsewhere.

Today's workers are managing their own careers as never before. According to Pat Milligan, a partner at Towers Perrin, a human resources consulting firm, the new attitude among companies is that "there will never be job security. You will be employed by us as long as you add value to the organization, and you are continuously responsible for finding ways to add value. In return, you have the right to demand interesting and important work, the freedom and resources to perform it well, pay that reflects your contribution, and the experience and training needed to be employable here or elsewhere."[35] The career path that many workers are now using is to constantly find ways to add value to themselves, thereby protecting themselves in this new business environment.

A survey of 1,000 employees revealed that workers are four times more likely to look for a new job within 12 months if there is a lack of growth opportunities, training, and education.[36] It might be called enlightened self-interest. A person must discover what companies need, then develop the necessary skills to meet these needs as defined by the marketplace. As one Avon executive stated, "Always be doing something that contributes significant, positive change to the organization. That's the ultimate job security."[37] Basically, the only tie that binds a worker to the company and vice versa is a common commitment to mutual success and growth.

▶ Regardless of the career pursued, today's workers need to develop a plan whereby they are viewed as continually *adding value* to their careers.

## Demotion

Demotions have long been associated with failure, but limited promotional opportunities in the future and the fast pace of technological change may make them more legitimate career options. If the stigma of demotion can be removed, more employees—especially older workers—might choose to make such a move. Working long hours for limited promotional opportunities loses its appeal to some, especially if the worker can financially afford the demotion. Also, some workers have no desire to change as technology changes, so lower-level jobs that

---

▶ *The Sky's the Limit*

Bob Allen and Thelma Gowen, both supervisors in the trust department of American Bank of New York, were in the employee lounge having a cup of coffee and discussing a point of mutual concern. Bob said, "I'm beginning to get frustrated. When I joined American four years ago, I really felt that I could make a career here. Now I'm not so sure. I spoke with the boss last week about where I might be in the next few years and all she kept saying was, 'There are all kinds of possibilities.' I need more than that. I'd like to know what specific opportunities might be available if I continue to do a good job. I'm not sure if I want to spend my career in the trust department. There may be better chances for advancement in other areas. This is a big bank."

Thelma replied, "I'm having the same trouble. She told me that 'the sky's the limit.' I'd also like to know where I might progress if I decide to stay with American. I wonder what 'the limit' means to her."

*In today's work environment, is there a problem with Bob and Thelma's expectations?*

require less technological savvy might be more suitable. In certain instances, this approach might open up a clogged promotional path and at the same time permit a senior employee to escape unwanted stress without being viewed as a failure.

## CAREER DEVELOPMENT

**Career development tools**
Skills, education, and experiences, as well as behavioral modification and refinement techniques that allow individuals to work better and add value.

As previously mentioned, career development is a formal approach taken by the organization to ensure that people with the proper qualifications and experiences are available when needed. Career development benefits both the organization and the employee because properly developed employees are better prepared to add value both to themselves and to the company. Thus, career development includes exposure to any and all activities that prepare a person for satisfying the present and future needs of the firm. **Career development tools** consist of skills, education, and experiences, as well as behavioral modification and refinement techniques that allow individuals to work better and add value. Specific methods were discussed in Chapter 8 under the heading "Training and Development Methods." The methods can apply to employee training and development at all levels, even nonmanagerial. Once only managers were thought to need developing, but the current move toward a team-based environment has created the need for a wider range of worker development. Developmental efforts, therefore, are also often quite important for nonmanagerial employees.

Although skills, education, and experiences are very important, the behaviors that accomplish work are becoming more important as the workforce diversifies and becomes more interdependent. Therefore, the need for organizational development (discussed in Chapter 8) is often essential. Organizational development is important because it helps develop appropriate employee behaviors. Organizational development efforts include a number of interventions such as survey feedback, quality circles, sensitivity training, and team building.

Many key individuals must work together if an organization is to have an effective career development program. Management must first make a commitment to support the program by making policy decisions and allocating resources to the program. Human resource professionals often provide the necessary information, tools, and guidance. The worker's immediate supervisor is responsible for providing support, advice, and feedback. Through the supervisor, a worker can find out how supportive of career development the organization actually is. Finally, individual employees are ultimately responsible for developing their own careers.[38] In today's environment, workers may be more in tune with what is needed for their career development than the company. If they do not see the career development efforts of the company matching their specific needs, a change in jobs often is forthcoming.

## CAREER PLANNING AND DEVELOPMENT METHODS

There are numerous methods for career planning and development. Some currently utilized methods, most of which are used in various combinations, are discussed next.

### Discussions with Knowledgeable Individuals

In a formal discussion, the superior and subordinate may jointly agree on what type of career planning and development activities are best. The resources made available to achieve these objectives may also include developmental programs. In some organizations, human resource professionals are the focal point for providing assistance on the topic. In other instances, psychologists and guidance counselors provide this service. In an academic setting, colleges and universities often provide career planning and development information to students. Students often go to their professors for career advice.

## Company Material

Some firms provide material specifically developed to assist their workers in career planning and development. Such material is tailored to the firm's special needs. In addition, job descriptions provide valuable insight for individuals to personally determine if a match exists between their strengths and weaknesses and specific positions.

## Performance Appraisal System

The firm's performance appraisal system can also be a valuable tool in career planning and development. Noting and discussing an employee's strengths and weaknesses with his or her supervisor can uncover developmental needs. If overcoming a particular weakness seems difficult or even impossible, an alternate career path may be the solution.

## Workshops

Some organizations conduct workshops lasting two or three days for the purpose of helping workers develop careers within the company. Employees define and match their specific career objectives with the needs of the company. [39] At other times, the company may send workers to workshops available in the community, or workers may initiate the visit themselves. Consider just a few of the developmental activities that recently appeared in Atlanta, Georgia:

- The Peachtree Spectrum Chapter of the American Business Women's Association meeting. Participants learn new skills, the importance of networking, and how to seek new directions for personal achievement.
- Atlanta Multicultural Diversity Career Fair. Individuals meet face to face with major metro Atlanta corporations that have numerous career opportunities from entry-level to technical to professional.
- Career Development Center of the Southeast. One-on-one career assessment and counseling is provided. Programs are available for adults and college and high school students.
- Career Direction. A Job Search/Career Change Skills Workshop is offered.[40]

## Personal Development Plans (PDPs)

Many employers encourage employees to write their own personal development plans. This is a summary of a person's personal development needs and an action plan to achieve them. Workers are encouraged to analyze their strengths and weaknesses, as previously described in this chapter. A PDP could be the nucleus of a wider career plan such as setting out alternative long-term strategies, identifying one's long-term learning needs, and setting out a plan of self-development.[41]

## Software Packages

Some software packages assist employees in navigating their careers. For example, Self-SkillView Technologies has developed a program that permits a person to assess his or her information technology skills. To build skill profiles, the worker is rated on a list of skills. Ratings range from *no ability* to *complete mastery*. For an employee looking ahead at his or her career path, the software can compare the employer's organizational chart with the employee's skill profile to show the employee's readiness to move up. The user can click to see a listing of all the jobs in the company and his or her degree of fit for each, such as a "60.1 percent fit for Vice President, Information Systems." Users can see a variety of reports on their skills that show gaps, provide a development plan, and—of particular interest to managers—outline a succession plan.[42]

## Career Planning Web Sites

Numerous Web sites provide career planning and career counseling as well as career testing and assessment. Two such sites are CareerPlanner.com and Suite101.com. Although these are paid sites, there is considerable free information available on each site.

## USING THE INTERNET FOR CAREER PLANNING AND DEVELOPMENT AT TEXAS INSTRUMENTS

Job seeking students across America can now use the career Web site of Texas Instruments (TI) at www.ti.com/recruit to help plan their careers. The Web site introduces graduating college students to the career planning process, from developing a personal job profile and résumé building to actually choosing a career. With this free service, students can test their aptitude for jobs and match their skills and interests to a variety of opportunities. For graduating engineering students, the Cyber Recruiter answers questions about online job searching, getting résumés noticed, and working at TI. TI recognizes the importance of using the Internet as a career tool so students can learn more about themselves and about securing the right job. This Web site offers graduating students practical advice about their job search so they can weigh their options and make better informed choices.

The first step in the job search is TI's *Engineer Your Career.* Through a series of exercises and information, students can design a personal blueprint for a successful job search. *Engineer Your Career* includes a handy reference guide to landing a job, including self assessment, marketplace assessment, developing and using the résumé, developing a marketing plan, job search tools, job interviewing, and handling job offers. The TI site offers other career tools, such as the following:

- ▶ *Career Mapper*—A comprehensive survey that provides students with a practical, hands-on personal profile for their job search.
- ▶ *Résumé Builder*—Students input information about their education, employment experience, and personal skills and produce a professionally prepared résumé.
- ▶ *Campus Visit Schedule*—A schedule of job fairs and university visits by TI campus recruiters. TI recruits a number of talented individuals directly from colleges and universities in the United States.
- ▶ *Fit Check*—An interactive quiz that lets engineering graduates determine if TI's work environment suits their needs.
- ▶ *Ask the Cyber Recruiter*—Students can ask questions online about TI's hiring practices, work-life programs, and jobs offered. A TI professional responds within 24 hours via e-mail.[43]

Career planning and development are essential for the continual evolution of the labor force and the success of organizations, as well as individuals. Certain groups of employees are unique because of the specific characteristics of the work they do or who they are. Several groups including Generation X employees and the *new* factory workers are first discussed. Because of certain differences between these groups and more traditional workers and because of differences in the methods of accomplishing work, each group must be developed in rather unique ways. Although generalizations about a group are risky, these generalizations are offered simply to provide additional insight into what some members of each group may require developmentally. Generation Y and Generation I individuals are also briefly described as unique segments of the workforce of the future.

## Generation X Employees

**Generation X** is the label affixed to the 40 million American workers born between 1965 and 1976.[44] They are one of the most widely misunderstood phenomena facing the HR professional today. According to a University of Michigan study, Generation Xers are responsible for 70 percent of all the new start-ups in America. A CNN/Time poll found that three out of five Xers aspire to be their own bosses, and *Forbes* magazine called them the most entrepreneurial generation in American history.[45] Generation Xers do indeed differ from previous generations in some significant ways including their natural affinity for technology and their entrepreneurial spirit. Job instability and the breakdown of traditional employer-employee relationships in today's era of restructuring brought a realization to Generation Xers that the world of work is different for them than for past generations.

Managers who understand how these circumstances have shaped Generation Xers' outlook on career issues can begin to develop a positive relationship with young workers and harness their unique abilities. In fact, a company's success in the coming decades will depend on its ability to turn the extraordinary promise of Generation Xers into reality. Developing Generation X employees requires supporting their quest to acquire skills and expertise. Given the demise of the old employment contract, Generation Xers recognize that their careers cannot be founded securely on a relationship with any one employer. They think of themselves more as free agents in a mobile workforce and expect to build career security, not job security, by acquiring marketable skills and expertise. Fortunately, the surest way to gain Xers' loyalty is to help them develop self-building career security. When a company helps them expand their knowledge and skills—in essence, preparing them for the job market—Xers will often want to stay on board to learn those very skills. The result should be lower turnover rates and greater commitment from Generation Xers, thereby benefiting everyone.[46]

To support Xers' career development goals, the organization must provide them with opportunities to learn new skills, processes, and technologies. Generation Xers recognize the value of formal training and development programs that support individualized career goals and welcome both regular and ad hoc opportunities to learn on the job, as well as mentoring relationships. Also, since Generation Xers are independently motivated to learn and grow professionally, they are especially good at the lateral moves that are becoming more common. Supporting Xers in building self-based career security is also the key to recruiting the best young talent today.

**Generation X**
The label affixed to the 40 million American workers born between 1965 and 1976.

Basically, the developmental program must have self-building security as one of its main goals. First managers must understand that Xers expect to develop career security by acquiring marketable job skills and expertise. Second, an implicit contract should exist whereby the company fully supports Xers' pursuit of marketable skills and expertise and, in exchange, receives their commitment to the company's vision and goals during their tenure with the firm.[47]

## The <u>New</u> Factory Workers

Today, life on the factory line requires more brains than brawn, so laborers are taking evaluation examinations to identify skill and educational strengths and weaknesses and adaptability. After being evaluated, *new* factory workers are heading for development in the form of training, classroom lectures, computer-aided learning, organizational development techniques, and so on. Tens of thousands of factory workers across America are going back to school. These days, in an economy where even factory work increasingly is defined by blips on a computer screen, more schooling is the road to success.

Over the past decade, the thinned-out ranks of managers have been equipping factory workers with industrial robots and teaching them to use computer controls to operate technologically advanced manufacturing processes. At the same time, managers are funneling information through the computers, thereby bringing employees into the data loop. Workers are trained to watch inventories and to know suppliers and customers, as well as be aware of costs and prices. Knowledge that long separated brain workers from brawn workers is now available from computers on the factory floor.

The trend toward high-skills manufacturing began with innovative companies such as Corning, Motorola, and Xerox. They replaced rote assembly-line work with an industrial vision that requires skilled and nimble workers to think while they work. Large, old-line companies have learned that investments in people boost productivity, often at less cost than capital investments. Indeed, the old formula of company loyalty, a strong back, and showing up on time no longer guarantees job security or even a decent paycheck. Today, industrial workers will thrive only if they use their wits and keep adding to their skills base by continual development. Closing the skills gap requires carefully considered career development programs to ensure that workers can compete in the factory of the future. More companies are recognizing that they cannot afford *not* to develop employees and are therefore willing to develop employees who fit the profile of a lifelong learner.

## Generation Y as Future Employees

They have never wound a watch, dialed a rotary phone, or plunked the keys of a manual typewriter. But without a thought they format disks, download music from the Internet, and set the clock on a videocassette recorder. These teenagers are the leading edge of a generation that promises to be the richest, smartest, and savviest ever. These Generation Yers, often referred to as *Echo Boomers,* are the coddled, confident offspring of post–World War II baby boomers. Generation Y individuals are a most privileged generation, who came of age during the hottest domestic economy in memory. In many cities, job offers are abundant, from lifeguarding to baby-sitting to burger flipping.

They have also been exposed to some of the worst things in life: schoolyard shootings, drug use, and the Clinton sex scandal. Yet they are far more optimistic than baby boomers and Generation Xers.[48] **Generation Y** are the sons and

**Generation Y**
The sons and daughters of boomers; people who were born between 1979 and 1994.

daughters of boomers and were born between 1979 and 1994. They are the largest group to surface on the American scene since the 72 million baby boomers.[49] Much of the research regarding Generation Y concerns marketing and the impact they will have on the market. But, ultimately Yers will have careers, become managers, and be studied just as the boomers and Generation Xers are now. Remember that most college students today are Generation Yers, and they too will require unique developmental efforts.

## Generation I as Future Employees

First it was Generation X, and then came Generation Y. Bill Gates, the chairman of Microsoft Corporation, recently referred to children born after 1994 as Generation I. Specifically, **Generation I** are Internet-assimilated children, born after 1994. According to Gates, "These kids will be the first generation to grow up with the Internet. The Web will change Generation I's world as much as television transformed our world after World War II. That is why it is so critical to ensure that new teachers understand how to incorporate technology into their instruction and that teachers have the technological training they want and need. We cannot afford to have any teacher locked out of the greatest library on earth—the Internet."[50]

**Generation I**
Internet-assimilated children, born after 1994.

---

### Bringing Them Home

Much has been written about the importance of training and developing employees prior to their taking a global assignment. Unfortunately, the same amount of effort is not spent when they are brought home. According to Michael McCallum, international chair of the Society for Human Resource Management's Area I Leadership Committee, national director of business development, and training consultant for HR for Berlitz International Inc. in Princeton, New Jersey, "About 50 percent of repats leave their companies within two years of repatriation." Recruitment, selection, and orientation for a global assignment are often neglected, as are repatriation efforts.

Usually, the cause of these poor retention rates is simply that companies do a poor job of repatriating employees. "Many people think all it consists of is moving household goods and making travel arrangements," says McCallum. McCallum's views are supported by the International Assignee Research Project, a recent joint study by Berlitz International and the Institute for International Human Resources. The study revealed that 77 percent of international transferees received no career counseling from their employers upon returning from global assignments, and only 6 percent were offered reentry training. Training is important when sending employees abroad, but it is just as important when they return. Terry Hogan, vice president of client services for Cendant International Assignment Services in Danbury, Connecticut, believes that "you want to capitalize on the investment you're making" in employees. "You don't want them to take what they've gained from the experience and bring it to a competitor." When employers do not assist workers returning from overseas assignments, it makes it easier for other companies to attract them. HR professionals must realize that returning repatriates may need help adjusting to domestic surroundings that they have not experienced in several years. Unfortunately, what is obvious to the repatriate may not be as obvious to the HR professional.[51]

# ► Summary

**①  Define *career planning* and *career development*.**

Career planning is an ongoing process whereby an individual sets career goals and identifies the means to achieve them. Career development is a formal approach taken by the organization to ensure people with the proper qualifications and experience are available when needed.

**②  Distinguish between job security and career security.**

Job security is protection against job loss within the company. Career security is the development of marketable skills and expertise that helps ensure employment within a range of careers.

**③  Describe career-impacted life stages and career anchors.**

The main life stages of the career cycle include growth, exploration, establishment, maintenance, and decline. The career anchors are managerial competence, technical/functional competence, security, creativity, autonomy and independence, and technical competence.

**④  Explain individual and organizational career planning.**

Through career planning, a person continuously evaluates his or her abilities and interests, considers alternative career opportunities, establishes career goals, and plans practical developmental activities. In organizational career planning, the organization identifies paths and activities for individual employees as they develop.

**⑤  Describe the various types of career paths.**

Types of career paths include the traditional career path, the network career path, the lateral skill path, and the dual career path, as well as adding value to one's career and demotions.

**⑥  Explain the importance of career development.**

Career development benefits both the organization and the employee because properly developed employees are better prepared to add value both to themselves and to the company.

**⑦  Describe career planning and development methods.**

Methods include discussion with knowledgeable individuals, company material, performance appraisal system, workshops, personal development plans (PDPs), software packages, and career planning Web sites.

**⑧  Describe unique segments of the workforce that need to be developed.**

Some unique segments include Generation X employees, the *new* factory workers, and Generation Y and Generation I as future employees.

# ► Questions for Review

1. Define the following terms:

    a. *Career*
    b. *Career planning*
    c. *Organizational career planning*
    d. *Career path*
    e. *Career development*

2. What is the difference between job security and career security?

3. Identify and discuss the basic career-impacted life stages that people pass through.

4. List and briefly define the types of career anchors.

5. How should a strength/weakness balance sheet and a likes and dislikes survey be prepared?

6. What objectives are career planning programs expected to achieve?

7. What are the types of career paths? Briefly describe each.

8. Identify and describe some of the methods of organizational career planning and development.

9. Explain the nature of the following:

   a. Generation X employees
   b. The *new* factory workers
   c. Generation Y individuals
   d. Generation I individuals

*We invite you to visit the Mondy homepage on the Prentice Hall Web site at*
**www.prenhall.com/mondy**
*for updated information, Web-based exercises, and links to other HR-related sites.*

TAKE IT TO
THE NET

## Developing HRM Skills

### An Experiential Exercise

Career planning and development is extremely important to many individuals. Workers want to know how they fit into the future of the organization. Employees who believe that they have a future with the company are often more productive than those who do not. This exercise is designed to assist in understanding what it takes for a certain human resource professional to climb the organizational ladder. This climb is partially dependent on the individual's self-perceptions and perceptions of past experiences with the company. This exercise provides one method of individual career planning.

Everyone in the class can participate in this exercise. Your instructor will provide the participants with additional information necessary to complete the exercise.

## HRM INCIDENT 1

### There Is No Future Here!

"Could you come to my office for a minute, Bob?" asked Terry Geech, the plant manager.

"Sure, be right there," said Bob Glemson. Bob was the plant's quality control director. He had been with the company for four years. After completing his degree in mechanical engineering, he worked as a production supervisor and then as a maintenance supervisor prior to moving to his present job. Bob thought he knew what the call was about.

"Your letter of resignation catches me by surprise," began Terry. "I know that Wilson Products will be getting a good person, but we sure need you here, too."

"I thought about it a lot," said Bob, "but there just doesn't seem to be a future for me here."

"Why do you say that?" asked Terry.

"Well," replied Bob, "the next position above mine is yours. Since you're only 39, I don't think it's likely that you'll be leaving soon."

"The fact is that I *am* leaving soon," said Terry. "That's why it's even more of a shock to learn that you're resigning. I think I'll be moving to the corporate office in June of next year. Besides, the company has several plants that are larger than this one, and we need good people in those plants from time to time, both in quality control and in general management."

"Well, I heard about an opening in the Cincinnati plant last year," said Bob, "but by the time I checked, the job had already been filled. We never know about opportunities in the other plants until we read about the incumbent in the company paper."

"All this is beside the point now. What would it take to get you to change your mind?" asked Terry.

"I don't think I will change my mind now," replied Bob, "because I've given Wilson Products my word that I'm going to join them."

### Questions

1. Evaluate the career planning and development program at this company.
2. What actions might have prevented Bob's resignation?

---

▶ **HRM INCIDENT 2**

#### Adding Value

J. D. Wallace, a 30-year-old employee with Bechtel Engineering, headquartered in Houston, Texas, describes his assessment of career development.

*My present job is to work with an engineering software design program, Plant Design System (PDS), that is used to create a three-dimensional model of a petro-chem refinery. PDS is the fastest-growing and most demanded skill in my industry. The system has grown into a major design system that clients prefer. It has become very difficult for designers to find new jobs or keep their current job if they do not have the ability to run this system. Unfortunately, a lot of the designers have been caught with their pants down. They didn't see the need to get new skills. They believe, "I've done it this way for 20 years and I have not needed computer skills. Computers will never replace board drafting. This company needs me and they will not be able to replace me because of my many years of experience."*

*On the other hand, some designers realize the importance of learning new technology. These designers can, for the most part, write their own ticket. They have become the highest paid and most sought after employees. I believe that it is very important to constantly increase your value to the company. For example, my college degree opened the door for me. Once the door opened, it was up to me to keep learning. I had to continue to train, retrain, and learn new systems. Some of the systems I have invested time learning have quickly become obsolete. However, I have not lost anything in the process. Improving skills is never a waste of time. It is amazing how fast the industry can change. Skills that you obtain and thought you would never use, can be the only reason you have a job tomorrow.*

*Workers today must do whatever it takes to get the training needed to keep their jobs. Some of the things you could do include going back to school, or changing companies to get the necessary training. Very few companies spend the time and money needed to give workers all the training they need. Everybody must realize that they must stay current or they will be left behind.*

*In the last year alone the market for designers with PDS training has grown so fast that companies can no longer be assured of having an adequate work pool to draw from. The pay scale has expanded rapidly and is still growing. A good friend of mine has recently quit his present job for a 35 percent pay increase. Another company has lost many of their 10-year-plus employees for huge salary offers. Workers with the needed skills now have a lot of options. They can (for the most part) pick the company they want—by location, benefits, permanent staff, or contract. They currently have a lot of leverage. Workers without those skills have very limited choices because they do not add value to their companies.*

## Questions

1. Do you agree with J.D.'s assessment of what it takes to be successful in today's workplace? Discuss.
2. Do you agree with J.D.'s statement that "improving your skills is never a waste of time," considering that he has learned systems which quickly became obsolete? Discuss.

## Notes

1. Adapted from a real case presented in an article by Stephen Baker and Larry Armstrong, "Special Report—The New Factory Worker," *Business Week* (September 30, 1996): 59.
2. Julie Rawe, "What Will Be the 10 Hottest Jobs?. . . and What Jobs Will Disappear?" *Time* 155 (May 22, 2000): 73.
3. Richard L. Knowdell, "Specialized Occupations That Changed Radically or Fell by the Wayside," *The Futurist* 32 (June/July 1998): 20.
4. Jenny C. McCune, "HR's Top Concerns," *HR Focus* 74 (March 1997): 6.
5. "Development Is Hot, Resolutions Are Not, Personnel Decisions International Survey Says," *PR Newswire* (December 21, 1999): 1.
6. "IPD Publication Urges Employers to Wise Up to Career Development," *Management Services* 44 (April 2000): 4.
7. Julie Newberg, "Workers Today Placing More Importance on Job, Not Career," *The Arizona Republic* (October 13, 1998): WT3.
8. Phillip Schofield, "Your Career Path Can Lead You Anywhere," *Independent on Sunday* (September 6, 1998): 2.
9. "Career Evolution," *The Economist* 354 (January 2000).
10. Robert McGarvey, "Loyal Following: Bringing Employee Loyalty Back from the Dead," *Entrepreneur Magazine* 26 (May 1998): 86.
11. Louis S. Richman, "How to Get Ahead in America," *Fortune* 129 (May 14, 1994): 46.

12. Jonathan Sidener, "Pace of Net Technology Means Redefining Jobs Quickly," *The Arizona Republic* (May 14, 2000): S13.

13. Bill Breen, "Money Isn't Everything," *Fast Company* (April 1, 1998): 231.

14. Richard L. Knowdell, "The 10 New Rules for Strategizing Your Career," *The Futurist* 32 (June 1998): 1.

15. Bill Leonard, "Employee Loyalty Continues to Wane," *HRMagazine* 45 (January 2000): 21.

16. Edgar Schein, *Career Dynamics: Matching Individual and Organizational Needs* (Reading, MA: Addison-Wesley, 1978); and Thomas A. Kochan and Thomas A. Barocci, *Human Resource Management and Industrial Relations: Text, Readings, & Cases* (Glenview, IL: Scott, Foresman, & Company, 1985): 105.

17. Edgar Schein, "How 'Career Anchors' Hold Executives to Their Career Paths," *Personnel* 52 (May-June 1975): 11–24.

18. Richard Ream, "Changing Jobs? It's a Changing Market," *Information Today* 17 (February 2000): 18.

19. Schofield, "Your Career Path Can Lead You Anywhere."

20. Ream, "Changing Jobs? It's a Changing Market."

21. John H. Sheriday, "Ready for the Revolution," *Industry Week* 249 (January 24, 2000): 89.

22. Iris Randall, "Focus on Your Goal," *Black Enterprise* 30 (December 1999): 72.

23. Bob Lewis, "Formal Career Planning? Get Real! Here's a Better Way to Achieve Your Goals," *InfoWorld* 20 (August 3, 1998): 78.

24. Barbara Moses, "Career Intelligence: The 12 New Rules for Success," *The Futurist* 33 (August 1999): 28–35.

25. Lewis Carroll, *Through the Looking Glass* (New York: Norton, 1971): 127.

26. Gina Imperato, "Get Your Career in Site," *Fast Company* (March 2000): 322.

27. Ibid.

28. Milan Moravec, "A Cost-Effective Career Planning Program Requires a Strategy," *Personnel Administrator* 27 (January 1982): 29.

29. Donald L. Caruth, Robert M. Noe III, and R. Wayne Mondy, *Staffing the Contemporary Organization* (Westport, CT: Quorum Books, 1988): 42.

30. Anne Fisher, "Six Ways to Supercharge Your Career," *Fortune* 135 (January 13, 1997): 46+.

31. "Career Evolution," *The Economist* 354 (January 2000).

32. Milan Moravec and Beverly McKee, "Designing Dual Career Paths and Compensation," *Personnel* 67 (August 1990): 5.

33. Barb Cole-Gomolski, "Dual Career Paths Reduce Turnover Practicing," *Computerworld* 33 (February 22, 1999): 24.

34. Fisher, "Six Ways to Supercharge Your Career."

35. Brian O'Reilly, "The New Deal: What Companies and Employees Owe One Another," *Fortune* 129 (June 13, 1994): 44.

36. "Saratoga Institute: The 1999 Emerging Workforce Study," *M2 PressWIRE* (March 25, 1999): 1.

37. Richman, "How to Get Ahead in America," 49.

38. Loretta D. Foxman and Walter L. Polsky, "Aid in Employee Career Development," *Personnel Journal* 69 (January 1990): 22.

39. Robert McLuham, "There Are No Dead Ends, Only Crossroads," *Independent on Sunday* (November 22, 1998): 2.

40. "Career Calendar: A Schedule You Can Use for Advancement," *The Atlanta Journal and Constitution* (May 30, 1999): R2.

41. Schofield, "Your Career Path Can Lead You Anywhere."

42. Jim Meade, "Self-Assessment Tool Helps Target Training," *HRMagazine* 45 (May 2000): 167.

43. "Texas Instruments Web Site Helps College Students Choose Their Career," *M2 PressWIRE* (January 27, 1999).

44. "Key to Marketing Successfully to Gen X and Y? Break all the Rules," *Card News* (February 10, 2000).

45. Meredith Bagby, "The New Generation GAP/Generation X Generates Its Own Way," *Newsday* (September 16, 1999): A49.

46. Bruce Tulgan, "Managing Generation X," *HR Focus* 72 (November 1995): 22–24.

47. Ibid.

48. Chris Woodyard, "Generation Y: The Young and the Boundless Are Taking Over Pop Culture," *USA Today* (October 6, 1998): 1A.

49. Ellen Neuborne and Kathleen Kerwin, "Generation Y," *Business Week* (February 15, 1999): 80.

50. Bill Leonard, "After Generations X and Y Comes I," *HRMagazine* 45 (January 2000): 21.

51. Andrea C. Poe, "Welcome Back," *HRMagazine* 45 (March 2000): 94–105.

 Objectives

- Define *performance appraisal*.
- Identify the uses of performance appraisal.
- Describe the performance appraisal process.
- Explain performance appraisal environmental factors.
- Identify the aspect of a person's performance that an organization should evaluate.
- Identify who may be responsible for performance appraisal and the performance period.
- Identify the various performance appraisal methods used.
- List the problems that have been associated with performance appraisal.
- Explain the characteristics of an effective appraisal system.
- Describe the legal implications of performance appraisal.
- Explain how the appraisal interview should be conducted.

# Performance Appraisal

Marco Ghignoni, vice president of production for Block and Becker exclaimed, "Doug, we simply must increase our productivity. If we don't, the foreign competition is going to 'eat our lunch.' Worker productivity hasn't declined much, but our people seem to have little incentive to work together to improve it."

"I agree with you, Marco," said Doug Overbeck, vice president for human resources. "We really don't have a good system for evaluating team results while at the same time recognizing differences in individual performance. I'm convinced that our team approach in manufacturing is sound. But, it does bring us new problems with performance appraisal and our reward system. We need to take some action in these areas, and fast!"

# Key Terms

Performance appraisal (PA) 279
Performance management 280
360-degree feedback 288
Rating scales method 289
Critical incident method 292
Essay method 292
Work standards method 292

Ranking method 292
Paired comparison 292
Forced distribution method 293
Forced-choice performance report 293
Weighted checklist performance report 293

Behaviorally anchored rating scales (BARS) 293
Halo error 295
Leniency 295
Strictness 295
Central tendency 296

$\text{M}$arco and Doug had begun to realize a need for identifying both team and individual performance. When a performance appraisal system is geared totally toward individual results, it is not surprising that employees show little interest in working in teams. On the other hand, individual contributions must also be taken into account.

We begin this chapter by defining *performance appraisal* and identifying the uses of performance appraisal. We then explain environmental factors affecting performance appraisal and the performance appraisal process. Then, we identify the aspect of a person's performance that should be evaluated, who will be responsible for appraisal, and the appraisal period. Next, we discuss the various performance appraisal methods, problems associated with performance appraisal, and characteristics of an effective appraisal system. The final portions of the chapter deal with legal implications of performance appraisal and how the appraisal interview should be conducted.

## PERFORMANCE APPRAISAL DEFINED

As emphasized before, virtually every American business firm is affected by global competition. For survival and success, it is imperative that these organizations remain competitive in this new environment. Continued competence can be maintained only through ceaseless development of human resources. Employee performance appraisal is a potential mechanism for this growth. It is vital for managers to realize that performance appraisal must be comprehensive and that it is a continuous process, rather than an event that occurs once a year. **Performance appraisal (PA)** is a system of review and evaluation of an individual's or team's job performance. While the performance of teams should also be evaluated, the focus of PA in most firms remains on the individual employee. Regardless of the emphasis, an effective system evaluates accomplishments and develops plans for individual and team development, goals, and objectives.

Conducting performance appraisals is often a frustrating human resource management task. One management guru, Edward Lawler, noted the considerable documentation showing that performance appraisal systems neither motivate individuals nor effectively guide their development. Instead, he maintains, they create conflict between supervisors and subordinates and lead to dysfunctional behaviors.[1] A bit of advice to the team-oriented workgroups in the twenty-first century: "De-emphasize elaborate individual performance evaluations; use more informal feedback."[2] These caveats are important, for it is certain that if a performance appraisal system has a faulty design or is improperly administered, the employees will dread receiving appraisals and the managers will despise giving them. In fact, some managers have always loathed the time, paperwork, difficult choices, and discomfort that often accompany the appraisal process.[3] Going through the procedure cuts into a manager's high-priority workload, and the experience can be quite unpleasant when the employee in question has not been toeing the line.[4]

**Performance appraisal (PA)**
A formal system of periodic review and evaluation of an individual's or team's job performance.

Because performance appraisal is so often perceived as a negative, disliked activity and one that seems to elude mastery, why don't organizations just drop the whole thing? Actually, some might do just that if managers did not have to make decisions about developmental needs, promotions, pay raises, terminations, transfers, admission to training programs, and—on top of all these considerations—be concerned about legal ramifications. Indeed, performance appraisal serves many purposes[5] and improved results and efficiency are increasingly critical in today's globally competitive marketplace. Therefore, shucking the only program with "performance" in its name and employees as its focus would seem to be an ill-advised overreaction.

Developing an effective performance appraisal system has been and will continue to be a high priority of human resource management. Regardless of the criticism this management process has received, America's best-managed corporations consider performance appraisal to be no joke; with them it is serious business.[6] Remember that performance appraisal is not an end in itself, but rather the means to impact performance. **Performance management** is a business process that significantly affects organizational success by having managers and employees work together. It can serve as the key to change that boosts both individual and team accomplishment.[7] Performance management requires planning to determine specific job responsibilities and performance measurements and uses coaching and training to develop needed skills and capabilities.[8] Finally, performance management reviews accomplishments and provides the basis for individual or team performance evaluation.

According to one study, firms that have effective performance management processes in place outperformed those without such systems on several critical measures including profits, cash flow, and stock market performance.[9] In striving to learn more about performance management, many managers take to the Web for information. While many Web sites display advertisements only for their fee-based products, CYBERManagement Inc. (cyberm.com) and Zigon Performance Group (zigonperf.com) serve as excellent sources of free information.[10]

Performance appraisal is only one technique designed to enhance performance management. Mentoring and coaching (discussed in Chapter 8), along with other training and development activities, are as critical. However, PA is a crucial component. It is also one of many human resource activities that must be essentially owned by line managers. Human resource professionals play an important role in developing and coordinating appraisal systems. However, a cross section of managers and employees who will use the system should be involved in developing it.[11] Approached in this manner, performance appraisal has the best chance for successful implementation.

**Performance management**
A process that significantly affects organizational success by having managers and employees work together to set expectations, review results, and reward performance.

## USES OF PERFORMANCE APPRAISAL

For many organizations, the primary goal of an appraisal system is to improve performance. Other goals may be sought as well, however. A potential problem—and possible cause of much dissatisfaction with PA—is expecting too much from one appraisal plan. For example, a plan that is effective for developing employees may not be the best for determining how pay increases should be administered. Yet, a system that is properly designed and communicated can help achieve organizational objectives and enhance employee performance. In fact, PA data are potentially valuable for use in virtually every human resource functional area, including the following.

# Human Resource Planning

In assessing a firm's human resources, data must be available that describe the promotability and potential of all employees, especially key executives. Management succession planning (discussed in Chapter 4) is a key concern for all firms. A well-designed appraisal system provides a profile of the organization's human resource strengths and weaknesses to support this effort.

# Recruitment and Selection

Performance evaluation ratings may be helpful in predicting the performance of job applicants. For example, it may be determined that successful managers in a firm (identified through performance evaluations) exhibit certain behaviors when performing key tasks. These data may then provide benchmarks for evaluating applicant responses obtained through behavioral interviews (discussed in Chapter 7). Also, in validating selection tests, employee ratings may be used as the variable against which test scores are compared. In this instance, determination of the selection test's validity would depend on the accuracy of appraisal results.

# Training and Development

A performance appraisal should point out an employee's specific needs for training and development (T&D). For instance, if Matrese Celestine's job requires skill in technical writing and her evaluation reveals a deficiency in this factor, she may need additional training in written communication. If the human resource manager finds that a number of first-line supervisors are having difficulty in administering discipline, training sessions addressing this problem may be suggested. By identifying deficiencies that adversely affect performance, human resource and line managers are able to develop T&D programs that permit individuals to build on their strengths and minimize their deficiencies. An appraisal system does not guarantee that employees will be properly trained and developed. However, the task of determining training and development needs is assisted when appraisal data are available.

# Career Planning and Development

Career planning and development may be viewed from either an individual or organizational viewpoint. In either case, performance appraisal data are essential in assessing an employee's strengths and weaknesses and in determining the person's potential. Managers may use such information to counsel subordinates and assist them in developing and implementing their career plans.

# Compensation Programs

Performance appraisal results provide a basis for rational decisions regarding pay adjustments. Most managers believe that outstanding job performance should be rewarded tangibly with pay increases. They believe that *the behaviors you reward are the behaviors you get*. To encourage good performance, a firm should design and implement a fair performance appraisal system and then reward the most productive workers and teams accordingly.

# Internal Employee Relations

Performance appraisal data are also frequently used for decisions in several areas of internal employee relations, including motivation, promotion, demotion, termination, layoff, and transfer. For example, self-esteem is essential for motivation.

Therefore, appraisal systems must be designed and implemented in a way to maintain and build employees' self-esteem. PA systems that result in brutally frank descriptions of performance may demotivate people. On the other hand, ignoring deficiencies in performance may hinder an individual's opportunity to improve and achieve his or her potential. Of course, the organization will also suffer if inept employees are retained in the firm.

An employee's performance in one job may be useful in determining his or her ability to perform another job on the same level, as is required in the consideration of transfers. When the performance level is unacceptable, demotion or even termination may be appropriate. When employees working under a labor agreement are involved, employee layoff is typically based on seniority. However, when management has more flexibility, an employee's performance record is generally a more relevant criterion.

## Assessment of Employee Potential

Some organizations attempt to assess employee potential as they appraise their job performance. The best predictors of future behavior are said to be past behaviors. However, an employee's past performance in a job may not accurately indicate future performance in a higher-level or different position. The best salesperson in the company may not have what it takes to become a successful district sales manager. The best computer programmer may, if promoted, be a disaster as an information technology manager. Overemphasizing technical skills and ignoring other equally important skills is a common error in promoting employees into management jobs. Recognition of this problem has led some firms to separate the appraisal of performance—which focuses on past behavior—from the assessment of potential, which is future oriented. These firms have established *assessment centers*, which were discussed in Chapter 7 as a selection method and will be mentioned again later in this chapter as an adjunct to appraisal.

## PERFORMANCE APPRAISAL ENVIRONMENTAL FACTORS

Many of the external and internal environmental factors discussed in Chapter 2 can influence the appraisal process. For example, legislation requires that appraisal systems be nondiscriminatory. In the case of *Mistretta v Sandia Corporation* (a subsidiary of Western Electric Company, Inc.), a federal district court judge ruled against the company, stating, "There is sufficient circumstantial evidence to indicate that age bias and age based policies appear throughout the performance rating process to the detriment of the protected age group." The *Albermarle Paper v Moody* case supported validation requirements for performance appraisals, as well as for selection tests. Organizations should avoid using any appraisal method that results in a disproportionately negative impact on a protected class.

The labor union is another external factor that might affect a firm's appraisal process. Unions have traditionally stressed seniority as the basis for promotions and pay increases. They may vigorously oppose the use of a management-designed performance appraisal system that would be used for these purposes.

Factors within the internal environment can also affect the performance appraisal process. For instance, the type of corporate culture can assist or hinder the process. In today's dynamic organizations, which increasingly utilize teams to perform jobs, overall team results as well as individual contributions must be recognized. A closed, nontrusting culture does not provide the environment needed to encourage high performance by either individuals or teams. In such an atmosphere, performance will suffer even though employees may try to do a good job.

## THE PERFORMANCE APPRAISAL PROCESS

As shown in Figure 10-1, identification of specific goals is the starting point for the PA process. An appraisal system probably cannot effectively serve every desired purpose. Therefore, management should select those specific appraisal goals it

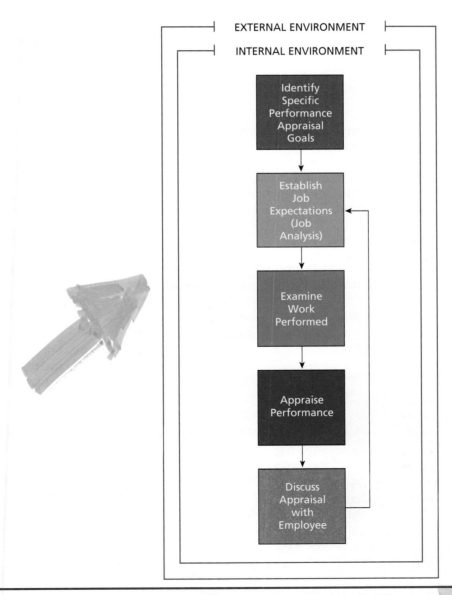

**The Performance Appraisal Process**     Figure 10-1

believes to be most important and realistically achievable. For example, some firms may want to stress employee development, whereas other organizations may want to focus on administrative decisions, such as pay adjustments. Too many PA systems fail because management expects too much from one method and does not determine specifically what it wants the system to accomplish.

After specific appraisal goals have been established, workers and teams must understand what is expected of them in their task accomplishments. This understanding is greatly facilitated when employees have had input into the established goals. At the end of the appraisal period, the appraiser and the employee together review work performance and evaluate it against established performance standards. This review helps determine how well employees have met these standards, determines reasons for deficiencies, and develops a plan to correct the problems. The discussion also establishes goals for the next evaluation period.

## WHAT TO EVALUATE

What aspect of a person's performance should an organization evaluate? In practice, the most common appraisal criteria are traits, behaviors, task outcomes, and improvement potential.

### Traits

Some employees are evaluated on the basis of certain traits such as *attitude, appearance, initiative*, and so on. However, many of these commonly used traits are subjective and may be either unrelated to job performance or virtually impossible to define. In such cases, inaccurate evaluations may occur and create legal difficulties for the organization. At the same time, certain traits may be related to job performance and, if this connection can be established, using traits may be satisfactory.

### Behaviors

When an individual's task outcome is difficult to determine, it is common to evaluate the person's task-related behavior. For example, an appropriate behavior to evaluate for a manager might be *leadership style*. For individuals working in teams, *developing others, teamwork and cooperation,* or *customer service orientation* might be appropriate.

The importance of organizational fit was discussed in Chapter 7. At San Francisco–based Air Touch Communications, this point is emphasized to employees from their first day on the job. The employees are drilled about the company's values on ethics, integrity, customer satisfaction, leadership, teamwork, innovation, and the ability to think and act like owners. Then, to reinforce behavior that is consistent with these organizational values, the employees are evaluated on how they adhere to them.[12]

Stability provides another example of behavior that may be important for organizational planning. If so, it should be measured in performance appraisals of executives as well as mid-level managers and front-line supervisors.[13] Desired behaviors may be appropriate as evaluation

www.techjobbank.com
*Source:* TechJobBank.

criteria because of the belief that if recognized and rewarded, they will be repeated. In addition, firms pay people salaries for behaving in certain ways that produce results. People do not perform traits; they perform behaviors.

## Task Outcomes

If ends are considered more important than means, task outcomes become the more appropriate factor to evaluate. This approach is followed when a goals-oriented process is used. The outcomes established should be within the control of the individual or team and should be those results that lead to the firm's success. At upper levels, the goals might deal with financial aspects of the firm, such as profit or cash flow, and market considerations, such as market share or position in the market. At lower organizational levels, the outcomes might be meeting the customer's quality requirements and delivering according to the promised schedule.[14]

A problem might occur when a firm fails to recognize the difference between productivity and quality of output. Overemphasizing productivity may result in such a frenzied work pace that mistakes are passed on to the customer. On the other hand, a total focus on quality may generate fantastic products, but also botched delivery dates. The obvious answer is to balance the requirement for speed with the need to do the job right. Evaluation criteria are not mutually exclusive. In fact, many appraisal systems are a hybrid of these approaches.[15]

## Improvement Potential

When an employee's performance is evaluated, the criteria used focus on the past. From a performance management viewpoint, the problem is that the past cannot be changed. Unless a further step is taken, the evaluation data become merely historical documents. Therefore, some attention must be given to the future and the behaviors and outcomes that are needed to not only develop the employee, but also achieve the firm's goals. This involves an assessment of the employee's potential.[16] In this light, the manager needs to provide specific examples of how the employee can further his or her development and achieve specific goals.[17] A consensus should be reached as to the employee's goals for the next evaluation period and the assistance and resources to be provided by the manager. This aspect of employee appraisal should be the most positive element in the entire process and help the employee focus on behavior that will produce positive results for all concerned.

## RESPONSIBILITY FOR APPRAISAL

In most organizations, the human resource department is responsible for coordinating the design and implementation of performance appraisal programs. However, it is essential that line managers play a key role from beginning to end. These individuals will likely have responsibility for actually conducting the appraisals, and they must directly participate in the program if it is to succeed. Several possibilities exist as to who will actually rate the employee, and these are presented next.

## Immediate Supervisor

An employee's immediate supervisor has traditionally been the most common choice for evaluating performance. This continues to be the case, and there are several reasons for this approach. In the first place, the supervisor is usually in an excellent position to observe the employee's job performance. Another reason is that the supervisor has the responsibility for managing a particular unit. When the task of evaluating subordinates is given to someone else, the supervisor's authority may be undermined. Finally, subordinate training and development is an important element in every manager's job and, as previously mentioned, appraisal programs and employee development are often closely related.

On the negative side, the immediate supervisor may emphasize certain aspects of employee performance and neglect others. Also, managers have been known to manipulate evaluations to justify their pay increases and promotions. In project or matrix organizations, the functional supervisor may not have the opportunity to observe performance sufficiently to evaluate it. However, in most instances, the immediate supervisor will probably continue to be involved in evaluating performance. Organizations will seek alternatives, however, because of the organizational innovations that have occurred and a desire to broaden the perspective of the appraisal.

## Subordinates

Historically, evaluation by subordinates has been viewed negatively in our culture.[18] However, in the past 10 years or so, this thinking has changed. Some firms have concluded that evaluation of managers by subordinates is not only feasible but needed. They reason that subordinates are in an excellent position to view their superior's managerial effectiveness. Advocates of this approach believe that supervisors will become especially conscious of the work group's needs and will do a better job of managing. Critics are concerned that the manager will be caught up in a popularity contest or that employees will be fearful of reprisal. If this approach has a chance for success, one thing is clear: Anonymity of the evaluators must be guaranteed. Assuring this might be particularly difficult in a small department—especially if demographic data that could identify raters are included in the evaluation.

## Peers

A major strength of using peers to appraise performance is that they work closely with the evaluated employee and probably have an undistorted perspective on typical performance, especially in team assignments.[19] Organizations are increasingly using teams, including those that are self-directed. The rationale for evaluations conducted by team members includes the following:

- Team members know each other's performance better than anyone and can, therefore, evaluate performance more accurately.
- Peer pressure is a powerful motivator for team members.
- Members who recognize that peers within the team will be evaluating their work show increased commitment and productivity.
- Peer review involves numerous opinions and is not dependent on one individual.

Problems with peer evaluations include the reluctance of people who work closely together, especially on teams, to criticize each other. On the other hand, peers who interact infrequently, as is the case with boards of directors, often lack the information needed to make an accurate assessment.[20] In some cases, team members may have little or no appraisal training. Training in performance appraisal is obviously needed for team members as it is for anyone evaluating performance.

Peer evaluation works best in a participative culture. However, the approach is not always satisfactory even in this type of environment. Quaker Oats had such a plan in one of its plants for 10 years before it failed. An explanation for its demise was that there was no incentive for people to be strict about it. One of the success stories comes from W. L. Gore of Newark, Delaware. Gore associates (employees) are organized in work teams that handle performance problems. They also perform other traditional human resource functions, such as hiring and firing.[21] As the popularity of self-directed work teams increases, use of peer appraisal will likely increase.

## Self-Appraisal

If employees understand the objectives they are expected to achieve and the standards by which they are to be evaluated, they are in a good position to appraise their own performance. Many people know what they do well on the job and what they need to improve. If they are given the opportunity, they will criticize their own performance objectively and take action needed to improve it. Also, because employee development is self-development, employees who appraise their own performance may become more highly motivated. Even if a self-appraisal is not a part of the system, the employee should at least be asked for a list of his or her most important accomplishments and contributions over the appraisal period. This will prevent the manager from being blind-sided when the employee complains, perhaps justifiably, "You didn't even mention the Bandy contract I landed last December!"[22]

As a complement to other approaches, self-appraisal has great appeal to managers who are primarily concerned with employee participation and development. For compensation purposes, however, its value is considerably less. It is well known that some individuals attribute good performance to their own efforts and poor performance to someone else's.

## Customer Appraisal

Customer behavior determines a firm's degree of success. Therefore, some organizations believe it is important to obtain performance input from this critical source. Organizations use this approach because it demonstrates a commitment to the customer, holds employees accountable, and fosters change. Customer-related goals for executives generally are of a broad, strategic nature, while targets for lower-level employees tend to be more specific. For example, an objective might be to improve the rating for accurate delivery or reduce the number of dissatisfied customers by half. It is important to have employee participation in setting goals and to include only those factors within the employees' control.

# THE APPRAISAL PERIOD

Formal performance evaluations are usually prepared at specific intervals. While there is nothing magic about the periods, in most organizations, they are made either annually or semiannually. In high-tech organizations, however, the speed of change mandates that a performance period be shorter—perhaps three or four months. The need is to link performance communication to the actual work cycle. Discussions of accomplishments can then keep pace with new goals and priorities. In the current business climate, it may be well for all firms to consider monitoring performance often. Changes occur so fast that employees need to look at objectives and their own role throughout the year to see if they need to be altered. A study by Hewitt Associates found that companies conducting multiple performance reviews had better results in terms of total shareholder return, return on equity, sales growth, and cash flow.[23]

Some organizations use the employee's date of hire to determine the rating period. However, in the interest of consistency, it may be advisable to perform evaluations on a calendar basis, not on anniversaries.[24] If the appraisals are not done at the same time, it may not be feasible to make needed comparisons between employees.[25]

## PERFORMANCE APPRAISAL METHODS

Managers may choose from among a number of appraisal methods. The type of performance appraisal system utilized depends on its purpose. If the major emphasis is on selecting people for promotion, training, and merit pay increases, a traditional method such as rating scales may be appropriate. Collaborative methods—including input from the employees themselves—may prove to be more suitable for helping employees become more effective.

### The 360-Degree Evaluation

**360-degree feedback**
A multirater evaluation that involves input from multiple levels within the firm and external sources as well.

The **360-degree feedback**, or multirater evaluation is an increasingly popular appraisal method that involves input from multiple levels within the firm and external sources as well. This method has been introduced in most *Fortune* 1,000 companies and continues to spread, even among smaller firms.[26] Businesses using 360-degree feedback include McDonnell-Douglas, AT&T, Allied Signal, Dupont, Honeywell, Boeing, and Intel. These firms use their 360-degree feedback to provide evaluations for conventional uses. However, for many other firms this process is used strictly for developmental purposes, and only the managers being rated see the feedback.[27]

Unlike traditional approaches, 360-degree feedback focuses on skills needed across organizational boundaries. Also, by shifting the responsibility for evaluation from one person, many of the common appraisal errors can be reduced or eliminated. Thanks to computer networks, the people who provide the ratings can do so quickly and conveniently because many rating instruments can now be administered online.[28] The 360-degree feedback method may provide a more objective measure of a person's performance. Including the perspective of multiple sources results in a broader view of the employee's performance and helps minimize biases that result from limited views of behavior.[29] Personal development requires good, honest, well-expressed, and specific feedback, which is essential in the workplace.[30]

Having multiple raters also makes the process more legally defensible. The raters, or stakeholders, can be senior managers, the employee himself or herself, immediate managers, peers, team members, and customers. All parties should know the strategic competencies to be evaluated, the methods for gathering and summarizing the feedback, and how the feedback will be used with the evaluation system. This involvement is critical to ensure

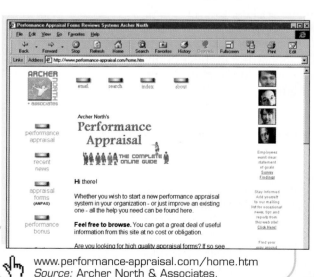

www.performance-appraisal.com/home.htm
*Source:* Archer North & Associates.

stakeholder support of and commitment to the feedback process.[31] An appraisal system involving numerous evaluators will naturally take more time and, therefore, be more costly. Nevertheless, the way firms are being organized and managed may require innovative alternatives to traditional top-down appraisals.

Some experts feel that 360-degree feedback should be used only for developmental purposes. Their rationale stems from a concern that when raters believe others will be hurt by what they say in the evaluation, they will not be honest. An opposing view is that input from peers, who may be competitors for raises and promotions, might intentionally distort the data. Yet, many firms want to use 360-degree feedback as an appraisal approach, and some that have done so have found ways to avoid the pitfalls.[32]

## Rating Scales

The **rating scales method** is a widely used appraisal approach that rates employees according to defined factors. Using this approach, judgments about performance are recorded on a scale. The scale is divided into categories—normally five to seven in number—that are often defined by adjectives, such as *outstanding, meets expectations,* or *needs improvement.* While an overall rating may be provided, the method generally allows for the use of more than one performance criterion. One reason for the popularity of the rating scales method is its simplicity, which permits many employees to be evaluated quickly. When the ratings are quantified, the method facilitates comparison of employees' performances.

The factors chosen for evaluation are typically of two types: job-related and personal characteristics. Note that in Figure 10-2, job-related factors include quality and quantity of work, whereas personal factors include such behaviors as interpersonal skills and traits such as adaptability. The rater (evaluator) completes the form by indicating the degree of each factor that is most descriptive of the employee and

**Rating scales method**
A widely used performance appraisal method that rates employees according to defined factors.

---

### ▶ United Parcel's 360-Degree Evaluation System

TRENDS &
INNOVATIONS

United Parcel Service's (UPS's) airline operations headquarters in Louisville, Kentucky, uses an automated 360-degree process every six months that measures skills such as customer focus, financial and internal business process knowledge, people skills, business values, and leadership. Prior to implementing this process, HR trainers simply explain the purpose and the process to participants. Employees can also download information about the process from the company's intranet. The managers themselves initiate the process twice a year, asking their peers, supervisors, and others to evaluate them. They are rated on a scale from one to seven, and the scores are then reviewed with supervisors and direct reports. Based on the feedback, the employee sets goals for the next six months with HR available to offer training if needed. The employee rechecks his or her improvements and results again six months later.

Hope Zoeller Stith, trainer in the HR learning and development department, emphasizes the importance of ongoing communication as well as individual feedback. To ensure that this feedback occurs, UPS uses two main strategies; an in-house course to help managers give and receive feedback and informal meetings, called "Talk, Listen, Act" or TLAs. In these meetings, supervisors and their direct reports are encouraged to talk about any work-related concern. These meetings are scheduled at least twice a year but may be conducted any time.[33]

| Name | Job Title |
|---|---|
| Supervisor/Manager | Department |
| Appraisal Period: From | To |

Evaluate the performance in each of the following factors on a scale of 1 to 5:
**5 = Outstanding,** consistently exceeds expectations for this factor.
**4 = Above Expectations,** consistently meets and occasionally exceeds expectations.
**3 = Meets Expectations,** consistently meets expectations.
**2 = Below Expectations,** occasionally fails to meet expectations.
**1 = Needs Improvement,** consistently fails to meet expectations.

**Part 1—Task Outcomes (Weighted 80% of total score)**
List mutually agreed-to performance factors from the job description and goals established from the preview performance review. **Points**

- ______________________________ ____
- ______________________________ ____
- ______________________________ ____
- ______________________________ ____
- ______________________________ ____
- Quality of work ____
- Quantity of work ____

**Total Points** ____
**Average Score (Divide total points by number of factors used)** ____ Multiplied by **16** = ____
**Comments** ______________________________

**Part 2—Personal Behaviors (10% of total score)**

- Leadership ____
- Interpersonal skills ____
- Developing others ____
- Customer service ____
- Teamwork ____

**Total Points** ____
**Average Score (Divide total points by number of applicable factors)** ____ Multiplied by **2** = ____
**Comments** ______________________________

**Figure 10-2** **Rating Scales Method of Performance Appraisal**

his or her performance. The points in each part are totaled and then averaged. This average is multiplied by a factor representing the weight given each section. The final score (total points) for the employee is the total of each section's points.

Some firms provide space for the rater to comment on the evaluation given for each factor. This practice may be especially encouraged, or even required, when the rater gives either the highest or lowest rating. For instance, if an employee is rated *needs improvement* (a 1 on the sample form) on *teamwork*, the rater provides written justification for this low evaluation. The purpose of this requirement is to discourage arbitrary and hastily made judgments.

Part 3—Personal Traits (10% of total score)
- Adaptability _____
- Judgment _____
- Appearance _____
- Attitude _____
- Initiative _____

Total Points _____

Average Score (Divide total points by 5) _____ Multiplied by **2** = _____

Comments _____

_____

_____

Points from Part 1 _____ + Part 2 _____ + Part 3 _____ = Total Points _____

Performance goals for next appraisal period:
- _____
- _____
- _____
- _____
- _____

Self-development activities for this employee

_____

_____

Employee comments

_____

_____

| Evaluated By: | Title | Date |
|---|---|---|
| Approved | Title | Date |
| Employee's Signature (Does not necessarily indicate agreement) | Title | Date |

**Rating Scales Method of Performance Appraisal (*continued*)**    Figure 10-2

In order to receive an *outstanding* rating for a factor such as *quality of work*, a person must consistently go beyond the prescribed work requirements. While the sample form falls short in this respect, the more precisely the various factors and degrees are defined, the more accurately the rater can evaluate worker performance. When the various performance levels are described merely as *above expectations* or *below expectations* without further elaboration, what has the employee really learned? These generalities do not provide the guidance needed for improving performance.[34] Evaluation agreement throughout the organization is achieved when each rater interprets the factors and degrees in the same way. This ability may be acquired through performance appraisal training. Many rating scale performance appraisal forms also provide for considering future behavior. Notice that the form shown in Figure 10-2 has space for performance goals for the next period and self-development activities for the next appraisal period.

## Critical Incidents

**Critical incident method**
A performance appraisal technique that requires a written record of highly favorable and highly unfavorable employee work.

The **critical incident method** requires that written records be kept of highly favorable and highly unfavorable work actions. When such an action affects the department's effectiveness significantly—either positively or negatively—the manager writes it down. It is called a *critical incident*. At the end of the appraisal period, the rater uses these records along with other data to evaluate employee performance. With this method, the appraisal is more likely to cover the entire evaluation period and not focus on the last few weeks or months.

## Essay

**Essay method**
A performance appraisal method in which the rater writes a brief narrative describing an employee's performance.

In the **essay method**, the rater simply writes a brief narrative describing the employee's performance. This method tends to focus on extreme behavior in the employee's work rather than routine day-to-day performance. Ratings of this type depend heavily on the evaluator's writing ability. Because of their excellent writing skills, some supervisors can make even a marginal worker sound like a top performer. Comparing essay evaluations might be difficult because no common criteria exist. However, some managers believe that the essay method is not only the most simple but also an acceptable approach to employee evaluation.

## Work Standards

**Work standards method**
A performance appraisal method that compares each employee's performance to a predetermined standard or expected level of output.

The **work standards method** compares each employee's performance to a predetermined standard or expected level of output. Standards reflect the normal output of an average worker operating at a normal pace. Work standards may be applied to virtually all types of jobs, but they are most frequently used for production jobs. Several methods may be utilized in determining work standards, including time study and work sampling. An obvious advantage of using standards as appraisal criteria is objectivity. However, in order for employees to perceive that the standards are objective, they should understand clearly how the standards were set. It follows that the rationale for any changes to the standards must also be carefully explained.

## Ranking

**Ranking method**
A job evaluation method in which the rater simply places all employees from a group in rank order of overall performance.

**Paired comparison**
A variation of the ranking method of performance appraisal in which the performance of each employee is compared with that of every other employee in the group.

In using the **ranking method**, the rater simply places all employees from a group in rank order of overall performance. For example, the best employee in the group is ranked highest, and the poorest is ranked lowest. This procedure is followed until all employees have been ranked. A difficulty occurs when individuals have performed at comparable levels.

**Paired comparison** is a variation of the ranking method in which the performance of each employee is compared with every other employee in the group. The comparison is often based on a single criterion, such as overall performance. The employee who receives the greatest number of favorable comparisons is ranked highest. Some professionals in the field argue for using a comparative approach, such as ranking, whenever human resource decisions are made. For example, they feel that employees are promoted not because they achieve their objectives, but because they achieve them better than others in their work group. Such decisions go beyond a single individual's performance and, therefore, should be considered on a broader basis.

## Forced Distribution

In the **forced distribution method**, the rater is required to assign individuals in the work group to a limited number of categories similar to a normal frequency distribution. As an example, employees in the top 10 percent are placed in the highest group, the next 20 percent in the next group, the next 40 percent in the middle group, the next 20 percent in the second-to-lowest group, and the remaining 10 percent in the lowest category. This approach is based on the questionable assumption that all groups of employees will have the same distribution of excellent, average, and poor performers. In short, this method makes no sense unless employees have been selected randomly. If a department has done an outstanding job in selecting people with the result that 20 percent should be rated in the top group, the 10 percent left out will probably become unhappy at best and leave for greener pastures at worst.

**Forced distribution method**
An appraisal approach in which the rater is required to assign individuals in a work group to a limited number of categories similar to a normal frequency distribution.

## Forced-Choice and Weighted Checklist Performance Reports

The **forced-choice performance report** requires that the appraiser choose from a series of statements about an individual those that are most or least descriptive of the employee. One difficulty with this method is that the descriptive statements may be virtually identical. Using the **weighted checklist performance report**, the rater completes a form similar to the forced-choice performance report, but the various responses have been assigned different weights. The form includes questions related to the employee's behavior, and the evaluator answers each question either positively or negatively. The evaluator is not aware of each question's weight, however. As with forced-choice performance reports, the weighted checklist is expensive to design. Both methods strive for objectivity, but the evaluator does not know which items contribute most to successful performance. Employee development, therefore, cannot result from this approach.

**Forced-choice performance report**
A performance appraisal technique in which the rater is given a series of statements about an individual and indicates which items are most or least descriptive of the employee.

**Weighted checklist performance report**
A performance appraisal technique in which the rater completes a form similar to a forced-choice performance report except that the various responses have been assigned different weights.

## Behaviorally Anchored Rating Scales

The **behaviorally anchored rating scales (BARS)** method combines elements of the traditional rating scales and critical incident methods.[35] Using BARS, job behaviors derived from critical incidents—effective and ineffective behavior—are described more objectively. Individuals familiar with a particular job identify its major components. They then rank and validate specific behaviors for each of the components. Because BARS typically requires considerable employee participation, supervisors and subordinates accept it more readily.

In BARS, various performance levels are shown along a scale and described in terms of an employee's specific job behavior. In evaluating a group of employees working as interviewers, for example, suppose the factor chosen for evaluation is *Ability to Absorb and Interpret Policies*. On the *very positive* end of this factor might be, "This interviewer could be expected to serve as an information source concerning new and changed policies for others in the organization." On the *very negative* end of this factor might be, "Even after repeated explanations, this interviewer would be unable to understand new procedures." There might be several levels in between the very negative and very positive level.

**Behaviorally anchored rating scales (BARS) method**
A performance appraisal method that combines elements of the traditional rating scale and critical incident methods.

BARS differs from rating scales because instead of using adjectives at each scale point, BARS uses behavioral anchors related to the criterion being measured. This modification clarifies the meaning of each point on the scale and reduces rater bias and error by anchoring the rating with specific behavioral examples based on job analysis information.[36] Instead of providing a space for entering a rating figure for a category such as *Above Expectations*, the BARS method provides examples of such behavior. This approach facilitates discussion of the rating because specific behaviors can be addressed. It was developed to overcome weaknesses in other evaluation methods. Regardless of apparent advantages of BARS, reports on its effectiveness are mixed, and it does not seem to be superior to other methods in overcoming rater errors or in achieving psychometric soundness. A specific deficiency is that the behaviors used are activity oriented rather than results oriented. Also, the method may not be economically feasible since each job category requires its own BARS. On the positive side, because the system is job related, it is relatively invulnerable to legal challenge.[37]

## Results-Based Systems

The manager and the subordinate jointly agree on objectives for the next appraisal period in a results-based system. In such a system one objective might be, for instance, to cut waste by 1 percent. At the end of the appraisal period, an employee's evaluation is based on how well this objective was accomplished. One distinct advantage of this approach is that it provides a measure of achievement against predetermined objectives. However, since performance outcomes do not indicate how to change, the method may be less helpful in employee development. Nevertheless, a results-oriented approach remains a popular technique to evaluate employees, especially managers.[38]

## Assessment Centers

The primary use of assessment centers is to identify and select employees for higher-level positions, as discussed in Chapter 7. They may also be used as part of a management system that focuses on employee development. Some performance appraisals attempt to not only evaluate performance, which essentially focuses on the past, but also determine an individual's potential for advancement, which is future oriented. Recognizing the differences in purposes and the difficulty that a PA system will have in achieving both aims, some firms opt to use an assessment center as an adjunct to their appraisal system.

Finding the best performance evaluation system seems to be an unending challenge for most organizations. Some, however, appear to be taking a more strategic approach to the process. Instead of using the familiar "check the box, write a comment" ritual, some organizations are integrating the company's mission statement, vision, and values in their PA systems.[39]

## PROBLEMS IN PERFORMANCE APPRAISAL

As indicated at the beginning of this chapter, performance appraisal has come under a heavy barrage of criticism. The rating scales method seems to have been the most popular target. In all fairness, many of the problems commonly mentioned are not inherent in this method but, rather, reflect improper usage. For example, raters may be inadequately trained, or the appraisal criteria used may be too subjective and not job related. The following section highlights some of the more common problem areas.

## Lack of Objectivity

A potential weakness of traditional performance appraisal methods is that they lack objectivity. In the rating scales method, for example, commonly used factors such as attitude, loyalty, and personality are difficult to measure. In addition, these factors may have little to do with an employee's job performance. Some subjectivity will always exist in appraisal methods. However, employee appraisal based primarily on personal characteristics may place the evaluator and the company in untenable positions with the employee and equal employment opportunity guidelines. The firm may be hard pressed to show that these factors are job related.

## Halo Error

**Halo error** occurs when a manager generalizes one positive performance feature or incident to all aspects of employee performance.[40] For example, Freddie Flores, accounting supervisor, placed a high value on *neatness*, a factor used in the company's performance appraisal system. As Freddie was evaluating the performance of his senior accounting clerk, Jack Hicks, he noted that Jack was a very neat individual and gave him a high ranking on this factor. Also, consciously or unconsciously, Freddie permitted the high ranking on neatness to carry over to other factors, giving Jack undeserved high ratings on all factors. Of course, if Jack had not been neat, the opposite could have occurred. Either way, the halo error distorts the appraisal.

**Halo error**
Occurs when a manager generalizes one positive performance factor or incident to all aspects of employee performance.

## Leniency/Strictness

Giving undeserved high ratings is referred to as **leniency**. This behavior is often motivated by a desire to avoid controversy over the appraisal. It is most prevalent when highly subjective (and difficult to defend) performance criteria are used, and the rater is required to discuss evaluation results with employees. One research study found that when managers know they are evaluating employees for administrative purposes, such as pay increases, they are likely to be more lenient than when evaluating performance to achieve employee development.[41] Leniency may result in failure to recognize deficiencies that should be corrected. The practice may also deplete the merit budget and reduce the reward available for superior employees. In addition, an organization will find it difficult to terminate employees who cannot achieve acceptable performance levels.

**Leniency**
Giving an undeserved high performance appraisal rating to an employee.

Few people enjoy delivering bad news to employees, but good managers understand that doing so, when deserved, is crucial to an organization's long-term success. Not tolerating unsatisfactory performance can also be a tonic for top performers who relish working in an environment free of noncontributors. A climate that openly tolerates mediocrity demoralizes this group of employees.[42]

Being unduly critical of an employee's work performance is referred to as **strictness**. Many firms make it extremely difficult for managers to rate more than a very few of their employees as outstanding. They are relentless in making sure that *evaluation inflation* does not creep into the process. But, what happens when a manager has five superstars yet is told that only three are eligible for the bonus pool? It is one thing to have a system that demotivates average performers, but to demotivate your top performers is the height of self-destructive folly.[43]

**Strictness**
Being unduly critical of an employee's work performance.

Although leniency is usually more prevalent than strictness, some managers—on their own—apply an evaluation more rigorously than the company standard. This behavior may be due to a lack of understanding of various evaluation factors. The worst situation is when a firm has both lenient and strict managers and nothing is done to level the inequities. Here, the weak performers get relatively high pay increases and promotions from a lenient boss, while stronger employees are under-rewarded by the strict manager. This can have a devastating effect on the morale and motivation of the top-performing people.[44]

## Central Tendency

Central tendency
A common error in performance appraisal that occurs when employees are incorrectly rated near the average or middle of the scale.

**Central tendency** is a common error that occurs when employees are incorrectly rated near the average or middle of the scale. This practice may be encouraged by some rating scale systems that require the evaluator to justify in writing extremely high or extremely low ratings. With such a system, the rater may avoid possible controversy or criticism by giving only average ratings.

## Recent Behavior Bias

Anyone who has observed the behavior of young children several weeks before Christmas can readily identify with the problem of recent behavior bias. All of a sudden, it seems, the wildest kids in the neighborhood develop angelic personalities in anticipation of the rewards they hope to receive from Old Saint Nick. Individuals in the workforce are not children, but they are human. Virtually every employee knows precisely when he or she is scheduled for a performance review. Although his or her actions may not be conscious, an employee's behavior often improves and productivity tends to rise several days or weeks before the scheduled evaluation. It is only natural for a rater to remember recent behavior more clearly than actions from the more distant past. However, performance appraisals generally cover a specified period of time, and an individual's performance over the entire period should be considered. Maintaining records of performance throughout the appraisal period helps avoid this problem.

## Personal Bias

Supervisors doing performance appraisals may have biases related to their employees' personal characteristics such as race, religion, gender, disability, or age. While existing legislation protects such employees, discrimination continues to be an appraisal problem. Discrimination in appraisal can be based on many factors in addition to those mentioned. For example, mild-mannered employees may be appraised more harshly simply because they do not seriously object to the results. This type of behavior is in sharp contrast to the *hell raisers*, who often confirm the adage, "the squeaky wheel gets the grease." In another example, one study concluded that people perceived to be smokers received lower performance evaluations than nonsmokers—the implication being that if they stopped smoking, they would get higher ratings.[45]

## Manipulating the Evaluation

In some instances, supervisors control virtually every aspect of the appraisal process and are therefore in a position to manipulate the system. For example, a supervisor may want to give a pay raise to a certain employee. In order to justify this action, the supervisor may give the employee a high performance evaluation. Or, the supervisor may want to get rid of an employee and so may give the individual a low rating. In either instance, the system is distorted and the goals of performance appraisal cannot be achieved. Additionally, in the latter example, if the

### Inflated Ratings

▶ The belief that accurate ratings would have a damaging effect on the subordinate's motivation and performance
▶ The desire to improve an employee's eligibility for merit raises
▶ The desire to avoid airing the department's dirty laundry
▶ The wish to avoid creating a negative permanent record of poor performance that might hound the employee in the future
▶ The need to protect good performers whose performance was suffering because of personal problems
▶ The wish to reward employees displaying great effort even when results are relatively low
▶ The need to avoid confrontation with certain hard-to-manage employees
▶ The desire to promote a poor or disliked employee up and out of the department

### Lowered Ratings

▶ To scare better performance out of an employee
▶ To punish a difficult or rebellious employee
▶ To encourage a problem employee to quit
▶ To create a strong record to justify a planned firing
▶ To minimize the amount of the merit increase a subordinate receives
▶ To comply with an organization edict that discourages managers from giving high ratings

*Source:* Clinton Longenecker and Dean Ludwig, "Ethical Dilemmas in Performance Appraisal Revisited," *Journal of Business Ethics* 9 (December 1990): 963. Reprinted by permission of Kluwer Academic Publishers.

employee is a member of a protected group, the firm may wind up in court. If the evaluation given cannot be adequately supported, the firm may suffer significant financial loss.

One study revealed that over 70 percent of responding managers believe that inflated and lowered ratings are intentionally given to subordinates. Table 10-1 shows these managers' explanations for their rationale. The results suggest that the validity of many performance appraisal systems is flawed, although another study indicated that appraisal data is valid 75 percent of the time.[46] Evaluator training should be provided to emphasize the negative consequences of rater errors.

---

### ▶ The Pressure Is There

**HRM IN ACTION**

"Gina, I need your advice on a problem," said Marvin Alexander, production supervisor for Service International to Gina Magdaleno, the HR manager. "Tom Esprit has worked for me for four years. He is likable and never misses a day of work. However, he is strictly mediocre at his job, despite numerous retraining attempts, conferences, and even incentives. I hear that the company is preparing for a reduction in force. As I was working on Tom's appraisal this morning, he stuck his head in the door, handed me three cigars, and said that his wife had just had triplets. That sure puts pressure on me."

*If you were Gina, how would you respond?*

HR WEB WISDOM

▶ *Appraisal Tips*

**www.prenhall.com/mondy**

Ways to improve performance appraisal are provided at this Web site.

## CHARACTERISTICS OF AN EFFECTIVE APPRAISAL SYSTEM

The basic purpose of a performance appraisal system is to improve performance of individuals, teams, and the entire organization. The system may also assist in making administrative decisions such as pay increases, transfers, or terminations. In addition, the appraisal system must be legally defensible. Although a perfect system does not exist, every system should possess certain characteristics. An accurate assessment of performance should be sought that permits developing a plan to improve individual and group performance. The system must honestly inform people how they stand with the organization. The following factors assist in accomplishing this purpose.

### Job-Related Criteria

Job relatedness is perhaps the most basic criterion in employee performance appraisal. The *Uniform Guidelines* and court decisions are quite clear on this point. More specifically, evaluation criteria should be determined through job analysis. Subjective factors such as initiative, enthusiasm, loyalty, and cooperation are obviously important; however, unless they can be clearly shown to be job related, they should not be used.

### Performance Expectations

Managers and subordinates must agree on performance expectations in advance of the appraisal period. How can employees function effectively if they do not know what they are being measured against? On the other hand, if the expectations are clearly understood, employees can evaluate their own performance and make timely adjustments as they perform their jobs without having to wait for the formal evaluation.[47] The establishment of highly objective work standards is relatively simple in many areas, such as manufacturing, assembly, and sales. For numerous other types of jobs, however, this task is more difficult. Still, evaluation must take place, and performance expectations—however elusive—should be defined in understandable terms.

### Standardization

Employees in the same job category under the same supervisor should be appraised using the same evaluation instrument. Also important is that appraisals be conducted regularly for these employees and that they cover similar periods of time. Although annual evaluations are most common, many successful firms evaluate their employees more frequently. Feedback sessions and appraisal interviews should be regularly scheduled for all employees.

Formal documentation of appraisal data serves several purposes including protection against possible legal action. Employees should sign their evaluations. If the employee refuses to sign, the manager should document this behavior. Records should also include a description of employee responsibilities, expected performance results, and the way these data will be viewed in making appraisal decisions. While performance appraisal is important for small firms, they are not expected to maintain performance appraisal systems that are as formal as those used by large organizations. Courts have reasoned that objective criteria are not as important in firms with fewer than 30 employees because a smaller firm's top managers are more intimately acquainted with their employees' work.

## Trained Appraisers

Responsibility for evaluating employee performance is often assigned to the individual or individuals who directly observe at least a representative sample of job performance. Usually, this person is the employee's immediate supervisor. However, as previously discussed, other approaches are gaining in popularity.

Situations that lessen the immediate supervisor's ability to appraise performance objectively include those found in matrix organizations. In these firms, certain employees may be formally assigned to a supervisor but actually work under various project managers. Also, a new supervisor may initially have insufficient knowledge of employee performance. In such instances, multiple raters may be used as in 360-degree feedback.

A common deficiency in appraisal systems is that the evaluators seldom receive training on how to conduct effective evaluations.[48] The training should be an ongoing process in order to ensure accuracy and consistency. The training should cover how to rate employees and (for supervisors) how to conduct appraisal interviews. Instructions should be rather detailed and stress the importance of making objective and unbiased ratings. A training module posted on the Internet or company intranet may serve to provide information for managers as needed.

## Continuous Open Communication

Most employees have a strong need to know how well they are performing. A good appraisal system provides highly desired feedback on a continuing basis. There should be very few surprises in the performance review. Daily performance problems are best handled when they occur and should not be allowed to pile up for six months or a year and then be addressed during the performance appraisal interview.[49] When something totally new surfaces, the manager probably did not do a good enough job communicating with the employee throughout the appraisal period.[50] Even though the interview presents an excellent opportunity for both parties to exchange ideas, it should never serve as a substitute for the day-to-day communication and coaching required by performance management.

## Performance Reviews

In addition to the need for continuous communication between managers and their employees, a special time should be set for a specific discussion of the employee's performance. Many appraisal systems are designed to improve performance; therefore, withholding appraisal results would be absurd. Employees would be severely handicapped in their developmental efforts if denied access to this information. Also, a performance review allows them to detect any errors that may have been made. Or, an employee may simply disagree with the evaluation and want to challenge it.

Constant employee performance documentation is vitally important for accurate performance appraisals. Although the task can be tedious and boring for managers, maintaining a continuous record of observed and reported incidents is essential in building a useful appraisal.[51] The appraisal interview is discussed in a later section.

## Due Process

Ensuring due process is vital. If a formal grievance procedure does not exist, one should be developed to permit employees to appeal appraisal results that they consider inaccurate or unfair. They must have a procedure for pursuing their grievances and having them addressed objectively.

# LEGAL IMPLICATIONS

A review of court cases makes it clear that legally defensible performance appraisal systems should be in place. Perfect systems are not expected, and neither is it anticipated that supervisory discretion should be removed from the process. However, the courts normally require these conditions:

▶ Either the absence of adverse impact on members of certain groups or validation of the process.
▶ A system that prevents one manager from directing or controlling a subordinate's career. The performance appraisal should be reviewed and approved by someone or some group in the organization.
▶ The rater must have personal knowledge of and contact with the employee's job performance.
▶ Formal appraisal criteria that limit the manager's discretion must be used. A system is needed that forces managers to base evaluations on certain predetermined criteria.

Mistakes in appraising performance and decisions based on invalid results can have serious repercussions. For example, discriminatory allocation of money for merit pay increases can result in costly legal action. In settling cases, courts have held employers liable for back pay, court costs, and other costs related to training and promoting certain employees in protected classes. Amtrak recently agreed to settle a racial discrimination lawsuit by paying $8 million. Without admitting liability, the firm said it would change its hiring, promotion, and performance appraisal procedures to make them more evenhanded.[52] An employer may also be vulnerable to a negligent retention claim if an employee who continually receives unsatisfactory ratings in safety practices, for example, is kept on the payroll and he or she causes injury to a third party. In this instance, the firm's liability might be reduced if the substandard performer had received training designed to overcome the deficiencies.

Performance appraisals definitely have the potential for discrimination. For example, a female employee who was due for promotion sued the firm when her promotion was denied. She claimed she was the victim of unlawful sex discrimination under the Civil Rights Act. Her supervisor had noted in her appraisal that she needed to "take a course in a charm school, walk more femininely, talk more femininely, dress more femininely, wear makeup, and wear jewelry."[53] While the tone of these remarks is troublesome, the firm would have been in a much better position to defend itself if the appraisal had read differently, perhaps stating that the employee lacked interpersonal skills rather than implying gender in the remarks.

It is unlikely that any appraisal system will be totally immune to legal challenge. However, systems that possess the characteristics previously discussed are apparently more legally defensible. At the same time, they can provide a more effective means for achieving performance management goals.

▷ *Appraisal News*

**www.prenhall.com/mondy**

Performance appraisal news and general PA information are provided.

## THE APPRAISAL INTERVIEW

The appraisal interview is the Achilles' heel of the entire evaluation process. In fact, employee appraisal review sessions often create hostility and can do more harm than good to the employee-manager relationship. To minimize the possibility of hard feelings, the face-to-face meeting and the written review must have performance improvement—not criticism—as their goal.[54] The reviewing manager must utilize all the tact he or she can muster in discussing areas needing improvement. Employees should be made to understand that they are not the only ones under the gun. Rating managers should emphasize their own responsibility for the employees' development and guarantee to provide support.

The appraisal interview definitely has the potential for confrontation and undermining of the goal of motivating employees.[55] The situation can be helped considerably if input is received from several sources, including perhaps the employee's own self-appraisal. Regardless of the system used, employees will not trust a system they do not understand. Secrecy will invariably breed suspicion and thereby thwart efforts to obtain employee participation.

### Scheduling the Interview

Supervisors usually conduct a formal appraisal interview at the end of an employee's appraisal period. Employees usually know when their interview should take place, and their anxiety tends to increase when it is delayed. Interviews with top performers are often pleasant experiences for all concerned. However, supervisors may be reluctant to meet face to face with poor performers. They tend to postpone these anxiety-provoking interviews.

### Interview Structure

A successful appraisal interview should be structured in a way that allows both the supervisor and the subordinate to view it as a problem-solving session rather than a fault-finding session. The manager should consider three basic purposes when planning an appraisal interview:

1. Discussing the employee's performance
2. Assisting the employee in setting objectives and personal development plans
3. Suggesting means for achieving established objectives, including support to be provided by the manager and firm

▷ The appraisal interview is the Achilles' heel of the entire evaluation process.

For instance, a worker may receive an average rating on a factor such as *quality of production*. In the interview, both parties should agree to the *specific*

improvement needed during the next appraisal period and *specific* actions that each should take.

The amount of time devoted to an appraisal interview varies considerably with company policy and the position of the evaluated employee. Although costs must be considered, there is merit in conducting separate interviews for discussing (1) employee performance and development and (2) pay increases. Many managers have learned that as soon as pay is mentioned in an interview, it tends to dominate the conversation with performance improvement taking a back seat. Rhone-Poulenc Rorer Inc. (RPR), one of the world's top-ranked pharmaceutical companies, learned that, once employees heard their rating number and knew what it meant in terms of pay increases, discussions of performance issues were stalled.[56] For this reason, it might be advisable to defer pay discussions for one to several weeks after the appraisal interview.

## Use of Praise and Criticism

As suggested at the beginning of this chapter, conducting an appraisal interview requires tact and patience on the part of the evaluator. Praise should be provided when warranted, but it can have only limited value if not clearly deserved. Criticism, even if warranted, is especially difficult to give. The employee may not perceive it as being constructive. It is important that discussions of these sensitive issues focus on the deficiency, not the person. Threats to the employee's self-esteem should be minimized whenever possible. Several points about criticizing employees are worth considering:[57]

▶ Emphasize the positive aspects of performance.
▶ Criticize actions, not the person.
▶ Avoid making any criticism destructive or too personal.
▶ Do not surprise the employee by bringing up a problem that should have been dealt with previously.
▶ Ask the employee how he or she would change things to improve the situation.
▶ Avoid supplying all the answers.
▶ Be specific and give alternatives for the criticized behavior.
▶ When criticizing, concentrate on developing the employee.
▶ Try to turn the interview into a win-win situation so that all concerned gain.

## Employees' Role

From the employees' side, two weeks or so before the review, they should go through their diary or files and make a note of every project worked on, regardless of whether they were successful or not. This information should be given to the appraising manager well before the review. Employees can help their cause by reminding the boss just what each event has done to improve personal and team development and also how the firm itself has benefited. Reminding managers of information they may have missed should help in developing a more objective and accurate appraisal.[58]

## Use of Software

Computer software is available for recording the appraisal data. As an example, KnowledgePoint's *Performance Now* provides a standardized, yet thorough set of templates for the review. The rater begins by adding employees in a tabbed dialog box, selecting a specific category of job such as clerical, management, or manufacturing. *Performance Now* then adds the appropriate performance categories to the review, along with dummy text for each category. The rater edits the text in the built-in word processor. A toolbar button provides context-sensitive advice, including suggestions for how to improve employee performance. This software simplifies reviews and provides not only consistency, but also a professional appearance.[59]

## Concluding the Interview

Ideally, employees will leave the interview with positive feelings about management, the company, the job, and themselves. The prospects for improved performance will be bleak if the employee's ego is deflated. Past behavior cannot be changed, but future performance can. Specific plans for the employee's development should be clearly outlined and mutually agreed on. Employees who obviously require additional training should be assured that it will be forthcoming and that they will have the full support of their supervisor. Managers must make an effort to salvage marginal employees. Individuals in this category should, however, be told specifically the consequences if their performance does not reach an acceptable level.

Conducting performance appraisal in the United States presents significant challenges to domestic managers. But, the technique offers even greater problems in the global human resources arena, as "A Global Perspective" illustrates.

**①** Define *performance appraisal.*

Performance appraisal (PA) is a system of review and evaluation of an individual's or team's job performance.

**②** Identify the uses of performance appraisal.

Performance appraisal data are potentially valuable for use in numerous human resource functional areas including human resource planning, recruitment and selection, training and development, career planning and development, compensation programs, internal employee relations, and assessment of employee potential.

**③** Describe the performance appraisal process.

The steps in the performance appraisal process include identifying the specific performance appraisal goals, establishing job expectations (job analysis), examining work performed, appraising performance, and discussing the appraisal with the employee.

**④** Explain performance appraisal environmental factors.

Many of the external and internal environmental factors discussed in Chapter 2 can influence the appraisal process. For example, legislation requires that appraisal systems be nondiscriminatory.

**⑤** Identify the aspect of a person's performance that an organization should evaluate.

The aspects of a person's performance that an organization should evaluate include traits, behaviors, and task outcomes.

**⑥** Identify who may be responsible for performance appraisal and the performance period.

People usually responsible for performance appraisal include immediate supervisors, subordinates, peers, self-appraisal and customers, and—in the 360-degree feedback method—perhaps all of the above. Formal performance evaluations are usually prepared at specific intervals. While there is nothing magic about the periods, in most organizations they are made either annually or semiannually.

**⑦** Identify the various performance appraisal methods used.

Performance appraisal methods include 360-degree feedback, rating scales, critical incidents, essay, work standards, ranking, forced distribution, forced-choice and weighted checklist performance reports, behaviorally anchored rating scales, results-oriented approaches, and assessment centers.

**⑧** List the problems that have been associated with performance appraisal.

The problems associated with performance appraisal include the lack of objectivity, halo error, leniency/strictness, central tendency, recent behavior bias, personal bias, and manipulating the evaluation.

**⑨** Explain the characteristics of an effective appraisal system.

Characteristics include job-related criteria, performance expectations, standardization, trained appraisers, continuous open communication, performance reviews, and due process.

**⑩** Describe the legal implications of performance appraisal.

It is unlikely that any appraisal system will be totally immune to legal challenge. However, systems that possess certain characteristics are more legally defensible.

**⑪** Explain how the appraisal interview should be conducted.

A successful appraisal interview should be structured in a way that allows both the supervisor and the subordinate to view it as a problem-solving session rather than a fault-finding session.

1. Define *performance appraisal* and briefly discuss its basic purposes.
2. What are the basic steps in the performance appraisal process?
3. What aspect of a person's performance should an organization evaluate?
4. Many different people can conduct performance appraisals. Briefly describe the various alternatives.
5. Briefly describe each of the following methods of performance appraisal:
   - a. Rating scales
   - b. Critical incidents
   - c. Essay
   - d. Work standards
   - e. Ranking
   - f. Forced distribution
   - g. Forced-choice and weighted checklist performance reports
   - h. Behaviorally anchored rating scales
   - i. Results-based systems
   - j. 360-degree feedback
6. What are the various problems associated with performance appraisal? Briefly describe each.
7. What are the characteristics of an effective appraisal system?
8. What are the legal implications of performance appraisal?
9. Explain why the following statement is often true: "The Achilles' heel of the entire evaluation process is the appraisal interview itself."

*We invite you to visit the Mondy homepage on the Prentice Hall Web site at*

**www.prenhall.com/mondy**

*for updated information, Web-based exercises, and links to other HR-related sites.*

TAKE IT TO
THE NET

---

### An Experiental Exercise

Performance appraisal (PA) is an essential aspect of human resource management. It is a formal system that provides a periodic review and evaluation of an individual's or team's job performance. Developing an effective performance appraisal system is difficult. However, some managers do not take performance appraisal as seriously as they should. Such attitudes are counterproductive, and they frequently lower individual and group productivity.

Larry Beavers, supervisor of an electrical department, and Alex Martin, one of his employees, meet today for Alex's performance appraisal interview. When these two get together, it will be a meeting of two quite different minds; in all likelihood, the meeting will be filled with disagreement, dissatisfaction, and maybe even hard feelings. This exercise will require active participation from two of you.

One person will play the supervisor conducting the performance appraisal, and the other will be the evaluated employee. Only two can play; the rest of you should observe carefully. Your instructor will provide the participants with additional information necessary to complete the exercise.

## ▶ HRM INCIDENT 1

### These Things Are a Pain

"There, at last it's finished," thought Rajiv Chaudhry as he laid aside the last of 12 performance appraisal forms. It had been a busy week for Rajiv, who supervises a road maintenance crew for the Georgia Department of Highways.

In passing through Rajiv's district a few days earlier, the governor had complained to the area superintendent that repairs were needed on several of the highways. Because of this, the superintendent assigned Rajiv's crew an unusually heavy workload. In addition, Rajiv received a call from the personnel office that week telling him that the performance appraisals were late. Rajiv explained his predicament, but the personnel specialist insisted that the forms be completed right away.

Looking over the appraisals again, Rajiv thought about several of the workers. The performance appraisal form had places for marking *quantity of work, quality of work*, and *cooperativeness*. For each characteristic, the worker could be graded *outstanding, good, average, below average*, or *unsatisfactory*. As Rajiv's crew had completed all of the extra work assigned for that week, he marked every worker *outstanding* in *quantity of work*. He marked Joe Blum *average* in *cooperativeness* because Joe had questioned one of his decisions that week. Rajiv had decided to patch a pothole in one of the roads, and Joe thought the small section of road surface ought to be broken out and replaced. Rajiv didn't include this in the remarks section of the form, though. As a matter of fact, he wrote no remarks on any of the forms.

Rajiv felt a twinge of guilt as he thought about Roger Short. He knew that Roger had been sloughing off, and the other workers had been carrying him for quite some time. He also knew that Roger would be upset if he found that he had been marked lower than the other workers. Consequently, he marked Roger the same to avoid a confrontation. "Anyway," Rajiv thought, "these things are a pain, and I really shouldn't have to bother with them."

As Rajiv folded up the performance appraisals and put them in the envelope for mailing, he smiled. He was glad he would not have to think about performance appraisals for another six months.

### Question

1. What weaknesses do you see in Rajiv's performance appraisals?

## ▶ HRM INCIDENT 2

### Performance Appraisal?

As the production supervisor for Sweeny Electronics, Mike Mahoney was generally well regarded by most of his subordinates. Mike was an easygoing individual who tried to help his employees in any way he could. If a worker needed a small loan until payday, he would dig into his pocket with no questions asked. Should an employee need some time off to attend to a personal problem, Mike would not dock the individual's pay; rather, he would take up the slack himself until the worker returned.

Everything had been going smoothly, at least until the last performance appraisal period. One of Mike's workers, Bill Overstreet, had been experiencing a large number of personal problems for the past year. Bill's wife had been sick much of the time and her medical expenses were high. Bill's son had a speech impediment and the doctors had recommended a special clinic. Bill, who had already borrowed the limit the bank would loan, had become upset and despondent over his general circumstances.

When it was time for Bill's annual performance appraisal, Mike decided he was going to do as much as possible to help him. Although Bill could not be considered more than an average worker, Mike rated him outstanding in virtually every category. Because the firm's compensation system was heavily tied to the performance appraisal, Bill would be eligible for a merit increase of 10 percent in addition to a regular cost-of-living raise.

Mike explained to Bill why he was giving him such high ratings, and Bill acknowledged that his performance had really been no better than average. Bill was very grateful and expressed this to Mike. As Bill left the office, he was excitedly looking forward to telling his friends about what a wonderful boss he had. Seeing Bill smile as he left gave Mike a warm feeling.

## Questions

1. From Sweeny Electronics's standpoint, what difficulties might Mike Mahoney's performance appraisal practices create?
2. What can Mike do now to diminish the negative impact of his evaluation of Bill?

---

## Notes

1. Edward E. Lawler III, "Performance Management: The Next Generation," *Compensation & Benefits Review* 26 (May/June 1994): 16.
2. Jean Lipman Bluman and Harold J. Leavitt, "Hot Groups and the HR Manager: How to Fire Up Your Employees," *HR Focus* 76 (August 1999): 11.
3. Marilyn Moats Kennedy, "The Case against Performance Appraisals," *Across the Board* 36 (January 1999): 51.
4. Raymond Dreyfack, "Money-Saving Ideas for the Profit-Minded Supervisors," *Supervision* 59 (August 1998): 22.
5. "Getting the Most Out of the Review Process," *HR Focus* 74 (January 1997): 15.
6. Dick Grote, "The Secrets of Performance Appraisal," *Across the Board* 37 (May 2000): 14.
7. Milan Moravec, "Bringing Performance Management Out of the Stone Age," *Management Review* 85 (February 1996): 38.
8. Samuel Greengard, "Putting HR Software to Work," *Workforce* 78 (September 1999): 10.
9. Robert B. Campbell and Lynne M. Garfinkel, "Performance Management: Strategies for Success," *HRMagazine* 41 (June 1996): 98.
10. Noah P. Barsky and Christopher D. Flick, "Look at the Net! Performance Management Resources Are Out There," *Strategic Finance Magazine* 81 (December 1999): 26–27.
11. Karen Hildenbrand, "Performance Appraisals: Waste of Time or Boost to the Bottom Line?" *Colorado Business Magazine* (November 1997): 1.

12. "Censored!" 'Free' Speech at Work," *Workforce* 79 (September 1999): 34.

13. Roger E. Herman, "Stability Is Watchword for Effective Workforce," *HR Focus*, Special Report on Recruitment & Retention (June 1999): S1.

14. Jack Zigon, "Is Your Performance Appraisal System Team-Friendly?" *Zigon Performance Group* zigonperf.com/Articles/Team_Friendly.htm (July 3, 2000).

15. Stephen E. Gross, *Compensation for Teams* (New York: American Management Association, 1995): 90.

16. Assessment Centers were discussed as a method for selecting employees in Chapter 7. They may also be used as an adjunct to a performance appraisal system in assessing potential.

17. David K. Lindo, "Where's My Raise?" *Supervision* 60 (April 1, 1999): 6.

18. George T. Milkovich and Jerry M. Newman, *Compensation*, 6th ed. (Boston: Irwin McGraw-Hill, 1999): 353.

19. Ibid., 352.

20. Jay A. Conger, Edward E. Lawler III, and David Finegold, "Evaluating Individual Directors," *Directors & Boards* (Winter 1998): 51–54.

21. Mathew Budman and Berkley Rice, "The Rating Game," *Across the Board* 31 (February 1994): 34–38.

22. Dick Grote, "Painless Performance Appraisals Focus on Results, Behaviors," *HRMagazine* 43 (October 1998): 52.

23. Michelle Neely Martinez, "Rewards Given the Right Way," *HRMagazine* 42 (May 1997): 116.

24. David C. Martin and Kathryn M. Bartol, "Performance Appraisal: Maintaining System Effectiveness," *Public Personnel Management* 27 (Summer 1998): 223.

25. "Steps to Maximize Consistency," *HRMagazine* www.shrm.org/hrmagazine/articles/10steps.html (July 1, 1997).

26. Dennis E. Coates, "Don't Tie 360 Feedback to Pay," *Training* 35 (September 1998): 68.

27. Leanne Atwater and David Waldman, "Accountability in 360 Degree Feedback; Is it Time to Take the 360-Degree Feedback Method to Its Next Step?" *HRMagazine* 43 (May 1, 1998): 96.

28. Coates, "Don't Tie 360 Feedback to Pay."

29. Richard Lepsinger and Anntoinette D. Lucia, "360(Degree) Feedback and Performance Appraisal," *Training* 34 (September 1997): 63.

30. Jane L. Wilson, "360 Appraisals," *Training and Development* 51 (June 1997): 44.

31. Scott Wimer and Kenneth M. Nowack, "13 Common Mistakes Using 360-Degree Feedback," *Training and Development* 52 (May 1998): 69.

32. Lepsinger and Lucia, "360(Degree) Feedback and Performance Appraisal."

33. Susan J. Wells, "A New Road: Traveling Beyond 360-Degree Evaluation," *HRMagazine* 44 (September 1999): 82–91.

34. David K. Lindo, "Can You Answer Their Questions?" *Supervision* 58 (October 1997): 12.

35. Joseph Maiorca, "How to Construct Behaviorally Anchored Rating Scales (BARS) for Employee Evaluations," *Supervision* 58 (August 1997): 15.

36. Ibid.

37. James S. Bowman, "Performance Appraisal: Verisimilitude Trumps Veracity," *Public Personnel Management* 28 (Winter 1999): 560.

38. Ibid., 561.

39. Dick Grote, "Staff Performance Advice for CPAs," *Journal of Accountancy* 188 (July 1999): 51.

40. Charles N. Painter, "Ten Steps for Improved Appraisals," *Supervision* 60 (June 1999): 12.

41. "Research on Performance Appraisals Wins Award," *HR News* 16 (July 1997): 13.

42. Grote, "The Secrets of Performance Appraisal."

43. Michael Schrage, "How the Bell Curve Cheats You," *Fortune* 141 (February 21, 2000): 296.

44. John Mariotti, "Tough Bosses, Easy Bosses: Easy Graders Undermine Appraisal Systems—and Morale," *Industry Week* 246 (January 20, 1997): 57.

45. G. Ronald Gilbert, Edward L. Hannan, and Kevin B. Lowe, "Is Smoking Stigma Clouding the Objectivity of Employee Performance Appraisal?" *Public Personnel Management* 27 (Fall 1998): 285.

46. Iris Randall, "Performance Appraisal Anxiety," *Black Enterprise* 25 (January 1995): 60.

47. Lindo, "Can You Answer Their Questions?"

48. Robert D. Ramsey, "How to Write Better Employee Evaluations," *Supervision* 59 (June 1998): 5.

49. Thomas C. Timmreck, "Developing Successful Performance Appraisals through Choosing Appropriate Words to Effectively Describe Work," *Health Care Management Review* 23 (June 22, 1998): 46.

50. Paul Falcone, "Rejuvenate Your Performance Evaluation Skills," *HRMagazine* 44 (October 1999): 129–131.

51. Painter, "Ten Steps for Improved Appraisals."

52. "Amtrak Pays $8 Million to Settle Racial Discrimination Lawsuit," *Jet* 96 (July 19, 1999): 6.

53. William E. Lissy, "Performance Appraisals Can Be a Weapon for Employees," *Supervision* 58 (March 1997): 17.

54. Ted Pollock, "Make Your Criticism Pay Off," *Supervision* 59 (October 1, 1998): 24.

55. Falcone, "Rejuvenate Your Performance Evaluation Skills," 126.

56. Martinez, "Rewards Given the Right Way."

57. Donald J. Klein and Suzanne M. Crampton, "Helpful Hints for Sending Criticism," *Workforce* 78 (May 1999): 9.

58. Stephen Kindel, "The No-Beg Bonus," *Esquire* 133 (February 2000): 48.

59. David Haskin, "Performance Now 3.0," *Computing* 17 (November 1999): 101.

60. Fons Trompenaars and Charles Hampden-Turner, *Riding the Waves of Culture: Understanding Diversity in Global Business* (Toronto: Irwin Professional Publishing, 1998).

Few of us are really good at hearing bad news about ourselves. Because performance evaluations are usually closely tied to salary increases and career advancement, they are important events for most employees. Evaluation interviews are often difficult for managers, too. While rewarding good work and motivating happy employees is easy and enjoyable, helping someone face the fact of poor performance can be a painful experience. When an evaluation interview becomes confrontational, not only do both parties suffer emotionally, but also an opportunity for communicating ways to improve job performance is lost.

For these reasons, as Chapter 10 explains, it pays for the manager to have clear and objective standards that are applied uniformly across the organization. These standards usually appraise employee traits, behaviors, task outcomes, and improvement potential. Where more than one manager has input to an employee evaluation, as at Quicktakes, they should all share a clear understanding of what the standards are, what the criteria mean, and how these are to be applied. For all employees, whether they are performing well or poorly, the manager should keep careful written records of how their work contributions meet, exceed, or fail these standards. Further, the manager should be in frequent informal contact with each employee about his or her performance throughout the year, not just at evaluation time. The best evaluation systems are those that yield no surprises.

In this video we see how Tom Bailey's evaluation is finalized by Hal Boylston and Janet Mason, post-production supervisor and Tom's immediate superior, after being drafted by a management committee that also makes salary recommendations. One member of the committee is Quicktakes' co-owner and director of sales, Karen Jarvis.

Tom is a problem employee. His performance is erratic and his commitment to the job is in question. He is often late and his attitude is poor. Janet is clearly unhappy with him, and she is willing to let him know by giving him a poor evaluation.

Observe the process by which Hal and Janet come to a decision about Tom, and note whether there are any flaws in it. Do you think the process yields similar results for good performers at Quicktakes?

Janet must give the bad news to Tom. You'll undoubtedly spot communication mistakes made by both parties in their discussion. Perhaps these are inevitable, given Tom's negative feelings about his job and Janet's impatience with his poor attitude. Watch, however, for any point at which the conversation could have been turned around. Was there any possibility for a different outcome?

### Discussion Questions

1. Janet and Hal both feel that the members of the salary review committee are less familiar with certain job requirements and the performance of individual employees than they themselves are. Is there any advantage in having such a committee? If so, how can Hal and Janet make better use of it? How can they address the potential flaws in Quicktakes' evaluation system?
2. Is Janet making any mistakes in forming her evaluation of Tom? What are they, and what can she do to prevent them?
3. Does Janet bear any responsibility for Tom's poor performance? If so, why?
4. Tom apparently sees money as a motivator, while Janet uses it as a reward. How does this difference in viewpoint add to the difficulty of determining Tom's raise?
5. What did Janet and Tom each do to contribute to the hostile nature of the evaluation meeting? What, specifically, could Janet have done to improve the tone of the meeting and its outcome?

c h a p t e r
chapterchapterchapterchapterchapterchapter

# 11

# Compensation

objectivesobjectivesobjectivesobjectives

## Objectives

- Describe the various forms of compensation.
- Explain the concept of equity in financial compensation.
- Identify the determinants of financial compensation.
- Identify organizational factors that should be considered as determinants of financial compensation.
- Describe factors that should be considered when the labor market is a determinant of financial compensation.
- Explain how the job is a determinant of financial compensation.
- Explain the various forms of job evaluation.
- Identify factors related to the employee that are essential in determining financial compensation.
- Describe *job pricing*.
- Explain how executive compensation is determined and the types of executive compensation

**E** arl Lewis and his wife are full of excitement and anticipation as they leave their home for a shopping trip. Earl had just learned that his firm was implementing a new variable pay system and that his ability to perform at a high level would finally pay off. He looked forward to the opportunity to increase his income so he could purchase some needed items for a new home.

Inez Scoggin's anxiety over scheduled minor surgery was somewhat relieved. Her supervisor has assured her that a major portion of her medical and hospitalization costs will be covered by the firm's health insurance plan.

Trig Ekeland, executive director of the local YMCA, returns home dead tired from his job each evening no earlier than six o'clock. His salary is small compared to the salaries of many other local managers who have similar responsibilities. Yet Trig is an exceptionally happy person who believes that his work with youth, civic leaders, and other members of the community is extremely important and worthwhile.

Joanne Abrahamson has worked for a large manufacturing company for eight years. Although her pay is not what she would like it to be, her firm's flexible work hours make it possible for her to take care of important personal business. She also appreciates the ability to tailor much of her benefits program to fit her particular needs.

**M**oney and financial benefits are obviously important to Earl Lewis and Inez Scoggin, as they are to most employees. However, for Trig Ekeland and Joanne Abrahamson, other factors in a total compensation package assume great importance. These components include satisfaction with having a meaningful job to perform and a work/life situation that accommodates personal needs. Compensation administration is one of management's most difficult and challenging human resource areas because it has many elements and a far-reaching impact on performance.

We begin this chapter with an overview of compensation and an explanation of compensation equity. Next, we discuss determinants of individual financial compensation and the organization as a determinant of financial compensation. This is followed by a discussion of the labor market, the job, and the employee as determinants of financial compensation. Finally, job pricing and executive compensation are presented.

## COMPENSATION: AN OVERVIEW

**Compensation**
The total of all rewards provided employees in return for their services.

**Direct financial compensation**
Pay that a person receives in the form of wages, salary, bonuses, and commissions.

**Indirect financial compensation**
All financial rewards that are not included in direct compensation.

**Compensation** is the total of all rewards provided employees in return for their services. The components of a total compensation program are shown in Figure 11-1. **Direct financial compensation** consists of the pay that a person receives in the form of wages, salary, bonuses, and commissions. Earl Lewis just received word that by continuing his high level of performance, he may now increase the size of his paycheck. **Indirect financial compensation** (benefits) includes all financial rewards that are not included in direct compensation. Inez Scoggin will receive indirect financial compensation because her company pays for a major portion of her medical and hospital costs. As you can see in Figure 11-1, this form of compensation includes a wide variety of rewards that are normally received indirectly by the employee. Providing a perfect pay package is not possible. However, a growing number of firms apparently feel that people should be allowed to customize their own compensation packages as much as is technically, legally, financially, and organizationally desirable.[1]

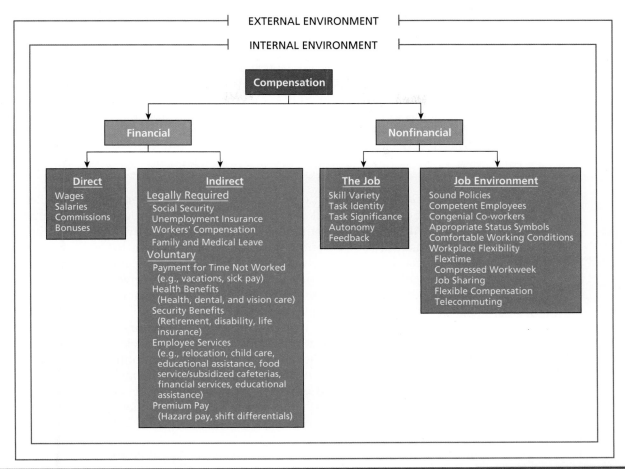

EXTERNAL ENVIRONMENT

INTERNAL ENVIRONMENT

**Compensation**

**Financial**

**Nonfinancial**

**Direct**
Wages
Salaries
Commissions
Bonuses

**Indirect**
Legally Required
  Social Security
  Unemployment Insurance
  Workers' Compensation
  Family and Medical Leave
Voluntary
  Payment for Time Not Worked
    (e.g., vacations, sick pay)
  Health Benefits
    (Health, dental, and vision care)
  Security Benefits
    (Retirement, disability, life
    insurance)
  Employee Services
    (e.g., relocation, child care,
    educational assistance, food
    service/subsidized cafeterias,
    financial services, educational
    assistance)
  Premium Pay
    (Hazard pay, shift differentials)

**The Job**
Skill Variety
Task Identity
Task Significance
Autonomy
Feedback

**Job Environment**
Sound Policies
Competent Employees
Congenial Co-workers
Appropriate Status Symbols
Comfortable Working Conditions
Workplace Flexibility
  Flextime
  Compressed Workweek
  Job Sharing
  Flexible Compensation
  Telecommuting

**Components of a Total Compensation Program**   **Figure 11-1**

**Nonfinancial compensation** consists of the satisfaction that a person receives from the job itself or from the psychological and/or physical environment in which the person works. Trig Ekeland and Joanne Abrahamson are receiving important forms of nonfinancial compensation. Trig is extremely satisfied with the job he performs. This type of nonfinancial compensation consists of the satisfaction received from performing meaningful tasks. Joanne's job permits her to handle her personal affairs with a minimum of hassle and to maximize her benefits package. This aspect of nonfinancial compensation involves both psychological and physical factors within the firm's working environment.

All such rewards comprise a *total compensation program.* Historically, compensation practitioners have focused primarily on financial compensation and benefits. However, this has changed over time and in 2000, the expanded emphasis was reflected in the name change of this field's professional organization. The American Compensation Association, as noted in Chapter 1, is now known as WorldatWork, the Professional Association for Compensation, Benefits and *Total Rewards.*[2] This new model now includes characteristics of nonfinancial compensation.

The rewards employees receive in a total compensation program may be based on several factors including membership in the organization, seniority, or other elements. To remain competitive, organizations are increasingly rewarding performance outcomes that are required to achieve their key goals. In determining effective rewards, the uniqueness of employees must be considered. People

**Nonfinancial compensation**
The satisfaction that a person receives from the job itself or from the psychological and/or physical environment in which the person works.

have different reasons for working, and the most appropriate compensation package depends in large measure on those reasons. When individuals are being stretched to provide food, shelter, and clothing for their families, money may well be the most important reward. However, some people work long hours each day, receive relatively little pay, and yet love their work because it is interesting or provides an environment that satisfies other needs. To a large degree, adequate compensation is in the mind of the receiver. It is often more than the financial compensation received in the form of a paycheck.

## EQUITY IN FINANCIAL COMPENSATION

**Equity**
The perception by workers that they are being treated fairly.

**External equity**
Payment of employees at rates comparable to those paid for similar jobs in other firms.

**Internal equity**
Payment of employees according to the relative value of their jobs within an organization.

**Employee equity**
A condition that exists when individuals performing similar jobs for the same firm are paid according to factors unique to the employee, such as performance level or seniority.

**Team equity**
Payment of more productive teams in an organization at a higher rate than less productive teams.

Organizations must attract, motivate, and retain competent employees. Because achievement of these goals is largely accomplished through a firm's financial compensation system, organizations must strive for equity. **Equity**, in the context of financial compensation, means fair pay treatment for employees. As we shall see, fairness can be viewed from several perspectives. Ideally, compensation will be evenhanded to all parties concerned and be perceived as such. However, this is a very elusive goal. As you read this section, remember that nonfinancial factors can alter one's perception of equity.

**External equity** exists when a firm's employees are paid comparably to workers who perform similar jobs in other firms. Trig Ekeland did not receive a salary comparable to other local managers with similar responsibilities. Compensation surveys help organizations determine the extent to which external equity is present. **Internal equity** exists when employees are paid according to the relative value of their jobs within the same organization. Job evaluation is a primary means for determining internal equity. Joanne Abrahamson may not believe that there is internal equity regarding salary, but her total work environment is such that she forgoes other opportunities. **Employee equity** exists when individuals performing similar jobs for the same firm are paid according to factors unique to the employee, such as performance level or seniority. **Team equity** is achieved when more productive teams are rewarded more than less productive teams. Performance levels may be determined through appraisal systems, which were discussed in the previous chapter.

Inequity in any category can result in morale problems. If employees feel they are being compensated unfairly, they may leave the firm. Even greater damage may result for the firm if the employees do not leave but stay and restrict their efforts. In either event, the organization's overall performance is damaged. Regarding employee equity, for example, suppose that two accountants in the same firm are performing similar jobs, and one is acknowledged to be far superior to the other in performance. If both workers receive equal pay increases, employee equity does not exist, and the more productive employee is likely to be unhappy. Most workers are concerned with both internal and external pay equity. From an employee relations perspective, internal pay equity may be more important simply because employees have more information about pay matters within their own organization, and these data are used to form perceptions of equity. On the other hand, an organization must be competitive in the labor market to remain viable. In the current competitive environment—and especially for high-tech employees—it becomes clear that the market is of primary importance. IBM's experience makes this point.

IBM's *old* culture was most apparent in the company's strong emphasis on internal equity over external equity. In any given salary grade, accountants, development engineers, HR professionals, programmers, and manufacturing managers

## ▶ Equity?

"It's just not fair!" screamed Dikran Jebejian to Lili Sugandi, the HR manager for IBX Electronics. "I just found out that Veronique Ligerot makes $100 more a month than I do and she was just hired. What are you going to do about this? I can't live with her making more than I do." Lili knew that Dikran had been with IBX for five years and had been a good, solid worker. But, because of the tight job market, the company was forced to pay Veronique more than Dikran.

*How should Lili respond?*

would be paid comparably off the same salary structure, regardless of what market data revealed about trends for each job family. This approach was established during the years when IBM virtually dominated its industry. The program was sound in that environment, as it was hard to be overly concerned with compensation competitiveness when the firm was larger than its seven largest rivals combined. The focus on internal equity made sense. However, times have changed dramatically. This model could not survive in a new generation that lives under constant pressure to win against relentless competition.[3]

## DETERMINANTS OF INDIVIDUAL FINANCIAL COMPENSATION

Compensation theory has never been able to provide a completely satisfactory answer to what an individual's service performing jobs is worth. While no scientific approach is available, a number of relevant factors are typically used to determine individual pay. These determinants are shown in Figure 11-2. Historically, the organization, the labor market, the job, and the employee all have impacted job pricing and the ultimate determination of an individual's financial compensation. These

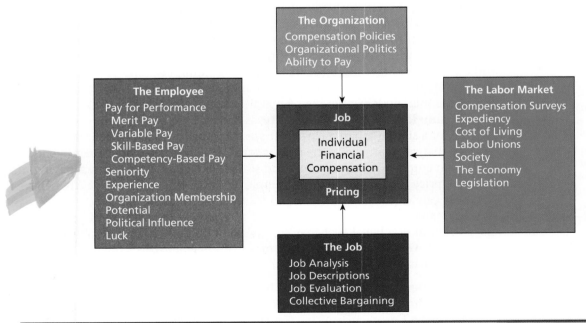

**Primary Determinants of Individual Financial Compensation**   **Figure 11-2**

factors continue to play an important role. However, for more and more business firms, the world has become the marketplace. As global economics increasingly establish the cost of labor, the global labor market grows in importance as a determinant of financial compensation for individuals.

# THE ORGANIZATION AS A DETERMINANT OF FINANCIAL COMPENSATION

Managers tend to view financial compensation as both an expense and an asset. It is an expense in the sense that it reflects the cost of labor. In service industries, for example, labor costs account for more than 50 percent of all expenses. However, financial compensation can be viewed as an asset when it induces employees to put forth their best efforts and to remain in their jobs. Compensation programs have top management's attention because they have the potential to influence employee work attitudes and behavior that lead to improved organizational performance.

A study sponsored by the American Management Association determined the chief compensation interests of HR professionals. These were the top six concerns:[4]

- Hiring and retaining top talent
- Developing and improving systems that effectively communicate compensation and benefits programs to employees to maximize their effectiveness
- Variable pay; whether it works and under what conditions
- Expatriate and global issues
- Creating attractive stock options and other incentive programs
- Health care costs

These issues will have the greatest influence on employers as they develop their financial compensation programs.

## Compensation Policies

Corporate culture has a major effect on an individual's financial compensation. An organization often formally or informally establishes compensation policies that determine whether it will be a pay leader, a pay follower, or strive for an average position in the labor market. **Pay leaders** are organizations that pay higher wages and salaries than competing firms. Using this strategy, they feel that they will be able to attract high-quality, productive employees and so achieve lower per-unit labor costs. Higher-paying firms usually attract more and better qualified applicants than do lower-paying companies in the same labor market.

The **market rate**, or **going rate**, is the average pay that most employers provide for a similar job in a particular area or industry. Many organizations have a policy that calls for paying the market rate. In such firms, management believes that it can employ qualified people and still remain competitive by not having to raise the price of goods or services. Employers with this policy evidently believe that they can acquire the skills needed for their particular operations.

Companies that choose to pay below the market rate because of poor financial condition or a belief that they simply do not require highly capable employees are **pay followers**. Difficulties often occur when this policy is followed. Consider the case of Melvin Denney.

Melvin Denney managed a large, but financially strapped farming operation in the Midwest. Although no formal policies had been established, Melvin had a practice of paying the lowest wage possible. One of his farmhands, George McMillan, was paid minimum wage. During a period of three weeks, George wrecked a tractor, severely damaged a combine,

**Pay leaders**
Those organizations that pay higher wages and salaries than competing firms.

**Market (going) rate**
The average pay that most employers provide for the same job in a particular area or industry.

**Pay followers**
Companies that choose to pay below the market rate because of a poor financial condition or a belief that they simply do not require highly capable employees.

and tore out the transmission in a new pickup truck. George's actions prompted Melvin to remark, "George is the most expensive darned employee I've ever had."

As Melvin discovered, paying the lowest wage possible did not save money—actually, the practice was quite expensive. In addition to hiring unproductive workers, organizations that are pay followers may have a high turnover rate as their most qualified employees leave to join organizations that pay more. Equally important, in situations where incompetent or disgruntled employees come in contact with customers, they may not provide the kind of customer service management desires. If management does not treat its employees well, customers may also suffer, and this spells disaster for any firm in today's environment.

The organizational level in which compensation decisions are made can also have an impact on pay. These decisions are often made at a high management level to ensure consistency. However, there are advantages to making pay decisions at lower levels where better information may exist regarding employee performance. And, extreme pressure to retain top performers may override the desire to maintain consistency in the pay structure. Exceptions are increasingly being made for just this reason.

## Organizational Politics

Take another look at Figure 11-2 and you will see that compensation surveys, job analysis, job evaluation, and employee performance are all involved in setting base pay. Political considerations may also enter into the equation in the following ways:

- Determination of firms included in the compensation survey. Managers could make their firm appear to be a wage leader by including in the survey those organizations that are *pay followers*.
- Choice of compensable factors for the job evaluation plan. Again, the job value determined by this process could be manipulated.
- Emphasis placed on either internal or external equity.
- Results of employee performance appraisal. Remember from Chapter 10 the various reasons rating supervisors may intentionally distort the ratings.

A sound, objective compensation system can be destroyed by organizational politics. Managers should become aware of this possibility and take appropriate action.

## Ability to Pay

An organization's assessment of its ability to pay is also an important factor in determining pay levels. Financially successful firms tend to provide higher-than-average compensation. However, an organization's financial strength establishes only the upper limit of what it will pay. To arrive at a specific pay level, management must consider other factors.

## THE LABOR MARKET AS A DETERMINANT OF FINANCIAL COMPENSATION

Potential employees located within the geographic area from which employees are recruited comprise the **labor market**. Labor markets for some jobs extend far beyond the locality of a firm's operations. An aerospace firm in Seattle, for example, may be concerned about the labor market for engineers in Wichita, Kansas, or Orlando, Florida. Managerial and professional employees are often recruited from a wide geographic area. In fact, some firms engage in global recruitment for certain

**Labor market**
The geographic area from which employees are recruited for a particular job.

**www.prenhall.com/mondy**

Various compensation and benefit issues including compensation surveys are addressed.

skills and top executives. Telecommuting—discussed in the next chapter—makes a global labor market feasible for numerous jobs.

Pay for the same job in a different labor market may vary considerably. Secretarial jobs, for example, may carry an average salary of over $30,000 per year in a large, urban community but only $18,000 or less in a smaller town. Compensation managers must be aware of these differences in order to compete successfully for employees. The market rate is an important guide in determining pay. Many employees view it as the standard for judging the fairness of their firm's compensation practices.

## Compensation Surveys

**Compensation survey**
A means of obtaining data regarding what other firms are paying for specific jobs or job classes within a given labor market.

A **compensation survey** strives to obtain data regarding what other firms are paying for specific jobs or job classes within a given labor market. Virtually all compensation professionals use compensation surveys either directly or indirectly. They may be purchased, outsourced to a consulting firm, or conducted by the organization itself.[5] Organizations use surveys for two basic reasons: to identify their relative position with respect to the chosen competition in the labor market and to provide input in developing a budget and compensation structure.[6] Of all the wage criteria, market rates remain the most important standard for determining pay. In a competitive environment, the marketplace determines economic worth, and this is *the* critical factor.

Large organizations routinely conduct compensation surveys to determine market pay rates within labor markets. These surveys typically provide the low, high, and average salaries for a given position. The market rate, or going rate, may be defined as the 25th to 75th percentile range of pay for jobs rather than a single, specific pay point. They give a sense of what other companies are paying employees in various jobs.

A primary difficulty in conducting a compensation survey involves determining comparable jobs. Surveys that have brief job descriptions are far less helpful than surveys that provide detailed and comprehensive descriptions.[7] As the scope of jobs becomes broader, this difficulty grows. Employees are increasingly being paid for skills and competencies they bring to the job rather than for performing traditional job descriptions. Therefore, compensation levels must be matched to these broader roles. Although the specific information a company requires depends upon its business needs, for many firms this trend changes the nature of the data needed and makes the task of conducting a compensation survey more complex.

Compensation surveys provide information for establishing both direct and indirect compensation. Before a compensation survey is conducted, the following determinations must be made:

▶ The geographic area of the survey
▶ The specific firms to contact
▶ The jobs to include

The geographic area to involve in the survey is often determined from employment records. Data from this source may indicate maximum distance or time that employees are willing to travel to work. Also, the firms to be contacted in the survey may be product line competitors or competitors for certain skilled employees. However, only 50 to 75 percent of the firms may be willing to share data.[8] Because obtaining data on all jobs in the organization may not be feasible, compensation surveys often include only benchmark jobs. A **benchmark job** is one that is well known in the company and industry and one performed by a large number of employees.

**Benchmark job**
A well-known job in the company and industry and one performed by a large number of employees.

In addition to surveys, there are other ways to obtain compensation data. Some professional organizations, such as WorldatWork and the Society for Human Resource Management periodically conduct surveys, as do several industry associations. Consulting firms including Hewett Associates, Towers Perrin, Hay Associates, and William M. Mercer, Inc. also conduct surveys. The U.S. Bureau of Labor Statistics conducts the following five surveys that may be valuable:

- Area wage surveys
- White-collar pay survey
- Employee benefits in small private establishments
- Employee benefits in medium and large private establishments
- Employee benefits in state and local governments[9]

The National Compensation Survey, conducted by the Bureau of Labor Statistics, is a new concept. It provides statistically valid, comprehensive, and interrelated data on wages and employee benefits for all American workers. The survey attempts to respond to these common questions from employers: What is the average salary for secretaries in my area? How have wage costs changed over the past year? How have benefit costs—and specifically health care costs—changed over the past year? What is the average employer cost for a defined benefit plan as opposed to a defined contribution plan? The goal of the National Compensation Survey is to be able to answer these questions and many more.[10]

## Expediency

While compensation surveys assist organizations in developing logical pay structures, there are times that the data derived from such efforts are ignored. In this high-tech, dot-com environment, the competition for valued employees is so intense in some labor markets that managers must at times be left to their own devices. For example, Disney has given certain managers the authority to award salary increases on the spot. Managers at FedEx have also been delegated the authority to reward employees with instant raises and bonuses.[11] While the decisions these managers make are likely within certain guidelines provided by the firms' policies, the historical pressure to maintain consistency (internal equity) throughout a firm may be long gone for many employers.

## Cost of Living

Although not a problem in recent years, the logic for using cost of living as a pay determinant is simple: When prices rise over a period of time and pay does not, *real pay* is actually lowered. A pay increase must be roughly equivalent to the increased cost of living if a person is to maintain a previous level of real wages. For instance, if someone earns $42,000 during a year in which the average rate of inflation is 5 percent, a $175-per-month pay increase will be necessary merely to maintain that person's purchasing ability.

People living on fixed incomes (primarily the elderly and the poor) are especially hard hit by inflation, but they are not alone; most employees also suffer financially. Recognizing this problem, some firms index pay increases to the inflation rate. In fact, in a questionable practice, some organizations sacrifice merit pay to provide across-the-board increases designed to offset the results of inflation.

## Labor Unions

An excerpt from the Wagner Act, which is discussed in Chapter 14, prescribes the areas of mandatory collective bargaining between management and unions as "wages, hours, and other terms and conditions of employment." These broad bargaining areas obviously have great potential impact on compensation decisions. When a union uses comparable pay as a standard in making compensation demands, the employer must obtain accurate labor market data. When a union emphasizes cost of living, management may be pressured to include a cost-of-living allowance. A **cost-of-living allowance (COLA)** is an escalator clause in the labor agreement that automatically increases wages as the U.S. Bureau of Labor Statistics cost-of-living index rises.

**Cost-of-living allowance (COLA)**
An escalator clause in a labor agreement that automatically increases wages as the U.S. Bureau of Labor Statistics' cost-of-living index rises.

Unions may also attempt to create, preserve, or even destroy pay differentials between wages for craft workers and unskilled workers. The politics of a given situation will determine the direction taken. For instance, if the unskilled workers have the largest union membership, an attempt may be made to minimize pay differentials. Management may want to use incentive plans to encourage greater productivity. However, decisions to implement such plans may be scrapped if the union strongly opposes this approach. Employee acceptance of such a plan is essential for successful implementation, and union opposition may make it unworkable.

## Society

Compensation paid to employees often affects a firm's pricing of its goods or services. For this reason, consumers may also be interested in compensation decisions. At times in the past, the government has responded to public opinion and stepped in to encourage businesses to hold down wages and prices.

Businesses in a local labor market are also concerned with the pay practices of new firms locating in their area. For instance, local civic leaders confronted the management of a large electronics firm when it announced plans to locate a branch plant in their small community. Their questions largely concerned the wage and salary rates that would be paid. Subtle pressure was applied to keep the company's wages in line with other wages in the community.

## The Economy

The economy definitely affects financial compensation decisions. For example, a depressed economy generally increases the labor supply. This, in turn, serves to lower the market rate. Historically, the cost of living rises as the economy expands. Recently, however, the inflation rate has been both low and stable even as the economy has grown. This condition serves to minimize the prevalence of cost-of-living increases.

## Legislation

Federal and state laws can also affect the amount of compensation a person receives. Equal employment legislation—including the Civil Rights Act, the Age Discrimination in Employment Act, the Americans with Disabilities Act, and the Family and Medical Leave Act—all prohibit discrimination against specified groups in employment matters, including compensation. The same is true for federal government contractors or subcontractors who are covered by Executive Order 11246 and the Rehabilitation Act. States and municipal governments also have laws that affect compensation practices. Our focus in the next section, however, is on the federal legislation that provides broad coverage and specifically deals with compensation issues.

**Davis-Bacon Act of 1931.** The Davis-Bacon Act of 1931 was the first national law to deal with minimum wages. It requires federal construction contractors with projects valued in excess of $2,000 to pay at least the prevailing wages in the area. The Secretary of Labor has the authority to make this determination, and the prevailing wage is often the average local union rate.

> **Davis - Bacon and related Acts**
> U.S. DOL
>
> SURVEYS  FORMS  HELP  REGIONS
> CONTACT DBRA  SEARCH  RELATED LINKS  SITE MAP
> SECURITY  DISCLAIMER  ACCESSIBILITY
>
> The Davis-Bacon and related Acts (**DBRA**) web information service provides public access to Davis-Bacon information and supports the user in filling out the Report of Construction Contractor's Wage Rates (WD-10) Form. The type of information that you will find here includes information about the Schedule of Surveys being conducted to make wage determinations; regional office information; and, help. We also provide a WD-10 Form that you can view.
>
> NEW! The WD-10 instructions are now available. There are three ways you can view it:
> - on the web
> - Microsoft Word version
> - Microsoft PowerPoint version (for download only)
>   - Section I - How Davis-Bacon Prevailing Wage Rates are Determined
>   - Section II - Instructions for Completing the Report of Construction Contractor's Wage Rates Davis-Bacon Wage Survey
>
> Additional information about some of this site's features has been provided on the Features Page.

www.dol.gov/dol/esa/public/programs/dbra/index.html

**Walsh-Healy Act of 1936.** The Walsh-Healy Act of 1936 requires companies with federal supply contracts exceeding $10,000 to pay prevailing wages. The act also requires one-and-a-half times the regular pay rate for hours over eight per day or 40 per week.

**Fair Labor Standards Act of 1938, as Amended (FLSA).** The most significant law affecting compensation is the Fair Labor Standards Act of 1938 (FLSA). It establishes a minimum wage, requires overtime pay and record keeping, and provides standards for child labor. The Wage and Hour Division of the U.S. Department of Labor (DOL) administers this act. The act currently provides for a minimum wage of not less than $5.15 an hour.[12] It also requires overtime payment at the rate of one-and-one-half times the employee's regular rate after 40 hours of work in a 168-hour period. Although most organizations and employees are covered by the act, certain classes of employees are specifically exempt from overtime provisions. However, nonexempt employees—many of whom are paid salaries—must receive overtime pay.

**Exempt employees** are categorized as executive, administrative, and professional employees and outside salespersons. An *executive employee* is essentially a manager (such as a production manager) with broad authority over subordinates. An *administrative employee,* while not a manager, occupies an important staff position in an organization and might have a title such as systems analyst or assistant to the president. A *professional employee* performs work requiring advanced knowledge in a field of learning, normally acquired through a prolonged course of specialized instruction. This type of employee might have a title such as company physician, legal counsel, or senior statistician. *Outside salespeople* sell tangible or intangible items away from the employer's place of business. Employees in jobs not conforming to the above definitions are considered nonexempt.

**Exempt employees**
Those categorized as executive, administrative, or professional employees and outside salespersons.

For medium and large organizations with many white-collar employees, the most common violations of the FLSA involve incorrectly identifying jobs as exempt. Another common violation relates to the failure of employers to include payments such as bonuses and other forms of compensation in calculating the pay rate for overtime purposes. If firms offer employees a bonus for achieving a certain goal, therefore giving up discretion as to whether it will be received, the bonus payment must be included in figuring the regular rate of pay for overtime purposes. Special-occasion bonuses given at the employer's discretion do not need to be included.

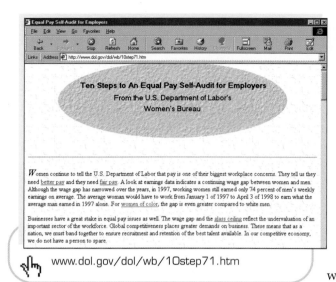

Ten Steps to An Equal Pay Self-Audit for Employers

From the U.S. Department of Labor's
Women's Bureau

*W*omen continue to tell the U.S. Department of Labor that pay is one of their biggest workplace concerns. They tell us they need better pay and they need fair pay. A look at earnings data indicates a continuing wage gap between women and men. Although the wage gap has narrowed over the years, in 1997, working women still earned only 74 percent of men's weekly earnings on average. The average woman would have to work from January 1 of 1997 to April 3 of 1998 to earn what the average man earned in 1997 alone. For women of color, the gap is even greater compared to white men.

Businesses have a great stake in equal pay issues as well. The wage gap and the glass ceiling reflect the undervaluation of an important sector of the workforce. Global competitiveness places greater demands on business. These means that as a nation, we must band together to ensure recruitment and retention of the best talent available. In our competitive economy, we do not have a person to spare.

www.dol.gov/dol/wb/10step71.htm

Still another problem relates to the FLSA's prohibiting private employers from docking an *exempt* worker's pay for less than a full day's absence. If an employer improperly docks even one exempt employee and the practice is discovered, the Labor Department can assume all employees in this exempt category are being treated as nonexempt workers. The firm can then lose the exempt status for all its exempt employees.[13]

Most violations result from ignorance of the law and can be resolved at an early stage of an investigation. If an employer has doubts about any aspect of complying with the FLSA, it may be advisable to check with the Wage-Hour Division. This practice may insulate the employer from violations without raising a red flag. The absolute worst thing an employer can do is try to conceal a problem.

Business and professional groups, such as SHRM, are urging Congress to update FLSA and revise rules written for a bygone era. For example, the law requires that workers in nonexempt jobs be paid time-and-a-half for any hours worked over 40 hours a week. Bills that are up for consideration would allow workers to choose pay or compensatory time off for overtime at their discretion. Workers would be able to bank a certain number of hours each pay period or each year that could then be taken as paid days off to extend a vacation, care for a sick child, take in an afternoon soccer game, or visit the dentist. Sponsors of the bill say there are safeguards built into the bill that prevent abuses including coercion by employers who want employees to take time off during slack periods in lieu of paying out cash during crunch times.[14] The current law also conflicts with some applications of flextime (discussed in the next chapter) that might benefit both employees and employers. Yet another problem centers on the salary requirements in determining exempt employees. The salaries have not been adjusted since they were established in 1975. The result is that many employees earning as little as $12,500 per year in salary may be classified as "exempt" and therefore deprived of being paid overtime.[15] The FLSA is so riddled with problems that Congress will probably take action soon to bring the act into the twenty-first century.

**Equal Pay Act of 1963.** The Equal Pay Act of 1963 (an amendment to the FLSA) prohibits an employer from paying an employee of one gender less money than an employee of the opposite gender if both employees do work that is the same or substantially the same. Jobs are considered *substantially the same* when they require equal skill, effort, and responsibility and are performed under similar working conditions.

The act covers work within the same physical place of business. For example, an employer could pay a female working in San Francisco more than a male working in the same position in Slippery Rock, Pennsylvania, even if the jobs were substantially the same. Also, a male working in a position that requires five years' experience may legally be paid more than a female who is in a position that requires only three years' experience. The EPA permits pay distinctions based on the following factors:[16]

▶ Unequal responsibility
▶ Dissimilar working conditions

- Differences due to seniority
- Differences resulting from a merit pay system
- Differences based on quantity or quality of production

The EPA also includes a catchall provision that permits pay differentials based on any factor other than sex. One issue that the courts have found does *not* warrant differential pay is basing the current pay solely on the employees' earnings at a previous employer.

Recent studies show that women still earn only 75 cents for every dollar that men earn. While pay inequities obviously exist and no doubt reflect gender discrimination to some degree, there may be legitimate reasons for part of the problem. According to economist Dr. Bette Tokar of Holy Family College, supply-and-demand factors help explain pay inequity's persistence. Traditionally, many women held occupations such as schoolteacher, secretary, social worker, nurse, waitress, and other low-paying jobs. Men often did not consider these jobs because of the lack of prestige and pay. Dr. Tokar feels this situation will change as women increasingly enter jobs that were once male dominated.[17]

One thing is certain: The Equal Pay Act has teeth and they will get sharper because the U.S. Department of Labor is aggressively enforcing the act and seeking harsher penalties against companies that violate it. For example, in 1999, following a Department of Labor audit, Texaco agreed to pay a record $3.1 million to female employees who had been consistently paid less than their male counterparts. The settlement included $2.2 million in back pay and interest and $900,000 in salary increases.[18]

Since 1992, the Labor Department has collected an average of $32 million annually from government contractors for violations—or alleged violations—of the act. The bulk of that amount is back-pay settlements resulting from routine payroll audits. Most often, employers agree to big settlements because they lack the documentation to explain pay discrepancies, some of which may be legitimate.[19]

To prove a violation of the Equal Pay Act, an employee must show that a male and a female worker employed by the same firm are paid different wages, on the basis of sex, for equal work. The burden then shifts to the employer, who may rebut any of the allegations or prove that the unequal pay resulted from an exception to the EPA. The points an HR professional needs to keep in mind are these:[20]

- Understand that the EPA is limited strictly to pay differences based on gender.
- Remember that nothing would prevent males from claiming pay inequality (although such instances have been rare).
- Treat *red-circle* rates with care (these rates are discussed later in the chapter).
- Make sure that supervisory titles accurately reflect job duties and responsibilities.

## THE JOB AS A DETERMINANT OF FINANCIAL COMPENSATION

The individual employee and market forces have become most prominent as wage criteria in some firms. However, the job itself continues to be a factor, especially in those firms that have internal pay equity as a primary consideration. These organizations pay for the value they attach to certain duties, responsibilities, and other job-related factors such as working conditions. Management techniques utilized for determining a job's relative worth include job analysis, job descriptions, and job evaluation. When present in a firm, unions normally prefer to determine compensation through the process of collective bargaining, a topic covered in Chapter 15.

HR WEB WISDOM

*Wage and Salary Information*

**www.prenhall.com/mondy**

Numerous Web sites related to wage and salary information are provided.

## Job Analysis and Job Descriptions

Before an organization can determine the relative difficulty or value of its jobs, it must first define their content. Normally, it does so by analyzing jobs. Recall from Chapter 4 that job analysis is the systematic process of determining the skills and knowledge required for performing jobs. Remember also that the primary by-product of job analysis is the job description—a written document that describes job duties or functions and responsibilities. Job descriptions are used for many different purposes, including job evaluation. They are essential to all job evaluation methods that depend largely on their accuracy and clarity for success.

## Job Evaluation

**Job evaluation** is that part of a compensation system in which a firm determines the relative value of one job in relation to another. The basic purpose of job evaluation is to eliminate internal pay inequities that exist because of illogical pay structures. For example, a pay inequity exists if the mailroom supervisor earns more money than the accounting supervisor. Obviously, organizations prefer internal pay equity. However when a pay rate ultimately determined following job evaluation conflicts with the market rate, the latter is almost surely to take precedence. Job evaluation measures job worth in an administrative rather than an economic sense. The latter can be determined only by the marketplace via compensation surveys. Nevertheless, many firms continue to use job evaluation for the following purposes:

> To identify the organization's job structure
> To bring equity and order to the relationships among jobs
> To develop a hierarchy of job value that can be used to create a pay structure

The human resource department is typically responsible for administering job evaluation programs. However, committees often perform actual evaluations. A typical committee might include the chief human resource executive and representatives from other functional areas such as finance, production, information technology, and marketing. If a labor union is present, representation from this group might also be involved if the union is not opposed to the concept of job evaluation. The composition of the committee usually depends on the type and level of the jobs that are being evaluated. In all instances, it is important for the committee to keep personalities out of the evaluation process and to remember it is the job that should be evaluated, not the person(s) performing the job.

Small- and medium-sized organizations often lack job evaluation expertise and may elect to use an outside consultant. When employing a qualified consultant, management should require that the consultant not only develop the job evaluation system but also train company employees to administer it properly.

The four traditional job evaluation methods are the ranking, classification, factor comparison, and point methods. There are innumerable versions of these methods, and a firm may choose one and modify it to fit its particular purposes. Another option is to purchase a proprietary method such as the Hay Plan. This

**Job evaluation**
That part of a compensation system in which a company determines the relative value of one job in relation to another.

system, a variation of the point method, is also discussed in this section. The ranking and classification methods are nonquantitative, whereas the factor comparison and point methods are quantitative approaches.

Ranking Method. The ranking method is the simplest of the four job evaluation methods. In the **job evaluation ranking method**, the raters examine the description of each job being evaluated and arrange the jobs in order according to their value to the company. The procedure is essentially the same as that discussed in Chapter 10 regarding the ranking method for evaluating employee performance. The only difference is that jobs—not people—are being evaluated. The first step in this method, as with all the methods, is conducting job analysis and writing job descriptions.

Classification Method. The **classification method** involves defining a number of classes or grades to describe a group of jobs. In evaluating jobs by this method, the raters compare the job description with the class description. Class descriptions are prepared that reflect the differences between groups of jobs at various difficulty levels. The class description that most closely agrees with the job description determines the classification for that job. For example, in evaluating the job of word processing clerk, the description might include these duties:

1. Data-enter letters from prepared drafts
2. Address envelopes
3. Deliver completed correspondence to unit supervisor

Assuming that the remainder of the job description includes similar routine work, this job would most likely be placed in the lowest job class.

If the class descriptions are too specific, the evaluation's reliability may be improved, but the variety of jobs that can easily be classified may be limited. On the other hand, vaguely written descriptions leave a lot of room for "judgment."[21] Probably the best-known illustration of the classification method is the federal government's 18-class evaluation system.

Factor Comparison Method. The factor comparison method is somewhat more involved than the two previously discussed qualitative methods. In the **factor comparison method**, raters need not keep the entire job in mind as they evaluate it; instead, they make decisions on separate aspects or factors of the job. A basic underlying assumption is that there are five universal job factors:

▸ Mental requirements, which reflect mental traits, such as intelligence, reasoning, and imagination
▸ Skills, which pertain to facility in muscular coordination and training in the interpretation of sensory impressions
▸ Physical requirements, which involve sitting, standing, walking, lifting, and so on
▸ Responsibilities, which cover areas such as raw materials, money, records, and supervision
▸ Working conditions, which reflect the environmental influences of noise, illumination, ventilation, hazards, and hours

The committee first ranks each of the selected benchmark jobs on the relative degree of difficulty of each of the five factors. The committee then allocates the total pay rates for each job to each factor based on the importance of the respective factor to the job. This step is probably the most difficult to explain satisfactorily to employees because the decision is highly subjective.

**Job evaluation ranking method**
A method in which the raters examine the description of each job being evaluated and arrange the jobs in order according to their value to the company.

**Classification method**
A job evaluation method in which classes or grades are defined to describe a group of jobs.

**Factor comparison method**
A job evaluation method in which raters need not keep an entire job in mind as they evaluate it; instead, they make decisions on separate aspects or factors of the job.

| | Mental | Skill | Physical | Responsibility | Working Conditions |
|---|---|---|---|---|---|
| $8.00 | Systems Analyst | | | Systems Analyst | |
| 7.50 | (Programmer Analyst) | | | | |
| 7.00 | | | | | |
| | Programmer | Systems Analyst | | | |
| 6.00 | | | | Programmer | |
| 5.00 | Console Operator | | | | |
| | | Console Operator Programmer | | | |
| 4.00 | | | | Console Operator | |
| 3.00 | | Data Entry Clerk | | | Data Entry Clerk Console Operator Systems Analyst Programmer |
| | Data Entry Clerk | | | | |
| 2.00 | | | Data Entry Clerk Systems Analyst Programmer Console Operator | Data Entry Clerk | |
| 1.00 | | | | | |
| 0 | | | | | |

**Figure 11-3.** Job Comparison Scale

A job comparison scale, reflecting rankings and money allocations, is developed next (see Figure 11-3). All jobs shown, except for programmer analyst, are original benchmark jobs. The scale is then used to rate other jobs in the group being evaluated. The raters compare each job, factor by factor, with those appearing on the job comparison scale. Then, they place the jobs on the chart in an appropriate position. For example, assume that the committee is evaluating the job of *programmer analyst*. The committee determines that this job has fewer mental requirements than that of *systems analyst* but more than those of *programmer*. The job would then be placed on the chart between these two jobs at a point agreed on by the committee. In this example, the committee evaluated the mental requirements factor at $7.50 (a point between the $8.00 and $6.50 values that had been allocated to the benchmark jobs of systems analyst and programmer, respectively). The committee repeats this procedure for the remaining four factors and then for all jobs to be evaluated. Adding the values of the five factors for each job yields the total value for the job.

The factor comparison method provides a systematic approach to job evaluation. However, at least two problems with it should be noted. The assumption that the five factors are universal has been questioned because certain factors may be more appropriate to some job groups than others. Also, while the steps are not overly complicated, they are somewhat detailed and may be difficult to explain to employees.

Point Method. In the **point method**, raters assign numerical values to specific job components, and the sum of these values provides a quantitative assessment of a job's relative worth. Historically, some variation of the point plan has been the most popular option.

The point method requires selection of job factors according to the nature of the specific group of jobs being evaluated. Because job factors vary from one group to another, a separate plan for each group of similar jobs (job clusters) is appropriate. Production jobs, clerical jobs, and sales jobs are examples of job clusters. The procedure for establishing a point method is illustrated in Figure 11-4. After determining the group of jobs to be studied, analysts conduct job analysis and write job descriptions if current descriptions are not available. The job evaluation committee will later use these descriptions as the basis for making evaluation decisions.

Next, the committee selects and defines the factors to be used in measuring job value. These factors become the standards used for the evaluation of jobs. They can best be identified by individuals who are thoroughly familiar with the

**Point method**
An approach to job evaluation in which numerical values are assigned to specific job components, and the sum of these values provides a quantitative assessment of a job's relative worth.

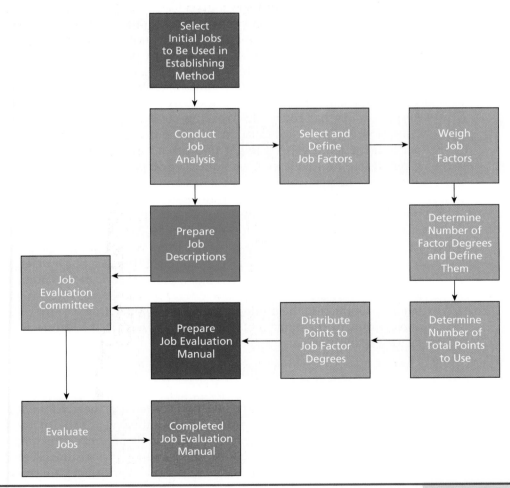

**Procedure for Establishing the Point Method of Job Evaluation**   Figure 11-4

content of the jobs under consideration. Education, experience, job knowledge, mental effort, physical effort, responsibility, and working conditions are examples of factors. Each should be significant in helping to differentiate jobs. Factors that exist in equal amounts in all jobs within a cluster obviously would not serve this purpose. As an example, in evaluating a company's clerical jobs, the working conditions factor would be of little value in differentiating jobs if all jobs in the cluster had approximately the same working conditions. The number of factors used varies with the job cluster under consideration. It is strictly a subjective judgment.

The committee must establish factor weights according to their relative importance in the jobs to be evaluated. For example, if experience is considered quite important for a particular job cluster, this factor might be weighted as much as 35 percent. Physical effort (if used at all as a factor in an office cluster) would likely be low—perhaps less than 10 percent.

The next consideration is to determine the number of degrees for each job factor and define each degree. Degrees represent the number of distinct levels associated with a particular factor. The number of degrees needed for each factor depends on job requirements. If jobs in a particular cluster required similar levels of experience, for example, a smaller number of degrees would be appropriate compared to some clusters that required a broad range of experience.

The committee then determines the total number of points to be used in the plan. The number may vary, but 500 or 1,000 points may work well. The use of a smaller number of points (for example, 50) would not likely provide the proper distinctions among jobs, whereas a larger number (such as 50,000) would be unnecessarily cumbersome. The total number of points in a plan indicates the maximum points that any job could receive.

The next step is to distribute point values to job factor degrees (see Table 11-1). As you can see, Education and Physical effort each have five degrees; Responsibility has four; and Working conditions has three. Degree 1 under Education might, for example, indicate the need for a high school education to perform the job. Degree 5 might mean that a master's degree is required. A job given degree 1 for Education would receive 50 points, whereas a job that required a graduate degree would receive 250 points, or the maximum for that factor. Maximum points for each factor are easily calculated by multiplying the total points in the system by the assigned weights. For example, the maximum points any job could receive for Education would be 250 (50 percent weight multiplied by 500 points). If the interval between factors is to be a constant number, points for the minimum degree may take the value of the percentage weight assigned to the factor. For instance, the percentage weight for education is 50 percent, so the minimum number of points would also be 50. The degree interval may be calculated by subtracting the minimum number of points from the maximum number and dividing by the number of degrees used minus 1. For example, the interval for factor 1 (Education) is:

$$\text{Interval} \quad = \quad \frac{250 - 50}{5 - 1} \quad = \quad 50$$

As you can see in Table 11-1, the interval between each degree for Education is 50.

This approach to determining the number of points for each degree is referred to as *arithmetic progression*. An arithmetic progression is simple to understand and explain to employees. In the example, it is assumed that the factors have been defined so that the intervals between the degrees are equal. However, if this is not the case, another method—such as a geometric progression—may be more appropriate.

| Job Factor | Weight | Degree of Factor | | | | |
|---|---|---|---|---|---|---|
| | | 1 | 2 | 3 | 4 | 5 |
| 1. Education | 50% | 50 | 100 | 150 | 200 | 250 |
| 2. Responsibility | 30% | 30 | 70 | 110 | 150 | |
| 3. Physical effort | 12% | 12 | 24 | 36 | 48 | 60 |
| 4. Working conditions | 8% | 8 | 24 | 40 | | |

The next step involves preparing a job evaluation manual. Although there is no standard format, the manual often contains an introductory section, factor and degree definitions, and job descriptions. As a final step, the job evaluation committee then evaluates jobs in each cluster by comparing each job description with the factors in the job evaluation manual. Point plans require time and effort to design. Historically, a redeeming feature of the method has been that, once developed, the plan was useful over a long period of time. In today's environment, the shelf life may be considerably less. In any event, as new jobs are created and the contents of old jobs substantially changed, job analysis must be conducted and job descriptions rewritten. The job evaluation committee evaluates the jobs and updates the manual. Only when job factors change, or for some reason the weights assigned become inappropriate, does the plan become obsolete.

**The Hay Guide Chart-Profile Method (Hay Plan).**[22] The **Hay guide chart-profile method** is a refined version of the point method. The Hay Plan uses the compensable factors of know-how, problem solving, accountability, and additional compensable elements. Point values are assigned to these factors to determine the final point profile for any job.

> **Hay guide chart-profile method (Hay Plan)**
> A highly refined version of the point method of job evaluation that uses the factors of know-how, problem solving, accountability, and additional compensable elements.

*Know-how* is the total of all knowledge and skills needed for satisfactory job performance. It has three dimensions including the amount of practical, specialized, or scientific knowledge required; the ability to coordinate many functions; and the ability to deal with and motivate people effectively.

*Problem solving* is the degree of original thinking required by the job for analyzing, evaluating, creating, reasoning, and making conclusions. Problem solving has two dimensions: the thinking environment in which problems are solved (from strict routine to abstractly defined) and the thinking challenge presented by the problems (from repetitive to uncharted). Problem solving is expressed as a percentage of know-how, since people use what they know to think and make decisions.

*Accountability* is the responsibility for action and accompanying consequences. Accountability has three dimensions including the degree of freedom the job incumbent has to act, the job impact on end results, and the extent of the monetary impact of the job. The fourth factor, *additional compensable elements,* addresses exceptional conditions in the environment in which the jobs are performed. Because the Hay Plan is a job evaluation method used by employers worldwide, it facilitates job comparison among firms. Thus, the method serves to determine both internal and external equity.

## THE EMPLOYEE AS A DETERMINANT OF FINANCIAL COMPENSATION

In addition to the organization, the labor market, and the job, factors related to the employee are also essential in determining pay equity. Although the 1990s were prosperous years for the American economy, the average worker's pay has

▶ Factors related to the employee are essential in determining pay equity.

not kept pace with other indicators. For example, average workers' wages rose by 27 percent, while corporate profits increased by 105 percent and the average pay for CEOs improved by a whopping 163 percent in firms with revenues of $10 billion or more.[23] The disparity between CEO pay increases and those received by average workers provides another illustration of labor market impact. Still, other factors play a role in determining financial compensation, including the employee. Just how individual employees influence their own pay is covered next.

## Performance-Based Pay

As previously discussed, individual financial compensation may be influenced by many factors. The factor most controllable by employees is their performance on the job. This performance is typically determined through performance appraisal. Appraisal data provide the input for such approaches as merit pay, variable pay, skill-based pay, and competency-based pay. Each of these plans is discussed in the following sections.

**Merit pay**
Pay increase given to employees based on their level of performance as indicated in the appraisal.

**Merit Pay.** In theory, **merit pay** is a pay increase given to employees based on their level of performance as indicated in the appraisal. In practice, however, it is often merely a cost-of-living increase in disguise. For example, the average annual merit increases over an 11-year period, adjusted for the Consumer Price Index, have not exceeded 2 percent.

From the employer's viewpoint, a primary disadvantage to the typical merit pay increase is that it is added to an employee's base pay. It is therefore received each year the person is on the payroll regardless of later performance levels. How can you justify merit pay increases based on a previous employment period but added perpetually to base pay?

A survey of compensation professionals determined that merit pay is seen as being *marginally successful* in influencing pay satisfaction and performance. It indicated that merit pay should play a more limited role and be used to support alternative reward strategies such as gainsharing, team-based pay, and profit sharing. While the use of merit pay is declining, it is still the most frequently used method of determining pay increases for exempt employees.[24]

While many companies continue with their merit pay plans, others seek to control fixed costs by using variable pay. Actually, the two approaches are not mutually exclusive; in fact, they are often used together. Merit pay, which increases base salary, may be used to recognize lasting contributions of employees; variable pay, including lump sum bonuses, may be used to recognize annual accomplishments.

**Variable pay**
Compensation based on performance.

**Bonus (lump sum payment)**
A one-time award that is not added to employees' base pay.

**Variable Pay.** **Variable pay** is compensation based on performance. Growing foreign competition is giving a boost to this compensation approach that is designed to improve productivity. The most common type of variable pay for performance is the bonus. The **bonus**, or **lump sum payment**, is a one-time award that is not added to employees' base pay. Firms are pushing these forms of pay, once reserved for high-ranking executives, down through the ranks. According to a Hewitt

Associates study, the most successful variable pay plans have three main qualities in common: clear employee communication, annual plan reviews, and performance targets that *stretch* employees without breaking them. The study also indicates that 77 percent of companies with an annual communication plan felt that their variable compensation plans were effective in improving business results.[25]

The typical large firm spends an average of more than $30 million a year on performance-based compensation. At least 20 percent of American companies use variable pay plans of some type where growing numbers of middle managers and nonmanagers are included.[26]

Some firms pay bonuses for work that wins patents. High-tech firms, particularly, must have innovative employees to survive. In Motorola's program, inventors may receive a lump sum ranging from $10,000 to $40,000, depending on the estimated value of the patent. Although Motorola awarded over 1,400 patents in 1998, it ranked only fourth among U.S. firms granting patents. If a firm funds a patent bonus program, there must be a clear understanding about who owns the patent rights. Although the patent may be issued in the name of the inventor, the employer is the owner.[27]

With increasing domestic and international competition, maintaining high performance levels and controlling labor costs are essential. Variable pay addresses these requirements by rewarding and therefore encouraging high performance. It is cost effective in that the rewards provided for one period are not added to base pay. Therefore, they are not automatically carried over into subsequent periods unless performance is maintained. As previously stated, there are potential advantages to using a two-component approach including merit pay but emphasizing variable pay. Among the advantages of such a system are the following:[28]

- It reduces fixed payroll expenses.
- It reduces benefits costs since many benefits are tied to base salary, including life insurance, disability insurance, and retirement.
- It supports employee development initiatives.
- It provides motivational rewards (by reducing merit increases, firms will be able to provide greater funds for variable pay).

Variable rewards allow for significant upside potential if performance exceeds the standard. However, they also allow for reduced rewards if performance is below par. The insecurity inherent in variable pay may adversely affect employees' sense of financial security. In turn, the result may have negative consequences for their attitude toward their work and their employer. Perhaps this potential problem explains why many firms consider variable pay a supplement to rather than a replacement for merit pay.

A prerequisite for any pay system tied to performance is a sound performance appraisal program. A valid means of determining varying performance levels is absolutely essential. Managers say that performance-based pay is a win-win situation because it boosts production and efficiency and gives employees some control over their earning power. However, labor unions call it nothing more than a current version of the *carrot-and-stick philosophy.* According to Steven E. Gross, who analyzes employee compensation for William M. Mercer, Inc., "The issue of individual variation of pay is really the antithesis of the union, which says it will treat everybody the same."[29]

**Skill-Based Pay.** **Skill-based pay** is a system that compensates employees on the basis of the job-related skills and knowledge they possess, not for their job titles. It is based on the belief that employees who know more are more valuable

**Skill-based pay**
A system that compensates employees on the basis of job-related skills and the knowledge they possess.

to the firm and therefore should be rewarded accordingly. The purpose of this approach is to encourage employees to gain additional skills that will increase their value to the organization and improve its competitive position. Typically, skill pay is used in settings where the work tends to be more procedural and less varied, such as skills of assembly or responding to customer service questions.

When employees obtain additional job-relevant skills, both individuals and the departments they serve benefit. Employees may receive both tangible and intangible rewards: pay increases, job security, greater mobility, and the satisfaction of being more valuable. Acquiring additional skills also allows employees the opportunity to increase their earnings without the necessity of being moved permanently to a higher-level job. This factor gains additional importance in a highly competitive environment in which promotional opportunities are more limited than in the past. Organizational units are also provided with a greater degree of versatility in dealing with absenteeism and turnover.

Skill-based pay is often used with autonomous work groups or other job enrichment programs. A high commitment to human resource development is necessary to implement such a program successfully. In addition, employees involved in skill-based pay programs must have the desire to grow and increase their knowledge and skills.

While skill-based pay appears to have advantages for both employer and employee, there are some challenges for management. Adequate training opportunities must be provided or else the system can become a demotivator. Since research has revealed that it takes an average of only three years for a worker to reach a maximum level in a skill-based pay system, what will keep employees motivated? One answer has been coupling the plan with a pay-for-performance system. An additional challenge associated with skill-based pay is that payroll costs will escalate. It is conceivable that a firm could have, in addition to high training and development costs, a very expensive workforce possessing an excess of skills. In spite of these negative possibilities, a number of firms have achieved lower operating costs and other benefits with their pay-for-skills programs.

**Competency-based pay**
A compensation plan that rewards employees for their demonstrated expertise.

**Competency-Based Pay.** **Competency-based pay** is a compensation plan that rewards employees for their demonstrated expertise. Competencies include skills but also involve other factors such as motives, traits, values, attitudes, and self-concepts.[30] While core competencies may be unique to each company, one service firm identified the following:

▸ *Team-centered.* Builds productive working relationships at levels within and outside the organization
▸ *Results-driven.* Is focused on achieving key objectives
▸ *Client-dedicated.* Works as a partner with internal and external clients
▸ *Innovative.* Generates and implements new ideas, products, services, and solutions to problems
▸ *Fast cycle.* Displays a bias for action and decisiveness[31]

Pay for performance focuses on end results; competency-based pay examines how an employee accomplishes the objectives. Although competencies may relate to performance, it appears that they would be more difficult to evaluate than results.

## Seniority

The length of time an employee has been associated with the company, division, department, or job is referred to as *seniority*. While management generally prefers performance as the primary basis for compensation changes, labor unions tend to favor seniority. They believe the use of seniority provides an objective and fair basis for pay increases. Many union leaders consider performance evaluation systems as being too subjective, permitting management to reward favorite employees arbitrarily. As previously mentioned, labor unions normally prefer collective bargaining for achieving their compensation goals, and seniority will usually be the preferred criterion.

## Experience

Regardless of the nature of the task, experience has potential for enhancing a person's ability to perform. However, this possibility can only be realized if the experience acquired is positive. Knowledge of the basics is usually a prerequisite if a person's experience is to be put to effective use. This is true for a person starting to play golf, learn a foreign language, or manage people in organizations. People who express pride in their long tenure as managers may be justified in their sentiments, but only if their experience has been beneficial. Those who have been bull-of-the-woods autocrats for a dozen years or so would likely not find their experience highly valued by a Malcolm Baldrige Award–winning firm. Nevertheless, experience is often indispensable for gaining the insights necessary for performing many tasks.

A relatively new aspect of experience related to organizational value stems from the creation of a new economy. How do you best do things in a dot-com world as opposed to the old economy? As previously pointed out by the mentoring relationship between Jack Welch of General Electric and Scott McNealy of Sun Microsystems, experience in both areas is essential. Employees are often compensated on the basis of their experience. This practice is justified if the experience is positive and relevant to the work.

## Membership in the Organization

Some components of individual financial compensation are given to employees without regard to the particular job they perform or their level of productivity. These rewards are provided to all employees simply because they are members of the organization. For example, an average performer occupying a job in pay grade 1 may receive the same number of vacation days, the same amount of group life insurance, and the same reimbursement for educational expenses as a superior employee working in a job classified in pay grade 10. In fact, the worker in pay grade 1 may get more vacation time if he or she has been with the firm longer. Rewards based on organizational membership are intended to maintain a high degree of stability in the workforce and to recognize loyalty.

## Potential

Potential is useless if it is never realized. However, organizations do pay some individuals based on their potential. In order to attract talented young people to the firm, for example, the overall compensation program must appeal to those with no experience or any immediate ability to perform difficult tasks. Many young employees are paid well, perhaps not because of their ability to make an immediate contribution, but because they have the potential to add value to the firm as a professional, first-line supervisor, manager of compensation, vice president of marketing, or possibly even chief executive officer.

## Political Influence

Political influence is a factor that obviously should not be used to determine financial compensation. However, to deny its existence would be unrealistic. There is an unfortunate element of truth in the statement, "It's not *what* you know, it's *who* you know." To varying degrees in business, government, and not-for-profit organizations, a person's *pull* or political influence may sway pay and promotion decisions. It may be natural for a manager to favor a friend or relative in granting a pay increase or promotion. Nevertheless, if the person receiving the reward is not deserving of it, this fact will soon become known throughout the work group. The result may be devastating to employee morale.

## Luck

You have undoubtedly heard the expression, "It helps to be in the right place at the right time." There is more than a little truth in this statement as it relates to compensation. Opportunities are continually presenting themselves in firms. Realistically, there is no way for managers to foresee many of the changes that occur. For instance, who could have known that the purchasing agent, Joe Flynch, an apparently healthy middle-aged man, would suddenly die of a heart attack? Although the company may have been grooming several managers for Joe's position, none may be capable of immediately assuming the increased responsibility. The most experienced person, Tommy Loy, has been with the company only six months. Tommy had been an assistant buyer for a competitor for four years. Because of his experience, Tommy receives the promotion and the increased financial compensation. Tommy Loy was lucky; he was in the right place at the right time.

When asked to explain their most important reasons for success and effectiveness as managers, two chief executives responded candidly. One said, "Success is being at the right place at the right time *and being recognized as having the ability to make timely decisions.* It also depends on having good rapport with people, a good operating background, and the knowledge of how to develop people." The other replied, "My present position was attained by being in the right place at the right time *with a history of getting the job done.*" Both executives recognize the significance of luck combined with the ability to perform. Their experiences lend support to the idea that luck works primarily for the efficient.

## Special Employee Classes

Compensation for several employee groups merits special attention. These include executives, discussed in a later section, and professionals and sales employees. Here we will mention the unique aspects of professionals and sales representatives.

**Compensation for Professionals.** According to the definition in the Fair Labor Standards Act, a professional is any person who has received special training of a scientific or intellectual nature and whose job does not entail supervisory responsibilities for more than 20 percent of the time. Scientists and engineers are included in this category. They are initially paid for the knowledge they bring to the organization. Gradually, however, much of this knowledge becomes obsolete, and this is reflected in the salaries they receive. At times, this encourages professionals to enter management to make more money. The problem is that many are not suited for this role. To deal with this potential dilemma, some organizations have created a dual compensation track (discussed in Chapter 9). This approach provides a separate pay structure for professionals, which overlaps the managerial pay structure. With this system, high-performing professionals are not required to enter management to obtain greater pay. Some firms face serious organizational problems when a highly competent and effective professional feels compelled to become a manager for more pay and is unable to perform well in this capacity.

The unstable nature of professional jobs and their salaries results in a heavy emphasis on market data for job pricing. This has resulted in the use of maturity curves that reflect the relationship between professional compensation and years of experience. Such maturity curves reveal a rapid increase in pay for roughly 15 years, but a leveling off or even some decline in pay after that point.[32]

**Compensation for Sales Employees.** Designing compensation programs for sales employees involves unique considerations. For this reason, this task may be assigned to the sales staff rather than to human resources. However, many general compensation practices apply to sales jobs. For example, job content, relative job worth, and job market value should be determined.

The *straight salary* approach is one extreme in sales compensation. In this method, salespersons receive a fixed salary regardless of their sales levels. Organizations use straight salary primarily to stress continued product service after the sale. For instance, sales representatives who deal largely with the federal government are often compensated in this manner.

At the other extreme, the person whose pay is totally determined as a percentage of sales is on *straight commission*. If no sales are made, the person working on straight commission receives no pay. On the other hand, highly productive sales representatives can earn a great deal of money under this plan.

Between these extremes is the endless variety of *part-salary, part-commission* combinations. The possibilities increase when various types of bonuses are added to the basic compensation package. The emphasis given to either commission or salary depends on several factors, including the organization's philosophy toward service, the nature of the product, and the amount of time required to close a sale.

In addition to salary, commissions, and bonuses, salespersons often receive other forms of compensation that are intended to serve as added incentives. Sales contests that offer products such as VCRs, DVDs, or all-expenses-paid vacations to exotic locations are common. If any one feature sets sales compensation apart from other programs, it is the emphasis on incentives. Sales volume can usually be related to specific individuals, a situation that encourages payment of incentive compensation. Also, experience in sales compensation practices over the years has supported the concept of directly relating rewards to performance.

The headache so long associated with calculating various bonuses disappears when packaged software automates the process. A firm with 400 salespeople will have to shell out a lot of money to buy it. But, users taking the plunge apparently feel the cost is worth it to achieve a simplified system of setting up, managing, and tracking incentive compensation plans.[33]

Computer software has also made it possible to measure sales performance much more precisely. This development gives firms the ability to measure things like gross profits per line of billing, profitability per customer, profitability per product, and sales costs as a percentage of gross profit per territory. Technology has made it feasible to more closely align the sales reward system with corporate strategy and to reward the behaviors that impact the bottom line.

## JOB PRICING

The primary considerations in pricing jobs are the organization's policies, the labor market, and the job itself. If allowances are to be made for individual factors, they too must be considered. Recall that the process of job evaluation results in a job hierarchy. It might reveal, for example, that the job of senior accountant is more valuable than the job of computer operator, which, in turn, is more valuable than the job of senior invoice clerk. At this point, the relative value of these jobs to the company is known, but their absolute value is not. Placing a dollar value on the worth of a job is called **job pricing**. It takes place after the job has been evaluated and the relative value of each job in the organization has been determined. Firms often use pay grades and pay ranges in the job pricing process.

## Pay Grades

A **pay grade** is the grouping of similar jobs to simplify pricing jobs. It is much more convenient for organizations to price 15 pay grades rather than 200 separate jobs. The simplicity of this approach is similar to a college or university's practice of grouping grades of 90 to 100 into an A category, grades of 80 to 89 into a B, and so on. A false implication of preciseness is also avoided. While job evaluation plans may be systematic, none is scientific.

Plotting jobs on a scatter diagram is often useful to managers in determining the appropriate number of pay grades for a company. In Figure 11-5, each dot on the scatter diagram represents one job as it relates to pay and evaluated points, which reflect its worth. When this procedure is used, a certain point spread will probably work satisfactorily (100 points was used in this illustration). Each dot represents one job but may involve dozens of individuals who fill that one job. The large dot at the lower left represents the job of data entry clerk, which was evaluated at 75 points. The data entry clerk's hourly rate of $12.90 represents either the average wage currently being paid for the job or its market rate. This decision depends on how management wants to price its jobs.

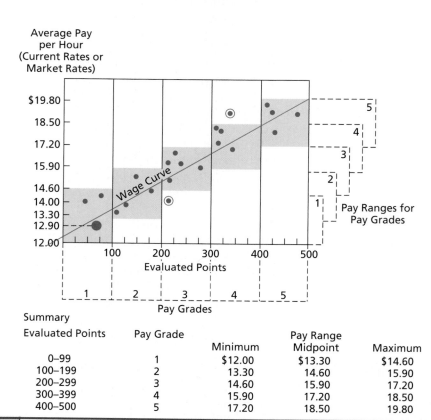

| Summary Evaluated Points | Pay Grade | Pay Range | | |
|---|---|---|---|---|
| | | Minimum | Midpoint | Maximum |
| 0–99 | 1 | $12.00 | $13.30 | $14.60 |
| 100–199 | 2 | 13.30 | 14.60 | 15.90 |
| 200–299 | 3 | 14.60 | 15.90 | 17.20 |
| 300–399 | 4 | 15.90 | 17.20 | 18.50 |
| 400–500 | 5 | 17.20 | 18.50 | 19.80 |

**Figure 11-5** **Scatter Diagram of Evaluated Jobs Illustrating the Wage Curve, Pay Grades, and Pay Ranges**

A **wage curve** (or pay curve) is the fitting of plotted points to create a smooth progression between pay grades. The line that is drawn to minimize the distance between all dots and the line—a line of best fit—may be straight or curved. However, when the point system is used (normally considering only one job cluster), a straight line is the usual result, as in Figure 11-5. This wage line can be drawn either freehand or by using a statistical method.

## Pay Ranges

After pay grades have been determined, the next decision is whether all individuals performing the same job will receive equal pay or whether pay ranges will be used. A **pay range** includes a minimum and maximum pay rate with enough variance between the two to allow for a significant pay difference. Pay ranges are generally preferred over single pay rates because they allow employees to be paid according to length of service and performance. Pay then serves as a positive incentive. When pay ranges are used, a method must be developed to advance individuals through the range.

Referring again to Figure 11-5, note that anyone can readily determine the minimum, midpoint, and maximum pay rates per hour for each of the five pay grades. For example, for pay grade 5, the minimum rate is $17.20, the midpoint is $18.50, and the maximum is $19.80. The minimum rate is normally the *hiring in* rate that a person receives when joining the firm. The maximum pay rate represents the maximum that an employee can receive for that job, regardless of how well the job is performed. A person at the top of a pay grade will have to be promoted to a job in a higher pay grade in order to receive a pay increase unless (1) an across-the-board adjustment is made or (2) the job is reevaluated and placed in a higher pay grade. This situation has caused numerous managers some anguish as they attempt to explain the pay system to an employee who is doing a tremendous job but is at the top of a pay grade. Consider this situation:

> Everyone in the department realized that Beth Smithers was the best secretary in the company. At, times she appeared to do the job of three people. Bob Marshall, Beth's supervisor, was especially impressed. Recently, he had a discussion with the human resource manager to see what could be done to get a raise for Beth. After Bob described the situation, the human resource manager's only reply was, "Sorry, Bob. Beth is already at the top of her pay grade. There is nothing you can do except have her job upgraded or promote her to another position."

Situations such as Beth's present managers with a perplexing problem. Many would be inclined to make an exception to the system and give Beth a salary increase. However, this action would violate a traditional principle, which holds that every job in the organization has a maximum value, regardless of how well it is performed. The rationale is that making exceptions to the compensation plan would result in widespread pay inequities. We should recognize that many traditional concepts are being challenged today as firms make decisions necessary to retain top-performing employees. For example, if Beth Smithers worked for Microsoft or Motorola, she might get a raise.

The rate ranges established should be large enough to provide an incentive to do a better job. At times, pay differentials may need to be greater to be meaningful, especially at higher levels. There may be logic in having the rate range become increasingly wide at each consecutive level. Consider, for example, what a $200-per-month salary increase would mean to a file clerk earning $2,000 per month (a 10 percent increase) and to a senior cost accountant earning $5,000 per month (a 4 percent increase). Assuming an inflation rate of 4 percent, the accountant's *real pay* would remain unchanged.

## Broadbanding

The pressure on U.S. business firms to do things better, faster, and less expensively has brought all internal systems under close scrutiny. Compensation in particular has received attention because of its ability to affect job behavior. Responding to this need, an approach termed *broadbanding* was devised. **Broadbanding** is a technique that collapses many pay grades (salary grades) into a few wide bands to improve organizational effectiveness. Organizational downsizing and restructuring of jobs create broader job descriptions, with the result that employees perform more diverse tasks than they did previously. Broadbanding creates the basis for a simpler compensation system that de-emphasizes structure and control and places greater importance on judgment and flexible decision making. In a recent year, one survey indicated that 21 percent of large companies had instituted broadbanding programs, up from 6 percent five years earlier and practically zero a few years before that.[34] The rapid growth in the use of broadbanding suggests that numerous benefits may be derived from its use. These benefits may include improved ability to do the following:[35]

- Provide flexibility in the way work is performed
- Promote lateral development of employees
- Support business goals
- Develop employee skills and encourage a team focus
- Direct employee attention away from vertical promotional opportunities

The decreased emphasis on job levels should encourage employees to make cross-functional moves to jobs that are on the same or even lower level because their pay rate would remain unchanged. The problem previously mentioned concerning employees at the top of their pay grade would also be minimized. Moving an employee's job to a new band would occur only when there was a significant increase in accountability. However, considerable advancement in pay is possible within each band. This is particularly important in firms with flatter organizational

TRENDS & INNOVATIONS
@

## ▶ Broadbanding at Georgia-Pacific Corporation

When the compensation group at Atlanta-based Georgia-Pacific realized that the firm's system with 27 grades between entry level and vice president had become counterproductive, it started to consider broadbanding. George Murphy, director of corporate compensation, said, "We found that in today's environment, jobs are no longer very segmented. You can't take a cookie-cutter approach that a controller is a controller is a controller."

The firm has plans to move away from the incremental advancement that dominates employees' career planning. Murphy continues, "We're hiring bright people who want to be challenged, but when you have these narrow salary structures and job-evaluation systems, you have difficulty getting people to do what you want them to do—and allowing them to do what they can do. The inherent message in a traditional structure is that we can measure the minute differences in positions, and that the way to move up is to move to the next higher position. A broadbanding structure doesn't deliver that message."[36]

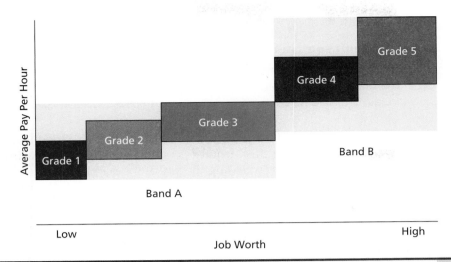

**Broadbanding and Its Relationship to Traditional Pay Grades and Ranges**

*Source:* Adapted from Joseph J. Martocchio, *Strategic Compensation* (Upper Saddle River, NJ: Prentice Hall, 1998): 36.

**Figure 11-6**

structures that offer fewer promotional opportunities. Figure 11-6 illustrates broadbanding as it relates to pay grades and rate ranges.

Broadbanding is not the only means for improving the effectiveness and efficiency of a compensation system and is not appropriate for every organization. However, it is an approach that should be considered in light of the potential benefits. For example, even massive General Electric has managed to place all its exempt jobs into five bands.[37] Although broadbanding has been implemented successfully in some organizations, the practice is not without pitfalls. Since each band consists of a broad range of jobs, the market value of these jobs may also vary considerably. Unless carefully monitored, employees in jobs at the lower end of the band could progress to the top of the range and become overpaid.

## Single-Rate System

Pay ranges are not appropriate for some workplace conditions such as some assembly-line operations. For instance, when all jobs within a unit are routine, with little opportunity for employees to vary their productivity, a single-rate system (or fixed-rate system) may be more applicable. When single rates are used, everyone in the same job receives the same base pay, regardless of seniority or productivity. This rate may correspond to the midpoint of a range determined by a compensation survey.

## Adjusting Pay Rates

When pay ranges have been determined and jobs assigned to pay grades, it may become obvious that some jobs are overpaid and others underpaid. Underpaid jobs are normally brought to the minimum of the pay range as soon as possible. Referring again to Figure 11-5, you can see that a job evaluated at about 225 points and having a rate of $14.00 per hour is represented by a circled dot immediately below pay grade 3. The job was determined to be difficult enough to fall in pay grade 3 (200–299 points). However, employees working in the job are being paid 60 cents per hour less than the minimum for the pay grade ($14.60 per hour). If one or more female employees should be in this circled job, the employer

HR WEB
WISDOM

▶ *Compensation Link*

**www.prenhall.com/mondy**

Compensation Link was designed by compensation professionals for those working in the compensation area.

might soon learn more than desired about the Equal Pay Act. Good management
practice would be to correct this inequity as rapidly as possible by placing the job
in the proper pay grade and increasing the pay of those in that job.

Overpaid jobs present a different problem. An overpaid job for pay grade 4 is
illustrated in Figure 11-5 (note the circled dot above pay grade 4). Employees in
this job earn $19.00 per hour, or 50 cents more than the maximum for the pay
grade. This type of overpayment, as well as the kind of underpayment discussed
earlier, is referred to as *red circle rate*.

An ideal solution to the problem of an overpaid job is to promote the
employee to a job in a higher pay grade. This is a good idea if the employee is
qualified for a higher-rated job and a job opening is available. Another possibility would be to bring the job rate and employee pay into line through a pay cut.
While this decision may appear logical, it is not consistent with good management practice. This action would punish employees for a situation they did not
create. Somewhere in between these two possible solutions is a third: to freeze
the rate until across-the-board pay increases bring the job into line. In an era
where this type of increase is declining in popularity, it might take a long time
for this to occur.

Pricing jobs is not a romp on the beach. It requires effort that never ends. As
shown in the next section, executive compensation is even more complex. The
job of an executive is quite different from most others in a firm, especially in
terms of responsibility. This uniqueness is reflected in executive compensation—a
topic that is discussed next.

## EXECUTIVE COMPENSATION

Executive skill largely determines whether a firm will prosper, survive, or fail.
Therefore, providing adequate compensation for these managers is vital. A company's program for compensating executives is a critical factor in attracting and
retaining the best available managers.

## Determining Executive Compensation

In determining executive compensation, firms typically prefer to relate salary
growth for the highest-level managers to overall corporate performance, including
the firm's market value. For the next management tier, they tend to integrate overall corporate performance with market rates and internal considerations to come up
with appropriate pay. For lower-level managers, salaries are often determined on the
basis of market rates, internal pay relationships, and individual performance.

In general, the higher the managerial position, the greater the flexibility managers have in designing their jobs. Management jobs are often difficult to define
because of their diversity. When they are defined, they are often described in
terms of anticipated results rather than tasks or how the work is accomplished.
Thus, market pricing may be the best general approach to use in determining

executive pay for several reasons. For one thing, such jobs are critically important to the organization, and the people involved are highly skilled and difficult to replace. In addition, the firm often has a considerable investment in developing managers. Even though the market may support a high salary for a manager, the amount may still seem extremely large. However, managers represent a relatively small percentage of the total workforce, and the overall impact on total labor costs is small.

In using market pricing, organizations utilize compensation survey data to determine pay levels for a representative group of jobs. These data may be obtained from such sources as William M. Mercer, WorldatWork, Towers Perrin, Hay Associates, and Hewett Associates.

## Types of Executive Compensation

Executive compensation often has five basic elements: (1) base salary, (2) short-term (annual) incentives or bonuses, (3) long-term incentives and capital appreciation plans, (4) executive benefits, and (5) perquisites.[38] The way an executive compensation package is designed is partially dependent on ever-changing tax legislation.

Base Salary. Although it may not represent the largest portion of the executive's compensation package, salary is obviously important. It is a factor in determining the executive's standard of living. Salary also provides the basis for other forms of compensation. For example, the amount of bonuses and certain benefits may be based on annual salary.

Short-Term Incentives or Bonuses. Payment of bonuses reflects a managerial belief in their incentive value. Today, these incentives on average comprise over 70 percent of executive compensation.[39] The popularity of this compensation component has risen rapidly in recent years, and virtually all executives receive incentives or bonuses.

Long-Term Incentives and Capital Appreciation. The stock option is a long-term incentive designed to further integrate the interests of management with those of the organization. To ensure this integration, some boards of directors require their top executives to hold some of the firm's stock. While the motivational value of stock ownership seems logical, research on the subject has not been conclusive.

There are various types of plans, but the typical **stock option plan** gives the manager the option to buy a specified amount of stock in the future at or below the current market price. This form of compensation is advantageous when stock prices are rising. However, there are potential disadvantages to stock option plans. A manager may feel uncomfortable investing money in the same organization in which he or she is building a career. As with profit sharing, this method of compensation is popular when a firm is successful, but during periods of decline when stock prices fall, the participants may become disenchanted. Nevertheless, there are several bona fide reasons for including stock ownership in executive compensation plans. In addition to aligning employees' interests with those of shareholders, retention of top executives is also a factor. For example, since 1997 AT&T has boosted its stock options to stem the tide in executive resignations. The firm's compensation committee approved a new option plan that will permit executives to exercise 25 percent of the options each year after they receive them and an additional 25 percent every year thereafter. Previously, managers had to wait five years to exercise the options.[40]

Stock option plan
An incentive plan in which managers can buy a specified amount of stock in their company in the future at or below the current market price.

**Indexed stock option plan**
A stock option plan that holds executives to a higher standard and requires that increased stock compensation be tied to outperforming peer groups or a market index.

An **indexed stock option plan** holds executives to a higher standard and requires that increased stock compensation be tied to outperforming peer groups or a market index. The true superstars can still have huge earnings as their company's stock outperforms the index. Federal Reserve Chairman Alan Greenspan supports such a plan, but indexed stock options remain quite unpopular, perhaps for obvious reasons.[41]

**Executive Benefits.** Executive benefits are similar to but usually more generous than those received by other employees because they are tied to managers' higher salaries. However, current legislation (ERISA) does restrict the value of executive benefits to a certain level above that of other workers.

**Perquisites (perks)**
Special benefits provided by a firm to a small group of key executives to give them something extra.

**Perquisites.** **Perquisites (perks)** are any special benefits provided by a firm to a small group of key executives and designed to give the executives something extra. In addition to conveying status, these rewards are either not considered as earned income or taxed at a lower level than ordinary income.[42] An executive's perks may include some of the following:

- A company-provided car
- Accessible, no-cost parking
- Limousine service; the chauffeur may also serve as a bodyguard
- Kidnapping and ransom protection
- Counseling service, including financial and legal services
- Professional meetings and conferences
- Spouse travel
- Use of company plane and yacht
- Home entertainment allowance
- Special living accommodations away from home
- Club memberships
- Special dining privileges
- Season tickets to entertainment events
- Special relocation allowances
- Use of company credit cards
- Medical expense reimbursement; coverage for all medical costs
- Reimbursement for children's college expenses
- No- and low-interest loans[43]

**Golden parachute contract**
A perquisite provided that protects executives in the event that another company acquires their firm or they are forced to leave the firm for other reasons.

A **golden parachute contract** is a perquisite that protects executives in the event that another company acquires their firm or the executive is forced to leave the firm for other reasons. Today's severance package for CEOs is typically three times annual salary and bonus and accelerated vesting of options. The reason for such generosity is the competition for top executives provided by dot-com companies. Because the competition is so severe, in many cases CEOs have to commit a serious crime such as rape or murder to be ineligible for severance.

An interesting example of severance pay is the experience of Jill Barad as the top executive at Mattel. Her separation contract called for five years' salary and bonuses worth $26.4 million. She also had the option to buy her office furniture for $1; free financial counseling services; forgiveness of a $4.2 million personal loan; forgiveness of a $3 million home loan; and also $3.31 million to cover the taxes she owed on the forgiveness of her home loan. All this totaled about $47 million, not counting options.[44]

Extreme competition for executive talent is the rationale given for such generosity. The liberality of executive perks grew to such proportions during the

1980s that Congress imposed penalties on excess payments in the form of a nondeductible excise tax on individuals and a cap on a company's tax deductibility.[45]

The high level of compensation for top executives has received increased attention in recent years. For example, Charles Wang, CEO of Computer Associates International, received total compensation of $655,424,000 in 1999. This award prompted a dozen lawsuits and a barrage of criticism. In fact, Wang has announced that he plans to give some of the money back as a settlement. While Wang's pay was extraordinary, consider that the 20 highest-paid American executives averaged $112.9 million in total compensation. The vast majority of total compensation for all these executives was not salary, but long-term compensation. For example, the second-highest-paid CEO, L. Dennis Kozlowski of Tyco International, received $4,550,000 in salary and bonuses and $165,446,000 in long-term compensation, a total of $169,996,000.[46]

High compensation for top executives is apparently acceptable to shareholders when firms are performing well. Many feel it is absolutely essential to reward them highly to retain them. This seems especially true today, when the dot-com firms are raiding so many organizations' top people. However, the practice of paying megabucks to executives when their companies are performing poorly is another matter. For example, Stephen Case, CEO of America Online, Inc. and the fifth-highest-paid executive in 1999, earned over $117 million while his firm's return on investment was negative 119 percent.[47]

**A GLOBAL PERSPECTIVE**

## Why Global Rates for Top Talent Are Converging

Designing total compensation packages for expatriates and local nationals is often quite complex, and at some companies such as Unilever, always changing. At Unilever, an Anglo-Dutch food and household-goods conglomerate, Brian Dive, the head of remuneration, must deal with the problem of how to pay his 20,000 managers in 90 countries from Bangladesh to Britain. In the past, the boss of a region or a big country determined pay, but now at Unilever, as with many other multinationals, brand managers in different countries are determining pay. Recently, Unilever moved from a narrow grading structure to five global work levels. Managers' pay is still based on the country they work in, but Dive thinks there will be regional convergence. In time, "we will have a pan-European rate."

According to Jonathan Baines of the London headhunter firm Baines Gwinner, there is a global converging of compensation. Managers in any of the time zones are increasingly rewarded the same way. But, because the main source of people with technical skills is New York, pay for the moment tends to move up to the New York level. As New York drags up London, so London drags up Europe. To keep talented people in France, says Marina Eloy, who is in charge of global human resources at Paribas, a French bank, Paribas must pay British prices. "As soon as someone has an international side, you have to give them double the domestic equivalent." In Canada and Mexico, compensation committees routinely look at American boardroom pay in deciding what to offer their chief executives, because they know how easily good managers can move across the border for more. The market rate for top talent in various industries will converge as it has done in finance, as more senior executives speak English and have experience working in several countries.[48]

**①** **Describe the various forms of compensation.**

Compensation is the total of all rewards provided employees in return for their services. Forms of compensation include direct financial compensation, indirect financial compensation (benefits), and nonfinancial compensation.

**②** **Explain the concept of equity in financial compensation.**

Equity is workers' perceptions that they are being treated fairly. Forms of compensation equity include external equity, internal equity, employee equity, and team equity.

**③** **Identify the determinants of financial compensation.**

The organization, the labor market, the job, and the employee all have an impact on job pricing and the ultimate determination of an individual's financial compensation.

**④** **Identify organizational factors that should be considered as determinants of financial compensation.**

Organizational factors that should be considered include compensation policies, organizational politics, and ability to pay.

**⑤** **Describe factors that should be considered when the labor market is a determinant of financial compensation.**

Factors that should be considered include compensation surveys, expediency, cost of living, labor unions, society, the economy, and certain federal and state legislation.

**⑥** **Explain how the job is a determinant of financial compensation.**

Management techniques utilized for determining a job's relative worth include job analysis, job descriptions, and job evaluation.

**⑦** **Explain the various forms of job evaluation.**

Forms of job evaluation include the ranking method, the classification method, factor comparison method, the point method, and the Hay Plan.

**⑧** **Identify factors related to the employee that are essential in determining financial compensation.**

The factors include performance-based pay, seniority, experience, membership in the organization, potential, political influence, luck, and special employee classes.

**⑨** **Describe job pricing.**

Placing a dollar value on the worth of a job is job pricing.

**⑩** **Explain how executive compensation is determined and the types of executive compensation.**

In determining executive compensation, firms typically prefer to relate salary growth for the highest-level managers to overall corporate performance. Executive compensation often has five basic elements: (1) base salary, (2) short-term (annual) incentives or bonuses, (3) long-term incentives and capital appreciation plans, (4) executive benefits, and (5) perquisites.

---

## ► Questions for Review

1. Define each of the following terms:

    a. *compensation*
    b. *direct financial compensation*
    c. *indirect financial compensation*
    d. *nonfinancial compensation*

2. Distinguish among external equity, internal equity, employee equity, and team equity.

3. What are the primary determinants of individual financial compensation? Briefly describe each.

4. What organizational factors should be considered as determinants of financial compensation?

5. What factors should be considered when the labor market is a determinant of financial compensation? ~~320~~

6. How has government legislation affected compensation?

7. What factors should be considered when the job is a determinant of financial compensation?

8. Give the primary purpose of job evaluation.

9. Distinguish between the following job evaluation methods: the ranking, classification, factor comparison, and point methods.

10. Describe the Hay guide chart-profile method of job evaluation.

11. Define each of the following:
    a. *merit pay*
    b. *bonus*
    c. *skill-based pay*
    d. *competency-based pay*

12. Describe the various factors relating to the employee in determining pay and benefits.

13. What is the purpose of job pricing? Discuss briefly.

14. State the basic procedure for determining pay grades.

15. What is the purpose of establishing pay ranges? ~~337~~

16. Define *broadbanding*.

17. What are the various types of executive compensation?

*We invite you to visit the Mondy homepage on the Prentice Hall Web site at*
**www.prenhall.com/mondy**
*for updated information, Web-based exercises, and links to other HR-related sites.*

**TAKE IT TO THE NET**

## Developing HRM Skills ◀

### An Experiential Exercise

In the future, one of the key issues concerning pay may be comparable worth. If comparable worth should become federal law, organizations will have to base salaries and wages on job evaluation scores. Salaries and wages will be determined by the requirements of the job itself, skills required, knowledge required, effort required, working conditions, and responsibilities, rather than the workings of the labor market. Then, equal pay for different jobs of the same value will have to be determined by looking not at the *going rate* in the marketplace, but rather at the job's difficulty, importance, and the training required to properly perform it. This exercise has been developed to impart an understanding and appreciation of the concept of comparable worth.

## ► HRM INCIDENT 1

### You're Doing a Great Job, Though

During a Saturday afternoon golf game with his friend Randy Dean, Harry Neil discovered that his department had hired a recent university graduate as a systems analyst at a starting salary almost as high as Harry's. Although Harry was good natured, he was bewildered and upset. It had taken him five years to become a senior systems analyst and attain his current salary level at Trimark Data Systems. He had been generally pleased with the company and thoroughly enjoyed his job.

The following Monday morning, Harry confronted Dave Edwards, the human resource director, and asked if what he had heard was true. Dave apologetically admitted that it was and attempted to explain the company's situation. "Harry, the market for systems analysts is very tight, and in order for the company to attract qualified prospects, we have to offer a premium starting salary. We desperately needed another analyst, and this was the only way we could get one."

Harry asked Dave if his salary would be adjusted accordingly. Dave answered, "Your salary will be reevaluated at the regular time. You're doing a great job, though, and I'm sure the boss will recommend a raise." Harry thanked Dave for his time, but left the office shaking his head and wondering about his future.

#### Questions

1. Do you think Dave's explanation was satisfactory? Discuss.
2. What action do you believe the company should have taken with regard to Harry?

## ► HRM INCIDENT 2

### The Controversial Job

David Rhine, compensation manager for Farrington Lingerie Company, was generally relaxed and good natured. Although he was a no-nonsense, competent executive, David was one of the most popular managers in the company. This Friday morning, however, David was not his usual self. As chairperson of the company's job evaluation committee, he had called a late morning meeting at which several jobs were to be considered for reevaluation. The jobs had already been rated and assigned to pay grade 3. But the office manager, Ben Butler, was upset that one was not rated higher. To press the issue, Ben had taken his case to two executives who were also members of the job evaluation committee. The two executives (production manager Bill Nelson and general marketing manager Betty Anderson) then requested that the job ratings be reviewed. Bill and Betty supported Ben's side of the dispute, and David was not looking forward to the confrontation that was almost certain to occur.

The controversial job was that of receptionist. Only one receptionist position existed in the company, and it was held by Beth Smithers. Beth had been with the firm 12 years, longer than any of the committee members. She was extremely efficient, and virtually all the executives in the company—including the president—

had noticed and commented on her outstanding work. Bill Nelson and Betty Anderson were particularly pleased with Beth because of the cordial manner in which she greeted and accommodated Farrington's customers and vendors, who frequently visited the plant. They felt that Beth projected a positive image of the company.

When the meeting began, Dave said, "Good morning. I know that you're busy, so let's get the show on the road. We have several jobs to evaluate this morning and I suggest we begin . . ." Before he could finish his sentence, Bill interrupted, "I suggest we start with Beth." Betty nodded in agreement. When David regained his composure, he quietly but firmly asserted, "Bill, we are not here today to evaluate Beth. Her supervisor does that at performance appraisal time. We're meeting to evaluate jobs based on job content. In order to do this fairly, with regard to other jobs in the company, we must leave personalities out of our evaluation." David then proceeded to pass out copies of the receptionist job description to Bill and Betty, who were obviously very irritated.

### Questions

1. Do you feel that David was justified in insisting that the job, not the person, be evaluated? Discuss.
2. Do you believe that there is a maximum rate of pay for every job in an organization, regardless of how well the job is being performed? Justify your position.
3. Assume that Beth is earning the maximum of the range for her pay grade. In what ways could she obtain a salary increase?

## Notes

1. Michael Schrage, "Cafeteria Benefits? Ha! You Deserve a Richer Banquet," *Fortune* 141 (April 3, 2000): 274.

2. "ACA Name Change to WorldatWork Reflects Changes in the Profession," *WorldatWork: The Professional Association for Compensation, Benefits and Total Rewards.* www.worldatwork.org/home/generic/html/namechange.html (July 30, 2000).

3. Andrew S. Richter, "Compensation Management and Cultural Change at IBM: Paying the People in Black at Big Blue," *Compensation & Benefits Review* 30 (May/June 1998): 51–59.

4. "Top 10 Compensation and Benefits Concerns," *HR Focus* 75 (November 1998): S1.

5. Steve Werner, Robert Konopaske, and Chris Touhey, "Ten Questions to Ask Yourself About Compensation Surveys," *Compensation & Benefits Review* 31 (May/June 1999): 54.

6. John H. Davis, "The Future of Salary Surveys When Jobs Disappear," *Compensation & Benefits Review* 29 (January/February 1997): 18–26.

7. Werner, Konopaske, and Touhey, "Ten Questions to Ask Yourself About Compensation Surveys." 54.

8. Donald G. McDermott, "Case Studies: Gathering Information for the New Age of Compensation," *Compensation & Benefits Review* 29 (March/April 1997): 57–63.

9. Joseph J. Martocchio, *Strategic Compensation* (Upper Saddle River, NJ: Prentice Hall, 1998): 202–203.

10. William Wiatrowski, "A Formidable New Compensation Tool: Bureau of Labor Statistics' New National Compensation Survey," *Compensation & Benefits Review* 30 (September/October 1998): 29.

11. Devin Leonard, "They're Coming to Take You Away," *Fortune* 41 (May 29, 2000): 106.

12. The Small Business Protection Act of 1996, an amendment to the FLSA, raised the minimum wage to $5.15 effective September 1, 1997.

13. Joan M. Eagle, "Wage and Hour Traps for the Unwary," *Journal of Property Management* 64 (March/April 1999): 94.

14. David A. Andelman, "Work for Time," *Management Review* 86 (March 1997): 44.

15. Robert W. Thompson, "Battle Brewing Over FLSA White-Collar Exemptions," *HR News* 19 (June 2000): 23.

16. Timothy S. Bland, "Equal Pay Enforcement Heats Up," *HRMagazine* 44 (July 1999): 140–145.

17. Teresa Brady, "How Equal Is Equal Pay?" *Management Review* 87 (March 1998): 59.

18. Bland, "Equal Pay Enforcement Heats Up," 138.

19. Marc Adams, "Fair and Square," *HRMagazine* 44 (May 1, 1999): 38.

20. Brady, "How Equal Is Equal Pay?"

21. George T. Milkovich and Jerry M. Newman, *Compensation,* 6th ed. (Boston: Irwin McGraw-Hill, 1999): 115.

22. Martocchio, *Strategic Compensation,* 184.

23. Kim Clark, Joellen Perry, and Marissa Melton, "Why It Pays to Quit," *U.S. News & World Report* 127 (November 1, 1999): 76.

24. Don Eskew and Robert L. Heneman, "A Survey of Merit Pay Plan Effectiveness: End of the Line for Merit Pay or Hope for Improvement," *Human Resource Planning* 19 (1996): 12.

25. Larry Reynolds, "Variable Pay Laws May Benefit Employers," *HR Focus* 75 (December 1998): 3.

26. Carrie Mason-Draffen, "Companies Find New Ways to Pay," *Newsday* (January 5, 1997): F8.

27. Betty Sosnin, "A Pat(ent) on the Back," *HRMagazine* 45 (March 2000): 107–108.

28. R. Bradley Hill, "The Advantages of a Two-Component Approach to Compensation," *Personnel Journal* 72 (May 1993): 154–161.

29. Sandy Shore (Associated Press), "Companies Find Merit in Merit Pay; Proponents Call It a Win-Win Situation that Boosts Efficiency and Gives Workers Control," *Denver Rocky Mountain News* (October 11, 1998): 10.

30. Steven E. Gross, *Compensation for Teams* (New York: American Management Association) 1995: 47.

31. Steven E. Gross, "When Jobs Become Team Roles, What Do You Pay For?" *Compensation & Benefits Review* 29 (January/February 1997): 48–51.

32. Milkovich and Newman, *Compensation,* 463–465.

33. Craig Stedman, "Complex Sales Commission Process Automated," *Computerworld* 33 (July 5, 1999): 38.

34. Mathew Budman, "Mixed Results," *Across the Board* 35 (June 1998): 23.

35. Kenan S. Abosch, "The Promise of Broadbanding," *Compensation & Benefits Review* 27 (January/February 1995): 55–56.

36. Budman, "Mixed Results."

37. Gross, *Compensation for Teams,* 66.

38. Milkovich and Newman, *Compensation,* 458.

39. Ibid., 460.

40. "The Talent Drain at AT&T," *Business Week* (March 13, 2000): 94–96.

41. Jennifer Reingold, "An Options Plan Your CEO Hates," *Business Week* (February 28, 2000): 82.

42. Since the late 1970s, the IRS has required firms to place a value on more perks and has recognized them as imputed income.

43. Richard I. Henderson, *Compensation Management in a Knowledge-Based World,* 7th ed. (Upper Saddle River, NJ: Prentice Hall, 1997): 508–509.

44. Suzanne Koudsi, "Why CEOs Are Paid So Much to Beat It," *Fortune* 141 (May 29, 2000): 34.

45. George B. Paulin, "Executive Compensation and Changes in Control: A Search for Fairness," *Compensation & Benefits Review* 29 (March/April 1997): 30.

46. Jennifer Reingold, "Executive Pay," *Business Week* (April 17, 2000): 106.

47. Ibid., 102.

48. "No Man Is An Island: Why Global Rates For Top Talent Are Converging," *The Economist* 351 (May 8, 1999): NA(1).

# 12

# Benefits and Other Compensation Issues

 Objectives

- Define benefits.
- Describe legally required benefits.
- Identify the basic categories of voluntary benefits.
- Describe the Consolidated Omnibus Budget Reconciliation Act (COBRA), the Health Insurance Portability and Accountability Act, the Employee Retirement Income Security Act (ERISA), and the Older Workers Benefit Protection Act (OWBPA).
- Describe the importance of communicating information about the benefits package.
- Explain the various forms of incentive compensation.
- Describe how the job environment is a component of nonfinancial compensation.
- Explain how factors related to workplace flexibility are a component of nonfinancial compensation.
- Describe the concepts of severance pay, comparable worth, pay secrecy, and pay compression.

John Hicks, a college dropout, is a senior credit clerk at Ajax Manufacturing Company. A bright young man, John has been with Ajax for four years. He has received excellent performance ratings in each of the several positions he has held with the firm. However, during his last appraisal interview, John's supervisor implied that promotion to a higher-level job would require additional formal education. Because John appeared to be receptive to the idea, his supervisor suggested that he check with human resources to learn the details of Ajax's educational assistance policy. When John checked the specifics of the educational assistance program, he found it covered 90 percent of tuition and the cost of required textbooks. Ajax's educational program and its other benefit programs were top notch, which is very important to John and his family.

## ▶ Key Terms

Arnold Anderson, Bob Minnis, and Mason Kearby are all employed as shipping clerks for Mainstreet Furniture Company. Arnold and Bob are energetic young people who consistently work hard each day. Mason is a "good ole boy" who spends most of his time flipping quarters with dockworkers and talking with anyone who will listen. They all earn about $14.50 per hour, plus benefits. Yesterday, work was piling up in the department, and Arnold and Bob were working furiously to keep up. Mason was nowhere to be found. "Arnold," Bob said disgustedly, "the pay here just isn't fair. We do twice as much work as Mason, yet he makes as much as we do."

"I know," Arnold acknowledged, "but we all punch in and out at the same time. Besides, I understand that management is looking into an incentive plan where we sign each shipment that we are responsible for bringing to the loading area. We'll be given a bonus, over our hourly wage, for the number of shipments we handle above an established norm."

"Good," said Bob. "Now they'll find out how little Mason does."

**A**lthough these anecdotes may seem to have little in common, each relates to the broad area of compensation. John is investigating the possibility of continuing his education through his company's educational assistance program. Arnold and Bob are disgusted because a less productive worker makes as much money as they do.

We begin the chapter with a discussion of benefits, both mandated and voluntary. Then, legislation related to benefits and the proper communication of information about benefit packages is discussed. Next, we present various types of incentive compensation and describe nonfinancial compensation and the job as a total compensation factor. The job environment as a total compensation factor is then discussed. The final portion of the chapter is devoted to a discussion of workplace flexibility and other compensation issues.

▶ *International Foundation of Employee Benefit Plans*

**www.prenhall.com/mondy**

Current news regarding employee benefit plans is available.

HR WEB
WISDOM

# BENEFITS (INDIRECT FINANCIAL COMPENSATION)

**Benefits**
All financial rewards that generally are not paid directly to an employee.

Most organizations recognize that they have a responsibility to their employees to provide them with insurance and other programs for their health, safety, security, and general welfare (see Figure 12-1). These programs are called **benefits** and include all financial rewards that generally are not paid directly to the employee. Benefits cost the firm money, but employees usually receive them indirectly. For example, an organization may spend $3,200 a year as a contribution to the health insurance premiums for each nonexempt employee. The employee does not receive money but does obtain the benefit of health insurance coverage. This type of compensation has two distinct advantages: (1) it is generally nontaxable to the employee, and (2) the cost of some benefits may be much less for large groups of employees than for individuals.

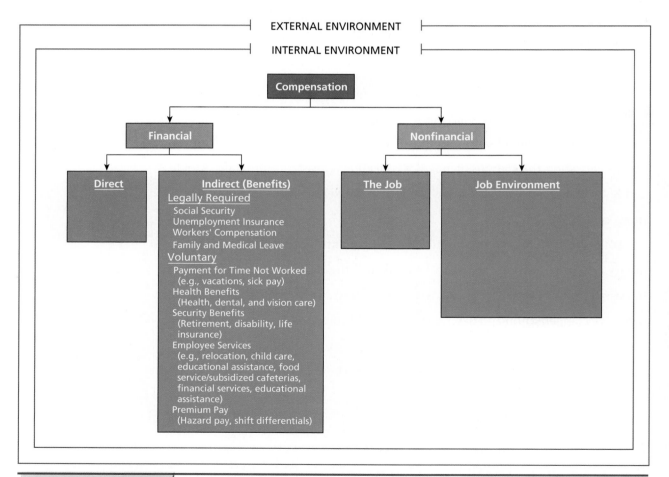

**Figure 12-1** **Benefits in a Total Compensation Program**

Generally speaking, benefits are provided to employees because of their membership in the organization. For example, John and his family received benefits, as did all other Ajax employees and their families. Benefits are typically not related to employee productivity; therefore, while they may be valuable in recruiting and retaining employees, they do not serve as motivation for improved performance. Legislation mandates some benefits, and employers voluntarily provide others.

An equitable and effective incentive plan should help organizations attract, retain, and motivate qualified employees. Such a plan will create a more evenhanded situation for Arnold and Bob at the Mainstreet Furniture Company. Mason will probably improve his performance or leave the firm, either voluntarily or otherwise.

The cost of benefits is high and is growing rapidly. Recently, employers spent an average of between $3,000 and $5,000 for each full-time employee for *mandated* benefits. The average cost for *discretionary* benefits was $11,506 per employee.[1] A typical worker who earns $30,000 per year will receive approximately $11,700 (almost 40 percent) indirectly in total benefits. The magnitude of this expenditure no doubt accounts for the less frequent use of the term *fringe benefits*. In fact, the benefits that employees receive today are significantly different from those of just a few years ago. As benefit dollars compete with financial compensation, some employers move away from paternalistic benefits programs. They may shift more responsibilities to employees as with 401(k) retirement plans, discussed later. However, in a tight labor market, other firms—especially those in high-tech industries—are careful to provide desired benefits to attract and retain employees with critical skills.

www.benefitslink.com/index.shtml
*Source:* Benefits Link.

## Mandated (Legally Required) Benefits

Most employee benefits are provided at the employer's discretion, but the law requires others. These required benefits currently account for about 10 percent of total compensation costs. They include Social Security, workers' compensation, unemployment insurance, and family and medical leave. The future comparative importance of these benefits will depend on how the United States deals with rising health care costs and with long-term custodial care for elderly citizens.

## Social Security

The Social Security Act of 1935 created a system of retirement benefits. The act established a federal payroll tax to fund unemployment and retirement benefits. It also established the Social Security Administration. Employers are required to share equally with employees the cost of old age, survivors', and disability insurance. Employers are required to pay the full cost of unemployment insurance.

Subsequent amendments to the act added other forms of protection, such as disability insurance, survivors' benefits, and, most recently, Medicare. Medicare spending per beneficiary has doubled in real terms in the past two decades. The increase has been attributed to greater use of post–acute care services such as skilled nursing, home health care, and rehabilitation facilities. However, there is concern that in the poorly monitored home health care industry, there may be outright fraud.[2]

Disability insurance protects employees against loss of earnings resulting from total disability. Survivors' benefits are provided to certain members of an employee's family when he or she dies. These benefits are paid to the widow or widower and unmarried children of the deceased employee. Unmarried children may be eligible for survivors' benefits until they are 18 years old. In some cases, students retain eligibility until they are 19. Medicare provides hospital and medical insurance protection for individuals 65 years of age and older and for those who have become disabled.

While employees must pay a portion of the cost of Social Security coverage, the employer makes an equal contribution. It is the employer's part that is considered a benefit. The 2000 tax rate was 6.2 percent for the Social Security portion and 1.45 percent for Medicare. The total tax rate of 7.65 percent applied to a maximum taxable wage of $76,200. The rate for Medicare, 1.45 percent, applied to all earnings. Today, approximately 95 percent of the workers in this country pay into and may draw Social Security benefits.

Beginning with employees who reached age 62 in 2000, the retirement age will be increased gradually until 2009, when it reaches age 66. After stabilizing at this age for a period of time, it will again increase in 2027, when it reaches age 67. These changes will not affect Medicare, with full eligibility under this program holding at age 65.

## Unemployment Compensation

An individual laid off by an organization covered by the Social Security Act may receive unemployment compensation for up to 26 weeks. While the federal government provides certain guidelines, unemployment compensation programs are administered by the states, and the benefits vary by state. A payroll tax paid solely by employers funds the unemployment compensation program. The tax burden may approximate 6.2 percent of the first $7,000 earned by each employee. However, each company's actual rate is dependent on its experience with unemployment.

## Workers' Compensation

Workers' compensation benefits provide a degree of financial protection for employees who incur expenses resulting from job-related accidents or illnesses. As with unemployment compensation, the various states administer individual programs, which are subject to federal regulations. Employers pay the entire cost of workers' compensation insurance, and their premium expense is directly tied to their past experience with job-related accidents and illnesses. These circumstances should encourage employers to actively pursue health and safety programs, which are topics discussed in Chapter 13.

## Family and Medical Leave Act of 1993 (FMLA)

The Family and Medical Leave Act applies to private employers with 50 or more employees and to all governmental employers regardless of the number of employees. The act provides for up to 12 workweeks of unpaid leave per year for absences due to the employee's own serious health condition or the need to care for a newborn or newly adopted child or a seriously ill child, parent, or spouse.

FMLA rights apply only to employees who have worked for the employer for at least 12 months and who have at least 1,250 hours of service during the 12 months immediately preceding the start of the leave. The FMLA guarantees that health insurance coverage is maintained during the leave and also that the employee has the right to return to the same or an equivalent position after a leave. The leave can be taken intermittently under certain circumstances. Defining these circumstances often presents a challenge to employers. It may be difficult to determine whether an absence is FMLA related, which therefore complicates management's ability to monitor and discipline employees for attendance matters.[3]

The FMLA prohibits employers from taking any adverse or discriminatory action against employees who exercise their rights under the FMLA. Absence on FMLA leave cannot be used as a negative factor in any employment action, including performance appraisals, promotions, or bonuses unrelated to individual production. It is important for firms and individual managers to realize that they might be held liable for FMLA violations. A federal court in Ohio held an HR manager personally liable for an employee's damages under the FMLA.[4]

▶ Organizations voluntarily provide numerous benefits.

The Department of Labor recently issued a report that suggests the cost and inconvenience of the FMLA have been insignificant. However, a study by Business and Legal Reports, Inc., revealed significant problems associated with complying with the law. Nearly half the employers responding to the survey reported incurring additional administrative expenses as a result of FMLA compliance. A few firms even indicated the need to hire additional personnel to meet the increased administrative load. In addition, FMLA reportedly makes maintaining attendance standards more difficult for employers. One-fourth of the respondents to the survey reported increased absenteeism as a serious problem; for example, employees with poor attendance habits have learned that the FMLA can shield them from discipline. According to these sources, this behavior frustrates and demoralizes the rest of the workforce.[5]

While the Clinton administration asserted that the FMLA should be amended to protect more workers and generally expand the law, employers have preferred to cut back on its scope. Business groups feel that Department of Labor regulations and court decisions have pushed the law well beyond its original simple formula and appear to be encouraging workers to increasingly invoke FMLA in marginal disputes. According to Philadelphia lawyer Michael J. Ossip, chairman of the American Bar Association's FMLA Committee, a seemingly expanding definition of what *serious health condition* means is the biggest problem for health administrators.[6]

## DISCRETIONARY (VOLUNTARY) BENEFITS

Organizations voluntarily provide numerous benefits. Generally speaking, such benefits are not legally required. They may result from unilateral management decisions in some firms and from union-management negotiations in others.

# Payment for Time Not Worked

In providing payment for time not worked, employers recognize that employees need time away from the job for many purposes. Included in this category are paid vacations, payment for holidays not worked, sick pay, and payment for jury duty, National Guard or other military reserve duty, voting time, and bereavement time.[7] It is also common for organizations to provide payments to assist employees in performing civic duties. Some payments for time not worked are provided for time off routinely taken during work hours. Common benefits in this area include rest periods, coffee breaks, lunch periods, cleanup time, and travel time.

**Paid Vacations.** Payment for time not worked serves important compensation goals. For instance, paid vacations provide workers with an opportunity to rest, become rejuvenated, and—one hopes—become more productive. They may also encourage employees to remain with the firm. Paid vacation time typically increases with seniority. For example, employees with six months' service might receive one week of vacation; employees with one year of service, two weeks; ten years' service, three weeks; and fifteen years' service, four weeks.

Vacation time may also vary with organizational rank. For instance, a senior-level executive, regardless of time with the firm, may be given a month of vacation. With an annual salary of $120,000, this manager would receive a benefit of approximately $10,000 each year while not working. A junior accountant earning $36,000 a year might receive two weeks of vacation time worth about $1,500.

**Sick Pay.** Each year many firms allocate to each employee a certain number of days of sick leave, to be used when ill. Employees who are too sick to report to work continue to receive their pay up to the maximum number of days accumulated. As with vacation pay, the number of *sick leave* days often depends on seniority.

Some sick leave programs have been severely criticized. At times, individuals have abused the system by calling in sick when all they really wanted was additional paid vacation. According to a study conducted by CCH Inc. of Chicago, more than three-quarters of the time when workers call in sick, they are not. There may be several explanations for this phenomenon. First, Americans log more hours at work than their counterparts in any other industrialized nation in the world. In addition, many employees are working in an environment with reduced staffs due to downsizing or are dealing with disadvantages associated with the use of temporary employees. Some employees may feel they deserve more pay than they are receiving and therefore seek equity in other ways. One way may be to take a day off—a sick day off.[8]

One way to deal with the problem of unscheduled absences is to provide more flexibility. In lieu of sick leave, vacation time, and a personal day or two, a growing number of companies are providing **paid time off (PTO)**—a certain number of days each year that employees can use for any purpose they deem necessary. According to surveys, up to 27 percent of American firms now have such plans. Maureen Brookband, benefits vice president at Marriott, which has such a plan, says that employees tell her, "It's very nice, there's no guilt. You don't have to use a sick day when you aren't really sick."[9] Some critics of the plan feel there is still a need for sick leave. And, as one expert pointed out, a prominent reason for taking sick days is stress, and this factor is not really dealt with. The impact of stress is examined in the next chapter.

**Paid time off (PTO)**
A means of dealing with the problem of unscheduled absences by providing a certain number of days each year that employees can use for any purpose they deem necessary.

# Health Benefits

Health benefits are often included as part of an employee's indirect financial compensation. Specific areas include health care and dental and vision care.

**Health Care.** Benefits for health care represent the most expensive cost in the area of indirect financial compensation. A number of factors have combined to create this situation: an aging population, a growing demand for medical care, increasingly expensive medical technology, a lack of price controls, and inefficient administrative processes. It is increasingly important for firms to hold the line on health care costs. What do you think is the most expensive component of a Chrysler vehicle? It is not steel; it is not plastic; it is health care. Between 1986 and 1999, DaimlerChrysler's health care costs doubled to $1.4 billion.[10]

Managed care systems have been the general response to medical costs that are inching into double digits again and increasing at a rate three times higher than general inflation.[11] These networks are comprised of doctors and hospitals that agree to accept negotiated prices for treating patients. Employees are given financial incentives to use the facilities within the network. Today, a majority of all insured employees in the United States participate in some kind of managed care plan, and the growth of these plans continues.

In addition to *self-insurance* (in which firms provide benefits directly from their own assets) and *traditional commercial insurers* (which supply indemnity insurance covering bills from any health care provider), employers may utilize one of several managed care options. **Health maintenance organizations (HMOs)** cover all services for a fixed fee. However, control is exercised over which doctors and health facilities a member may use. **Preferred provider organizations (PPOs)** are a more flexible managed care system. Incentives are provided to members to use services within the system, but out-of-network providers may be utilized at greater cost. An SHRM benefits survey indicated that 78 percent of the respondents use PPOs and 58 percent have HMOs. **Point-of-service (POS)** permits a member to select a provider within the network or, for a lower level of benefits, go outside the network. **Exclusive provider organizations (EPOs)** offer a smaller PPO provider network and usually provide little, if any, benefits when an out-of-network provider is used. Only 9 percent of respondents to a recent survey indicated their firm used an EPO.[12] Each of these forms of managed care systems appears to be losing its uniqueness. For example, HMOs are developing more flexible products, and many offer POS and PPOs. Large, independent PPO companies are providing programs that resemble HMOs. Regardless of the precise form, managed care systems strive to control health care costs.

**Capitation**, typically the reimbursement method used by primary care physicians,[13] is an approach to health care where providers negotiate a rate for health care for a covered life over a period of time. It presumes that doctors have an incentive to keep patients healthy and avoid costly procedures when they are paid for each patient rather than for each service. This approach, long the domain of HMOs, is moving into other managed care systems. Capitation appears to control costs, reduce paperwork, and require providers to work within a budget. It also shifts some of the financial risk to the doctors. If providers' costs exceed the cost of providing care, doctors suffer a loss. This system shifts the incentive for physicians away from providing care toward limiting care. This change has prompted some critics to fear that the plans compromise the quality of health care.

In a **defined contribution health care system**, companies give each employee a set amount of money annually with which to purchase health care coverage. In this proposed health care system, employees could shop around, probably

**Health maintenance organizations (HMOs)**
Insurance programs provided by companies that cover all services for a fixed fee but control is exercised over which doctors and health facilities may be used.

**Preferred provider organizations (PPOs)**
A flexible managed care system in which incentives are provided to members to use services within the system; out-of-network providers may be utilized at greater cost.

**Point-of-service (POS)**
A managed care option that permits a member to select a health care provider within the network or—for a lower level of benefits—outside the network.

**Exclusive provider organizations (EPOs)**
A managed care option that offers a smaller preferred provider network and usually provides few, if any, benefits when an out-of-network provider is used.

**Capitation**
An approach to health care in which providers negotiate a rate for health care for a covered life over a period of time.

**Defined contribution health care system**
A system in which each employee is given a set amount of money annually with which to purchase health care coverage.

using online services, for plans that meet their individual needs. The Internet contains a wealth of health information, and it is frequently accessed. For example, health care content sites are one of the top three in terms of Internet popularity.

The defined contribution system is based on the belief that consumers are in the best position to know what kind of health care they need and how much they want to spend for it. In this plan, employees could choose to buy less expensive plans and put the difference into a medical savings account. Or, they could add personal funds to the employers' contribution and purchase more deluxe coverage. While on the surface there are advantages to this type of plan, one primary difficulty is that the amount of money contributed by the employer would be fully taxed under current law.

Among other firms, Xerox is experimenting with an approach similar to the defined contribution system in which employees are given an allowance to choose from an array of plans selected by the company. On the bet that businesses will make the move to defined contribution plans with all health care decisions in the hands of employees, many online companies are being formed. SimplyHealth.com is one of these new online vendors. This firm allows individuals and groups to evaluate and purchase health plans. Eventually, the site will allow individual purchasers to be pooled together into risk groups, making it possible for them to receive more favorable risk ratings.[14]

In addition to doctor office visits, health insurance typically includes hospital room and board costs, service charges, and surgical fees. These benefits may be paid partially, or totally, by the employer. *Medical flexible spending accounts* and *prescription programs* are also frequently provided benefits. Many plans provide for *major medical benefits* to cover extraordinary expenses that result from long-term or serious health problems. The use of *deductibles* is a common feature of medical benefits. For example, the employee may have to pay the first $400 of medical bills before the insurance takes over payment. In order to control health care costs, a number of firms have increased the amount of deductibles and/or reduced the scope of insurance coverage.

Health insurance premiums alone amount to a sizable portion of an employer's total payroll. In a further attempt to curb medical costs, many firms use some type of utilization review service. **Utilization review** is a process that scrutinizes medical diagnoses, hospitalization, surgery, and other medical treatment and care prescribed by doctors. The reviewer—often a registered nurse—explores alternatives to the treatment provided, such as outpatient treatment or admission on the day of surgery. The objective of this process is, of course, to hold down costs.

With the high cost of medical care, an individual without health care insurance is quite vulnerable. The Consolidated Omnibus Budget Reconciliation Act of 1985 (COBRA) was enacted to give employees the opportunity to temporarily continue their coverage if they would otherwise lose it because of termination, layoff, or other change in employment status. The act applies to employers with 20 or more employees. Under COBRA, individuals may keep their coverage, as well as coverage for their spouses and dependents, for up to 18 months after their employment ceases. Certain qualifying events can extend this coverage for up to 36 months. The individual, however, must pay for this health insurance.

The Health Insurance Portability and Accountability Act of 1996 provided new protections for approximately 25 million Americans who move from one job to another, who are self-employed, or who have preexisting medical conditions. The law focuses on limiting exclusions for preexisting medical conditions, prohibiting discrimination against employees and dependents based on their health

**Utilization review**
A process that scrutinizes medical diagnoses, hospitalization, surgery, and other medical treatment and care prescribed by doctors.

status, guaranteeing availability of health insurance to small employers, and guaranteeing renewability of insurance to all employers regardless of size.[15] Among the provisions of the act, employers with 50 or fewer employees and self-employed individuals can establish tax-favored *medical savings accounts (MSAs)*. This portion of the act is limited to a four-year demonstration period.[16]

**Dental and Vision Care.** Dental and vision care are popular benefits in the health care area. The *2000 SHRM Benefits Survey* indicated that 96 percent of the respondents' firms provide dental insurance and 62 percent furnish vision insurance.[17] Both types of plans are typically paid for entirely by the employer except for a deductible, which may amount to $50 or more per year. Dental plans may cover, for example, 70 to 100 percent of the cost of preventive procedures (including semiannual examinations) and 50 to 80 percent of restorative procedures (including crowns, bridgework, etc.). Some plans also include orthodontic care. Vision care plans may cover all or part of the cost of eye examinations and glasses. Other company programs that provide health benefits for employees include employee assistance programs (EAPs), wellness programs, and physical fitness programs. These topics are discussed in the next chapter.

## Security Benefits

Security benefits include retirement plans, disability protection, supplemental unemployment benefits, and life insurance. These important benefits are discussed next.

**Retirement Plans.** Retirement is currently a hot topic because the baby boomer generation is nearing retirement. This huge segment of our population is starting to take retirement seriously not only because of their age but also because of the long bull stock market and a strained Social Security system. Employers are right in the middle of this challenge, since they are one of our society's primary providers of retirement income.[18]

Retirement plans are generally either defined benefit plans or defined contribution plans. In a **defined benefit plan**, the employer agrees to provide a specific level of retirement income that is either a fixed dollar amount or a percentage of earnings. An employee's seniority or rank in the firm may determine the precise figure. Plans that are considered generous typically provide pensions equivalent to 50 to 80 percent of an employee's final earnings. Use of this type of retirement plan is declining. However, 47 percent of firms responding to a recent survey indicated that a defined benefit retirement plan was still in use. Even so, the same survey reported that 72 percent of the companies utilized a newer approach—a defined contribution plan, which is discussed next.[19]

A **defined contribution plan** is a retirement plan that requires specific contributions by an employer to a retirement or savings fund established for the employee. While employees will know in advance how much their retirement income will be under a defined benefit plan, the amount of retirement income from a defined contribution plan will depend upon the investment success of the pension fund.

A **401(k) plan** is a defined contribution plan in which employees may defer income up to a maximum amount allowed. Employers typically match employee contributions 50 cents for each dollar deferred. As 401(k) plans become the primary retirement income design, sponsoring firms are making them more flexible by permitting more frequent transfers between investment accounts. They are also providing more investment choices for employees. According to a study conducted by the Profit Sharing/401(k) Council of America, three-fourths of participating

**Defined benefit plan**
A retirement plan in which an employer agrees to provide a specific level of retirement income that is either a fixed dollar amount or a percentage of earnings.

**Defined contribution plan**
A retirement plan that requires specific contributions by an employer to a retirement or savings fund established for the employee.

**401(k) plan**
A defined contribution retirement plan in which employees may defer income up to a certain maximum amount.

firms offered five or more options in 1995, up from 16 percent only five years earlier. As an indication of their acceptance by employees, almost 90 percent of those who are eligible to participate in 401(k) plans are doing so.[20]

More firms are starting to provide financial planning for all their employees, not just their top executives. The explosion of 401(k) retirement plans has required 23 million employees to become *investment managers,* and they often look to their employers for help. Federal law requires employers to give guidance on these plans but forbids their recommending specific investments. Of course, this is just what employees want and need. The employers' role is to get financial planners from firms such as Fidelity and Charles Schwab to provide this advice. Firms must also obtain means for defenses in potential lawsuits if workers lose money.[21] This protection is critically important because poor investment decisions could force individuals to delay retirement or require those already retired to rejoin the workforce.

A **cash contribution plan** is a hybrid retirement plan with elements of both defined benefit plans and defined contribution plans. It resembles a defined contribution plan in that it uses an account balance to communicate the benefit amount. However, it is actually a defined benefit plan because the employer normally funds it and maintains investment control. Contributions by the employer to each participant's account are normally made on an annual basis, and investment earnings are at a set amount. If the fund's investment earnings exceed this set amount, the plan sponsor benefits from the performance. If the trust fund does not perform well, the plan sponsor needs to make contributions to fund the shortfall.[22]

In designing an appropriate retirement system, some sources suggest that the terms *defined benefit* and *defined contribution* be ignored. Instead, the focus should be on a plan that meets specific objectives. In other words, a hybrid system may more effectively achieve the firm's compensation goals.[23]

Profit sharing—if the distribution of funds is deferred until retirement—is another form of defined contribution plan. It will also be discussed later in this chapter.

An **employee stock option plan (ESOP)** is a defined contribution plan in which a firm contributes stock shares to a trust. The trust then allocates the stock to participating employee accounts on the basis of employee earnings. Many of the benefits of profit-sharing plans have also been cited for ESOPs. Specifically, ESOP advocates have promoted employee ownership plans as a means to align the interests of workers and their companies to stimulate productivity. This practice, long reserved for executives, has in more recent years included employees working at lower levels in the firm.

While the potential benefits of ESOPs are attractive, some employees want the ability to sell their shares prior to retirement, which ESOPs do not allow. A lot of people simply do not want to take the chance that the stock is going to be valuable when they retire. Periods of wild rides in the stock market also dampen worker enthusiasm for ESOPs.[24] Although the potential advantages of ESOPs are impressive, the other side of the coin is the danger of having all your eggs in one basket.

Disability Protection. Workers' compensation protects employees from job-related accidents and illnesses. Some firms, however, provide additional protection that is more comprehensive. A firm's sick leave policy may provide full salary for short-term health problems; when these benefits expire, a short-term disability plan may become operative and provide pay equivalent to 50 to 100 percent of regular pay.[25] Short-term disability plans may cover periods up to six months.

**Cash contribution plan**
A hybrid retirement plan with elements of both defined benefit plans and defined contribution plans.

**Employee stock option plan (ESOP)**
A defined contribution plan in which a firm contributes stock shares to a trust.

When the short-term plan runs out, a firm's long-term plan may become active; such a plan may provide 50 to 70 percent of an employee's wages.[26] Only about 35 percent of American businesses are estimated to provide long-term disability insurance, and the plans that exist pay for periods from two years to the life of the employee.[27]

**Supplemental Unemployment Benefits (SUB).** Supplemental unemployment benefits first appeared in auto industry labor agreements in 1955. They are designed to provide additional income for employees receiving unemployment insurance benefits. These plans have spread to many industries and are usually financed by the company. They tend to benefit newer employees since layoffs are normally determined by seniority. For this reason, employees with considerable seniority are often not enthusiastic about these benefits.

**Life Insurance.** Group life insurance is a benefit commonly provided to protect the employee's family in the event of his or her death.[28] Although the cost of group life insurance is relatively low, some plans call for the employee to pay part of the premium. Coverage may be a flat amount (for instance, $50,000) or based on the employee's annual earnings. For example, a worker earning $30,000 per year may have $60,000 worth of group life coverage.

## Employee Services

Organizations offer a variety of benefits that can be termed *employee services*. These benefits encompass a number of areas including relocation benefits, child care, educational assistance, food services/subsidized cafeterias, and financial services.

**Relocation.** **Relocation benefits** include shipment of household goods and temporary living expenses that cover all or a portion of the real estate costs associated with buying a new home and selling the previously occupied home. Seventy-nine percent of firms with over 5,000 employees provide some *relocation benefits,* according to an SHRM benefits survey. Sixty percent of all respondents to the survey provide relocation benefits, and 19 percent provide spousal relocation assistance.[29]

While a transfer used to be viewed as a step up, employees are now taking a closer look at not only the economic impact of the move, but also what it does to quality of life. This concern has broadened the scope of relocation services to include providing information about crime statistics, kids' sports teams, tutors, churches, and doctors.[30] Relocation can be as stressful for employees as a death in the family, divorce, or loss of a job. Not only are job-related factors considered, but also the disruption of the familiar patterns of daily life, such as commuting, cultural and recreational opportunities, and school and church affiliations. A 1998 Atlas Van Lines survey found family ties were the main reason for rejecting a move for about 75 percent of respondents. The spouse's employment was the second most prominent reason, given by about 55 percent of the respondents.[31]

> **Relocation benefits** Company-paid shipment of household goods and temporary living expenses, covering all or a portion of the real estate costs associated with buying a new home and selling the previously occupied home.

**Child Care.** Another benefit offered by some firms is subsidized *child care.* Here, the firm may provide an on-site child care center, support an off-site center, or subsidize the costs of child care. Twelve percent of respondents to an SHRM survey indicated that they follow one of these alternative approaches to child care.[32] This benefit is an effective recruitment aid and helps to reduce absenteeism. The need for such programs is emphasized by the facts that about 70 percent of working parents missed at least one day in the past year because of child-related problems, and U.S. businesses lose $3 billion a year because of child-care-related absences.[33]

**Educational Assistance.** According to a recent benefits survey, 81 percent of firms have *educational benefits* that reimburse employees for college tuition and books.[34] NYNEX, the $13 billion telecommunications company, has a plan that is hard to top. The firm pays employees to attend college one workday a week with a guaranteed raise upon graduation. In addition to springing for tuition and books, NYNEX gives each participant a laptop computer. This program provides employees with enhanced telecommunications and communications skills that will provide them with job security. The firm believes its investment will strengthen its workforce and provide a bottom-line payoff.[35]

**Food Services/Subsidized Cafeterias.** There is generally no such thing as a free lunch. However, firms that provide *food services* or *subsidized cafeterias* provide an exception to this rule. What they hope to gain in return is increased productivity, less wasted time, enhanced employee morale, and—in some instances—a healthier workforce. Most firms that offer free or subsidized lunches feel that they get a high payback in terms of employee relations. Hewitt Associates, Northwestern Mutual Life, and Alliance Capital Management Corporation are among the firms that provide this benefit. Keeping the lunch hour to a minimum is an obvious advantage, but employees also appreciate the opportunity to meet and mix with people they work with. Making one entree a heart-healthy choice and listing the calories, fat, cholesterol, and sodium content in food is also appealing to a large number of employees. Healthy meals may also result in a payoff. At Alliance, for example, lunch costs $5 to $6 per employee per day. However, the firm has seen about a 20 percent reduction in medical claims and its insurance premiums have not increased since it began the subsidized lunch program.[36]

**Financial Services.** Some firms offer various types of financial services. One *financial benefit* that is growing in popularity permits employees to purchase different types of insurance policies through payroll deduction. Using this approach, the employer can offer a benefit at almost no cost and employees can save money by receiving a deeply discounted rate. Firms can offer discounts to employers because the plans usually eliminate the middlemen. Administrative costs are also drastically reduced. For example, the insurance company sends one statement to the business and receives one premium check. Otherwise, dozens or even hundreds of individual transactions might be involved. It is also possible for employers to offer employees discounted policies on automobile or homeowner's insurance. In fact, many other benefits may be offered through payroll deduction plans.

**Unique Benefits.** A tight labor market gives birth to creativity in providing benefits. Victoria's Secret offers gift certificates and discounts to its employees, and the Men's Warehouse literally dresses its employees. These firms are merely reacting to an era where recruitment and retention are difficult. Some firms in the high-tech industry go even further. For example, a computer systems and software company allows all 55 of its employees from the receptionist to top managers free use of leased BMWs. Another firm covers lawn care costs, dry cleaning, and pet care.[37]

## Premium Pay

**Premium pay** is compensation paid to employees for working long periods of time or working under dangerous or undesirable conditions. As we mentioned in Chapter 11, payment for overtime is required for nonexempt employees who work more than 40 hours in a given week. However, some firms pay overtime for hours worked beyond eight in a given day and pay double time, or even more, for

**Premium pay**
Compensation paid to employees for working long periods of time or working under dangerous or undesirable conditions.

work on Sundays and holidays. Bonuses are also sometimes given for performing at a level above an established norm.

**Hazard Pay.** Additional pay provided to employees who work under extremely dangerous conditions is called **hazard pay**. A window washer for skyscrapers in New York City might well be given extra compensation because of dangerous working conditions. Military pilots receive extra money in the form of flight pay because of the risks involved in the job.

**Shift Differentials.** A **shift differential** is paid to employees for the inconvenience of working less desirable hours. This type of pay may be provided on the basis of additional cents per hour. For example, employees who work the second shift *(swing shift)*, from 4:00 P.M. until midnight, might receive $0.75 per hour above the base rate for that job. The third shift *(graveyard shift)* often warrants an even greater differential; for example, an extra $0.90 per hour may be paid for the same job. Shift differentials are sometimes based on a percentage of the employee's base rate.

**Hazard pay**
Additional pay provided to employees who work under extremely dangerous conditions.

**Shift differential**
Additional money paid to reward employees for the inconvenience of working undesirable hours.

## Benefits for Part-Time Employees[38]

Part-time employees currently comprise 13.6 percent of the workforce, or about 19 million people. Recent studies indicate that employers are offering this group more benefits than ever. Growth in the number of part timers is due to the aging of the workforce and also to an increased desire by more employees to balance their lives between work and home.

According to studies conducted by Hewitt and RewardsPlus, a majority of employers provide some benefits to their part-time workers. Both studies found that more than 80 percent of employers provide vacation, holiday, and sick leave benefits and that more than 70 percent offered some form of health care benefits. Most employers who provide benefits to their part-time employees prorate them. Smaller firms often lack the resources to provide a wide selection of benefits even to their full-time employees.

## OTHER BENEFIT-RELATED LEGISLATION

The Employee Retirement Income Security Act of 1974 (ERISA) was passed to strengthen existing and future retirement programs. Mismanagement of retirement funds was the primary spur for this legislation. Many employees were entering retirement only to find that the retirement income they had counted on was not available. The act's intent was to ensure that when employees retire, they receive deserved pensions. The purpose of the act is described here:

> It is hereby declared to be the policy of this Act to protect . . . the interests of participants in employee benefit plans and their beneficiaries . . . by establishing standards of conduct, responsibility and obligations for fiduciaries of employee benefit plans, and by providing for appropriate remedies, sanctions, and ready access to the federal courts.[39]

Note that the word *protect* is used here because the act does not force employers to create employee benefit plans. It does set standards in the areas of participation, vesting of benefits, and funding for existing and new plans. Numerous existing retirement plans have been altered in order to conform to this legislation.

The Older Workers Benefit Protection Act (OWBPA) is a 1990 amendment to the Age Discrimination in Employment Act and extends its coverage to all employee benefits. Employers must offer benefits to older workers that are equal to or greater than the benefits given to younger workers, with one exception. The act does not require employers to provide equal or greater benefits to older workers when the cost to do so is greater than for younger workers.[40]

## COMMUNICATING INFORMATION ABOUT THE BENEFITS PACKAGE

Employee benefits can help a firm recruit and retain a top-quality workforce. In keeping the program current, management depends on an upward flow of information from employees to determine when benefit changes are needed. In addition, because employee awareness of benefits is often limited, the program information must be communicated downward.

The Employee Retirement Income Security Act provides still another reason for communicating information about a firm's benefits program. This act requires organizations with a pension or profit-sharing plan to provide employees with specific data at specified times. The act further mandates that the information be presented in an understandable manner. With the advent of the Internet and individual intranets, many firms will have little difficulty in achieving the desired communication with employees about anything, including their benefits.

A vast majority of organizations go far beyond what is legally required in benefits. In fact, there seems to be no end to the types of benefits firms offer. This trend accelerates during periods of tight employment as firms develop strategies designed to attract and retain high-quality employees. A corporation that is in tune with the needs of its workers might provide a broad range of employee benefits such as those shown in Figure 12-2.

## INCENTIVE COMPENSATION

**Incentive compensation**
A payment program that relates pay to productivity.

To survive and prosper in a global economy, firms have paid increased attention to productivity and how to improve it. Although compensation is often determined by how much time an employee spends at work, compensation programs that relate pay to productivity are referred to as **incentive compensation**. The basic purpose of all incentive plans is to improve employee productivity in order to gain a competitive advantage. To do this, the firm must utilize various rewards and focus on the needs of employees as well as the firm's business goals.

Productive workers such as Arnold Anderson and Bob Minnis (mentioned at the beginning of the chapter) probably would prefer to be paid on the basis of their output. In fact, they may not maintain their high performance level for long if they are not paid in this way. Money can serve as an important motivator for those who value it; and many of us do. However, employees must see a clear relationship between performance and pay if money is to serve as an effective motivator. Firms may have incentive pay plans that focus on either individuals or teams. Some plans are even companywide. These three approaches are discussed in the sections that follow.

### Individual Incentive Plans

**Piecework**
An incentive pay plan in which employees are paid for each unit produced.

Pay for performance was generally discussed in the preceding chapter. A specific form of performance-based pay is an individual incentive plan called **piecework**. Through the years, many forms of incentive pay plans have been used. However, the piecework plan is the most simple and most commonly used, especially in production/operations. In such a plan, employees are paid for each unit they produce.

**Personal Benefits:**
> *Medical Plans:* Two options as well as various HMOs are available.
> *Dental Plans:* Two options as well as various Dental Maintenance Alternatives (DMAs) and the MetLife Preferred Dentist Program (PDP) are available.

**Work and Personal Life Balancing:**
> *Vacation:* 1 to 4 years service—10 days per year
> 5 to 9 years service (or age 50–59)—15 days
> 10 to 19 years service or age 60 and over—20 days
> 20 years or more—25 days
> *Holidays:* 12 days per year (6 observed nationally; other 6 vary with at least one personal choice).
> *Life Planning Account:* $250 of taxable financial assistance each year, with certain conditions.
> *Flexible Work Schedules, Telecommuting, and Workweek Balancing:* (with local management approval).

**Capital Accumulation, Stock Purchase, and Retirement:**
> *401(K) Plan:* Employees may contribute up to 12 percent of eligible compensation, which is matched 50 percent on the first 6 percent.
> *Stock Purchase Plan:* Employees may contribute up to 10 percent of eligible compensation each pay period for the purchase of company stock (pay 85 percent of average market price per share on date of purchase).
> *Retirement Plan:* Competitive, company-paid retirement benefit plan with vesting after 5 years of continuous service.

**Income and Asset Protection:** Some of the plans offered include:
> *Sickness and Accident Income Plans*
> *Long-Term Disability Plan*
> *Group Life Insurance*
> *Travel Accident Insurance*
> *Long-Term Care Insurance*

**Skills Development:**
> *Tuition Refund:* If aligned with business needs and approved.
> *Educational Leaves of Absence:* Under appropriate circumstance and approved by management.

**Additional Employee Programs:**
> *Site Offerings:* Many sites offer programs including
> > *Fitness Centers*
> > *Educational Courses*
> > *Award Programs*
> > *Career Planning Centers*
> *Clubs:* These clubs organize recreational leagues, company-sponsored trips, and a variety of classes and programs.

---

**An Example of a Corporation's Benefit Program**    **Figure 12-2**

Requirements for the plan include developing output standards for the job and being able to measure the output of a single employee. A piecework plan would not be feasible for many jobs.

A basic question that should precede the introduction of any incentive plan is this: "What effect will it have on productivity and quality?" Although success cannot be guaranteed, results are often positive, as indicated by the following account.

Safelite Glass Corporation, the nation's largest installer of automobile glass, implemented a system for determining the exact rate of installations done by each worker as well as a piecework system that would allow a productivity bonus on top of the guaranteed hourly pay rate. The workers performed individual tasks that could be counted and rewarded, and the firm had hard numbers of the output both before and after the new system went into effect. The results of the piecework system were as follows:

- Productivity jumped 36 percent.
- The average worker's pay increased from $25,000 a year to $27,000, but very able workers had the potential to make $40,000.
- Absenteeism dropped, and paid sick hours fell by 61 percent.
- Turnover among the most efficient workers decreased.
- While pay for the average worker rose by 10 percent, productivity rose by 20 percent.
- Customer satisfaction increased from a 90 percent to a 95 percent rate.[41]

Safelite's production operation lends itself almost perfectly to a piecework plan. Obviously, many other jobs do not. However, Safelite's experience does give credibility to the notion that financial incentives have the potential to motivate performance in a positive way.

## Team-Based Compensation Plans

Team performance consists of individual efforts. Therefore, individual employees should be recognized and rewarded for their contributions. However, if the team is to function effectively, a reward based on the overall team performance should be provided as well.

Nucor, a high-performing steel company, divides its production workers into work groups of 25 to 35 people and pays work group members a bonus based on their group's production over a certain predetermined standard. If they produce 50 percent above the standard, they receive a 50 percent bonus; if they produce 100 percent above the standard, they receive a 100 percent bonus. During the past decade, Nucor's sales grew 850 percent and its profits grew 1,250 percent. While most of the U.S. steel industry laid off workers, Nucor laid off none.[42]

Team incentives have both advantages and disadvantages. On the positive side, firms find it easier to develop performance standards for groups than for individuals. For one thing, there are fewer standards to determine. Also, the output of a team is more likely to reflect a complete product or service. Another advantage is that employees may be more inclined to assist others and work collaboratively if the reward is based on the team's output.

A potential disadvantage for team incentives relates to exemplary performers. If individuals in this category consistently do more than others in the group, they may become disgruntled and leave. A solution to this situation might be to base part of the employees' compensation on individual performance and part on the overall team results. Aid Association for Lutherans (AAL), a fraternal benefits society, tries to cover all bases in compensating its insurance service teams. Its plan allows the firm to accomplish the following:[43]

- *Recognize individual accomplishments.* Outstanding individual achievement is recognized through a lump sum payment once a year. It may be worth as much as 6 percent of the individual's compensation.
- *Reward team productivity.* The entire team is awarded an annual bonus based on productivity, customer satisfaction, and quality of work.
- *Compensate employees for the acquisition of new skills.* A skill-based pay system compensates individuals for each additional skill they acquire in an effort to help the team.
- *Remain competitive with its salary structure.* The company uses market data to ensure that employees are paid a competitive wage.

Before implementing the team structure, AAL was organized on a functional basis, according to type of product. The rationale for moving to teams was the desire to have employees see the whole job, not just a part of it. The company also wanted its employees to learn additional jobs that would help the team as a whole and to boost overall performance. Does this plan work? After five years, productivity has increased by 40 percent, and surveys indicate that 90 percent of the firm's customers are satisfied with the service provided.

Hallmark Cards put team members' pay at risk by cutting base pay between 5 and 10 percent but also provided opportunities to earn *more* than base pay if the team met its targets. Hallmark integrated fixed and variable components into its existing pay structure to assure the plan's effectiveness and encourage employees' acceptance. Today, the system applies to numerous teams, many of which concentrate on specific retail market segments—anywhere a customer might buy a card or gift. These teams consist of more than just salespeople; they include people from finance, information systems, and administration.[44]

Unisys has made dramatic changes in the way people work. Today, there are more than 140 people organized into 10 teams at the firm's Bismarck, North Dakota, office. These teams handle various accounting functions, such as the firm's accounts payable and employees' business travel reimbursements. Each team takes care of an entire process, from opening mail to issuing checks, and seeks solutions internally to any problems it encounters. And while every individual gets a wage base, people also get paid for the performance of the team.[45]

## Companywide Plans

In baseball, an outstanding pitcher or a great outfield is not the standard by which a team is judged. The standard is the team's overall win-loss record. The criterion for success focuses on overall team performance, not the batting average of a star outfielder. In business, companywide plans offer a feasible alternative to the incentive plans previously discussed. Companywide plans may be based on the organization's productivity, cost savings, or profitability. To illustrate the concept of companywide plans, we discuss profit sharing and a gain-sharing plan known as the Scanlon Plan.

Profit Sharing. **Profit sharing** is a compensation plan that results in the distribution of a predetermined percentage of the firm's profits to employees. Many firms use this type of plan to integrate the employees' interests with those of the company—a goal also sought through the use of ESOPs, another companywide plan previously discussed. Profit-sharing plans can aid in recruiting, motivating, and retaining employees, which usually enhances productivity.

**Profit sharing**
A compensation plan that distributes a predetermined percentage of a firm's profits to its employees.

There are several variations of profit-sharing plans, but two basic kinds of plans are widely used today: current profit sharing and deferred profit sharing.[46]

- *Current plans* provide payment to employees in cash or stock as soon as profits have been determined.
- *Deferred plans* involve placing company contributions in an irrevocable trust to be credited to the account of individual employees. The funds are normally invested in securities and become available to the employee (or his or her survivors) at retirement, termination, or death.

These two plans are not mutually exclusive. *Combination plans* permit employees to receive payment of part of their share of profits on a current basis, while payment of part of their share is deferred.

Normally, most full-time employees are included in a company's profit-sharing plan after a specified waiting period. Vesting determines the amount of profit an employee actually owns in his or her account and is often established on a graduated basis. For example, an employee may become 25 percent vested after being in the plan for two years; 50 percent vested after three years; 75 percent vested after four years; and 100 percent vested after five years. This gradual approach to vesting may tend to reduce turnover by encouraging employees to remain with the company.

Profit sharing is another compensation plan that tends to tie employees to the economic success of the firm. Reported results include increased efficiency and lower costs. In recent years, however, the increased popularity of employee thrift plans has slowed the growth of profit-sharing plans. Also, variations in profits may present a special problem. When employees have become accustomed to receiving added compensation from profit sharing and then there is no profit to share, they may become disgruntled.

Problems with a profit-sharing plan stem from the recipients' seldom knowing precisely how they helped generate the profits, beyond just doing their jobs. If employees continue to receive a payment, they will come to expect it and depend on it. If they do not know what they have done to deserve it, they may view it as an entitlement program. The results may be just the opposite of what is desired. The intended *ownership attitude* may not materialize.

Gain Sharing. **Gain sharing** plans are designed to bind employees to the firm's performance by providing an incentive payment based on improved company performance. Improved performance can take the form of increased productivity, increased customer satisfaction, lower costs, or better safety records.[47] Gain sharing plans (also known as *productivity incentives, team incentives,* and *performance-sharing incentives*) generally refer to incentive plans that involve many or all employees in a common effort to achieve a firm's performance objectives.

Joseph Scanlon developed the first gain-sharing plan during the Great Depression, and it continues to be a successful approach to group incentive, especially in smaller firms. The **Scanlon plan** provides a financial reward to employees for savings in labor costs that result from their suggestions. Employee-management committees evaluate these suggestions. Savings are calculated as a ratio of payroll costs to the sales value of what that payroll produces. If the company is able to reduce payroll costs through increased operating efficiency, it shares the savings with its employees.

The Scanlon plan embodies employee participation, management-labor cooperation, collaborative problem solving, teamwork, trust, gain sharing, open-book management, and servant leadership. The four basic principles emphasized are the following:[48]

1. *Identity.* To focus on employee involvement, the firm's mission or purpose must be clearly articulated.
2. *Competence.* The plan requires the highest standards of work behavior and a continual commitment to excellence.
3. *Participation.* The plan provides a mechanism for using the ideas of knowledgeable employees and translating these into productivity improvements.
4. *Equity.* Equity is achieved when three primary stakeholders—employees, customers, and investors—share financially in the productivity increases resulting from the program.

Such firms as Herman Miller, Ameritech, Martin Marietta, Donnelly Mirrors, Motorola, and Boston's Beth Israel Hospital are realizing benefits from the Scanlon plan. They have created formal participative means for soliciting suggestions and are sharing the revenue resulting from increases in productivity.

Gain-sharing studies indicate that firms using these plans increase their productivity from 10 to 12 percent a year.[49]

## NONFINANCIAL COMPENSATION

Historically, compensation departments in organizations have not dealt with nonfinancial factors. However, as indicated in the previous chapter, the new model of WorldatWork indicates that this is changing. One thing is clear: Nonfinancial compensation can be a very powerful factor in the compensation equation. Consider this situation:

> The workplace atmosphere is highly invigorating. Roy, Ann, Jack, Sandra, Walton, and Patsy are excited as they try to keep up with double-digit growth in sales orders. They do whatever it takes to get the job done, wearing multiple hats that would be difficult to cover in a job description. Their jobs have no salary grades, and their performance is never formally reviewed. This doesn't worry them, however, because they enjoy the camaraderie and teamwork at their firm. They have complete trust in the firm's highly visible management, and they have total confidence their

### ▶ *The Same Old Debits and Credits*

**HRM IN
ACTION**

Linda Nelson, the accounts receivable clerk for Delta Services, had finally made up her mind to quit. She had been with Delta for six years and knew that she was doing a good job. But, to Linda, the work was boring. There was never anything new to do. It was the same old debits and credits five days a week, eight hours a day. She felt that a trained chimpanzee could do her work. Linda scheduled an appointment with her supervisor, Bruce Young, for 10:00 A.M. to tell him of her decision. As she knocked on Bruce's door, Linda was nervous but knew that she had made the right decision. Bruce cordially invited her in and asked what she needed. "Mr. Young, I feel that I must turn in my resignation," she said.

Bruce was shocked and quickly asked, "Aren't you being paid enough?" Linda nodded that she was. "We have the best fringe benefits anywhere in our industry. Why, you wouldn't be able to get three weeks' vacation until you had been with our competitor for ten years. We give it in five. Delta is known for trying to keep its employees happy. I just don't understand," Bruce said.

"The job is just so repetitive," Linda replied. "I just don't feel that I ever do anything new. I appreciate everything that Delta has done for me, but I just feel that it's in my best interest to find something that would be more challenging."

After Linda left, Bruce picked up the phone and called June Swann, the personnel manager. "June," Bruce said, "you had better start looking for another accounts receivable clerk. Just had another one quit. I don't understand why she's leaving, though. We give them so much."

*What aspect of compensation had Bruce neglected?*

leaders will do what's right for them and the company. Believe it or not, it is a real-life scene from a real-life company, and thousands of firms like it exist across the country.[50]

As discussed earlier, money—provided directly or indirectly—is far from being the sole factor in a firm's reward system. The components of nonfinancial compensation consist of the job and the total environment in which the job is performed. A number of work arrangements are included in this environment. They are designed to create a flexible workplace and a more desirable work life for employees.

## The Job as a Total Compensation Factor

Some jobs can be so exciting that the incumbent can hardly wait to get to work each day. At the evening meal, details of what happened on the job are shared with a spouse who, hopefully, has the same level of enthusiasm. A person in this type of job would not trade his or her employment with anyone in the world. Given the prospect of getting a generous raise by leaving this job, this worker quickly says no to the opportunity. Unwillingness to change jobs for additional money suggests that the job itself is indeed an important reward.

On the other hand, a job may be so boring or distasteful that an individual dreads going to work. This condition is very sad considering the time a person devotes to his or her job.

Most of us spend a large part of our lives, not on the beach, but working. When work is a drag, life may not be very pleasant and, as we discuss in Chapter 13, the stressed person involved may eventually become emotionally or physically ill.

The job itself is a central issue in many theories of motivation, and it is also a vital component of a total compensation program. Job characteristic theory goes a long way in explaining the importance of the job itself in determining compensation. According to job characteristic theory, employees experience intrinsic compensation when their jobs rate high on the five core job dimensions of skill variety, task identity, task significance, autonomy, and feedback. These characteristics create the potential for increased performance, lower absenteeism and turnover, and higher employee satisfaction.[51]

### Skill Variety

**Skill variety**
The extent to which work requires a number of different activities for successful completion.

The extent to which work requires a number of different activities for successful completion is called **skill variety**. This factor is similar to the concept of job enlargement previously discussed in Chapter 4. Some workers enjoy variety in their jobs, and if so, it serves as compensation. One only has to visualize work on an assembly line where an individual is more like a machine to realize the importance of skill variety. Expanding the number of job activities is quite important to some workers. Therefore, skill variety must be considered a compensation factor for some people.

### Task Identity

**Task identity**
The extent to which the job includes an identifiable unit of work that is carried out from start to finish.

**Task identity** is the extent to which the job includes an identifiable unit of work that is carried out from start to finish. As a product rolls off the assembly line, the worker might say, "I made that widget." Some individuals enjoy the added responsibility provided by a project that permits involvement to its completion. For example, an author who, upon publication of a new book, reads it over and over knowing that those words came out of her thoughts alone provides an example of task identity. No one else can claim responsibility for the content of the book. Task identity is similar to job enrichment, also discussed in Chapter 4.

## Task Significance

The impact that the job has on other people is referred to as **task significance**. A manager who enjoys helping other people and seeing them grow and develop provides an example. When a job has impact on others, employees often realize a sense of achievement. Jim Stahl, director of wellness for a regional university, designed hundreds of exercise and diet regimens for clients. When these clients would later achieve their personal goals such as weight loss or a reduction in cholesterol level, they would be grateful and Jim would have the feeling of performing important work. His success in changing lifestyles for the better emphasized that his job was truly significant.

**Task significance**
The impact that the job has on other people.

## Autonomy

**Autonomy** is the extent of individual freedom and discretion employees have in performing their jobs. Jobs that provide autonomy often lead employees to feel responsible for outcomes of work. Most workers do not want someone standing over their shoulders all day long just waiting for them to make the slightest error. These individuals know what needs to be done and want the freedom to get the job done their way. Autonomy is at the very heart of self-directed work teams. Some of these groups have been given the authority to make decisions such as who to hire, who to promote, work schedules, and methods to follow. This freedom of action creates a sense of responsibility that probably cannot be achieved in any other manner.

**Autonomy**
The extent of individual freedom and discretion employees have in performing their jobs.

## Feedback

**Feedback** is the amount of information employees receive about how well they have performed the job. For some, it is exhilarating to hear the boss or a respected co-worker say, "You did an excellent job." In fact, most people have a strong need to know how they are doing in their jobs. Top salespersons, for example, want and obtain rapid feedback from securing a sale. When a sale is made, they get their reward in the form of a commission check.

**Feedback**
The amount of information employees receive about how well they have performed the job.

These five tasks are vitally important in considering compensation regarding the job. It is without question an important component of compensation. The job as a component of compensation is important whether performed by regular employees, temps, part timers, consultants, contract workers, or teams. As long as employees are required by organizations, a major management objective will be to match job requirements with employee abilities and aspirations. There is no question that as the scope of many jobs expands and they become more complex, this challenge will also increase in difficulty.

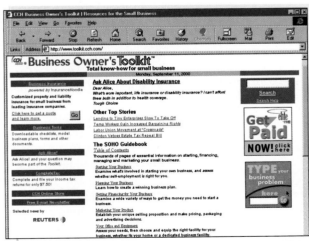

www.toolkit.cch.com
*Source:* Reproduced with permission from CCH Business Owner's Toolkit™ published and copyrighted by CCH Incorporated.

## Cyberwork

Technology has created an assortment of possibilities that will be rewarding for some individuals, but not for others. Development of the Internet has had significant implications for the job. For example, cyberspace engineers are intent on giving users anywhere, anytime access to the Internet. The wireless industry, whose market has already surpassed that of personal computers, has created the potential for **cyberwork**—the possibility of a never-ending workday created through the use of technology. Cell phones and the Internet have stretched work at both ends. What will employees scattered across the globe do when their managers need information from them at an inconvenient hour—wait until 8:00 A.M. their time? Obviously, this would be an option. Individuals could turn off their smart phones, notebooks, or pocket devices to prevent such inconvenient intrusions. However, many people who want to advance will not make this decision simply because they are competing with others for promotions and bonuses; these individuals will choose to be available when needed.[52] Basically, some employees will jump at the chance to be maximally involved, while others will place greater value on their privacy and off-duty time.

**Cyberwork**
The possibility of a never-ending workday created through the use of technology.

# THE JOB ENVIRONMENT AS A TOTAL COMPENSATION FACTOR

Performing a challenging, responsible job in a pigsty would not be rewarding to most people. The job environment must also be satisfactory. Employees can draw satisfaction from their work through several nonfinancial factors such as sound policies, competent employees, congenial co-workers, appropriate status symbols, and pleasant working conditions.

## Sound Policies

Human resource policies and practices reflecting management's concern for its employees can serve as positive rewards. If a firm's policies show consideration rather than disrespect, fear, doubt, or lack of confidence, the result can be rewarding to both the employees and the organization. Policies that are arbitrary and too restrictive can really turn people off.

To assist in meeting the challenges of attracting and retaining the right employees in today's tight labor market, some firms have articulated the goal of *having fun* in their mission or value statements. A new survey by William M. Mercer Inc. shows:[53]

- Eight percent of employers surveyed include the goal of incorporating humor into the work environment.
- Among firms without a formal statement, 29 percent say fun is encouraged as part of the work culture.
- Sixty-two percent of the surveyed firms believe encouraging fun or humor in communications or management style benefits employees and the firm as a whole. Of these, 55 percent say fun and humor reduce workplace stress.

## Competent Employees

Successful organizations emphasize continuous development and assure that competent managers and nonmanagers are employed. Today's competitive environment and the requirement for teamwork will not permit otherwise. "Bad apples," as described by Libby Sartain, vice president of human resources for Southwest Airlines, can disrupt any organization.

## Congenial Co-Workers

Although a few individuals in this world may be quite self-sufficient and prefer to be left alone, they will become lonely indeed in the team-oriented organizations that exist today. The American culture has historically embraced individualism, yet most people possess, in varying degrees, a desire to be accepted by their work group. It is very important that management develop and maintain compatible work groups.

## Appropriate Status Symbols

**Status symbols** are organizational rewards that take many forms such as office size and location, desk size and quality, private secretaries, floor covering, and title. Some firms make liberal use of these types of rewards; others tend to minimize them. This latter approach reflects a concern about the adverse effect they may have on creating and maintaining a team spirit among members at various levels in the firm. This is true within many workplaces, where the corner office and private washroom have given way to more democratic arrangements. For example, Andy Grove, former CEO of Intel Corporation, occupied a cubicle inside the company's headquarters because he did not care for the *mahogany row* syndrome.[54]

**Status symbols**
Organizational rewards that take many forms such as office size and location, desk size and quality, private secretaries, floor covering, and title.

## Working Conditions

The definition of *working conditions* has been broadened considerably during the past decade. At one time, a reasonably safe and healthy workplace that was air conditioned was deemed satisfactory. Today, numerous additional factors are considered essential by many organizations; these are often included under the heading of *workplace flexibility*. American and European human resource executives, responding to a Towers Perrin survey, overwhelmingly included *work environment* as a key element in a total rewards system (along with pay, benefits, and learning and development opportunities).[55] A flexible workplace featuring such practices as flextime and telecommuting definitely enhances the nonfinancial compensation package. These topics are discussed in the following section.

## WORKPLACE FLEXIBILITY

Flexible work arrangements do more than just help new mothers return to full-time work. They comprise an aspect of nonfinancial compensation that allows families to manage a stressful work/home-juggling act. As labor markets become tighter, it will be important—if not crucial for survival—for firms to find and sustain a balance between quality of life for employees and organizational goals.[56]

For employers, workplace flexibility can be a key strategic factor in attracting and retaining the most talented employees. And, there is a strong statistical correlation between employee satisfaction and increased company profits, according to a nationwide survey of U.S. workers released by the Gallup Organization and Carlson Marketing Group. This survey indicates that nearly seven out of ten employees say nonmonetary forms of recognition provide the best motivation.[57]

In an attempt to meet working parents' needs, firms such as Johnson & Johnson, Eli Lilly and Company, InfoMart, and Texas Instruments are offering benefits heretofore unheard of. Examples include paid time off when children are home sick, paid time off when parents volunteer at a child's school, a referral and resource service that offers parenting advice 24 hours a day, college counseling for children, summer camps for older children who are too old for day care, and Parents' Night Out programs.[58]

Eli Lilly contracted with the YMCA in developing a camp for children ages 5 to 12. While the camp is located on the firm's premises, it is operated by the YMCA. In addition to providing swimming and games, the program also emphasizes science. While the company pays for program development, equipment, and grounds maintenance, parents pay $75 a week to the YMCA, a fee below market rates.[59]

Benefits claimed for these innovative programs include increased productivity, improved recruitment and retention of employees, and enhanced company image. Other programs that provide workplace flexibility are discussed in the following sections. These include flextime, a compressed workweek, job sharing, flexible compensation, telecommuting, part-time work, and modified retirement.

## Flextime

**Flextime**

The practice of permitting employees to choose their own working hours, within certain limitations.

**Flextime** is the practice of permitting employees to choose their own working hours, within certain limitations. For many *old economy* managers who think they must see their employees every minute to make sure they are working, this may be hard to stomach. However, over half of the firms responding to the 2000 SHRM Benefits Survey indicated that they used flextime.[60] And, the Bureau of Labor Statistics estimates that the percentage of workers on a flexible schedule nearly doubled within the past six years.[61]

In a flextime system, employees work the same number of hours per day as they would on a standard schedule. However, they are permitted to work these hours within what is called a *bandwidth,* which is the maximum length of the workday (see Figure 12-3). *Core time* is that part of the day when all employees must be present. *Flexible time* is the time period within which employees may vary their schedules. A typical schedule permits employees to begin work between 6:00 A.M. and 9:00 A.M. and to complete their workday between 3:00 P.M. and 6:00 P.M.

After conducting numerous focus groups and interviews with managers, Baxter International, a global medical products and services firm, confirmed the need to support workers' attempts to balance work and home. This intensive investigation resulted in a formalized process to help employees develop solutions for themselves by tinkering with their work arrangements. The program has been embraced to the point that nearly 20 percent of Baxter's employees take advantage of some form of alternative work schedule. This does not include the many managers who vary their work hours informally on an as-needed basis. Griffin Lewis, vice president of logistics, says that the program pays off in boosted morale, more effective recruiting, better stress management, and increased productivity.[62]

Flexible hours are highly valued in today's society. Therefore, a flexible work schedule gives employers an edge in recruiting new employees and retaining scarce qualified employees. In addition, organizations using flextime schedules have reported an average increase of 1 percent to 5 percent in productivity. The reasons for this increased productivity include the following:[63]

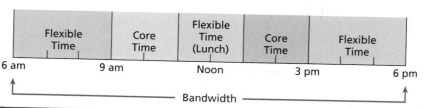

**Figure 12-3** **Illustration of Flextime**

- Short-term absences are reduced because of greater control over schedules.
- Tardiness is reduced since the workday begins when the employee arrives.
- Morning coffee breaks are reduced due to staggered hours.
- Employees are more likely to work during their most productive hours: mornings for early birds, evenings for night owls.
- Workers are more focused on doing the job as opposed to spending time in the office.
- Businesses can offer more flexible service to customers.
- Supervisors are forced to communicate more effectively since employees are not always in the office.

In addition to these benefits, employees are generally happy and grateful. They are better able to fit family, community, and social commitments into their schedules and they appreciate that. In addition, flextime allows employees to expand their opportunities. For example, continuing their education may be easier than with a traditional work schedule.

The public also seems to reap benefits from flextime. Transportation services, recreational facilities, medical clinics, and other services can be better utilized as a result of reduced competition for service at conventional peak times. Yet, flextime is not suitable for all types of organizations. For example, its use may be severely limited in assembly-line operations and companies utilizing multiple shifts.

In spite of limitations and potential hurdles, flextime is feasible in many situations, benefiting the employee, the employer, and the public. Clearly, flextime and other similar plans are compatible with the desire of employees (especially younger ones) to have greater control over their work situations.

## The Compressed Workweek

The **compressed workweek** is an arrangement of work hours that permits employees to fulfill their work obligation in fewer days than the typical five-day workweek. A common compressed workweek is four 10-hour days. Working under this arrangement, employees have reported greater job satisfaction. In addition, the compressed workweek offers the potential for better use of leisure time for family life, personal business, and recreation. Employers in some instances have cited advantages such as increased productivity and reduced turnover and absenteeism. In other firms, however, work scheduling and employee fatigue problems have been encountered. In some cases, these problems have resulted in lower product quality and reduced customer service. Nevertheless, it is apparent that a number of organizations feel the advantages of compressed workweeks outweigh the disadvantages. A study by William M. Mercer of 800 firms with 1,000 or more employees found that 34 percent use compressed workweeks for some part of their workforce and an additional 14 percent are considering this approach.[64]

**Compressed workweek**
Any arrangement of work hours that permits employees to fulfill their work obligation in fewer days than the typical five-day workweek.

## Job Sharing

Job sharing is an approach to work that is attractive to people who want to work fewer than 40 hours per week. In **job sharing**, two part-time people split the duties of one job in some agreed-on manner and are paid according to their contributions. A recent survey by SHRM revealed that 22 percent of the respondents offered job sharing.[65] Sharing jobs has potential benefits that include the broader range of skills the partners bring to the job. For job sharing to work, however, the partners must be compatible, have good communication skills, and have a bond of trust with their manager.

**Job sharing**
The filling of a job by two part-time people who split the duties of one full-time job in some agreed-on manner and are paid according to their contributions.

### ▶ A Work/Life Program You Won't Believe

Software giant SAS Institute Inc. has a culture that gives it a powerful competitive edge. The environment and benefits provided for employees are out of sight. To begin, the company's main campus offers day care as inexpensively as $250 per month, free access to a 36,000-square-foot gym, a putting green, sky-lit meditation rooms, and the services of a full-time in-house eldercare consultant. The café has a pianist at noon and baby seats so children in day care can lunch with their parents. Also available is all the free juice and soda that employees want. There are subsidized cafeterias, casual dress every day, profit sharing (which has been 15 percent every year for 23 years), domestic partner benefits, unlimited sick days, free health insurance, an on-site medical clinic staffed by doctors and nurse practitioners, and free laundering of sweaty gym clothes overnight. There are soccer fields, baseball diamonds, coed work-out areas, separate workout areas for men and women, and pool tables. Every white-collar employee has a private office and flexible work schedule, with a standard 35-hour workweek. All employees have three weeks' paid vacation plus the week off from Christmas to New Year's. After 10 years with the firm, employees get an additional week of paid vacation. As if this is not enough, SAS expects to add financial planning services to the lineup, and there is a process for adding still more benefits, including a test for whether a suggested benefit should be approved.

What does all this amount to? SAS has a turnover rate that is never more than 5 percent a year compared to the industry average of over 20 percent. *Harvard Business Review* recently figured that SAS's low turnover saves the company $75 million a year. SAS has been in the top 10 of *Fortune's* "100 Best Companies to Work For" three years running.[66]

---

Job sharing normally occurs below executive ranks. However, this is not always the case. Is it hard to believe, but Sandra Cavanah and Kathleen Layendecker share the job of vice president of affiliate development and market-ing for an Internet media company. The scenario becomes believable when you examine their résumés, which include—for Sandra—a Harvard M.B.A. and—for Kathleen—a degree from Yale's School of Management. These mothers of young children have their families as a first priority but also wanted to participate in today's exciting business world.

Initially skeptical about a high-level job share, their employer later stated, "I was wrong. I thought a job share would only work in a project-oriented setting. But, any job can function as a job share. It all depends on how well the two indi-viduals work together."

While each job sharer spends just three days in the office, those days are long—sometimes stretching to 12 hours. And, they also meet informally twice a week for one to three hours. From this experience, it appears that while a success-ful job share is difficult to pull off, especially at this level, it can be done. It requires professional soulmates, trusted individuals possessing about the same skills and work ethic. And—oh yes—as you may have guessed, the job sharers must be extremely well organized.[67]

## Flexible Compensation (Cafeteria Compensation)

**Flexible compensation plans**
A method that permits employees to choose from among many alternatives in deciding how their finan-cial compensation will be allocated.

**Flexible compensation plans** permit employees to choose from among many alternatives in deciding how their financial compensation will be allocated. Employees are given considerable latitude in determining, for example, how much they will take in the form of salary, life insurance, pension contributions, and other benefits. Cafeteria plans permit flexibility in allowing each employee to determine the compensation package that best satisfies his or her particular needs.

Twenty years ago or so firms offered a uniform package that generally reflected a *typical* employee. Today, the workforce has become considerably more heterogeneous, and this prototype is no longer representative. To accommodate such diversity, flexible compensation plans appear to provide a satisfactory solution. Recent studies suggest that flexible compensation programs are becoming increasingly popular among employers.

The rationale behind cafeteria plans is that employees have individual needs and preferences. A 60-year-old man would not need maternity benefits in an insurance plan. At the same time, a 25-year-old woman who regularly jogs three miles each day might not place a high value on a parking space near the firm's entrance. Some of the possible compensation vehicles utilized in a cafeteria approach are shown in Table 12-1.

Obviously, organizations cannot permit employees to select all their financial compensation vehicles. For one thing, benefits required by law must be provided. In addition, it is probably wise to require that each employee have core benefits, especially in areas such as retirement and medical insurance. Some guidelines would likely be helpful for most employees in the long run. However, the freedom to select highly desired benefits would seem to maximize the value of an individual's compensation. Employees' involvement in designing their own compensation plans should also effectively communicate to them the cost of their benefits.

The existing information regarding employee satisfaction with flexible compensation plans is limited. However, from the evidence available after flexible plans have been implemented, it appears that overall job satisfaction, pay satisfaction,

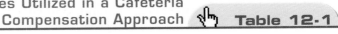

## Compensation Vehicles Utilized in a Cafeteria Compensation Approach    Table 12-1

| | |
|---|---|
| Accidental death, dismemberment insurance | Health maintenance organization fees |
| Birthdays (vacation) | Home health care |
| Bonus eligibility | Hospital-surgical-medical insurance |
| Business and professional membership | Incentive growth fund |
| Cash profit sharing | Interest-free loans |
| Club memberships | Long-term disability benefit |
| Commissions | Matching educational donations |
| Company medical assistance | Nurseries |
| Company-provided automobile | Nursing home care |
| Company-provided housing | Outside medical services |
| Company-provided or -subsidized travel | Personal accident insurance |
| Day care centers | Price discount plan |
| Deferred bonus | Recreation facilities |
| Deferred compensation plan | Resort facilities |
| Dental and eye care insurance | Sabbatical leaves |
| Discount on company products | Salary continuation |
| Education costs | Savings plan |
| Educational activities (time off) | Scholarships for dependents |
| Free checking account | Severance pay |
| Free or subsidized lunches | Sickness and accident insurance |
| Group automobile insurance | Stock appreciation rights |
| Group homeowners' insurance | Stock bonus plan |
| Group life insurance | Stock purchase plan |

and understanding of benefits have increased. These outcomes are desirable, as they often lead to reduced absenteeism and turnover.[68]

Development and administrative costs for flexible compensation plans exceed those for more traditional plans. For example, a firm with 10,000 employees might incur developmental costs of about $500,000.[69] Even though flexible compensation programs add to the organization's administrative burden, advantages seem to greatly outweigh shortcomings. Therefore, systems of this type will likely become more common in the future.

## Telecommuting

**Telecommuting**
A procedure allowing workers to remain at home (or otherwise away from the office) and perform their work over data lines tied to a computer.

**Telecommuting** is a work arrangement whereby employees, called *teleworkers* or *telecommuters,* are able to remain at home (or otherwise away from the office) and perform their work using computers and other electronic devices that connect them with their offices. Modern communications and data processing technologies permit people to work just about anywhere they want. The number of telecommuters has skyrocketed, growing from 4 million in 1990, to 8 million in 1995, to 11 million in 1997. By the year 2000, there were more than 14 million home-based workers.[70] In a survey of 300 North American senior executives, the William Olsten Center for Workforce Strategies found 51 percent of respondents allow telecommuting, either through pilot or ongoing programs.[71] Ford Motor Company and Delta Air Lines are currently providing employees with personal computers for home use, and this practice is expected to become common.[72]

Telecommuters generally are information workers. They accomplish jobs that require, for example, analysis, research, writing, budgeting, data entry, or computer programming. Teleworkers also include illustrators, loan executives, architects, attorneys, and desktop publishers.[73] Both training and job duties are carried out without loss of efficiency and quality by using a personal computer located away from the office and connected to a computer network. Advantages of telecommuting accrue to the company, the employee, and the community. These advantages are shown in Figure 12-4.

Another advantage of telecommuting is that it eliminates the need for office space. As one manager put it, "The expense of an employee is not just the person, it's also the fact that I pay $90,000 a year for the office that person sits in." Also, commuting distances are not a factor for teleworkers. Therefore, firms may hire

| For the Company | For the Employee | For the Community |
|---|---|---|
| Aids recruitment and retention | Provides work/life flexibility | Decreases traffic congestion |
| Broadens labor market (e.g., worker location not a factor; caters to employees with disabilities) | Reduces transportation and clothing costs | Conserves energy and reduces pollution |
| Reduces sick time and absenteeism | Reduces stress of travel | Relieves public transportation of "rush hour" problems |
| Improves job satisfaction and productivity | Caters to most productive hours for both "early birds" and "night owls" | Reduces peak-time congestion for many service organizations (e.g., retail and health care) |
| Saves costs for office space and utilities | | |

**Figure 12-4** **Advantages of Telecommuting**

the best available employees located virtually anywhere. The labor market is broadened through the increased ability to utilize disabled workers and workers with small children. The ability to expand the workforce globally, as mentioned in Chapter 11, has unlimited potential.

While telecommuting has many advantages, it also has some potential pitfalls. For example, ties between employees and their firms may be weakened, and successful programs will require a higher degree of trust between employees and their supervisors. And, while telecommuting does not involve additional pay, it is often viewed as a benefit because of the advantages of working at home. Therefore, diversity goals should be kept in mind. Firms should try to avoid the perception that telecommuting is a form of special treatment. This could easily arise when telecommuters in a work group are mostly of one race, gender, or ethnicity.[74]

Firms considering telecommuting will need to think about changes in other policy areas as well. Questions such as the following will need to be addressed:

- Will compensation and benefits be affected? If so, how?
- Who will be responsible for workers injured at home?
- What about the responsibility for purchasing and providing insurance coverage for equipment?
- How will taxes be affected by telecommuting?
- Will overtime be allowed?
- Will security be provided for the telecommuter's work? How?
- Will the firm have safety requirements for the home? Will OSHA be involved?

These kinds of questions seem to suggest that telecommuting poses insurmountable problems. Yet, there are sufficient examples of successful telecommuting to suggest that it can work effectively in certain environments.

## Part-Time Work

As mentioned earlier in this chapter, use of part-time workers on a regular basis has begun to gain momentum in the United States. This approach adds many highly qualified individuals to the labor market by permitting both employment and personal needs to be addressed. For many reasons, some people do not either want or need full-time employment. Unfortunately, part-time employees have historically been regarded as second-class workers. This perception is apparently changing as must be the case if part-time programs are to be successful.

## Modified Retirement

**Modified retirement** is an option that permits older employees to work fewer than their regular hours for a certain period of time preceding retirement. This option allows an employee to avoid an abrupt change in lifestyle and move gracefully into retirement.

To prosper with a diverse workforce, organizations need to develop workplace flexibility. Apparently, some firms resist this shift. For example, the view that *presence equals productivity* remains part of many corporate cultures. Flexible options seem to work best in environments characterized by freedom, trust, responsibility, and respect. It is encouraging that some organizations are altering traditional approaches to jobs and work, not only to cut costs, but also to ease conflicts between work and family responsibilities and to attract and retain qualified people. If these goals are achieved, it seems reasonable that organizations will become more productive and more competitive globally.

**Modified retirement**
An option that permits older employees to work fewer than their regular hours for a certain period of time preceding retirement.

Several issues that relate to compensation deserve mention. These issues include severance pay, comparable worth, pay secrecy, and pay compression. They are examined next.

## Severance Pay

**Severance pay** Compensation designed to assist laid-off employees as they search for new employment.

**Severance pay** is compensation designed to assist laid-off employees as they search for new employment. This factor was especially prominent during the years of downsizing, which has subsided in recent years. Nowadays, although some firms are trimming the amount of severance pay offered, they typically offer one to two weeks of severance pay for every year of service, up to some predetermined maximum. Severance pay is generally shaped according to the organizational level of the employee. For example, nonmanagers may get eight or nine weeks of pay even if their length of service is greater than eight or nine years. Middle managers may receive twelve to sixteen weeks, and top executives receive payment to cover nine months to a year of employment. The rationale for enhanced severance for executives is that it takes longer for an executive to secure another position. The subject of golden parachutes, a form of severance pay for executives, was discussed in the previous chapter.

## Comparable Worth

**Comparable worth** A determination of the values of dissimilar jobs (such as company nurse and welder) by comparing them under some form of job evaluation, and the assignment of pay rates according to their evaluated worth.

The comparable worth, or pay equity, theory extends the concept of the Equal Pay Act. While the act requires equal pay for equal work, comparable worth advocates prefer a broader interpretation of requiring equal pay for comparable worth, even if market rates vary and job duties are considerably different. **Comparable worth** requires the value for dissimilar jobs, such as company nurse and welder, to be compared under some form of job evaluation and pay rates for both jobs to be assigned according to their evaluated worth. Although the Supreme Court has ruled that the law does not require comparable worth, a number of state and local governments—along with some jurisdictions in Canada—have passed legislation that mandates this version of pay equity.

The concept of comparable worth has been around for about 40 years. When the Kennedy administration first proposed legislation requiring equal pay for comparable work, Congress rejected the legislation. In fact, this body of lawmakers has rejected every effort since then to pass such legislation.

In the business world, comparable worth would create numerous difficulties. To implement such a system, a reliable way would be required to determine when completely different jobs have a comparable value. Experts cannot agree on any system that would intelligently do this. Remember that in the point system of job evaluation, separate job clusters were considered necessary because of the difficulty relating dissimilar jobs in the *same company*. Comparable worth advocates envision comparing dissimilar jobs even *between industries*.

In addition, the concept of comparable worth is antithetical to our nation's free market economic system. In this system, the market allocates scarce resources according to supply and demand. To implement comparable worth, a bureaucratic government would artificially establish pay levels for jobs it deems *comparable*. If the wages for scarce male-dominated jobs were artificially set below the level that the market would demand, labor shortages would result.

Despite problems that are obvious to practitioners, the Clinton administration pushed the concept of comparable worth. The proposed Paycheck Fairness Act (S. 74 and H.R. 541) would implement comparable worth concepts. In addition, the OFCCP is enforcing comparable worth concepts during compliance reviews of federal contractors, resulting in multimillion-dollar settlements.[75]

The goal of nondiscriminatory pay practices is one that every organization should seek to achieve for ethical and legal reasons. Whether comparable worth is an appropriate solution remains to be seen. If the past is any indication, comparable worth will be debated as long as there is a disparity between the compensation of men and women.

## Pay Secrecy

Some organizations tend to keep their pay rates secret for various reasons. If a firm's compensation plan is illogical, secrecy may indeed be appropriate because only a well-designed system can stand careful scrutiny. An open system would almost certainly require managers to explain the rationale for pay decisions to subordinates. Secrecy, however, can have some negative side effects including a

---

### Stock Options as a Benefit

**A GLOBAL PERSPECTIVE**

When Daimler-Benz AG and Chrysler Corporation merged last year, it was learned that Chrysler head Robert Eaton was paid more than seven times as much as Daimler chairman and CEO Jurgen Schrempp. Although the two CEOs had similar salaries, the American CEO took home a reported total of $16.1 million, while his German counterpart made a comparatively paltry $1.9 million. The $14.2 million disparity came mostly from Eaton's stock options.

"Salary translations in Europe and America are not significantly different enough to cause heartburn. The issue that always causes consternation is long-term incentives," says Robert Freedman, principal at New York–based consulting firm Towers Perrin. Up to now, compensating executives using stock options has been primarily an American phenomenon. In 1998, the average CEO received four times his base salary in stock options. All countries do not support stock options as in the United States. In Poland, before options can be purchased, approval may have to be sought from the Polish Central Bank. In Japan, if a U.S. multinational has more than 50 employees, in general the company must go through a cumbersome yearly notification process with the ministry of finance. In Holland, because unconditional options may be taxed when they are granted, some executives must pay taxes even if they never exercise their stock options. Companies often feel the burden of these differences.

Not every company supports across-the-board stock option grants. Deere & Company even reversed its policy. "Up until 1994, we had a global stock option program," says Stephen P. Jarnecke, international HR programs manager. "Since then, we have differentiated. If there is not a practice of offering stock options in a given country, we no longer automatically extend a U.S. program." His reasoning? "Part of it is a cultural shift. We're now stepping back and saying, does it really make sense to deliver stock options in places like China where it is not tax advantageous?" Instead, Deere follows local compensation norms, using market practice to determine whether to offer such benefits as stock, extra vacation time, cars, or cash.

As American corporations expand their global reach and as capital becomes increasingly global, companies are being forced to give stock to stay competitive. Towers Perrin's Freedman says that without competitive programs, companies are having difficulty attracting and retaining the right employees. "They're not on a level playing field," he says. It's possible, then, that over the next 10 or 15 years, the American way of compensating may become the standard.[76]

distortion of the actual rewards people receive. Secrecy also spawns a low-trust environment in which people have trouble understanding the relationship between pay and performance. It may, therefore, cause an otherwise sound compensation system to be ineffective.[77]

## Pay Compression

**Pay compression** is created in several ways, including the hiring of new employees at pay rates comparable to or higher than those of current employees who have been with the firm for several years and who may hold the same or even higher-rated jobs. Pay compression may also occur when pay adjustments are made at the lower end of the job hierarchy without commensurate adjustments at the top. The explanation for this action may be the firm's need to meet market prices in retaining or hiring people with scarce skills and an inability to make needed adjustments elsewhere in the pay structure. Pay compression is a serious problem in many areas of our economy including nursing, engineering, and higher education. Unfortunately, no easy solution is available if a firm lacks the resources to maintain internal equity or believes that external equity should be of primary concern.

**Pay compression**
A situation that occurs when workers perceive that the pay differential between their pay and that of employees in jobs above or below them is too small.

## ▶ Summary

**①  Define *benefits*.**
Benefits include all financial rewards that generally are not paid directly to the employee.

**②  Describe legally required benefits.**
Legally required benefits include Social Security retirement benefits, disability insurance, and survivors' benefits; Medicare; unemployment compensation; workers' compensation benefits; and unpaid leave, mandated by the Family and Medical Leave Act.

**③  Identify the basic categories of voluntary benefits.**
Voluntary benefits include payment for time not worked, health benefits, security benefits, employee services, premium pay, and benefits for part-time employees.

**④  Describe the Consolidated Omnibus Budget Reconciliation Act (COBRA), the Health Insurance Portability and Accountability Act, the Employee Retirement Income Security Act (ERISA), and the Older Workers Benefit Protection Act (OWBPA).**
The Consolidated Omnibus Budget Reconciliation Act of 1985 (COBRA) was enacted to give employees the opportunity to temporarily continue their coverage if they would otherwise lose it because of termination, layoff, or other change in employment status. The Health Insurance Portability and Accountability Act of 1996 provides new protections for approximately 25 million Americans who move from one job to another, who are self-employed, or who have preexisting medical conditions. The Employee Retirement Income Security Act of 1974 (ERISA) was passed to strengthen existing and future retirement programs. The Older Workers Benefit Protection Act (OWBPA) is a 1990 amendment to the Age Discrimination in Employment Act and extends its coverage to all employee benefits.

**⑤  Describe the importance of communicating information about the benefits package.**
Employee benefits can help a firm recruit and retain a high-quality workforce. The Employee Retirement Income Security Act requires organizations with a pension or profit-sharing plan to provide employees with specific data at specified times.

**6** **Explain the various forms of incentive compensation.**
Compensation programs that relate pay to productivity are referred to as *incentive compensation*. The three basic forms are individual, team-based, and companywide incentive compensation.

**7** **Describe how the job environment is a component of nonfinancial compensation.**
Employees can draw satisfaction from their work through nonfinancial factors such as pleasant working conditions and competent co-workers.

**8** **Explain how factors related to workplace flexibility are a component of nonfinancial compensation.**
Workplace flexibility factors such as flextime, the compressed workweek, job sharing, flexible compensation plans, part-time work, telecommuting, and modified retirement are components of nonfinancial compensation.

**9** **Describe the concepts of severance pay, comparable worth, pay secrecy, and pay compression.**
Compensation designed to assist laid-off employees as they search for new employment is referred to as severance pay. Comparable worth requires the value for dissimilar jobs, such as company nurse and welder, to be compared under some form of job evaluation, and pay rates for both jobs to be assigned according to their evaluated worth. With pay secrecy, organizations tend to keep their pay rates secret for various reasons. Pay compression occurs when workers perceive that the pay differential between their pay and that of employees in jobs above or below them is too small.

## Questions for Review ◀

1. Define *benefits*. 352 - 353

2. What are the legally required benefits? 353 - 354

3. What are the basic categories of voluntary benefits? Describe each.

4. Define each of the following laws:
   a. *Consolidated Omnibus Budget Reconciliation Act of 1985 (COBRA)*
   b. *Health Insurance Portability and Accountability Act of 1996*
   c. *Employee Retirement Income Security Act of 1974 (ERISA)*
   d. *Older Workers Benefit Protection Act (OWBPA)*

5. Why is it crucial to effectively communicate information regarding a worker's benefit package?

6. What is meant by the term *incentive compensation?* What are the basic forms of incentive compensation?

7. What factors are related to the job as a total compensation factor?

8. What compensation factors are related to the job environment?

9. Define the following:
   a. *severance pay*
   b. *comparable worth*
   c. *pay compression*

10. What are some means that organizations have used to achieve workplace flexibility? 378 - 379

## ▶ Developing HRM Skills

### *An Experiential Exercise*

Because of a downward trend in business and resulting financial constraints over the last two years, Straight Manufacturing Company has been able to grant only cost-of-living increases to its employees. However, the firm has just signed a lucrative three-year contract with a major defense contractor. As a result, management has formed a salary review committee to award merit increases to deserving employees. Members of the salary review committee have only $13,500 of merit money; therefore, deciding who will receive merit increases will be difficult. Louis Convoy, Sharon Kubiak, J. Ward Archer, Ed Wilson, C. J. Sass, and John Passante have been recommended for raises.

Six students will serve on the salary review committee. While the committee would like to award significant merit increases to all those who have been recommended, there are limited funds available for raises. The committee must make a decision as to how the merit funds will be distributed. Your instructor will provide the participants with additional information necessary to complete the exercise.

## ▶ HRM INCIDENT 1

### *A Benefits Package Designed for Whom?*

Wayne McGraw greeted Robert Peters, his next interviewee, warmly. Robert had an excellent academic record and appeared to be just the kind of person Wayne's company, Beco Electric, was seeking. Wayne is the university recruiter for Beco and had already interviewed six graduating seniors at Centenary College.

Based on the application form, Robert appeared to be the most promising candidate to be interviewed that day. He was 22 years old and had a 3.6 grade point average with a 4.0 in his major field, industrial management. Not only was Robert the vice president of the Student Government Association, but he was also activities chairman for Kappa Alpha Psi, a social fraternity. The reference letters in Robert's file revealed that he was both very active socially and a rather intense and serious student. One of the letters, from Robert's employer during the previous summer, expressed satisfaction with Robert's work habits.

Wayne knew that discussion of pay could be an important part of the recruiting interview. But he did not know which aspects of Beco's compensation and benefits program would appeal most to Robert. The company has an excellent profit-sharing plan, although 80 percent of profit distributions are deferred and included in each employee's retirement account. Health benefits are also good. The company's medical and dental plan pays almost 100 percent of costs. A company lunchroom provides meals at about 70 percent of outside prices, although few managers take advantage of this. Employees get one week of paid vacation after the first year and two weeks after two years with the company. In addition, there are 12 paid holidays each year. Finally, the company encourages advanced education, paying for tuition and books in full, and often allowing time off to attend classes during the day.

**Questions**

1. What aspects of Beco's compensation and benefits program are likely to appeal to Robert? Explain.
2. In today's work environment, what additional benefits might be more attractive to Robert? Explain.

**HRM INCIDENT 2** ◀

## A Motivated Worker!

Bob Rosen could hardly wait to get back to work Monday morning. He was excited about his chance of getting a large bonus. Bob is a machine operator with Ram Manufacturing Company, a Wichita, Kansas, maker of electric motors. He operates an armature-winding machine. The machine winds copper wire onto metal cores to make the rotating elements for electric motors.

Ram pays machine operators on a graduated piece-rate basis. Operators are paid a certain amount for each part made, plus a bonus. A worker who produces 10 percent above standard for a certain month receives a 10 percent additional bonus. For 20 percent above standard, the bonus is 20 percent. Bob realized that he had a good chance of earning a 20 percent bonus that month. That would be $587.

Bob had a special use for the extra money. His wife's birthday was just three weeks away. He was hoping to get her a new Chevrolet. He had already saved $1,000, but the down payment on the car was $1,500. The bonus would enable him to buy the car.

Bob arrived at work at seven o'clock that morning, although his shift did not begin until eight. He went to his workstation and checked the supply of blank cores and copper wire. Finding that only one spool of wire was on hand, he asked the forklift truck driver to bring another. Then, he asked the operator who was working the graveyard shift, "Sam, do you mind if I grease the machine while you work?"

"No," Sam said, "that won't bother me a bit."

After greasing the machine, Bob stood and watched Sam work. He thought of ways to simplify the motions involved in loading, winding, and unloading the armatures. As Bob took over the machine after the eight o'clock whistle, he thought, "I hope I can pull this off. I know the car will make Kathy happy. She won't be stuck at home while I'm at work."

**Question**

1. Explain the advantages and disadvantages of a piecework pay system such as that at Ram.

**Notes** ◀

1. Joseph J. Martocchio, *Strategic Compensation* (Upper Saddle River, NJ: Prentice Hall, 1998): 254, 274.
2. Gene Koretz, "Medical Costs of the 'Old Old,'" *Business Week* (January 31, 2000): 34.

3. Maria Greco Danaher, "Intermittent Leave Under the FMLA," *Workforce Online* www.workforce.com/feature/00/04/81 (May 2000).

4. Stephanie M. Cerasano, "Managers Beware: You Can Be Personally Liable for FMLA Violations," *Arizona Employment Law Letter* 6 (October 1999): 1.

5. Ronald J. Andrykovitch and Jeffrey A. VanDoren, "Legal Update: Family and Medical Leave Act's Real Impact," *Getting Results . . . For the Hands-On Manager* 42 (January 1, 1997): 7.

6. Daniel B. Moskowitz and Nancy Rowell, "Struggling With FMLA's Scope," *Business and Health* 17 (September 1999): 45–46.

7. A 1998 survey indicated that firms provide an average of less than 3½ days of bereavement leave. Kathryn Tyler, "Giving Time to Grieve," *HRMagazine* 44 (November 1999): 66–73.

8. Elizabeth Chang, "Flexibility Can Cure Problems with Sick Pay," *St. Louis Post-Dispatch* (May 11, 2000): C7.

9. Ibid.

10. Susan J. Wells, "Avoiding the Health Care Squeeze," *HRMagazine* 45 (April 2000): 46–52.

11. Shari Caudron, "Employee, Cover Thyself," *Workforce* 79 (April 2000): 34–42.

12. *2000 Benefits Survey,* Society for Human Resource Management (2000): 17.

13. Manfred J. Nowacki, Douglas A. Collet, Shellie A. Stoddard, and Elizabeth A. Runge, "Prognosis, Guarded," *Best's Review—Life/Health Insurance Edition* (January 1997): 68–70.

14. Caudron, "Employee, Cover Thyself."

15. "HCFA Issues Regulations Under Health Insurance Portability and Accountability Act: Fact Sheet." *US Newswire* www3.elibrary.com/getdoc.cgi?id=76...D002&Form= RL&pubname=US_Newswire&puburl=0 (August 1, 1997).

16. Health Insurance Portability and Accountability Act of 1996. Washington, DC: HHS, Press Office. www.os.dhhs.gov/news/press/1996pres/960821.html (August 1, 1997).

17. *2000 Benefits Survey,* 17.

18. R. Evan Inglis and Steven G. Vernon, "A Better Retirement Plan," *HRMagazine* 44 (August 1999): 91.

19. *2000 Benefits Survey,* 24.

20. Jenny C. McCune, "HR News Capsules: Downsizing on the Downswing," *HR Focus* 74 (January 1997): 6–7.

21. Anne Willette, "Firms Adding Financial Planning to List of All Workers' Benefits," *USA Today* (March 24, 1997): 1A.

22. R. Evan Inglis and Richard R. Joss, "Smoothing the Way for Cash Balance Plans," *HRMagazine* 44 (December 1999): 77–78.

23. Inglis and Vernon, "A Better Retirement Plan," 91–93.

24. Michael Arndt and Aaron Bernstein, "From Milestone to Millstone?" *Business Week* (March 20, 2000): 120, 122.

25. Martocchio, *Strategic Compensation,* 278.

26. Ibid.

27. George T. Milkovich and Jerry M. Newman, *Compensation,* 6th ed. (Boston: Irwin McGraw-Hill, 1999): 440.

28. According to the *2000 Benefits Survey* conducted by the Society for Human Resource Management, 95 percent of the responding firms reported providing life insurance.

29. *2000 Benefits Survey,* 15.

30. Carla Joinson, "Relocation Counseling Meets Employees' Changing Needs," *HRMagazine* 43 (February 1998): 68–70.

31. Howard R. Mitchell III, "When a Company Moves: How to Help Employees Adjust," *HRMagazine* 44 (January 1999): 61.

32. *2000 Benefits Survey,* 11.

33. Hillary Chura, "Careers/Fresh Starts; Companies Lend Parents a Hand," *Los Angeles Times* Home Edition (January 27, 1997): D2.

34. *2000 Benefits Survey,* 24.

35. David Fischer and Kevin Whitelaw, "A New Way to Shine Up Corporate Profits," *U.S. News & World Report* 120 (April 15, 1996): 54.

36. Julie Cohen Mason, "Whoever Said There Was No Such Thing as a Free Lunch?" *Management Review* 83 (April 1994): 60–62.

37. Bruce Shutan, "HR Review? You Bet Your Bottom Line," *Employee Benefit News* (December 1998): 23.

38. Bill Leonard, "Recipes for Part-Time Benefits," *HRMagazine* 45 (April 2000): 56–62.

39. *U.S. Statutes at Large* 88, Part I, 93rd Congress, 2nd Session, 1974: 833.

40. Martocchio, *Strategic Compensation,* 63.

41. Geoffrey Loftus, "Ultimate Pay for Performance," *Across the Board* 31 (January 1997): 9–10.

42. James Martin, "HR in the Cybercorp," *HR Focus* 74 (April 1997): 3–4.

43. Shari Caudron, "Master the Compensation Maze," *Personnel Journal* 72 (June 1993): 64G–64I.

44. Steven E. Gross, "When Jobs Become Team Roles, What Do You Pay For?" *Compensation and Benefits Review* 29 (January/February 1997): 48–51.

45. Ibid.

46. Martocchio, *Strategic Compensation,* 121.

47. Ibid., 115.

48. Chris Lee, "So Long, 20th Century," *Training* 36 (December 1999): 30–36.

49. Carrie Mason-Draffen, "Companies Find New Ways to Pay/Worker's Performance Tied to Stock Options, Bonuses, Raises," *Newsday* (January 5, 1997): F8.

50. Adapted from Craig J. Cantoni, "Learn to Manage Pay and Performance Like an Entrepreneur," *Compensation & Benefits Review* 29 (January/February 1997): 52–58.

51. Martocchio, *Strategic Compensation.*

52. "The Wireless Internet," *Business Week* (May 29, 2000): 136–144.

53. "Employers Stress Workplace Fun," *National Underwriter (Property & Casualty/Risk & Benefits Management)* 103 (May 17, 1999): 25.

54. Shari Caudron, "The New Status Symbols," *Industry Week* 248 (June 21, 1999): 24.

55. Emmet Seaborn, "Strengthen Links between Benefits and Strategy," *HR Focus* (June 1999): 11.

56. Andrea C. Poe, "Parenting Programs Take Off," *HRMagazine* 44 (November 1999): 42–50.

57. "Recognition Plus Performance Measurement Equals Happy Workers," *HR Focus* 76 (April 1999): 5.

58. Poe, "Parenting Programs Take Off."

59. Ibid.

60. *2000 Benefits Survey,* 11.

61. "HR News Capsules," *HR Focus* (June 1999): 5.

62. Shelly Reese, "Working Around the Clock," *Business & Health* 18 (April 2000): 71–72.

63. Brian Gill, "Flextime Benefits Employees and Employers," *American Printer* 220 (February 1998): 70.

64. Fay Hansen, "Introduction: Experts Debate the Future of the FLSA and the NLRA," *Compensation & Benefits Review* 28 (July/August 1996): 6.

65. *2000 Benefits Survey,* 11.

66. Charles Fishman, "Moving toward a Balanced Work Life," *Workforce* 79 (March 2000): 39–40.

67. Patricia Nakache, "One VP, Two Brains," *Fortune* 140 (December 20, 1999): 327–328.

68. Martocchio, *Strategic Compensation.*

69. Ibid., 299.

70. Linda Micco, "Telecommuting Increase Found," *HR News* 16 (August 1997): 23.

71. "Telecommuters Welcome," *HR Focus* 75 (February 1998): 6.

72. Leigh Rivenbark, "Employees Want More Opportunities to Telecommute, Report Reveals," *HR News* 19 (April 2000): 14.

73. Mary Molina Fitzer, "Managing from Afar: Performance and Rewards in a Telecommuting Environment," *Compensation & Benefits Review* 29 (January/February 1997): 65–73.

74. "Telecommuting: The Basics of a Successful Telework Network," *HR Focus* 76 (June 1999): 10.

75. Timothy S. Bland, Thomas H. Nail, and David P. Knox, "OFCCP, White House Push Comparable Worth," *HR News* 19 (May 2000): 22.

76. Shirley Fung, "How Should We Pay Them?" *Across the Board* 36 (June 1999): 36–41.

77. Edward E. Lawler, "The New Pay: A Strategic Approach,"*Compensation & Benefits Review* 27 (July/August 1995): 14–22.

Perhaps it is only natural for most of us to feel, as does one of the characters in this video, that we deserve more than we are paid. Still, when such feelings meet a loosely organized pay plan, they can create pay inequity within an organization, with resulting problems for the firm that far outweigh the original employee's dissatisfaction.

Equity is only one of four factors that influence the formulation of pay plans. The other three are legislation (such as the Fair Labor Standards Act, which sets the minimum wage), union agreements and contracts, and company compensation policies that govern everything from overtime policies to criteria for pay increases.

Job evaluation is the part of the compensation system that determines the relative value of each job in relation to the others. You should recall from Chapter 11 that many firms use job evaluation to:

1. Identify the organization's job structure
2. Bring equity and order to the relationships among jobs
3. Develop a hierarchy of job value that can be used to create a pay structure

A company does not have to grow very large before it faces the problems of setting salary levels for comparable jobs, paying for different skill levels in the same job, and compensating long-term employees who may experience the kind of inequity discussed in Chapter 11. Equity is still an important goal of any good pay plan. It is no defense of an inequitable pay plan to say that people *can* be paid unfairly because they don't *know* that they are.

Karen Jarvis, director of sales, and Hal Boylston, president, have responded to Kim's request for a meeting. (You may recall meeting Kim, one of Quicktakes' writers, in Segment 1.) Kim has been with the firm for a long time, and she has begun to feel underpaid as her own living expenses begin to climb. As you listen to her conversation with Hal and Karen, ask yourself whether Kim is making a good business argument for the raise she demands. Compare Hal and Karen's response, in their private conversation after Kim leaves the room, with the salary review committee's reaction to Tom Bailey in Part 4. Are the two reactions based on the same kind of evidence?

## Discussion Questions

1. Kim makes three arguments for the raise she wants. Identify them. Do you find them persuasive? How can they be objectively evaluated? Are any of them based on her job performance?
2. Hal's first reaction is to note that Kim is one of the highest paid employees in the firm. Should that make any difference to the way her request is handled? Why or why not? Would it change your answer to take into consideration the fact that Kim has been on staff for many years?
3. Hal admits to not knowing what the competition is paying people like Kim. How does that affect his judgment in this incident?
4. Once he decides to give Kim a raise, Hal tries to persuade Karen by saying, "What we need to focus on is her value to the company." Comment on this remark.
5. Could Kim have made a better case for a raise, and could she have presented her case differently? If you answered yes to either, what advice would you give her for improvement? Assuming Kim took your advice, what effect would you expect her revised proposal to have on Karen and Hal?
6. Hal is probably right that if news of Kim's raise gets out, there will be trouble with other members of the staff. What is the best way for Quicktakes to avoid such trouble in the future?

chapter
chapterchapterchapterchapterchapterchapter

# 13

# A Safe and Healthy Work Environment

D ionne Moore, safety engineer for Sather Manufacturing, was walking through the plant when she spotted a situation that immediately caught her attention. Several employees had backed out of a room where several chemicals were used in a critical manufacturing process. Dionne inspected the room but could not determine that anything was wrong or even different from any other day. She was puzzled as to why the workers were reluctant to resume their tasks. As it turned out, the employees were not only hesitant to return to work; they were adamant in maintaining that conditions in the room were unhealthy. Dionne and the group's supervisor discussed the situation and wondered whether they should order the people to resume work since the department was already behind schedule.

Bob Byrom, CEO for Aztec Enterprises, is concerned about his vice president for marketing, 38-year-old Cecil Pierce. The two had just returned from a short walk to the corporate attorney's office to discuss plans for an overseas joint venture. As they returned to Bob's office, Cecil's face was flushed, he was breathing hard, and he had to sit down and rest. This really alarmed Bob because he didn't think that such a brief bit of exercise should tire anyone, especially someone as apparently healthy as Cecil. Bob knew that the firm could not afford to do without Cecil's expertise—even for a short time—during its expansion plans.

**D**ionne and Bob are each involved with only a few of the many critical areas related to employee safety and health. Dionne realizes that safety is a major concern in her organization and that she must constantly strive to maintain a safe and healthy work environment. Bob's experience has caused him to confront the serious ramifications of losing a key executive to illness or even death.

We begin this chapter by describing the nature and role of safety and health and provide an overview of the Occupational Safety and Health Act. Then, we discuss the focus of safety programs in business operations and explain ergonomics and the consequences of repetitive stress injuries. Next, the effect on business of workplace violence and domestic violence is described. Wellness programs, stress, and burnout are then explained. The importance of physical fitness programs, alcohol and drug abuse programs, and employee assistance programs is described next. The chapter ends with discussions of smoking in the workplace and AIDS.

## THE NATURE AND ROLE OF SAFETY AND HEALTH

In our discussion, **safety** involves protecting employees from injuries caused by work-related accidents. Obviously, several Sather Manufacturing employees view one phase of a critical manufacturing process as unsafe. Dionne Moore and the group's supervisor now have a dilemma: If they ignore the workers' concerns, the group will continue to balk at working in this environment. If they address the employees' safety concerns, the company may have to modify the existing manufacturing process or reengineer this phase of the work environment. Either path will lead to further production delays.

**Safety**
The protection of employees from injuries caused by work-related accidents.

▶ *SHRM-HR Links*

**www.prenhall.com/mondy**

Various safety and health issues including AIDS/HIV in the workplace, employee assistance plans, ergonomics, mental health, substance abuse, and workplace violence are addressed at this site.

HR WEB WISDOM

www.osha.gov

**Health** refers to employees' freedom from physical or emotional illness. Cecil Pierce, marketing vice president for Aztec Enterprises, is obviously not as healthy as one might expect a 38-year-old to be. Bob Byrom, CEO of Aztec, started worrying about Cecil's health when, after only a short walk, Cecil started breathing hard, had a flushed face, and needed rest. Managers such as Dionne Moore and Bob Byrom are vitally concerned with safety and health. Problems in these areas seriously affect the productivity and quality of work life. They can dramatically lower a firm's effectiveness and employee morale. In fact, job-related injuries and illnesses are more common than most people realize. They cost the nation far more than AIDS or Alzheimer's disease. Job-related injuries and illnesses are grossly underestimated as a contributor to health care costs in the United States.[1]

> **Health**
> An employee's freedom from physical or emotional illness.

Although line managers are primarily responsible for maintaining a safe and healthy work environment, human resource professionals provide staff expertise to help them deal with these issues. In addition, the human resource manager is frequently responsible for coordinating and monitoring specific safety and health programs.

## THE OCCUPATIONAL SAFETY AND HEALTH ACT

The most important federal legislation in the safety and health area is the Occupational Safety and Health Act of 1970. The purpose of this act is to assure a safe and healthful workplace for every American worker. There is little doubt that the act's intent is justified. Organizations must meet these goals if they are to reach their full productive potential.

The act's enforcement by the Occupational Safety and Health Administration (OSHA) dramatically altered management's role in the area of safety and health. Financial penalties serve as pointed reminders to industry of the benefits of maintaining safe and healthy working conditions. Skyrocketing costs for workers' compensation insurance, the expense of training new workers, and the fact that risky jobs command higher pay also keep safety and health issues on managers' minds.

In implementing the act, OSHA has changed the way it selects sites to inspect. Previously, an employer was more likely to be inspected if it was part of an industry with high injury and illness rates, regardless of its own record. Today, OSHA targets inspections more narrowly, aiming at specific work sites rather than entire industries. This change of focus means that OSHA spends more time inspecting sites with potential problems and less time inspecting those with good records. The so-called "Hit List" is shown in Table 13-1. You can see that problems related to scaffolding head the list of areas considered most dangerous. Of course, a complaint or accident will still trigger an inspection regardless of the safety record.[2]

OSHA oversees from six to seven million businesses but has only 1,242 inspectors. Sharing the responsibility for oversight of workplace safety and health are 25 states that run their own OSHA programs with 1,246 inspectors.[3] Even with assistance from these states, the average employer will not likely see an OSHA inspector unless an employee instigates an inspection. When OSHA inspectors come to a site, the employer has the option of denying the inspector access to the

OSHA inspectors consider violations of all types. However, those deemed most serious are the ones inspectors are most likely to target. Recently, the 10 most frequently found serious violations related to problems in the following areas:

| Rank | Area of Concern | Serious Violations |
|---|---|---|
| 1 | Scaffolding | 5,539 |
| 2 | Fall protection | 3,862 |
| 3 | Hazard communication | 3,274 |
| 4 | Lockout/tagout | 3,532 |
| 5 | Machine guarding | 2,266 |
| 6 | Power presses | 2,230 |
| 7 | Mechanical power | 2,151 |
| 8 | Electrical | 1,902 |
| 9 | Excavation (construction) | 1,399 |
| 10 | Machine guarding (abrasive wheels) | 1,338 |

*Lockout/tagout* refers to electrical repairs, during which switches for power must be shut off, locked, or tagged so power cannot be turned on while an electrical system is being repaired.

*Hazard communication* refers to the proper use of safety sheets for chemical products at a worksite.

*Source:* Occupational Safety and Health Administration.

work site. In such cases, OSHA would be required to get a warrant to proceed with the inspection. If the employer refuses access to view certain documents, OSHA would be required to get an administrative subpoena. As a result of OSHA inspections, a total of $79 million in penalties were levied in 1998, and the figure grew even higher in 1999, resulting from an estimated 34,000 inspections.[4]

Roughly 70 percent of OSHA inspections have resulted from employee complaints. As you recall from the incident at the beginning of this chapter, employees at Sather Manufacturing Company refused to work in an environment they considered hazardous. Under the Occupational Safety and Health Act, an employee can legally refuse to work when the following conditions exist:

▶ The employee reasonably fears death, disease, or serious physical harm.
▶ The harm is imminent.
▶ There is too little time to file an OSHA complaint and get the problem corrected.
▶ The worker has notified the employer about the condition and asked that it be corrected, but the employer has not taken action.

Since its inception, OSHA has revised its mission. The current thrust is to give employers a choice between partnership and traditional enforcement, to inject common sense into regulation and enforcement, and to eliminate red tape. The overall purpose, of course, is to reduce injuries, illnesses, and fatality rates. To help small businesses, OSHA is expanding its assistance, reducing penalties, and putting more of its informational materials in electronic formats, including CD-ROMs and Internet sites.[5] OSHA's director has emphasized that these firms will not be punished for violations if they seek OSHA's assistance in correcting problems.

## SAFETY: THE ECONOMIC IMPACT

Job-related deaths and injuries of all types extract a high toll in terms of not only human misery, but also economic loss. The significant financial costs are often passed along to the consumer in the form of higher prices. Thus, everyone is

The true cost to the nation, to employers, and to individuals of work-related deaths and injuries is much greater than the cost of workers' compensation insurance alone. The figures presented below show the National Safety Council's estimates of the total costs of occupational deaths and injuries. Cost estimating procedures were revised for the 1993 edition of *Accident Facts™*. In general, cost estimates are not comparable from year to year. As additional or more precise data become available, they are used from that year forward. Previously estimated figures are not revised.

**Total cost in 1997 . . . . . $127.7 billion**
Includes wage and productivity losses of $63.4 billion, medical costs of $20.7 billion, and administrative expenses of $26.5 billion. Includes employer costs of $11.9 billion such as the money value of time lost by workers

other than those with disabling injuries, who are directly or indirectly involved in injuries, and the cost of time required to investigate injuries, write up injury reports, etc. Also includes damage to motor vehicles in work injuries of $2.0 billion and fire losses of $3.2 billion.

**Cost per worker . . . . . . . . . . . . . $980**
This figure indicates the value of goods or services each worker must produce to offset the cost of work injuries. It is *not* the average cost of a work injury.

**Cost per death . . . . . . . . . . . $890,000**
**Cost per disabling injury . . . . $28,000**
These figures include estimates of wage losses, medical expenses, administrative expenses, and employer costs and exclude property damage costs except to motor vehicles.

*Source: Accident Facts* (Chicago, IL: National Safety Council, 1998): 51.

affected, directly or indirectly, by job-related deaths and injuries. The National Safety Council estimated the total costs of job-related injuries in 1997 to be almost $128 billion (see Table 13-2).[6] Some people may be surprised to discover that motor vehicle accidents are the number one cause of death on the job. As you can see in Table 13-3, transportation incidents result in more than twice the number of deaths caused by assaults and violent acts, the second leading cause of death.

## THE FOCUS OF SAFETY PROGRAMS

Faulty management safety policies and decisions, personal factors, and environmental factors are the basic causes of accidents. If defective, these factors result in unsafe working conditions and unsafe employee actions. Direct causes of accidents stem from unplanned releases of energy and/or hazardous material. Regardless of the cause, the result is an accident (see Figure 13-1). Safety programs may be designed to accomplish their purposes in two primary ways: one focusing on *unsafe employee actions* and the other on *unsafe working conditions*.

The first approach in a safety program is to create a psychological environment and employee attitudes that promote safety. Accidents can be reduced when workers consciously or subconsciously think about safety. This attitude must permeate the firm's operations, and a strong company policy emphasizing safety and health is crucial. For example, a major chemical firm's policy states: "It is the policy of the company that every employee be assigned to a safe and healthful place

| | |
|---|---|
| Transportation incidents | 12,890 |
| Assaults and violent acts | 6,355 |
| Contact with objects and equipment | 4,987 |
| Falls | 3,218 |
| Exposure to harmful substances and environments | 2,970 |
| Fires, explosions, and other | 1,147 |
| Total fatalities | 31,567 |

*Source:* Carla Joinson, "Controlling Hostility," *HRMagazine* 43 (August 1998): 65.

to work. We strongly desire accident prevention in all phases of our operations. Toward this end, the full cooperation of all employees will be required." As the policy infers, no one person is assigned the task of making the workplace safe. While there is danger that everyone's responsibility will become no one's responsibility, a truly safe environment takes the effort of everyone from top management to the lowest-level employee. While every individual in a firm should be encouraged to come up with solutions to potential safety problems, the firm's managers must take the lead. Management's unique role is clear since OSHA places primary responsibility for employee safety on the employer.

The second approach to safety program design is to develop and maintain a safe physical working environment. Here, the environment is altered to prevent accidents. Even if Joe, a machine operator, has been awake all night with a sick child and can barely keep his eyes open, the safety devices on his machine will help protect him. Attempts are made to create a physical environment in which accidents cannot occur. It is in this area that OSHA has had its greatest influence.

## Developing Safety Programs

Workplace accident prevention requires safety program planning. Plans may be relatively simple, as for a small retail store, or more complex and highly sophisticated, as for a large automobile assembly plant. Regardless of the organization's

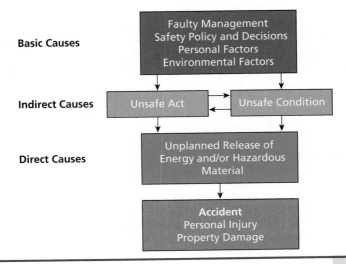

**Accident Causes** | **Figure 13-1**

*Source:* Occupational Safety and Health Administration

size, the support of top management is essential if safety programs are to be effective. Top executives in a firm should be aware of the tremendous economic losses that can result from accidents.

Some of the reasons for top management's support of a safety program are listed in Table 13-4. These data show that the lost productivity of a single injured worker is not the only factor to consider. Every phase of human resource management is involved. For instance, the firm may have difficulty in recruitment if it gains a reputation for being an unsafe place to work. Employee relations may be seriously eroded if workers believe that management does not care enough about them to make their workplace safe. Compensation may also be affected if the firm must pay a premium to attract qualified applicants and retain valued employees. Maintaining a stable workforce may become very difficult if the workplace is perceived as hazardous, as was the case with Sather Manufacturing.

**Job Hazard Analysis.** The main goal of safety and health professionals is to prevent job-related injuries and illnesses. This goal is achieved by educating workers in the hazards associated with their work, installing engineering controls, defining safe work procedures, and prescribing appropriate personal protective equipment. Identifying job hazards in a Job Hazard Analysis (JHA) is key to determining and implementing the necessary controls, procedures, and training. The JHA is a common tool for identifying hazards and for developing appropriate controls to ensure the job is performed safely. OSHA publication 3071, *Job Safety Hazard Analysis* is a good primer on performing a Job Hazard Analysis.[7]

**The Superfund Amendments Reauthorization Act, Title III (SARA).** SARA requires businesses to communicate more openly about the hazards associated with the materials they use and produce and the wastes they generate. Although SARA has been around for several years, many firms do not yet have a satisfactory program for it in place. The hazard communication standard often leads the list of

---

**Table 13-4** Reasons for Management Support of a Safety Program

▸ **Personal loss.** The physical pain and mental anguish associated with injuries are always unpleasant and may even be traumatic for an injured worker. Of still greater concern is the possibility of permanent disability or even death.

▸ **Financial loss to injured employees.** Most employees are covered by company insurance plans or personal accident insurance. However, an injury may result in financial losses not covered by insurance.

▸ **Lost productivity.** When an employee is injured, there will be a loss of productivity for the firm. In addition to obvious losses, there are often hidden costs. For example, a substitute worker may need additional training to replace the injured employee. Even when another worker is available to move into the injured employee's position, efficiency may suffer.

▸ **Higher insurance premiums.** Workers' compensation insurance premiums are based on the employer's history of insurance claims. The potential for savings related to employee safety provides a degree of incentive to establish formal programs.

▸ **Possibility of fines and imprisonment.** Since the enactment of the Occupational Safety and Health Act, a willful and repeated violation of its provisions may result in serious penalties for the employer.

▸ **Social responsibility.** Many executives feel responsible for the safety and health of their employees. A number of firms had excellent safety programs years before OSHA existed. They understand that a safe work environment is not only in the best interests of the firm; providing one is the right thing to do.

OSHA violations. Dealing with this standard appears to be relatively simple and inexpensive, except when its provisions are ignored.

**Employee Involvement.** One way to strengthen a safety program is to include employee input, which provides workers with a sense of accomplishment. To prevent accidents, each worker must make a personal commitment to safe work practices. A team concept, where employees watch out for each other as a moral obligation, is a worthy goal. Supervisors can show support for the safety program by conscientiously enforcing safety rules and by closely conforming to the rules themselves. Participation in such teams helps form positive attitudes, and employees develop a sense of ownership of the program. The committee may become involved with not only safety issues but also ways to improve productivity.

In many companies, one staff member coordinates the overall safety program. Some major corporations have *risk management departments* that anticipate losses associated with safety factors and prepare legal defenses in the event of lawsuits. Such titles as *safety director* and *safety engineer* are common. One of the safety director's primary tasks is to provide safety training for company employees. This involves educating line managers about the merits of safety and recognizing and eliminating unsafe situations. Although the safety director operates essentially in an advisory capacity, a well-informed and assertive director may exercise considerable influence in the organization.

## Accident Investigation

Accidents can happen even in the most safety-conscious firms. Whether or not it results in an injury, each accident should be carefully evaluated to determine its cause and to ensure it does not recur. The safety engineer and the line manager jointly investigate accidents. One of the responsibilities of any supervisor is to prevent accidents. To do so, the supervisor must learn—through active participation in the safety program—why accidents occur, how they occur, where they occur, and who is involved. Supervisors gain a great deal of knowledge about accident prevention by helping prepare accident reports. Safety should also be emphasized during the training and orientation of new employees. The early months of employment are often critical because work injuries decrease with length of service.

## Evaluation of Safety Programs

Perhaps the best indicator that a safety program is succeeding is a reduction in the frequency and severity of injuries and illnesses. Therefore, statistics including the number of injuries and illnesses (frequency rate) and the amount of work time lost (severity rate) are often used in program evaluation. In addition to program evaluation criteria, an effective reporting system is needed to ensure that accidents are recorded. When a new safety program is initiated, the number of accidents may decline significantly. However, some supervisors may be failing to report certain accidents to make the statistics for their units look better. Proper evaluation of a safety program depends on the accurate reporting and recording of data.

To be of value, the conclusions derived from an evaluation must be used to improve the safety program. Gathering data and permitting this information to collect dust on the safety director's desk will not solve problems or prevent accidents. The results of the evaluation must be transmitted upward to top management and downward to line managers in order to generate improvements. Most employers will also mail or electronically transmit records of occupational injuries and illnesses directly to OSHA.

# Rationale for Safety and Health Trends

Organizations are giving increased attention to safety. In addition to legal requirements, the reasons for this concern include the following business issues:

▶ *Profitability.* Employees can only produce while they are on the job. In addition to payouts related to medical costs, other factors—such as lost production and increased recruiting and training requirements—add to a firm's expense when an employee is injured or becomes ill.

▶ *Employee and Public Relations.* A good safety record may well provide companies with a competitive edge. Firms with good safety records have an effective vehicle for recruiting and retaining good employees.

▶ *Reduced Liability.* An effective safety program can reduce corporate and executive liability for charges when employees are injured.

▶ *Marketing.* A positive safety record can help firms win contracts.

▶ *Productivity.* An effective safety program may boost morale and productivity while simultaneously reducing rising costs.

## ERGONOMICS

**Ergonomics**
The study of human interaction with tasks, equipment, tools, and the physical work environment.

One specific safety and health approach that has become prominent is the emphasis on ergonomics. **Ergonomics** is the study of human interaction with tasks, equipment, tools, and the physical environment. Through ergonomics, an attempt is made to fit the machine and work environment to the person, rather than require the person to make the adjustment. Ergonomics includes all attempts to structure work conditions so that they maximize energy conservation, promote good posture, and allow workers to function without pain or impairment. Failure to address ergonomics issues results in repetitive stress injuries, with carpal tunnel syndrome being the most common type.

## REPETITIVE STRESS INJURIES (RSIs)

The Occupational Health and Safety Administration forecasts that one in six heavy computer users—those who spend more than 50 percent of their time on computers—will develop a repetitive stress injury. According to OSHA, the cost per claim can reach $50,000 depending on whether surgery is needed. The U.S. Bureau of Labor Statistics reports that repetitive stress injuries account for 25 percent of cases involving days away from work. The Bureau also stated that disorders associated with repeated trauma account for nearly 60 percent of all work-related illness.[8]

**Carpal tunnel syndrome**
A condition caused by pressure on the median nerve in the wrist due to repetitive flexing and extension of the wrist.

**Carpal tunnel syndrome**, the most commonly reported repetitive stress injury, is caused by pressure on the median nerve in the wrist due to repetitive flexing and extension of the wrist. People developing this RSI may experience pain, numbness or tingling in the hands or wrist, a weak grip, the tendency to drop objects, sensitivity to cold, and—in later stages—muscle deterioration, especially in the thumb.

People who use their hands and wrists repeatedly in the same way tend to develop carpal tunnel syndrome. Illustrators, carpenters, assembly-line workers, and of course those whose jobs involve work on personal computers are the most likely affected.[9] Carpal tunnel syndrome injuries, described as the *plague of the Information Age,* are also among the most expensive workers' compensation claims. They exceed the cost of claims from injuries due to sprains, strains, and fractures. If a carpal tunnel case requires surgery, it will cost $20,000 to $30,000, including lost wages, medical, and administration costs.[10]

The increased frequency of repetitive stress injuries is attributed to the growth of computer use and an aging population that is more vulnerable to such injuries. Also related to increased workers' compensation claims is the increased recognition that such injuries are compensable. As great as the risk of carpal tunnel syndrome has become, it can be prevented or at least reduced. Managers can provide ergonomic furniture, especially chairs, and ensure that computer monitors are set at eye level and keyboards at elbow level. Employees can also cooperate by reporting early symptoms of RSIs and by taking the following actions:

▶ Keep wrists straight.
▶ Take exercise breaks.
▶ Alternate tasks.
▶ Shift positions periodically.
▶ Adjust chair height.
▶ Work with feet flat on the floor.
▶ Be conscious of posture.
▶ Use padded wrist supports.

These voluntary actions may soon be supplemented by governmental intervention. After eight years of debate, the Department of Labor has proposed a set of rules for addressing repetitive stress injuries in industry. Labor unions such as the AFL-CIO have pushed for aggressive regulations.[11] The draft outlines a strict set of rules and regulations for firms to develop ergonomic programs. Such programs would involve informing employees of hazards; establishing procedures for employees to report problems; pinpointing the causes of problems; training employees on how to avoid injury; providing medical care; and keeping written records of actions taken and injury rates. If adopted as law, these rules will give OSHA more authority to enforce ergonomics at companies.[12]

The business community is quite upset about the proposed rules and regulations and views them as being vaguely worded, entrenched in faulty science, and too comprehensive and costly to implement. Under the proposal, qualifying employees would be eligible for as many as six months of restricted duty with full pay and other benefits. According to critics, the new rule involves OSHA in making rules about individual responses to routine chores. One legal expert expressed the view that OSHA would be "literally regulating every fiber of your body."[13] Representatives from the steel industry also decried the ergonomics rule as confusing, misguided, and unnecessary. Steel industry representatives had three basic complaints about the standard. Specifically, they believe the standard is vague and confusing, key terms are not defined, and the source of data on which the standard is premised is flawed. "The whole premise for these proceedings is mistaken," said James W. Stanley, vice president of safety and health for AK Steel Corporation and former OSHA compliance officer and regional officer. Stanley noted that AK Steel has an OSHA-recordable rate of less than two musculoskeletal disorders (MSDs) for every 100 workers. "That's hardly an epidemic," he stated.[14]

Once again, there is a problem that needs to be fixed. The question is whether legislation is needed or the private sector is up to the task. It is clear, however, that there is a payoff in using ergonomics. For example, since Compaq introduced its health and safety standards in the early 1990s, injury rates have decreased 175 percent although its workforce has tripled to 68,000. Today, its rates are one-third the industry average. Other companies have also discovered that improving the work environment boosts morale, lowers injury rates, and yields a positive return on investment (ROI). Employee input in the design and implementation of safety and health programs may well increase the chances for success of such programs.[15]

## WORKPLACE VIOLENCE

In the workplace, homicide is the leading cause of on-the-job death for women and the number two cause of death for men. But, homicide accounts for only a small percentage of the overall incidence of workplace violence. During the decade of the 1990s, yearly averages of workplace violence included 1.48 million simple assaults (verbal threats and arguments), 395,500 aggravated assaults, 50,000 sexual assaults, and 1,000 murders. Fellow workers committed almost 20 percent of the murders. The cost to employers for all workplace incidents was more than $4.2 billion annually.[16] However, when lost time, lower productivity, and litigation costs as well as medical, disability, and workers' compensation payments are included, the costs balloon to around $36 billion.[17] Additionally, there is no way to estimate the physical and psychological damage to other employees, who are only onlookers to the violence.

While employers must take steps to reduce the potential for employee homicides, they must also take action against more pervasive problems that can inflict havoc day in and out. These include bullying, verbal threats, harassment, intimidation, pushing, shoving, slapping, kicking, and fistfights. The vast majority of these types of assaults and other forms of aggression do not show up in the statistics, as they go unreported.[18]

### Vulnerable Employees

Employees at gas stations and liquor stores, taxi drivers, and police officers working overnight shifts face the greatest danger from violence. Ninety percent of the time these workers are threatened by armed criminals, not disgruntled co-workers.[19] Taxi and delivery drivers are 60 times more likely than other workers to be murdered while on the job. The National Institute for Occupational Safety and Health (NIOSH) identified the following factors that put drivers at risk:[20]

- working with the public
- working with cash
- working alone
- working at night
- working in high-crime areas

While these factors increase risk, no workplace is immune from violence. In addition to taxi and delivery drivers, certain businesses are more susceptible to it. The characteristics of a high-risk workplace, according to the National Safe Workplace Institute, include the following:

- Chronic labor/management disputes
- Frequent grievances filed by employees
- A large number of workers' compensation injury claims, especially for psychological injury
- Understaffing and excessive demands for overtime in an authoritarian management style[21]

There are numerous reasons for violent acts committed by employees or former employees. Among the most common are personality conflicts, marital or family problems, drug or alcohol abuse, and firings or layoffs.

# Legal Consequences of Workplace Violence

In addition to the horror of workplace violence, there is also the ever-present threat of legal action. Civil lawsuits claiming *negligent hiring* or *negligent retention* account for more than half of the estimated $36 billion a year in costs to businesses. Just having a standard workplace violence policy supports a firm's position should it wind up in court.[22] Other legal consequences of workplace violence include discrimination lawsuits, workers' compensation claims, third-party claims for damages, invasion of privacy actions, and OSHA violation charges.[23] Under OSHA's general duty clause, employers are required to "furnish, to each employee, employment and place of employment that is free from recognizable hazards that are causing, or likely to cause, death or serious harm to the employee."[24]

Even today, few firms are adequately prepared to deal with the threat of workplace violence. A typical approach has been to screen out applicants with histories of violent tendencies during the selection process. However, the profile developed for a typical attacker is not helpful: "A middle-aged white man who has worked for several years at his company and was dissatisfied with his career status." Firms trying to dig deeper into personality traits can run into difficulty with the Americans with Disabilities Act, which makes it difficult to reject applicants on the basis of psychological tests.

## Individual and Organizational Characteristics to Monitor

Some firms that have had extensive experience with workplace violence are trying an alternative approach. Instead of trying to screen out violent people, they are attempting to detect employees who commit minor aggressive acts and exhibit certain behaviors. These individuals often go on to engage in more serious behaviors. Once identified, these people are required to meet with trained members of the human resources staff for counseling as long as needed. This approach may require more commitment on the part of the firm, but the alternative cost of violence may make this expenditure reasonable in the long run.[25]

Robert Martin, vice president of Gavin de Becker Inc., a company involved with violence prevention, says, "In every case of workplace violence I've seen, there have always been pre-incident indicators." Although every case is different, Martin states that usually a series of exchanges or posturing takes place before the incident.[26] Some warning signs for employees include behavior such as the following:

- Screaming
- Explosive outbursts over minor disagreements
- Making off-color remarks
- Crying
- Decreased energy or focus
- Deteriorating work performance and personal appearance
- Becoming reclusive

A study of 395 human resource managers and security managers conducted by the University of Southern California's Center for Crisis Management found that violence was linked to an uncertain economy or a prolonged recession. Workplace violence was attributed to such organizational deficiencies as inadequate training programs to handle stress, substance abuse, insufficient background screening checks of employees, poor communications, and general organizational instability.[27]

## Preventive Actions

There is no way an employer can completely avoid risk when it comes to violence. Incidences of some unbalanced person coming in and shooting people right and left happen so randomly that not much can be done to anticipate or prevent them. However, firms should consider the following actions both to minimize violent acts and to avoid lawsuits:

- Implement policies that ban weapons on company property, including parking lots.
- Under suspicious circumstances, require employees to submit to searches for weapons or examinations to determine their mental fitness for work.
- Have a policy stating that the organization will not tolerate any incidents of violence or even threats of violence.
- Have a policy that encourages employees to report all suspicious or violent activity to management.
- Develop relationships with mental health experts who may be contacted for recommendations in dealing with emergency situations.
- Train managers and receptionists to recognize the warning signs of violence and techniques to diffuse violent situations.
- Equip receptionists with panic buttons to permit them to alert security officers instantly.[28]

Domestic violence generally occurs away from the workplace. Nevertheless, it is a significant workplace issue and is discussed next.

## DOMESTIC VIOLENCE

Spillover from domestic violence is an unexpected threat to both women and their companies. If a woman is being abused at home, there is a 70 percent chance she will be harassed at work. If she finally leaves her abuser, that is when the real workplace exposure begins.[29] The Office of Criminal Justice calculates that three to four million women are battered each year. The U.S. Surgeon General's office reports that domestic violence is the most widespread cause of injury for women between 15 and 44 years of age. While women in traditional relationships are the most common victims by far, children and men are also affected. The most tragic aspects of domestic violence affect the home, but a shocking toll is also exacted from the workplace in terms of lost productivity, increased health care costs, absenteeism, and sometimes even workplace violence. The Bureau of National Affairs estimates the price tag of domestic violence to corporate America to be from $3 billion to $5 billion a year.[30]

There are indications that domestic violence has decreased in recent years. A Justice Department study found that instances of domestic violence have dropped 21 percent in recent years, falling from an estimated 1.1 million cases in 1993 to about 876,000 cases in 1998.[31] While this short-term trend provides a degree of optimism, it is obvious that this type of behavior remains at an unacceptable level. Business organizations have a huge stake in the problem of violence. The courts apparently agree, as they have ruled that employers owe a duty of care for their employees, customers, and business associates to take reasonable steps to prevent violence on their premises.

In 1990, Joe Leutzinger, director of health promotion at Union Pacific Railroad, found that 29 percent of the costs of medical care could be attributed to lifestyle choices such as diet, exercise, smoking, and stress. At that time, medical claims costs per employee averaged $6,000 per year. Leutzinger gathered data from medical forms that revealed the medical conditions resulting in days lost to illness. From these data, the loss in productivity, as well as total medical costs, could be determined. After assessing needs and conducting a pilot program, Union Pacific implemented "Health Track," a preventive care program, to improve the health of its 58,000 employees. The program includes activities to help employees lower their blood pressure and cholesterol, stop smoking, lose weight, and manage stress. Educational mailings and one-on-one coaching are also provided. Over five years, the costs of medical claims associated with lifestyle choices dropped to 19 percent of medical care costs and medical claims costs per employee dropped to $4,000 a year. However, Leutzinger suggests that in selling a wellness program, it may not be best to focus on cost savings alone. He recommends that wellness be promoted on the basis of its impact on growth in workforce productivity.[32]

## WELLNESS PROGRAMS

The traditional view that health is dependent on medical care and is simply the absence of disease is changing. Today, it is clear that optimal health can generally be achieved through environmental safety, organizational changes, and different lifestyles. Infectious diseases, over which a person has little control, are not the problem they once were. For example, from 1900 to 1970, the death rate from major infectious diseases dropped dramatically. However, the death rate from major chronic diseases—such as heart disease, cancer, and stroke—has significantly increased. It is quite possible that Cecil Pierce, the marketing vice president for Aztec Enterprises, is a candidate for a heart attack or stroke. When a 38-year-old person cannot walk a short distance without getting flushed, breathing hard, and needing to rest, that individual has a problem. Today, heart disease and stroke are the top two killers worldwide. Chronic obstructive pulmonary disease and lung cancer are expected to move up to the number 3 and 4 spots, respectively, by the year 2000. All of these causes of death may be partly prevented by lifestyle measures such as not smoking, eating healthy foods, and exercising more.[33]

In order to address the appropriate health needs of employees, a firm should conduct an assessment of needs before implementation of a wellness program. After outcome goals are established, the following data should be collected:

▶ Medical records such as blood pressure checks, height-to-weight ratios, and cholesterol levels
▶ Facility assessments, focusing on the health and safety of the work environment
▶ Absenteeism rates
▶ Health risk appraisals, including employee health habits and family histories

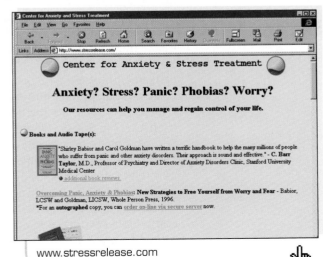

www.stressrelease.com
*Source:* Stressrelease.com

HR WEB
WISDOM

> *Stress Busters*

**www.prenhall.com/mondy**

This site offers thoughts for reducing work stress as well as stress-related beliefs.

To protect employee privacy, composite data only should be analyzed. While these data will indicate possible areas of health needs, it is also important to measure employee interest. This information can be obtained using surveys, focus groups, e-mails, or meetings.[34]

Chronic lifestyle diseases are much more prevalent today than ever before. The good news is that people have a great deal of control over many of them. These are diseases related to smoking, excessive stress, lack of exercise, obesity, and alcohol and drug abuse. Increased recognition of this has prompted employers to become actively involved with their employees' health and establish wellness programs. A 2000 benefits survey conducted by SHRM showed that 49 percent of responding firms have wellness programs.[35] Quite possibly, Cecil would benefit greatly from participating in such a program. Physical fitness continues to be an important component of most major programs. However, there has been a shift toward a more holistic approach to improving health. Wellness programs often expand their focus to include other health issues such as diet, stress, alcohol and drug abuse, employee assistance programs, and smoking. Stress—one of the top concerns in wellness—is discussed next.

## THE NATURE OF STRESS

**Stress**
The body's nonspecific reaction to any demand made on it.

**Stress** is the body's nonspecific reaction to any demand made on it. It affects people in different ways and is therefore a highly individual condition. Certain events may be quite stressful to one person but not to another. Moreover, the effect of stress is not always negative. For example, mild stress actually improves productivity, and it can be helpful in developing creative ideas. Although everyone lives under a certain amount of stress, if it is severe enough and persists long enough, it can be harmful. In fact, stress can be as disruptive to an individual as any accident. It can result in poor attendance, excessive use of alcohol or other drugs, poor job performance, or even overall poor health. There is increasing evidence indicating that severe, prolonged stress is related to the diseases that are the leading causes of death, including coronary heart disease, stroke, hypertension, cancer, emphysema, diabetes, and cirrhosis; stress may even lead to suicide. Stress costs U.S. industry billions of dollars each year in lost wages and treatment of related disorders. To further illustrate the problem, according to the American Institute on Stress, 78 percent of Americans describe their jobs as stressful. Seventy-five to 90 percent of visits to doctors are for stress-related ailments.[36]

The National Institute for Occupational Safety and Health has studied stress as it relates to work. This organization's research indicates that some jobs are generally perceived as being more stressful than others. The 12 most stressful jobs are listed in Table 13-5. The common factor among these jobs is lack of employee control over work. Workers in such jobs may feel that they are trapped, treated more like machines than people. Workers who have more control over their jobs, such as college professors and master craftspersons, hold some of the least stressful jobs.

### The 12 Jobs with the Most Stress

1. Laborer
2. Secretary
3. Inspector
4. Clinical lab technician
5. Office manager
6. Supervisor
7. Manager/administrator
8. Waitress/waiter
9. Machine operator
10. Farm owner
11. Miner
12. Painter

### Other High-Stress Jobs (in Alphabetical Order)

| | |
|---|---|
| Bank teller | Nurse's aide |
| Clergy member | Plumber |
| Computer programmer | Policeperson |
| Dental assistant | Practical nurse |
| Electrician | Public relations worker |
| Firefighter | Railroad switchperson |
| Guard | Registered nurse |
| Hairdresser | Sales manager |
| Health aide | Sales representative |
| Health technician | Social worker |
| Machinist | Structural-metal worker |
| Meat cutter | Teacher's aide |
| Mechanic | Telephone operator |
| Musician | Warehouse worker |

*Source:* From a ranking of 130 occupations by the federal government's National Institute for Occupational Safety and Health.

The fact that certain jobs are identified as more stressful than others has important managerial implications. Managers are responsible for recognizing significantly deviant behavior and referring employees to health professionals for diagnosis and treatment. Some signs that may indicate problems include impaired judgment and effectiveness, rigid behavior, medical problems, increased irritability, excessive absences, emerging addictive behaviors, lowered self-esteem, and apathetic behavior. In addition, managers should monitor their employees' progress and provide them with a supportive environment. They should ensure that employees are aware there are rewards for lifestyle changes and that the advantages of such changes are greater than the costs involved. Stress can generally be handled successfully, but where it cannot, burnout may occur. This phenomenon is discussed next.

## BURNOUT

**Burnout**, while rarely fatal, is an incapacitating condition in which individuals lose a sense of the basic purpose and fulfillment of their work. While some stress is healthy, when the ability to cope with it begins to fail, burnout may be on the horizon. People burn out when they lose interest in what they are doing—when their passion for their work leaves and they do not want to get out of bed in the morning. When stress relief tactics fail to work, that is the time to seek professional help.[37]

Stress is a major cause of low productivity, high absenteeism, poor decisions, and low morale. People become physically and psychologically weakened from trying to combat it. When they become burned out, they are more likely to complain,

**Burnout**
An incapacitating condition in which individuals lose a sense of the basic purpose and fulfillment of their work.

attribute their errors to others, and become highly irritable. The alienation they feel often drives them to think about quitting their jobs.[38]

Burnout is often associated with a midlife or mid-career crisis, but it can happen at different times to different people. When this occurs, they may lose their motivation to perform. Although some employees try to hide their problems, shifts in their behavior may indicate dissatisfaction. They may start procrastinating or go to the opposite extreme of taking on too many assignments. They may lose things and become increasingly scatterbrained. Individuals who are normally amiable may turn irritable. They may become cynical, disagreeable, pompous, or even paranoid.

Individuals in the helping professions, such as teachers and counselors, seem to be susceptible to burnout because of their jobs, whereas others may be vulnerable because of their upbringing, expectations, or personalities. Burnout is frequently associated with people whose jobs require working closely with others under stressful and tension-filled conditions. However, any employee may experience burnout, and no one is exempt. The dangerous part of burnout is that it is contagious. A highly cynical and pessimistic burnout victim can quickly transform an entire group. Therefore, dealing with the problem quickly is very important. Once it has begun, it is difficult to stop. Ideally, burnout should be dealt with before it occurs. To do this, managers must be aware of potential sources of stress. These sources exist both within and outside the organization.

## SOURCES OF STRESS

Regardless of its origin, stress possesses devastating potential. While work-related factors are controllable to varying degrees, others may not be. Three general areas from which stress may emanate include the organization—including the firm's culture, the jobs people perform, and working conditions. Personal factors focus around the family and financial problems. Finally, the general environment also contains elements that may produce stress. These factors are discussed next.

## Organizational Factors

Many factors associated with a person's employment can be potentially stressful. These include the firm's culture, the individual's job, and general working conditions.

**Corporate Culture.** Corporate culture, introduced in Chapter 2, has a lot to do with stress. The CEO's leadership style often sets the tone. An autocratic CEO who permits little input from subordinates may create a stressful environment. A weak CEO may encourage subordinates to compete for power, resulting in internal conflicts. Policies that emanate from the top of the organization may also have a negative effect when it comes to stress. For example, requiring employees to wear white shirts and ties to work may produce discomfort in those who dislike such formality. Even in the healthiest corporate culture, stressful relationships among employees can occur. Employee personality types vary, and combined with differing values and belief systems, they may so impair communication that stress is inevitable. Also, competition encouraged by the organization's reward system for promotion, pay increases, and status may add to the problem.

**The Job Itself.** A number of factors related to the job people perform may produce excessive stress. As previously noted, some jobs are generally perceived as being more stressful than others due to the nature of the tasks involved. Managerial work may itself be a source of stress. Responsibility for people, conducting performance appraisals, coordinating and communicating layoffs, and conducting outplacement counseling can create a great deal of stress for some people. Other sources of stress related to the job include role ambiguity, role conflict, workload variance, and working conditions.

**Role ambiguity** exists when an employee does not understand the content of the job. The employee may feel stress when he or she does not perform certain duties expected by the supervisor, or when he or she attempts to perform tasks that are a part of someone else's job. Role ambiguity is a condition that can easily lead to conflict with one's boss or co-workers. It can be quite threatening to an employee and can produce feelings of insecurity.

**Role conflict** exists when an individual is placed in the position of having to pursue opposing goals. For example, a manager may be expected to increase production while at the same time decreasing the size of the workforce. Attaining both goals may be impossible, and stress is likely to result.

**Workload variance** involves dealing with both job overload and job underload. When employees are given more work than they can reasonably handle, they become victims of **job overload**. A critical aspect of this problem is that the best performers in the firm are often the ones most affected. These individuals have proven that they can perform more, so they are often given more to do. At its extreme, work overload results in burnout.

**Job underload** may occur when employees are given menial, boring tasks to perform. Individuals who constantly seek challenge in their jobs may experience stress when this happens.

**Working Conditions.** Working conditions, including the physical characteristics of the workplace and the machines and tools used, can also create stress. Overcrowding, excessive noise, poor lighting, poorly maintained work stations, and equipment that does not work properly can all adversely affect employee morale and increase stress. Working conditions that do not provide workplace flexibility, as discussed in the previous chapter, may also produce excessive stress.

## Personal Factors

Stress factors outside the job and job environment also may affect job performance. Although these are usually far less controllable by management, managers should recognize that they do exist and may have implications for job performance. Factors in this category include the family and financial problems.

**The Family.** Although a frequent source of happiness and security, the family can also be a significant stressor. As a result, over one-half of all marriages end in divorce, which in itself is generally quite stressful. When divorce leads to single parenthood, the difficulties may be compounded. Contrary to conventional wisdom, women feel no more anxiety on the job because they are mothers than do men because they are fathers. However, concern about their children can cause either parent to suffer stress-related health problems. When trouble exists both at home and at work, a double dose of stress exists. On the positive side, a healthy home life provides a protective buffer against work-related stressors such as an overbearing boss. An increasingly common circumstance involving a change in traditional roles is the dual-career family, discussed in Chapter 2, in which both husband and wife have jobs and family responsibilities. What happens when one partner is completely content with a job, and the other is offered a desired promotion requiring transfer to a distant city? At best, these circumstances are beset with difficulties.

**Role ambiguity**
A condition that exists when employees do not understand the content of their jobs.

**Role conflict**
A condition that occurs when an individual is placed in the position of having to pursue opposing goals.

**Workload variance**
Both job overload and job underload.

**Job overload**
A condition that exists when employees are given more work than they can reasonably handle.

**Job underload**
A condition that occurs when employees are given menial, boring tasks to perform.

**Financial Problems.** Problems with finances may place an unbearable strain on the employee. For some, these problems are persistent and never quite resolved. Unpaid bills and bill collectors can create great tension and play a role in divorce or poor work performance.

## The General Environment

Stress is a part of everyone's everyday life; its potential lurks not only in the workplace and the home, but also in our general environment. The long commute in rush-hour traffic, the unrelenting rain, the oppressive heat or chilling cold—all can create stress. Excessive noise can also create extreme stress in some people. While stress is seemingly ubiquitous, there are ways that it can be dealt with. Some suggestions that may be helpful in dealing with stress are discussed in the following sections.

## MANAGING STRESS

Experts emphasize that some stress is healthy, and moderate stress is the key to survival. Yet, excessive, prolonged stress must be dealt with, and both the individual and organizations have a responsibility to take appropriate measures.

## Individual Coping Approaches

There are a number of ways that individuals may control excessive stress. The Canadian Mental Health Association recommends the following approaches:

- Recognize your symptoms of stress.
- Look at your lifestyle and see what can be changed.
- Use relaxation techniques.
- Exercise.
- Manage your time well.
- Aim for a diet with a balance of fruits, vegetables, whole grains, and foods high in protein but low in fat.
- Get enough rest and sleep.
- Talk with others: friends, professional counselors, and support groups.
- Help others.
- Engage in volunteer work.
- Get away for a while.
- Ease up on criticism of others.
- Don't be too competitive.
- Make the first move to be friendly.
- Have some fun.[39]

Individuals can utilize several specific techniques to deal with stress. These methods include hypnosis, biofeedback, and transcendental meditation.

**Hypnosis** is an altered state of consciousness that is artificially induced and characterized by increased receptiveness to suggestions. A person in a hypnotic state may, therefore, respond to the hypnotist's suggestion to relax. Hypnosis can help many people cope with stress. The serenity achieved through dissipation of anxieties and fears can restore an individual's confidence. A principal benefit of hypnotherapy is that peace of mind continues after the person awakens from a hypnotic state. This tranquility continues to grow, especially when the person has been trained in self-hypnosis.

**Hypnosis**
An altered state of consciousness that is artificially induced and characterized by increased receptiveness to suggestions.

**Biofeedback** is a method that can be used to control involuntary bodily processes, such as blood pressure or heart rate. For example, using equipment to provide a visual display of blood pressure, individuals may learn to lower their systolic blood pressure levels.

**Transcendental meditation (TM)** is a stress-reduction technique in which an individual, comfortably seated, silently repeats a secret word or phrase (mantra) provided by a trained instructor. Repeating the mantra over and over helps prevent distracting thoughts. Transcendental meditation has successfully produced physiologic changes such as decreased oxygen consumption, decreased carbon dioxide elimination, and a decreased breathing rate. This technique results in a decreased metabolic rate and a restful state.

**Biofeedback**
A method of learning to control involuntary bodily processes, such as blood pressure or heart rate.

**Transcendental meditation (TM)**
A stress-reduction technique in which an individual, comfortably seated, silently repeats a secret word or phrase (mantra) provided by a trained instructor.

## Organizational Coping Approaches

A number of programs and techniques may effectively prevent or relieve excessive stress. General organizational programs, while not specifically designed to cope with stress, may nevertheless play a major role. The programs listed in Table 13-6 are discussed in the chapters indicated. Their effective implementation will achieve the following results:

▸ A corporate culture that holds anxiety and tension to an acceptable level is created. Employee inputs are sought and valued, employees are given greater control over their work, and communication is emphasized.

▸ Each person's role is defined as clearly as possible in today's environment, with encouragement given to risk takers and to those who want to assume greater responsibility.

▸ Individuals are given the training and development they need to successfully perform current and future tasks. Equal consideration is given to achieving personal and organizational goals. Individuals are trained to work as effective

**Organizational Programs and Techniques That Can be Helpful in Coping with Stress**  🖐  **Table 13-6**

| General Organizational Programs Addressed in This Book | Chapter |
|---|---|
| Corporate Culture (effective communication, motivation, and leadership styles) | 2 |
| Job Analysis | 4 |
| Training and Development | 8 |
| Organization Development | 8 |
| Career Planning and Development | 9 |
| Performance Appraisal | 10 |
| Compensation and Benefits | 11, 12 |
| **Specific Techniques** | |
| Hypnosis | 13 |
| Transcendental Meditation | 13 |
| Biofeedback | 13 |
| **Specific Organizational Programs** | |
| Physical Fitness | 13 |
| Alcohol and Drug Abuse | 13 |
| Employee Assistance Programs | 13 |

> Thousands of U.S. business firms have exercise programs designed to help keep their workers physically fit.

team members and to develop an awareness of how they and their work relate to others.

> Employees are assisted in planning for career progression.

> Employees participate in making decisions that affect them. They know what is going on in the firm, what their particular roles are, and how well they are performing their jobs.

> Employees' financial and nonfinancial needs are met through an equitable reward system.

Table 13-6 also lists specific programs that are designed to deal with stress and related problems. These include physical fitness programs, alcohol and drug abuse programs, and employee assistance programs.

## PHYSICAL FITNESS PROGRAMS

According to an SHRM study, 19 percent of responding firms have on-site physical fitness centers and 24 percent provide fitness center/gym subsidies.[40] In addition, thousands of U.S. business firms have exercise programs designed to help keep their workers physically fit. Cecil Pierce, the vice president introduced earlier, obviously needs medical attention and probably would benefit greatly from a physician-supervised fitness program. From management's viewpoint, this effort makes a lot of sense. Loss of productivity resulting from coronary heart disease alone costs U.S. businesses billions of dollars annually. Company-sponsored fitness programs often reduce absenteeism, accidents, and sick pay. There is increasing evidence that if employees stick to company fitness programs, they will experience better health, and the firm will have lower costs. A study at Steelcase, an office equipment manufacturer, found that participants in a corporate fitness program had 55 percent lower medical claims costs over a six-year period than did nonparticipants.[41]

## ALCOHOL AND DRUG ABUSE PROGRAMS

**Alcoholism**
A treatable disease characterized by uncontrolled and compulsive drinking that interferes with normal living patterns.

**Alcoholism** is a disease characterized by uncontrolled and compulsive drinking that interferes with normal living patterns. It is a significant problem that affects people at every level of society, and it can both result from and cause excessive stress. As a person starts to drink excessively, the drinking itself produces greater stress. A vicious cycle is created as this increased stress is dealt with by more drinking. Early signs of alcohol abuse are especially difficult to identify. Often the symptoms are nothing more than an increasing number of absences from work. Although our society attaches a stigma to alcoholism, in 1956 the American Medical Association described it as a treatable disease.

Drug users are increasingly gravitating to the workplace, which is an ideal place to sell drugs. Since 95 percent of *Fortune* 500 companies conduct preemployment drug screening, 60 percent of employed drug users work for smaller businesses, many of which do not use drug testing. Many young drug users, whose lifestyle includes an unprecedented level of comfort with drug use, will be moving into the workforce, adding a new dimension to the problem.[42]

In certain industries—transportation, for example—drug use on the job is especially hazardous and potentially devastating to the firm. Think of the damage that can be done by a 40-ton truck careening out of control. Under ideal conditions, a fully loaded truck in daylight on a dry road cannot stop in less than 300 feet, or the length of a football field.

All illegal drugs have some adverse effects. Although some claim that marijuana is innocuous, another source estimates that the use of marijuana and other illegal drugs costs approximately $100 billion per year in lost productivity in American companies.[43] Prescription drugs can also be as addictive, impairing, and destructive as common street drugs. According to drug enforcement agencies, at least 25–30 percent of drug abuse in the workplace involves prescription drugs. And, standard drug screens do not always detect these drugs. Currently, Vicodin—a painkiller—is the drug of choice, but other abused drugs include Demerol, Darvon, Tylenol with codeine, anti-anxiety drugs such as Xanax and Valium, and stimulants such as Ritalin.[44]

Chemically dependent employees exhibit behaviors that distinguish them from drug-free workers. In one study, employees who had a positive drug test but were hired anyway missed 50 percent more time from work than other employees. They also had a 47 percent higher chance of being fired. According to the NIDA, one Utah power company found that drug-positive employees were five times more likely than other employees to cause an on-the-job accident. Substance abuse involving either alcohol or drugs increases employee theft, lowers morale, and reduces productivity.[45]

The Drug Free Workplace Act of 1988 requires firms with large government contracts or grants to make a good faith effort to maintain a *drug free workplace*. Because substance abuse is so expensive, all firms should have the same objective. Drug testing as a component in an organization's selection process is one means of achieving this goal. However, since a large percentage of substance abusers are already employed, this is obviously not the solution to the problem. For one thing, managers must learn to recognize impaired or intoxicated employees and those who may be addicted. Signs that suggest that an employee may be impaired are shown in Table 13-7. Remember that none of the signs alone necessarily means that an employee is impaired. Also, it is necessary to observe behavior over a long period of time.

## Signs Suggesting Employee Impairment because of Substance Abuse  Table 13-7

- Tardiness, poor attendance, or problems performing the job.
- Accident proneness and multiple workers' compensation claims.
- Physical appearance; e.g., dilated or constricted pupils.
- Lack of coordination.
- Mood swings.
- Psychomotor agitation or retardation. Alcohol, marijuana, and opioids can all cause fatigue. Cocaine, amphetamines, and hallucinogens can cause anxiety.
- Thought disturbances. Cocaine, alcohol, PCP, amphetamines, and inhalants often cause grandiosity or a subject sense of profound thought.
- Other indicators. Cocaine, PCP, and inhalants can all cause aggressive or violent behavior. Alcohol and other sedatives reduce inhibition. Marijuana increases appetite, whereas stimulants decrease it. Both types of drugs cause excessive thirst.

*Source:* Deanna Kelemen, "How to Recognize Substance Abuse in the Workplace," *Supervision* 56 (September 1995): 4.

## HR WEB WISDOM

▶ *EAPs*

**www.prenhall.com/mondy**

Information on program design, implementation, counseling, and evaluation is included.

Many firms have tackled the drug abuse problem head on by establishing a drug-free workplace program. Such an approach might include the following:[46]

▶ A clear, consistent zero tolerance policy
▶ Education and training for workers and supervisors
▶ A drug-testing program
▶ An employee assistance program to help employees with substance abuse problems

At Texas Instruments, the policy is simple and straightforward: "There will be no use of any illegal drug. There will be no illicit use of a legal drug." The difficult part is not formulating the policy, but rather implementing it. Also, remember that the Americans with Disabilities Act protects an employee in a substance abuse rehabilitation program.

## EMPLOYEE ASSISTANCE PROGRAMS (EAPs)

**Employee assistance program (EAP)**
A comprehensive approach that many organizations have taken to deal with burnout, alcohol and drug abuse, and other emotional disturbances.

An **employee assistance program (EAP)** is a comprehensive approach that many organizations have taken to deal with numerous problem areas, including marital or family difficulties, job performance problems, stress, emotional or mental health issues, financial troubles, alcohol and drug abuse, and grief. Most programs are created to control substance abuse or mental health costs. Some have also become concerned with HIV and AIDS, eldercare, workplace violence, and natural disasters such as earthquakes, floods, and tornadoes.

In an EAP, a firm either provides in-house professional counselors or refers employees to an appropriate community social service agency. Currently, a tug-of-war exists that pits the traditional workplace-focused *assessment and referral (A&R)* model against the *counseling* model. The workplace-based A&R approach might feature a greater workplace presence, more supervisor contact, and an emphasis on management referrals. This approach holds that EAP professionals should see clients only long enough to identify the basic problem, then motivate them to seek outside help if necessary. A counseling approach is more likely to be external to the firm and involves prolonged therapeutic intervention and an emphasis on self-referrals. A problem with this model is that the staffs of some organizations

## HRM IN ACTION

▶ *Is There Substance to This?*

"I just don't know what to do about Robert Lewis," said Marty Fagetti, the production supervisor, to Eli Richard, the human resource manager. "Lately I've noticed that Robert has missed work frequently. Even when he shows up, he is usually late and looks like hell warmed over. He gets angry real easy these days, and he seems to move in slow motion. He also doesn't hang around with the old gang anymore. Again, today, he didn't show up for work."

*If you were Eli, what action would you suggest?*

lack specialized training and have no EAP-specific certification. To rectify this situation, two states—North Carolina and Tennessee—have passed licensing laws for EAPs; five other states have bills under consideration. The Employee Assistance Professionals Association (EAPA) has a certification program for individuals, and the Employee Assistance Society of North America has an accreditation program for EAP programs.[47]

In either EAP model, most or all of the costs (up to a predetermined amount) are borne by the employer. The EAP concept includes a response to personal psychological problems that interfere with both an employee's well-being and overall productivity. The purpose of assistance programs is to provide emotionally troubled employees with the same consideration and assistance given employees with physical illnesses.

Since 1999, Florida Power and Light employees have used their computers as an outlet for handling emotional turmoil. The firm pays for its 10,600 employees to log on to the Web site MasteringStress.com to use its software to deal with bouts of depression, anger, and other emotional turmoil.[48]

The Drug Free Workplace Act of 1988 requires federal employees and employees of firms under government contract to have access to employee assistance program services. As you can imagine, EAPs grew rapidly in number following that act. However, many firms have determined that there are other advantages to be derived from EAPs and have implemented them voluntarily. In 1958, fewer than 50 American firms offered employee assistance counseling. In 2000, a study by SHRM indicated that 97 percent of responding firms with over 5,000 employees had an employee assistance program. Even in small firms with fewer than 100 employees, 48 percent had EAPs.[49] These programs are being set up primarily to increase worker productivity and reduce costs. Utah Power and Light's EAP program receives a $3.73 return on every dollar invested. This return stems from less time off required by employees and reduced medical costs for the EAP users. R.R. Donnelley & Sons found a return of $1.61 for each dollar invested in the first year its employee assistance program was in operation.[50] Returns on investment will vary, but one executive estimates that a mature, well-run program will return a minimum of three dollars for every dollar spent on it. This level of return will not happen, however, unless the employer is committed to promoting the program, educating employees and managers about its purpose, and eliminating any stigma from seeking help. Advantages claimed for EAPs include lower absenteeism, decreases in workers' compensation claims, and fewer accidents.

A primary concern is getting employees to use the program. Some employees perceive that there is a stigma attached to needing help. Supervisors must receive training designed to provide specialized interpersonal skills for recognizing troubled employees and encouraging them to utilize the firm's employee assistance program. Addicted employees are often experts at denial and deception, and they can fool even experienced counselors.

Two additional health issues of concern to management include smoking and AIDS. These topics are dealt with in the next sections of the chapter.

## SMOKING IN THE WORKPLACE

An important health issue facing employers today is environmental tobacco smoke (ETS). Although some smokers and advocates remain adamant that passive cigarette smoke is not harmful, the Environmental Protection Agency has determined that ETS is a class A carcinogen—a category reserved for the most dangerous cancer-causing agents in humans. Secondhand smoke kills an estimated 35,000 to

65,000 nonsmoking Americans each year, mostly by causing heart attacks and lung cancer. In fetuses, it increases the risk of low birth weight, and it is responsible for up to 300,000 cases of childhood bronchitis and pneumonia, according to a new government report. It is also linked to childhood asthma and sudden infant death syndrome.[51] In fact, smoking is the leading cause of preventable death, resulting in more deaths than the combined toll from AIDS, cocaine, heroin, alcohol, fire, automobile accidents, homicide, and suicide. These data will likely strengthen efforts to ban smoking. Smoking bans have already been enacted in businesses and public buildings nationwide. OSHA has proposed banning smoking or limiting it to separately ventilated areas in six million U.S. businesses.

Numerous studies have concluded that workplace smoking is not only hazardous to employees' health, but is also detrimental to the firm's financial health. Employers have begun to develop ways to eliminate smoking in the workplace because the costs associated with tobacco use are staggering. According to public health reports, expenditures in the United States directly related to smoking total $72 billion per year. Costs not related to health but caused by tobacco use include property losses from fires caused by cigarettes or cigars, work productivity losses, and the costs of extra cleaning and maintenance required because of tobacco smoke, smokeless tobacco, and tobacco-related litter. These costs amount to over $44 billion annually.[52] One research study indicated that by the year 2002, no less than 96 percent of the companies surveyed had a goal to be smoke free.[53] A Gallup survey indicated that a vast majority of Americans—94 percent—favored some type of restriction on workplace smoking.[54]

When tough smoking policies prove ineffective, some employers think it is time to quit battering morale by booting smokers out into blizzards or heat waves. Companies are also concerned about lost productivity. Smoking breaks taken some distance away from the workplace eat up a lot of time. To deal with this, State Farm Insurance will soon have a covered smoking area near the main building. For this firm, a two-year-old edict prohibiting smoking anywhere on company property was reversed. At the other end of the continuum, Motorola is making smoking even tougher. This firm has started enforcing a policy at four plants that prohibits employees from smoking anywhere on company property, including in their own cars parked in the Motorola parking lot.[55] Another approach is being taken by an increasing number of firms. Nearly 25 percent of large companies charge smokers higher premiums than nonsmoking co-workers for health insurance. U-Haul and Texas Instruments add an extra $10 to $50 a month, and a group of more aggressive firms is charging double.[56]

Regardless of the twist a firm's smoking policy takes, the company will have to maintain fresh indoor air for its employees. The alternative will be a backlash from nonsmokers and lawsuits from survivors of those who may one day die from secondhand smoke.

## AIDS IN THE WORKPLACE

**AIDS (acquired immune deficiency syndrome)**
A disease that undermines the body's immune system, leaving the person susceptible to a wide range of fatal diseases.

**AIDS (acquired immune deficiency syndrome)** is a disease that undermines the body's immune system, leaving the person susceptible to a wide range of fatal diseases. AIDS is a blood-borne virus with very limited avenues of transmission. Humans acquire HIV infection by having unprotected sex with an infected partner, by sharing contaminated needles, by being born to an infected mother, or by receiving a contaminated blood product.

AIDS is definitely a workplace issue and one that impacts productivity. Employees fearful of associating with those infected with the virus create an atmosphere that is not conducive to efficiency. A challenge to management is to educate all employees about the disease, how to deal with it, and that it cannot be transmitted through casual contact. Outside of the health care arena, workplace exposure to blood is rare. Therefore, there is no rational reason for employees to fear working with someone who has AIDS or has been exposed to the virus. Unfortunately, the vast majority of employers have not provided workplace AIDS education for their employees and few companies have AIDS policies, according to the Centers for Disease Control and Prevention.

Management cannot automatically assume that the infected individual will have anything other than a normal life span in the workplace. This situation is different from the assumption only a few years ago, when an individual with AIDS was presumed to have a short work life. For the infected employee, the Americans with Disabilities Act requires that reasonable accommodations be made. They may include, for example, equipment changes, work station modifications, adjustments to work schedules, or assistance accessing the facility.

## Summary

**❶ Describe the nature and role of safety and health.**
Safety involves protecting employees from injuries due to work-related accidents. Health refers to the employees' freedom from physical or emotional illness.

**②  Explain the purpose of the Occupational Safety and Health Act.**
The purpose of this act is to assure a safe and healthful workplace for every American worker.

**③  Describe the focus of safety programs in business operations.**
Safety programs may be designed to accomplish their purposes in two primary ways. The first approach is to create a psychological environment and attitudes that promote safety. The second approach to safety program design is to develop and maintain a safe physical working environment.

**④  Explain the purpose of ergonomics.**
Through ergonomics, an attempt is made to fit the machine and work environment to the person, rather than require the person to make the adjustment.

**⑤  Describe the consequences of repetitive stress injuries.**
The Occupational Health and Safety Administration forecasts that one in six heavy computer users—those who spend more than 50 percent of their time on computers—will develop a repetitive stress injury.

**⑥  Explain the effect on businesses of workplace and domestic violence.**
The fastest-growing form of homicide is killing in the workplace. Homicide is the leading cause of on-the-job death for women and the number two cause of death for men. Spillover from domestic violence is an unexpected threat to both women and their companies.

**⑦  Describe the purposes of wellness programs.**
The traditional view is changing. No longer is health considered to be dependent on medical care and simply the absence of disease. Today, the prevailing opinion is that optimal health can generally be achieved through environmental safety, organizational changes, and changed lifestyles.

**⑧  Describe stress and burnout.**
Stress is the body's nonspecific reaction to any demand made on it. Burnout, while rarely fatal, is an incapacitating condition where individuals lose a sense of the basic purpose and fulfillment of their work.

**⑨  Explain sources of stress and means of coping with stress.**
Three general areas from which stress may emanate include the organization (including the firm's culture), the jobs people perform, and working conditions. Personal factors focus on the family and financial problems. Finally, the general environment also contains elements that may produce stress. Stress may be coped with through individual or organizational means.

**⑩  Describe the importance of physical fitness programs.**
Many U.S. business firms have exercise programs designed to help keep their workers physically fit. These programs often reduce absenteeism, accidents, and sick pay.

**⑪  Explain alcohol abuse and drug abuse programs.**
Alcohol, cocaine, and other mind-altering drugs have impacted the workplace. Numerous firms have recognized that these problems pervade our society and have taken positive action to deal with them. Many firms have tackled the drug abuse problem head-on by establishing a drug-free workplace program.

**⑫  Describe employee assistance programs.**
An employee assistance program (EAP) is a comprehensive approach that many organizations develop to deal with numerous problem areas, including marital or family problems, job performance problems, stress, emotional or mental health issues, financial troubles, alcohol and drug abuse, and grief.

**⑬  Describe the possible impact of smoking in the workplace.**
Workplace smoking is not only hazardous to employees' health but is also detrimental to the firm's financial health.

**14** **Explain the possible impact of AIDS in the workplace.**
AIDS is a disease that undermines the body's immune system, leaving the person susceptible to a wide range of fatal diseases. AIDS is definitely a workplace issue and one that impacts productivity.

## Questions for Review ◄

1. Define *safety* and *health*. 391-392
2. What is the purpose of the Occupational Safety and Health Act? 393
3. What effect does workplace violence have on an organization?
4. What are the primary ways in which safety programs are designed? Discuss.
5. What is carpal tunnel syndrome? 398 - 400
6. What are the purposes of wellness programs? 404
7. Why should a firm attempt to identify stressful jobs? What could an organization do to reduce the stress associated with a job?
8. Why should a firm be concerned with employee burnout? 405
9. What are the major sources of stress? 406 - 407
10. What are the means of managing stress? 408
11. Why should alcohol and drug abuse programs be established?
12. Explain why employee assistance programs are being established. 413
13. What concerns should a manager have regarding smoking in the workplace?

*We invite you to visit the Mondy homepage on the Prentice Hall Web site at*
**www.prenhall.com/mondy**
*for updated information, Web-based exercises, and links to other HR-related sites.*

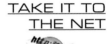

TAKE IT TO
THE NET

## Developing HRM Skills ◄

### An Experiential Exercise

At times, workers have personal problems that negatively influence their work and that may make the workplace unsafe. When this occurs, both managers and human resource professionals may be required to become involved to maintain a safe and healthy work environment. Dealing with one's own personal problems is often difficult, and assisting employees in dealing with their personal problems can be even more taxing on managers. However, since a problem employee can have a negative effect on workforce productivity, such a situation must be addressed by individuals involved in human resource management. This exercise should provide a better understanding of how to handle a most difficult issue: that of resolving employee problems.

If you are a sensitive person, you may want to play a role in this exercise. Two students will actively participate. One will play Annette and one will play Walter.

The rest of you should observe carefully. Your instructor will provide any additional information necessary to participate.

► HRM INCIDENT 1

### A Commitment to Safety?

Wanda Zackery was extremely excited a year ago when she joined Landon Electronics as its first safety engineer. She had graduated from Florida State University with a degree in electrical engineering and had a strong desire to enter business. Wanda had selected her job at Landon Electronics over several other offers. She believed that it would provide her with a broad range of experiences that she could not receive in a strictly engineering job. Also, when she was interviewed by the company's president, Mark Lincoln, he promised her that the firm's resources would be at her disposal to correct any safety-related problems.

Her first few months at Landon were hectic but exciting. She immediately identified numerous safety problems. One of the most dangerous involved a failure to install safety guards on all exposed equipment. Wanda carefully prepared her proposal, including expected costs, to make needed minimum changes. She estimated that it would take approximately $50,000 to complete the necessary conversions. Wanda then presented the entire package to Mr. Lincoln. She explained the need for the changes to him, and Mr. Lincoln cordially received her presentation. He said that he would like to think it over and get back to her.

But that was six months ago! Every time Wanda attempted to get some action on her proposal, Mr. Lincoln was friendly but still wanted some more time to consider it. In the meantime, Wanda had become increasingly anxious. Recently, a worker had barely avoided a serious injury. Some workers had also become concerned. She heard through the grapevine that someone had telephoned the regional office of OSHA.

Her suspicions were confirmed the very next week when an OSHA inspector appeared at the plant. No previous visits had ever been made to the company. Although Mr. Lincoln was not overjoyed, he permitted the inspector access to the company. Later he might have wished that he had not been so cooperative. Before the inspector left, he wrote violations for each piece of equipment that did not have the necessary safety guards. The fines would total $5,000 if the problems were not corrected right away. The inspector cautioned that repeat violations could cost $50,000 and possible imprisonment.

As the inspector was leaving, Wanda received a phone call. "Wanda, this is Mark. Get up to my office right now. We need to get your project under way."

**Questions**

1. Discuss Mr. Lincoln's level of commitment to occupational safety.
2. Is there a necessary trade-off between Landon's need for low expenses and the workers' need for safe working conditions? Explain.

► HRM INCIDENT 2

### What a Change!

"Just leave me alone and let me do my job," said Manuel Gomez. Dumbfounded, Bill Brown, Manuel's supervisor, decided to count to 10 and not respond to

Manuel's comment. As he walked back to his office, Bill thought about how Manuel had changed over the past few months. He had been a hard worker and extremely cooperative when he started working for Bill two years earlier. The company had sent Manuel to two training schools and had received glowing reports about his performance in each of them.

Until about a year ago, Manuel had a perfect attendance record and was an ideal employee. At about that time, however, he began to have personal problems, which resulted in a divorce six months later. Manuel had requested a day off several times to take care of personal business. Bill attempted to help in every way he could without getting directly involved in Manuel's personal affairs. But, Bill was aware of the strain Manuel must have experienced as his marriage broke up, and he and his wife engaged in the inevitable disputes over child custody, alimony payments, and property.

During the same time period, top management initiated a push for improving productivity. Bill found it necessary to put additional pressure on all his workers, including Manuel. He tried to be considerate, but he had to become much more performance oriented, insisting on increased output from every worker. As time went on, Manuel began to show up late for work and actually missed two days without calling Bill in advance. Bill attributed Manuel's behavior to extreme stress. Because Manuel had been such a good worker for so long, Bill excused the tardiness and absences, only gently suggesting that Manuel should try to do better.

Sitting at his desk, Bill thought about what might have caused Manuel's outburst a few minutes earlier. Bill had simply suggested to Manuel that he shut down the machine he was operating and clean up the surrounding area. This was a normal part of Manuel's job and something he had been careful to do in the past. Bill felt the disorder around Manuel's machine might account for the increasing number of defects in the parts he was making. "This is a tough one. I think I'll talk to the boss about it," thought Bill.

### Questions

1. What do you think is likely to be Manuel's problem? Discuss.
2. If you were Bill's boss, what would you recommend that he do?

## Notes ◀

1. "Job Related Injuries, Illness Take Heavy Toll," *Houston Chronicle* (July 28, 1997): A1.

2. William Atkinson, "When OSHA Comes Knocking," *HRMagazine* 44 (October 1999): 36–38.

3. "OSHA Facts: New Ways of Working," Occupational Safety and Health Administration www.osha-slc.gov/OSHAFacts/OSHAFacts2_3_00.pdf (July 1, 2000).

4. Atkinson, "When OSHA Comes Knocking."

5. Linda Micco, "OSHA Reform Legislation Premature, Official Says," *HR News* 16 (August 1997): 11.

6. "Job Related Injury Costs," *Accident Facts* (Chicago: National Safety Council, 1998): 51.

7. Michael J. Blotzer, "Job Hazard Analysis and More," *Occupational Hazards* 60 (July 1, 1998): 25.

8. Amanda Levin, "Ergonomic Software Used to Reduce RSI," *National Underwriter* 104 (March 13, 2000): 15.

9. Phyllis G. Cooper, "Carpal Tunnel Syndrome," *Clinical Reference Systems* (July 1, 1999): 232.

10. John G. Spooner, "RSI: More Stress for IT," *PC Week* (March 1, 1999): 39.

11. Linda Rosencrance, "OSHA Proposal Requires IT Action," *Computerworld* 33 (November 29, 1999): 1.

12. Spooner, "RSI: More Stress for IT."

13. John Elvin, "OSHA Wants to Regulate Your Body," *Insight on the News* (October 4, 1999): 34.

14. "Steel Industry Condemns Ergonomics Proposal," *CCH NetNews: Employment Safety and Workers' Compensation* (May 8, 2000): 3.

15. Robert J. Grossman, "Make Ergonomics Go," *HRMagazine* 45 (April 2000): 38–41.

16. James E. Crockett, "Minimizing the Risk of Workplace Violence," *Business Insurance* 33 (July 1999): 35.

17. Stephanie Schroeder, "The High Cost of Workplace Violence," *Risk Management* 46 (November 1999): 54.

18. William Atkinson, "The Everyday Face of Violence in the Workplace," *Risk Management* 47 (February 2000): 12.

19. Kevin Dobbs, "The Lucrative Menace of Workplace Violence," *Training* 37 (March 2000): 54–62.

20. "Risk Factors and Protective Measures for Taxi and Livery Drivers," U.S. Department of Labor, Occupational Safety and Health Administration www.osha.gov/OSHAFacts/ taxi-livery-drivers.pdf (May 2000).

21. Crockett, "Minimizing the Risk of Workplace Violence."

22. Dobbs, "The Lucrative Menace of Workplace Violence."

23. Crockett, "Minimizing the Risk of Workplace Violence."

24. Atkinson, "The Everyday Face of Violence in the Workplace," 14.

25. John T. Landry, "Workplace Violence: Preventing the Unthinkable," *Harvard Business Review* 75 (January/February 1997): 11–12.

26. Carla Joinson, "Controlling Hostility," *HRMagazine* 43 (August 1998): 66.

27. "Workplace Violence Linked to WC Claims, EAP Usage," *National Underwriters, Property & Casualty Risk & Benefits Management Edition* (January 8, 1996): 15.

28. Patrick Mirza, "Tips Offered on Minimizing Workplace Violence," *HR News* 16 (July 1997): 15.

29. Schroeder, "The High Cost of Violence."

30. Charlene Marmer Solomon, "Talking Frankly About Domestic Violence," *Personnel Journal* 74 (April 1995): 64.

31. Eric Lichtblau, "Violence against Women by Partners Decreasing," *The Dallas Morning News* (May 18, 2000): 1A.

32. Martinez, "Using Data to Create Wellness Programs That Work."

33. "Longevity Facts," *The Johns Hopkins Medical Letter: Health After 50* 9 (September 1997): 1.

34. Michelle Neely Martinez, "Using Data to Create Wellness Programs That Work," *HRMagazine* 44 (November 1999): 110–113.

35. *2000 Benefits Survey,* Society for Human Resource Management, 17.

36. Jane Stahl, "Stress Busters," *Successful Meetings* 48 (November 1999): 67.

37. Lin Grensing-Pophal, "HR, Heal Thyself," *HRMagazine* 44 (March 1999): 83–88.

38. John Yuen and Maryjane Martin, "Creative Ways for Managing Work-Place Tension," *Communication World* 15 (August 18, 1998): 18.

39. Ibid.

40. *2000 Benefits Survey,* Society for Human Resource Management, 17.

41. Michael Barrier, "How Exercise Can Pay Off," *Nation's Business* 85 (February 1997): 41.

42. Jane Easter Bahls, "Drugs in the Workplace," *HRMagazine* 43 (February 1998): 84–85.

43. Charles R. Schwenk, "Marijuana and Job Performance: Comparing the Major Streams of Research," *Journal of Drug Issues* 28 (Fall 1998): 941.

44. Bahls, "Drugs in the Workplace," 83.

45. Deanna Kelemen, "How to Recognize Substance Abuse in the Workplace," *Supervision* 56 (September 1995): 3.

46. Bahls, "Drugs in the Workplace," 85.

47. Rudy M. Yandrick, "The EAP Struggle: Counselors or Referrers?" *HRMagazine* 43 (August 1998): 91–94.

48. Ron Shinkman, "Utility Workers Plug into Online Therapy," *Modern Healthcare* 29 (October 18, 1999): 46.

49. *2000 Benefits Survey,* Society for Human Resource Management, 18.

50. Gillian Flynn, "Nice Companies Don't Finish Last: A Look at Assistance That Works," *Personnel Journal* 74 (October 1995): 176.

51. "Living by the Numbers: How to Gauge Your Risks," *University of California, Berkeley, Wellness Letter: The Newsletter of Nutrition, Fitness, and Self-Care* 16 (June 2000): 4.

52. Lin Grensing-Pophal, "Smokin' in the Workplace," *HRMagazine* 44 (May 1999): 60–62.

53. Anne Rochell, "Secondhand Smoke Hits 9 of 10, CDC Says," *The Atlanta Journal* (April 24, 1996): 38.

54. Pophal, "Smokin' in the Workplace," 64.

55. Del Jones, "Breathing Room for Smokers: Employers Are Bringing Them in from the Cold," *USA Today* (July 10, 1996): 1B.

56. "More Employers Charge Smokers Higher Premiums," *USA Today* (July 28, 1997): 1.

57. Nancy Breuer, "AIDS Threatens Global Business," *Workforce* 79 (February 2000): 52–55.

In this video we leave Quicktakes temporarily and look in on a situation faced by Mia Cipriano, founder of a Web site for working women called allaboutself.com. There are two possible outcomes to the dilemma Mia confronts. Your instructor will choose one of these for you to view and discuss.

Researchers believe that fulfilling work is one of the things that make most people happy. But what about stressful work? Too much work? Work done under impossible deadlines? While most of us can and do cope with occasional stressors, and some people may even be stimulated by certain kinds of pressure, a constant diet of stress can take a toll on our productivity and our health.

There may be few stresses in a manager's life to equal the realization that a trusted subordinate is performing poorly. Seldom, however, is the problem a simple one. The manager who lets the problem accumulate to the crisis stage is only adding to his or her own burden. If the manager's only solution is to do the work him or herself, then stress, not sound management practice, may be in play. Some stress, however, may be inevitable. How should we deal with it?

The stress we can't avoid *can* be managed. Keeping yourself in good health—eating well, getting enough sleep, exercising regularly—prepares your mind and body to react less severely to the ordinary stresses of life. The energy and well-being we derive from feeling fit and refreshed are effective weapons against the downward tug of stress. Don't underestimate the value of having a few close friends to talk to, and of taking occasional short breaks during the day when you can get away from your desk for a few quiet moments. Finally, choose the right things to worry about (those you can actually influence), and nurture your sense of humor.

In this video Mia is caught off guard by a poorly done assignment she had delegated to Joan. Under deadline pressure, she is feeling severely stressed because Joan's article isn't good enough to post on the Web site as written, and she feels it can't be postponed because it has been promoted already and must be available when promised. Mia has two options: she can take the evening off to be with a friend and get away from a stressful situation, or she can work late rewriting the article and confront Joan the next day.

### Discussion Questions

1. Why do you think Mia is in the position of redoing someone else's work the night before the deadline? How could she have avoided being in this situation?
2. Do you think time management and organization are Mia's only problem? Does she have any personality characteristics that fuel her need to stay late at the office?
3. What kind of message is Mia sending Joan by trying to redo her work?

### Additional discussion questions for Option 1

4. Do you think Chris offers Mia good advice? Why or why not? Did Mia make the right decision about how to spend the evening?
5. What do you think Mia should try to achieve when she talks to Joan in the morning? How should she approach the conversation?

### Additional discussion questions for Option 2

6. Did Mia make the right decision about how to spend the evening?
7. How well do you think she handled her conversation with Joan the next morning? What do you think she should have done differently?

**Part Seven**

*Employee and Labor Relations*

 ## Objectives

- Describe the labor movement prior to 1930.
- Identify the major labor legislation that was passed after 1930.
- Describe the state of unions today.
- Describe union growth strategies.
- Describe the relationship between teams and organized labor.
- Explain unionization in the public sector.
- Identify union objectives and the reasons why employees join unions.
- Describe the basic structure of the union.
- Identify the steps involved in establishing the collective bargaining relationship.
- Explain union decertification.
- Describe union-free strategies and tactics.

# chapter

# 14

# The Evolution of Labor Unions

R obert Bandy, president of United Technologies, was disturbed and disappointed. The National Labor Relations Board had just informed him that a majority of his employees had voted to have the union represent them. The past months had been difficult ones, with charges and countercharges being made by both management and labor. The vote had been close, with only a few votes tipping the scales in favor of labor instead of maintaining a union-free environment.

Robert looked at the human resource manager, Marthanne Bello, and said, "I don't know what to do. The union will demand so much we can't possibly be competitive. One of their main demands will be for more full-time employees. I know they don't understand that we can't make our part timers full-time employees. We don't fire people, but when we need to reduce the size of our workforce, part timers give us the flexibility we need."

 ## Key Terms

Conspiracy 425
Injunction 425
Yellow-dog contract 425
Right-to-work laws 428
Individual representation 431
Union salting 431
Flooding the community 432

Corporate labor campaigns 432
Pay-equalization rules 439
Local union 441
Craft union 441
Industrial union 441
National union 441
Collective bargaining 443

Bargaining unit 443
Authorization card 444
Decertification 447
Open-door policy 450
Grievance procedure 451
Ombudsperson 452

Marthanne replied, "Just because the union has won the right to be represented doesn't mean that we have to accept all their terms. I believe that a reasonable contract can be negotiated. I know many of those guys, and I am sure that we can work out a contract that will be fair to both sides."

**R**obert Bandy is not only troubled but also misinformed as to the necessary impact of unionization and, specifically, collective bargaining. Employees have decided to move from a union-free workplace to a unionized one, but that in no way mandates management's acceptance of contractual terms that would adversely impact the health and profitability of the company.

We begin this chapter with a history of the labor movement in the United States before and after 1930. Then we describe unions in today's environment. Union growth strategies, teams and organized labor, and unionism in the public sector are then explained. Next, we discuss union objectives, why employees join unions, and union structure. We then address the steps used to establish a collective bargaining relationship. Finally, we review decertification and union-free strategies and tactics.

## THE LABOR MOVEMENT BEFORE 1930

Unions are not a recent development in American history. The earliest unions originated toward the end of the eighteenth century, about the time of the American Revolution. Although these early associations had few characteristics of present-day labor unions, they did bring workers in craft or guild-related occupations together to consider problems of mutual concern. These early unions were local in nature and usually existed for only a short time.[1]

Development of the labor movement has been neither simple nor straightforward. Instead, unionism has experienced as much failure as success. Employer opposition, the impact of the business cycle, the growth of American industry, court rulings, and legislation have exerted their influence in varying degrees at different times. As a result, the history of the labor movement has somewhat resembled the swinging of a pendulum. At times, the pendulum has moved in favor of labor and, at other times, it has swung toward the advantage of management.

HR WEB WISDOM

▶ *Labor Law*

**www.prenhall.com/mondy**

Numerous sites related to labor history are hot linked.

Prior to the 1930s, the trend definitely favored management. The courts strongly supported employers in their attempts to thwart the organized labor movement. This was first evidenced by the use of criminal and civil conspiracy doctrines derived from English common law. A **conspiracy**, generally defined, is the combination of two or more persons who band together to prejudice the rights of others or of society (e.g., by refusing to work or demanding higher wages). An important feature of the conspiracy doctrine is that an action by one person, though legal, may become illegal when carried out by a group. In 1806, the year in which the conspiracy doctrine was first applied to labor unions, the courts began to influence the field of labor relations.[2] From 1806 to 1842, 17 cases charging labor unions with conspiracies went to trial. These cases resulted in the demise of several unions and certainly discouraged other union activities. The conspiracy doctrine was softened considerably by the decision in the landmark case *Commonwealth v Hunt* in 1842. In that case, Chief Justice Shaw of the Supreme Judicial Court of Massachusetts contended that labor organizations were legal. Thus, in order for a union to be convicted under the conspiracy doctrine, it had to be shown that the union's objectives were unlawful or the means employed to gain a legal end were unlawful. To this day, the courts continue to exert a profound influence on both the direction and character of labor relations.

Other tactics used by employers to stifle union growth were injunctions and yellow-dog contracts. An **injunction** is a prohibiting legal procedure used by employers to prevent certain union activities, such as strikes and unionization attempts. A **yellow-dog contract** was a written agreement between the employee and the company made at the time of employment that prohibited a worker from joining a union or engaging in union activities. Each of these defensive tactics, used by management and supported by the courts, severely limited union growth.

In the latter half of the nineteenth century, the American industrial system started to grow and prosper. Factory production began to displace handicraft forms of manufacturing. The Civil War gave the factory system a great boost. Goods were demanded in quantities that only mass production methods could supply. The railroads developed new networks of routes spanning the continent and knitting the country into an economic whole. Employment was high, and unions sought to organize workers in both new and expanding enterprises. Most unions during this time were small and rather weak, and many did not survive the economic recession of the 1870s. Union membership rose to 300,000 by 1872 and then dropped to 50,000 by 1878.[3] This period also marked the rise of radical labor activity and increased industrial strife as unions struggled for recognition and survival.[4]

Out of the turbulence of the 1870s emerged the most substantial labor organization that had yet appeared in the United States. The Noble Order of the Knights of Labor was founded in 1869 as a secret society of the Philadelphia garment workers. After its secrecy was abandoned and workers in other areas were invited to join, it grew rapidly, reaching a membership of more than 700,000 by the mid-1880s. Internal conflict among the Knights' leadership in 1881 gave rise to the nucleus of a new organization that would soon replace it on the labor scene.[5] That organization was the American Federation of Labor (AFL).

Devoted to what is referred to as either *pure and simple unionism* or *business unionism*, Samuel Gompers of the Cigarmakers Union led some 25 labor groups representing skilled trades to found the AFL in 1886. Gompers was elected the first president of the AFL, a position he held until his death in 1924 (except for one year, 1894–1895, when he adamantly opposed tangible support for the strikers of the Pullman group). He is probably the single most important individual in

**Conspiracy**
The combination of two or more persons who band together to prejudice the rights of others or of society (such as by refusing to work or demanding higher wages).

**Injunction**
A prohibiting legal procedure used by employers to prevent certain union activities, such as strikes and unionization attempts.

**Yellow-dog contract**
A written agreement between an employee and a company made at the time of employment that prohibits a worker from joining a union or engaging in union activities.

American trade union history. The AFL began with a membership of some 138,000 and doubled that number during the next 12 years.

In 1890, Congress passed the Sherman Anti-Trust Act, which marked the entrance of the federal government into the statutory regulation of labor organizations. Although the primary stimulus for this act came from public concern over business's monopoly power, court interpretations soon applied its provisions to organized labor. Later, in 1914, Congress passed the Clayton Act (an amendment to the Sherman Act), which, according to Samuel Gompers, was the Magna Carta of Labor. The intent of this act was to remove labor from the purview of the Sherman Act. Again, judicial interpretation nullified that intent and left labor even more exposed to lawsuits.[6] Nonetheless, as a result of industrial activity related to World War I, the AFL grew to almost 5 million members by 1920.[7]

During the 1920s, labor faced legal restrictions on union activity and unfavorable court decisions. The one exception to such repressive policies was the passage and approval of the Railway Labor Act of 1926. Passage of this legislation marked the first time that the government declared without qualification the right of private employees to join unions and bargain collectively through representatives of their own choosing without interference from their employers. It also set up special machinery for the settlement of labor disputes. Although the act covered only employees in the railroad industry (a later amendment extended coverage to the airline industry), it foreshadowed the extension of similar rights to other classes of employees in the 1930s.

## THE LABOR MOVEMENT AFTER 1930

The 1930s found the United States in the midst of the worst depression in its history. The unemployment rate rose as high as 25 percent.[8] The sentiment of the country began to favor organized labor as many people blamed business for the agony that accompanied the Great Depression. The pendulum began to swing away from management and toward labor. This swing was assisted by several acts and actions that supported the cause of unionism.

### Anti-Injunction Act (Norris-LaGuardia Act)—1932

The Great Depression caused a substantial change in the public's thinking about the role of unions in society. Congress reflected this thinking in 1932 with the passage of the Norris-LaGuardia Act. It affirms that U.S. public policy sanctions collective bargaining and approves the formation and effective operation of labor unions. While this act did not outlaw the use of injunctions, it severely restricted the federal courts' authority to issue them in labor disputes. It also made yellow-dog contracts unenforceable in the federal courts.[9]

### National Labor Relations Act (Wagner Act)—1935

In 1933, Congress made an abortive attempt to stimulate economic recovery by passing the National Industry Recovery Act (NIRA). Declared unconstitutional by the U.S. Supreme Court in 1935, the NIRA did provide the nucleus for legislation that followed it. Section 7a of the NIRA proclaimed the right of workers to organize and bargain collectively. Congress did not, however, provide procedures to enforce these rights.

Undeterred by the Supreme Court decision and strongly supported by organized labor, Congress speedily enacted a comprehensive labor law, the National Labor Relations Act (Wagner Act). This act, approved by President Roosevelt on July 5, 1935, is one of the most significant labor-management relations statutes ever enacted. Drawing heavily on the experience of the Railway Labor Act of 1926 and Section 7a of the NIRA, the act declared legislative support, on a broad scale, for the right of employees to organize and engage in collective bargaining. The spirit of the Wagner Act is stated in Section 7, which defines the substantive rights of employees:

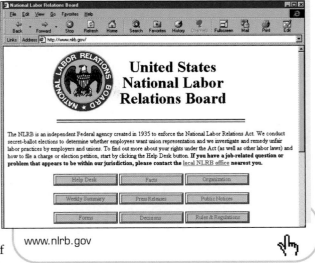

www.nlrb.gov

> Employees shall have the right to self-organization, to form, join, or assist labor organizations, to bargain collectively through representatives of their own choosing, and to engage in other concerted activities, for the purpose of collective bargaining or other mutual aid or protection.

The rights defined in Section 7 were protected against employer interference by Section 8, which detailed and prohibited five management practices deemed to be unfair to labor:

1. Interfering with or restraining or coercing employees in the exercise of their right to self-organization
2. Dominating or interfering in the affairs of a union
3. Discriminating in regard to hire or tenure or any condition of employment for the purpose of encouraging or discouraging union membership
4. Discriminating against or discharging an employee who has filed charges or given testimony under the act
5. Refusing to bargain with chosen representatives of employees

The National Labor Relations Act created the National Labor Relations Board (NLRB) to administer and enforce the provisions of the act. The NLRB was given two principal functions: (1) to establish procedures for holding bargaining-unit elections and to monitor the election procedures, and (2) to investigate complaints and prevent unlawful acts involving unfair labor practices. Much of the NLRB's work is delegated to 33 regional offices throughout the country.

Following passage of the Wagner Act, union membership increased from approximately 3 million to 15 million between 1935 and 1947.[10] The increase was most conspicuous in industries utilizing mass production methods. New unions in these industries were organized on an industrial basis rather than a craft basis, and members were primarily unskilled or semiskilled workers. An internal struggle developed within the AFL over the question of whether unions should be organized to include all workers in an industry or strictly on a craft or occupational basis. In 1935, a new group was formed by ten AFL-affiliated unions and the officers of two other AFL unions. Called the Committee for Industrial Organization, its purpose was to promote the organization of workers in mass production and unorganized industries. The controversy grew to the point that in 1938 the AFL expelled all but one of the Committee for Industrial Organization unions. In November 1938, the expelled unions held their first convention in Pittsburgh, and reorganized as a federation of unions under the name of Congress of Industrial Organizations (CIO). The new federation included the nine unions expelled from the AFL and 32 other groups established to recruit workers in various industries. John L. Lewis, president of the United Mine Workers, was elected the first president of the CIO.

The rivalry generated by the two large federations stimulated union organizing efforts in both groups. With the ensuing growth, the labor movement gained considerable influence in the United States. However, many individuals and groups began to feel that the Wagner Act favored labor too much. This shift in public sentiment was in part related to a rash of costly strikes following World War II. Whether justified or not, much of the blame for these disruptions fell on the unions.

## Labor-Management Relations Act (Taft-Hartley Act)—1947

In 1947, with public pressure mounting, Congress overrode President Truman's veto and passed the Labor Management Relations Act (Taft-Hartley Act). The Taft-Hartley Act extensively revised the National Labor Relations Act and became Title I of that law. A new period began in the evolution of public policy regarding labor. The pendulum had begun to swing toward a more balanced position between labor and management.

Some of the important changes introduced by the Taft-Hartley Act include the following:

1. Modifying Section 7 to include the right of employees to refrain from union activity as well as engage in it
2. Prohibiting the closed shop (the arrangement requiring that all workers be union members at the time they are hired) and narrowing the freedom of the parties to authorize the union shop (the situation in which the employer may hire anyone he or she chooses, but all new workers must join the union after a stipulated period of time)
3. Broadening the employer's right of free speech
4. Providing that employers need not recognize or bargain with unions formed by supervisory employees
5. Giving employees the right to initiate decertification petitions
6. Providing for government intervention in *national emergency strikes*

Another significant change extended the concept of unfair labor practices to unions. Labor organizations were to refrain from the following:

1. Restraining or coercing employees in the exercise of their guaranteed collective bargaining rights
2. Causing an employer to discriminate in any way against an employee in order to encourage or discourage union membership
3. Refusing to bargain in good faith with an employer regarding wages, hours, and other terms and conditions of employment
4. Engaging in certain types of strikes and boycotts
5. Requiring employees covered by union-shop contracts to pay initiation fees or dues in an amount which the Board finds excessive or discriminatory under all circumstances
6. *Featherbedding,* or requiring that an employer pay for services not performed

**Right-to-work laws**
Laws that prohibit management and unions from entering into agreements requiring union membership as a condition of employment.

One of the most controversial elements of the Taft-Hartley Act is Section 14b, which permits states to enact right-to-work legislation. **Right-to-work laws** are laws that prohibit management and unions from entering into agreements requiring union membership as a condition of employment. Twenty-one states, located primarily in the South and West, have adopted such laws, which are a continuing source of irritation between labor and management.[11] The National Right to Work Committee, based in Springfield, Virginia, provides much of the impetus behind the right-to-work movement.

For about 10 years after the passage of the Taft-Hartley Act, union membership expanded at about the same rate as nonagricultural employment. But all was not well within the organized labor movement. Since the creation of the CIO, the two federations had engaged in a bitter and costly rivalry. Both the CIO and the AFL recognized the increasing need for cooperation and reunification. In 1955, following two years of intensive negotiations between the two organizations, a merger agreement was ratified, the AFL-CIO became a reality, and George Meany was elected president. In the years following the merger, the labor movement faced some of its greatest challenges.

## Labor-Management Reporting and Disclosure Act (Landrum-Griffin Act)— 1959

Corruption had plagued organized labor since the early 1900s. Periodic revelations of graft, violence, extortion, racketeering, and other improper activities aroused public indignation and invited governmental investigation. Even though the number of unions involved was small, every disclosure undermined the public image of organized labor as a whole.[12] Corruption had been noted in the construction trades and Laborers, Hotel and Restaurant, Carpenters, Painters, East Coast Longshoremen, and Boilermakers unions.

Scrutiny of union activities is a focal point in today's labor environment, but it began to intensify immediately after World War II. Ultimately, inappropriate union activities led to the creation in 1957 of the Senate Select Committee on Improper Activities in the Labor or Management Field, headed by Senator McClellan of Arkansas. Between 1957 and 1959, the McClellan Committee held a series of nationally televised public hearings that shocked and alarmed the entire country. As evidence of improper activities mounted—primarily against the Teamsters and Longshoremen/Maritime unions—the AFL-CIO took action. In 1957, the AFL-CIO expelled three unions (representing approximately 1.6 million members) for their practices. One of them, the Teamsters, was the largest union in the country.

In 1959, largely as a result of the recommendations of the McClellan Committee, Congress enacted the Labor-Management Reporting and Disclosure Act (Landrum-Griffin Act). This act marked a significant turning point in the involvement of the federal government in internal union affairs. The Landrum-Griffin Act spelled out a *Bill of Rights for Members of Labor Organizations* designed to protect certain rights of individuals in their relationships with unions. The act requires extensive reporting on numerous internal union activities and contains severe penalties for violations. Employers are also required to file reports when they engage in activities or make expenditures that might undermine the collective bargaining process or interfere with protected employee rights. In addition, the act amended the Taft-Hartley Act by adding additional restrictions on picketing and secondary boycotts.[13]

In 1974, Congress extended coverage of the Taft-Hartley Act to private, not-for-profit hospitals. This amendment brought within the jurisdiction of the

It is the union practice of vigorous action and involvement as a means of achieving recruitment goals by activities such as demonstrations and protests.

National Labor Relations Board some two million employees. Proprietary (profit-making) health care organizations were already under NLRB jurisdiction. The amendment does not cover government-operated hospitals; it applies only to the private sector.

## UNIONS TODAY

Overall, the fall of Big Labor since the 1970s has been dramatic. Despite the reaffiliation of the Teamsters with the AFL-CIO, union membership dropped from about one-third of the nonfarm workforce in 1950 to 13.9 percent in 1999.[14] Total union membership increased by 266,000 in 1999—the largest annual increase for organized labor in more than two decades. With the U.S. economy expanding, however, that increase was only good enough to keep the percentage of workers who are unionized steady.[15] As shown in Figure 14-1, the unionized share of the private-sector workforce has shrunk to about 9.5 percent.[16]

According to AFL-CIO President John J. Sweeney, "We're turning the corner, but we're not at our destination yet." But in the same breath, he admits that "labor will become irrelevant if it doesn't begin to build its ranks."[17] The good news for unions is that 43 percent of employees surveyed in a Peter D. Hart Research poll would vote for a union in their workplace, an increase from 39 percent in the mid-1990s.[18]

According to Rutgers economist Leo Troy, distinguished professor of economics, unionism today is healthy only in the public sector. Even though unionized companies pay 15 to 20 percent higher wages than comparable nonunion

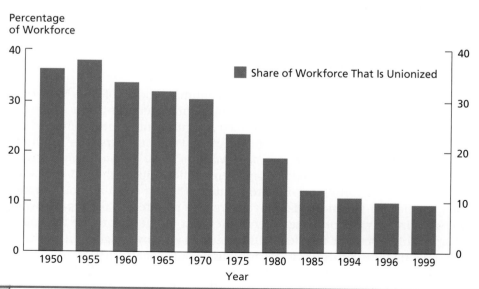

**Figure 14-1** **Percentage of the Private Workforce That is Unionized**
*Source:* Labor Department

firms, workers have stopped joining unions. Ever since President Reagan's dismissal of the striking air traffic controllers, labor clout has seriously diminished. Reasons vary, but the concept of **individual representation**, in which people prefer to bargain for themselves and ignore the interests of the collective members of the workforce, is becoming more common (this will be discussed further in the "Labor-Management Relations and Individual Bargaining" section of Chapter 15). Some workers do not like paying union dues, some do not like pay-equalization rules, and some believe that unionized firms might be less competitive and could go out of business (not a problem for public-sector workers).[19]

**Individual representation**
A situation in which people prefer to bargain for themselves and ignore the interests of the collective members of the workforce.

## UNIONS' GROWTH STRATEGIES

Organized labor has a renewed emphasis on recruiting, similar to that seen in the early 1900s. Remember that AFL-CIO President John J. Sweeney said, "Labor will become irrelevant if it doesn't begin to build its ranks." Sweeney has pushed affiliated unions to devote more resources to broadening their organizing efforts.[20] The key to this stronger movement is a union that is "stronger in voice, stronger in membership, [and] stronger in perception."[21]

Organized labor's new strategies for a stronger movement involve practices such as greater political involvement, union salting, flooding the community with organizers, corporate labor campaigns, building organizing funds, organizing students, activism and focus, forming coalitions, and the AFL-CIO cyberunion.

### Political Involvement

Political involvement now means more than simply endorsing candidates at all levels of politics, and then attempting to deliver the union membership's vote. Unions are giving money to candidates who pledge to help pass pro-labor legislation. The AFL-CIO's Sweeney made political action a top priority and has pumped millions of dollars into political activities that include the training of political organizers and politicians in labor issues. Some believe that the AFL-CIO is moving too far to the Left politically and is associating with the wrong groups. The AFL-CIO has abandoned its historic stance of political independence in favor of strategic alliances with liberal special-interest groups such as the NAACP and the National Organization for Women. Much of organized labor now openly aligns itself with the Democratic Party and has moved from the center to the Left. The AFL-CIO is now embracing concepts such as affirmative action to encourage workforce diversity, and it endorsed the notion that women's wages should no longer be determined by the marketplace but by comparable worth.[22]

### Union Salting

**Union salting** is the process of training union organizers to apply for jobs at a company and, once hired, work to unionize employees. Although salting is primarily used by blue-collar labor unions within the construction and building industry, it's a strategy labor unions are also using in other sectors, such as the hotel and restaurant industries.[23] The U.S. Supreme Court has ruled that employers cannot discriminate against union salts *(NLRB v Town & Electric Inc.)*. Therefore, a company cannot terminate these employees solely because they also work for a union.[24] The practice is on the rise and being supported by AFL-CIO President John Sweeney. "We will be training at least a thousand organizers a year, pouring $20 million into organizing programs, and organizing from the Sunbelt to the Rust Belt and from the health care industry to the high-tech field," said Sweeney.[25]

**Union salting**
The process of training union organizers to apply for jobs at a company and, once hired, work to unionize employees.

# Flooding Communities with Organizers

**Flooding the community** is the process of the union inundating communities with organizers to target a particular business. With their flooding campaigns, unions typically choose companies in which nonunionized employees have asked for help in organizing. Generally, organizers have been recruited and trained by the national union. They are typically young, ambitious, college-educated people with a passion for the American labor movement. Organizers meet with employees in small groups and even visit them at home. They know every nuance of a company's operations and target weak managers' departments as a way to appeal to dissatisfied employees who may be willing to organize.

## Corporate Labor Campaigns

**Corporate labor campaigns** involve labor maneuvers that do not coincide with a strike or organizing campaign to pressure an employer for better wages, benefits, and the like. Increasingly, these campaigns are used as an alternative to strikes because more employers are willing to replace their striking employees. Employers have less recourse against labor campaigns that involve joining political and community groups that support union goals or picketing homes of a company's board of directors. They are also defenseless in dealing with the union's initiating proxy challenges to actions negative to labor, writing letters to the editor of the local newspaper, and filing charges with administrative agencies such as OSHA, the Department of Labor, and the NLRB. These types of public awareness campaigns, which are not tied directly to labor gains, are often effective methods of developing union leverage. Also, fighting such campaigns is time consuming and costly for companies.[26]

## Building Organizing Funds

To encourage workers to come together, the AFL-CIO asked its affiliates to increase organizing funds to 30 percent of their budgets by 2000. The federation also increased funding to its Organizing Institute, which trains organizers, and even launched an advertising campaign to create wider public support for unions.[27] National unions are also creating organizing funds. For example, the United Steelworkers of America (USWA) will create a $40 million fund for organizing. According to George Becker, USWA's president, "Our greatest challenge is organizing. Our ability to organize and grow the union bears directly on our effectiveness at the bargaining table and in the political arena."[28]

## Organizing Students

The AFL-CIO recruiting plans include the unusual steps of organizing students, encouraging activism against sweatshops, and supporting the organizing efforts of graduate students. An organization of high school students known as the International Student Activism Alliance has 160 chapters and 1,200 members in the United States and does most of its work via the Internet, battling such issues as mandatory drug testing of students, zero-tolerance policies, and the lack of low-cost federal college loans. Unions hope to gain in the future when these individuals enter the workforce, hopefully remembering the support and encouragement given to them by organized labor.[29]

## Activism and Focus

Activism and focus are some of the weapons of choice of AFL-CIO President John J. Sweeney. These involve the union practice of vigorous action and involvement as a means of achieving recruitment goals through such activities as demonstrations and protests. Activism and focus resulted in the recruiting of 2,700 new members at the Las Vegas MGM Grand, the world's largest hotel. It took dedication to wage a three-year activism campaign of street demonstrations, mass arrests, and attacks on the company's business record to help oust the stridently anti-labor CEO. Soon after, the MGM Grand recognized the union without an election. Another group was victorious at New York, New York, a new Las Vegas hotel that acceded to the unionization of 900 workers without a certification election.

Such victories have turned Local 226 of the Hotel Employees & Restaurant Employees International Union into one of the country's fastest-growing local unions. The local's ranks have doubled in the past decade, to 40,000 members, and it now represents virtually every major Las Vegas hotel.[30] Much of this success lies with the spirited rank and file. When meetings end, the largely black, Hispanic, and female crowds jump to their feet, clap, and shout "Unions, yes!" Some members even meet the following morning, on their day off, to sign up recruits outside the New York, New York hiring office. According to Edelisa Wolf, an $11.25-an-hour waitress at the MGM Grand, "I spend a day a week volunteering for the union because otherwise, we would earn $7.50 an hour and no benefits." A combination of in-your-face activism and a single-minded focus on recruitment apparently has been quite successful. Utilizing this approach has doubled the membership of the Service Employees International Union (SEIU) to 1.1 million members.

## Forming Coalitions

Organized labor is also forming coalitions with unlikely partners, such as religious groups. In October, the AFL-CIO cosponsored a five-day meeting in Los Angeles with Christian, Jewish, and Muslim religious leaders and seminary students to encourage religious organizations to use their political clout to further union goals. This type of association is unusual given the traditional, often hostile relationship between these groups.[31] For example, leaders of the Roman Catholic church, Catholic health care, and organized labor have reached a pact that is intended to govern labor relations in Catholic health care organizations. The pact calls for management and unions to use restraint in pursuing their aims.[32]

## AFL-CIO—Cyberunion

The AFL-CIO is now offering members Internet access in an effort to create a Web-based community and give itself more political clout. The service, called Workingfamilies.com, provides union members with low-cost access as well as full financing for low-cost computers. The goal is to bring families online for under $30 per month. According to John Sweeney, "With Workingfamilies.com, we're helping bridge the growing gap between the technological 'haves' and 'have-nots,' and we're also giving working families new ways to connect with one another and to make their voices heard. This is a twenty-first-century communications tool that will help co-workers share information, help our unions mobilize our members, and hold policy makers more accountable to working families."

Some believe that the networking of organized labor will help revitalize the political power that unions once wielded.[33]

## TEAMS AND ORGANIZED LABOR

According to Labor Secretary Alexis Herman, "Labor-management relations are evolving to include more partnerships and fewer confrontations."[34] However, as is discussed in Chapter 15, unions appear to be more comfortable with past adversarial relationships, as they continue to fight cooperative labor-management legislation like the TEAM Act. Organized labor's strategic plan is to reestablish itself in the workplace through expanded recruiting efforts. Because of these renewed efforts by organized labor, HR professionals must create and maintain environments that eliminate the need for union representation.

Modern business managers try to forge cooperative workplace cultures in which employees work together and with management to solve problems, increase productivity, and improve quality. The old top-down mentality in which the boss issues orders and subordinates snap to attention is obsolete. To be globally competitive, most organizations must utilize cohesive teams that take maximum advantage of the physical and mental capacities of each employee. Unfortunately, the 1935 National Labor Relations Act prohibits such arrangements because some companies could establish management-labor teams as *sham unions* to avert union organizing. In 1992, the National Labor Relations Board (NLRB) ruled that a system of teams or committees implemented by a company is analogous to a company-dominated union, which is prohibited by law.

The Teamwork for Employees and Management Act (TEAM Act), which would have amended the 1935 National Labor Relations Act's ban on company or sham

### TRENDS & INNOVATIONS

▶ **The "Buy American" Slogan May No Longer Make Sense to Unions**

One surprising impact of the Daimler-Benz takeover of Chrysler appears to be the possible demise of the long-standing "Buy American" campaign by organized labor in the United States. Replacing it will probably be a more realistic emphasis on American jobs, regardless of where corporate profits end up. Basically, Toyotas may now be welcome in union parking facilities because they are made in the United States and create U.S. jobs.

For years, the national labor movement and groups representing workers urged the public to "Buy American" as a patriotic way to support domestic union jobs. But now, because of the largest industrial takeover ever—one in which the German automaker Daimler-Benz will be a dominant force—there is widespread agreement that the "Buy American" slogan makes little sense in the United States, where transnational ownership is increasingly common. According to labor professor Robert Bruno of the University of Illinois in Chicago, "This notion of 'Buy American' is really more confusing than educational, and it's been that way for some time." United Auto Workers spokesperson Bobbie Barbee believes that the "Buy American" slogan may be finished as a union byline because so many companies are becoming intermingled, like Ford and Mazda and Jaguar, that it's very hard to buy American. There is general agreement that maintaining American jobs, regardless of who owns the company and gets the profits, is most important. According to AFL-CIO Director of Corporate Affairs Ron Blackwell, "It's where the product is made [that matters]."[35]

unions by allowing nonunion companies to set up worker-management groups that could address matters of mutual interest but not negotiate contracts, was opposed by unions. In 1996, both houses of Congress passed identical versions of the TEAM Act, but President Clinton vetoed it, even though the legislation expressly excludes unionized companies from coverage. Congress later revived the TEAM Act and attempted once again to bring the nation's labor laws into the modern age, but union resistance and President Clinton's veto once again derailed their efforts.[36]

Organized labor believes such legislation, which gives legal status to an already widespread practice, would make it far more difficult to persuade employees to vote for union representation. The TEAM Act would have allowed selected workers and managers to discuss wages, hours, and working conditions in a nonunion setting, a practice now illegal under the National Labor Relations Act.[37] Union resistance to management-labor teams is undermining the best efforts of corporations to become more competitive globally and more progressive in terms of dealing with employee needs. This prohibition even forbids managers and employees from discussing safety and quality-of-life issues.

Employers believe the TEAM Act is necessary to allow employers and employees to work together as a team to assure a mutually better future. Organized labor believes it is union-busting legislation.[38] Under the current law, nonunion, management-controlled committees can discuss only certain issues, such as product quality and sales. Worker group involvement in determining terms and conditions of employment must be free of employer control.[39]

## THE PUBLIC SECTOR

Government (public-sector) employees are generally considered a class apart from private-sector workers. This is reflected in their exclusion from coverage of general labor legislation.[40] However, unlike their counterparts in private industry, government employees have demonstrated a persistence in organizing in order to gain an effective voice in the terms and conditions of their employment. Unionism is healthy in the public sector and has remained so ever since John F. Kennedy's 1963 decision to allow federal workers to organize. Presently, public-sector unions have about 38 percent of government employees, a figure that exceeds their private-sector peak (36 percent, in 1953).[41] Although AFL-CIO officials are pleased with these gains in membership among civil servants, serious problems loom. A new generation of fiscally conservative governors and mayors has set out to reduce the role of government and the size of its workforce. Most of these officials do not have close relations with local union establishments. More often than not, they regard unions as impediments to reform. Seeking ways to reduce the cost of government services, they increasingly look to privatization schemes that turn decision-making power over to employers less constrained than municipal governments in resisting union demands.[42]

For many years the federal government had no well-defined policy on labor-management relations regarding its own employees. In order to address this situation, President Kennedy issued Executive Order 10988 in 1962. Section 1(a) of the order stated:

> Employees of the federal government shall have, and shall be protected in the exercise of, the right, freely and without fear of penalty or reprisal, to form, join and assist any employee organization or to refrain from any such activity.

For the first time in the history of the federal civil service, a uniform, comprehensive policy of cooperation between employee organizations and management in the executive branch of government was established. Employees were permitted to organize and negotiate human resource policies and practices and matters affecting working conditions that were within the administrative discretion of the agency officials concerned. However, Public Law 84-330, passed in 1955, made it a felony for federal employees to strike against the U.S. government.[43]

Executive Order 10988 established the basic framework for collective bargaining in federal government agencies. Subsequent EOs revised and improved this framework and brought about a new era of labor relations in the public sector.[44] In fact, the federal government codified the provisions of those orders and transferred them to Title VII of the Civil Service Reform Act of 1978. This act regulates most of the labor-management relations in the federal service. It establishes the Federal Labor Relations Authority (FLRA), which is modeled on the National Labor Relations Board. The intent of the FLRA is to bring the public-sector model in line with that of the private sector. Requirements and mechanisms for recognition and elections, dealing with impasses, and handling grievances are covered in the act.

The U.S. Postal Service is not subject to Title VII of the Civil Service Reform Act of 1978. It was given independent government agency status by the Postal Reorganization Act of 1970. Postal employees were given collective bargaining rights comparable to those governing private industry. National Labor Relations Board rules and regulations controlling representation issues and elections are applicable to the postal service. Unfair labor practice provisions are also enforced by the NLRB. However, the right to strike is prohibited, and union-shop arrangements are not permitted.

## Labor Relations and Bargaining Patterns

There is no uniform pattern to state and local labor relations and bargaining rights. Some states have no policy at all, whereas a haphazard mixture of statutes, resolutions, ordinances, and civil service procedures exists in others. However, the passage of public-employer legislation by state and local governments accelerated noticeably after the issuance of EO 10988 in 1962.[45] Forty-one states and the District of Columbia have collective bargaining statutes covering all or some categories of public employees. Also, 38 states have some form of legislation that obligates state agencies and local governments to permit their public employees to join unions and to recognize bona fide labor organizations. However, the diversity of state labor laws makes it difficult to generalize about the legal aspects of collective bargaining at the state and local levels.

## Employee Associations

In the past, employee associations were concerned primarily with the professional aspects of employment and avoided any semblance of unionism. In recent years, this approach has changed as public- and private-sector unions have actively organized both professional and government employees. Many employee associations now enthusiastically pursue collective bargaining relationships. The National Education Association (NEA) is the largest public-sector union in the United States, with 2.5 million members.[46]

The greater public-sector penetration of unions in recent years indicates that the process of unionization in the public sector differs from that in the private labor market. One factor that accounts for membership gains is clearly the role played by government employee associations, particularly at the state and local level. Challenged by established unions, the associations either merged with unions or transformed themselves into collective bargaining organizations. Many are becoming de facto unions.

The labor movement has a long history in the United States. Although each union is a unique organization seeking its own objectives, several broad objectives characterize the labor movement as a whole:

1. To secure and, if possible, improve the living standards and economic status of its members
2. To enhance and, if possible, guarantee individual security against threats and contingencies that might result from market fluctuations, technological change, or management decisions
3. To influence power relations in the social system in ways that favor and do not threaten union gains and goals
4. To advance the welfare of all who work for a living, whether union members or not[47]
5. To create mechanisms to guard against the use of arbitrary and capricious policies and practices in the workplace

The underlying philosophy of the labor movement is that of organizational democracy and an atmosphere of social dignity for working men and women. To accomplish these objectives, most unions recognize that they must strive for continued growth and power. Although growth and power are related, we will discuss them separately to identify the impact of both factors on unionization.

## Growth

To maximize its effectiveness, a union must strive for continual growth. Members pay dues, which are vital to promoting and achieving union objectives. Obviously, the more members the union has, the more dues they pay to support the union and the labor movement. Thus, an overall goal of most unions is continued growth. However, the percentage of union members in the workforce is declining, even though the number of union members increased in 1999. Most union leaders are concerned about this trend. Much of a union's ability to accomplish its objectives is derived from strength in numbers. For this reason, unions continue to explore new sources of potential members. Unions are now directing much of their attention to organizing the service industries, professional employees, and government employees. Specifics related to growth issues were addressed earlier in the union strategies section of this chapter.

Unions have had some success in organizing jobs that do not require a hard hat. In 1999, 45,000 doctors were union members, but most doctors could not join unions because they are self-employed and antitrust laws ban collective bargaining by the self-employed. There is an on-going effort to change the law; if changed, union membership for doctors could be 650,000.[48] In addition, 75,000 home health aide workers unionized in California.[49] Also, the summer of 2000 was a hotbed of strikes against hospitals.[50] As previously mentioned, in 1999, total union membership in all industries increased by 266,000, the largest annual increase for organized labor in more than two decades.[51] Obviously, unions want to continue this trend, which should prove to be quite challenging.

## Power

We define *power* here as the amount of external control that an organization is able to exert. A union's power is influenced to a large extent by the size of its membership and the possibility of future growth. However, we also have to consider other factors when assessing the future power base of unions. The importance of the jobs held by union members significantly affects union power. For instance, an entire plant may have to be shut down if unionized machinists performing critical jobs decide to strike. Thus, a few strategically located union members may exert a disproportionate amount of power. The type of firm that is unionized can also determine a union's power. Unionization of truckers, steel-workers, or farmworkers can affect the entire country and, subsequently, enhance the union's power base. Through control of key industries, a union's power may extend to firms that are not unionized.

By achieving power, a union is capable of exerting its force in the political arena. The political arm of the AFL-CIO is the Committee on Political Education (COPE). Founded in 1955, its purpose is to support politicians who are friendly to the cause of organized labor. The union recommends and assists candidates who will best serve its interests. Union members also encourage their friends to support those candidates. The larger the voting membership, the greater the union's influence with politicians. With friends in government, the union is in a stronger position to maneuver against management.

Reduced union strength contributes to weaker unions at the bargaining table, and therefore, labor leaders will continually strive to increase their political clout. This slowdown in union gains, coupled with declining union membership as a percentage of the workforce, caused unions to compensate by attempting to increase their political activity. Even though unions have taken their political knocks over the past decade, they remain a potent political force.

## WHY EMPLOYEES JOIN UNIONS

Individuals join unions for many different reasons, which tend to change over time. They may involve job, personal, social, or political considerations. It would be impossible to discuss them all, but the following are some of the major reasons: dissatisfaction with management, compensation, job security, management's attitude, the need for a social outlet, the opportunity for leadership, forced unionization, and peer pressure.

## Dissatisfaction with Management

Every job holds the potential for real dissatisfactions. Each individual has a boiling point that can trigger him or her to consider a union as a solution to real or perceived problems. Unions look for arbitrary or unfair management decisions then emphasize the advantages of union membership as a means of solving these problems. Some of the other common reasons for employee dissatisfaction are described in the following paragraphs.

**Compensation.** Employees want their compensation to be fair and equitable. Wages are important to them because they provide both the necessities and pleasures of life. If employees are dissatisfied with their wages, they may look to a union for assistance in improving their standard of living. However, the ability of unions to make satisfactory gains in income has been severely hampered in the past few years.

An important psychological aspect of compensation involves the amount of pay an individual receives in relation to that of other workers performing similar work. If an employee perceives that management has shown favoritism by paying someone else more to perform the same or a lower-level job, the employee will likely become dissatisfied. Union members know precisely the basis of their pay and how it compares with others'. Historically, union members have accepted pay inequities if seniority was the criterion used. Basically, the 15 to 20 percent higher wage rates of unionized workers are often offset by **pay-equalization rules**, where every worker is rewarded equally when pay or benefit gains are realized, based on seniority rather than worker productivity.[52]

**Pay-equalization rules** Rules under which every worker is rewarded equally when pay or benefit gains are realized, based on seniority rather than worker productivity.

**Job Security.** Historically, young employees have been less concerned with job security than older workers. The young employee seemed to think, "If I lose this job, I can always get another." But as young employees have witnessed management consistently terminating older workers to make room for younger, more aggressive employees, they may have begun to think about job security. If the firm does not provide its employees with a sense of job security, workers may turn to a union. Robert Bandy of UT believes that the main reason the union barely won in its organizing attempt is UT's refusal to allow part timers to achieve full-time employment status under normal circumstances. Generally speaking, employees are more concerned than ever about job security because of a decline in employment in such key industries as automobiles, rubber, and steel. The General Motors strike was conducted simply to temporarily protect the jobs of workers at two old-line Flint, Michigan, plants. Unfortunately for the union, many believe that cooperative employers rather than unions can provide job security.

**Attitude of Management.** People like to feel that they are important. They do not like to be considered a commodity that can be bought and sold. Thus, employees do not like to be subjected to arbitrary and capricious actions by management. In some firms, management is insensitive to the needs of its employees. In such situations, employees may perceive that they have little or no influence in job-related matters. Workers who feel that they are not really part of an organization are prime targets for unionization.

Management's attitude may be reflected in such small actions as how bulletin board notices are written. Memos addressed "To All Employees" instead of "To *Our* Employees" may indicate that managers are indifferent to employee needs. Such attitudes likely stem from top management, but they are noticed initially by employees in the actions of first-line supervisors. Workers may notice that supervisors are judging people entirely on what they can do, how much they can do, and when they can do it. Employees may begin to feel they are being treated more as machines than people. Supervisors may fail to give reasons for unusual assignments and may expect employees to dedicate their lives to the firm without providing adequate rewards. The prevailing philosophy may be: "If you don't like it here, leave." A management philosophy such as this, which does not consider the needs of employees as individuals, makes the firm ripe for unionization. Management must keep in mind that unions would never have gained a foothold if management had not abused its power.

## A Social Outlet

By nature, many people have strong social needs. They generally enjoy being around others who have similar interests and desires. Some employees join a union for no other reason than to take advantage of union-sponsored recreational and social activities that members and their families find fulfilling. Some unions

▶ *Using Her Influence?*

Sandy Marshall, one of the workers in the plant, has just come to see the human resource manager, Lonnie Miller, for advice. Apparently, a union organizer approached her yesterday and asked her to help with the union organizing effort. Lonnie knows that lately there have been growing tensions and a lot of talk about unions. He has even seen what appears to be authorization cards being passed around. Lonnie knows that if Sandy starts working for the union, she will have a lot of influence. She seems to be a natural leader, and Lonnie thinks she is supervisory material.

*What advice should Lonnie give Sandy?*

now offer day care centers and other services that appeal to working men and women and increase their sense of solidarity with other union members. People who develop close personal relationships, whether in a unionized or union-free organization, will likely stand together in difficult times.

## Opportunity for Leadership

Some individuals aspire to leadership roles, but it is not always easy for an operative employee to progress into management. However, employees with leadership aspirations can often satisfy them through union membership. As with the firm, the union also has a hierarchy of leadership, and individual members have the opportunity to work their way up through its various levels. Employers often notice employees who are leaders in the union, and it is not uncommon for them to promote such employees into managerial ranks as supervisors.

## Forced Unionization

Requiring an individual to join a union prior to employment is generally illegal. However, in the 29 states without right-to-work laws, it is legal for an employer to agree with the union that a new employee must join the union after a certain period of time (generally 30 days) or be terminated. This is referred to as a *union-shop agreement.*

## Peer Pressure

Some individuals will join a union simply because they are urged to do so by other members of the work group. Friends and associates may constantly remind an employee that he or she is not a member of the union. In extreme cases, union members have threatened nonmembers with physical violence and sometimes have carried out these threats.

## UNION STRUCTURE

The labor movement has developed a multilevel organizational structure. This complex of organizations ranges from local unions to the principal federation, the AFL-CIO. Each level has its own officers and ways of managing its affairs. Many national unions have intermediate levels between the national and the local levels. In this section, however, we describe only the three basic elements of union organization: the local union, the national union, and the federation, or AFL-CIO.

## The Local Union

The basic element in the structure of the U.S. labor movement is the **local union** (or simply, the *local*). To the individual union member, it is the most important level in the structure of organized labor. Through the local, the individual deals with the employer on a day-to-day basis. A local union may fill a social role in the lives of its members, sponsoring dances, festivals, and other functions. It may be the focal point of the political organization and activity of its members.[53]

There are two basic kinds of local unions: craft and industrial. A **craft union**, such as the Carpenters and Joiners union, is typically composed of members of a particular trade or skill in a specific locality. Members usually acquire their job skills through an apprenticeship training program. An **industrial union** generally consists of all the workers in a particular plant or group of plants. The type of work they do and the level of skill they possess are not a condition for membership in the union. An example of an industrial union is the United Auto Workers.

The local union's functions are many and varied. Administering the collective bargaining agreement and representing workers in handling grievances are two very important activities. Other functions include keeping the membership informed about labor issues, promoting increased membership, maintaining effective contact with the national union, and—when appropriate—negotiating with management at the local level.

**Local union**
The basic element in the structure of the U.S. labor movement.

**Craft union**
A bargaining unit, such as the Carpenters and Joiners union, that is typically composed of members of a particular trade or skill in a specific locality.

**Industrial union**
A bargaining unit that generally consists of all the workers in a particular plant or group of plants.

## The National Union

The most powerful level in the union structure is the national union. As we stated previously, most locals are affiliated with national unions. A **national union** is composed of local unions, which it charters. As such, it is the parent organization to local unions. The local union—not the individual worker—holds membership in the national union. Each local union provides financial support to the national union based on its membership size.

The national union is governed by a national constitution and a national convention of local unions, which usually meets every two to five years. Elected officers, aided by an administrative staff, conduct the day-to-day operation of the national union. The national union is active in organizing workers within its jurisdiction, engaging in collective bargaining at the national level, and assisting its locals in their negotiations. In addition, the national union may provide numerous educational and research services for its locals, dispense strike funds, publish the union newspaper, provide legal counsel, and actively lobby at national and state levels.

**National union**
An organization composed of local unions, which it charters.

## The AFL-CIO

The American Federation of Labor and Congress of Industrial Organizations (AFL-CIO) is the central trade union federation in the United States. It is a voluntary federation of 68 national and international labor unions representing approximately

▶ *The AFL-CIO*

**www.prenhall.com/mondy**

Current news about union activities, political candidate positions, health and safety laws, and quizzes ("How Well Do You Know Your Rights @ Work?") are offered at this Web site.

HR WEB
WISDOM

13 million members.[54] It represents the interests of labor and its member national unions at the highest level. The federation does not engage in collective bargaining; however, it provides the means by which member unions can cooperate to pursue common objectives and attempt to resolve internal problems faced by organized labor. The federation is financed by its member national unions and is governed by a national convention, which meets every two years.

As shown in Figure 14-2, the structure of the AFL-CIO is complex. The federation is active in all states and Puerto Rico. In addition, national unions can affiliate

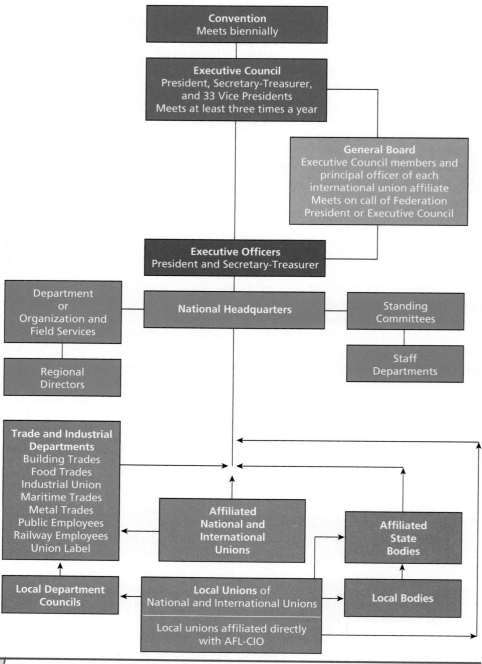

**Figure 14-2** **The Structure of the AFL-CIO**

*Source:* Bureau of Labor Statistics, *Directory of National Unions and Employee Associations.*

with one or more of the trade and industrial departments. These departments seek to promote the interests of specific groups of workers who are in different unions but have common interests. The federation's major activities include the following:

1. Improving the image of organized labor
2. Extensive lobbying on behalf of labor interests
3. Politically educating constituencies and others through COPE
4. Resolving disputes between national unions
5. Policing internal affairs of member unions

The AFL-CIO is a loosely knit organization of national unions that has little formal power or control.[55] The member national unions remain completely autonomous and decide their own policies and programs. Not all national unions are members of the federation.

The fastest-growing segment of the AFL-CIO is the service workers' union. The Hotel Employees and Restaurant Employees International Union (HERE) has some 300,000 members across the United States and Canada. The members primarily work in the hospitality trades industry, but HERE represents some clerical and university employees as well. There are 118 local unions in 14 districts. The local unions range in size from a few hundred members to more than 40,000 members in Las Vegas.[56]

## ESTABLISHING THE COLLECTIVE BARGAINING RELATIONSHIP: UNION CERTIFICATION

Before a union can negotiate a contract, it must first be certified. Recently, unions won 1,653 representation elections, or 51.2 percent out of 3,229 elections, possibly signaling increased worker interest and more collective bargaining activity in the future.[57] The primary law governing the relationship of companies and unions is the National Labor Relations Act, as amended. Collective bargaining is one of the key parts of the act. Section 8(d) of the act defines **collective bargaining** as follows:

> The performance of the mutual obligation of the employer and the representative of the employees to meet at reasonable times and confer in good faith with respect to wages, hours, and other terms and conditions of employment, or the negotiation of an agreement, or any question arising thereunder, and the execution of a written contract incorporating any agreement reached if requested by either party, but such obligation does not compel either party to agree to a proposal or require the making of a concession.

The act further provides that the designated representative of the employees shall be the exclusive representative for all the employees in the unit for purposes of collective bargaining. A **bargaining unit** consists of a group of employees—not necessarily union members—recognized by an employer or certified by an administrative agency as appropriate for representation by a labor organization for purposes of collective bargaining. A unit may cover the employees in one plant of an employer, or it may cover employees in two or more plants of the same employer. Although the act requires the representative to be selected by the employees, it does not require any particular procedure to be used so long as the choice clearly reflects the desire of the majority of the employees in the bargaining unit. The employee representative is normally chosen in a secret ballot election conducted by the NLRB. When a union desires to

**Collective bargaining**
The performance of the mutual obligation of the employer and the representative of the employees to meet at reasonable times and confer in good faith with respect to wages, hours, and other terms and conditions of employment, or the negotiation of an agreement, or any question arising thereunder, and the execution of a written contract incorporating any agreement reached if requested by either party, but such obligation does not compel either party to agree to a proposal or require the making of a concession.

**Bargaining unit**
A group of employees—not necessarily union members—recognized by an employer or certified by an administrative agency as appropriate for representation by a labor organization for purposes of collective bargaining.

HR WEB WISDOM

⟩ *Collective Bargaining*

**www.prenhall.com/mondy**

This site offers various quotations related to negotiations and collective bargaining during labor's history.

become the bargaining representative for a group of employees, several steps leading to certification have to be taken (see Figure 14-3).

## Signing of Authorization Cards

**Authorization card**
A document indicating that an employee wants to be represented by a labor organization in collective bargaining.

A prerequisite to forming a recognized bargaining unit is to determine whether there is sufficient interest on the part of employees to justify the unit. Evidence of this interest is expressed when at least 30 percent of the employees in a work group sign an authorization card. The **authorization card** is a document indicating that an employee wants to be represented by a labor organization in collective bargaining. Most union organizers will not proceed unless at least 50 percent of the workers in the group sign cards. An authorization card used by the International Association of Machinists and Aerospace Workers is shown in Figure 14-4.

## Petition for Election

After the authorization cards have been signed, a petition for an election may be made to the appropriate regional office of the NLRB. When the petition is filed, the NLRB will conduct an investigation. The purpose of the investigation is to determine, among other things, the following:

1. Whether the Board has jurisdiction to conduct an election
2. Whether there is a sufficient showing of employee interest to justify an election
3. Whether a question of representation exists (for example, the employee representative has demanded recognition, which has been denied by the employer)
4. Whether the election will include appropriate employees in the bargaining unit (for instance, the Board is prohibited from including plant guards in the same unit with the other employees)
5. Whether the representative named in the petition is qualified (for example, a supervisor or any other management representative may not be an employee representative)

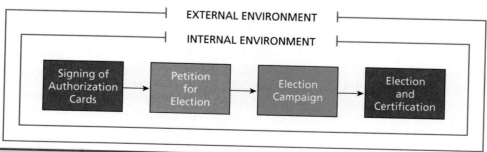

**Figure 14-3** ⟩ **The Steps That Lead to Forming a Bargaining Unit**

```
┌─────────────────────────────────────────────────────────────┐
│       ┌──────────────────────────────────────────────┐       │
│       │          YES, I WANT THE IAM                  │       │
│       └──────────────────────────────────────────────┘       │
│                                                               │
│              I, the undersigned, an employee of               │
│       ┌──────────────────────────────────────────────┐       │
│       │ (Company) _____      │       │
│       │                                               │       │
│       │ hereby authorize the International Association│       │
│       │ of Machinists and                             │       │
│       │ Aerospace Workers (IAM) to act as my          │       │
│       │ collective bargaining                         │       │
│       │ agent with the company for wages, hours, and  │       │
│       │ working                                       │       │
│       │ conditions.                                   │       │
│       │                                               │       │
│       │ NAME (print) _____ DATE _____ │       │
│       │                                               │       │
│       │ ADDRESS (print) _____ │       │
│       │                                               │       │
│       │ CITY _____ STATE _____ ZIP _____  │       │
│       │                                               │       │
│       │ DEPT. _____ SHIFT _____ PHONE _____   │       │
│       │                                               │       │
│       │ Classification _____ │       │
│       │                                               │       │
│       │ SIGN HERE X _____ │       │
│       │                                               │       │
│       │ NOTE: THIS AUTHORIZATION IS TO BE SIGNED AND  │       │
│       │ DATED IN                                      │       │
│       │ EMPLOYEE'S OWN HANDWRITING. YOUR RIGHT TO SIGN│       │
│       │ THIS CARD                                     │       │
│       │ IS PROTECTED BY FEDERAL LAW.                  │       │
│       └──────────────────────────────────────────────┘       │
└─────────────────────────────────────────────────────────────┘
```

**An Authorization Card**   **Figure 14-4**

Source: The International Association of Machinists and Aerospace Workers.

6. Whether there are any barriers to an election in the form of existing contracts or prior elections held within the past 12 months[58]

If these conditions have been met, the NLRB will ordinarily direct that an election be held within 30 days. Election details are left largely to the agency's regional director. Management is prohibited from making unusual concessions or promises that would encourage workers to vote against union recognition.

## Election Campaign

When an election has been ordered, both union and management usually promote their causes actively. Unions will continue to encourage workers to join the union, and management may begin a campaign to tell workers the benefits of remaining union free. The supervisor's role during the campaign is crucial. Supervisors need to conduct themselves in a manner that avoids violating the law and committing unfair labor practices. Specifically, they should be aware of what can and cannot be done in the preelection campaign period. In many cases, it is not so much what is said by the supervisor as how it is said.[59] Throughout the campaign, supervisors should keep upper management informed about employee attitudes.

Theoretically, both union and management are permitted to tell their stories without interference from the other side. At times, the campaign becomes quite intense. Election results will be declared invalid if the campaign was marked by conduct that the NLRB considers to have interfered with the employees' freedom of choice. Examples of such conduct include the following:

▶ An employer or a union threatens loss of jobs or benefits to influence employees' votes or union activities.
▶ An employer or a union misstates important facts in the election campaign when the other party does not have a chance to reply.

- Either an employer or a union incites racial or religious prejudice by inflammatory campaign appeals.
- An employer fires employees to discourage or encourage their union activities or a union causes an employer to take such an action.
- An employer or a union makes campaign speeches to assembled groups of employees on company time within 24 hours of an election.

## Election and Certification

The NLRB monitors the secret-ballot election on the date set. Its representatives are responsible for making sure that only eligible employees vote and for counting the votes. Following a valid election, the board will issue a certification of the results to the participants. If a union has been chosen by a majority of the employees voting in the bargaining unit, it will receive a certificate showing that it is now the official bargaining representative of the employees in the unit. However, the right to represent employees does not mean the right to dictate terms to management that would adversely affect the organization. The bargaining process does not require either party to make concessions; it only compels them to bargain in good faith. Robert Bandy of United Technologies is misinformed in his belief that the company has to accept all of the terms outlined by the union.

## Union Strategies in Obtaining Bargaining Unit Recognition

Unions may use various strategies to obtain recognition by management. Unions generally try to make the first move because this places management in the position of having to react to union maneuvers. The search for groups of employees to organize involves a continuous effort by union leaders. To begin a drive, unions often look for areas of dissatisfaction. Union organizers are aware that an overall positive attitude toward management among employees generally indicates that organizing employees will be extremely difficult.

Some situations indicate that employees are ripe for organizing:

- A history of management's unjustified and arbitrary treatment of employees
- Compensation below the industry average
- Management's lack of concern for employee welfare

A union does not normally look at isolated conditions of employee unrest. Rather, it attempts to locate general patterns of employee dissatisfaction. Whatever the case, the union will probably not make a major attempt at organizing unless it believes that it has a good chance of success.

The union may take numerous approaches to getting authorization cards signed. One effective technique is to first identify workers who are not only dissatisfied but also influential in the firm's informal organization. These individuals can assist in developing an effective organizing campaign. Information is obtained through the grapevine regarding who was hired, who was fired, and management mistakes in general. Such information is beneficial to union organizers as they approach company employees. Statements such as this are common: "I hear Bill Adams was fired today. I also understand that he is well liked. No way that would have happened if you had a union."

Ultimately, the union must abandon its secret activities. Sooner or later management will discover the organizing attempt. At this point, union organizers may station themselves and other supporters at company entrances and pass out *throwsheets*—campaign literature proclaiming the benefits of joining the union and emphasizing management weaknesses. They will talk to anyone who will listen in their attempt to identify union sympathizers. Employees who sign an authorization card are then encouraged to convince their friends to sign one also. The effort often mushrooms, yielding a sufficient number of signed authorization cards before management has time to react.

Union efforts continue even after the NLRB has approved the election petition. Every attempt is made by the organizers to involve as many workers from the firm as possible. The outside organizers would prefer to take a back seat and let company employees convince their peers to join the union. Peer pressure typically has a much greater effect on convincing a person to join a union than outside influence does. Whenever possible, unions utilize peer pressure to encourage and expand unionization.

## UNION DECERTIFICATION: REESTABLISHING THE INDIVIDUAL BARGAINING RELATIONSHIP

Until 1947, once a union was certified, it was certified forever. However, the Taft-Hartley Act made it possible for employees to decertify a union. This action results in a union losing its right to act as the exclusive bargaining representative of a group of employees. **Decertification** is essentially the reverse of the process that employees must follow to be recognized as an official bargaining unit. The outcome of decertification elections is of increasing concern to unions. Employees have used decertification petitions with increasing frequency and success. In 1965, only 200 decertification elections were held, 64 percent of which the unions lost. Between 1987 and 1991, an average of 636 decertification elections were held each year, resulting in an average union loss rate of 72 percent. Recently, 485 decertification elections were held and the union was ousted in 69 percent of those elections.[60]

**Decertification**
Election by a group of employees to withdraw a union's right to act as their exclusive bargaining representative; the reverse of the process that employees must follow to be recognized as an official bargaining unit.

## Decertification Procedure

The rules established by the NLRB spell out the conditions for filing a decertification petition. At least 30 percent of the bargaining unit members must petition for an election. As might be expected, this task by itself may be difficult because union supporters are likely to oppose the move strongly. Unfortunately, few employees know about decertification and fewer still know how to start the process.[61] Also, although the petitioners' names are supposed to remain confidential, many union members are fearful that their signatures on the petition will be discovered. Timing of the NLRB's receipt of the decertification petition is also critical. The petition must be submitted between 60 and 90 days prior to the expiration of the current contract. When all these conditions have been met, the NLRB regional director will schedule a decertification election by secret ballot.

The NLRB carefully monitors the events leading up to the election. Current employees must initiate the request for the election. If the NLRB determines that management initiated the action, it will not certify the election. After a petition has been accepted, however, management can support the decertification election attempt. If a majority of the votes cast are against the union, the employees will be free from the union. Strong union supporters are all likely to vote. Thus, if a substantial number of employees are indifferent to the union and choose not to vote, decertification may not occur.

## Management and Decertification

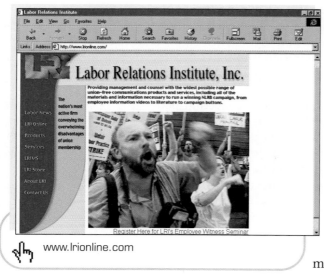

www.lrionline.com

When management senses employee discontent with the union, it often does not know how to react. Many times, management decides to do nothing, reasoning that it is best not to get involved or that doing so may even be illegal. But if it does want to get involved, management can use a variety of legal tactics. If management really wants the union decertified, it must learn how to be active rather than passive.

Meetings with union members to discuss the benefits of becoming union free have proven beneficial. In fact, such discussions are often cited as being the most effective campaign tactic. These meetings may be with individual employees, small groups, or even entire units. Management explains the benefits and answers employees' questions.

Management may also provide workers with legal assistance in preparing for decertification. Because the workers probably have never been through a decertification election, this type of assistance may prove invaluable. For example, the NLRB may not permit an election if the paperwork has not been properly completed. Management must always remember that it cannot initiate the decertification action; that is the workers' responsibility.

The most effective means of accomplishing decertification is to improve the corporate culture so workers no longer feel the need to have a union. This cannot be done overnight, as mutual trust and confidence must be developed between workers and the employer. If decertification is to succeed, management must eliminate the problems that initially led to unionization. Although many executives believe that pay and benefits are the primary reasons for union membership, other factors are probably more important. For example, failure to treat employees as individuals is often the primary reason for unionization. The real problems often stem from practices such as failing to listen to employees' opinions, dealing with workers unfairly and dishonestly, and treating employees as numbers and not as people. Employers who desire to remain or become union free can employ certain strategies and tactics that benefit both employers and employees, but not unions.

## UNION-FREE STRATEGIES AND TACTICS

Employers who adhere to certain union-free strategies and tactics can remain or become union free.[62] Some managers believe that the presence of a union is evidence of management's failure to treat employees fairly. While this is true in certain cases, the factors that the AFL-CIO believes will significantly reduce chances of unionizing are notable and are therefore listed in Table 14-1. According to a report published in *Unions in Transition,* certain similar characteristics help organizations remain union free: competitive pay and strong benefits, a team environment, open communication, a pleasant work environment, and the avoidance of layoffs.[63]

If a firm's goal is to remain union free, it should establish its strategy long before a union-organizing attempt begins. The development of long-term strategies

1. A conviction by employees that the boss is not taking advantage of them.
2. Employees who have pride in their work.
3. Good performance records kept by the company. Employees feel more secure on their jobs when they know their efforts are recognized and appreciated.
4. No claims of high-handed treatment. Employees respect firm but fair discipline.
5. No claim of favoritism that's not earned through work performance.
6. Supervisors who have good relationships with subordinates. The AFL-CIO maintains that this relationship of supervisors with people under them—above all—stifles organizing attempts.

*Source:* "What to Do When the Union Knocks," *Nation's Business* 54 (November 1966): 107.
Copyright 1977 by Nation's Business. Reprinted by permission.

and effective tactics for the purpose of remaining union free is crucial because the employees' decision to consider forming a union is usually not made overnight. Negative attitudes regarding the company are typically formed over a period of time and well in advance of any attempt at unionization.

If a firm desires to remain union free, it must borrow some of the union's philosophy. Basically, management must be able and willing to offer workers equal or better conditions than they could expect with a union. Weakness in any critical area may be an open invitation to a union. As shown in Figure 14-5, all aspects of an organization's operations are involved in maintaining its union-free status.

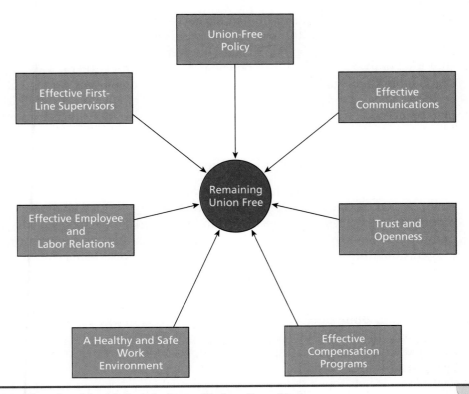

**Factors Involved in Maintaining a Union-Free Status**

Figure 14-5

## Effective First-Line Supervisors

Extremely important to an organization's ability to remain union free is the overall effectiveness of its management, particularly its first-line supervisors. These supervisors represent the first line of defense against unionization.[64] Their supervisory ability often determines whether unionization will be successful. The supervisor assigns work, evaluates each individual's performance, and provides praise and punishment. The manner in which he or she communicates with the employee in these and other matters can affect the individual's attitude toward the firm. Even though the first-line supervisor is the lowest level of management in the workplace, this individual usually has more influence over employees than any other manager.

## Union-Free Policy

The fact that the organization's goal is to remain union free should be clearly and forcefully communicated to all its members. Such a policy statement might read as follows:

> Our success as a company is founded on the skill and efforts of our employees. Our policy is to deal with employees as effectively as possible, respecting and recognizing each of them as individuals. In our opinion, unionization would interfere with the individual treatment, respect, and recognition the company offers. Consequently, we believe a union-free environment is in the employees' best interest, the company's best interest, and the interest of the people served by the corporation.[65]

This type of policy evolves into a philosophy that affects everyone in the organization. All employees, from the lowest-paid worker to top management, must understand it. No major human resource–related decision should be made without asking, "How will this affect our union-free status?" The union-free policy should be repeatedly communicated to every worker. Workers must be told why the company advocates the policy and how it affects them. This involves much more than sending a memo each year to all employees stating that the company's goal is to remain union free. Every means of effective communication may be needed to convince employees that the organization intends to remain union free.

## Effective Communication

To remain union free, one of the most important actions a company can take is to establish credible and effective communication. A very positive by-product of the participative management, cooperation, and teamwork is open and effective communication. Employees must be given the information they need to perform their jobs and then be provided feedback on their performance. Management should openly share information with workers concerning activities taking place within the organization.

One approach taken to encourage open communication is the open-door policy. The **open-door policy** gives employees the right to take any grievance to the person next in the chain of command if the problem cannot be resolved by the immediate supervisor. Creating a genuine open-door policy in a company can be facilitated by using certain ongoing communications tactics. Delta Air Lines is well known for its open-door policy, which enables employees to express their grievances. An effective open-door policy represents an attitude of openness and

**Open-door policy**
A company policy allowing employees the right to take any grievance to the person next in the chain of command if a satisfactory solution cannot be obtained from their immediate supervisor.

trust among people within the organization. It is counterproductive to state that an open-door policy exists, then punish an employee for bypassing his or her immediate supervisor. The employee must not fear that talking to the manager next in line will be detrimental to his or her career. Although it might seem that an open-door policy would result in wasted time for upper and middle managers, in most instances this has not proven to be the case. The mere knowledge that an employee can move up the chain of command with a complaint without fear of retribution often encourages the immediate supervisor and the employee to work out their differences.

## Trust and Openness

Openness and trust on the part of managers and employees alike are important for an organization to remain union free. The old expression, "Actions speak louder than words," is certainly valid for such an organization. Credibility, based on trust, must exist between labor and management, and this trust develops only over time. If employees perceive that the manager is being open and receptive to ideas, feedback is likely to be encouraged. Managers need this feedback to do their jobs effectively. However, if managers give the impression that their directives should never be questioned, communication will be stifled and credibility lost.

## Effective Compensation Programs

The financial compensation that employees receive is the most tangible measure they have of their worth to the organization. If an individual's pay is substantially below that provided for similar work in the area, the employee will soon become dissatisfied. Compensation must remain relatively competitive if the organization expects to remain union free.

## A Healthy and Safe Work Environment

An organization that gains a reputation for failing to maintain a safe and healthy work environment leaves itself wide open for unionization. For years, unions have campaigned successfully by convincing workers that the union will provide them with a safer work environment. In fact, labor organizations were leading advocates of the Occupational Safety and Health Act, and they continue to support this type of legislation. Union cooperation on matters of safety and health, the establishment of a joint local labor-management safety and health committee, protective clothing, and safety "dos and don'ts" are the most frequently appearing subjects in collective bargaining agreements.[66]

## Effective Employee and Labor Relations

No organization is free from employee disagreements and dissatisfaction. Therefore, a means of resolving employee complaints, whether actual or perceived, should be available. The **grievance procedure** is a formal, systematic process that permits employees to complain about matters affecting them and their work. Most labor-management agreements contain formal grievance procedures, and union members regard handling grievances as one of the most important functions of a labor union. In North American unionized workplaces, formal grievance procedures are typically used to resolve alleged violations of rights to which employees or employers are entitled by collective agreements.[67] These violations often reflect differences over the interpretation and application of collective bargaining agreements.

**Grievance procedure**
A formal, systematic process that permits employees to complain about matters affecting them and their work.

## Global Union Membership Declines

The future of unionism abroad seems brighter than domestic unionism. However, according to the International Labor Office (ILO), unions must change because the world is changing around them. The ILO reports that out of 92 countries surveyed, 72 showed membership declines over a 10-year period. In 48 countries, fewer than 20 percent of all workers are in a union today.[68] Unionism is also declining in Canada, Western Europe, and Japan.[69] As the world economy becomes more global, unions in all countries are under increasing pressure because of globalization, slowing productivity, lower economic growth, rapid technological changes, and a shift toward a free market system.[70]

In many industries, managers respond to global competition by telling unions that labor must restrain demands for wage increases and benefits in order to save jobs. If restraint is not used, the company may move to other countries. Mercedes-Benz's decision to locate outside of Germany and in the United States, China, and India to escape Germany's strict work rules and extremely high union wage rates is probably indicative of the future of unionism. Mercedes-Benz is reinventing itself outside of Germany because the labor situation in Germany is not conducive to competitiveness. This turn of events surprised many people, especially in Germany. The United States is the recipient of these jobs, which is a reversal of recent history.[71]

Until recently, grievance procedures were not so common in union-free organizations. However, many nonunion firms have started grievance procedure programs. When employees do not have ways to voice their complaints and have them resolved, even small gripes may grow into major problems. A formal grievance procedure is needed for effective human resource management.[72]

One means of resolving grievances in union-free organizations is through the use of ombudspersons. This approach has been used for some time in Europe, and the practice is now popular in the United States for a multitude of jobs.[73] An **ombudsperson** is a complaint officer with access to top management who hears employees' complaints, investigates them, and sometimes recommends appropriate action.[74] Because of their access to top management, ombudspersons can often resolve problems swiftly.

At times, the ombudsperson has assumed the additional duties of helping uncover scandals within organizations. Large defense contractors, such as McDonnell Douglas and General Electric, have used ombudspersons to respond to questions raised regarding product design safety or defense contract billings. Workers who believe that a problem exists can now bypass the supervisor and talk to the ombudsperson.[75]

**Ombudsperson**
A complaint officer with access to top management who hears employees' complaints, investigates them, and sometimes recommends appropriate action.

## ▶ Summary

**①** **Describe the labor movement prior to 1930.**
Prior to 1930, the trend definitely favored management. The courts strongly supported employers in their attempts to thwart the organized labor movement.

**②** **Identify the major labor legislation that was passed after 1930.**
Major legislation included the Anti-Injunction Act of 1932, the National Labor Relations Act, the Labor-Management Relations Act, and the Labor-Management Reporting and Disclosure Act.

**3** **Describe the state of unions today.**

Overall, the fall of Big Labor has been dramatic since the 1970s.

**4** **Describe union growth strategies.**

Organized labor's new strategies for a stronger movement include greater political involvement, union salting, flooding communities with organizers, corporate labor campaigns, building organizing funds, organizing students, activism and focus, forming coalitions, and the AFL-CIO cyberunion.

**5** **Describe the relationship between teams and organized labor.**

To be globally competitive, most organizations must utilize cohesive teams that take maximum advantage of the physical and mental capacities of each employee. However, the 1935 National Labor Relations Act prohibits such arrangements.

**6** **Explain unionization in the public sector.**

Employees are permitted to organize and negotiate human resource policies and practices and matters affecting working conditions within the administrative discretion of the agency officials concerned. However, it is a felony for federal employees to strike against the U.S. government.

**7** **Identify union objectives and the reasons why employees join unions.**

Union objectives are growth and power. Reasons that employees join unions include dissatisfaction with management, need for a social outlet, opportunities for leadership, forced unionization, and social pressure from peers.

**8** **Describe the basic structure of the union.**

The basic element in the structure of the American labor movement is the local union. The national union is the most powerful level, and the American Federation of Labor and Congress of Industrial Organizations (AFL-CIO) is the central trade union federation in the United States.

**9** **Identify the steps involved in establishing the collective bargaining relationship.**

The steps involved include signing authorization cards, petitioning for election, campaigning, winning the election, and being certified.

**10** **Explain union decertification.**

Decertification is essentially the reverse of the process that employees must follow to be recognized as an official bargaining unit.

**11** **Describe union-free strategies and tactics.**

Tactics employers can use to remain union free include effective first-line supervision, a union-free policy, effective communication, trust and openness, effective compensation programs, a healthy and safe work environment, and effective employee and labor relations.

---

## Questions for Review ◀

1. Describe the development of the labor movement in the United States before 1930.

2. What major labor legislation was passed after 1930?

3. List the unfair labor practices that were prohibited by management by the Wagner Act.

4. What union actions were prohibited by the Taft-Hartley Act?

5. What growth strategies are currently being used by unions?

6. In what way does unionization of the public sector differ from unionization of the private sector?

7. Why would unions strive for continued growth and power? Discuss.

8. What are the primary reasons for employees joining labor unions?

9. Describe the union structure in the United States.

10. What steps must a union take in attempting to form a bargaining unit? Briefly describe each step.

11. What are ways unions might go about gaining bargaining unit recognition?

12. What are the steps in decertification?

13. What are strategies and tactics to remain union free?

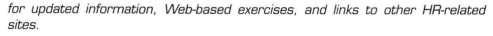

<u>TAKE IT TO</u>
<u>THE NET</u>

*We invite you to visit the Mondy homepage on the Prentice Hall Web site at*
**www.prenhall.com/mondy**

*for updated information, Web-based exercises, and links to other HR-related sites.*

# ▶ Developing HRM Skills

### An Experiential Exercise

Unionization is often met with mixed feelings by all concerned. Management is usually opposed to such efforts. Beth Morrison, the production manager of the heavy motors division of MNP Corporation, knows that upper management does not care much for unions. Senior officials believe the unionizing effort MNP faces is not good for anybody involved with the company and that the union wants to turn employees against them. Upper management also feels that a union will destroy the company's competitive edge—something that has happened to many other firms. The firm must do everything possible to circumvent this union-organizing effort, but it must do so in line with NLRB guidelines.

If you are either in favor of or opposed to unions, there is a role for you here. One of you will play the production manager, and another will play the supervisor. The rest of you should observe carefully. Your instructor will provide the participants with additional information.

# ▶ HRM INCIDENT 1

### Open the Door

Barney Cline, the new human resource manager for Ampex Utilities, was just getting settled in his new office. He had recently moved from another firm to take his new job. Barney had been selected over several in-house candidates and numerous other applicants because of his record of getting things done. He had a good reputation for working through people to get the job accomplished.

Barney's phone rang. The person on the other end of the line asked, "Mr. Cline, could I set up an appointment to talk with you?" "Certainly," Barney said, "when do you want to get together?" "How about after work? It might be bad if certain people saw me speaking to anyone in management," said the caller.

Barney was a bit puzzled, but he set up an appointment for 5:30 P.M., when nearly everyone would be gone. At the designated time there was a knock on his door; it was Mark Johnson, a senior maintenance worker who had been with the firm for more than 10 years.

After the initial welcome, Mark began by saying, "Mr. Cline, several of the workers asked me to talk to you. Rumor has it that you're a fair person. The company says it has an open-door policy, but we're afraid to use it. Roy Edwards, one of the best maintenance workers in our section, tried it several months ago. They hassled him so much that he quit last week. We just don't know what to do to get any problems solved. There has been talk of organizing a union. We really don't want that, but something has to give."

Barney thanked Mark for his honesty and promised not to reveal the conversation. In the weeks following the conversation with Mark, Barney was able to verify that the situation was just as Mark had described. There was considerable mistrust between managers and the operative employees.

### Questions

1. What are the basic causes of the problems confronting Ampex Utilities?
2. How should Barney attempt to resolve these problems?

---

**HRM INCIDENT 2**

### You Are out of What?

Marcus Ned eagerly drove his new company pickup onto the construction site. He had just been assigned by his employer, Kelso Construction Company, to supervise a crew of 16 equipment operators, oilers, and mechanics. This was the first unionized crew Marcus had supervised, and he was unaware of the labor agreement in effect that carefully defined and limited the role of supervisors. As he approached his work area, he noticed one of the cherry pickers (a type of mobile crane with an extendable boom) standing idle with the operator beside it. Marcus pulled up beside the operator and asked, "What's going on here?"

"Out of gas," the operator said.

"Well, go and get some," Marcus said.

The operator reached to get his thermos jug out of the toolbox on the side of the crane and said, "The oiler's on break right now. He'll be back in a few minutes."

Marcus remembered that he had a five-gallon can of gasoline in the back of his pickup. So he quickly got the gasoline, climbed on the cherry picker, and started to pour it into the gas tank. As he did so, he heard the other machines shutting down in unison. He looked around and saw all the other operators climbing down from their equipment and standing to watch him pour the gasoline. A moment later, he saw the union steward approaching.

### Questions

1. Why did all the operators shut down their machines?
2. If you were Marcus, what would you do now?

# ► Notes

1. *Brief History of the American Labor Movement,* Bulletin 1000 (Washington, DC: U.S. Department of Labor Statistics, 1970): 1.

2. Benjamin J. Taylor and Fred Witney, *Labor Relations Law,* 5th ed. (Upper Saddle River, NJ: Prentice-Hall, 1987): 12–13.

3. *Brief History of the American Labor Movement,* 9.

4. Foster Rhea Dulles, *Labor in America,* 3rd ed. (New York: Crowell, 1966): 114–125.

5. Ibid., 126–149.

6. E. Edward Herman, Alfred Kuhn, and Ronald L. Seeber, *Collective Bargaining and Labor Relations* (Upper Saddle River, NJ: Prentice-Hall, 1987): 32–34.

7. *Brief History of the American Labor Movement,* 27.

8. *Historical Statistics of the United States, Colonial Times to 1970,* bicentennial ed., part I (Washington, DC: U.S. Bureau of the Census, 1975): 126.

9. Taylor and Witney, *Labor Relations Law,* 78–81.

10. *Brief History of the American Labor Movement,* 65.

11. Right-to-work states include Alabama, Arizona, Arkansas, Florida, Georgia, Idaho, Iowa, Kansas, Louisiana, Mississippi, Nebraska, Nevada, North Carolina, North Dakota, South Carolina, South Dakota, Tennessee, Texas, Utah, Virginia, and Wyoming.

12. Dulles, *Labor in America,* 382–383.

13. *Brief History of the American Labor Movement,* 58–61.

14. James Worsham, "Unions Gain Members But Lose Ground Nonetheless," *Nation's Business* 87 (March 1999): 12.

15. Chuck Hutchcraft and Scott Hume, "Union Watch," *Restaurant and Institutions* 110 (April 15, 2000): 46.

16. John E. Lyncheski and Joseph M. McDermott, "Unions Employ New Growth Strategies," *HR Focus* 73 (September 1996): 22; and Worsham, "Unions Gain Members But Lose Ground Nonetheless."

17. Kevin Galvin, "Rising Global Job Market Has Dimmed the Nation's Stake in Labor Strikes: Changing Times Have Unions Organizing to Rejuvenate the Ranks in Solidarity," *Minneapolis Star Tribune* (July 31, 1998): 3D.

18. William H. Miller, "Labor on the Rebound?" *Industry Week* (July 5, 1999): 10–13.

19. Dan Seligman, "Driving the AFL-CIO Crazy," *Forbes Magazine* 164 (November 1, 1999): 102–108.

20. Galvin, "Rising Global Job Market Has Dimmed the Nation's Stake in Labor Strikes."

21. James Worsham, "Labor Comes Alive," *Nation's Business* 84 (February 1996): 16

22. Arch Puddington, "Is Labor Back? (Trouble in the AFL-CIO)," *Commentary* 3 (January 1998): 39–43.

23. Cory R. Fine, "Covert Union Organizing: Beware the Trojan Horse," *Workforce* 77 (May 1998): 44.

24. Lyncheski and McDermott, "Unions Employ New Growth Strategies."

25. Fine, "Covert Union Organizing: Beware the Trojan Horse."

26. Galvin, "Rising Global Job Market Has Dimmed the Nation's Stake in Labor Strikes."

27. Sharon Leonard, "Unions Could Be Staging a Comeback," *HRMagazine* 44 (December 1999): 207.

28. "USWA Will Form $40 Million Organizing Fund," *Iron Age New Steel* 14 (September 1998): 40.

29. Leonard, "Unions Could Be Staging a Comeback."

30. Kathy Seal, "Hotel Union's New Boss Heightens Expectations," *Hotel and Motel Management* 213 (October 1998): 58.

31. Ibid.

32. J. Duncan Moore Jr., "Modern Healthcare," *Chicago* (September 27, 1999): 10.

33. Cynthia G. Wagner, "Cyberunions: Organized Labor Goes Online," *The Futurist* 34 (January/February 2000): 7.

34. Galvin, "Rising Global Job Market Has Dimmed the Nation's Stake in Labor Strikes."

35. Philip Dine, "'Buy American' Slogan May Stop Making Sense: Labor's New Emphasis Could Be on Domestic Jobs—Unions Welcome Chrysler's Buyout," *St. Louis Post-Dispatch* (May 8, 1998): A14.

36. "Team Act," *Journal for Quality and Participation* 21 (January/February 1998): 7.

37. Faye Fiore and Martha Groves, "Bill to Curb Union Power Passes Senate; Veto Likely," *Los Angeles Times* (July 11, 1996): A-1.

38. Richard Lesher, "Management and Labor Work Best as Cohesive Teams," *Human Events* (March 7, 1997): 27.

39. Peter Szekely, "TEAM Act: New Political Hot Potato," *Reuters* (May 8, 1996): 1.

40. Examples include the Social Security Act, the Fair Labor Standards Act, and the National Labor Relations Act, as amended.

41. Seligman, "Driving the AFL-CIO Crazy"; and Worsham, "Unions Gain Members but Lose Ground Nonetheless."

42. Puddington, "Is Labor Back? (Trouble in the AFL-CIO)."

43. Section 305 of the Labor Management Relations Act of 1947 also makes it unlawful for government employees to participate in any strike.

44. They are Executive Order 11491 (effective January 1, 1970), EO 11616 (effective November 1971), EO 11636 (effective December 1971), and EO 11828 (effective May 1975).

45. Herman, Kuhn, and Seeber, *Collective Bargaining and Labor Relations,* 407.

46. www.nea.org/aboutnea (July 3, 2000).

47. Edwin F. Beal and James P. Begin, *The Practice of Collective Bargaining,* 5th ed. (Homewood, IL: Richard D. Irwin, 1982): 91.

48. Jay Thomas Rex, "Bill Aimed at Fighting HMOs: Bargaining Rights Given to Doctors by Proposal," *The Arlington Morning News* (March 28, 2000): 1C.

49. www.aflcio.org/voice/at work/morejoin.htm (July 9, 2000).

50. Ibid.

51. Hutchcraft and Hume, "Union Watch."

52. Seligman, "Driving the AFL-CIO Crazy."

53. Michael R. Carrell and Christina Heavrin, *Labor Relations and Collective Bargaining,* 5th ed. (Upper Saddle River, NJ.: Prentice Hall, 1998): 95.

54. See the AFL-CIO homepage at www.aflcio.org/about/meet.

55. Miller, "Labor on the Rebound?"

56. For more information about the Hotel Employees & Restaurant Employees (HERE) International Union, see www.hereunion.org.

57. Miller, "Labor on the Rebound?"

58. *A Guide to Basic Law and Procedures under the National Labor Relations Act* (Washington, DC: U.S. Government Printing Office, October 1978): 11–13.

59. Art Bethke, R. Wayne Mondy, and Shane R. Premeaux, "Decertification: The Role of the First-Line Supervisor," *Supervisory Management* 31 (February 1986): 21–23.

60. Catherine Meeker, "Union Decertification under the National Labor Relations Act," *The University of Chicago Law Review* 66 (Summer 1999): 999.

61. Ibid.

62. Mark A. Spognardi, "Conducting a Successful Union-Free Campaign," *Employee Relations Law Journal* 24 (Autumn 1998): 35.

63. Alexander B. Trowbridge, "A Management Look at Labor Relations," in *Unions in Transition* (San Francisco: ICS Press, 1988): 415–416.

64. Jonathan A. Segal, "Unshackle Your Supervisors to Stay Union Free," *HRMagazine* 43 (June 1998): 77–184.

65. James F. Rand, "Preventive Maintenance Techniques for Staying Union-Free," *Personnel Journal* 59 (June 1980): 497.

66. George R. Grey, Donald W. Myers, and Phyllis S. Myers, "Collective Bargaining Agreements: Safety and Health Provisions," *Monthly Labor Review* 121 (May 1998): 13.

67. Dean Tjosvold and Motohiro Morishima, "Grievance Resolution: Perceived Goal Interdependence and Interaction Patterns," *Relations Industrielles* 54 (Summer 1999): 527.

68. Jeffrey H. Epstein, "Reinventing Labor Unions," *The Futurist* 32 (August 1, 1998): 13.

69. Seligman, "Driving the AFL-CIO Crazy."

70. Worsham, "Labor Comes Alive."

71. Donald W. Nauss, "It's Fun, It's Useful, It's a Mercedes?" *Los Angeles Times* (May 18, 1997): A-1.

72. Donald Caruth and Gail Handlogten, "Avoiding HR Lawsuits," *Credit Union Executive Journal* 39 (November-December 1999): 25.

73. Lucia Moses, "All (Ombuds)men Are Not Created Equal," *Editor & Publisher* 133 (January 2000): 26.

74. Stephen L. Hayford, "Alternative Dispute Resolution," *Business Horizons* (January/February): 2.

75. Michael Brody, "Listen to Your Whistleblower," *Fortune* 124 (November 1986): 77–78.

chapter

# 15

# Labor-Management Relations

## Objectives

- Explain labor-management relations and individual bargaining.
- Describe labor-management relations and collective bargaining.
- Explain the psychological aspects of collective bargaining.
- Describe the factors involved in preparing for negotiations.
- Explain typical bargaining issues.
- Describe the process of negotiating the agreement.
- Identify ways to overcome breakdowns in negotiations.
- Describe what is involved in ratifying the agreement.
- Explain factors involved in administering the agreement.
- Describe collective bargaining for federal employees.

abor-management relations changed significantly after MBI, Inc. became unionized. Individual bargaining was replaced by a collective bargaining relationship. Barbara Washington, the chief union negotiator, was meeting with company representatives on a new contract. Both the union team and management had been preparing for this encounter for a long time. Barbara's deep concern was whether union members would support a strike vote if one were called. Sales for the industry were generally down because of imports. In fact, there had even been some layoffs at competing firms. The union members' attitude could be described as, "Get what you can for us, but don't rock the boat." She hoped, however, that skillful negotiating could win concessions from management.

In the first session, Barbara's team presented its demands to management. The team had determined that pay was the main issue, and a 20 percent increase spread over three years was demanded.

## Key Terms

Employment at will 461
Mandatory bargaining issues 465
Permissive bargaining issues 465
Prohibited bargaining issues 465
Closed shop 470
Union shop 470
Agency shop 470

Open shop 470
Checkoff of dues 470
Seniority 471
Beachhead demands 474
Mediation 474
Arbitration 474
Rights arbitration 474

Interest arbitration 474
Strike 475
Boycott 477
Secondary boycott 477
Lockout 478

Management countered by saying that since sales were down it could not afford to provide any pay raises. After much heated discussion, both sides agreed to reevaluate their positions and meet again in two days. Barbara met with her negotiating team in private, and they decided to decrease the salary demand slightly. The team felt that the least they could accept was a 15 percent raise.

At the next meeting, Barbara presented the revised demands to management. They were not well received. Bill Thompson, the director of industrial relations, began by saying, "We cannot afford a pay increase in this contract, but we will make every attempt to ensure that no layoffs occur. Increasing wages at this time will virtually guarantee a reduction in the workforce."

Barbara's confidence collapsed. She knew that there was no way that the general membership was willing to accept layoffs and that a strike vote would be virtually impossible to obtain. She asked for a recess to review the new proposal. Barbara is experiencing the negotiating crunch that has existed for several years in the United States. The power pendulum has swung in favor of management, making it very difficult for union negotiators to bargain effectively with management on certain issues, including pay increases.

**W**e devote the first portion of the chapter to labor-management relations involving both individual and collective bargaining. Then, we describe the psychological aspects of collective bargaining and preparing for negotiations. Next, we address bargaining issues, negotiating the agreement, and breakdowns in negotiations. Then, we describe what is involved in ratifying and administering the agreement. Collective bargaining for federal employees is the final section in the chapter.

HR WEB WISDOM

▷ *SHRM-HR Links*

**www.prenhall.com/mondy**

Various labor relations issues are addressed.

# LABOR-MANAGEMENT RELATIONS AND INDIVIDUAL BARGAINING

We previously stated that approximately 9.5 percent of the private workforce is unionized.[1] Therefore, over 90 percent of the private workforce base their labor-management relations on individual bargaining.[2] We also mentioned in Chapter 14 that one of the goals of a union is to gain power, which is largely dependent on the size of union membership. In individual negotiations, however, the worker is alone in negotiating with company representatives. Even so, negotiations can still be on a power basis, depending on the value of the individual to the company. An employee who continuously adds value to himself or herself is in a position of power. Should an individual desire a raise or other tangible evidence of value, negotiations will likely receive positive results if the company values the worker. Otherwise, the worker can join another company. Seniority means little in this environment. Negotiations are ineffective unless the worker has a positive value component.

Another factor influencing individual negotiations is the concept of supply and demand. In 2000, with unemployment hovering around 4 percent, workers skilled in certain employment areas—such as information technology (IT)—were in *great* demand. These workers could demand promotions and raises and, if not forthcoming, move easily to another position with another company. Thus, negotiations on an individual basis are more effective when demand for workers is high and supply is low.

An individual negotiator usually falls under the concept of employment at will. **Employment at will** is an unwritten contract created when an employee agrees to work for an employer but includes no agreement as to how long the parties expect the employment to last. Historically, because of a century-old common law precedent in the United States, employment of indefinite duration could, in general, be terminated at the whim of either party.[3] Employment at will is discussed in greater detail in Chapter 16.

**Employment at will**
An unwritten contract that is created when an employee agrees to work for an employer but includes no agreement as to how long the parties expect the employment to last.

One might think that an individual employee would be extremely vulnerable when dealing with individual negotiations. As our society becomes more legalistic, more and more individual rights are protected. Think back to Chapter 3, which detailed the many laws and court decisions that exist to protect individual rights. In the past, many of these protections were based on union representation. Individual negotiators now possess many of these rights. As you will see in the next chapter, even the concept of employment at will has eroded somewhat in recent years because of state court decisions.

Even though most workers in the U.S. economy are not unionized, if a firm desires to remain union free, its management must maintain an environment that discourages unionizing attempts. The old saying that *management gets what it deserves* is never truer than when a union successfully organizes a group of employees. After the union successfully organizes, management usually recognizes the avoidable mistakes that led to unionization. However, a well-conceived and implemented employee relations plan could reduce the likelihood of unionization.[4] When unionization occurs, collective bargaining follows, as the union becomes a third party within the corporate setting.

# LABOR-MANAGEMENT RELATIONS AND COLLECTIVE BARGAINING

The collective bargaining process is fundamental to management–organized labor relations in the United States. Most labor-management agreements in the United States are for a three-year period. Thus, on average, one-third of collective bargaining agreements occur each year.

# Forms of Bargaining Structures and Union-Management Relationships

The bargaining structure can affect the conduct of collective bargaining. The four major structures are one company dealing with a single union, several companies dealing with a single union, several unions dealing with a single company, and several companies dealing with several unions.

Most contract bargaining is carried out under the first type of structure, as was the case with MBI, Inc. The process can become quite complicated when several companies and unions are involved in the same negotiations. However, even when there is only one industry involved and one group of workers with similar skills, collective bargaining can be very difficult.

The type of union-management relationship that exists can have a major impact on the collective bargaining process. When a group of workers decide they want union representation, changes occur in the organization. Sloane and Witney list six types of union-management relations that may exist in an organization:

1. *Conflict.* Each challenges the other's actions and motivation; cooperation is nonexistent, and uncompromising attitudes and union militancy are present.
2. *Armed truce.* Each views the other as antagonistic but tries to avoid head-on conflict; bargaining obligations and contract provisions are strictly interpreted.
3. *Power bargaining.* Management accepts the union; each side tries to gain advantage from the other.
4. *Accommodation.* Each tolerates the other in a *live and let live* atmosphere and attempts to reduce conflict without eliminating it.
5. *Cooperation.* Each side accepts the other, and both work together to resolve human resource and production problems as they occur. Although the National Labor Relations Act of 1935 prohibits management domination of unions, cooperation is allowed if prescribed in the collective bargaining agreement.
6. *Collusion.* Both cooperate to the point of adversely affecting the legitimate interests of employees, other businesses in the industry, and the consuming public; this involves conniving to control markets, supplies, and prices illegally and/or unethically.[5]

The nature and quality of union-management relations vary over time. Today, many employers appear unwilling to accept unions.[6] This attitude has created an adversarial relationship with labor. Basically, during the past years, U.S. industry has conducted one of its most successful antiunion wars ever, and many managers appear eager to continue their assault on labor. According to the National Labor Relations Board, companies are increasingly using every weapon—legal or not—to thwart attempts to organize their workers. Some of the tactics that unions have accused management of using include harassing and firing pro-union workers as well as management coercion that intimidates workers. According to National Association of Manufacturers Vice President Patrick J. Cleary, managers are merely "exercising their First Amendment rights to give [workers] facts about unions" when they campaign against unions. Others believe that there is a disturbing trend of management coercion that inhibits workers.[7]

Today, many believe that to counteract management tactics, organized labor has been using an old-style adversarial collective bargaining relationship. As evidence, they cite strikes in 1998 at Northwest Airlines, General Motors Corp., and Bell Atlantic. In 1999, the pilots at American Airlines staged a 10-day *sick-out* that forced the airline to cancel more than 6,600 flights. Saturn employees also voted out all local union leaders, who had made Saturn one of the country's most prominent experiments in labor relations. They voted in United Auto Worker leaders who advocated a more traditional relationship with management. The new leaders believe that Saturn should stop linking pay to productivity and should adopt many of the work rules that are in place at other GM factories. Pay and productivity issues will continue to be of prime concern to unionized companies.[8] There is also a long-running battle between *San Diego Union-Tribune* pressroom employees, who have been without a new contract or raises since 1992, and a management group accused of driving out three other unions in five years. Recently, union leaders launched a TV campaign promoting a newspaper boycott.[9]

Some people believe that this new adversarial relationship is because union leaders need a tougher position at the bargaining table to get higher visibility for organizing purposes. A tougher stance and highly visible strikes help the labor organizing movement.[10] Other hostile relationships existed between labor and management during the summer of 2000. Medical personnel even struck major hospitals in the San Francisco area. The Hollywood actors' strike against advertisers stretched into a third month. Medical doctors were also attempting to unionize.[11] Whether this adversarial relationship will increase union membership is still unknown.

## The Collective Bargaining Process

Regardless of the current state of labor-management relations, the general aspects of the collective bargaining process are the same and are illustrated in Figure 15-1. Depending on the type of relationship encountered, the collective bargaining process may be relatively simple or it may be a long, tense struggle for both parties. Regardless of the complexity of the bargaining issues, the ability to reach agreement is the key to any successful negotiation.

As you can see, both external and internal environmental factors can influence the process. The first step in the collective bargaining process is preparing for negotiations. This step is often extensive and ongoing for both the union and management. After the issues to be negotiated have been determined, the two sides confer to reach a mutually acceptable contract. Although breakdowns in negotiations can occur, both labor and management have at their disposal tools and arguments that can be used to convince the other side to accept their views. Eventually, however, management and the union usually reach an agreement that defines the rules of the game for the duration of the contract. The next step is for the union membership to ratify the agreement. Note the feedback loop from "Administration of the Agreement" to "Preparing for Negotiation" in Figure 15-1. Collective bargaining is a continuous and dynamic process, and preparing for the next round of negotiations often begins the moment a contract is ratified.

### PSYCHOLOGICAL ASPECTS OF COLLECTIVE BARGAINING

Prior to collective bargaining, both management and union teams have to prepare positions and accomplish certain tasks. Vitally important for those involved are the psychological aspects of collective bargaining. Psychologically, the collective bargaining process is often difficult because it is an adversarial situation and must be approached as such.[12] It is a situation that is fundamental to law, politics, business, and government, because out of the clash of ideas, points of view, and interests come agreement, consensus, and justice.

In effect, those involved in the collective bargaining process will be matching wits with the competition, will experience victory as well as defeat, and will usually

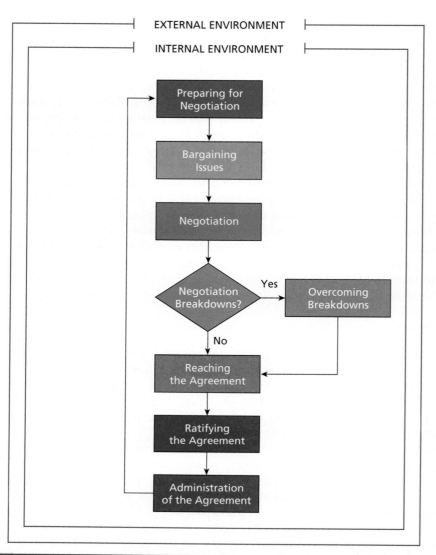

EXTERNAL ENVIRONMENT

INTERNAL ENVIRONMENT

Preparing for
Negotiation

Bargaining
Issues

Negotiation

Negotiation
Breakdowns?

Yes → Overcoming
Breakdowns

No

Reaching
the Agreement

Ratifying
the Agreement

Administration
of the Agreement

**Figure 15-1** **The Collective Bargaining Process**

resolve problems, resulting in a contract. The role of those who meet at the bargaining table essentially involves the management of aggression in a manner that allows them to hammer out a collective bargaining agreement. The personalities of those involved have a major impact on the negotiation process. The attitudes of those who will be negotiating have a direct effect on what can be accomplished and how quickly a mutually agreed-on contract can be finalized. Problems are compounded by differences in the experiences and educational backgrounds of those involved in the negotiation process. Finally, the longer, more involved, and intense the bargaining sessions are, the greater will be the psychological strain on all concerned. As psychological pressures intensify, the gap between labor and management can easily widen, further compounding the problem of achieving mutual accommodation.

Scare tactics intensify the psychological pressures of collective bargaining. Labor may threaten to strike; management may threaten a lockout. Most likely, neither side wants either a strike or a lockout. But, the psychological impact of the threat is hoped to bring the other side back to the bargaining table.

Because of the complex issues facing labor and management today, the negotiating teams must carefully prepare for the bargaining sessions. Prior to meeting at the bargaining table, the negotiators should thoroughly know the culture, climate, history, present economic state, and wage and benefits structure of both the organization and similar organizations. Because the length of a typical labor agreement is three years, negotiators should develop a contract that is successful both now and in the future. This consideration should prevail for both management and labor, although it rarely does. During the term of an agreement, the two sides usually discover contract provisions that need to be added, deleted, or modified. These items become proposals to be addressed in the next round of negotiations.

Bargaining issues can be divided into three categories: mandatory, permissive, and prohibited. **Mandatory bargaining issues** fall within the definition of wages, hours, and other terms and conditions of employment (see Table 15-1). These issues generally have an immediate and direct effect on workers' jobs. A refusal to bargain in these areas is grounds for an unfair labor practice charge. In many industries, collective bargaining toward new wage, rules, and benefits agreements typically drags on for a long time.[13]

**Permissive bargaining issues** may be raised, but neither side may insist that they be bargained over. For example, the union may want to bargain over health benefits for retired workers or union participation in establishing company pricing policies, but management may choose not to bargain over either issue.[14] A new collective bargaining weapon in management's arsenal is the ability, under certain circumstances, to terminate health benefits for retirees during a lapse in collective bargaining. In *Joyce et al. v Curtiss-Wright Corporation,* the U.S. Court of Appeals for the Second Circuit ruled that an employer did not violate ERISA when it terminated retirement health benefits during a period when there was no collective bargaining agreement in effect providing such benefits.[15]

The AFL-CIO has vowed to emphasize work-family issues, particularly child care, in bargaining. According to the head of the AFL-CIO's Department of Working Women, "Despite the fact that over half the women with young children work outside the home, as a country, we still cling to the 'every woman for herself attitude' and dare to call it a solution to the country's child care crisis." This is a critical issue because fewer than 10 percent of Americans feel that the country's child care system meets the essential child care criteria.[16]

**Prohibited bargaining issues**, such as the issue of the closed shop, are statutorily outlawed. The Taft-Hartley Act made the closed shop illegal. However, the act was modified 12 years later by the Landrum-Griffin Act to permit a closed shop in the construction industry. This is the only exception allowed.

The union must continuously gather information regarding membership needs to isolate areas of dissatisfaction. The union steward is normally in the best position to collect such data. Because stewards are usually elected by their peers, they should be well informed regarding union members' attitudes. The union steward constantly funnels information up through the union's chain of command,

**Mandatory bargaining issues**
Bargaining issues that fall within the definition of wages, hours, and other terms and conditions of employment; refusal to bargain in these areas is grounds for an unfair labor practice charge.

**Permissive bargaining issues**
Issues that may be raised by management or a union; neither side may insist that they be bargained over.

**Prohibited bargaining issues**
Issues that are statutorily outlawed from collective bargaining.

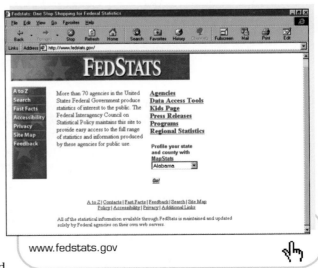

www.fedstats.gov

**Table 15-1** Mandatory Bargaining Issues

| | |
|---|---|
| Wages | Change in operations resulting in reclassifying workers from incentive to straight time, or a cut in the work-force, or installation of cost-saving machinery |
| Hours | |
| Discharge | |
| Arbitration | |
| Paid holidays | |
| Paid vacations | Price of meals provided by company |
| Duration of agreement | Group insurance—health, accident, life |
| Grievance procedure | Promotions |
| Layoff plan | Seniority |
| Reinstatement of economic strikers | Layoffs |
| Change of payment from hourly base to salary base | Transfers |
| | Work assignments and transfers |
| Union security and checkoff of dues | No-strike clause |
| Work rules | Piece rates |
| Merit wage increase | Stock purchase plan |
| Work schedule | Workloads |
| Lunch periods | Change of employee status to independent contractors |
| Rest periods | |
| Pension plan | Motor carrier-union agreement providing that carriers use own equipment before leasing outside equipment |
| Retirement age | |
| Bonus payments | |
| Cancellation of seniority upon relocation of plant | |
| | Overtime pay |
| Discounts on company products | Agency shop |
| Shift differentials | Sick leave |
| Contract clause providing for supervisors keeping seniority in unit | Employer's insistence on clause giving an arbitrator the right to enforce an award |
| Procedures for income tax withholding | |
| Severance pay | Management rights clause |
| Nondiscriminatory hiring hall | Plant closing |
| Plant rules | Job posting procedures |
| Safety | Plant reopening |
| Prohibition against supervisor doing unit work | Employee physical examination |
| | Arrangement for negotiation |
| Superseniority for union stewards | Change in insurance carrier and benefits |
| Partial plant closing | Profit-sharing plan |
| Hunting on employer's forest reserve where previously granted | Company houses |
| | Subcontracting |
| Plant closedown and relocation | Production ceiling imposed by union |

*Source:* Reed Richardson, "Positive Collective Bargaining," Chapter 7.5 of ASPA *Handbook of Personnel and Industrial Relations,* 7–121. Copyright 1979 by The Bureau of National Affairs, Inc., Washington, DC. Reprinted by permission.

where the data are compiled and analyzed. Union leadership attempts to uncover any areas of dissatisfaction because the general union membership must approve any agreement before it becomes final. Because they are elected, union leaders will lose their positions if the demands they make of management do not represent the desires of the general membership.

Management also spends long hours preparing for negotiations. The many interrelated tasks that management must accomplish are presented in Figure 15-2. In this example, the firm allows approximately six months to prepare for negotiations. All aspects of the current contracts are considered, including flaws that should be corrected. When preparing for negotiations, management should listen carefully to first-line managers. These individuals administer the labor agreement on a day-to-day basis and must live with errors made in negotiating the contract.

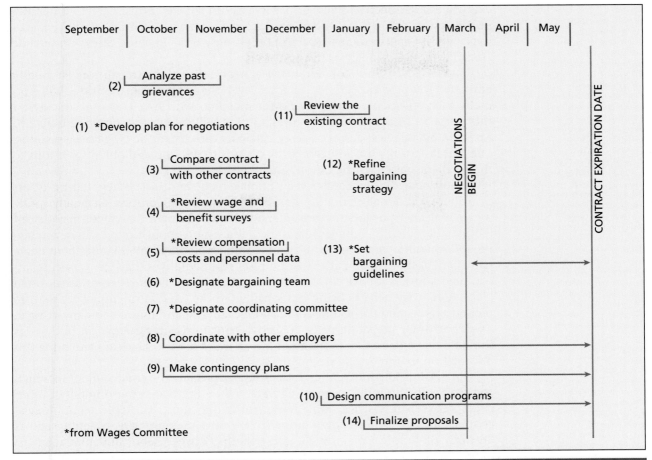

**An Example of Company Preparations for Negotiations**

Figure 15-2

*Source:* Adapted from Ronald L. Miller, "Preparations for Negotiations," *Personnel Journal,* Vol. 57, 38.
Copyright January 1978. Reprinted with permission.

An alert line manager is also able to inform upper management of the demands unions may plan to make during negotiations.

Management also attempts periodically to obtain information regarding employee attitudes. Surveys are often administered to workers to determine their feelings toward their jobs and job environment. Union and management representatives like to know as much as possible about employee attitudes when they sit down at the bargaining table.

Another part of preparation for negotiations involves identifying various positions that both union and management will take as the negotiations progress. Each side usually takes an initially extreme position, representing the conditions union or management would prefer. The two sides will likely determine absolute limits to their offers or demands before a breakdown in negotiations occurs. They also usually prepare fallback positions based on combinations of issues. Preparations should be detailed because cool heads often do not prevail during the heat of negotiations.

A major consideration in preparing for negotiations is selecting the bargaining teams. The makeup of the management team usually depends on the type of organization and its size. Normally, bargaining is conducted by labor relations specialists, with the advice and assistance of operating managers. Sometimes, top executives are directly involved, particularly in smaller firms. Larger companies utilize staff specialists (a human resource manager or industrial relations executive), managers of principal operating divisions, and—in some cases—an outside consultant, such as a labor attorney.

The responsibility for conducting negotiations for the union is usually entrusted to union officers. At the local level, the bargaining committee will normally be supplemented by rank-and-file members who are elected specifically for this purpose. In addition, the national union will often send a representative to act in an advisory capacity or even participate directly in the bargaining sessions. The real task of the union negotiating team is to develop and obtain solutions to the problems raised by the union's membership.

Traditional differences between management and union negotiating teams contribute additional friction to the collective bargaining process. Generally speaking, management negotiators are older and better educated than labor negotiators. From management's point of view, its people are more sophisticated and have a better understanding of the issues at hand than does labor's team. Management negotiators are likely to be impatient with union representatives they view as being less educated and less knowledgeable. On the other hand, labor representatives often perceive management as being less sensitive to the feelings of employees than to property rights and the realities of economic survival and future company growth. As part of their preparation for collective bargaining, negotiators on both sides should fully appraise the strengths and weaknesses of the other team and bring this information to bear during negotiations.

Finally, it is imperative that both groups appreciate the environment in which companies in the industry must operate. While there are environmental differences between industries, some basic similarities do exist. Rapid technological changes and ever-increasing competitive global pressures are sweeping across Western economies, making the partnership between labor and management more essential than ever. Labor must keep in mind that it is often at a bargaining disadvantage because of lower union membership rates, outmoded labor laws, and management inclination to transfer lower-skilled and/or labor-intensive jobs overseas. More and more, the jobs remaining in the United States require specific skills, adaptability, and flexibility—traits that many traditional core union members historically lacked. Lastly, worker involvement is a reality, not just an option, for larger corporations.

## Bargaining Issues

The document that emerges from the collective bargaining process is known as a *labor agreement* or *contract*. It regulates the relationship between employer and employees for a specified period of time. Collective bargaining basically determines the relationship between labor and management. It is still an essential but difficult task because each agreement is unique, and there is no standard or universal model. Despite much dissimilarity, certain topics are included in virtually all labor agreements. These include recognition, management rights, union security, compensation and benefits, a grievance procedure, employee security, and job-related factors.

### Recognition

This section usually appears at the beginning of the labor agreement. Its purpose is to identify the union that is recognized as the bargaining representative and to describe the bargaining unit, that is, the employees for whom the union speaks. A typical recognition section might read as follows:

HRM IN
ACTION
ACTION
ACTION
ACTION
ACTION
ACTION

### ▶ *Don't Do That!*

Brad Carpet, general manager for Royal Airlines, was visibly upset. He had just walked through the Royal terminal and accidentally heard one of the supervisors severely reprimanding an employee in front of co-workers. Brad called the supervisor aside and said, "We're a union-free organization and hope to remain that way. What you just did was one of the fastest ways to create a feeling among our employees that they need a union."

*Do you agree with Brad's assessment of the situation?*

> The XYZ Company recognizes the ABC Union as the sole and exclusive representative of the bargaining unit employees for the purpose of collective bargaining with regard to wages, hours, and other conditions of employment.

## Management Rights

A section that is often but not always written into the labor agreement spells out the rights of management. If no such section is included, management may reason that it retains control of all topics not described as bargainable in the contract. The precise content of the management rights section will vary by industry, company, and union. When included, management rights generally involve three areas:

1. Freedom to select the business objectives of the company
2. Freedom to determine the uses to which the material assets of the enterprise will be devoted
3. Power to discipline for cause

In a brochure the company publishes for all its first-line managers, AT&T describes management's rights when dealing with the union, including the following:

> You should remember that management has all such rights except those restricted by law or by contract with the union. You either make these decisions or carry them out through contact with your people. Some examples of these decisions and actions are:
>
> ▶ To determine what work is to be done and where, when, and how it is to be done.
> ▶ To determine the number of employees who will do the work.
> ▶ To supervise and instruct employees in doing the work.
> ▶ To correct employees whose work performance or personal conduct fails to meet reasonable standards. This includes administering discipline.
> ▶ To recommend hiring, dismissing, upgrading, or downgrading of employees.
> ▶ To recommend employees for promotion to management.[17]

## Union Security

Union security is typically one of the first items negotiated in a collective bargaining agreement. The objective of union security provisions is to ensure that the union continues to exist and perform its functions. A strong union security provision makes it easier for the union to enroll and retain members. We describe some basic forms of union security clauses in the following paragraphs.

**Closed Shop.** A **closed shop** is an arrangement whereby union membership is a prerequisite. Remember that, except for the construction and maritime industries, the closed shop is illegal.

**Union Shop.** As we mentioned in Chapter 14, a **union shop** arrangement requires that all employees become members of the union after a specified period of employment (the legal minimum is 30 days) or after a union shop provision has been negotiated. Employees must remain members of the union as a condition of employment.[18] The union shop is generally legal in the United States, except in states that have right-to-work laws.

**Maintenance of Membership.** Employees who are members of the union at the time the labor agreement is signed or who later voluntarily join must continue their memberships until the termination of the agreement, as a condition of employment. This form of recognition is also prohibited in most states that have right-to-work laws.

**Agency Shop.** An **agency shop** provision does not require employees to join the union; however, the labor agreement requires that, as a condition of employment, each nonunion member of the bargaining unit pay the union the equivalent of membership dues as a kind of tax, or service charge, in return for the union acting as the bargaining agent.[19] Remember that the National Labor Relations Act requires the union to bargain for all members of the bargaining unit, including nonunion employees. The agency shop is outlawed in most states that have right-to-work laws. Also, there could be judicial and legislative problems with permitting agency shops to exist in the public sector.[20]

**Exclusive Bargaining Shop.** Thirteen of the 21 states having right-to-work laws allow only exclusive bargaining shop provisions. Under this form of recognition, the company is legally bound to deal with the union that has achieved recognition, but employees are not obligated to join or maintain membership in the union or to contribute to it financially.

**Open Shop.** An open shop describes the absence of union security, rather than its presence. The **open shop**, strictly defined, is employment that has equal terms for union members and nonmembers alike. Under this arrangement, no employee is required to join or contribute to the union financially.[21]

**Dues Checkoff.** Another type of security that unions attempt to achieve is the checkoff of dues. A checkoff agreement may be used in addition to any of the previously mentioned shop agreements. Under the **checkoff of dues** provision, the company agrees to withhold union dues from members' paychecks and to forward the money directly to the union. Because of provisions in the Taft-Hartley Act, each union member must voluntarily sign a statement authorizing this deduction. Dues checkoff is important to the union because it eliminates much of the expense, time, and hassle of collecting dues from each member every pay period or once a month.

## Compensation and Benefits

This section typically constitutes a large portion of most labor agreements. Virtually any item that can affect compensation and benefits may be included in labor agreements. Some of the items frequently covered include the following.

---

**Closed shop**
An arrangement making union membership a prerequisite for employment.

**Union shop**
A requirement that all employees become members of the union after a specified period of employment (the legal minimum is 30 days) or after a union shop provision has been negotiated.

**Agency shop**
A labor agreement provision requiring, as a condition of employment, that each nonunion member of a bargaining unit pay the union the equivalent of membership dues as a kind of tax, or service charge, in return for the union acting as the bargaining agent.

**Open shop**
Employment that has equal terms for union members and nonmembers alike.

**Checkoff of dues**
An agreement by which a company agrees to withhold union dues from members' paychecks and to forward the money directly to the union.

**Wage Rate Schedule.** The base rates to be paid each year of the contract for each job are included in this section. At times, unions are able to obtain a cost-of-living allowance (COLA), or escalator clause, in the contract in order to protect the purchasing power of employees' earnings. These clauses are generally related to the Consumer Price Index (CPI) prepared by the Bureau of Labor Statistics. However, the average COLA has increased at a smaller percentage in recent years. Currently, increases in pay remain scarce in key sectors of the economy because employers cannot simply raise prices to compensate for higher wages.

Even with the strong economy in 2000, wage-fringe settlements were expected to remain about the same.[22] According to Kenneth Deavers, chief economist for the Employment Policy Foundation in Washington, D.C., a business-supported research organization, "Clearly unions are winning a few more elections. But, we see a change in the issues they're bargaining on. They're much less likely to bargain on wage issues, because they're not winning them. So they're concentrating on other issues such as scheduling, outsourcing, and job security."[23]

**Overtime and Premium Pay.** Another section of the agreement may cover hours of work, overtime pay, hazard pay, and premium pay, such as shift differentials (discussed in Chapter 12).

**Jury Pay.** For some firms, jury pay amounts to the employee's entire salary when he or she is serving jury duty. Others pay the difference between the amount employees receive from the court and the compensation that would have been earned. The procedure covering jury pay is typically stated in the contract.

**Layoff or Severance Pay.** The amount that employees in various jobs and/or seniority levels will be paid if they are laid off or terminated is a frequently included item.

**Holidays.** The holidays to be recognized and the amount of pay that a worker will receive if he or she has to work on a holiday are specified. In addition, the pay procedure for times when a holiday falls on a worker's normal day off is provided.

**Vacation.** This section spells out the amount of vacation that a person may take, based on seniority. Any restrictions as to when the vacation may be taken are also stated.

**Family Care.** This is a benefit that has been included in recent collective bargaining agreements, with child care expected to be a hot bargaining issue in the near future.

## Grievance Procedure

A portion of most labor agreements is devoted to a grievance procedure. It contains the means whereby employees can voice dissatisfaction with and appeal specific management actions. Also included in this section are procedures for disciplinary action by management and the termination procedure that must be followed.

## Employee Security

This section of the labor agreement establishes the procedures that cover job security for individual employees. Seniority is a key topic related to employee security. **Seniority** is the length of time that an employee has worked in various capacities with the firm. Seniority may be determined companywide, by division, by department, or by job. Agreement on seniority is important because the person with the most seniority, as defined in the labor agreement, is typically the last to be laid off and the first to be recalled. The seniority system also provides a basis for promotion

**Seniority**
The length of time that an employee has worked in various capacities with the firm.

decisions. When qualifications are met, employees with the greatest seniority will likely be considered first for promotions to higher-level jobs.

Recent labor negotiations have dramatically focused on the security issue. Since 1990, labor agreements with the then–"Big Three" auto makers have included provisions to protect employee security. Settlements with the Big Three provided lower wage rate changes than those negotiated in the contracts they replaced, but the firms did fully restore the funding for job security and supplemental unemployment benefits provided in previous agreements.[24]

Competitive forces and technology are reshaping industries and trimming both production jobs and management ranks. Anheuser-Busch is battling increased competition in an industry that is growing slowly. Anheuser-Busch management says job security is there, but only for current workers. Specifically, the company will not promise to hire replacements for each worker who leaves. Continued automation means fewer people are needed in an industry that is growing slowly. Management has been trimmed by 500 jobs in the past year, and more than 450 full-time jobs were cut from the production department during the last contract. At the beginning of 2000, the company employed 8,357 full-time production workers, about 8,000 of whom are Teamsters. The company acknowledges that at least 600 more full-time jobs will be eliminated during the life of the new contract. Job security for future employees may soon be a thing of the past.[25]

## Job-Related Factors

Many of the rules governing employee actions on the job are also included. Some of the more important factors are company work rules, work standards, and rules related to safety.[26] This section varies, depending on the nature of the industry and the product manufactured. Work rules are vitally important to both employers and employees, with companies tending to favor less restrictive work rules.

▶ It is important for union and management negotiators to strive to develop and maintain clear and open lines of communication.

## NEGOTIATING THE AGREEMENT

There is no way to ensure speedy and mutually acceptable results from negotiations. At best, the parties can attempt to create an atmosphere that will lend itself to steady progress and productive results. For example, the two negotiating teams usually meet at an agreed-on neutral site, such as a hotel. When a favorable relationship can be established early, eleventh hour (or last-minute) bargaining can often be avoided. It is equally important for union and management negotiators to strive to develop and maintain clear and open lines of communication. Collective bargaining is a problem-solving activity; consequently, good communication is essential to its success. Negotiations should be conducted in the privacy of the conference room, not in the news media. If the negotiators feel that publicity is necessary, joint releases to the media may avoid unnecessary conflict.

The negotiating phase of collective bargaining begins with each side presenting its initial demands.

Because a collective bargaining settlement can be expensive for a firm, the cost of various proposals should be estimated as accurately as possible. Some changes can be quite expensive, and others cost little or nothing, but the cost of the various proposals being considered must always be carefully deliberated. The term *negotiating* suggests a certain amount of give-and-take, the purpose of which is to lower the other side's expectations. For example, the union might bargain to upgrade its members' economic and working conditions, and the company might negotiate to maintain or enhance profitability.

One of the most costly components of any collective bargaining agreement is a wage increase provision. An example of the negotiation of a wage increase is shown in Figure 15-3. In this example, labor initially demands a 40¢ per hour increase. Management counters with an offer of only 10¢ per hour. Both labor and management—as expected—reject each other's demand. Plan B calls for labor to lower its demand to a 30¢ per hour increase. Management counters with an offer of 20¢. The positions in plan B are feasible to both sides, as both groups are in the bargaining zone. Wages within the bargaining zone are those that management and labor can both accept—in this case, an increase of between 20¢ and 30¢ per hour. The exact amount will be determined by the power of the bargaining unit and the skills of the negotiators.

The realities of negotiations are not for the weak of heart and, at times, are similar to a high-stakes poker game. A certain amount of bluffing and raising the ante takes place in many negotiations. The ultimate bluff for the union is when a negotiator says, "If our demands are not met, we are prepared to strike." Management's version of this bluff would be to threaten a lockout. We will discuss each of these tactics later as a form of power politics. The party with the greater leverage can expect to extract the most concessions.

Even though one party in the negotiating process may appear to possess the greater power, negotiators often take care to keep the other side from losing face. They recognize that the balance of power may switch rapidly. By the time the next round of negotiations occurs, the pendulum may be swinging back in favor of the other side. Even when management appears to have the upper hand, it may make minor concessions that will allow the labor leader to claim gains for the

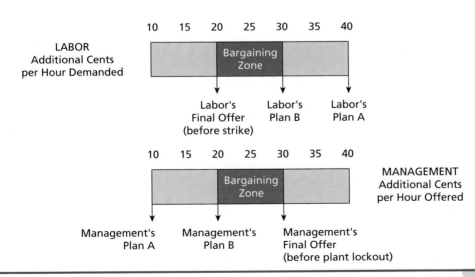

**An Example of Negotiating a Wage Increase**   **Figure 15-3**

union. For example, management may demand that workers pay for lost grease rags (assuming that the loss has become excessive). In order to obtain labor's agreement to this demand, management may agree to provide new uniforms for the workers if the cost of these uniforms would be less than the cost of lost rags. Thus, labor leaders, although forced to concede to management's demand, could show the workers that they have obtained a concession from management.

Each side usually does not expect to obtain all the demands presented in its first proposal. However, management must remember that a concession may be difficult to reverse in future negotiations. For instance, if management agreed to provide dental benefits, withdrawing these benefits in the next round of negotiations would be difficult. Labor, on the other hand, can lose a demand and continue to bring it up in the future. Demands for benefits that the union does not expect to receive when they are first made are known as **beachhead demands**.

**Beachhead demands**
Demands for benefits that the union does not expect management to meet when they are first made.

## BREAKDOWNS IN NEGOTIATIONS

At times negotiations break down, even though both labor and management may sincerely want to arrive at an equitable contract settlement. Several means of removing roadblocks may be used in order to get negotiations moving again. Breakdowns in negotiations can be overcome through third-party intervention, union strategies, and management strategies.

### Third-Party Intervention

Often an outside person can intervene to provide assistance when an agreement cannot be reached and the two sides reach an impasse. The reasons behind each party's position may be quite rational, or the breakdown may be related to emotional disputes that tend to become distorted during the heat of negotiations. Regardless of the cause, something must be done to continue the negotiations. The two basic types of third-party intervention are mediation and arbitration.

**Mediation.** In **mediation**, a neutral third party enters a labor dispute when a bargaining impasse occurs. A mediator basically acts like a facilitator. The objective of mediation is to persuade the parties to resume negotiations and reach a settlement. A mediator has no power to force a settlement but can help in the search for solutions, make recommendations, and work to open blocked channels of communication. Successful mediation depends to a substantial degree on the tact, diplomacy, patience, and perseverance of the mediator. The mediator's fresh insights are used to get discussions going again. Mediation skills are becoming more important in labor relations and other management areas. Unlike binding arbitration, mediation is voluntary at every step of the process. The mediator serves as an informal coach, helping ensure that the discussions are fair and effective.

**Mediation**
A process in which a neutral third party enters and attempts to resolve a labor dispute when a bargaining impasse occurs.

**Arbitration**
A process in which a dispute is submitted to an impartial third party for a binding decision.

**Rights arbitration**
Arbitration that involves disputes over the interpretation and application of the various provisions of an existing contract.

**Interest arbitration**
Arbitration that involves disputes over the terms of proposed collective bargaining agreements.

**Arbitration.** In **arbitration**, a dispute is submitted to an impartial third party for a binding decision; an arbitrator basically acts as a judge and jury.[27] There are two principal types of union-management disputes: rights disputes and interests disputes. Those that involve disputes over the interpretation and application of the various provisions of an existing contract are submitted to **rights arbitration**. This type of arbitration is used in settling grievances. Grievance arbitration is common in the United States. The other type of arbitration, **interest arbitration**, involves disputes over the terms of proposed collective bargaining agreements. In the private sector, the use of interest arbitration as an alternative procedure for impasse resolution is not a common practice. Unions and employers rarely agree to submit the basic terms of a contract (such as wages, hours, and working conditions) to a neutral party for disposition. They prefer to rely on collective bargaining and the threat of economic pressure (such as strikes and lockouts) to decide these issues.

In the public sector, most governmental jurisdictions prohibit their employees from striking. As a result, interest arbitration is used to a greater extent than in the private sector. Although there is no uniform application of this method, 14 states have legislation permitting the use of interest arbitration to settle unresolved issues for public employees. In a number of states, compulsory arbitration of interest items is required at various jurisdictional levels. A procedure used in the public sector is *final-offer arbitration,* which has two basic forms: package selection and issue-by-issue selection. In package selection, the arbitrator must select one party's entire offer on all issues in dispute. In issue-by-issue selection, the arbitrator examines each issue separately and chooses the final offer of one side or the other on each issue. Final-offer arbitration is often used to determine the salary of a professional baseball player. Both the player and management present a dollar figure to an arbitrator. The arbitrator chooses one or the other figure.[28]

www.adr.org/contents2.htm

The principal organization involved in mediation efforts, other than some state and local agencies, is the Federal Mediation and Conciliation Service (FMCS).[29] In 1947, the Taft-Hartley Act established the FMCS as an independent agency. Either one or both parties involved in negotiations can seek the assistance of the FMCS, or the agency can offer its help if it feels that the situation warrants it. Federal law requires that the party wishing to change a contract must give notice of this intention to the other party 60 days prior to the expiration of a contract. If no agreement has been reached 30 days prior to the expiration date, the FMCS must be notified.

In arbitration, the disputants are free to select any person as their arbitrator, so long as they agree on the selection. Most commonly, however, the two sides make a request for an arbitrator to either the American Arbitration Association (AAA) or the FMCS. The AAA is a nonprofit organization with offices in many cities.[30] Both the AAA and the FMCS maintain lists of arbitrators. Only people who can show, through references, experience in labor-management relations and acceptance by both labor and management as neutral parties are selected for inclusion on these lists.[31]

## Union Strategies for Overcoming Negotiation Breakdowns

There are times when a union believes that it must exert extreme pressure to get management to agree to its bargaining demands. Strikes, boycotts, and activism are the primary means that the union may use to overcome breakdowns in negotiations.

**Strikes.** When union members refuse to work in order to exert pressure on management in negotiations, their action is referred to as a **strike**. A strike halts production, resulting in lost customers and revenue, which the union hopes will force management to submit to its terms. In reality, the United States has always

**Strike**
An action by union members who refuse to work in order to exert pressure on management in negotiations.

had the lowest percentage of days lost due to strikes of all industrialized nations. There are fewer strikes today than at any time since such statistics were gathered. Strikes involving 1,000 or more workers have declined sharply since 1970. In 1970 there were 381 strikes involving 1,000 or more workers; in 1975, 235; in 1980, 187; in 1985, 54; in 1990, 44; in 1996, 37 strikes; and, since 1997, the nation has had fewer strikes than in any of the past 50 years.[32]

The timing of a strike is important in determining its effectiveness. An excellent time is when business is thriving and the demand for the firm's goods or services is expanding. However, the union might be hard pressed to obtain major concessions from a strike if the firm's sales are down and it has built up a large inventory. In this instance, the company would not be severely damaged. Timing-based work stoppages like CHAOS (Create Havoc Around Our System) have been as effective as strikes in the airline industry.

Contrary to many opinions, unions prefer to use the strike only as a last resort. In recent years, many union members have been even more reluctant to strike because of the fear of being replaced. When a union goes on an economic strike and the company hires replacements, the company does not have to lay off these individuals at the end of the strike. In 1995, in an attempt to reverse this position on striker replacements, President Clinton issued Executive Order 12954. This order authorized the federal government to disqualify employers who hired replacement workers from receiving certain federal contracts. The U.S. Chamber of Commerce challenged the executive order, and the U.S. Supreme Court ruled that it was preempted by federal labor laws and was therefore illegal.[33]

With the threat of replacement looming and union membership declining, organized labor is quite cautious about striking. Even General Motors, which for

## TRENDS & INNOVATIONS

▶ **CHAOS May Be the Key to Resuming Collective Bargaining**

Capitalizing on timing, the 2,400 flight attendants of America West Airlines used the time-sensitive approach called CHAOS (Create Havoc Around Our System ), in which selected flights are targeted at the last minute. America West Airlines calls the tactic illegal because it violates the Railway Labor Relations Act, which bars intermittent work stoppages. However, in a similar situation, a federal judge has ruled that Alaska Airlines flight attendants could use the tactic and that they could not be fired or suspended. Organized labor believes that such disruptions are as effective as the Alaska Airlines intermittent strike, which disrupted only seven flights in two months. Because of the last-minute approach of CHAOS, management does not have time to adjust and, therefore, flights are disrupted and customers suffer. CHAOS was effective in forcing Alaska Airlines back to the bargaining table because bookings of its flights dropped 20 percent due to customer apprehension about possible flight disruptions. This strategy was developed after the 1986 TWA strike, in which 6,000 flight attendants were replaced. Basically, CHAOS succeeds because the company loses revenue and is forced back to the bargaining table. As the United States moves more toward a service economy, such timed strikes could be a very effective method of encouraging collective bargaining.[34]

years has backed down to organized labor, is beginning to draw the line against striking employees. General Motors held fast during a 17-day strike in Ohio and Canada and won the right to slash up to one-fifth of its 26,000 Canadian jobs.[35] Even in the latest General Motors strike, the major gain was to temporarily protect the jobs at two old-line Flint, Michigan, plants.[36]

The United Automobile Workers (UAW) has employed the strike effectively to gain additional bargaining power. When General Motors (GM) would not meet union demands at one of its automobile assembly plants, the union called a strike at GM's Warren, Michigan, transmission and parts plant, effectively shutting down six GM car assembly plants. This increased union leverage and brought GM back to the bargaining table, resulting in settlements.[37]

A union's treasury is often depleted by payment of strike benefits to its members. In addition, members suffer because they are not receiving their normal pay. Striking workers during the latest General Motors strike got paid about $150 a week strike pay instead of the roughly $1,000 a week that they might be taking home with all of their overtime.[38] Although strike benefits help, union members certainly cannot maintain a normal standard of living from these minimal amounts. Sometimes during negotiations (especially at the beginning), the union may want to strengthen its negotiating position by taking a strike vote. Members often give overwhelming approval to a strike. This vote does not necessarily mean that there will be a strike, only that the union leaders now have the authority to call one if negotiations reach an impasse. A favorable strike vote can add a sense of urgency to efforts to reach an agreement.

Successful passage of a strike vote has additional implications for union members. Virtually every national union's constitution contains a clause requiring the members to support and participate in a strike if one is called. If a union member fails to comply with this requirement, he or she can be fined. Therefore, union members place themselves in jeopardy if they cross a picket line without the consent of the union. Fines may be as high as 100 percent of wages for as long as union pickets remain outside the company. However, the Supreme Court has ruled that an employee on strike may resign from the union during a strike and avoid being punished by the union. Union members have used more subtle measures—such as sick-outs and work slowdowns—to successfully avoid the impact of a strike while still bringing pressure on the company to meet union demands.

**Boycotts.** The boycott is another of labor's weapons to get management to agree to its demands. A **boycott** involves an agreement by union members to refuse to use or buy the firm's products. A boycott exerts economic pressure on management, and the effect often lasts much longer than that of a strike. Once shoppers change buying habits, their behavior will likely continue long after the boycott has ended. At times, significant pressures can be exerted on a business when union members, their families, and their friends refuse to purchase the firm's products. This approach is especially effective when the products are sold at retail outlets and are easily identifiable by brand name. For instance, the boycott against Adolph Coors Company was effective because the product—beer—was directly associated with the company.[39] The latest round of sparring between the Union-Tribune Publishing Company and Graphic Communications International Union has resulted in a boycott of this newspaper. The union claims that the boycott caused a circulation loss of about 2,000 Sunday papers.[40]

The practice of a union attempting to encourage third parties (such as suppliers and customers) to stop doing business with the company is known as a **secondary boycott**. The Taft-Hartley Act declared this type of boycott to be illegal.

**Boycott**
Refusal by union members to use or buy their firm's products.

**Secondary boycott**
A union's attempt to encourage third parties (such as suppliers and customers) to stop doing business with a firm.

HR WEB
WISDOM

▶ *Labor and Industrial Relations*

**www.prenhall.com/mondy**

Numerous sites related to labor and industrial relations are hot linked.

## Management's Strategies for Overcoming Negotiation Breakdowns

**Lockout**
A management decision to keep employees out of the workplace and to operate with management personnel and/or temporary replacements.

Management may also use various strategies to encourage unions to come back to the bargaining table. One form of action that is somewhat analogous to a strike is called a **lockout**. In a lockout, management keeps employees out of the workplace and may run the operation with management personnel and/or temporary replacements. Unable to work, the employees do not get paid. Although the lockout is used rather infrequently, the fear of a lockout may bring labor back to the bargaining table. A lockout is particularly effective when management is dealing with a weak union, when the union treasury is depleted, or when the business has excessive inventories. The lockout is also used to inform the union that management is serious regarding certain bargaining issues. This was the case with BC Railroad and a union group. Apparently the union wanted a complete rollover of its contract and did not want to make concessions. Within days of a threatened lockout, a tentative contract was reached.[41]

Another course of action that a company can take if the union goes on strike is to operate the firm by placing management and nonunion workers in the striking workers' jobs. The type of industry involved has considerable effect on the impact of this maneuver. If the firm is not labor intensive and if maintenance demands are not high, such as at a petroleum refinery or a chemical plant, this practice may be quite effective. When appropriate, management may attempt to show how using nonunion employees can actually increase production. For example, when unionized employees at Southwestern Bell Telephone Company went on strike, the company continued to provide virtually uninterrupted service to consumers. At times, management personnel will actually live in the plant and have food and other necessities delivered to them.

Another way management can continue operating a firm during a strike is to hire replacements for strikers. Hiring replacements on either a temporary or a permanent basis is legal when the employees are engaged in an economic strike—that is, one that is part of a collective bargaining dispute. However, a company that takes this course of action risks inviting violence and creating bitterness among its employees, which may adversely affect the firm's performance long after the strike ends. This was the case with Davidson Aluminum & Metal Corporation, which hired permanent replacements for 56 workers who struck the company's Deer Park plant rather than accept a contract slashing their wages for the second time in five years.[42]

## RATIFYING THE AGREEMENT

Most collective bargaining leads to an agreement without a breakdown in negotiations or disruptive actions. Typically, agreement is reached before the current contract expires. After the negotiators have reached a tentative agreement on all contract terms, they prepare a written agreement covering those terms, complete with the effective and termination dates. The approval process for management is often easier than for labor. The president or CEO has usually been briefed regularly on the progress of negotiations. Any difficulty that might have stood in the way of obtaining approval has probably already been resolved with top management by the negotiators.

However, the approval process is more complex for the union. Until a majority of members voting in a ratification election approve it, the proposed agreement is not final. At times, union members reject the proposal and a new round of negotiations must begin. Many of these rejections might not have occurred if union negotiators had been better informed of the desires of the membership.

## ADMINISTRATION OF THE AGREEMENT

Negotiating, as it relates to the total collective bargaining process, may be likened to the tip of an iceberg. It is the visible phase, the part that makes the news. The larger and perhaps more important part of collective bargaining is administration of the agreement, which the public seldom sees. The agreement establishes the union-management relationship for the duration of the contract. Usually, neither party can change the contract's language until the expiration date, except by mutual consent. However, the main problem encountered in contract administration is uniform interpretation and application of the contract's terms. Administering the contract is a day-to-day activity. Ideally, the aim of both management and the union is to make the agreement work to the benefit of all concerned. Often, this is not an easy task.

Management is primarily responsible for explaining and implementing the agreement. This process should begin with meetings or training sessions not only to point out significant features but also to provide a clause-by-clause analysis of the contract. First-line supervisors, in particular, need to know their responsibilities and what to do when disagreements arise. Additionally, supervisors and middle managers should be encouraged to notify top management of any contract modifications or new provisions required for the next round of negotiations.

The human resource manager or industrial relations manager plays a key role in the day-to-day administration of the contract. He or she gives advice on matters of discipline, works to resolve grievances, and helps first-line supervisors establish good working relationships within the terms of the agreement. When a firm becomes unionized, the human resource manager's function tends to change rather significantly and may even be divided into separate human resource and industrial relations departments. In such situations, the vice president of human resources may perform all human resource management tasks with the exception of industrial relations. The vice president of industrial relations would likely deal with all union-related matters. As one vice president of industrial relations stated:

> My first challenge is, wherever possible, to keep the company union free and the control of its operations in the hands of corporate management at all levels. Where unions represent our employees, the problem becomes one of negotiating collective bargaining agreements which our company can live with, administering these labor agreements with the company's interests paramount (consistent with good employee relations), and trying to solve all grievances arising under the labor agreement short of their going to arbitration, without giving away the store.

Collective bargaining for federal unions such as the American Federation of Government Employees (AFGE) (the largest federal union), the National Air Traffic Controllers (NATCA), and National Treasury Employees Union (NTEU) has traditionally been quite different from private-sector bargaining because wages were off the table. Title V of the U.S. Code—the law that dictates personnel rules for federal employees—did not allow bargaining over wage issues, except for the U.S. Postal Service. With the exception of the postal service, federal managers, policy makers, and politicians have managed to keep pay off the negotiating table for the 40-year history of modern federal labor relations started by President Kennedy. However, the key to building union membership is the ability to deliver concrete benefits to workers—in particular, additional wages.

Now the 40-year legacy of keeping wages off the bargaining table is beginning to change. In a deal signed in August of 1998, the NATCA succeeded in placing pay issues on the bargaining table. It won a collective $200 million raise over three years, adding as much as $10,000 a year to the salaries of controllers in high-traffic centers. Money for the raises came in large part from reductions in supervisory ranks to decrease ratios of managers to front-line personnel from 1-to-7 to 1-to-10. The negotiation was a remarkable first, but now the NTEU has also earned the right to address wage issues. The NTEU recently won a significant compensation coup for workers at the IRS. NTEU parlayed the congressional IRS overhaul into an opportunity to indirectly bargain over pay. Job classifications determine

## A GLOBAL PERSPECTIVE

### Labor Relations Are Different in Other Countries

The fate of workers around the globe is at risk as many employees are being intimidated, threatened, and even murdered for their efforts to form trade unions to bargain for their collective rights, according to a report by the International Labor Organization (ILO). Juan Somavia, the director general of the ILO, says, "A global economy in which people do not have the rights to organize will lack social legitimacy. People organize themselves to make their voices heard so they can express such fundamental rights as their human rights and their developmental rights."

This report comes out strongly against oil-rich Arab nations such as Oman, Saudi Arabia, and the United Arab Emirates for the "outright prohibitions on trade unions." In nearby countries such as Bahrain and Qatar, government constraints have denied committees of workers or labor councils the opportunity to form independent workers' organizations.

Violence against labor rights activists has prevailed in several developing countries. In countries ranging from Ecuador and Guatemala in Latin America to Zimbabwe and Sudan in Africa, physical assaults have been a common form of intimidation. In China, El Salvador, Morocco, and Pakistan, arrests and detention have been evident. In Nicaragua, Lebanon, and Senegal, trade union premises and property have been attacked. During the past 10 years, the report declares, the ILO has also documented allegations of the murder of trade unionists in Colombia, the Dominican Republic, Ecuador, Guatemala, and Indonesia. The current crop of export-processing zones (EPZs) also came under the critical gaze of the ILO report for antiunion acts, which include "harassment, blacklisting, and massive dismissals" of the labor force. EPZs in Bangladesh, the Philippines, and Sri Lanka were singled out for ignoring basic labor rights in an effort to attract foreign investments.[43]

job grades, and job grades determine salary levels, and now the NTEU can negotiate job classification upgrades. The ability to bargain over pay is a big part of what has made unions such as the NATCA, the Postal Service, and the NTEU so healthy. What distinguishes NATCA and NTEU from AFGE and other federal unions is that they have aggressively and successfully fought for the right to bargain over wages and benefits for their members.[44]

## Summary ◀

**1** **Explain labor-management relations and individual bargaining.**
In individual negotiations, the worker is negotiating with the company representative.

**2** **Describe labor-management relations and collective bargaining.**
Regardless of the current state of labor-management relations, the general aspects of the collective bargaining process are the same. Even though collective bargaining is widely practiced, there is no precise format for what to do or how to do it.

**3** **Explain the psychological aspects of collective bargaining.**
Psychologically, the collective bargaining process is often difficult for both labor and management because an adversarial situation may exist.

**4** **Describe the factors involved in preparing for negotiations.**
Because of the complex issues facing labor and management today, the negotiating teams must carefully prepare for the bargaining sessions. Prior to meeting at the bargaining table, the negotiators should thoroughly know the culture, climate, history, present economic state, and wage and benefits structure of both the organization and similar organizations. Because the length of a typical labor agreement is three years, negotiators should develop a contract that is successful both now and in the future. This consideration should prevail for both management and labor, although it rarely does. During the term of an agreement, the two sides usually discover contract provisions that need to be added, deleted, or modified. These items become proposals to be addressed in the next round of negotiations.

**5** **Explain typical bargaining issues.**
Mandatory bargaining issues are those issues that fall within the definition of wages, hours, and other terms and conditions of employment. Permissive bargaining issues are those issues that may be raised, but neither side may insist that they be bargained over.

**6** **Describe the process of negotiating the agreement.**
There is no way to ensure speedy and mutually acceptable results from negotiations. At best, the parties can attempt to create an atmosphere that will lend itself to steady progress and productive results.

**7** **Identify ways to overcome breakdowns in negotiations.**
Breakdowns in negotiations can be overcome through third-party intervention, union tactics, and management recourse.

**8** **Describe what is involved in ratifying the agreement.**
The president of the organization can make the decision for the firm. However, until a majority of union members voting in a ratification election approve it, the proposed agreement is not final.

**9** **Describe what is involved in administering the agreement.**
Ideally, the aim of both management and the union is to make the agreement work to the mutual benefit of all concerned. Management is primarily responsible for explaining and implementing the agreement. The human resource manager or industrial relations manager plays a key role in the day-to-day administration of the contract.

**10** Describe collective bargaining for federal employees.

Collective bargaining for federal unions has traditionally been quite different from private-sector bargaining because wages were off the table.

## ▶ Questions for Review

1. Describe the negotiation process for a worker in a nonunion environment.

2. Describe the basic steps involved in the collective bargaining process.

3. Distinguish among mandatory, permissive, and prohibited bargaining issues.

4. What are the topics included in virtually all labor agreements?

5. Define each of the following:

   a. *Closed shop*
   b. *Union shop*
   c. *Agency shop*
   d. *Maintenance of membership*
   e. *Checkoff of dues*

6. What are the primary means by which breakdowns in negotiations may be overcome? Briefly describe each.

7. What is involved in the administration of a labor agreement?

8. How is the collective bargaining process different for federal employees?

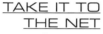

TAKE IT TO THE NET

*We invite you to visit the Mondy homepage on the Prentice Hall Web site at*

**www.prenhall.com/mondy**

*for updated information, Web-based exercises, and links to other HR-related sites.*

## ▶ Developing HRM Skills

### *An Experiential Exercise*

A major part of the human resource manager's job is to advise managers at all levels regarding HR matters. The human resource manager's knowledge and experience are often required in dealing with union matters, especially in handling situations that have an impact on future unionization. This exercise provides additional insight into the importance of properly handling employee problems in a unionized environment.

Three individuals will participate in this exercise: one to serve as the human resource manager, one to serve as the supervisor, and another to play the role of union steward. Your instructor will provide the participants with additional information necessary to complete the exercise.

## ▶ HRM INCIDENT 1

### *Break Down the Barrier*

Yesterday, Bill Brown was offered a job as an operator trainee with GEM Manufacturing. He had recently graduated from Milford High School in a small town in the Midwest. Since Bill had no college aspirations, upon graduation he moved to Chicago to look for a job.

Bill's immediate supervisor spent only a short time with him before turning over Bill to Gaylord Rader, an experienced operator, for training. After they had talked for a short time, Gaylord asked, "Have you given any thought to joining our union? You'll like all of our members."

Bill had not considered this. Moreover, he had never associated with union members and his parents had never been members either. At Milford High, his teachers had never really talked about unions. The fact that this union operated as an open shop meant nothing to him. Bill replied, "I don't know. Maybe. Maybe not."

The day progressed much the same way, with several people asking Bill the same question. They were all friendly, but there seemed to be a barrier that separated Bill from the other workers. One worker looked Bill right in the eyes and said, "You're going to join, aren't you?" Bill still did not know, but he was beginning to lean in that direction.

After the buzzer rang to end the shift, Bill went to the washroom. Just as he entered, David Clements, the union steward, also walked in. After they exchanged greetings, David said, "I hear that you're not sure about joining our union. You, and everyone else, reap the benefits of the work we've done in the past. It doesn't seem fair for you to be rewarded for what others have done. Tell you what, why don't you join us down at the union hall tonight for our beer bust? We'll discuss it more then."

Bill nodded yes and finished cleaning up. "That might be fun," he thought.

## Questions

1. Why does Bill have the option of joining or not joining the union?
2. How are the other workers likely to react toward Bill if he chooses not to join? Discuss.

---

### How about a Strike Vote?

Christina Wilkes, the chief union negotiator, was meeting with management on a new contract. The union team had been preparing for this encounter for a long time. Christina felt that she was on top of the situation. Her only worry was whether the union members would support a strike vote if one were called. Because of the recession, there was high unemployment in the area. The members' attitude was: "We are generally pleased, but get what you can for us." She believed, however, that skillful negotiating could keep the union team from being placed in a position where the threat of a strike would be needed.

In the first session, Christina's team presented its demands to management. Pay was the main issue, and a 30 percent increase spread over three years was demanded. Management countered with an offer of a 10 percent raise over three years. After some discussion, both sides agreed to reevaluate their positions and meet again in two days.

Christina met with her negotiating team in private, and it was the consensus that they would decrease the salary demand slightly. They felt that the least they could accept was a 25 percent increase.

At the next meeting, Christina presented the revised demands to management. They were not well received. Sam Waterson, the director of industrial relations, began by saying: "Our final offer is a 15 percent increase over three years. Business has been down, and we have a large backlog of inventory. If you feel that it is in your best interest to strike, go ahead."

Christina was confident that there was no way that a strike vote could be obtained. Management had accurately read the mood of the workers, and Christina quickly asked for additional time to consider the new information.

### Questions

1. How important is the threat of a strike to successful union negotiations?
2. What do you recommend that Christina do when she next confronts management?

▶ **Notes**

1. James Worsham, "Unions Gain Members But Lose Ground Nonetheless," *Nation's Business* (March 1999): 12.
2. Hoyt N. Wheeler, "Viewpoint: Collective Bargaining Is a Fundamental Human Right," *Industrial Relations* (July 2000): 535.
3. Paul Falcone, "A Legal Dichotomy?" *HRMagazine* 44 (May 1999): 110.
4. Mark A. Spognardi, "Conducting a Successful Union-Free Campaign," *Employee Relations Law Journal* 24 (Autumn 1998): 35.
5. Arthur A. Sloane and Fred Witney, *Labor Relations,* 4th ed. (Upper Saddle River, NJ: Prentice Hall, 1981): 28–35.
6. Joe Strupp, "Union-Tribune Local Airs Boycott Ad," *New York* 132 (December 18, 1999): 9; Joe Laws Thomas and Li-Ping Tang, "Japanese Transplants and Union Membership: The Case of Nissan Motor Manufacturing Corporation," *S.A.M. Advanced Management Journal* 64 (Spring 1999): 16–25; "Contractor Actions Were Not Antiunion Motivated," *ENR* 242 (May 3, 1999): 24; Aaron Bernstein, "All's Not Fair in Labor Wars," *Business Week* (July 19, 1999): 43; and Aaron Bernstein and Peter Galuszka, "How Ltv's Grand Scheme Hit the Smelter," *Business Week* (September 27, 1999): 103.
7. Aaron Bernstein, "All's Not Fair in Labor Wars," *Business Week* (July 19, 1999): 43.
8. Neil Campbell and Neil Vousden, "Import Competition and Worker Productivity in Unionized Firms," *Review of International Economics* (May 2000): 193–207.
9. Strupp, "Union-Tribune Local Airs Boycott Ad."
10. Stephenie Overman, "Unions: New Activism or Old Adversarial Approach?" *HR Focus* 76 (May 1999): 7–8.
11. Jill Wechsler, "Doctors Win Antitrust Skirmish But Might Lose War," *Managed Healthcare* (May 2000): 16–18.
12. Frank N. Wilner, "Interest-based Bargaining," *Traffic World* (November 1, 1999): 13–14.
13. Frank N. Wilner, "Relative Peace," *Railway Age* (May 2000): 47–48.
14. Sue Burzawa, "Health Benefits Issues For Collectively-bargained Plans," *Employee Benefit Plan Review* (May 2000): 12–13.
15. "Employer Could Terminate Retiree Health Benefits During Lapse in Bargaining Contracts," *Employee Benefit Plan Review* (July 1999): 62.
16. Larry Reynolds, "Washington Update: A Crisis in Childcare?" *HR Focus* 74 (May 1997): 2.
17. *Management/Employee/Union Relations* (Dallas, TX: Southwestern Bell Telephone Company): 3.
18. "The CIO's Drive for the Checkoff, Closed Shops, and Straight Seniority," *Iron Age New Steel* (April 1999): 11–15.

19. Aron Gregg, "The Constitutionality of Requiring Annual Renewal of Union Fee Objections in an Agency Shop," *Texas Law Review* (April 2000): 1159–1180.

20. Kathleen Masters and James K. McCollum, "Agency Shop for Baltimore County: No More Free Lunch?" *Journal of Collective Negotiations in the Public Sector* (1999): 153–164.

21. Sherie Winston, "Labor: When Contractors Are Organized," *ENR* (December 20, 1999): 30–32.

22. Sherie Winston, "Labor: Union Wages Staying Steady," *ENR* 244 (March 27, 2000): 106–107.

23. Ira B. Lobel, "Is Interest Based on Bargaining Really New?" *Dispute Resolution Journal* 55 (February 2000): 8–17.

24. Bill Vlasic and Aaron Bernstein, "Workplace: Unions: Why Ford Is Riding Shotgun for the UAW," *Business Week* (March 17, 1997): 11; William Symonds and Kathleen Kerwin, "Labor: So Much for Hardball," *Business Week* (November 4, 1996): 48.

25. Al Stamborski, "Teamsters Uneasy about 'Common Sense' Job Stance," *St. Louis Post-Dispatch* (April 12, 1998): A1.

26. Terence K. Huwe and Janice Kimball, "Collective Bargaining for Health and Safety: A Handbook for Unions," *Industrial Relations* (July 2000): 547–551.

27. Martin J. Oppenheimer and John F. Fullerton III, "The Role of the Union in the Arbitration of Statutory Employment Claims," *Dispute Resolution Journal* (May-July 2000): 70–78.

28. Jason Micah Ross, "Baseball Litigation: A New Calculus for Awarding Damages in Tort Trials," *Texas Law Review* 78 (December 1999): 439.

29. For additional information regarding the Federal Mediation and Conciliation Service, see www.fmcs.gov

30. For additional information regarding the American Arbitration Association, see www.adr.org.

31. Donald Austin Woolf, "Arbitration in One Easy Lesson: A Review of Criteria Used in Arbitration Awards," *Personnel* 55 (September/October 1978): 76; and Bill Leonard, "Groups Adopt New Arbitration Procedural Rules," *HRMagazine* 41 (July 1996): 8.

32. National Labor Relations Board and Kevin Galvin, "Rising Global Job Market Has Dimmed the Nation's Stake in Labor Strikes/Changing Times Have Unions Organizing to Rejuvenate the Ranks in Solidarity," *Minneapolis Star Tribune* (July 31, 1998): 3D.

33. Peter Corbett, "Union Strategy: Chaos for AMWEST\Strikes to Target Selected Flights," *The Arizona Republic* (March 7, 1999): D1.

34. Michael R. Carrell and Christina Heavrin, *Labor Relations and Collective Bargaining,* 5th ed. (Upper Saddle River, NJ: Prentice Hall, 1998): 214.

35. Symonds and Kerwin, "Labor: So Much for Hardball."

36. Galvin, "Rising Global Job Market Has Dimmed the Nation's Stake in Labor Strikes."

37. Micheline Maynard, "Back to Work: GM, Workers Settle Strike," *USA Today* (July 28, 1997): 1A.

38. Don Gonyea and Daniel Zwerdling, "GM Strike Far from Over," National Public Radio's *Weekend All Things Considered* (July 12, 1998).

39. Sandra Atchison and Aaron Bernstein, "A Silver Bullet for the Union Drive at Coors?" *Business Week* (July 11, 1988): 61.

40. Strupp, "Union-Tribune Local Airs Boycott Ad."

41. John Gallagher, "Strike Zone," *Traffic World* 261 (January 2000): 31.

42. Kenneth C. Crowe, "Deer Park Plant Replaces Strikers," *Newsday* (May 6, 1997): A53.

43. "World's Trade Unions under Siege," *International Press English News Wire* (May 29, 2000).

44. Jonathan Walters, "The Power of Pay," *Government Executive* 31 (January 1999): 32–37.

# 16

objectivesobjectivesobjectives

## ▶ Objectives

- Describe internal employee relations.
- Explain discipline and disciplinary action.
- Explain how grievance handling is typically conducted under a collective bargaining agreement.
- Explain how grievance handling is typically conducted in union-free firms.
- Define alternative dispute resolution.
- Describe how termination conditions may differ with regard to nonmanagerial/nonprofessional employees, executives, managers, and professionals.
- Explain the concept of employment at will.
- Describe demotion as an alternative to termination.
- Explain downsizing and layoffs.
- Describe transfers, promotions, resignations, and retirements as factors involved in internal employee relations.
- Explain the importance of evaluating the human resource management functions.

# Internal Employee Relations

alvin Scott, the production supervisor for American Manufacturing, was mad at the world when he arrived at work. The automobile mechanic had not repaired his car on time the day before, and he had been forced to take a taxi to work this morning. Because no one was safe around Calvin today, it was not the time for Phillip Martin—a member of Local 264—to report for work late. Without hesitation, Calvin exploded, "You know our company cannot tolerate this type of behavior. I do not want to see you around here anymore. You are fired!" Just as quickly, Phillip replied, "You're way off base. Our contract calls for three warnings for tardiness. My steward will hear about this."

In another situation, Julio Barrios, a 10-year employee at Ketro Productions, arrived at the office of the human resource manager to turn in his letter of resignation. Julio was very upset with his supervisor, John Higgins. When the human resource manager, Robert Noll, asked what was wrong, Julio replied, "Yesterday, I made a mistake and set my machine up wrong. It was the first time in years that I had done that. My boss chewed me out in front of my friends. I would not take that from the president, much less a two-bit supervisor!"

These scenarios represent only two of the many situations that managers confront when dealing with internal employee relations. Calvin Scott has just been reminded that his power to fire Phillip Martin has limits. The resignation of Julio Barrios might have been avoided if his supervisor had not shown poor judgment and disciplined him in front of his friends.

In this chapter, we first describe internal employee relations. Next, we discuss discipline and disciplinary action. We then describe grievance handling under a collective bargaining agreement and for union-free organizations. This is followed by a review of alternative dispute resolution, termination, employment at will, and demotion as an alternative to termination. Next, downsizing and layoffs, transfers, promotion, resignation, and retirement are discussed. The last portion of the chapter is devoted to evaluating the human resource management functions.

## INTERNAL EMPLOYEE RELATIONS DEFINED

The status of most workers is not permanently fixed in an organization. Employees constantly move upward, laterally, downward, and out of the organization. To ensure that workers with the proper skills and experience are available at all levels, constant and concerted efforts are required to maintain good internal employee relations. **Internal employee relations** comprise the human resource management activities associated with the movement of employees within the organization. These activities include promotion, transfer, demotion, resignation, discharge, layoff, and retirement. Discipline and disciplinary action are also crucial aspects of internal employee relations.

Some people believe that equal employment opportunity legislation primarily affects individuals entering the company for the first time. Nothing could be further from the truth. The legal environment described in Chapter 3 applies to every aspect of internal employee relations.[1] The thrust of equal employment opportunity legislation is that all workers should receive equal treatment, and internal

**Internal employee relations**
Those human resource management activities associated with the movement of employees within the organization.

▶ **SHRM-HR Links**

**www.prenhall.com/mondy**

Various issues including arbitration, mediation, handbooks, and policies are addressed.

HR WEB
WISDOM

employee relations must reflect this principle. For instance, are blacks being fired at a higher rate than whites? Are women not receiving promotional opportunities? The same kinds of questions may be asked about demotions and layoffs.

## DISCIPLINE AND DISCIPLINARY ACTION

**Discipline**
The state of employee self-control and orderly conduct; indicates the extent of genuine teamwork within an organization.

**Disciplinary action**
The invoking of a penalty against an employee who fails to meet organizational standards or comply with organizational rules.

**Discipline** is the state of employee self-control and orderly conduct and indicates the extent of genuine teamwork within an organization. A necessary but often trying aspect of internal employee relations is the application of disciplinary action. **Disciplinary action** invokes a penalty against an employee who fails to meet established standards. Effective disciplinary action addresses the employee's wrongful behavior, not the employee as a person. Incorrectly administered disciplinary action is destructive to both the employee and the organization. Thus, disciplinary action should not be applied haphazardly. Both Calvin Scott and John Higgins were haphazard in their application of discipline, with the result that two difficult employee relations situations developed.

Disciplinary action is not usually management's initial response to a problem. Normally, there are more positive ways of convincing employees to adhere to company policies that are necessary to accomplish organizational goals. However, managers must administer disciplinary action when company rules are violated. Disciplinary policies afford the organization the greatest opportunity to accomplish organizational goals, thereby benefiting both employees and the corporation.

### The Disciplinary Action Process

The disciplinary action process is dynamic and ongoing. Because one person's actions can affect others in a work group, the proper application of disciplinary action fosters acceptable behavior by other group members. Conversely, unjustified or improperly administered disciplinary action can have a detrimental effect on other group members.

The disciplinary action process is shown in Figure 16-1. The external environment affects every area of human resource management, including disciplinary policies and actions. Changes in the external environment, such as technological innovations, may render a rule inappropriate and may necessitate new rules. Laws and government regulations that affect company policies and rules are also constantly changing. For instance, the Occupational Safety and Health Act has caused many firms to establish safety rules.

Unions are another external factor. Specific punishment for rule violations is subject to negotiation and inclusion in labor-management agreements. For example, the union may negotiate for three written warnings for tardiness before a worker is suspended instead of the two warnings a present contract might require. This was the case with American Manufacturing, where the labor-management agreement required three warnings for tardiness before termination.

▶ The disciplinary action process is dynamic and ongoing.

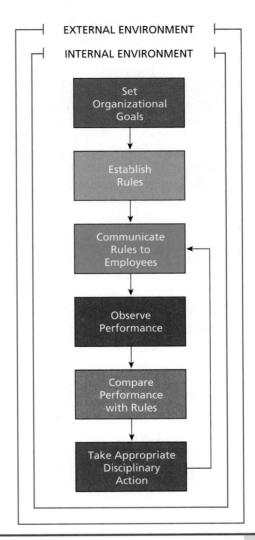

**The Disciplinary Action Process**    **Figure 16-1**

Changes in the internal environment of the firm can also alter the disciplinary process. Through organizational development, the firm may change its culture. As a result of this shift, first-line supervisors may handle disciplinary action more positively. Organization policies can also have an impact on the disciplinary action process. For instance, a policy of treating employees as mature human beings would significantly affect the process.

The disciplinary action process deals largely with infractions of rules. Rules are specific guides to behavior on the job. The dos and don'ts associated with accomplishing tasks may be highly inflexible. For example, a company rule may forbid employees from using the Internet for personal use at work.[2] In some firms, violation of this rule might result in immediate termination.

After management has established rules, it must communicate these rules to employees.[3] Individuals cannot obey a rule if they do not know it exists. As long as employee behavior does not vary from acceptable practices, there is no need for disciplinary action, but when an employee's behavior violates a rule, corrective action may be necessary. Disciplining someone often creates an uncomfortable psychological climate. Managers can still sleep well the night after firing a worker if the rules have been clearly articulated to everyone.[4] The purpose of disciplinary action is to alter behavior that can have a negative impact on achievement of organizational objectives—not to chastise the violator. The word *discipline* comes from the word *disciple,* and when translated from Latin, it means "to teach." Thus, the intent of discipline should be to ensure that the recipient sees the discipline as a learning process rather than as something that merely inflicts pain.[5]

Note that the process shown in Figure 16-1 includes feedback from the point of taking appropriate disciplinary action to communicating rules to employees. When appropriate disciplinary action is taken, employees should realize that certain behaviors are unacceptable and should not be repeated. However, if appropriate disciplinary action is not taken, employees may view the behavior as acceptable and repeat it.

## Approaches to Disciplinary Action

Several concepts regarding the administration of disciplinary action have been developed. Three of the most important concepts are the hot stove rule, progressive disciplinary action, and disciplinary action without punishment.

**The Hot Stove Rule.** One approach to administering disciplinary action is referred to as the *hot stove rule.* According to this approach, disciplinary action should have the following consequences, which are analogous to touching a hot stove:

1. *Burns immediately.* If disciplinary action is to be taken, it must occur immediately so that the individual will understand the reason for it. With the passage of time, people have the tendency to convince themselves that they are not at fault, which tends in part to nullify later disciplinary effects.
2. *Provides warning.* It is also extremely important to provide advance warning that punishment will follow unacceptable behavior. As individuals move closer to a hot stove, they are warned by its heat that they will be burned if they touch it; therefore, they have the opportunity to avoid the burn if they so choose.
3. *Gives consistent punishment.* Disciplinary action should also be consistent in that everyone who performs the same act will be punished accordingly. As with a hot stove, each person who touches it with the same degree of pressure and for the same period of time is burned to the same extent.
4. *Burns impersonally.* Disciplinary action should be impersonal. The hot stove burns anyone who touches it, without favoritism.[6]

Although the hot stove approach has some merit, it also has weaknesses. If the circumstances surrounding all disciplinary situations were the same, there would be no problem with this approach. However, situations are often quite different, and many variables may be present in each individual disciplinary case. For instance, does the organization penalize a loyal 20-year employee the same as an individual who has been with the firm less than six weeks? A supervisor often finds that he or she cannot be completely consistent and impersonal in taking disciplinary action. Because situations do vary, progressive disciplinary action may be more realistic and more beneficial to both the employee and the organization.

**Progressive disciplinary action**

An approach to disciplinary action designed to ensure that the minimum penalty appropriate to the offense is imposed.

**Progressive Disciplinary Action.** **Progressive disciplinary action** is intended to ensure that the minimum penalty appropriate to the offense is imposed. The goal of progressive discipline is to formally communicate problem issues to employees in a direct and timely manner so that they can improve their performance.[7] Its use involves answering a series of questions about the severity of the offense. The manager must ask these questions, in sequence, to determine the proper disciplinary action, as illustrated in Figure 16-2. After the manager has determined that disciplinary action is appropriate, the proper question is, "Does this violation warrant more than an oral warning?"[8] If the improper behavior is minor and has not previously occurred, perhaps only an oral warning will be sufficient. Also, an individual may receive several oral warnings before a *yes* answer applies. The manager follows the same procedure for each level of offense in the progressive disciplinary process. The manager does not consider termination until each lower-level question is answered *yes*. However, major violations—such as assaulting a supervisor or another worker—may justify immediate termination of the employee.

To assist managers in recognizing the proper level of disciplinary action, some firms have formalized the procedure. One approach is to establish progressive disciplinary action guidelines, as shown in Table 16-1. In this example, a worker who is absent without authorization will receive an oral warning the first time it happens and a written warning the second time; the third time, the employee will be terminated. Fighting on the job is an offense that normally results in immediate termination. However, specific guidelines for various offenses should be developed to meet the needs of the organization. For example, smoking in an unauthorized area may be grounds for immediate dismissal in an explosives factory. On the other hand, the same violation may be less serious in a plant producing concrete products. Basically, the penalty should be appropriate to the severity of the violation, and no greater.

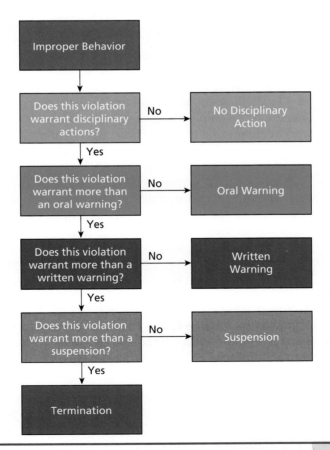

**The Progressive Disciplinary Approach**    **Figure 16-2**

**Table 16-1** Suggested Guidelines for Disciplinary Action

**Offenses Requiring First, an Oral Warning;
Second, a Written Warning; and Third, Termination**

Negligence in the performance of duties
Unauthorized absence from job
Inefficiency in the performance of job

**Offenses Requiring a Written Warning and Then Termination**

Sleeping on the job
Failure to report to work one or two days in a row without notification
Negligent use of property

**Offenses Requiring Immediate Discharge**

Theft
Fighting on the job
Falsifying time cards
Failure to report to work three days in a row without notification

**Disciplinary action
without punishment**
A process in which a
worker is given time off
with pay to think about
whether he or she wants
to follow the rules and
continue working for the
company.

*Disciplinary Action without Punishment.* The process of giving a worker time off with pay to think about whether he or she wants to follow the rules and continue working for the company is called **disciplinary action without punishment**. The approach is to throw out formal punitive disciplinary policies for dilemmas such as chronic tardiness or a crummy attitude in favor of affirming procedures that make employees want to take personal responsibility for their actions and be models for the corporate mission and vision.[9] When an employee violates a rule, the manager issues an oral reminder. Repetition brings a written reminder, and the third violation results in the worker having to take one, two, or three days off (with pay) to think about the situation. During the first two steps, the manager tries to encourage the employee to solve the problem. If the third step is taken, upon the worker's return, he or she and the supervisor meet to agree that the employee will not violate a rule again or the employee will leave the firm. When disciplinary action without punishment is used, it is especially important that all rules be explicitly stated in writing. At the time of orientation, new workers should be told that repeated violations of different rules will be viewed in the same way as several violations of the same rule. This approach keeps workers from taking undue advantage of the process.

## Problems in the Administration of Disciplinary Action

As you might expect, administering disciplinary actions is not a pleasant task. Although the manager is in the best position to take disciplinary action, many managers would rather avoid it.[10] The reasons managers want to avoid disciplinary action include the following issues.

1. *Lack of training.* The manager may not have the knowledge and skill necessary to handle disciplinary problems.
2. *Fear.* The manager may be concerned that top management will not support a disciplinary action.
3. *Being the only one.* The manager may think, "No one else is disciplining employees, so why should I?"

4. *Guilt.* The manager may think, "How can I discipline someone if I've done the same thing?"
5. *Loss of friendship.* The manager may believe that disciplinary action will damage a friendship with an employee or the employee's associates.
6. *Time loss.* The manager may begrudge the valuable time that is required to administer and explain disciplinary action.
7. *Loss of temper.* The manager may be afraid of losing his or her temper when talking to an employee about a rule violation.
8. *Rationalization.* The manager may think, "The employee knows it was the wrong thing to do, so why do we need to talk about it?"[11]

These reasons apply to all forms of disciplinary action—from an oral warning to termination. Managers often avoid disciplinary action, even when it is in the company's best interest.[12] Such reluctance often stems from breakdowns in other areas of the human resource management function. For instance, if a manager has consistently rated an employee high on annual performance appraisals, the supervisor's rationale for terminating a worker for poor performance would be weak. It is embarrassing to decide to fire a worker and then be asked why you rated this individual so highly on the previous evaluation. It could be that the employee's productivity has actually dropped substantially. It could also be that the employee's productivity has always been low, yet the supervisor may have trouble justifying to upper-level management that the person should be terminated. Rather than run the risk of a decision being overturned, the supervisor retains the ineffective worker.[13]

Finally, some managers believe that even attempting to terminate women and minorities is useless. However, the statutes and subsequent court decisions associated with women and minorities in the workplace were not intended to protect nonproductive workers. Anyone whose performance is below standard can, and should, be terminated after the supervisor has made reasonable attempts to salvage the employee.

A supervisor may be perfectly justified in administering disciplinary action, but there is usually a proper time and place for doing so. For example, disciplining a worker in the presence of others may embarrass the individual and actually defeat the purpose of the action. Even when they are wrong, employees resent disciplinary action administered in public. The scenario at the beginning of the chapter, in which Julio Barrios quit his job because he was disciplined in front of his peers, provides an excellent illustration. By disciplining employees in private, supervisors prevent them from losing face with their peers.

In addition, many supervisors may be too lenient early in the disciplinary action process and too strict later. This lack of consistency does not give the worker a clear understanding of the penalty associated with the inappropriate action. As a manager of labor relations for Georgia-Pacific Corporation once stated, "A supervisor will often endure an unacceptable situation for an extended period of time. Then, when the supervisor finally does take action, he or she is apt to overreact and come down excessively hard." However, consistency does not necessarily mean that the same penalty must be applied to two different workers for the same offense. For instance, employers would be consistent if they always considered the worker's past record and length of service. For a serious violation, a long-term employee might receive only a suspension, while a worker with only a few months' service might be terminated for the same act. This type of action could reasonably be viewed as being consistent.

To assist management in administering discipline properly, a "Code on Discipline Procedure" has been prepared by the Advisory, Conciliation and

**Table 16-2** Recommended Disciplinary Procedures

▶ All employees should be given a copy of the employers' rules on disciplinary procedures. The procedures should specify which employees they cover and what disciplinary actions may be taken, and should allow matters to be dealt with quickly.

▶ Employees should be told of complaints against them and given an opportunity to state their case. They should have the right to be accompanied by a trade union representative or fellow employee of their choice.

▶ Disciplinary action should not be taken until the case has been fully investigated. Immediate superiors should not have the power to dismiss without reference to senior management, and, except for gross misconduct, no employee should be dismissed for a first breach of discipline.

▶ Employees should be given an explanation for any penalty imposed, and they should have a right of appeal, with specified procedures to be followed.

▶ When disciplinary action other than summary dismissal is needed, supervisors should give a formal oral warning in the case of minor offenses or a written warning in more serious cases.

*Source:* "Code on Discipline Procedure," *Industrial Management* 7 (August 1977): 7. Used with permission.

Arbitration Service. The purpose of the code is to give practical guidance on how to formulate disciplinary rules and procedures and use them effectively. The code recommends the actions shown in Table 16-2. As you can see, it stresses communication of rules, telling the employee of the complaint, conducting a full investigation, and giving the employee an opportunity to tell his or her side of the story.

## GRIEVANCE HANDLING UNDER A COLLECTIVE BARGAINING AGREEMENT

If employees in an organization are represented by a union, workers who believe that they have been disciplined or dealt with unjustly can appeal through the grievance and arbitration procedures of the collective bargaining agreement. Obviously, Phillip Martin knew that the collective bargaining agreement negotiated by the union required three warnings for tardiness and he therefore could not be fired for being late one time. The grievance system encourages and facilitates the settlement of disputes between labor and management. A grievance procedure permits employees to express complaints without jeopardizing their jobs. It also assists management in seeking out the underlying causes of and solutions to grievances.

**HRM IN ACTION**

▶ *Is It Covered in the Contract?*

"I think I might have messed up this morning," said the maintenance supervisor, Carlos Chaves, to Doug Williams, the industrial relations manager. "One of the workers in my section wasn't doing the job exactly according to specs, and I blew up and told him, 'No more overtime for you!' Five minutes later the union steward was in the office reading me the riot act. She said situations such as this are covered in our contract and that I was violating it. I had never spoken to the worker before about that particular offense, and the steward said the contract called for both oral and written warnings before any penalty is assessed."

*How would you respond?*

# The Grievance Procedure

Virtually all labor agreements include some form of grievance procedure. A **grievance** can be broadly defined as an employee's dissatisfaction or feeling of personal injustice relating to his or her employment. A grievance under a collective bargaining agreement is normally well defined. It is usually restricted to violations of the terms and conditions of the agreement. There are other conditions that may give rise to a grievance, including the following:

- ▶ A violation of law
- ▶ A violation of the intent of the parties as stipulated during contract negotiations
- ▶ A violation of company rules
- ▶ A change in working conditions or past company practices
- ▶ A violation of health and/or safety standards

Grievance procedures have many common features. However, variations may reflect differences in organizational or decision-making structures or the size of a plant or company. Some general principles based on widespread practice can serve as useful guidelines for effective grievance administration:

- ▶ Grievances should be adjusted promptly.
- ▶ Procedures and forms used for airing grievances must be easy to utilize and well understood by employees and their supervisors.
- ▶ Direct and timely avenues of appeal from rulings of line supervision must exist.

The multiple-step grievance procedure shown in Figure 16-3 is the most common type. In the first step, the employee usually presents the grievance orally and informally to the immediate supervisor in the presence of the union steward. This step offers the greatest potential for improved labor relations, and a large majority of grievances are settled here. The procedure ends if the grievance can be resolved at this initial step. If the grievance remains unresolved, the next step involves a meeting between the plant manager or human resource manager and higher union officials, such as the grievance committee or the business agent or manager. Prior to this meeting, the grievance is written out, dated, and signed by the employee and the union steward. The written grievance states the events as the employee perceives them, cites the contract provision that allegedly has been violated, and indicates the settlement desired. If the grievance is not settled at this meeting, it is appealed to the third step, which typically involves the firm's top labor representative (such as the vice president of industrial relations) and high-level union officials. At times, depending on the severity of the grievance, the president may represent the firm. A grievance that remains unresolved at the conclusion of the third step may go to arbitration, if provided for in the agreement and the union decides to persevere.

Labor-relations problems can escalate when a supervisor is not equipped to handle grievances at the first step. Since the union steward, the aggrieved party, and the supervisor usually handle the first step informally, the supervisor must be fully prepared. The supervisor should obtain as many facts as possible before the meeting, because the union steward is likely to have done his or her homework.

The supervisor needs to recognize that the grievance may not reflect the real problem. For instance, the employee might be angry at the company for modifying its pay policies, even though the change was agreed to by the union. In order to voice discontent, the worker might file a grievance for an unrelated minor violation of the contract.

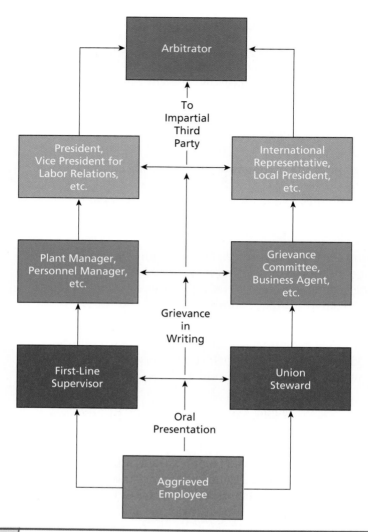

Figure 16-3  **A Multiple-Step Grievance Procedure**

*Source:* Robert W. Eckles et al., *Essentials of Management for First-Line Supervision* (New York: John Wiley & Sons, 1974): 529. Reprinted by permission of John Wiley & Sons, Inc.

## Arbitration

Arbitration is a grievance procedure that has successfully and peacefully resolved many labor-management problems. Arbitration is the final step in most grievance procedures. In arbitration, the parties submit their dispute to an impartial third party for resolution. Most agreements restrict the arbitrator's decision to application and interpretation of the agreement and make the decision final and binding on the parties. In a recent case, an arbitrator ruled that terminating an employee for violating a company's electronic communications policy was too severe a penalty.[14]

If the union decides in favor of arbitration, it notifies management. At this point, the union and the company select an arbitrator. Most agreements specify the selection method, although the choice is usually made from a list supplied by the Federal Mediation and Conciliation Service (FMCS) or the American Arbitration Association (AAA), both of which were discussed in Chapter 15. When considering potential arbitrators, both management and labor will study the candidates' previous decisions in an attempt to detect any biases. Obviously, neither party wants to select an arbitrator who might tend to favor the other's position.

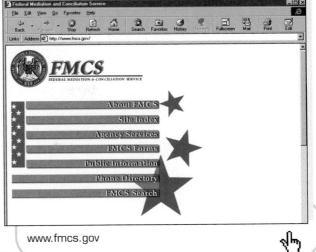

www.fmcs.gov

When arbitration is used to settle a grievance, a variety of factors may be used to evaluate the fairness of the management actions that caused the grievance. These factors include the following:

- Nature of the offense
- Due process and procedural correctness
- Double jeopardy
- Grievant's past record
- Length of service with the company
- Knowledge of rules
- Warnings
- Lax enforcement of rules
- Discriminatory treatment

The large number of interacting variables in each case makes the arbitration process difficult. The arbitrator must possess exceptional patience and judgment in rendering a fair and impartial decision.

After the arbitrator has been selected and has agreed to serve, a time and place for a hearing will be determined. The issue to be resolved will be presented to the arbitrator in a document that summarizes the question(s) to be decided. It will also point out any contract restrictions that prohibit the arbitrator from making an award that would change the terms of the contract.

At the hearing, each side presents its case. Arbitration is an adversarial proceeding, so a case may be lost because of poor preparation and presentation. The arbitrator may conduct the hearing much like a courtroom proceeding. Witnesses, cross-examination, transcripts, and legal counsel may all be used. The parties may also submit or be asked by the arbitrator to submit formal written statements. After the hearing, the arbitrator studies the material submitted and testimony given and is expected to reach a decision within 30 to 60 days. The decision is usually accompanied by a written opinion giving reasons for the decision.

The courts will generally enforce an arbitrator's decision unless (1) the arbitrator's decision is shown to be unreasonable or capricious in that it did not address the issues, (2) the arbitrator exceeded his or her authority, or (3) the award or decision violated a federal or state law. Such was the case with *Daily News L.P. v Newspaper & Mail Deliverers' Union of New York and Vicinity.* The court found that the arbitrator "manifestly disregarded evidence of the most critical nature" and vacated the award and held that the arbitration must be reopened.[15]

# Proof That Disciplinary Action Was Needed

Any disciplinary action administered may ultimately be taken to arbitration, when such a remedy is specified in the labor agreement. Employers have learned that they must prepare records that will constitute proof of disciplinary action and the reasons for it.[16] Although the formats of written warnings may vary, all should include the following information:

1. Statement of facts concerning the offense
2. Identification of the rule that was violated
3. Statement of what resulted or could have resulted because of the violation
4. Identification of any previous similar violations by the same individual
5. Statement of possible future consequences should the violation occur again
6. Signature and date

An example of a written warning is shown in Figure 16-4. In this instance, the worker has already received an oral reprimand. The individual is also warned that continued tardiness could lead to termination. It is important to document oral reprimands because they may be the first step in disciplinary action leading ultimately to arbitration.[17]

---

**Date:**      August 1, 2001

**To:**        Shane Boudreaux

**From:**      Wayne Sanders

**Subject:**   Written Warning

We are quite concerned because today you were thirty minutes late to work and offered no justification for this. According to our records, a similar offense occurred on July 25, 2001. At that time, you were informed that failure to report to work on time is unacceptable. I am, therefore, notifying you in writing that you must report to work on time. It will be necessary to terminate your employment if this happens again.

Please sign this form to indicate that you have read and understand this warning. Signing is not an indication of agreement.

_____
Name

_____
Date

---

**Figure 16-4** An Example of a Written Warning

# Weaknesses of Arbitration

Arbitration has achieved a certain degree of success in resolving grievances; however, it is not without weaknesses. Some practitioners claim that arbitration is losing its effectiveness because of the length of time between the first step of the grievance procedure and final settlement. Often, 100–250 days may elapse before a decision is made. The reason for the initial filing of the grievance may actually be forgotten before it is finally settled. Some people object to the cost of arbitration, which has been rising at an alarming rate. The cost of settling even a simple arbitration case can be quite high, even though labor and management typically share the expense. Forcing every grievance to arbitration could be used as a tactic to place either management or the union in a difficult financial position.

## GRIEVANCE HANDLING IN UNION-FREE ORGANIZATIONS

In the past, few union-free firms had formalized grievance procedures. Today, this is not the case as more and more firms have established formal grievance procedures and encouraged their use. Although the step-by step procedure for handling union grievances is a common practice, the means of resolving complaints in union-free firms vary. A well-designed grievance procedure ensures that the worker has ample opportunity to make complaints without fear of reprisal. If the system is to work, employees must be well informed about the program and convinced that management wants them to use it. Some employees are hesitant to formalize their complaints and must be constantly urged to avail themselves of the process. The fact that a manager says, "Our workers must be happy because I have received no complaints," does not necessarily mean that employees have no grievances. In a closed, threatening corporate culture, workers may be reluctant to voice their dissatisfaction to management.

Typically, an employee initiates a complaint with his or her immediate supervisor. However, if the complaint involves the supervisor, the individual is permitted to bypass the immediate supervisor and proceed to the employee-relations specialist or the manager at the next higher level. The grievance ultimately may be taken to the organization's top executive for a final decision. Brown & Root, a Houston-based engineering, construction, and maintenance company, has a unique dispute resolution program. Whenever workers feel they need to resolve a dispute, the program allows them to choose one or all four options including an open-door policy, a conference, mediation, or arbitration. "We wanted to give our employees several ports of entry to lodge a complaint if they wanted to," says Ralph Morales, manager of employee relations and administrator of the program.[18]

## ALTERNATIVE DISPUTE RESOLUTION

As the number of employment-related lawsuits increases, companies look for ways to protect themselves against the costs and uncertainties of the judicial system. **Alternative dispute resolution (ADR)** is a procedure whereby the employee and the company agree ahead of time that any problems will be addressed by an agreed-upon means. Some of these include arbitration, mediation, or mini-trials. The idea behind ADR is to resolve conflicts between employer and employee through means less costly and contentious than litigation. A successful program can save a company thousands of dollars in legal costs and hundreds of hours in managers' time. Just as important, perhaps, it can protect a company from the demoralizing tension and bitterness that employee grievances can spread through a workforce.[19]

**Alternative dispute resolution (ADR)**
A procedure agreed to ahead of time by the employee and the company for resolving any problems that may arise.

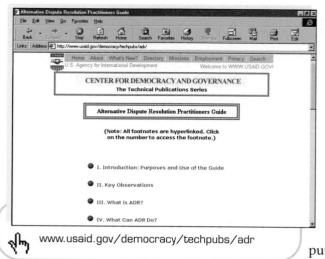

www.usaid.gov/democracy/techpubs/adr

Cases run the gamut from racial, gender, and age discrimination to unfair firings. Although ADR programs vary from employer to employer, many include informal methods that encourage workers to discuss their problem with their supervisor, a department head, or a panel of peers. The two best-known ADR methods are mediation and arbitration. Mediation is the preferred method for most people. When parties agree to mediate, they are able to reach a settlement in most of the cases.[20] In 1998, former President Clinton signed an executive order requiring that federal agencies must take steps to (1) promote greater use of mediation, arbitration, early neutral evaluation, agency ombudspersons, and other alternative dispute resolution techniques, and (2) promote greater use of negotiated rulemaking.[21]

The Supreme Court has endorsed arbitration as an effective and often preferable mechanism for resolving work-related disputes.[22] The court ruled that when there is a valid, binding arbitration agreement, such as the agreement signed by the employee, the EEOC may not sue on the behalf of the employee. In addition, the court found that Title VII does not require the EEOC to arbitrate a disagreement.[23] In another decision, an employee who signed the Form U-4, the Uniform Application for Securities Industry Registration or Transfer, cannot sue her employer for sex discrimination but must take her claim to arbitration as the U-4 specified. The employee worked as a securities trader for 10 years before resigning, claiming constructive discharge as the culmination of a pattern of sex bias throughout her tenure. She sued her employer, and a federal district court initially ruled in her favor, refusing to dismiss the case or to compel her to arbitrate her dispute. When the company appealed, however, the U.S. Court of Appeals for the Seventh Circuit backed the company and ordered the employee into arbitration.[24]

## TERMINATION

Termination is the most severe penalty that an organization can impose on an employee; therefore, it should be the most carefully considered form of disciplinary action. Calvin Scott, who tried to fire Phillip Martin for being late one time, did not carefully consider this decision. The experience of being terminated is traumatic for employees regardless of their position in the organization. They can experience feelings of failure, fear, disappointment, and anger.[25] It is also a difficult time for the person making the termination decision.[26] Knowing that termination may affect not only the employee but also an entire family increases the trauma. Not knowing how the terminated employee will react also

---

**HR WEB WISDOM**

▶ *Dispute Resolution, Arbitration, and Mediation*

**www.prenhall.com/mondy**

Numerous sites related to dispute resolution, arbitration, and mediation are hot linked.

may create considerable anxiety for the manager who must do the firing. Recall from Chapter 13 that an individual who is terminated may respond with violence in the workplace.

Termination is an extremely serious form of discipline and must therefore always be carefully considered and appropriate. It has even been determined that there is a *best* day to terminate someone. Mondays are best for terminated workers because they have some workdays (rather than a weekend, when everything is closed) to find a new job.[27] Furthermore, in today's business environment, companies need to be as concerned with the termination process as with the hiring process. Just as it is important to train recruiters to be effective, managers should also know how to terminate an employee.[28] Regardless of the similarities in the termination of employees at various levels, distinct differences exist with regard to nonmanagerial/nonprofessional employees, executives, managers, and professionals.

## Termination of Nonmanagerial/ Nonprofessional Employees

Individuals in this category are neither managers nor professionally trained individuals, such as engineers or accountants. They generally include such employees as steelworkers, truck drivers, salesclerks, and waiters. If the firm is unionized, the termination procedure is typically well defined in the labor-management agreement. For example, drinking on the job might be identified as a reason for immediate termination. Absences, on the other hand, may require three written warnings from the supervisor before termination action can be taken.

When the firm is union free, these workers can generally be terminated more easily. A history of unjustified terminations within a firm, however, may provide an opportunity for unionization. In some union-free organizations, violations justifying termination are included in the firm's employee handbook. At times—especially in smaller organizations—the termination process is informal, with the first-line supervisor telling workers what actions warrant termination. Regardless of the size of the organization, management should inform employees of the actions that warrant termination.

## Termination of Executives

Unlike individuals in most organization positions, CEOs do not have to worry about their jobs being eliminated. Their main concern is whether they themselves will become excess baggage. Increasingly, a CEO's status is related to the stock performance of his or her firm. According to a study of 476 companies in 50 industries and 25 countries, nearly half of all current CEOs have held their job for less than three years. In the past five years, nearly two-thirds of all companies have installed a new CEO.[29]

Executives usually have no formal appeal procedure. The decision to terminate an executive is normally made by the board of directors in the organization. In addition, the reasons for termination may not be as clear as those for lower-level employees. Some of the reasons include the following issues.

1. *Economic downturns.* At times, business conditions may force a reduction in the number of executives.
2. *Reorganization/downsizing.* In order to improve efficiency or as a result of merging with another company a firm may reorganize or downsize, resulting in the elimination of some executive positions.

3. *Philosophical differences.* A difference in philosophy of conducting business may develop between an executive and other key company officials. In order to maintain consistency in management philosophy, the executive may be replaced.
4. *Decline in productivity.* The executive may have been capable of performing satisfactorily in the past but, for various reasons, can no longer perform the job as required.

This list does not include factors related to illegal activities or actions taken that are not in the best interests of the firm. Under those circumstances, the firm has no moral obligation to the terminated executive.

An organization may derive positive benefits from terminating executives, but such actions also present a potentially hazardous situation for the company. Terminating a senior executive is an expensive proposition, often in ways more costly than just the separation package. The impact on the organization should be measured in relationships, productivity, strategic integrity, and investor confidence, as well as dollars. Many corporations are concerned about developing a negative public image that reflects insensitivity to the needs of their employees. They fear that such a reputation would impede their efforts to recruit high-quality managers. Also, terminated executives have, at times, made public statements detrimental to the reputation of their former employer.

## Termination of Middle and Lower-Level Managers and Professionals

In the past, the most vulnerable and perhaps the most neglected group of employees with regard to termination has been middle and lower-level managers and professionals, who are generally not union members and thus not protected by a labor-management agreement. Employees in these jobs also may not have the political clout that a terminated executive has. Termination may have been based on something as simple as the attitude or feelings of an immediate superior on a given day.

## EMPLOYMENT AT WILL

In approximately two of every three U.S. jobs, the worker's continued employment depends almost entirely on the continued goodwill of his or her employer. Individuals falling into this category are known as *at-will employees*. Generally, much of the U.S. legal system presumes that the jobs of such employees may be terminated at the will of the employer and that these employees have a similar right to leave their jobs at any time.[30] As mentioned in Chapter 15, employment at will is an unwritten contract created when an employee agrees to work for an employer but no agreement exists as to how long the parties expect the employment to last.[31] Historically, because of a century-old common-law precedent in the United States, employment of indefinite duration could, in general, be terminated at the whim of either party.

The concept of employment at will has eroded somewhat in recent years.[32] Some courts have decided that terminations of at-will employees are unlawful if they are contrary to general notions of acceptable *public policy* or if they are done in *bad faith*. Judges, legislators, and employees are increasingly willing to challenge rigid notions of unlimited employer discretion.

Employers can do certain things to help protect themselves against litigation for wrongful discharge based on a breach of implied employment contract. Statements in such documents as employment applications and policy manuals that suggest job security or permanent employment should be avoided if employers want to minimize charges of wrongful discharge. A person should not be employed without a signed acknowledgment of the at-will disclaimer. The policy manual should have it clearly stated in bold, larger than normal print, so it is very clear to the employee that this is an at-will relationship.[33] Other guidelines that may assist organizations in avoiding wrongful termination suits include clearly defining the worker's duties, providing good feedback on a regular basis, and conducting realistic performance appraisals on a regular basis.

## DEMOTION AS AN ALTERNATIVE TO TERMINATION

Termination frequently is the solution when a person is not able to perform his or her job satisfactorily. At times, however, demotions are used as an alternative to discharge, especially when a long-term employee is involved. The worker may have performed satisfactorily for many years, but his or her productivity may then begin to decline for a variety of reasons. Perhaps the worker is just not physically capable of performing the job any longer or no longer willing to work the long hours that the job requires.

**Demotion** is the process of moving a worker to a lower level of duties and responsibilities, which typically involves a reduction in pay. Emotions often run high when an individual is demoted. The demoted person may suffer loss of respect from peers and feel betrayed, embarrassed, angry, and disappointed.[34] The employee's productivity may also decrease further. For these reasons, demotion should be used very cautiously.

**Demotion**
The process of moving a worker to a lower level of duties and responsibilities; typically involves a pay cut.

If demotion is chosen over termination, efforts must be made to preserve the self-esteem of the individual. The person may be asked how he or she would like to handle the demotion announcement. A positive image of the worker's value to the company should be projected.

The handling of demotions in a unionized organization is usually spelled out clearly in the labor-management agreement. Should a decision be made to demote a worker for unsatisfactory performance, the union should be notified of this intent and given the specific reasons for the demotion. Often the demotion will be challenged and carried through the formal grievance procedure. Documentation is necessary for the demotion to be upheld. Even with the problems associated with demotion for cause, it is often easier to demote than to terminate an employee. In addition, demotion is often less devastating to the employee. For the organization, however, the opposite may be true if the demotion creates lingering ill will and an embittered employee.

As firms downsize and reduce the number of layers in the organizational structure, positions that may have been held by highly qualified employees may be eliminated. Rather than lose a valued employee, firms will at times offer this employee a lower-level position, often at the same salary.

## DOWNSIZING AND LAYOFFS

**Downsizing**, also known as *restructuring* and *rightsizing*, is essentially the reverse of a company growing and suggests a one-time change in the organization and the number of people employed. Typically, both the organization and the number of people in the organization shrink. Downsizing is still occurring in some firms. Despite near-optimal employment conditions, workers at some of the nation's top companies are finding themselves involuntarily thrust into the job market, even in the booming technology industry. Even when the U.S. stock market hovers near record levels, companies seem to feel more pressure than ever to cut costs in response to competitive pressures. In 1999, Compaq Computer Corporation said

**Downsizing**
A reduction in the number of people employed by a firm (also known as *restructuring* and *rightsizing*); essentially the reverse of a company growing; downsizing suggests a one-time change in the organization and the number of people employed.

it would eliminate up to 8,000 jobs, or 11 percent of its workforce. The same day, Electronic Data Systems Corporation announced that it would offer early retirement packages to 8,000 employees to reduce costs. Also, Eastman Kodak said it would cut 2,000 to 2,500 from its 83,500 head count.[35] Procter & Gamble Company said it would do away with 15,000 jobs, or 13 percent of its workforce, in the next few years. In 1999, announced layoffs by the prime employers in the U.S. economy were 36 percent ahead of the previous year's level, which had been the highest of the decade.[36]

In some cases downsizing has been successful. However, downsizing does not always turn a company around. The reason is that downsizing often does not solve the fundamental causes of problems. Some organizations have not developed an appropriate strategy for growth; instead, they focus on reducing costs, which is merely attacking a symptom of the problem. Management in these firms gave little thought to who would do the work after the firm had been downsized.[37]

One result of downsizing is that many layers are often pulled out of an organization, making advancement in the organization more difficult. In addition, when one firm downsizes, others in the same industry must follow if they are to be competitive. Thus, more and more individuals are finding themselves plateaued in the same job until they retire. To reinvigorate demoralized workers, some firms are providing additional training, lateral moves, short sabbaticals, and compensation based on a person's contribution, not his or her title.[38] Some firms are gaining enthusiasm from their employees by providing raises based on additional skills they acquire and use.

Another result of downsizing is that employee trust is often significantly reduced. For workers who remain after downsizing, the trust level is often low. These workers believe that it might happen to them the next time. A common pattern of thought is that "I must take care of myself, because the company will not." Employees who would never have considered changing jobs prior to downsizing may soon start thinking about this option, especially if their present company does not provide them with the necessary development to keep up with industry trends. One of the main goals of HR in today's environment is to reestablish this lost trust.[39] Another result of downsizing is that companies are using more contingent workers. In a recent survey conducted by Business and Legal Reports, more than 90 percent of the 1,110 respondents said contingent workers were part of their staffing mix, a 50 percent increase from five years ago. Almost 60 percent indicated they expected to be turning to contingents in increasing numbers over the next five years.[40]

The rush to downsize appears to be slowing down. Companies have learned that trimming a workforce is often harder than it appears. A recent survey of 500 HR executives by outplacement firm Lee Hecht Harrison based in Woodcliff Lake, New Jersey, illustrates this point. Just under one-third of those polled felt that their company had let go of too many workers. The survey also found that one-third of companies that downsized since 1994 restored jobs that had been cut. Nearly 75 percent refilled those slots with temporary or contract workers.[41]

Tied very closely to downsizing are layoffs—the primary difference being the magnitude of the number of workers no longer employed. Historically, the economic well-being of many companies has risen and fallen in cycles. Even in good economic times layoffs occur, as was the case in 1999–2000. There were 14,909 layoff events in 1999 involving a total of 1,572,399 initial claims for unemployment insurance in the 50 states and the District of Columbia.[42] Although being laid off is not the same thing as being fired, it has the same effect: The worker is unemployed. These workers provide a bonanza for the small- to medium-sized companies that have benefited most from a talent pool made available by layoffs at larger corporations.[43]

## Layoff/Recall Procedures

Even in this rapidly changing environment, recalls are necessary at times. Whether the firm is union free or unionized, carefully constructed layoff/recall procedures should be developed. Workers should understand when they are hired how the system will work in the event of a layoff. When the firm is unionized, the layoff procedures are usually stated clearly in the labor-management agreement. Seniority usually is the basis for layoffs, with the least senior employees laid off first. The agreement may also have a clearly spelled-out *bumping procedure*. When senior-level positions are eliminated, the people occupying them have the right to bump workers from lower-level positions, assuming that they have the proper qualifications for the lower-level job. When bumping occurs, the composition of the workforce is altered. Procedures for recalling laid-off employees are also usually spelled out in labor-management agreements. Again, seniority is typically the basis for worker recall, with the most senior employees being recalled first.

Regardless of a union-free firm's current stand on the issue of layoffs, it should establish layoff procedures prior to facing them. In union-free firms, seniority should also be an integral part of any layoff procedure; however, other factors are often considered more important. For example, productivity of the employee is typically a key consideration. When productivity is the primary factor, management must be careful to ensure that productivity—not favoritism—is the actual basis for the layoff decision. Workers may have an inaccurate perception of their own productivity level and that of their fellow employees. Therefore, it is important to define accurately both seniority and productivity considerations well in advance of any layoffs.

## Outplacement

Some organizations have established a systematic means of assisting laid-off or terminated employees in locating jobs. The use of outplacement began at the executive level, but it has also been used at other organizational levels. In **outplacement**, laid-off employees are given assistance in finding employment elsewhere. When downsizing was occurring at a rapid pace, mass layoffs often necessitated group outplacement. Through outplacement, the firm tries to soften the impact of displacement. Some of the services provided by group outplacement include the following:

**Outplacement**
A company procedure that assists a laid-off employee in finding employment elsewhere.

- A financial module that covers pension options, Social Security benefits, expenses for interviews, and wage/salary negotiations
- Career guidance, perhaps using aptitude/interest and personality profile tests and software
- Instruction in self-appraisal techniques, which help in the recognition of the skills, knowledge, experience, and other qualities recruiters may require
- Tutoring in personal promotional techniques, research, and gaining an entry to potential employers
- Help with understanding the techniques that lead to successful interviews
- Development of personal action plans and continuing support[44]

Outplacement may not be used as much as in the past. When the concept was first introduced, it dealt with specific individuals—usually executives. When it was introduced to address the needs of larger groups, it was still perceived to be in response to a one-time event. Today's college students are likely

**▶ Inplacement**

Opportunities for advancement have been severely curtailed in recent years because of downsizing. As downsizing was largely completed, employers became less concerned with getting rid of people. The new priority was making flexible and effective use of the survivors. But many of these individuals had watched colleagues lose their once-secure jobs, were now overworked, and had seen their promotion prospects evaporate. As a result, many were directionless and demotivated.

Outplacement firms needed a new role. They found it in helping the remaining executives define their career goals, identify how they needed to develop their skills, and learn to adapt to new ways of flexible working. The word *outplacement* was no longer appropriate, so helping people at work tends to be called *inplacement.* Consultants offering inplacement services now call themselves career-change consultants or career development consultants.

Top managers, including human resource managers, are realizing that people are confused at having to change from the traditional corporate structures, patterns of career development, and ways of working. According to John Ferguson, director of its Scotland division for Drake Beam Morin, "Companies like mine have been in outplacement for 20 years or so. And over the past 5 or 6 years we began to recognize the need for inplacement. When inplacement specialists are brought in, they may be called a coach or a counselor or a mentor. They provide individuals with a sense of direction. They are challenged on aspects related to their present activity and where they perceive their future activity to be."[45]

to have eight to ten jobs, and as many as three careers. The outplacement system was designed to guide people from job to similar job, not for the environment workers face today.[46]

# TRANSFERS, PROMOTIONS, RESIGNATIONS, AND RETIREMENTS

A major portion of internal employee relations relates to transfers, promotions, resignations, and retirements.

## Transfers

**Transfer**
The lateral movement of a worker within an organization.

The lateral movement of a worker within an organization is called a **transfer**. A transfer may be initiated by the firm or by an employee. The process does not and should not imply that a person is being either promoted or demoted. Transfers serve several purposes. First, firms often find it necessary to reorganize. Offices and departments are created and abolished in response to the company's needs. In filling positions created by reorganization, the company may have to move employees without promoting them. Relocations for transfers are much more common than for promotions.[47] A similar situation may exist when an office or department is closed. Rather than terminate valued employees, management may transfer them to other areas within the organization. These transfers may entail moving an employee to another desk in the same office or to a location halfway around the world.

A second reason for transfers is to make positions available in the primary promotion channels. Firms are typically organized into a hierarchical structure resembling a pyramid. Each succeeding promotion is more difficult to obtain because fewer positions exist. At times, very productive but unpromotable workers may clog promotion channels. Other qualified workers in the organization may find their opportunities for promotion blocked. When this happens, a firm's most capable future managers may seek employment elsewhere. To keep promotion channels open, the firm may decide to transfer employees who are unpromotable but productive at their organizational level.

Another reason for transfers is to satisfy employees' personal desires. The reasons for wanting a transfer are numerous. An individual may need to accompany a transferred spouse to a new location or work closer to home to care for aging parents, or the worker may dislike the long commute to and from work. Factors such as these may be of sufficient importance that employees may resign if a requested transfer is not approved. Rather than risk losing a valued employee, the firm may agree to the transfer.

Transfers may also be an effective means of dealing with personality clashes. Some people just cannot get along with one another. Because each of the individuals may be a valued employee, transfer may be an appropriate solution to the problem. But managers must be cautious regarding the *grass is always greener on the other side of the fence* syndrome. When some workers encounter a temporary setback, they immediately ask for a transfer before they even attempt to work through the problem.

Finally, because of a limited number of management levels, it is becoming necessary for managers to have a wide variety of experiences before achieving a promotion. Individuals who desire upward mobility often explore possible lateral moves so that they can learn new skills.

If the worker initiates the transfer request, it should be analyzed in terms of the best interests of both the firm and the individual. Disruptions may occur when the worker is transferred. For example, a qualified worker might not be available to step into the position being vacated. Management should establish clear policies regarding transfers. Such policies let workers know in advance when a transfer request is likely to be approved and what its ramifications will be. For instance, if the transfer is for personal reasons, some firms do not pay moving costs. Whether the organization will or will not pay these expenses should be clearly spelled out.

## Promotions

A **promotion** is the movement of a person to a higher-level position in the organization. The term *promotion* is one of the most emotionally charged words in the field of human resource management. An individual who receives a promotion normally receives additional financial rewards and the ego boost associated with achievement and accomplishment. Most employees feel good about being promoted. But for every individual who gains a promotion, there are probably others who were not selected. If these individuals wanted the promotion badly enough or their favorite candidate was overlooked, they may slack off or even resign. If the consensus of employees directly involved is that the wrong person was promoted, considerable resentment may result.

As discussed in Chapter 9, promotions will not be as available in the future as in the past. For one thing, many firms have reduced the number of levels in their hierarchies. As the number of middle management positions declined, fewer promotional opportunities were available. The effect of these changes is that more people will be striving for fewer promotion opportunities. Consequently, organizations must look for ways other than promotion to reward employees. One alternative is the dual-track system that we described in Chapter 9, whereby highly skilled technical workers can continue to receive financial rewards without progressing into management.

**Promotion**
The movement of a person to a higher-level position in an organization.

# Resignations

Even when an organization is totally committed to making its environment a good place to work, workers will still resign. Some employees cannot see promotional opportunities—or at least not enough—and will therefore move on. A certain amount of turnover is healthy for an organization and is often necessary to afford employees the opportunity to fulfill career objectives. When turnover becomes excessive, however, the firm must do something to slow it. The most qualified employees are often the ones who resign because they are more mobile.[48] On the other hand, marginally qualified workers never seem to leave. If excessive numbers of a firm's highly qualified and competent workers are leaving, a way must be found to reverse the trend.

**The Exit Interview: Analyzing Voluntary Resignations.** An **exit interview** is a means of revealing the real reasons employees leave their jobs, providing the organization with information on how to correct the causes of discontent, and reducing employee turnover.[49] Recently, it has been used as a means of protecting an organization against wrongful dismissal.[50] The most common reason individuals give for taking a job with another company is more money. This explanation, however, may not reveal other weaknesses in the organization. Upon investigation, it may be discovered that a weak manager is the cause of the resignation; perhaps an unqualified person had been placed in a management position.[51] Exit interviews can help the organization keep high-quality people by discovering and solving problems before they get out of control.[52]

When a firm wants to determine the real reasons that individuals decide to leave, it can use the exit interview and/or the postexit questionnaire. Often a third party conducts the exit interview because many former employees will not air their problems in the organization. The typical exit interview involves the following aspects:

- Establishing rapport
- Stating the purpose of the interview
- Exploring the employee's attitudes regarding the old job
- Exploring the worker's reasons for leaving
- Comparing old and new jobs
- Recording the changes recommended by the employee
- Concluding the interview[53]

Specific topics that might be covered by the interviewer during the exit interview are listed in Figure 16-5. Note that the interviewer is focusing on job-related factors and probing for the real reasons the person is leaving. Over a period of time, properly conducted exit interviews can provide considerable insight into why employees are leaving. Patterns are often identified that uncover weaknesses in the firm's human resource management system. Knowledge of the problem permits corrective action to be taken. Also, the exit interview helps to identify training and development needs, to create strategic planning objectives, and to identify those areas in which changes need to be made.

When a postexit questionnaire is used, it is sent to former employees several weeks after they leave the organization. Usually, they have already started work at their new companies. The questionnaire is structured to draw out the real reason the employee left. Ample blank space is provided so that a former employee can express his or her feelings about and perceptions of the job and the organization. One strength of this approach is that the individuals are no longer with the firm and may respond more freely to the questions. A weakness is that the interviewer is not present to interpret and probe for the real reasons the person left.

**Exit Interview Questions Related to General Job Factors**     Figure 16-5

*Source:* Wanda R. Embrey, R. Wayne Mondy, and Robert M. Noe, "Exit Interview: A Tool for Personnel Development." Reprinted from the May 1979 issue of *Personnel Administrator,* copyright 1979. Reprinted with permission from *HRMagazine* (formerly *Personnel Administrator*), published by the Society for Human Resource Management, Alexandria, Virginia.

**Attitude Surveys: A Means of Retaining Quality Employees.** Exit interviews can provide valuable information for improving human resource management practices. A more contented workforce should result. The problem is, however, that these approaches are reactions to events that are detrimental to the organization. The very people you want to save may be the ones being interviewed or completing questionnaires.

An alternative, proactive approach is administering attitude surveys (survey feedback was described in Chapter 8). **Attitude surveys** seek input from employees to determine their feelings about topics such as the work they perform, their supervisor, their work environment, flexibility in the workplace, opportunities for advancement, training and development opportunities, and the firm's compensation system. Since some employees will want their responses to be confidential, every effort should be made to guarantee their anonymity. To achieve this, it may be necessary to have the survey administered by a third party. Regardless of how the process is handled, it is clear that attitude surveys have the potential to improve management practices. For this reason, attitude surveys are widely used throughout industry today.[54]

**Attitude survey**
A survey of employees' feelings about topics such as the work they perform, their supervisor, their work environment, flexibility in the workplace, opportunities for advancement, training and development opportunities, and the firm's compensation system.

Employees should be advised of the purpose of the survey and also the results. The mere act of giving such a survey communicates to employees that management is aware that problems within the firm can be solved. Analyzing survey results of various subgroups and comparing them with the firm's total population may indicate areas that should be investigated and problems that need to be solved. Management must be willing to make needed changes, and if the survey does not result in some improvements, the process may be a real turn-off for employees.

**Advance Notice of Resignation.** Most firms would like to have at least two-weeks' notice of resignation from departing workers.[55] However, a month's notice may be desired from professional and managerial employees who are leaving. When the firm desires notice, the policy should be clearly communicated to all employees. If they want departing employees to give advance notice, companies have certain obligations. For instance, suppose that a worker who gives notice is terminated immediately. Word of this action will spread rapidly to other employees. Later, should they decide to resign, they will likely not give any advance notice.

In addition, treating departing employees as if they were second-class citizens should be avoided.[56] However, permitting a worker to remain on the job once a resignation has been submitted may create some problems. If bad feelings exist between the employee and the supervisor or the company, the departing worker may be a disruptive force. On a selective basis, the firm may wish to pay some employees for the notice time and ask them to leave immediately, especially to maintain control of business operations and staff planning.[57]

## Retirements

Many long-term employees leave an organization by retiring. Retirement plans may be based on attaining a certain age, working a certain number of years with the firm, or both. Upon retirement, former employees usually receive compensation either from a defined benefits plan or a defined contributions plan, both of which were discussed in Chapter 12.

Sometimes employees will be offered early retirement before reaching the organization's normal length-of-service requirement. Often retirement pay is reduced for each year that the retirement date is advanced. From an organization's viewpoint, early employee retirement has both positive and negative aspects.

Early retirement is often viewed as an attractive solution when staff reductions need to be made. Dayton, Ohio–based NCR Corporation recently offered an early retirement option to 1,200 of its most senior U.S. technical service employees. According to the company, it is making the early retirement offer due to an excess of highly skilled workers on its payroll.[58] If an extended layoff is expected, a product line is being discontinued, or a plant is being closed, early retirement may be a responsible solution to the problem of surplus employees.

From a negative viewpoint, valued employees may take advantage of the early retirement option and leave the organization. In addition, early retirement is often more expensive to the company than normal retirement. And early retirement decisions are often made on short notice, resulting in some disruption of a company's operations.

## EVALUATING THE HUMAN RESOURCE MANAGEMENT FUNCTION

Throughout this book, we have stressed that the HR function is now being measured just like any other department.[59] The success of any organization depends not only on the formulation and execution of superb plans but also on the continuous evaluation of progress toward the accomplishment of specified objectives. For an organization as a whole, evaluation may be performed in terms of profitability ratios, sales increases, market penetration, and a host of other factors.

How should an organization go about evaluating its human resource management function? An HR self-audit of the functional areas is a good place to start.[60] In this audit, the goal is to determine how well a function is being managed for value added. Are there particular measures or indicators that reveal how well this function is meeting its responsibilities and supporting the organization's efforts to reach its objectives? The two basic methods that may be used to evaluate human resource management activities are checklists and quantitative measures.

The checklist approach poses a number of questions that can be answered either *yes* or *no*. This method is concerned with determining whether important activities have been recognized and, if so, whether they are being performed.

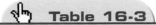
▶ Are all legally mandated reports submitted to requiring agencies on time?
▶ Have formalized procedures and methods been developed for conducting job analysis?
▶ Are forecasts for human resource requirements made at least annually?
▶ Is the recruiting process effectively integrated with human resource planning?
▶ Does the application form conform to applicable legal and affirmative action standards?
▶ Are all employees appraised at least annually?
▶ Are skills inventories maintained on all employees?
▶ Are career opportunities communicated clearly to all employees?

Essentially, the checklist is an evaluation of what should be done and the extent to which it is being done. Some typical human resource checklist questions are shown in Table 16-3. The more *yes* answers there are, the better the evaluation; *no* answers indicate areas or activities where follow-up or additional work is needed to increase HRM's effectiveness. Organizations deciding to use this evaluation approach will undoubtedly come up with many other questions to ask. The checklist method is purely an internal evaluation device and might be considered a first step in the audit.

The other method for evaluating the performance of human resource activities is a quantitative one. It relies on the accumulation of various types of numerical data and the calculation of certain ratios from them. Numerical data are useful primarily as an indicator of activity levels and trends. Ratios show results that are important in themselves but that also reveal (when maintained over a period of time) trends that may be even more important. Possible human resource areas to track include recruitment, turnover, absenteeism, salary levels, temporary help, overtime, unemployment, insurance, and workers' compensation. For instance, what is the cost of recruiting a particular skill? Is one recruitment method superior to another? Employment agencies are commonly used, but they are expensive, so could other methods be more cost effective?[61] Some examples of quantitative measures for human resource management are listed in Table 16-4.

▶ Women and minorities selection ratio
▶ Women and minorities promotion ratio
▶ Women and minorities termination ratio
▶ Minority and women hiring percentage
▶ Minority and women workforce percentage
▶ Requirements forecast compared to actual human resource needs
▶ Availability forecast compared to actual availability of human resources
▶ Average recruiting cost per applicant
▶ Average recruiting cost per employee hired
▶ Percentage of positions filled internally
▶ Average testing cost per applicant
▶ Percentage of required appraisals actually completed
▶ Percentage of employees rated in highest performance category
▶ Percentage of appraisals appealed
▶ Turnover percentage
▶ New-hire retention percentage
▶ Percentage of new hires lost

## Global Transfers and Spouse Relocation Packages

A trailing spouse resigns from his or her job and relocates with a spouse who has been transferred to a different country. This is hardly a unique concept today, but it has become a greater problem for families and employers in recent years and will likely continue as globalization becomes more common. Employers have to deal with the problems associated with trailing spouses if workers are to take global assignments.

Reasons for failure to relocate vary, but according to *Human Resources Executive* magazine, "Forty-two percent of the families surveyed reported a decreased standard of living after relocating." Subsequently, more companies are offering relocation packages to encourage workers to take global assignments. According to Linda Leslie, senior consultant at Lee Hecht Harrison, "Companies are realizing that employees are going to be happy if their families are happy." A relocation package can simply include literature and recommendations about a community's child care, schools, real estate services, recreation facilities, and other similar information. However, some companies also cover expenses associated with relocation, including moving costs, closing costs or expenses from the sale of a home, a stipend for incidentals, and the cost of rent while the employee shops for a house or apartment. A relocation package can also contain career counseling and hiring services for a trailing spouse.[62]

A detailed example of a quantitative analysis is provided next. To help compute a more precise figure so that companies can create benchmarks and properly assign resources for retention and recruitment, the consulting firm of Kepner-Tregoe, Inc. developed a formula for computing turnover cost. The Turnover Cost Formula involves the following measures:[63]

▶ Select a department or job function that has high turnover.
▶ Use an actual number or estimate the number of people who left during the past 12 months; write that number on line 4.
▶ The average cost of turnover is 25 percent of an employee's annual salary (line 1) plus the cost of the benefits (line 2). Typical benefits amount to about 30 percent of wages (the total cost of a complete benefits package on top of payroll). The total cost per employee (line 3) is the total of line 1 and line 2.

1. Annual wage: _____ × .25 = _____
2. Annual benefits: _____ × .30 = _____
3. Total turnover cost per employee (line 1 + line 2) = _____
4. Total number of employees who left = _____
5. Total cost of turnover (line 3 × line 4) = _____

Today, it is important for human resources to receive the same degree of cost evaluation as operations.

## ▶ Summary

### ❶ Describe internal employee relations.

Internal employee relations consists of the human resource management activities associated with the movement of employees within the firm after they have become organizational members. It includes the actions of promotion, transfer, demotion, resignation, discharge, layoff, and retirement. Discipline and disciplinary action are also included.

**② Explain discipline and disciplinary action.**

Discipline is the state of employee self-control and orderly conduct present within an organization. It indicates the extent of genuine teamwork that exists. Disciplinary action occurs when a penalty is invoked against an employee who fails to meet established standards.

**③ Explain how grievance handling is typically conducted under a collective bargaining agreement.**

Workers who believe that they have been disciplined or dealt with unjustly can appeal through the grievance and arbitration procedures of the collective bargaining agreement.

**④ Explain how grievance handling is typically conducted in union-free firms.**

The means of resolving complaints in union-free firms vary. A well-designed union-free grievance procedure ensures that the worker has ample opportunity to make complaints without fear of reprisal.

**⑤ Define *alternative dispute resolution.***

Alternative dispute resolution (ADR) is a procedure whereby the employee and the company agree ahead of time that any problems will be addressed by an agreed-upon means.

**⑥ Describe how termination conditions may differ with regard to nonmanagerial/nonprofessional employees, executives, managers, and professionals.**

The conditions for termination differ considerably with regard to nonmanagerial/nonprofessional employees, executives, managers, and professionals.

**⑦ Explain the concept of employment at will.**

Employment at will is an unwritten contract that is created when an employee agrees to work for an employer but there is no agreement as to how long the parties expect the employment to last.

**⑧ Describe demotion as an alternative to termination.**

At times demotions are used as an alternative to discharge, especially when a long-term employee is involved. Demotion is the process of moving a worker to a lower level of duties and responsibilities, which typically involves a reduction in pay. If demotion is chosen over termination, efforts must be made to preserve the self-esteem of the individual.

**⑨ Explain downsizing and layoffs.**

Downsizing, also known as restructuring and rightsizing, is essentially the reverse of a company growing and suggests a one-time change in the organization and the number of people employed. Tied very closely to downsizing are layoffs, which also reduce the number of people employed for a certain period of time.

**⑩ Describe transfers, promotions, resignations, and retirements as factors involved in internal employee relations.**

The lateral movement of a worker within an organization is called a transfer. A promotion is the movement of a person to a higher-level position in the organization. Even when an organization is totally committed to making its environment a good place to work, workers will still resign. One of the last phases of internal employee relations is retirements.

**⑪ Explain the importance of evaluating the human resource management functions.**

It is important for human resources to receive the same degree of cost evaluation as does operations.

# ▶ Questions for Review

1. Define *internal employee relations.*

2. Distinguish between discipline and disciplinary action.

3. Describe the following approaches to disciplinary action:

   a. hot stove rule
   b. progressive disciplinary action
   c. disciplinary action without punishment

4. In progressive disciplinary action, what steps are involved before employee termination?

5. What are the steps that should typically be followed in handling a grievance under a collective bargaining agreement?

6. Why is arbitration often used in the settlement of grievances in a unionized firm?

7. How would grievances typically be handled in a union-free firm? Describe briefly.

8. Define alternative dispute resolution (ADR). What is the purpose of ADR?

9. How does termination often differ with regard to nonmanagerial/nonprofessional employees, executives, managers, and professionals?

10. What is meant by the phrase *employment at will?*

11. Briefly describe the techniques available to determine the real reasons that an individual decides to leave the organization.

12. Distinguish between demotions, transfers, and promotions.

13. Why is it important to evaluate the human resource management function?

14. How should an organization go about evaluating its human resource management function?

TAKE IT TO THE NET    *We invite you to visit the Mondy homepage on the Prentice Hall Web site at*

**www.prenhall.com/mondy**

*for updated information, Web-based exercises, and links to other HR-related sites.*

# ▶ Developing HRM Skills

## *An Experiential Exercise*

Isadore Lamansky is the manager of the machine tooling operations at Lone Star Industries and has five supervisors who report to him. One of his employees is Susie Canton, a supervisor in maintenance. As Isadore comes to work this morning, his thoughts focus on Susie. "Today is the day that I must talk to Susie. I sure hate to do it. I know she is going to take it the wrong way. Ever since Susie was promoted to unit supervisor, she has had trouble maintaining discipline. She tries too hard to keep the men in line because she thinks they are continually trying to push her, and she lets the women get away with murder. Well, I guess I'll get this over with, since that's what I get paid for."

One person will play Susie, and another person will play Isadore. All others should observe carefully. The instructor will provide additional information to participants.

---

HRM INCIDENT 1 ◀

### To Heck with Them!

Isabelle Anderson is the North Carolina plant manager for Hall Manufacturing Company, a company that produces a line of relatively inexpensive painted wood furniture. Six months ago Isabelle became concerned about the turnover rate among workers in the painting department. Manufacturing plant turnover rates in that part of the South generally averaged about 30 percent, which was the case at Hall. The painting department, however, had experienced a turnover of nearly 200 percent in each of the last two years. Because of the limited number of skilled workers in the area, Hall had introduced an extensive training program for new painters, and Isabelle knew that the high turnover rate was very costly.

Isabelle conducted exit interviews with many of the departing painters. Many of them said that they were leaving for more money, others mentioned better benefits, and some cited some kind of personal reason for quitting. But there was nothing to help Isabelle pinpoint the problem. Isabelle had checked and found that Hall's wages and benefits were competitive with, if not better than, those of other manufacturers in the area. She then called in Nelson Able, the painting supervisor, to discuss the problem. Nelson's response was, "To heck with them! They will do it my way or they can hit the road. You know how this younger generation is. They work to get enough money to live on for a few weeks and then quit. I don't worry about it. Our old-timers can take up the slack." After listening to Nelson for a moment, Isabelle thought that she might know what caused the turnover problem.

#### Questions

1. Do you believe that the exit surveys were accurate? Explain your answer.
2. What do you believe was the cause of the turnover problem?

---

HRM INCIDENT 2 ◀

### I Wasn't Sleeping

As Norman Blankenship came to the office at Consolidated Coal Company's Rowland mine, near Clear Creek, West Virginia, he told the mine dispatcher not to tell anyone of his presence. Norman was the general superintendent of the Rowland operation. He had been with Consolidated for more than 23 years, having started out as a coal digger.

Norman had heard that one of his section bosses, Tom Serinsky, had been sleeping on the job. Tom had been hired two months earlier and assigned to the Rowland mine by the regional human resource office. He went to work as section boss, working the midnight to 8:00 A.M. shift. Because of his age and experience, Tom was the senior person in the mine on his shift.

Norman took one of the battery-operated jeeps used to transport workers and supplies in and out of the mine and proceeded to the area where Tom was assigned. Upon arriving, he saw Tom lying on an emergency stretcher. Norman stopped his jeep a few yards away from where Tom was sleeping and approached him. "Hey, you asleep?" Norman asked.

Tom awakened with a start and said, "No, I wasn't sleeping."

Norman waited a moment for Tom to collect his senses and then said, "I could tell that you were sleeping. But that is beside the point. You were not at your work station. You know that I have no choice but to fire you."

After Tom had left, Norman called his mine supervisor, who had accompanied him to the dispatcher's office, and asked him to complete the remainder of Tom's shift.

The next morning, Norman had the mine human resource officer officially terminate Tom. As part of the standard procedure, the mine human resource officer notified the regional human resource director that Tom had been fired and gave the reason for firing him. The regional director asked the human resource officer to put Norman on the line. When he did so, Norman was told, "Did you know that Tom is the brother-in-law of our regional vice president, Bill Frederick?"

"No, I didn't know that," replied Norman, "but it doesn't matter. The rules are clear, and I wouldn't care if he was the regional vice president's son."

The next day the regional director showed up at the mine just as Norman was getting ready to make a routine tour of the mine. "I guess you know what I'm here for," said the regional director.

"Yeah, you're here to take away my authority," replied Norman.

"No, I'm just here to investigate," said the regional director.

When Norman returned to the mine office after his tour, the regional director had finished his interviews. He told Norman, "I think we are going to have to put Tom back to work. If we decided to do that, can you let him work for you?"

"No, absolutely not," replied Norman. "In fact, if he works here, I go."

A week later Norman learned that Tom had gone back to work as section boss at another Consolidated coal mine in the region.

### Questions

1. What would you do now if you were Norman?
2. Do you believe that the regional director handled the matter in an ethical manner? Explain.

## ▶ Notes

1. Janine S. Pouliot, "Workers Are Not the Usual Suspects," *Nation's Business* 86 (February 1998): 48(1).

2. Shari Caudron, "Bashing HR on the Web," *Workforce* 78 (December 1999): 37.

3. Fred Elliott, "Basics of Head and Face Protection," *Occupational Health & Safety* 69 (March 2000): 60–63.

4. Charles Cresson Wood, "Integrated Approach Information Security," *Security* 37 (February 2000): 43–44.

5. Ed Lisoski, "Discipline Is for Children," *Supervision* 60 (May 1999): 3–5.

6. Herff L. Moore and Helen L. Moore, "Discipline + Help = Motivation," *Credit Union Management* 21 (August 1998): 33.

7. Paul Falcone, "Adopt a Formal Approach to Progressive Discipline," *HRMagazine* 43 (November 1998): 55–59.

8. Lauren M. Bernardi, "Progressive Discipline: Effective Management Tool or Legal Trap?" *Canadian Manager* 21 (January 1996): 9.

9. Lisa Leland, "Chat, Don't Chasten," *American Printer* 222 (February 1999): 94.

10. Gary A. Bielous, "Five Worst Disciplinary Mistakes (and How to Avoid Them)," *Supervision* (August 1998): 11–13.

11. Wallace Wohlking, "Effective Discipline in Employee Relations," *Personnel Journal* 54 (September 1975): 489.

12. Ed Lisoski, "Nine Common Mistakes Made When Disciplining Employees," *Supervision* 59 (October 1998): 12–14.

13. Kristen Gerencher, "Enterprise Careers: Tackling Terminations," *InfoWorld* 21 (March 1, 1999): 77–78.

14. "Firing for Pornographic e-mail Deemed Excessive by Arbitrator," *HR Focus* 77 (May 2000): 2.

15. Susan C. Zuckerman, "Labor: Manifest Disregard of the Evidence," *Dispute Resolution Journal* 55 (February 2000): 89–90.

16. Paul Falcone, "A Legal Dichotomy?" *HR Magazine* 44 (May 1999): 110–120.

17. "Avoiding Legal Pitfalls in the Disciplinary Process," *Association Management* 51 (March 1999): 81.

18. Jennifer Laabs, "Remedies for HR's Legal Headache," *Personnel Journal* 73 (December 1994): 69.

19. Michael Barrier, "A Working Alternative for Settling Disputes," *Nation's Business* 86 (July 1, 1998): 43–46.

20. "Up for Arbitration: How to Get the Most Out of Alternative Dispute Resolution," *Black Enterprise* 29 (January 31, 1999): 39.

21. "Memorandum on Agency Use of Alternate Means of Dispute Resolution and Negotiated Rulemaking" (Transcript), *Weekly Compilation of Presidential Documents* 34 (May 4, 1998): 749(2).

22. Adin C. Goldberg, "How to Craft Enforceable Arbitration Agreements," *HR Focus* 76 (October 1999): 10.

23. Christiaan M. Stone, "Arbitration Agreements Lessen EEOC's Power to Sue," *HR Focus* 77 (January 2000): 3.

24. "Agreement Binds Broker to Arbitrate Sex Bias Claim," *HR Focus* 76 (October 1999): 3.

25. "Firing: Letting People Go with Dignity Is Good for Business," *HR Focus* 77 (January 2000): 10.

26. Gerensher, "Enterprise Careers: Tackling Terminations."

27. "Another Day, Another Workplace Event," *Workforce* 79 (February 2000): 36.

28. Richard S. Deems, "When You Have to Fire Someone," *Executive Excellence* 16 (February 1999): 10.

29. "Goodbye, CEO," *Workforce* 79 (May 2000): 26.

30. Falcone, "A Legal Dichotomy?"

31. Gregg M. Bishop, "Discipline and Safety," *Occupational Health & Safety* 68 (May 1999): 16–20.

32. Del Jones, "Fired Workers Fight Back . . . and Win: Laws, Juries Shift Protection to Terminated Employees," *USA Today* (April 2, 1998): 1B.

33. Gillian Flynn, "How Do You Treat the At-Will Employment Relationship?" *Workforce* 79 (June 2000): 178–179.

34. Mark H. McCormack, "Boss Sends You a Message with Demotion," *The Arizona Republic* (October 1, 1998): 4.

35. "Kodak to Cut Workforce by up to 2,500," *Reuters Business Report* (July 21, 1999).

36. Simon Hirschfeld, "Focus-Corporate Layoffs Tied to Booming Economy," *Reuters Business Report* (August 9, 1999): 1.

37. Sherry Kuczynski, "Help! I Shrunk the Company!" *HRMagazine* 44 (June 1999): 40–45.

38. Jaclyn Fierman, "Beating the Midlife Career Crisis," *Fortune* 128 (September 6, 1993): 53.

39. Shari Caudron, "Rebuilding Employee Trust," *Training & Development* 50 (August 1996): 18.

40. Robert J. Grossman, "Short-Term Workers Raise Long-Term Issues: Greater Flexibility and Cost Savings Make Contingent Workers a Viable Strategy—But Watch Out for the Traps," *HR Magazine* 43 (April 1998): 80–89.

41. Kuczynski, "Help! I Shrunk the Company!"

42. "Fewer Mass Layoffs," *Monthly Labor Review* (March 2000): 2.

43. "Layoffs at Large Companies Help Small Ones Find Talent," *HR Focus* 76 (June 1999): S4.

44. Tony Simper, "Outplacement—A Justifiable Expense," *Insurance Brokers' Monthly and Insurance Advisor* 50 (June 2000): 31.

45. Philip Schofield, "Survivors of the Axe Get a Helping Hand," *Independent on Sunday* (March 21, 1999): 2.

46. William J. Morin, "Smart Managing/You Inc.: You Are Absolutely Positively on Your Own, Outplacement Is Dead, and Truth about Your Future Is Hard to Come by at Many Companies," *Fortune* 134 (December 9, 1996): 222.

47. "Lateral Moves Outweigh Promotions for Transferees," *HR Focus* 76 (October 1999): 16.

48. Marilyn Moats Kennedy, "What Managers Can Find Out from Exit Interviews," *Physician Executive* 22 (October 1996): 45.

49. Maureen Smith, "Getting Value from Exit Interviews," *Association Management* 52 (April 2000): 22.

50. Wes Spence, "Exit Interviews—A Key Ingredient to Successful Employee Relations," ent-net.com/collumns/employee (February 27, 2000).

51. Andrea C. Poe, "Make Foresight 20/20," *HRMagazine* 45 (February 2000): 74–80.

52. Rick Saia, "Parting Shots," *Computerworld* 33 (January 25, 1999): 58.

53. Wanda R. Embrey, R. Wayne Mondy, and Robert M. Noe, "Exit Interview: A Tool for Personnel Development," *Personnel Administrator* 24 (May 1979): 46.

54. Theodore Kunin, "The Construction of a New Type of Attitude Measure," *Personnel Psychology* 51 (Winter 1998): 823.

55. Paul Falcone, "Resignations," *HRMagazine* 44 (April 1999): 125.

56. Robin Kessler, "Employee Relations Say Good-Bye with Style: When Employers and HR Professionals Don't Leave Departing Employees with a Good Feeling, the Cost to the Organization Can Be Surprisingly High," *HR Magazine* 43 (June 1998): 171–174.

57. Falcone, "Resignations."

58. "NCR Offers Early Retirement to 1,200 Employees," *Employee Benefit Plan Review* (January 2000): 47.

59. Melody Jones, "Four Trends to Reckon with," *HR Focus* 73 (July 1996): 23.

60. "Is It Time to Try an Employment Practice Audit?" *HR Focus* 77 (June 2000): 9.

61. Nancy Sorensen, "Measuring HR for Success," *Training & Development* 49 (November 1995): 49.

62. Vicky Uhland, "If Mama's Not Happy . . . Employers Bear the Brunt of 'Trailing Spouses' Problem," *Denver Rocky Mountain News* (July 25, 1999): 1J.

63. "How Much Does Turnover Really Cost?" *HR Focus* 77 (May 2000): 9.

In this video we return to Quicktakes, the film production company introduced in Part 2.

Like many workers in specialized professions, the actors hired by Quicktakes in this video are union members. As you've learned from Chapter 14, labor unions in the United States have experienced periods of expansion and contraction throughout their history. After declining during the 1980s and 1990s, for example, union membership appears to be on the rise again, thanks in part to aggressive campaigns in traditionally nonunion industries.

Some managers fear any kind of interaction with labor unions. The threat of strikes, slowdowns, and job actions becomes very real when contract negotiations are strained or bogged down. While they are infrequent and represent the extreme of poor labor-management relations, these are still viewed as powerful negotiating strategies and often prove detrimental to the firm's morale, public image, and bottom line. But management can often contribute a great deal to creating a positive relationship with labor, and there are many specific actions, some outlined in Chapter 15, that managers can take to prevent minor disagreements from reaching the status of a grievance.

The first of these is to develop a work environment in which grievances don't need to occur. (Recall that a grievance is an employee's belief that the union contract has been violated by management. That initiates a formal procedure for determining whether a violation in fact took place.) From what you'll see of Quicktakes' oil company video operation in this video, you may be able to form an opinion about whether this kind of environment exists there.

You may also want to keep in mind the do's and don'ts for handling grievance procedures that are outlined in Chapter 16, since they are useful strategies for many kinds of interaction with unions. Some recommended actions include giving the employee a good and fair hearing, and holding grievance discussions in private. Actions to avoid include making arrangements inconsistent with the contract and refusing to admit it if the company is wrong. It will probably be clear to you from this video segment that acting hastily is also to be avoided.

The reason for guidelines like these is to protect the manager (and the firm) from making errors that could result in an escalation of the disagreement. It is thus important for managers to have a good understanding of any union contracts that are in effect at their firm and to master the skills of working successfully with union employees and their representatives.

Disciplinary measures and dismissal are major sources of grievances. Perhaps if Hal were aware of this, he might react differently in the situation you are about to see.

## Discussion Questions

1. Grievances are often merely a symptom of an underlying problem. Do you think this is the case here? If so, why? What do you think Jim's real problem is? What should he do about it?

2. Do you think Hal is doing everything he can to maintain a good relationship with the actors' union? Why or why not? If not, what more could he do, or what could he do differently?

3. Is Hal using good management techniques in dealing with Jim? Do you think Jim is a problem employee? What might Hal do differently in managing Jim?

4. What unintended effect will Hal's suspension of Jim have on Caitlin? What should Hal do about it?

5. Does Jim have good grounds for a grievance? Assuming he does, what actions should Hal take immediately, and what other, more extensive, preparations should be make?

# chapter

# 17

 ## Objectives

- Describe the evolution of global business.
- Explain the development of global human resource management.
- Describe the global human resource management functions.
- Explain possible barriers to effective global human resource management.
- Explain global equal employment opportunity.
- Describe the keys to global human resource management of expatriates.
- Explain the importance of maintaining corporate identity through corporate culture.

# Global Human Resource Management

n 1989, Boundless Technologies, headquartered in Hauppauge, Long Island, moved its network computer manufacturing operation to Hong Kong. Moving production to Hong Kong meant dealing with a new workforce, a new work environment, new pay structures, and a multitude of other global HR issues. High wage rates were the driving force behind the relocation decision, with Hong Kong wages being much less than those in Long Island. Unfortunately, the move was made primarily to escape high wage pressures, without regard to other HR issues.

Surprisingly, only a few years after moving to Hong Kong, Boundless returned to the United States, creating even more HR problems and requiring another massive HR effort. Failure to consider all of the problems that could result when relocating

globally caused major disruptions in Boundless Technologies' operations. Basically, Boundless returned to the United States to be closer to its consumer base and because the company could achieve high productivity rates here that could nearly offset the higher wage expense.

Globalization is multidimensional and must be considered with a strategic vision, taking into account all factors that impact business performance. Currently, management decisions focus on accomplishing the corporate mission rather than just zeroing in on factors such as cost savings. In line with that approach, Boundless recently bought a 70,000-square-foot manufacturing plant in Boca Raton, Florida. Having two U.S. plants diversifies its production capabilities and expands its geographic manufacturing base, while further complicating HR. Even with the expansion, Boundless will remain small and nimble, with the ability to quickly adapt to global market conditions.[1]

**B**oundless Technologies is a real company that actually did return to the United States and has been able to compete—even with higher U.S. wage rates—to the point of expanding by buying another plant in Boca Raton. If human resource issues had been carefully considered prior to the overseas move, it may have become evident that factors other than wage rates have equal or even greater importance. While an American-type factory can be constructed overseas, it will not necessarily operate as an American factory does. Managing people in global organizations is much more complex than ever, not only because of the rapidly changing and increasingly complicated global work environments, but also because these environments are often so different.

In the first part of this chapter, we discuss the evolution of global business and the development of global human resource management. Next, the global human resource management functions will be explained and possible barriers to effective global human resource management described. Global equal employment opportunity will then be discussed. The remainder of the chapter is devoted to describing keys to global HR management of expatriates and explaining the importance of maintaining corporate identity through corporate culture.

Without question, General Electric CEO Jack Welch's statement that "organizations must either globalize or they die" is a truth about the twenty first-century economy. Today, almost 50 percent of the U.S. economy is based on exports and imports. U.S. corporations have invested more than $1 trillion abroad and employ more than 100 million overseas workers.[2] More and more American companies are, like Coca-Cola, IBM, Ford, and General Motors, evolving into truly global corporations. For companies to grow in today's domestic economic environment, they must expand overseas. Global expansion is necessary for the continued existence of many firms, regardless of their size or the products and services they offer. Given the mature markets that exist in the United States and other countries, business growth depends on building new markets in developing countries.[3]

Twenty years ago, many U.S. multinational corporations had operations in Canada but not in many other countries. Today, most international corporations are becoming truly global. American companies still regularly do business in Canada, but many now have operations in Hong Kong, Singapore, Japan, the United Kingdom, France, Vietnam, and Germany, to name a few. More and more U.S. global corporations are doing business in former Eastern Bloc countries. This interdependence of national economies has created a global marketplace in which worldwide products and services are bought and sold. The globalization of the marketplace has created special human resource challenges that will endure well into the next century. Unfortunately, most HR managers have never worked abroad and are not adequately prepared to cope with the global environment.[4]

Normally, companies evolve to the point of being truly global over an extended period. Most companies initially become global without making substantial investments in foreign countries, by either exporting, licensing, or franchising. **Exporting** means selling abroad, either directly or indirectly, by retaining foreign agents and distributors. **Licensing** is an arrangement whereby an organization grants a foreign firm the right to use intellectual properties such as patents, copyrights, manufacturing processes, or trade names for a specific period of time. **Franchising** is a similar option, in which the parent company grants another firm the right to do business in a prescribed manner. Franchisees must follow stricter operational guidelines than do licensees. Licensing is usually limited to manufacturers, while franchising is popular with service firms such as restaurants and hotels.

Although exporting, licensing, and franchising are good initial entry options, in order to take full advantage of global opportunities, companies must make a substantial investment of their own funds in another country. Generally, global investment refers to operations in one country that are controlled by entities in another country. For example, Mercedes-Benz built its new sport utility vehicle production facility outside of Germany, in Vance, Alabama. Often, a foreign investment means acquiring control of more than 50 percent of a global operation, as did Daimler-Benz when it purchased the Chrysler Corporation, which became DaimlerChrysler.

Companies can vary greatly in their degree of global involvement, but an international business is any firm that engages in global trade and/or investment. The multinational corporation is one type of global business enterprise. A **multinational corporation (MNC)** is a firm that is based in one country (the parent or home country) and produces goods or provides services in one or more foreign countries (host countries). A multinational corporation directs manufacturing and marketing operations in several countries; these operations are coordinated by a parent

**Exporting**
Selling abroad, either directly or indirectly, by retaining foreign agents and distributors.

**Licensing**
A global arrangement whereby an organization grants a foreign firm the right to use intellectual properties such as patents, copyrights, manufacturing processes, or trade names for a specific period of time.

**Franchising**
A multinational option whereby the parent company grants another firm the right to do business in a prescribed manner.

**Multinational corporation (MNC)**
A firm that is based in one country (the parent or home country) and produces goods or provides services in one or more foreign countries (host countries).

**www.prenhall.com/mondy**

Various global issues including associations in many different countries are presented at this site.

company, usually based in the firm's home country. General Motors and Ford have evolved beyond being multinational corporations to become truly global.

A **global corporation (GC)** has corporate units in a number of countries that are integrated to operate as one organization worldwide. While the multinational corporation operates in a number of countries and adapts its products and practices to each, the global corporation operates as if the entire world were one entity. Global corporations sell essentially the same products in the same manner throughout the world with components that may be made and/or designed in different countries. Expectations are that as the world becomes more globally open, the globalization of corporations will become much more commonplace. **Globalization** is the creation of shareholder value worldwide through differentiation and competitive advantage. Going global places new demands on and creates new opportunities in each area of a firm, particularly HR.

**Global corporation (GC)**
An organization that has corporate units in a number of countries; the units are integrated to operate as one organization worldwide.

**Globalization**
The creation of shareholder value worldwide through differentiation and competitive advantage.

## THE DEVELOPMENT OF GLOBAL HUMAN RESOURCE MANAGEMENT

As one HR professional recently stated, "International human resource management quickly is becoming a management challenge of intercontinental proportions. Not only do you have to know HR well, but you also need a world of knowledge beyond that—literally."[5] Globally, human resource executives are strategic partners with line managers and actively participate in top-level business decisions. They bring human resource perspectives to the global management of a company.[6] Basically, the role of the global human resource executive is focused on being a strategic business partner and decision maker. Any human resource initiative must be based on maximizing productivity to best benefit the bottom line, and therefore a solid understanding of the total global system is essential.[7]

Just as global business enterprises evolve, so do the human resources that support them. According to the Council on Competitiveness in Washington, D.C., human resources are the key to global competitiveness.[8] Human resource management involves formulating and implementing HR policies, practices, and activities in global companies such as Coca-Cola and McDonald's. Such activities include selecting, training, and transferring parent-company personnel abroad and formulating policies and practices for the entire firm and for its foreign operations. However, most companies merely adapt their domestic HR policies and practices to the host country. This practice no doubt stems from the lack of global experience

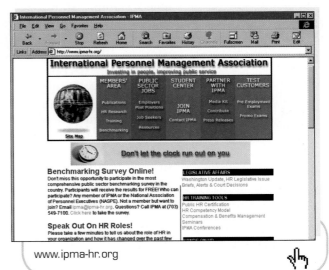

www.ipma-hr.org

> International human resource management quickly is becoming a management challenge of intercontinental proportions.

possessed by HR managers. Melissa DeCrane of the Corporate Resources Group believes that international expertise is an essential asset for human resources people because the global marketplace challenges every company.[9] Effectively dealing with global human resource issues is essential to achieve success in the global marketplace and to maximize profitability.[10]

Regardless of the nature of the global enterprise or the HR policies and practices in place, the basic goal of all global corporations is profitability, which is tied directly to productivity. The key to success and profitability is cost-effective productivity, and the key to ensuring cost-effective productivity is effective human resource management. Globally, productivity is much more than reducing wage pressures; it often requires overcoming other limitations resulting from abandoning a high-wage, highly trained workforce. Lower wages may be accompanied by a multitude of human resource problems that must be effectively dealt with to achieve acceptable global productivity. Apparently, Boundless Technologies could not overcome the problems it encountered in Hong Kong and made a rare retreat to the United States. However, in most cases, once the global move is made, HR must rise to the occasion and provide the support required for acceptable productivity levels.

## GLOBAL HUMAN RESOURCE MANAGEMENT

**Global human resource management (GHRM)**
The utilization of global human resources to achieve organizational objectives without regard to geographic boundaries.

Global human resource problems and opportunities are enormous and are expanding. **Global human resource management (GHRM)** is the utilization of global human resources to achieve organizational objectives without regard to geographic boundaries. Consequently, global managers are no longer able to simply strategize from the standpoint of domestic considerations but must think globally. Individuals dealing with global human resource matters face a multitude of challenges beyond that of their domestic counterparts. These considerations range from cultural barriers to political barriers to international aspects such as compensation. Before upper management decides on a global move, it is vitally important that the critical nature of human resource issues be considered. Failure to do so could result in problems, as well as lost opportunities, as was the case with Boundless Technologies.

Those engaged in the management of global human resources develop and work through an integrated global human resource management system similar to the one they experience domestically. As Figure 17-1 shows, the functional areas associated with effective global human resource management are the same

 **HR WEB WISDOM**

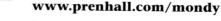 ▶ *International HR Organizations*

**www.prenhall.com/mondy**

International HR organizations are identified at this site.

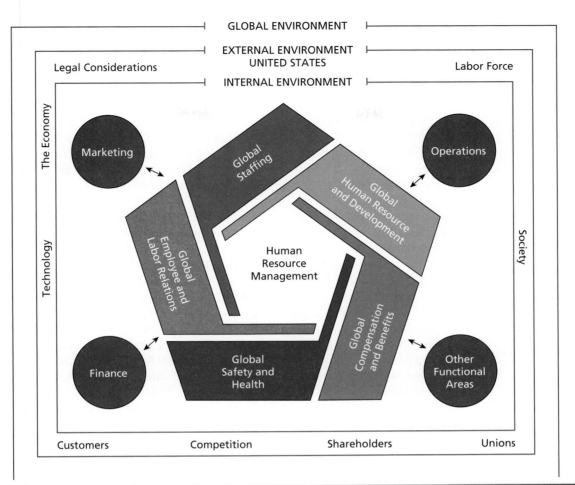

**Human Resource Management in the Global Environment** Figure 17-1

as those experienced domestically. Although the five areas are the same, how they are implemented may differ. Sound global human resource management practices are required for successful performance in each area. As with domestic human resources, the functional areas of GHRM are not separate and distinct but are highly interrelated.

# GLOBAL STAFFING

According to Bill Fontana, a veteran of many foreign assignments for Citibank and the vice president of the National Foreign Trade Council (NFTC), "There's no shortage of brain power [overseas]." Unfortunately, Fontana believes that there is "a shortage of people with the right mix of technical skills and a willingness to accept the Western style of business."[11] This could make global staffing quite difficult.[12]

A global organization must have qualified individuals in specific jobs at specific places and times in order to accomplish its goals. Before the staffing process for an international assignment begins, a thorough understanding of what is involved in the job should be developed. Individuals should be selected based upon the specific qualifications identified.

Selecting global assignees involves four distinct stages: self-selection, creating a candidate pool, technical skills assessment, and making a mutual decision. In the self-selection stage, employees determine if they are right for a global assign-ment, if their spouses and children are interested in relocating internationally, and if this is the best time for a move.[13] In the case of self-selection, the candidate will assess himself or herself on all of the relevant dimensions, then decide whether to pursue a global assignment. Basically, candidates must decide whether to go to the next step in the selection process.[14] Self-selection instruments includ-ing the SAGE (Self-Assessment for Global Endeavors) and the SAGE for Spouses (both by Caligiuri & Associates in Edison, New Jersey) can help employees and their families through the decision-making process. Some organizations—such as Texas-based EDS—develop a self-selection instrument, generally available on their company intranet, to encourage self-assessment among employees considering global assignments.

Stage two involves creating a candidate database organized according to the firm's staffing needs. Included in the database is information such as the year the employee is available to go overseas, the languages the employee speaks, the coun-tries the employee prefers, and the jobs for which the employee is qualified. During stage three, the database is scanned for all possible candidates for a given global assignment, then the list is forwarded to the assigning department. Then, each can-didate is assessed on technical and managerial readiness relative to the needs of the assignment. In the final stage, one person is identified as an acceptable candidate based on his or her technical or managerial readiness and is tentatively selected. To offer a preview of the country's environment, some organizations match repatriated families with the selected families. This allows the repatriated families to share experiences, as well as difficulties. In addition, many consulting firms offer thor-ough cross-cultural preparation for prospective global assignees and their families.[15] This process allows all aspects of the transfer to be considered.

If the decision is made to employ expatriates, certain selection criteria should be carefully considered in stages two and three. Expatriate selection criteria should include cultural adaptability, strong communication skills, technical com-petence, professional or operational expertise, global experience, country-specific experience, interpersonal skills, language skills, family flexibility, and country- or region-specific considerations.[16] One can only imagine the culture shock of the managers from Long Island who moved to Hong Kong. Boundless probably had few managers who had ever visited, much less worked in, Hong Kong.

Mercedes-Benz thoroughly planned every aspect of its move to the United States, including the human resources aspects. Its operation in Vance, Alabama, was used as the test bed to determine if its globalization should extend to Brazil, China, and India. Through effective planning, every desirable attribute of a Mercedes-Benz employee was isolated, with the most desirable trait—beyond gen-eral aptitude—being the ability to work in teams.[17] Mercedes-Benz was also able to attract a pool of 45,000 applicants to select from. Finally, the Mercedes-Benz selection process involved over 80 hours of applicant testing to help ensure the selection of the most qualified and appropriate applicants. Successful accomplish-ment of these three tasks is vital if the global organization is to achieve its mission effectively. Accomplishing these tasks resulted in the selection of the most quali-fied 900 employees from the applicant pool.[18] Thus far, Mercedes-Benz has been quite successful in the United States.

## Types of Global Staff Members

Companies like Mercedes-Benz must choose from various types of global staff mem-bers and may employ specific approaches to global staffing. Global staff members may be selected from among three different types: expatriates, host-country nationals, and third-country nationals. An **expatriate** is an employee who is not a citizen of the country in which the firm is located but is a citizen of the country in which the organization is headquartered. A **host-country national (HCN)** is an employee who is a citizen of the country where the subsidiary is located. An example would be a U.S. citizen working for a Japanese company in the United States. Normally, the bulk of employees in international offices will be host-country nationals. In most industries, local nationals comprise more than 98 percent of the workforce in the foreign operations of North American and Western European multinational companies.[19] According to Roberta Davis, expatriate services manager at Chubb & Sons Inc., "As a company develops its presence in a foreign market, . . . it's a wise strategy to be seen as a local company with a local staff."[20] This means that hiring local people and operating the company like local companies whenever possible is good business. A **third-country national (TCN)** is a citizen of one country, working in a second country, and employed by an organization headquartered in a third country. An example would be an Italian citizen working for a French company in Algeria.

## Approaches to Global Staffing[21]

Using the three basic types of global staff, there are four major approaches to global staffing: ethnocentric, polycentric, regiocentric, and geocentric staffing. These reflect how the organization develops its human resource policies and the preferred type of employees for different positions.

**Ethnocentric Staffing.** With **ethnocentric staffing**, companies primarily hire expatriates to staff higher-level foreign positions. This strategy assumes that home-office perspectives and issues should take precedence over local perspectives and issues and that expatriates will be more effective in representing the views of the home office. Corporate human resources is primarily concerned with selecting and training managers for foreign assignments, developing appropriate compensation packages, and handling adjustment issues when managers return home. Generally, expatriates are used to ensure that foreign operations are linked effectively with parent corporations. However, the use of expatriate employees must be carefully considered since the cost of an international assignment may be high both in terms of financial compensation and resentment on the part of the host-country employees.

**Polycentric Staffing.** When more host-country nationals are used throughout the organization, from top to bottom, it is referred to as **polycentric staffing**. The use of the polycentric staffing model is based on the assumption that host-country nationals are better equipped to deal with local market conditions. Organizations that use this approach will usually have a fully functioning human resource department in each foreign subsidiary responsible for managing all local human resource issues. Corporate human resource managers focus primarily on coordinating relevant activities with their counterparts in each foreign operation. Most global employees are usually host-country nationals because this helps clearly establish that the company is making a commitment to the host country and not just setting up a foreign operation. Compared to an outsider, host-country nationals often have much more thorough knowledge of the culture, the politics, and the laws of the locale, as well as how business is done.

**Regiocentric Staffing.** **Regiocentric staffing** is similar to the polycentric approach, but regional groups of subsidiaries reflecting the organization's strategy and structure work as a unit. There is some degree of autonomy in regional decision

---

**Expatriate**
An employee who is not a citizen of the country in which the firm is located but is a citizen of the country in which the organization is headquartered.

**Host-country national (HCN)**
An employee who is a citizen of the country in which a subsidiary is located, not of the country where the organization is headquartered.

**Third-country national (TCN)**
A citizen of one country, working in a second country, and employed by an organization headquartered in a third country.

**Ethnocentric staffing**
A staffing approach that assumes that home-office perspectives and issues should take precedence over local perspectives and issues and that expatriates will be more effective in representing the views of the home office.

**Polycentric staffing**
When more host-country nationals are used throughout the organization, from top to bottom.

**Regiocentric staffing**
An approach to staffing that is similar to the polycentric staffing approach, but regional groups of subsidiaries reflecting the organization's strategy and structure work as a unit.

making, and promotions are possible within the region but rare from the region to headquarters. Each region develops a common set of employment practices.

**Geocentric staffing**
A staffing approach that uses a worldwide integrated business strategy.

Geocentric Staffing. **Geocentric staffing** is a staffing approach that uses a worldwide integrated business strategy. The firm attempts to always hire the best person available for a position, regardless of where that individual comes from. The geocentric staffing model is most likely to be adopted and used by truly global firms such as Unilever. Usually the corporate human resource function in geocentric companies is the most complicated, since every aspect of HR must be dealt with in the global environment.

## GLOBAL HUMAN RESOURCE DEVELOPMENT

American companies spend more than $50 billion per year on workplace training, but little of that is allocated to global and cross-cultural programs. In that respect, the United States is far behind Asia and Europe. Consider the following:

- Seventy percent of American businesspeople who go abroad receive no cultural training or preparation.
- Fifty-nine percent of the T&D executives surveyed by ASTD reported there was no international training for staff taking assignments outside the United States, and another 5 percent did not know whether there was such training.
- American companies suffer more than $2 billion in losses yearly because of inadequate training and preparation of employees sent overseas.

Many U.S. businesses operate under the assumption that American ways and business practices are standard across the globe. Similarly, many T&D professionals believe that training and consulting principles and strategies that work for a U.S. audience can be equally effective abroad. Unfortunately, nothing could be further from the truth.[22] Many people responsible for the delivery of training and team organizational development programs in the United States assume that American corporate values and materials are transferable with little or no adaptation. Global training and development is needed because people, jobs, and organizations are often quite different globally.[23] Indications are that utilizing trainers who can deliver material in the local language, while translating the core message in a meaningful way that is more palatable to the other culture, increases the training success rate.[24]

## Expatriate Development

The development process should start as soon as the workforce is selected, even before beginning global operations if possible. Mercedes-Benz sent 165 early hires to Germany for their training. After receiving this training, these individuals—along with 70 Germans—conducted employee training in the United States.[25] Large-scale T&D programs like that of Mercedes-Benz are essential for most global relocations. The purpose of these development programs is to alter the environment within the firm to help global employees perform more productively in the host country.

Global expansion into China has been particularly difficult for McDonald's because the Cultural Revolution of the 1960s and 1970s closed most schools in China. As a result, an entire generation did not receive much education. McDonald's must personally develop these individuals. Bob Wilner, McDonald's director of international HR, says that McDonald's tries to develop local people in Asia, finding them more effective than expatriates because they better understand the Asian marketplace and customers.[26] David Hoff of Anheuser-Busch in Asia is

The Expatriate Preparation and Development Program    **Figure 17-2**

developing host-country nationals in a rather unique way. Hoff hires host-country nationals, develops their talents in the United States, and reassigns them abroad as local managers.[27]

Organizations are recognizing that expatriate employees and their families face special situations and pressures that training and development activities must prepare them to deal with.[28] Employees and their families must have an effective orientation program and a readjustment-training program. In addition, the employee must have a program of continual development. Figure 17-2 illustrates the ideal expatriate preparation and development program, which includes pre-move orientation and training, continual development, and repatriation orientation and training.

Pre-move orientation and training of expatriate employees and their families are essential before the global assignment begins. The pre-move orientation involves training and familiarization in language, culture, history, living conditions, and local customs and peculiarities.[29] Continuing employee development, in which the employee's global skills are fitted into career planning and corporate development programs, makes the eventual transition to the home country less disruptive. Continual development involves expanding both professional and operational skills, when appropriate, comprehensive career planning, and involvement in home-country development programs.

## Repatriation Orientation and Training

Orientation and training are also necessary prior to **repatriation**, which is the process of bringing expatriates home. Repatriation orientation and training are needed to prepare the employee and the family for a return to the home-country culture and to prepare the expatriate's new subordinates and supervisor for the return. As mentioned in Chapter 9, approximately 50 percent of repatriates leave their companies within two years of repatriation because most companies do a lousy job of repatriating employees.[30] Adjustments involve preparing the individual and the family, when appropriate, for returning to the U.S. lifestyle.

**Repatriation**
The process of bringing expatriates home.

## GLOBAL COMPENSATION AND BENEFITS

One reason that organizations relocate to other areas of the world is probably the high wage pressures that threaten their ability to compete on a global basis. Wage pressures and union inflexibility were the primary reasons that Mercedes-Benz

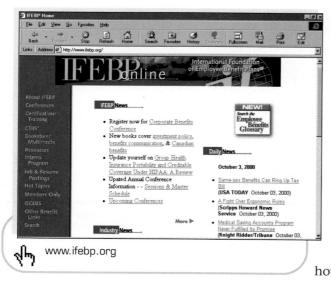

www.ifebp.org

located its sport utility plant in the United States.[31] Once wage pressures become so high they cannot be offset by increased productivity, the company will often make a global move. When the price of Mercedes-Benz luxury cars rose $15,000 above the competition, a global move was imminent.[32] On the other hand, Boundless returned to the United States despite the fact that salaries here were substantially higher than those in Hong Kong.

Globally, the question of what constitutes a fair day's pay is not as complicated as it is in the United States; normally, it is slightly above the prevailing wage rates in the area. Mercedes-Benz went global to avoid paying $30 an hour in Germany. Even though prevailing manufacturing wages in Alabama were $8 to $10, Mercedes-Benz paid about $13 an hour and, within two years, $18 an hour—only slightly below union wages for the Big Three automakers.[33]

The same is often true of benefits and nonfinancial rewards. Basically, compensation levels are usually much lower globally. However, variations in laws, living costs, tax policies, and other factors all must be considered when a company is establishing global compensation packages. Culture also plays a part. North American compensation practices encourage individualism and high performance; continental European programs typically emphasize social responsibility; the traditional Japanese approach considers age and company service as primary determinants of compensation.[34] There is no guarantee that additional compensation will ensure additional output. Some have found that, in some countries, additional pay has resulted in employees' working less. As soon as employees have earned enough to satisfy their needs, time spent with family or on other noncompany activities is perceived as more valuable than additional cash.[35]

American concepts such as employee stock ownership and linking executive compensation to corporate performance through equity and equity-based compensation techniques have caught on in an increasingly globalized marketplace.[36] Several Japanese companies, including Sony, have introduced radical foreign compensation practices such as employee stock options for their employees in Japan. In a like manner, many U.S.–based companies have adopted equally radical foreign approaches such as profit sharing and team-based and skill-based pay while often believing (erroneously) that these are purely homegrown innovations. No one country has a monopoly on the best practices, and those who believe they do are putting themselves at a serious competitive disadvantage.[37]

A country's culture can also impose significant constraints on the globalization of pay. Including bonus and long-term incentives, total compensation of a chief executive of a U.S. company typically exceeds the pay of that company's lowest-paid employee by a ratio of 60 to 1. In Sweden, the spread is likely to be closer to 8 to 1. While people in the United States derive great status from high pay, nations in large parts of Europe and Asia shun conspicuous wealth. In Italy, where teamwork is more valued than individual initiative, sales incentives for top sales professionals working in small teams can be demotivational. The recipient of a large award may feel awkward when receiving larger than a *fair share* of the reward pie.[38]

According to Roberta Davis of Chubb & Sons Inc., overcompensating expatriates is common: "Don't simply give whatever the expatriates ask for, but rather provide what they need." Trying to preserve the expatriate's home-country standard of living in a foreign country may not be practical.[39] On average, expatriates cost two to three times what they would in an equivalent domestic position. Paul Patt, director of business development at Runzheimer International, believes that companies should "try not to start out overly generous, because it is very, very difficult to scale back packages once they're in place."[40] A fully loaded expatriate package for an executive, including benefits and cost-of-living adjustments, costs anywhere from $300,000 to $1 million annually.[41]

For expatriate managers and professionals, the situation is more complex than simply paying at or slightly above local host-country compensation rates. Even minor changes in the value of the U.S. dollar may result in compensation adjustments for expatriates. Also, expatriate compensation packages must cover the extra costs of housing, education for children, and yearly transportation home for themselves and their family members. Additionally, compensation packages may include foreign service and hardship premiums, relocation and moving allowances, cost-of-living adjustments, and tax equalization payments. With regard to tax equalization payments, under Internal Revenue Service rules, U.S. citizens living overseas can exclude up to $70,000 of income earned abroad. Also, credits against U.S. income taxes are given for a portion of the foreign income taxes paid by U.S. expatriates beyond the $70,000 level.[42] All these factors make global compensation extremely complex.

## GLOBAL SAFETY AND HEALTH

Safety and health aspects of the job are important because employees who work in a safe environment and enjoy good health are more likely to be productive and yield long-term benefits to the organization than those in less desirable circumstances. For this reason, progressive global managers have long advocated adequate safety and health programs. U.S.–based global operations are often safer and healthier than host-country operations, but frequently not as safe as similar operations in the United States.[43] Safety and health laws and regulations often vary greatly from country to country. Such laws can range from virtually nonexistent to more stringent than those in the United States. In fact, the importance of workplace safety varies significantly among different countries.[44] Also, health care facilities across the globe vary greatly in their state of modernization.

Additional considerations specific to global assignments are emergency evacuation services and global security protection. Often, evacuating and caring for injured employees is done through private companies. Medical emergencies are frightening under any circumstances, but when an employee becomes sick or injured abroad, it can be a really frightening experience. If the travelers are assigned to more remote or less developed areas, companies should be aware that in many medical facilities needles are often reused, equipment is not properly used, and there is a lack of basic medical supplies. In these cases, purchasing a travel medical kit is recommended. Some common items found in these kits are gloves, sterile needles, a dental emergency kit, an IV administration kit, and bandages. Many of the items are necessary to ensure safe injections and other minor invasive procedures.[45] Also, employees and their families living abroad must constantly be aware of security issues. Many firms even provide bodyguards who escort executives everywhere. Some firms even have so-called "disaster plans" to deal with evacuating expatriates if natural disasters, civil conflicts, or even wars occur.

Companies may purchase insurance to assist expatriates. To help protect companies with international operations, CNA International has introduced a commercial policy that offers one-stop shopping for companies doing business abroad. It offers a host of coverage components, including property, business income, general liability, workers' compensation, and auto liability insurance, as well as confiscation, expropriation, and nationalization coverage. It also features kidnap and ransom coverage protection for employees who work and travel abroad. Additional services include international travel assistance, emergency medical referral and evacuation, emergency cash and messages, legal referral, and translation services.[46]

## GLOBAL EMPLOYEE AND LABOR RELATIONS

While unionism has waned in the United States, it has maintained much of its strength abroad. As stated in Chapter 1, total union membership in the United States is 13.9 percent of the workforce. In Sweden, the rate is 96 percent; it is 50 percent in the United Kingdom, 43 percent in Germany, 36 percent in Canada, and 28 percent in both Japan and France.[47] Although foreign unions are generally less adversarial with management and less focused on wage gains, globalization is a major threat to wage gains worldwide. This was definitely the situation when Mercedes-Benz dealt with German union inflexibility. When Mercedes-Benz decided to reinvent itself, the company decided to do it without union restrictions and subsequently went global.[48] The tide of union membership overseas may well be on a downturn, but unions are still quite influential around the globe. For this reason, HR policies and practices must be geared toward dealing with the global differences in collective bargaining.

Obviously, the strength and nature of unions differ from country to country, with unions ranging from nonexistent to relatively strong. Codetermination—requiring firms to have union or worker representatives on their boards of directors—is very common in European countries. Even though they face global competition, unions in several European countries have resisted changing their laws and removing government protections. In some South American countries, such as Chile, collective bargaining for textile workers, miners, and carpenters is prohibited. All negotiations are limited to the individual company. And unions are generally allowed only in companies of 25 workers or more. So businesses often split into small companies to avoid collective bargaining, leaving workers on their own.[49]

The North American Free Trade Agreement (NAFTA) between Canada, Mexico, and the United States facilitated the movement of goods across boundaries within North America. Labor relations took a major step forward, with a *side agreement* on labor designed to protect workers in all three countries from the effects of competitive economic pressures. NAFTA established a Commission for Labor Cooperation with offices in each country, which is governed by a council made up of labor ministers of Canada, Mexico, and the United States. Each country is accountable for complying with its own labor laws when dealing with occupational safety and health; child labor; migrant workers; human resource development; labor statistics; work benefits; social programs for workers; productivity improvements; labor-management relations; employment standards; the equality of men and women in the workplace; and forms of cooperation among workers, management, and government. A country that consistently fails to enforce its own labor laws could be fined up to $20 million per violation. If the offending nation is either the United States or Mexico, trade sanctions could be imposed between those two countries.[50] There are also a number of principles identifying broad areas of common agreement to protect the rights and interests of each workforce.

A global organization must cope with a multitude of unknowns. The management of HR functions globally is enormously complicated by the need to adapt HR policies and practices to different host countries. HR management must consider the potential impact of global differences on human resources. Differences in politics, law, culture, economics, labor-management relations systems, and other factors complicate the task of global human resource management. Figure 17-3 lists some of the possible barriers to effective global human resource management.

## Political and Legal Barriers

The nature and stability of political and legal systems vary throughout the globe. U.S. firms enjoy a relatively stable political and legal system. The same is true in many of the other developed countries, particularly in Europe. In other nations, however, the political and legal systems are much more unstable. Some governments are subject to coups, dictatorial rule, and corruption, and these can substantially alter the business environment, as well as the legal environment. Legal systems can also become unstable, with contracts suddenly becoming unenforceable because of internal politics. Also, because of restrictions imposed on U.S.–based firms by the Foreign Corrupt Practices Act, a gray area exists between paying legal agency fees and bribery, which is illegal. In the biggest ever case brought under the law, Lockheed Martin Corporation pleaded guilty to charges of bribe payments to a member of the Egyptian military to help sell aircraft to the Egyptian government.[51]

Additionally, HR regulations and laws vary greatly among countries. In many Western European countries, laws on labor unions and employment make it difficult to lay off employees. Equal employment legislation and sexual harassment laws exist to varying degrees but often differ significantly from U.S. laws and regulations. In other countries, religious or ethical differences make employment discrimination an acceptable practice. Because of political and legal differences, it is essential that a comprehensive review of the political and legal environment of the host country is conducted before beginning global operations.

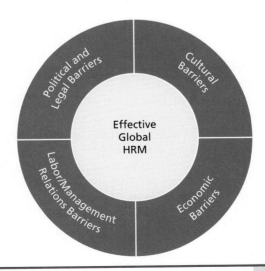

**Barriers To Effective Global Human Resource Management**  **Figure 17-3**

## HR WEB WISDOM

> *International Laws Affecting HR*

**www.prenhall.com/mondy**

This site is hot linked to numerous international law sites.

Americans may encounter laws that are routinely ignored by host countries, creating somewhat of a dilemma. For example, the laws in some countries that require a minimum age for factory workers are not enforced. Such practices are fairly common in countries such as Bangladesh, China, Pakistan, Brazil, India, Indonesia, Kenya, and the Philippines. At least 250 million children between the ages of five and fourteen work in organizations worldwide. Some believe that this estimate is low, and the real number of working children is actually much greater. More than 120 million of these children are employed full time, which means that they probably do not attend school.[52] According to a United Nations agency, the International Labor Organization (ILO), the number of children performing jobs instead of attending school is increasing throughout the world, both in absolute terms and as a proportion of the world's children. Competitive pressures have led individual countries to ignore their own laws on the minimum working age, even in hazardous industries such as manufacturing fireworks and glassware. Regardless of local laws, some countries in the global economy are clearly promoting child labor.

Also affecting the environment in which global companies operate are certain tariffs and quotas that can greatly impact business profitability. **Tariffs** are taxes collected on goods that are shipped across national boundaries. **Quotas** limit the number or value of goods that can be imported across national boundaries. Tariffs and quotas can affect human resources because the need for personnel varies based upon global corporate profitability.

**Tariffs**
Taxes collected on goods that are shipped across national boundaries.

**Quotas**
Policies that limit the number or value of goods that can be imported across national boundaries.

**Country's culture**
The set of values, symbols, beliefs, languages, and norms that guide human behavior within a country.

## Cultural Barriers

Cultural differences vary from country to country, with corresponding differences in HR practices. A **country's culture** is the set of values, symbols, beliefs, languages, and norms that guide human behavior within a country. For example, the cultural norms of Asia promote loyalty and teamwork in typical Japanese workers and influence how these people work. Japanese workers often expect lifetime employment in return for unquestioned loyalty. In Japan, the focus is on the work group, while in the United States, the focus is still on the individual. Obviously, such cultural differences have specific human resource implications. Employment practices must be adapted to local cultural norms, and therefore most human resource staff members in a foreign subsidiary should be drawn from host-country nationals.

However, just because certain cultural norms are restrictive does not mean that an attempt at change should not be made. In Japan, women rarely make it past the secretarial ranks. But that did not deter David Hoff, director of international resources for Anheuser-Busch. According to Hoff, Anheuser-Busch recruited women in Asia for its joint venture and discovered that Asian women are particularly effective in sales.[53] Also, Bank of America discovered that Japanese male employees opened up and shared their problems more readily with women, even expatriate women.[54] It is extremely important to preserve the desired corporate culture. Companies must bring in a critical mass of expatriates who carry the culture with them and always leave one or two behind to oversee locals and ensure

**▶ *It's the Culture, Stupid!***

As the new manager for the Mideast division office of Dester International, located in Damascus, Eric Ned is experiencing a bit of adjustment. Eric is a hard-working manager and was selected for his new assignment while working in the corporate headquarters in New York. There is one highly efficient and productive worker in Eric's office. When Eric requested a pay increase for this individual, he was told by his boss that merit increases are not permitted in this country. All employees must receive equal salary increases.

*What did Eric fail to take into consideration?*

that they are following corporate policies. The key is to accommodate local cultures while maintaining the critical nature of the corporate culture.[55]

## Economic Barriers

Differences in economic systems must also be thoroughly investigated. In a capitalist system, the overwhelming need for efficiency encourages human resource policies and practices that emphasize productivity. In a socialist system, human resource practices favor the prevention of unemployment, often at the expense of productivity and efficiency. In a competitive global economy, the results of this approach are ultimately unacceptable. Perhaps this explains why the countries in this world that embrace socialism are declining in number.

The impact of economic factors on pending global operations must be fully understood and accounted for prior to developing HR policies and practices. Probably one of the greatest economic factors is the difference in labor costs between the host country and the home country. Such variations could produce real differences in human resource policies and practices. Higher labor costs would likely encourage a firm to recruit and select more highly skilled employees and emphasize efficiency. Lower wage rates might result in a workforce that required more extensive training and development activities simply to ensure acceptable productivity levels. Even though wages may be much lower, some companies have discovered that performance is more like 40 percent or even 30 percent of the U.S. norm.[56]

## Labor-Management Relations Barriers

Unfortunately for American labor unions, globalization cannot be stopped, since the U.S. economy is in the midst of an economic boom that is based in part on globalization. Open borders have allowed new ideas and technology to flow freely around the globe, promoting productivity growth and helping U.S. companies become more competitive. The global economy is here to stay, and unless labor unions employ new organizing techniques, management will retain the negotiating power.[57]

The relationship between workers, unions, and employers varies dramatically from country to country and obviously has an enormous impact on human resource management practices. In the United States, HR policies on most matters involving compensation and benefits are determined by employers, at times with the intervention of labor unions. In other countries, the relations between employers and unions are not interfered with. Companies like General Electric, Volkswagen, and Volvo are attempting international bargaining that would

> **The Global Impact of the Internet**

Global e-business is conducted 24 hours a day on the Internet across traditional geo-graphic boundaries. The Internet tends to blur geographic boundaries, making e-busi-ness more seamless than traditional global business dealings. The Internet is impact-ing all aspects of business. Although North America has only about 5 percent of the world's population, it accounts for about half its online population. It is also projected that worldwide Internet access will increase during the next four years to about 10 percent, and that there will be more than 700 million Internet-connected devices by 2003, up from 200 million last year. Because the Internet blurs boundaries, con-ducting e-business subjects HR professionals to unfamiliar jurisdictions, laws, taxes, cultures, and even technologies. HR professionals are not alone in their concern over such issues, but the Internet has further complicated the already complex issue of going global.[58]

The Internet is allowing global companies to recruit more effectively. According to Reggie Barefield, executive director of Humana's Talent Resources and Technology Team, "The Internet is a job-lead generator and a global tool for creating a proactive recruiting team."[59] As mentioned in Chapter 6, in 2000, over 70 percent of the global *Fortune* 500 companies were using the Internet to recruit. Even though the Internet will not replace traditional recruiting methods soon, it does offer a viable, global route to the candidate pool.

require companies to adopt a global code of conduct. This global code of conduct would protect the rights of all employees globally.

## GLOBAL EQUAL EMPLOYMENT OPPORTUNITY (EEO)

Equal employment opportunity worldwide ranges from virtually nonexistent to highly sophisticated systems. Some countries have extensive EEO laws that they enforce vigorously. Other countries have similar laws that are not enforced, while others have no laws relating to EEO. Global companies operating in the United States are subject to an extensive and enforced set of laws that were discussed in Chapter 3. For example, when Honda is operating in the United States, it must adhere to all EEO laws.

Some U.S. labor laws extend to U.S. firms operating in other countries. The Civil Rights Act of 1991 and the Americans with Disabilities Act of 1990 are two primary ones. These laws apply to citizens working in other countries for covered employers, including foreign companies controlled by U.S.–based companies. However, the laws do not apply where compliance would violate local laws.

The global assignment of women and members of racial/ethnic minorities can involve legal issues, as these individuals may be protected by EEO regulations. Presently, it is estimated that women constitute 18 to 20 percent of the U.S. expa-triate managerial workforce. Unfortunately, these gains in female expatriate par-ticipation rates have not been equally distributed worldwide.[60] There are some countries in which the culture is so ingrained that certain groups would have extreme difficulty participating on equal footing with the majority population.

Sexual harassment is also a global problem. A disproportionate number of cross-cultural sexual harassment complaints involve perpetrators and victims from different ethnic, racial, or national-origin groups. When individuals from two different cultures interact, the potential for problems with sexual harassment is greater, not smaller. Some behaviors that violate U.S. cultural norms may not be perceived as a problem in another culture. In many Mediterranean and Latin countries, physical contact and sensuality are a common part of socializing. For example, one Brazilian senior HR executive was surprised when he was admonished for calling the women at work "girls." While this label was appropriate and acceptable in his native culture, it was insulting to North American women and could contribute to a *hostile or intimidating work environment* by U.S. standards.[61]

## EIGHT KEYS TO GLOBAL HR MANAGEMENT OF EXPATRIATES

The decision to enter foreign markets has profound implications on human resources, particularly when expatriates are used. Assigning and managing U.S. employees outside of the United States is a complex and sometimes overwhelming task. Global HR management of expatriates can be made simpler and more manageable by following eight steps, which are general guidelines for developing an expatriate workforce.

*First,* everyone involved must completely understand the global business plan. This knowledge will make it easier to determine how existing human resource policies can be adapted to accomplish global objectives.

*Second,* the company's foreign-service policy should be a set of guidelines, not rigid rules, for relocating employees and their families around the world while maintaining the domestic corporate culture.

*Third,* a global budget process should be developed so the overall cost of each expatriate global assignment can be estimated. This cost represents an enormous investment and should be carefully considered to determine whether expatriates, host-country nationals, or third-country nationals should be used.

*Fourth,* the candidate and his or her family should be profiled to determine whether he or she might be an effective selection for a global assignment. Often an entire family, not just an employee, must be considered in this determination.

*Fifth,* the terms and conditions of the global assignment should be clearly stated up front. Expatriates should be given both a verbal and written presentation of the terms and conditions of the assignment to ensure that they completely understand both the benefits and responsibilities of the assignment.

*Sixth,* expatriates and their families must be prepared for relocation with departure orientation and training. This should include language training, cultural training, and a general orientation as to everyday living and local customs.

*Seventh,* a continual development process must be designed and implemented to take advantage of the employee's global experiences. This will include career planning as well as home-country development during the global assignment period.

*Eighth,* returning expatriates and their families must receive repatriation orientation training, as discussed earlier in the chapter.

Unfortunately, according to David Hoff, Anheuser-Busch's director of international resources, "The cost of expatriates is enormous." Hoff recommends that as a long-term strategy, companies need alternatives, such as hiring foreign nationals, developing their talents in the United States, and reassigning them abroad as local managers.[62] While this may be an effective long-term solution, expatriates will probably always be used to some degree overseas, if for no other reason than to maintain ties with the home country.

# MAINTAINING CORPORATE IDENTITY THROUGH CORPORATE CULTURE

Maintaining an effective corporate culture that reflects the culture of the home country is essential for continuity worldwide; achieving this often requires innovative insight. Akio Morita, former chairman of the Sony Corporation, recently commented, "Culture may impact products, services, and operations by only 10 percent, but this is the most important 10 percent. This 10 percent determines success or failure."[63] It is a fact that people and organizations around the globe think, act, work, learn, and lead in different ways based on the cultural environment in which they were raised and now work.

When a U.S. company hires too many local people in its foreign offices, it risks losing the unique set of values and operating procedures that define its corporate culture. According to Bill Fontana, a veteran of many foreign assignments for Citibank and now vice president of NFTC, "If you rely too heavily on locals,

## A GLOBAL PERSPECTIVE

### Global HR Managers Must Carefully Consider Cultural Differences

Most managers think domestically, in that they are guided mostly by their domestic environment. In a global environment, the view of culture—particularly cultural differences between nations—probably should be of prime concern to HR managers. The cultural differences between nations can be described using five bipolar dimensions: power distance, individualism, masculinity, uncertainty avoidance, and Confucianism.

▶ *Power distance* is the degree of inequality in a country that is perceived to be normal. This can vary from relative equality, as in the United States, to extreme inequality, as in Indonesia.

▶ *Individualism* is the degree to which people in a country prefer to act as individuals rather than as part of a collective group. Highly individual countries like the United States expect people to "stand on their own two feet" and be prepared to fend for themselves; highly collectivist countries like Indonesia instill respect for the family group, which lasts a lifetime and incorporates both loyalty and protection.

▶ *Masculinity* is the degree to which traditionally "masculine" characteristics such as assertiveness, performance, success, and competition are preferred to more "feminine" traits such as an emphasis on personal relationships, quality of life, service, and care. In "masculine" societies like Japan, the role of women is very different from that in "feminine" societies like the Netherlands.

▶ *Uncertainty avoidance* is the degree to which people prefer clear rules and structure and avoid ambiguity. Countries with high uncertainty avoidance scores, such as Japan, might be referred to as rigid; those with low scores, such as Hong Kong, as flexible.

▶ *Confucianism* refers to differences in long-term and short-term orientations. A long-term culture, such as China, favors future-orientated values like savings and persistence, whereas a short-term culture, such as the United States, favors past and present values like those associated with respect.[64]

HR managers can use these five bipolar dimensions to develop a cultural profile of each nation where employees are deployed, thereby better preparing every employee who is about to embark on a global assignment in that nation.

you're going to have a local culture, not the corporate culture you want. . . . And the local culture may be totally foreign to the way you operate." To ensure a parallel corporate culture, firms should bring in a critical mass of expatriates who carry the culture with them at the beginning of the start-up. It is also critical that global corporations leave at least one or two expatriates behind to oversee the locals and ensure that they are following corporate policies.[65]

Often a global U.S. corporation forms an alliance with a company in the host country. In such situations, the corporate cultures and management styles of the partners must be blended together as quickly as possible. Long-term success means having a corporate culture that supports the goals of the global organization and effectively deals with the international business environment. As a firm becomes more and more global in nature, having a supportive corporate culture becomes more difficult. Alliances are useful for all partners because collaboration makes it possible to share the costs and risks of doing business and enables companies to share financial resources, technology, production facilities, marketing expertise, and—of course—human resources. However, problems may occur in international alliances when people from different organizations and national cultures work together.[66]

Regardless of whether an alliance exists, it is essential that the corporate culture focus on making a profit. Global firms must strive to create an effective corporate culture that effectively copes with the global environment and at the same time is profitable. Although it may be impossible to achieve, the ideal corporate culture of global corporations will closely parallel that of the home country.

## Summary

**❶ Describe the evolution of global business.**
Most companies initially become global without making substantial investments in foreign countries by either exporting, licensing, or franchising. A multinational corporation (MNC) is a firm that is based in one country (the parent or home country) and produces goods or provides services in one or more foreign countries (host countries). A global corporation (GC) has corporate units in a number of countries that are integrated to operate as one organization worldwide.

**❷ Explain the development of global human resource management.**
Human resource executives are strategic partners with line managers and actively participate in top-level business decisions. They bring human resource perspectives to the global management of a company.

**❸ Describe the global human resource management functions.**
The functions are global human resource planning, recruitment, and selection; global human resource development; global compensation and benefits; global safety and health; and global employee and labor relations.

**❹ Explain possible barriers to effective global human resource management.**
Possible specific barriers include political and legal factors, cultural factors, economic factors, and labor-management relations factors.

**❺ Explain global equal employment opportunity.**
The global assignment of women and racial or ethnic minorities can involve legal issues, as these individuals may be protected by equal employment opportunity (EEO) regulations.

**⑥ Describe the keys to global human resource management of expatriates.**
Assigning and managing U.S. employees outside of the United States is a complex and sometimes overwhelming task. Global HR management of expatriates can be made simpler and more manageable by following certain guidelines.

**⑦ Explain the importance of maintaining corporate identity through corporate culture.**
Maintaining an effective corporate culture that reflects the culture of the home country is essential for continuity worldwide; achieving this often requires innovative insight.

## ▶ Questions for Review

1. How has global business evolved?

2. How has global human resource management evolved?

3. What are the functional areas associated with effective global human resource management? Discuss each.

4. What are the various types of global staff members?

5. What are the approaches to global staffing?

6. Explain the expatriate development program.

7. Explain the general makeup of an expatriate compensation package.

8. What are the possible barriers to effective global human resource management?

9. Describe equal employment opportunity (EEO) and global human resource management.

10. What are the keys to global human resource management of expatriates?

TAKE IT TO THE NET

We invite you to visit the Mondy homepage on the Prentice Hall Web site at **www.prenhall.com/mondy** for updated information, Web-based exercises, and links to other HR-related sites.

## ▶ Developing HRM Skills

*An Experiential Exercise*

After studying this textbook, students should have a much better appreciation of the type of work human resource managers are involved in. In this exercise, participants will attempt to develop a profile of the attributes a human resource manager should possess. Knowledge gained throughout the course should be used in identifying necessary attributes. The result of this exercise should be a realistic profile of what attributes an effective human resource manager should possess.

## *Was There Enough Preparation?*

"Hi, Sam. How are the preparations going for your assignment in Japan?"

"Well, Elvis, I really feel prepared for the assignment, and the high level of apprehension I first experienced is gone."

"What exactly did the preparation program involve, Sam?"

"The experience was really exhaustive. First, I spend a good deal of time in a comprehensive orientation and training program. The program covered training and familiarization in the language, culture, history, living conditions, and local customs of Japan. Then, to make the transition home easier and better for my career, I have developed a plan with my boss that includes several trips back here to remain a key part of this operation. Also, my career development training will include the same training as the other managers in the home office. Finally, I was completely briefed on repatriation orientation and training that I would experience when I returned. Also, I was fully briefed on the compensation package, which appears to be fairly generous."

"That is great, Sam. Have you found a place to live yet?"

"Not yet, Elvis, but my wife and children are leaving in three days to meet with the company's relocation person to consider the various possibilities."

"How did the family like the orientation training, Sam?"

"Well, my wife ordered some Japanese language tapes, and I think she read all of the information that was covered in the class. She and the children will be fine because they have time to adapt; they don't have to hit the ground running like I do."

### Questions

1. Do you believe that Sam's family is adequately prepared for the move to Japan? Why or why not?
2. Should the company's orientation program have included training for Sam's family?
3. Is repatriation orientation and training necessary for Sam's family on their return to the United States?

## *Going to Russia*

"Bob, I just reviewed the global staffing plan and there must be a mistake. The plan requires a 100 percent expatriate workforce, including the staff, legal, and marketing areas. The technical people are also all expatriates, but that did not surprise me as much."

"I know, Robert. I was also surprised when I first reviewed the plan, but when I inquired I was told that since we would be involved in the creation of a wireless communication system in Russia, based on our super-secret technology, no outsiders are allowed."

"Well, Bob, I understand that the pirating of intellectual property is fairly common overseas, but we can protect our technical secrets and still have a support staff of host-country nationals in our Russian subsidiary."

"I understand your apprehension, Robert, but the decision has been made. Let's get ready to go global."

As Robert walked back to his office, he thought, "This is a big mistake."

### Questions

1. Why does Robert believe that excluding host-country nationals from the staff in Russia is a big mistake?
2. Do you believe that secrecy could have been maintained even with a staff of Russian nationals?

---

▶ **Notes**

1. This is an adaptation of the actual experiences of Boundless Technologies. Paul Krugman, "Lower Wages Weren't Enough to Keep U.S. Company Abroad," *USA Today* (June 16, 1997): 19A; and Mark Harrington, "Boundless Buys Florida for Undisclosed Sum," *Newsday* (January 26, 2000): A49.
2. Sabrina Hicks, "Successful Global Training," *Training & Development* 54 (May 2000): 95.
3. David E. Molnar, "Global Assignments: Seven Keys to International HR Management," *HR Focus* 74 (May 1997): 9.
4. J. Stewart Black and Hal B. Gregerson, "The Right Way to Manage Expats," *Harvard Business Review* 77 (March 1999): 52.
5. Jennifer J. Laabs, "Must-Have Global HR Competencies," *Workforce* 44 (March 1999): 30.
6. John Case, "HR Learns How to Open the Books: The Techniques of Open-Book Management Demonstrate How to Work on All Fronts in Pursuit of a Common Goal," *HRMagazine* 43 (May 1998): 70–76.
7. John F. Johnson, "HR Career: The 21st-Century HR Executive," *HR Focus* 74 (April 1997): 5.
8. Elizabeth Connor, "Will Our Human Resources Measure Up?" *HR Focus* 72 (October 1995): 22.
9. Stephenie Overman, "Is HR a Weak Link in the Global Chain?" *HRMagazine* 38 (June, 1994): 67–68.
10. Michael J. Lotito, "A Call to Action for U.S. Business and Education," *Employment Relations Today* 19 (Winter 1992/1993): 379–387.
11. Donald J. McNerney, "Global Staffing: Some Common Problems—And Solutions," *HR Focus* 73 (June 1996): 1–5.
12. Thomas A. Stewart, "Staying Smart/Managing: The Leading Edge: A Way to Measure Worldwide Success Going Global, Part II," *Fortune* 139 (March 15, 1999): 196+.
13. Valerie Frazee, "Selecting Global Assignees," *Workforce* 3 (July 1998): 28–30.
14. Paula Caligiuri, "Legal Issues in Selecting Global Assignees," *Workforce* 3 (July 1998): 29.
15. Frazee, "Selecting Global Assignees."
16. Charlene M. Soloman, "Success Abroad Depends on More than Job Skills," *Personnel Journal* 73 (April 1994): 51–59.
17. David Lawder, "Mercedes Mulls Expansion of U.S. Assembly Plant," *Reuters Business Report* (May 22, 1997): 1.
18. Ibid.
19. Calvin Reynolds, "Global Compensation and Benefits in Transition," *Compensation and Benefits Review* 32 (January/February 2000): 28.
20. McNerney, "Global Staffing: Some Common Problems—And Solutions."

21. This section was developed based on Anne Marie Francesco and Barry Allen Gold, *International Organizational Behavior* (Upper Saddle River, NJ: Prentice Hall, 1998): 165.

22. Hicks, "Successful Global Training."

23. Karen Roberts, Ellen Ernst, and Cynthia Ozeki, "Managing the Global Workforce: Challenges and Strategies" (Special Issue: Competitiveness and Global Leadership in the 21st Century), *The Academy of Management Executive* (November 1, 1998): 93.

24. Cynthia L. Kemper, "Global Training's Critical Success Factors," *Training & Development* 52 (February 1998): 35–37.

25. Donald W. Nauss, "It's Fun, It's Useful, It's a Mercedes?" *Los Angeles Times* (May 18, 1997): A-1.

26. Clifford C. Hebard, "Managing Effectively in Asia," *Training & Development* 50 (April 1996): 34.

27. Ibid.

28. Shirley Fishman, "Developing a Global Workforce," *Canadian Business Review* 23 (April 1996): 18.

29. Mark E. Mendelhall and Carolyn Wiley, "Strangers in a Strange Land: The Relationship between Expatriate Adjustment and Impression Management," *American Behavioral Scientist* (March/April 1994): 605–621.

30. Andrea C. Poe, "Welcome Back," *HRMagazine* 45 (March 2000): 94.

31. Nauss, "It's Fun, It's Useful, It's a Mercedes?"

32. Lawder, "Mercedes Mulls Expansion of U.S. Assembly Plant."

33. Ibid.

34. Reynolds, "Global Compensation and Benefits in Transition."

35. Ibid.

36. Arthur H. Kroll, "Equity Compensation in the Global Marketplace," *HR Focus* (August 1999): S4.

37. Reynolds, "Global Compensation and Benefits in Transition," 28–38.

38. Steven E. Gross and Per L. Wingerup, "Global Pay? Maybe Not Yet!" *Compensation and Benefits Review* 31 (July/August 1999): 25–34.

39. McNerney, "Global Staffing: Some Common Problems—And Solutions."

40. Ibid.

41. Black and Gregerson, "The Right Way to Manage Expats."

42. Brent M. Longnecker and Wendy Powell, "Executive Compensation in a Global Market," *Benefits & Compensation Solutions* (April 1996): 40–43.

43. M. Janssens, J. M. Brett, and F. J. Smith, "Confirmatory Cross-Cultural Research Testing the Viability of a Corporation-Wide Safety Policy," *Academy of Management Journal* 38 (June 1995): 364–380.

44. R. B. Palchak and R. T Schmidt, "Protecting the Health of Employees Abroad," *Occupational Health & Safety* 65 (February 1996): 53–56.

45. "Global Protection," *Occupational Health & Safety* 67 (October 1998): 182.

46. "Global Protection," *Risk Management* 46 (September 1999): 90.

47. M. E. Sharpe, "Labor's Future," *Challenge* 39 (March 1996): 65.

48. Lawder, "Mercedes Mulls Expansion of U.S. Assembly Plant."

49. Howard LaFranchi, "Protecting Workers in a Global Economy," *The Christian Science Monitor* (May 6, 1998): 5.

50. NAFTA Supplemental Agreements, Annex 1 (Washington, DC: U.S. Government Printing Office, 1993).

51. A. Macleans, Geo-JaJa, and Garth L. Mangum, "The Foreign Corrupt Practices Act's Consequences for U.S. Trade," *Journal of Business Ethics* 24 (April 2000): 245–255.

52. S. L. Bachman, "A New Economics of Child Labor: Searching for Answers Behind the Headlines," *Journal of International Affairs* 53 (Spring 2000): 545.

53. Hebard, "Managing Effectively in Asia."

54. Ibid.

55. McNerney, "Global Staffing: Some Common Problems—And Solutions."

56. Krugman, "Lower Wages Weren't Enough to Keep U.S. Company Abroad."

57. Aaron Bernstein, "Cover Story: Backlash: Behind the Anxiety over Globalization," *Business Week* (April 24, 2000): 38.

58. Leon A. Kappelman, "Behind the News: Working in the Global Village," *Information Week* (March 20, 2000):150.

59. Judith N. Mottl, "Managing Change: Employers Head to the Web," *Internet Week* (August 10, 1998): 29.

60. Nathan D. Kling, Joe F. Alexander, Denny E. McCorkle, and Rutilio Martinez, "Preparing for Careers in Global Business: Strategies for U.S. Female Students," *American Business Review* 17 (June 1999): 34–42.

61. Wendy Hardman and Jacqueline Heidelberg, "When Sexual Harassment is a Foreign Affair," *Personnel Journal* 75 (April 1996): 91.

62. Hebard, "Managing Effectively in Asia."

63. Hicks, "Successful Global Training."

64. Malcolm Smith, "Culture and Organizational Change," *Management Accounting* (July 17, 1998): 60–63.

65. McNerney, "Global Staffing: Some Common Problems—And Solutions."

66. Patricia M. Buhler, "The Impact of the Global Arena on Managers at All Organizational Levels," *Supervision* 60 (August 1999): 15–17.

Living abroad holds great appeal for many U.S. workers, who envision themselves leading glamorous lives on expense accounts in foreign capitals. Yet being an expatriate employee is not the same as being on vacation abroad. Work is still work, for one thing. Home office expectations may run high, and the stress of adjusting to their new environment often proves an insurmountable difficulty for transplanted employees and their families. Some firms with international operations therefore choose to hire locally, to avoid the problems inherent in training, maintaining, and repatriating their U.S. workers.

Whether hiring locally or not, however, all international firms face problems of compensating employees fairly when, due to location, some have higher living expenses than others. The cost of living in cities like London, New York, and Tokyo is notoriously high, and employees of international firms who transfer there face even greater adjustment problems if their salaries do not meet the expense of their new environments and their families' standard of living begins to drop.

Sometimes employees transfer to locales where living is far cheaper than at home, and the firm faces a different but equally difficult choice—should salary be adjusted downward during the employee's tenure abroad, to prevent pay inequities from arising in the overseas office?

Cultural differences, such as varying expectations for vacations, unfamiliar holidays, and different labor practices must also be acknowledged and dealt with fairly, as Hal is about to find out.

In this segment we meet the lone member of Quicktakes' London operation, and he is British. It would appear, then, that Quicktakes has solved one major problem that firms face when first expanding their operations overseas. Tim has no difficulty adjusting to working in Europe, he is multilingual, and he has no disenchanted family members wishing to return home to the United States.

In fact, all the problems between Tim and Quicktakes seem to flow the other way. It is the video producer's U.S. employees who are having trouble with Tim. His free spending on meals and amenities and his generous holiday allowance are well known in the home office. If that were not enough to cause dissatisfaction, Tim's sales are down. Now he appears at headquarters to ask Hal for a raise, and Hal must decide what to do.

## Discussion Questions

1. Are Tim's vacation time and expense account privileges inequitable? Why or why not? Justify your answer.
2. Is Tim justified in asking for a salary increase? Why or why not? If you answered no, would you allow him the time off instead? Why or why not?
3. Who do you think has the upper hand in the conversation between Tim and Hal? Why? Is this ideal for management?
4. Why do you think Tim came to see Hal before going to Eddie for his sales results?
5. Do you think Tim's threat to quit is sincere? What do you think he is really trying to accomplish by it?
6. What do you think of Hal's proposal that Tim become a freelancer and work for Quicktakes in that capacity? Discuss the advantages and disadvantages for Quicktakes of this proposal. Does it offer Tim anything?

# Glossary

**Adverse impact** A concept established by the *Uniform Guidelines;* it occurs if women and minorities are not hired at the rate of at least 80 percent of the best-achieving group.

**Advertising** A way of communicating the firm's employment needs to the public through media such as radio, newspaper, or industry publications.

**Affirmative action** Stipulated by Executive Order 11246, it requires covered employers to take positive steps to ensure employment of applicants and treatment of employees during employment without regard to race, creed, color, or national origin.

**Affirmative action program (AAP)** A program that an organization with government contracts develops to employ women and minorities in proportion to their representation in the firm's relevant labor market.

**Agency shop** A labor agreement provision requiring, as a condition of employment, that each nonunion member of a bargaining unit pay the union the equivalent of membership dues as a service charge in return for the union acting as the bargaining agent.

**AIDS (acquired immune deficiency syndrome)** A disease that undermines the body's immune system, leaving the person susceptible to a wide range of fatal diseases.

**Alcoholism** A treatable disease characterized by uncontrolled and compulsive drinking that interferes with normal living patterns.

**Alternative dispute resolution (ADR)** A procedure agreed to ahead of time by the employee and the company for resolving any problems that may arise.

**Apprenticeship training** A combination of classroom instruction and on-the-job training.

**Arbitration** A process in which a dispute is submitted to an impartial third party for a binding decision.

**Assessment center** A selection technique used to identify and select employees for positions in the organization that requires individuals to perform activities similar to those they might encounter in an actual job.

**Attitude survey** A survey of employees' feelings about topics such as the work they perform, their supervisor, their work environment, flexibility in the workplace, opportunities for advancement, training and development opportunities, and the firm's compensation system.

**Authorization card** A document indicating that an employee wants to be represented by a labor organization in collective bargaining.

**Autonomy** The extent of individual freedom and discretion employees have in performing their jobs.

**Availability forecast** A process of determining whether a firm will be able to secure employees with the necessary skills from within the company, from outside the organization, or from a combination of the two sources.

**Bargaining unit** A group of employees—not necessarily union members—recognized by an employer or certified by an administrative agency as appropriate for representation by a labor organization for purposes of collective bargaining.

**Beachhead demands** Demands that the union does not expect management to meet when they are first made.

**Behavioral interview** A structured interview that uses questions designed to probe the candidate's past behavior in specific situations.

**Behaviorally anchored rating scale (BARS) method** A performance appraisal method that combines elements of the traditional rating scale and critical incident methods.

**Behavior modeling** A training method that utilizes videotapes to illustrate effective interpersonal skills and how managers function in various situations.

**Benchmark job** A well-known job in the company and industry and one performed by a large number of employees.

**Benefits** All financial rewards that generally are not paid directly to an employee.

**Biofeedback** A method of learning to control involuntary bodily processes, such as blood pressure or heart rate.

**Board interview** A meeting in which one candidate is interviewed by several representatives of a company.

**Bonus (lump sum payment)** A one-time award that is not added to employees' base pay.

**Bottom-up approach** A forecasting method beginning with the lowest organizational units and progressing upward through an organization ultimately to provide an aggregate forecast of employment needs.

**Boycott** Refusal by union members to use or buy their firm's products.

**Broadbanding** A compensation technique that collapses many pay grades (salary grades) into a few wide bands in order to improve organizational effectiveness.

**Burnout** An incapacitating condition in which individuals lose a sense of the basic purpose and fulfillment of their work.

**Business games** Simulations that attempt to duplicate selected factors in a particular business situation, which are then manipulated by the participants.

**Capitation** An approach to health care in which providers negotiate a rate for health care for a covered life over a period of time.

**Career** A general course of action a person chooses to pursue throughout his or her working life.

**Career development** A formal approach taken by an organization to help people acquire the skills and experiences needed to perform current and future jobs.

**Career development tools** Skills, education, and experiences, as well as behavioral modification and refinement techniques that allow individuals to work better and add value.

**Career path** A flexible line of progression through which an employee may move during his or her employment with a company.

**Career planning** An ongoing process through which an individual sets career goals and identifies the means to achieve them.

**Career security** The development of marketable skills and expertise that help ensure employment within a range of careers.

**Carpal tunnel syndrome** A condition caused by pressure on the median nerve in the wrist due to repetitive flexing and extension of the wrist.

**Case study** A training method in which trainees are expected to study the information provided in the case and make decisions based on it.

**Cash contribution plan** A hybrid retirement plan with elements of both defined benefit plans and defined contribution plans.

**Central tendency** A common error in performance appraisal that occurs when employees are incorrectly rated near the average or middle of a scale.

**Checkoff of dues** An agreement by which a company agrees to withhold union dues from members' paychecks and to forward the money directly to the union.

**Classification method** A job evaluation method in which classes or grades are defined to describe a group of jobs.

**Closed shop** An arrangement making union membership a prerequisite for employment.

**Cognitive aptitude tests** Tests that measure general reasoning ability, memory, vocabulary, verbal fluency, and numerical ability.

**Collective bargaining** The performance of the mutual obligation of the employer and the representative of the employees to meet at reasonable times and confer in good faith with respect to wages, hours, and other terms and conditions of employment, or the negotiation of an agreement, or any question arising thereunder, and the execution of a written contract incorporating any agreement reached if requested by either party; such obligation does not compel either party to agree to a proposal or require the making of a concession.

**Comparable worth** A determination of the values of dissimilar jobs (such as company nurse and welder) by comparing them under some form of job evaluation, and the assignment of pay rates according to their evaluated worth.

**Compensation** The total of all rewards provided employees in return for their service.

**Compensation survey** A means of obtaining data regarding what other firms are paying for specific jobs or job classes within a given labor market.

**Competency-based pay** A compensation plan that rewards employees for their demonstrated expertise.

**Compressed workweek** Any arrangement of work hours that permits employees to fulfill their work obligation in fewer days than the typical five-day workweek.

**Computer-based training** A teaching method that takes advantage of the speed, memory, and data manipulation capabilities of the computer for greater flexibility of instruction.

**Concurrent validity** A validation method in which test scores and criterion data are obtained at essentially the same time.

**Conspiracy** The combination of two or more persons who band together to prejudice the rights of others or of society (such as by refusing to work or demanding higher wages).

**Construct validity** A test validation method to determine whether a selection test measures certain traits or qualities that have been identified as important in performing a particular job.

**Content validity** A test validation method whereby a person performs certain tasks that are actual samples of the kind of work a job requires or completes a paper-and-pencil test that measures relevant job knowledge.

**Contingent workers** Also known as part-timers, temporaries, and independent contractors, individuals who work for staffing companies or are classified as independent contractors.

**Corporate culture** The system of shared values, beliefs, and habits within an organization that interacts with the formal structure to produce behavioral norms.

**Corporate homepage** The initial page of the Web site used by an organization to present itself to viewers on the Internet.

**Corporate labor campaigns** Labor maneuvers that do not coincide with a strike or organizing campaign to pressure an employer for better wages, benefits, and the like.

**Corporate Web site** A virtual medium that presents information about the company, often including human resources information, and possibly even allowing individuals to apply for jobs.

**Cost-of-living allowance (COLA)** An escalator clause in a labor agreement that automatically increases wages as the U.S. Bureau of Labor Statistics' cost-of-living index rises.

**Country's culture** The set of values, symbols, beliefs, languages, and norms that guide human behavior within a country.

**Craft union** A bargaining unit, such as the Carpenters and Joiners union, that is typically composed of members of a particular trade or skill in a specific locality.

**Criterion-related validity** A test validation method that compares the scores on selection tests to some aspect of job performance determined, for example, by performance appraisal.

**Critical incident method** A performance appraisal technique that requires a written record of highly favorable and highly unfavorable employee work.

**Cyberwork** The possibility of a never-ending workday created through the use of technology.

**Decertification** Election by a group of employees to withdraw a union's right to act as their exclusive bargaining representative; the reverse of the process that employees must follow to be recognized as an official bargaining unit.

**Defined benefit plan** A retirement plan in which an employer agrees to provide a specific level of retirement income that is either a fixed dollar amount or a percentage of earnings.

**Defined contribution health care system** A system in which each employee is given a set amount of money annually with which to purchase health care coverage.

**Defined contribution plan** A retirement plan that requires specific contributions by an employer to a retirement or savings fund established for the employee.

**Demotion** The process of moving a worker to a lower level of duties and responsibilities; typically involves a pay cut.

**Development** Learning that goes beyond today's job; it has a more long-term focus.

**Direct financial compensation** Pay that a person receives in the form of wages, salary, bonuses, and commissions.

**Disciplinary action** The invoking of a penalty against an employee who fails to meet organizational standards or comply with organizational rules.

**Disciplinary action without punishment** A process in which a worker is given time off with pay to think about whether he or she wants to follow the rules and continue working for the company.

**Discipline** The state of employee self-control and orderly conduct; indicates the extent of genuine teamwork within an organization.

**Diversity** Any perceived difference among people: age, functional specialty, profession, sexual orientation, geographic origin, lifestyle, tenure with the organization, or position.

**Downsizing** A reduction in the number of people employed by a firm (also known as *restructuring* and *rightsizing*); essentially the reverse of a company growing; downsizing suggests a one-time change in the organization and the number of people employed.

**Dual-career family** A situation in which both husband and wife have jobs and family responsibilities.

**Dual career path** A method of rewarding technical specialists and professionals who can and should be allowed to continue to contribute significantly to a company without having to become managers.

**Employee assistance program (EAP)** A comprehensive approach that many organizations have taken to deal with burnout, alcohol and drug abuse, and other emotional disturbances.

**Employee enlistment** A recruitment method in which every employee becomes a company recruiter.

**Employee equity** A condition that exists when individuals performing similar jobs for the same firm are paid according to factors unique to the employee, such as performance level or seniority.

**Employee requisition** A document that specifies a particular job title, the appropriate department, and the date by which an open job should be filled.

**Employee stock option plan (ESOP)** A defined contribution plan in which a firm contributes stock shares to a trust.

**Employment agency** An organization that assists firms in recruiting employees and also aids individuals in their attempts to locate jobs.

**Employment at will** An unwritten contract that is created when an employee agrees to work for an employer but includes no agreement as to how long the parties expect the employment to last.

**Employment interview** A goal-oriented conversation in which an interviewer and an applicant exchange information.

**Equity** The perception by workers that they are being treated fairly.

**Ergonomics** The study of human interaction with tasks, equipment, tools, and the physical work environment.

**Essay method** A performance appraisal method in which the rater writes a brief narrative describing an employee's performance.

**Ethics** The discipline dealing with what is good and bad, or right and wrong, or with moral duty and obligation.

**Ethnocentric staffing** A staffing approach that assumes that home-office perspectives and issues should take precedence over local perspectives and issues and that expatriates will be more effective in representing the views of the home office.

**Exclusive provider organizations (EPOs)** A managed care option that offers a smaller preferred provider network and usually provides few, if any, benefits when an out-of-network provider is used.

**Executive** A top-level manager who reports directly to a corporation's chief executive officer or to the head of a major division.

**Executive order (EO)** Directive issued by the president that has the force and effect of a law enacted by the Congress.

**Executive search firms** Organizations retained by a company to search for the most qualified executive available for a specific position.

**Exempt employees** Those categorized as executive, administrative, or professional employees and outside salespersons.

**Exit interview** A means of revealing the real reasons employees leave their jobs, providing the organization with information on how to correct the causes of discontent, and reducing employee turnover.

**Expatriate** An employee who is not a citizen of the country in which the firm is located but is a citizen of the country in which the organization is headquartered.

**Exporting** Selling abroad, either directly or indirectly, by retaining foreign agents and distributors.

**External environment** Factors outside its boundaries that affect a firm's human resources.

**External equity** Payment of employees at rates comparable to those paid for similar jobs in other firms.

**Factor comparison method** A job evaluation method in which raters need not keep an entire job in mind as they evaluate it; instead, they make decisions on separate aspects or factors of the job.

**Feedback** The amount of information employees receive about how well they have performed the job.

**Flexible compensation plans** A method that permits employees to choose from among many alternatives in deciding how their financial compensation will be allocated.

**Flextime** The practice of permitting employees to choose their own working hours, within certain limitations.

**Flooding the community** The process of the union inundating communities with organizers to target a particular business.

**Forced-choice performance report** A performance appraisal technique in which the rater is given a series of statements about an individual and indicates which items are most or least descriptive of the employee.

**Forced distribution method** An appraisal approach in which the rater is required to assign individuals in a work group to a limited number of categories similar to a normal frequency distribution.

**401(k) plan** A defined contribution retirement plan in which employees may defer income up to a certain maximum amount.

**Franchising** A multinational option whereby the parent company grants another firm the right to do business in a prescribed manner.

**Functional job analysis (FJA)** A comprehensive approach to formulating job descriptions that concentrates on the interactions among the work, the worker, and the work organization.

**Gain sharing** A plan designed to bind employees to the firm's performance by providing an incentive payment based on improved company performance.

**Generalist** A person who performs tasks in a variety of human resource–related areas.

**Generation I** Internet-assimilated children, born after 1994.

**Generation X** The label affixed to the 40 million American workers born between 1965 and 1976.

**Generation Y** The sons and daughters of boomers; people who were born between 1979 and 1994.

**Genetic testing** Testing that can determine whether a person carries the gene mutation for certain diseases, including heart disease, colon cancer, breast cancer, and Huntington's disease.

**Geocentric staffing** A staffing approach that uses a worldwide integrated business strategy.

**Glass ceiling** The invisible barrier in organizations that prevents many women and minorities from achieving top-level management positions.

**Global corporation (GC)** An organization that has corporate units in a number of countries; the units are integrated to operate as one organization worldwide.

**Global human resource management (GHRM)** The utilization of global human resources to achieve organizational objectives without regard to geographic boundaries.

**Globalization** The creation of shareholder value worldwide through differentiation and competitive advantage.

**Golden parachute contract** A perquisite provided for the purpose of protecting executives in the event that another company acquires their firm or they are forced to leave the firm for other reasons.

**Grievance** An employee's dissatisfaction or feeling of personal injustice relating to his or her employment.

**Grievance procedure** A formal, systematic process that permits employees to complain about matters affecting them and their work.

**Group interview** A meeting in which several job applicants interact in the presence of one or more company representatives.

**Guidelines-oriented job analysis (GOJA)** A method that responds to the growing amount of legislation affecting employment decisions by utilizing a step-by-step procedure to describe the work of a particular job classification.

**Halo error** Occurs when a manager generalizes one positive performance factor or incident to all aspects of employee performance.

**Hay guide chart-profile method (Hay Plan)** A highly refined version of the point method of job evaluation that uses the factors of know-how, problem solving, accountability, and additional compensable elements.

**Hazard pay** Additional pay provided to employees who work under extremely dangerous conditions.

**Health** An employee's freedom from physical or emotional illness.

**Health maintenance organizations (HMOs)** Insurance programs provided by companies that cover all services for a fixed fee but control is exercised over which doctors and health facilities may be used.

**Host-country national (HCN)** An employee who is a citizen of the country in which a subsidiary is located, not of the country where the organization is headquartered.

**Human resource development** A major HRM function that consists not only of T&D but also individual career planning and development activities and performance appraisal.

**Human resource management (HRM)** The utilization of individuals to achieve organizational objectives.

**Human resource managers** Individuals who normally act in an advisory (or staff) capacity when working with other managers to help them deal with human resource matters.

**Human resource planning (HRP)** The process of systematically reviewing human resource requirements to ensure that the required number of employees with the required skills are available when and where they are needed.

**Hypnosis** An altered state of consciousness that is artificially induced and characterized by increased receptiveness to suggestions.

**In-basket training** A simulation in which the participant is given a number of business papers or e-mail messages including memoranda, reports, and telephone messages that would typically be sent to a manager or team leader.

**Incentive compensation** A payment program that relates pay to productivity.

**Indexed stock option plan** A stock option plan that holds executives to a higher standard and requires that increased stock compensation be tied to outperforming peer groups or a market index.

**Indirect financial compensation** All financial rewards that are not included in direct compensation.

**Individual representation** A situation in which people prefer to bargain for themselves and ignore the interests of the collective members of the workforce.

**Industrial union** A bargaining unit that generally consists of all the workers in a particular plant or group of plants.

**Informal organization** The set of evolving relationships and patterns of human interaction within an organization that are not officially prescribed.

**Injunction** A prohibiting legal procedure used by employers to prevent certain union activities, such as strikes and unionization attempts.

**Interest arbitration** Arbitration that involves disputes over the terms of proposed collective bargaining agreements.

**Internal employee relations** Those human resource management activities associated with the movement of employees within the organization.

**Internal environment** Factors inside a firm's boundaries that affect its human resources.

**Internal equity** Payment of employees according to the relative values of their jobs within an organization.

**Internet** The large system of many connected computers around the world that individuals and businesses use to communicate with each other.

**Internet recruiter** Also called *cyber recruiter;* a person whose primary responsibility is to use the Internet in the recruitment process.

**Internship** A special form of recruitment that involves placing students in temporary jobs with no obligation either by the company to hire the student permanently or by the student to accept a permanent position with the firm following graduation.

**Intranet** A system of computers that enables people within an organization to communicate with each other.

**Job** A group of tasks that must be performed if an organization is to achieve its goals.

**Job agent service site** Web site that permits job-seekers to specify parameters for their ideal job and to receive information on only the job opportunities that fit these restrictions.

**Job analysis** The systematic process of determining the skills, duties, and knowledge required for performing specific jobs in an organization.

**Job analysis schedule (JAS)** A systematic method of studying jobs and occupations; developed by the U.S. Department of Labor.

**Job bidding** A technique that permits individuals in an organization who believe that they possess the required qualifications to apply for a posted job.

**Job description** A document that provides information regarding the tasks, duties, and responsibilities of a job.

**Job design** A process of determining the specific tasks to be performed, the methods used in performing these tasks, and how the job relates to other work in an organization.

**Job enlargement** A change in the scope of a job so as to provide greater variety to a worker.

**Job enrichment** The restructuring of the content and level of responsibility of a job to make it more challenging, meaningful, and interesting to a worker.

**Job evaluation** That part of a compensation system in which a company determines the relative value of one job in relation to another.

**Job evaluation ranking method** A method in which the raters examine the description of each job being evaluated and arrange the jobs in order according to their value to the company.

**Job-knowledge tests** Tests designed to measure a candidate's knowledge of the duties of the job for which he or she is applying.

**Job overload** A condition that exists when employees are given more work than they can reasonably handle.

**Job posting** A procedure for communicating to company employees the fact that a job opening exists.

**Job pricing** Placing a dollar value on the worth of a job.

**Job rotation** A training method that involves moving employees from one job to another to broaden their experience.

**Job security** Protection against job loss within the company.

**Job sharing** The filling of a job by two part-time people who split the duties of one full-time job in some agreed-on manner and are paid according to their contributions.

**Job specification** A document that outlines the minimum acceptable qualifications a person should possess to perform a particular job.

**Job underload** A condition that occurs when employees are given menial, boring tasks to perform.

**Keyword résumé** A résumé that contains an adequate description of the jobseeker's characteristics and industry-specific experience presented in keyword terms in order to accommodate the electronic/computer search process.

**Keywords** Those words or phrases that are used for searches of databases for résumés that match.

**Labor market** The geographic area from which employees are recruited for a particular job.

**Lateral skill path** A career path that allows for lateral moves within the firm; these permit an employee to become revitalized and find new challenges.

**Learning organizations** Firms with the capacity to continuously adapt to change.

**Leniency** Giving an undeserved high performance appraisal rating to an employee.

**Licensing** A global arrangement whereby an organization grants a foreign firm the right to use intellectual properties such as patents, copyrights, manufacturing processes, or trade names for a specific period of time.

**Likes and dislikes survey** A procedure that helps individuals recognize restrictions they place on themselves.

**Local union** The basic element in the structure of the U.S. labor movement.

**Lockout** A management decision to keep employees out of the workplace and to operate with management personnel and/or temporary replacements.

**Management development** Learning experiences provided by an organization for the purpose of upgrading skills and knowledge required in current and future managerial positions.

**Management position description questionnaire (MPDQ)** A form of job analysis designed for management positions that uses a checklist method to analyze jobs.

**Mandatory bargaining issues** Bargaining issues that fall within the definition of wages, hours, and other terms and conditions of employment; refusal to bargain in these areas is grounds for an unfair labor practice charge.

**Market (going) rate** The average pay that most employers provide for the same job in a particular area or industry.

**Mediation** A process in which a neutral third party enters and attempts to resolve a labor dispute when a bargaining impasse has occurred.

**Merit pay** Pay increase given to employees based on their level of performance as indicated in the appraisal.

**Mission** The organization's continuing purpose or reason for being.

**Modified retirement** An option that permits older employees to work fewer than their regular hours for a certain period of time preceding retirement.

**Multimedia** An application that enhances computer-based learning with audio, animation, graphics, and interactive video.

**Multinational corporation (MNC)** A firm that is based in one country (the parent or home country) and produces goods or provides services in one or more foreign countries (host countries).

**National union** An organization composed of local unions, which it charters.

**Negligent hiring** The liability an employer incurs when it does not reasonably investigate an applicant's background and then assigns a potentially dangerous person to a position where he or she can inflict harm.

**Negligent referral** When a former employer fails to offer a warning about a particularly severe problem with a past employee.

**Negligent retention** When a company keeps persons on the payroll whose records indicate strong potential for wrongdoing.

**Network career path** A method of job progression that contains both vertical and horizontal opportunities.

**Niche sites** Web sites that cater to a specific profession.

**Nonfinancial compensation** The satisfaction that a person receives from the job itself or from the psychological and/or physical environment in which the person works.

**Norm** A frame of reference for comparing an applicant's performance with that of others.

**Objectivity** The condition that is achieved when all individuals scoring a given test obtain the same results.

**Ombudsperson** A complaint officer with access to top management who hears employees' complaints, investigates them, and sometimes recommends appropriate action.

**On-the-job training (OJT)** An informal approach to training in which an employee learns job tasks by actually performing them.

**Open-door policy** A company policy allowing employees the right to take any grievance to the person next in the chain of command if a satisfactory solution cannot be obtained from their immediate supervisor.

**Open shop** Employment that has equal terms for union members and nonmembers alike.

**Operative employees** All workers in an organization except managers and professionals, such as engineers, accountants, and professional secretaries.

**Organization development (OD)** An organizationwide application of behavioral science knowledge to the planned development and support of organizational strategies, structures, and processes for improving a firm's effectiveness.

**Organizational career planning** The process of the organization identifying paths and activities for individual employees as they develop.

**Organizational fit** Management's perception of the degree to which the prospective employee will fit in with the firm's culture or value system.

**Orientation** The initial T&D effort for new employees that strives to inform them about the company, the job, and the work group.

**Outplacement** A company procedure that assists a laid-off employee in finding employment elsewhere.

**Outsourcing** The process of transferring responsibility for an area of service and its objectives to an external provider.

**Paid time off (PTO)** A means of dealing with the problem of unscheduled absences by providing a certain number of days each year that employees can use for any purpose they deem necessary.

**Paired comparison** A variation of the ranking method of performance appraisal in which the performance of each employee is compared with that of every other employee in the group.

**Pay compression** A situation that occurs when workers perceive that the pay differential between their pay and that of employees in jobs above or below them is too small.

**Pay-equalization rules** Rules under which every worker is rewarded equally when pay or benefit gains are realized, based on seniority rather than worker productivity.

**Pay followers** Companies that choose to pay below the market rate because of a poor financial condition or a belief that they simply do not require highly capable employees.

**Pay grade** The grouping of similar jobs to simplify the job-pricing process.

**Pay leaders** Those organizations that pay higher wages and salaries than competing firms.

**Pay range** A minimum and maximum pay rate for a job, with enough variance between the two to allow for a significant pay difference.

**Performance appraisal (PA)** A formal system of periodic review and evaluation of an individual's job performance.

**Performance management** A process that significantly affects organizational success by having managers and employees work together to set expectations, review results, and reward performance.

**Permissive bargaining issues** Issues that may be raised by management or a union; neither side may insist that they be bargained over.

**Perquisites (perks)** Special benefits provided by a firm to a small group of key executives to give them something extra.

**Personality tests** Self-reported measures of traits, temperaments, or dispositions.

**Piecework** An incentive pay plan in which employees are paid for each unit produced.

**Point method** An approach to job evaluation in which numerical values are assigned to specific job components, and the sum of these values provides a quantitative assessment of a job's relative worth.

**Point-of-service (POS)** A managed care option that permits a member to select a health care provider within the network or—for a lower level of benefits—outside the network.

**Policy** A predetermined guide established to provide direction in decision making.

**Polycentric staffing** When more host-country nationals are used throughout the organization, from top to bottom.

**Position** The tasks and responsibilities performed by one person; there is a position for every individual in an organization.

**Position analysis questionnaire (PAQ)** A structured job analysis questionnaire that uses a checklist approach to identify job elements.

**Predictive validity** A validation method that involves administering a selection test and later obtaining the criterion information.

**Preferred provider organizations (PPOs)** A flexible managed care system in which incentives are provided to members to use services within the system; out-of-network providers may be utilized at greater cost.

**Premium pay** Compensation paid to employees for working long periods of time or working under dangerous or undesirable conditions.

**Proactive response** Taking action in anticipation of environmental changes.

**Profession** A vocation characterized by the existence of a common body of knowledge and a recognized procedure for certifying practitioners.

**Professional employer organization (PEO)** Off-site human resources department that puts a client firm's employees on its payroll, then leases the employees back to the company.

**Profit sharing** A compensation plan that distributes a predetermined percentage of a firm's profits to its employees.

**Progressive disciplinary action** An approach to disciplinary action designed to ensure that the minimum penalty appropriate to the offense is imposed.

**Prohibited bargaining issues** Issues that are statutorily outlawed from collective bargaining.

**Promotion** The movement of a person to a higher-level position in an organization.

**Promotion from within (PFW)** The policy of filling vacancies above entry-level positions with employees presently employed by a company.

**Psychomotor abilities tests** Aptitude tests that measure strength, coordination, and dexterity.

**Quality circles** Groups of employees who voluntarily meet regularly with their supervisors to discuss problems, investigate causes, recommend solutions, and take corrective action when authorized to do so.

**Quotas** Policies that limit the number or value of goods that can be imported across national boundaries.

**Ranking method** A job evaluation method in which the rater simply places all employees from a group in rank order of overall performance.

**Rating scales method** A widely used performance appraisal method that rates employees according to defined factors.

**Reactive response** Simply reacting to environmental changes after they occur.

**Realistic job preview (RJP)** A method of conveying both positive and negative job information to an applicant in an unbiased manner.

**Recruitment** The process of attracting individuals on a timely basis, in sufficient numbers and with appropriate qualifications, and encouraging them to apply for jobs with an organization.

**Recruitment methods** The specific means by which potential employees are attracted to an organization.

**Recruitment sources** Various locations in which qualified individuals are sought as potential employees.

**Reengineering** The fundamental rethinking and radical redesign of business processes to achieve dramatic improvements in critical, contemporary measures of performance such as cost, quality, service, and speed.

**Reference checks** A way to gain additional insight into the information provided by an applicant and to verify the accuracy of the information provided.

**Regiocentric staffing** Similar to the polycentric staffing approach, but regional groups of subsidiaries reflecting the organization's strategy and structure work as a unit.

**Relocation benefits** Company-paid shipment of household goods and temporary living expenses, covering all or a portion of the real estate costs associated with buying a new home and selling the previously occupied home.

**Reliability** The extent to which a selection test provides consistent results.

**Repatriation** The process of bringing expatriates home.

**Requirements forecast** An estimate of the numbers and kinds of employees an organization will need at future dates to realize its stated objectives.

**Résumé management systems** A process that scans résumés into databases, searches the databases on command, and ranks the résumés according to the number of resulting hits they receive.

**Rights arbitration** Arbitration involving disputes over the interpretation and application of the various provisions of an existing contract.

**Right-to-work laws** Laws that prohibit management and unions from entering into agreements requiring union membership as a condition of employment.

**Role ambiguity** A condition that exists when employees do not understand the content of their jobs.

**Role conflict** A condition that occurs when an individual is placed in the position of having to pursue opposing goals.

**Role playing** A training method in which participants are required to respond to specific problems they may actually encounter in their jobs.

**Safety** The protection of employees from injuries caused by work-related accidents.

**Scanlon plan** A gain-sharing plan designed to reward employees for savings in labor costs that result from their suggestions.

**Secondary boycott** A union's attempt to encourage third parties (such as suppliers and customers) to stop doing business with a firm.

**Selection** The process of choosing from a group of applicants those individuals best suited for a particular position and organization.

**Selection ratio** The number of people hired for a particular job compared to the total number of individuals in the applicant pool.

**Self-assessment** The process of learning about oneself.

**Seniority** The length of time that an employee has worked in various capacities with the firm.

**Sensitivity training** An organizational development technique that is designed to make people aware of themselves and their impact on others.

**Severance pay** Compensation designed to assist laid-off employees as they search for new employment.

**Shared service centers (SSCs)** Centers that take routine, transaction-based activities dispersed throughout the organization and consolidate them in one place.

**Shareholders** The owners of a corporation.

**Shift differential** Additional money paid to reward employees for the inconvenience of working undesirable hours.

**Simulation** A technique for experimenting with a real-world situation by means of a mathematical model that represents the actual situation.

**Simulators** Training devices of varying degrees of complexity that duplicate the real world.

**Skill-based pay** A system that compensates employees on the basis of job-related skills and the knowledge they possess.

**Skill variety** The extent to which work requires a number of different activities for successful completion.

**Social responsibility** The implied, enforced, or felt obligation of managers, acting in their official capacities, to serve or protect the interests of groups other than themselves.

**Special events** A recruitment method that involves an effort on the part of a single employer or group of employers to attract a large number of applicants for interviews.

**Specialist** An individual who may be a human resource executive, a human resource manager, or a nonmanager, and who is typically concerned with only one of the six functional areas of human resource management.

**Staffing** The process through which an organization ensures that it always has the proper number of employees with the appropriate skills in the right jobs at the right time to achieve the organization's objectives.

**Standardization** Uniformity of the procedures and conditions related to administering tests.

**Status symbols** Organizational rewards that take many forms such as office size and location, desk size and quality, private secretaries, floor covering, and title.

**Stock option plan** An incentive plan in which managers can buy a specified amount of stock in their company in the future at or below the current market price.

**Strategic planning** The determination of overall organizational purposes and goals and how they are to be achieved.

**Strength/weakness balance sheet** A self-evaluation procedure, developed originally by Benjamin Franklin, that helps people to become aware of their strengths and weaknesses.

**Stress** The body's nonspecific reaction to any demand made on it.

**Stress interview** A form of interview that intentionally creates anxiety to determine how a job applicant will react in certain types of situations.

**Strictness** Being unduly critical of an employee's work performance.

**Strike** An action by union members who refuse to work in order to exert pressure on management in negotiations.

**Structured interview** A process in which an interviewer consistently presents the same series of job-related questions to each applicant for a particular job.

**Succession development** The process of determining a comprehensive job profile of the key positions and then ensuring that key prospects are properly developed to match these qualifications.

**Succession planning** The process of ensuring that a qualified person is available to assume a managerial position once the position is vacant.

**Survey feedback** A process of collecting data from an organizational unit through the use of questionnaires, interviews, and objective data from other sources such as records of productivity, turnover, and absenteeism.

**Talent auction** In Web terminology, the process in which a person or persons place their qualifications on a site and have organizations bid for their services.

**Tariffs** Taxes collected on goods that are shipped across national boundaries.

**Task identity** The extent to which the job includes an identifiable unit of work that is carried out from start to finish.

**Task significance** The impact that the job has on other people.

**Team building** A conscious effort to develop effective work groups throughout an organization.

**Team equity** Payment of more productive teams in an organization at a higher rate than less productive teams.

**Telecommuting** A procedure allowing workers to remain at home or otherwise away from the office and perform their work over data lines tied to a computer.

**Third-country national (TCN)** A citizen of one country, working in a second country, and employed by an organization headquartered in a third country.

**360-degree feedback** A multirater evaluation that involves input from multiple levels within the firm and external sources as well.

**Total quality management (TQM)** A commitment to excellence by everyone in an organization that emphasizes excellence achieved by teamwork and a process of continuous improvement.

**Traditional career path** A vertical line of career progression from one specific job to the next.

**Training** Activities designed to provide learners with the knowledge and skill needed for their present jobs.

**Training and development** The heart of a continuous effort designed to improve employee competency and organizational performance.

**Transcendental meditation (TM)** A stress-reduction technique in which an individual, comfortably seated, mentally repeats a secret word or phrase (mantra) provided by a trained instructor.

**Transfer** The lateral movement of a worker within an organization.

**Union** A group of employees who have joined together for the purpose of dealing collectively with their employer.

**Union salting** The process of training union organizers to apply for jobs at a company and, once hired, work to unionize employees.

**Union shop** A requirement that all employees become members of the union after a specified period of employment (the legal minimum is 30 days) or after a union shop provision has been negotiated.

**Unstructured interview** A meeting with a job applicant during which the interviewer asks probing, open-ended questions.

**Utilization review** A process that scrutinizes medical diagnoses, hospitalization, surgery, and other medical treatment and care prescribed by doctors.

**Validity** The extent to which a test measures what it purports to measure.

**Variable pay** Compensation based on performance.

**Vestibule training** Training that takes place away from the production area on equipment that closely resembles the actual equipment used on the job.

**Virtual job fair** A recruitment method in which individuals meet recruiters face to face in interviews conducted over special computers that transmit head-and-shoulder images of both parties.

**Virtual reality** A unique computer-based approach that permits trainees to view objects from a perspective otherwise impractical or impossible.

**Vocational interest tests** A method of determining the occupation in which a person has the greatest interest and from which the person is most likely to receive satisfaction.

**Wage curve** The fitting of plotted points on a curve to create a smooth progression between pay grades (also known as the *pay curve*).

**Web (World Wide Web)** The system of connected documents on the Internet, which often contain color pictures, video, and sound and can be searched for information about a particular subject.

**Weighted checklist performance report** A performance appraisal technique in which the rater completes a form similar to a forced-choice performance report except that the various responses have been assigned different weights.

**Workload variance** Both job overload and job underload.

**Work-sample tests** Tests requiring an applicant to perform a task or set of tasks that are representative of a particular job.

**Work standards method** A performance appraisal method that compares each employee's performance to a predetermined standard or expected level of output.

**Yellow-dog contract** A written agreement between an employee and a company made at the time of employment that prohibits a worker from joining a union or engaging in union activities.

**Zero-base forecasting** A method for estimating future employment needs using the organization's current level of employment as the starting point.

# ▶ Name Index

# Company Index

# ▶ Subject Index

# ▶ Photo Credits

Chapter 1 FPG International LLC
Chapter 2 Bruce Ayers/Stone
Chapter 3 Mug Shots/The Stock Market
Chapter 4 Stewart Cohen/Index Stock Imagery, Inc.
Chapter 5 Mark Richards/PhotoEdit
Chapter 6 Steve Mason/PhotoDisc, Inc
Chapter 7 Ryan McVay/PhotoDisc, Inc
Chapter 8 Walter Hodges/Stone
Chapter 9 Tim Brown/Stone
Chapter 10 Keith Brofsky/PhotoDisc, Inc
Chapter 11 Bruce Ayers/Stone
Chapter 12 D. Sorey/Liaison Agency, Inc.
Chapter 13 Louis Psihoyos/Matrix International, Inc.
Chapter 14 Bill Haber/AP/Wide World Photos
Chapter 15 David H. Wells/The Image Works
Chapter 16 © John Coletti
Chapter 17 Greg Girard/Contact Press Images Inc.